ILLINOIS

A HISTORY OF THE PRAIRIE STATE

Abraham Lincoln

ILLINOIS

A HISTORY OF THE PRAIRIE STATE

by

Robert P. Howard

WILLIAM B. EERDMANS PUBLISHING COMPANY
Grand Rapids, Michigan

To Eleanor

Foreword

One may ask—and many have—what real differences there are between the various states of the Union. Obviously, in some cases, there are a great many. No one could put Alaska and Hawaii in the same basket, and California and Massachusetts are as dissimilar as night and day. (To these two, the reader can attach the label of his preference.) But what about Arizona and New Mexico? Or Washington and Oregon? Or at least three states of the Middle West: Ohio, Indiana, and Illinois?

There was a day when state pride burned fiercely in the United States. In 1861 Robert E. Lee, no secessionist, no advocate of slavery, decided without hesitation, though not without regret, that he owed his first allegiance to Virginia rather than to the nation. Many thousands followed his example. The Civil War was fought in part over the question of state sovereignty, a term which, though not synonymous with state pride, comes fairly close to it.

The Civil War scotched forever the concept of state sovereignty, and social and economic developments since then have diluted state pride. The American people have become highly mobile. Hardly anyone expects to live and die in the place of his birth. To be personal, I was born in Ohio and live in Illinois; my three brothers, also native Ohioans, live respectively in Pittsburgh, Pennsylvania; Bethesda, Maryland; and Santa Fe, New Mexico. Of my two children born in Springfield, Illinois, one now lives in the Chicago area, the other resides in New York City.

And yet there are many millions who, through the fact of residence for several years if not by nativity, have acquired interest in and affection for various states. That certainly has been the case with Robert P. Howard, author of this book. Born in Iowa, and graduating from college there, he did not come to Chicago until he was in his twenties, and there are at least five million people who will assert vigorously that Chicago is not Illinois. I suspect that Howard's affection for his adopted state really began about forty years ago when The Associated Press sent him to Springfield, the capital, as its legislative correspondent. Twenty-five years later he was stationed there permanently by the *Chicago Tribune.*

From Springfield as a base he traveled to other parts of the state as his duties required. Thus he came to know Illinois as no one whose life is confined to Cook County can know it. And the state fascinated him to the extent that he began building a library of books about it.

Howard saw that Illinois differed notably from its neighboring states of the Middle West. Historically it was the Prairie State, the first state encountered by the pioneers in their westward march where vast areas were covered by tall grass and flowers rather than towering trees and tangled underbrush. The pioneers were slow to recognize that the soil of the prairies was enormously rich, but when they did, Illinois became one of the great grain-producing regions of the North American continent.

The state had a range of climate that set it apart from adjacent states both east and west, stretching from the latitude of Boston, Massachusetts, on the north to that of Norfolk, Virginia, on the south. Pines grew along its northern border, cotton at its southern tip. A full month separated growing seasons, north and south. Its topography varied more than casual observers realized. To be sure, most of its surface was flat, but there were, and are, high hills in the northwestern corner and in the southern quarter, and a sizable segment of land between the Mississippi and the Illinois rivers had escaped the leveling effect of the glaciers. And underneath two-thirds of the surface lie the largest deposits of soft coal in the country.

Nature had destined Illinois to be the transportation center of the nation. Navigable rivers—the Mississippi and the Ohio—bordered it on two sides; the Illinois ran diagonally across the state from a point near Chicago to another near St. Louis, needing only a canal, built before too long, to enable it to carry heavy traffic from the Great Lakes to the Mississippi and thence to New Orleans, and in the other direction, from the Mississippi and Illinois valleys to Chicago and thence to the eastern seaboard. Chicago itself, the port near the southern tip of Lake Michigan, could not escape being the point of transshipment for waterborne commodities, and later, for the freight and passengers carried by the railroads that had their terminals there. (To this day, no cross-country railroad runs through Chicago. The eastern lines end there, and there the western lines begin.) In this modern age, Chicago continues to be the focal point for truck routes and airlines.

Howard discovered before long that the people of Illinois were anything but homogeneous. In part, as he points out in his narrative, their differences were the result of the process of settlement. The first American settlers in the state came from the South, principally from Kentucky and Tennessee, and for the most part stayed in the southern third of the state. Some moved into the central counties where they mingled with immigrants from the Atlantic states. Northern Illinois, peopled after the Black Hawk War and the opening of the Erie Canal, drew heavily from New England and New York. Some of these differences persist to this day in the soft, drawling speech of the "Egyptian" and in his steady, almost passionate devotion to the land where several generations of his family have lived. This is to say nothing of the heavy waves of immigrants—Irish, Germans, Swedes, Poles, Bohemians, and Italians—who sought new homes and opportunities in Illinois, principally in Chicago. And after World War I large numbers of Negroes would move up from the South, adding another element to a population already diverse.

Howard, imbued with a love of history in his youth, began to consider making a contribution of his own to the story of his adopted state. The centennial of Illinois in 1918 had been marked by the publication of six scholarly volumes, but within twenty-five years all went out of print. Besides, a great deal had happened in and to Illinois since 1918, all unreported by historians except in fragmentary fashion. After the Centennial History of Illinois only one general history of the state had been published, and that was a slender volume that emphasized the early years of statehood disproportionately, and ended with the year 1920. One chapter, added to a later edition, purported to cover the years 1920 to 1949, but did little to correct the imbalance of the original work.

Obviously, there was a need for a substantial one-volume history of Illinois covering all phases of the state's life, economic and social as well as political, and telling the story from the days of the Indians to the age of jets.

The Sesquicentennial of Illinois, celebrated in 1968, was marked by a resurgence of interest in the history of the state. An official program called for the preparation of various historical publications but not for a one-volume history for the general reader, since it was assumed that some enterprising writer would undertake this project on his own responsibility without a subsidy from the public treasury. Robert Howard decided that this was his opportunity. He had three advantages. His work for the *Tribune* kept him busy when the legislature was in session, but after the adjournment of that turbulent body he had considerable free time. At arm's length, in his own home, was a fine collection of Illinois books. And always at his command were the superb resources of the Illinois State Historical Library, indispensable to any serious worker in the field Howard had chosen.

So *Illinois: A History of the Prairie State* is the product of many years of reading, six years of intensive work, and first-hand acquaintance with every corner of the state. The author's qualifications for the task he set himself stand out on every page. If there is any event of more than evanescent significance he has missed I have not discovered it, and if there is any phase of life in this many-faceted state he has overlooked, I am unaware of it.

In fact, Howard has touched upon subjects that one might not expect to find in a one-volume general history. A case in point is his inclusion of the part played by Illinoisans in the formation and early years of the Grand Army of the Republic, which bore not only the most sonorous name ever attached to a veterans' organization, but also wielded more punch than any group in American politics. He has found a place for barbed wire, an Illinois invention that may have been as important as John Deere's steel plow and Cyrus McCormick's reaper. He has devoted several pages to the Chicago literary "renaissance," which threw in the face of the reading public such writers as Carl Sandburg, Vachel Lindsay, Edgar Lee Masters, and Harriet Monroe. Chicago's brief fling at movie-making has been noted, and one of Howard's most fascinating sections concerns the early preeminence of Illinois, and its subsequent failure, in the manufacture of automobiles.

Anyone who undertakes to write a history of Illinois faces

several difficult problems. In a sense, he must write about two states: Chicago and its metropolitan area, and what is colloquially, though not with geographical exactitude, called "downstate." He must also divide his attention between agriculture, manufacturing, transportation, mining, and other phases of the economy. Nor can he ignore, if he is to be honest, the fact that politics in Illinois has often had a rancid odor. This characteristic of the state he faces frankly, remarking that "Illinois has never been cited as an example of purity in governmental ethics," and documenting the statement with examples as recent as the year 1971.

In short, this is a fine book, comprehensive, detailed but not to the point of tedium, honest, and up to date. It should take its place immediately as the standard history of Illinois, and hold that distinction for many years to come.

Paul M. Angle

Contents

List of Maps

List of Illustrations

Introduction

This is a narrative of the struggles and accomplishments of the men and women who settled and civilized Illinois. To the extent that it is possible in one volume, it traces through three centuries the development of a complex society in which crowded cities have replaced Indian villages. In so doing, it seeks to explain why Illinois inevitably became one of the greatest of the American states and why most of its residents have found that the Prairie State is a good place in which to live.

Illinois has had a longer and more interesting history than any other state west of the Alleghenies. It was not accidental that the white settlement of the midcontinent began on the east bank of the Mississippi River and that the largest noncoastal city took root and flourished at the southwestern corner of Lake Michigan. As geographical and geological heritages, the flat prairie has soil of unusual fertility, convenient water routes, and readily available mineral resources. Because of them, the settlers came early, in increasing numbers, over several routes, and from varied national and racial backgrounds.

Illinois is Abraham Lincoln's state, but its history has much more than Lincoln. He is put in the context of his times while attention is given to other great personalities—to Jolliet and Marquette on unknown rivers in birchbark canoes, to the far-sighted but tragic La Salle with Tonti in his footsteps, to George Rogers Clark with a handful of woodsmen blocking British control of the

Old Northwest, to the intervention of Governor Edward Coles when Illinois almost became a slave state, and on through the panorama of the generations. The roster is lengthy and too many have been neglected.

During four decades as a close observer of Illinois, the writer has developed a deep affection for the state and its people. He also has accumulated a long list of debts that can be acknowledged but not repaid. This can be the occasion for a personal salute to Dr. John F. Snyder, John Moses, Alexander Davidson, Bernard Stuvé and others whose early histories provided entertaining reading and led to familiarity with later writers, of whom Clarence W. Alvord, Paul M. Angle, Paul Wallace Gates, Theodore C. Pease, and Milo Milton Quaife have been both scholarly and prolific. Many others have enriched the understanding of Illinois with biographies, regional histories, and specialized studies. An effort has been made to list most of them in the bibliography.

To the preparation of this work, Paul M. Angle contributed years of friendship, encouragement, and criticism. The suggestion that a history of Illinois be written came from Mr. Angle, Ralph G. Newman, and Clyde C. Walton in advance of the 1968 Illinois Sesquicentennial, but the project required much more time than they contemplated. It could not have been completed without proximity to the Illinois State Historical Library, the Illinois State Library, and the Lincoln Library of Springfield, and the assistance of their staffs. Over the years hundreds of news sources, friends, and at times total strangers have with kindness contributed to my knowledge of the state of Illinois. My thanks to all. To mention some individuals is to overlook many more. With apologies to the others, I acknowledge special debts to William K. Alderfer, Ralph A. Berkowitz, Margaret A. Flint, Johnson Kanady, William Lyons, Bruce McMillan, Fred Mohn, David E. Scherman, Mildred V. Schulz, George F. Schuppe, George H. Tagge, Alfred A. Von Behren, Lois Wilson, and Laurin A. Wollan, Jr. Mary Marada settled crises involving typing. The contributions of my daughters, Jane Howard and Ann Condon, included advice and enthusiasm. We regret that my wife, who gave invaluable help with much of this work, could not participate in its completion.

Robert P. Howard

Springfield, Illinois

1

PRAIRIE, PORTAGES, AND INDIANS

A STRANGE LAND, WITHOUT TREES

THE FLAT AND TREELESS PRAIRIES OF THE ILLINOIS COUNTRY astonished the white men who came as explorers and returned as settlers some three centuries ago. They had seen nothing like this beautiful and fertile land in Europe, where civilization developed in a timbered environment, or on their way through the forests of eastern Canada. Not until they reached Illinois did they encounter, at their eastern edge, the great central grasslands that as prairies and plains extend to the Rocky Mountains.

This prairie land, far richer than anything known in Europe or in the previously explored portions of North America, obviously could support prosperous populations. "No better soil can be found, either for corn, for vines, or for any other fruit whatever," said Louis Jolliet after his discovery expedition.[1] To him the region appeared "to be the most beautiful and most easily settled." Here a man could provide his own food and clothing, and ground could be plowed the day of arrival, without laboring ten years to cut down and burn trees. Father Marquette's journal of

---

[1] Reuben G. Thwaites (ed.), *The Jesuit Relations*, LXIII, 105-109.

their explorations said that "we have seen nothing like this river (the Illinois) that we enter, as regards its fertility of soil, its prairies and woods."[2] The great promise of Illinois also impressed La Salle and the generations that followed.

Nowhere else could they look to the far horizon without seeing either tree or shrub, and an impulse to assume that the land was sterile obviously was erroneous. Only a fertile soil could produce the blue-stem prairie grass, tall and coarse bearded, often as high as a mounted horseman, that rippled a golden yellow in the late summer breeze. Massed on the prairie, giving a patchwork effect, were tall flowers of many colors, a vivid garden springing from a sod so matted and tough that for decades it protected much of the rich loam from the bite of the wood-and-iron plow.

"In summer the prairie is covered with a tall grass, which is coarse in appearance, and soon assumes a yellow color, waving in the wind like a crop of corn," wrote Captain Basil Hall, who saw Illinois in 1827 and 1828. "In the early stages of its growth the grass is interspersed with little flowers, the violet, the strawberry blossom, and others of the most delicate structure. When the grass grows higher these disappear, and taller flowers displaying more lively colors take their place; and still later a series of still higher but less delicately formed flowers appear on the surface. While the grass is green these beautiful plains are adorned with every imaginable variety of color. It is impossible to conceive of a greater diversity .... In the summer the plants grow taller, and the colors more lively; in the autumn another generation of flowers arises which possesses less clearness and variety of color and less fragrance."[3]

The prairies covered most of Illinois and at Chicago touched the shore of Lake Michigan for a few miles. The northern border ran a few miles back from the lake to the vicinity of Milwaukee and then turned northwestward on a generally straight line past St. Paul. Beyond that line was solid forest. In the other direction the edge of the prairie curved eastward to take in a slice of Indiana and then make a great dip into lower Illinois before swinging back to cross the Mississippi River near Rock Island. Beyond the prairie,

---

2 *Ibid.*, LIX, 139-141, 161.

3 *Travels in North America*, quoted by Joan Hunter, "Prairie Splendors Lost," *Living Museum* (Springfield: Illinois State Museum, May, 1968).

virgin timber stretched eastward to the Atlantic Ocean and south-ward to the Gulf of Mexico.[4]

Strips of forest bisected the grassland and formed multiple prairies. Dense stands of trees, mostly hardwoods, grew along the watercourses, projected fingerlike into the open spaces, and at times encircled a sizable area. In most of central and northern Illinois the treeless region seemed almost continuous and a Grand Prairie extended from the Chicago vicinity far into the east-central section. There a man could travel three hundred miles as he went into Wisconsin and not encounter more than five miles of timber at a time. Jolliet gave this description: "There are prairies three, six, ten or twenty leagues in length, and three in width surrounded by forests of the same extent; beyond these the prairies begin again, so that there is as much of one sort of land as the other. Sometimes we saw grass very short, and, at other times, five or six feet high."

The timber, which originally covered about 42 percent of Illinois, was more extensive in the south. There prairies were small

[4] Walter P. Webb, *The Great Plains*, pp. 9, 29. *Grass*, U.S. Department of Agriculture Yearbook, 1948, pp. 20, 47-48, 651-652.

The Illinois prairie: the flowers and tall blue-stem grass of the original prairie, as shown by a diorama in the Illinois State Museum

Courtesy Illinois State Museum

enough to have individual names, such as "Looking Glass," and a man in whatever direction he gazed would almost certainly see trees. When he described Illinois in 1834, John Mason Peck wrote that the "prairies are comparatively small, varying in size from those of several miles in width, to those which contain only a few acres. As we go northward they widen and extend . . . from six to twelve miles in width. Their borders are by no means uniform. Long points of timber project into the prairies, and line the banks of streams . . . . In some cases there are copses of timber . . . like islands in an ocean."[5] Because of such patches of timber, the noun "grove" is part of the name of a number of Illinois communities. Some of the groves covered from one hundred to two thousand acres between Lake Michigan and the Sangamon River. In the generally flat terrain, the prairies varied in elevation and wetness. Soil scientists now question the original explanation that the prairies were the result of fires.[6] Fred Gerhard, who in 1857 wrote a guidebook for settlers, named and located 186 prairies, mostly in midstate.[7] Except for a few miscellaneous tracts, all have been turned over by the plow, which destroyed the colorful vegetation in the process of converting the native landscape into farms. The only survivor of consequence is the low-lying, eighteen-hundred-acre Goose Prairie in Grundy County. Originally it was a bit of the vast and untimbered Grand Prairie.

A screen of trees hid most of the prairie from explorers in canoes. Occasional bluffs and backwater flats provided variety. The major rivers had alluvial plains of great fertility, the most important of which acquired the name of the American Bottom. Frequently flooded, a breeding ground for malaria, it extended nearly one hundred miles along the east bank of the Mississippi, downstream from where the Missouri enters with its saturation of silt. On it the French would erect the strongest fort in the

[5] *A New Guide for Immigrants*, p. 264.

[6] Several theories have been advanced to explain the presence of the prairies. Fires could have been started by lightning and the Indians in their annual hunts burned the dry grass to stampede the wild game. Since only one year's growth was removed, a grass fire did less lasting damage than the burning of a tree. A possible explanation is that the dense root network of the perennial grass choked seedling trees. Other factors—temperature, wind, humidity, rainfall, and topography—may have played major roles in fixing the limits of the treeless area. Peter Farb, *Face of North America: The Natural History of a Continent*, pp. 206-210; Edith M. Poggi, *The Prairie Province of Illinois*, pp. 48, 67-70. See also J. E. Weaver, *North American Prairie*.

[7] *Illinois As It Is*, pp. 207-215.

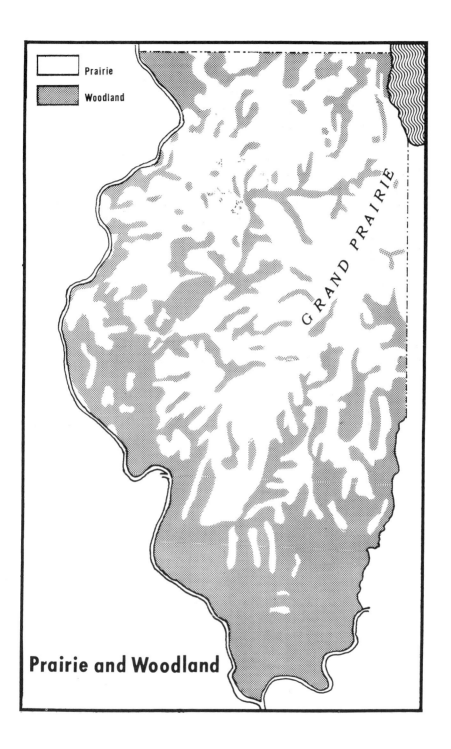

Prairie and Woodland

Prairie

Woodland

GRAND PRAIRIE

American interior. From it the first English-speaking settlers would spread word to the people back East about the value of Illinois land. The other rivers, chiefly the Wabash and the Illinois, had bottomlands of smaller extent, equal richness, and even more susceptibility to overflow.

The wild game of Illinois was more than adequate to feed the Indian tribes, and their food supply was supplemented by fish from the rivers and northeastern lakes. The last herds of buffalo, which the early French hoped to tame and use as oxen, would not be exterminated until after 1800, but deer, elk, and bears would be plentiful for years thereafter. The Illinois country also had foxes, raccoons, opossums, squirrels, and rabbits as game animals. Wild turkeys lived in the hills, and prairie chickens and quail were common. Flocks of wild pigeons obscured the sun, and masses of geese, ducks, herons, cranes, swans, and other birds congregated where there was water.

Life was not entirely a paradise. Some of the mosquito swarms carried malaria. The housefly did not exist in the wilderness, but hordes of stock flies swarmed from the woods and attacked animals until they bled. Because of them pioneer farmers often found it impossible to work in the heat of the day. Gnats and other insects pestered man and tormented animals. A traveler in 1842 reported that "in the middle of these large prairies is a perfect solitude, without a living thing, except such as one would rather want than have, viz., greenhead flies in thousands, snakes basking on the dusty track, and myriads of grasshoppers, some of them as large as the little finger, darting through the air like arrows, and sometimes coming full tilt against the face."[8]

The changeable weather, difficult to predict and at times violent, was an asset unappreciated in some seasons. The humid summers could be insufferably hot, and only a virile race, especially under the primitive conditions of early Illinois, could survive the winter's extreme cold and strong winds, with heavy snows followed by soaking rains. Tornadoes, whose destructiveness became more important as population and property holdings increased, were part of the frequently rapid weather changes. But in every season the unpleasant spells invariably gave way to longer periods of blue skies and sunny days, and the people of Illinois, then as now, found the temperate zone climate invigorating. The

[8] William Oliver, *Eight Months in Illinois*, p. 182.

growing season lasts from five to seven months and the continen-
tal-type climate provides seasonal changes in temperature and
lesser variations in precipitation. Droughts are infrequent, and
excessive rains fall only occasionally.[9] The climate, as well as the
natural resources and the location of Illinois, stimulated men to
develop farms and cities on its prairie soil.

THANK GOD FOR GLACIERS

   Geography and geology played important roles in the settlement and civilization of Illinois. The pioneers found the state
easily reachable over water and lake routes, and they recognized
that in Illinois, the center of an agricultural area that is richer than
any other region of comparable size elsewhere in the world, they
could better themselves. In some ways the land was inhospitable,
but because the soil possessed amazing fertility they came early
and remained to conquer the difficulties. Any explanation of why
Illinois is a great state must recognize the heritage of the glaciers.
   Fortunately, massive ice sheets invaded Illinois four times in its
comparatively recent geological history. Before that happened, the
land was hilly and the soil thinner, with better scenery but lower
productivity. A gradual change came as a result of prolonged cold
spells during which the summer sun didn't melt all of the winter
snow. The eventual result was the formation of glaciers. They
flattened the hills, filled in the valleys, and spread a deep and
intermixed layer of limestone and other rocks that had been
pulverized while being pushed slowly from central and eastern
Canada. In time the climate changed again and, when the glacial
ice melted, vast and shallow lakes and wide rivers were formed. In
the process they distributed a composite of the rock materials over
the low-lying regions. During the retreat of the last glacier, possibly fifteen thousand years ago, windstorms during a dry spell blew
a thick and fertile layer of topsoil, known as loess, over much of
the state. The pulverized rocks, both water-deposited and wind-
blown, became the present soil of Illinois as a result of centuries of

   [9] *Climate and Man,* U.S. Department of Agriculture Yearbook, 1941, pp. 841-851,
157-166. John L. Page, *Climate of Illinois,* University of Illinois Agricultural Experiment
Station *Bulletin,* No. 532 (Urbana, 1949). M. L. Fuller, "The Climate of Illinois: Its
Permanence," *Transactions of the Illinois State Historical Society,* XVII (1912), 54-62.
Poggi, *op. cit.,* pp. 11-16, 22-34, 48-56. Douglas C. Ridgley, *The Geography of Illinois,*
pp. 66-72, 85-91.

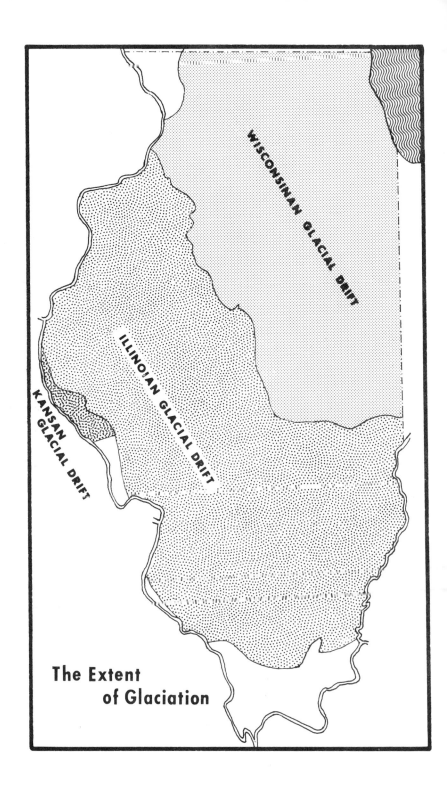

WISCONSINAN GLACIAL DRIFT

ILLINOIAN GLACIAL DRIFT

KANSAN GLACIAL DRIFT

The Extent
of Glaciation

weathering by rainfall, temperature changes, and other factors. Soil scientists have found that weathered glacial drift, whether loessial or alluvial, contains more soluble mineral matter, including valuable plant foods, than weathered bedrock. Fortunately the glacial deposits are comparatively young and level, and to date have lost little of their plant food from leaching. As a result, it is not coincidental that the midwestern corn belt, which has most of the best-producing land in the United States, corresponds with the area of recent glaciation.[10]

In the four periods of glaciation, approximately 90 percent of Illinois was covered by at least one ice sheet. The third, which was the most important and appropriately is known as the Illinoisan period, reached the state from one hundred to a hundred and fifty thousand years ago and pushed as far southward as Carbondale and Harrisburg, further than any other North American glacier. The deposits of the earlier Kansan and Nebraskan periods were obliterated by the Illinoian glacier, the only exception being that in the Quincy area some of the Kansan drift is still on the surface of the land. The most recent glacial period, the Wisconsinan, occurred from fifty to fifteen thousand years ago, which is quite recent by the geological measure of time. The Wisconsinan glacier covered most of the northern and eastern parts of the state but stopped at Peoria and Mattoon. Together the last two glaciers contributed the flat terrain and deep soil that give Illinois its agricultural eminence.[11]

The glaciated area ends in the southern portions of Jackson, Williamson, Saline, and Gallatin counties. Below that line is a spur of the Ozark Highland, with some good scenery and rough land adapted to fruit growing. Oddly the glaciers detoured the far northwestern corner, which left Galena with round knobs and lead deposits. Traces of the earliest glaciers have been eroded away at Calhoun County, the confluence of the Mississippi and Illinois rivers. In geological terms, those three regions are driftless areas, without the surface layer of finely pulverized rock material that was transported by ice and left behind when it melted. Elsewhere

[10] Poggi, op. cit., p. 48. Paul W. Gates, The Farmer's Age, pp. 179-180. Fred A. Shannon, The Farmer's Last Frontier, pp. 3-11. Climate and Man, op. cit., pp. 265-280.

[11] Guide to the Geologic Map of Illinois, Illinois State Geological Survey. Ridgley, op. cit., pp. 25-36. Soil, U.S. Department of Agriculture Yearbook, 1957, pp. 535-570. For a popular explanation of the geography of the far southern counties, see Baker Brownell, The Other Illinois, pp. 36-53.

the monotony of the level land is broken by moraines, shallow valleys, and some rough land where gullies portend serious erosion problems in future geological epochs. Modern Illinois can be thankful that the glaciers were here comparatively recently and that there hasn't been time for erosive forces to wash away the unleached topsoil.

Beneath the surface, the ancient sedimentary rock layers, mostly sandstone and limestone, also are relatively flat or only gently warped. Fortunately they contain multiple layers of valuable minerals. Mineable beds of bituminous coal, usually contaminated with sulphur and in some places fifteen feet thick, underlie about two-thirds of the state, which has the nation's largest coal reserves. The earliest extractive industries were the evaporation of salt brine near Shawneetown and the smelting of lead ore around Galena. Oil and gas later came into production. Fluorspar and tripoli mining attained localized importance. Small amounts of silver and iron ore were found, but not enough to aid appreciably in the development of the state. Of greater importance are sand and gravel, stone, cement, and clay, found in glacial deposits and deeper strata. They provide the raw materials for such prosaic but essential materials as bricks and concrete for buildings and pavement, tile for drainage, and limestone for soil improvement.[12]

VANISHED CIVILIZATIONS

At least ten thousand years ago, which was fairly soon after the last glacier retreated northward, prehistoric man reached the fortunate area that was destined to become known as Illinois. Occasional and scattered spear points of unique shape have been found within the borders of the present state and identified by archaeologists as the property of the first arrivals. Their Eurasian ancestors had crossed from Siberia to Alaska over a land bridge that appeared when a large portion of the world's supply of water was locked up in the ice sheets.[13] Known as Paleo-Indians, they spread through the Americans, living on edible plants and the mastodonic animals they pursued.

[12] The State Geological Survey's Educational Series of booklets combines popular reading with scholarship in *Guide to Rocks and Minerals of Illinois*, No. 5 (1959), and *History of Illinois Mineral Deposits*, No. 7 (1961).

[13] Peter Farb, *Man's Rise to Civilization*, pp. 191-221.

Climate, animal life, and vegetation underwent slow but drastic changes and as the centuries passed the descendants of the original Illinoisans became intermixed with new arrivals. The extermination of the long-haired bison and other mammoth animals forced the adoption of new techniques, and by necessity the early men changed their food supply to smaller animals and plants. Less nomadic, the so-called Archaic hunters invented a spear-thrower and snares, learned how to weave baskets, and used stones for grinding seeds. Evidence of their culture is found in many places along the prairie streams. Generation after generation they returned to a camp site under an overhanging rock ledge that overlooks the Mississippi River in Randolph County and is known as the Modoc Rock Shelter. There projectile points and other possessions became buried in debris and thus were preserved. [14] The careful sifting of the debris has helped archaeologists piece together the story of the unwritten past.

After 2,000 B.C., a new period opened with the advent of ceramics, the cultivation of plants, and the establishment of villages.[15] A millennium later, the first pottery appeared in Illinois during what is known as the Woodland phase. There is evidence that in an Eastern Woodland period the Indians in Illinois and eastward lived in villages of complex structure and achieved an intricate social system that included elaborate religious burials. The rich soil and invigorating climate of the midcontinent in time enabled them to acquire comparative wealth and some leisure. Meanwhile the rivers made Illinois a crossroad for trade routes and a meeting place for aboriginal cultures.

The fluctuating progress of mankind's struggle toward a better life reached one of its peaks between 500 B.C. and A.D. 500, when skilled craftsmen practiced a limited agriculture and buried their dead in mounds in the Illinois River valley and along other

[14] The Modoc site, where University of Chicago students first dug in 1932, is a comparatively new discovery. The approximate date of the eras in which campfires were lit and villages occupied is scientifically determined by a radioactive dating process. Accounts of archaeological discoveries in Illinois are found in Joseph R. Caldwell, *New Roads to Yesterday;* Thorne Deuel, *American Indian Ways of Life;* Fay-Cooper Cole and Thorne Deuel, *Rediscovering Illinois;* and Elaine A. Bluhm (ed.), *Illinois Archaeology.* For a more popular account, see Virginia S. Eifert, *Of Men and Rivers,* pp. 1-19.

Remains of Archaic camps have been located elsewhere in Illinois. One of the newest and most important is the Koster site near Kampsville.

[15] Charles R. DeBusk, "Dickson Mounds Prehistory," *The Explorer,* XI, No. 2 (1969).

streams. Known to scientists as Hopewellians, they also had major centers of development in Ohio and elsewhere. For reasons that are not fully understood, that culture faded away just as other civilizations have disappeared. The next layer of abandoned artifacts showed that the Hopewellians were followed by a people who had developed the bow and arrow but whose pottery had fewer aesthetic touches.

Spectacular mounds in Fulton County and outside East St. Louis were the work of a culture, now called Middle Mississippian, that by A.D. 900 flourished along the Illinois, Mississippi, Ohio, Wabash, and Tennessee rivers. Those people, who were the antecedents of southern Indian tribes, raised grain, traded with men from far regions, and built giant earthen mounds atop which they placed temples and the houses of their priests. Many of the mounds survive and some are owned by the state. Monks' Mound, near Cahokia, is the largest prehistoric earthwork on the North American continent. It covers seventeen acres and is 100 feet high, 710 feet wide, and 1,080 feet long. Around it clustered eighty-four other mounds, evidence that large numbers of people lived there for extended periods. Only a culture that relied on the growing of plants for food could support the large and comparatively permanent towns of which traces are found there and elsewhere in central and southern Illinois.[16]

For many of the hundred centuries of Illinois archaeology, men lived in scenic places along the Illinois River, and a state museum marks a major burial ground at Dickson Mounds. A string of towns, possibly satellites of Cahokia, extended up the Illinois valley. The Middle Mississippians built other mounds which seem less important or have been torn apart by the impatient bulldozer of the current civilization. Scientific digging at mound and village sites has been fairly widespread in Illinois in recent years. All of them testify that Illinois long has been populated by a succession of peoples.

About the time that Columbus discovered America, the Middle Mississippian culture came to an end for reasons that are not clear (it could have been the result of diseases imported from Europe). When the French began the recorded history of the upper Missis-

---

[16] For a short explanation of the evolution of prehistoric Indian cultures, the prize goes to a political scientist, David Kenney, *Basic Illinois Government, A Systematic Explanation*, pp. 2-13.

sippi valley, a different and less sophisticated Indian civilization hunted the game and fished the waters of Illinois.

LONG RIVERS AND SHORT PORTAGES

Buffalo trails became the first prairie roads, but for Illinois a greater asset was the network of bordering and interior rivers within easy reach of Lake Michigan. The rivers and the lake made it easy to explore the low-lying region and to return to develop it. For more than a century the waterways were the arteries of white commerce, as they had been for the Indians in the previous ages.

For commercial purposes the midcontinental location of Illinois was incomparable. The land was low and several river routes, all

Monks' Mound: largest prehistoric earthwork on the North American continent, from a model constructed by the Illinois State Museum
Courtesy Illinois State Museum

bordering or crossing the future state, almost reached streams that flowed into the Great Lakes. They made portaging easy for the early arrivals. Equally important, there were no physical barriers that had to be bypassed when it came time for railroad and highway construction. The blue lake would provide Chicago with more than a beautiful setting. It successively became the thoroughfare used by canoes, sailing vessels, steamers, and eventually the giant freighters that brought iron ore to steel mills that depended upon nearby coal fields. In the development of Illinois, Lake Michigan probably has been more important than the rivers.

The lake had convenient harbors at the shallow Chicago and Calumet rivers. The great Mississippi, flowing down the western border, was almost free of rapids, and the Ohio and Wabash rivers served as major transportation arteries on the south and part of the east sides. Tributary rivers, chiefly the broad Illinois, could be navigated by sizable boats. The Illinois, which angled in an almost straight line between the future cities of Chicago and St. Louis, was a union of smaller streams, the Des Plaines and the Kankakee, which played roles in history far exceeding their size. With great foresight after his one trip into Illinois, Jolliet pointed out that a short canal at the Chicago portage would enable a ship to go from the Great Lakes to the Gulf of Mexico.

The adventuresome French adopted the Indian's birchbark canoe, fabricated of forest materials and having the great advantage of being light enough for a man to carry on his back. As a result, travel routes were by water, on lakes that might be treacherous in storms and along meandering streams that might have dangerous rapids. Where the current was swift, the *voyageur* would jump waist deep into icy water to push his craft upstream. Around the big obstacles, such as waterfalls or deep rapids, or from one river to the next, portaging was required and cargo as well as craft had to be carried. Fortunately, rivers in the Illinois country had fewer rapids than those in Canada and the portages were shorter, requiring less labor. And there was a choice of routes.

One was the strategic portage between the Chicago and Des Plaines rivers.[17] In the spring floods it was a muddy lake flowing in both directions and a boat need not be unloaded. In dry seasons

---

[17] John Moses, *Illinois Historical and Statistical*, I, 77-79. Clarence W. Alvord, *The Illinois Country, 1673-1818*, pp. 4-8. Edward F. Dunne, *Illinois, the Heart of the Nation*, I, 2.

the land distance might not be more than four miles, but the Des Plaines was a difficult stream in the late summer and autumn, when French travelers might be forced to make as many as ten portages after reaching it. A few miles to the south the Calumet River afforded a short portage to the Des Plaines. The *voyageurs* had two choices—the Calumet River, which enters the lake in the present steel mill district on Chicago's south side, or the Little Calumet, the mouth of which is a dozen miles further east, in what is now Gary, Indiana. They joined south of Lake Calumet and almost reached the Des Plaines. In some early travel accounts it is impossible to know whether mention of the Chicago portage really meant the Calumet.[18]

Only one good travel route crossed Wisconsin, which appropriately has a city named Portage. It started at Green Bay, followed the Fox River to a short portage leading to the Wisconsin River, and reached the Mississippi at Prairie du Chien.

The long way around often was the fastest and most convenient in the wilderness. Many explorers preferred to reach the Illinois by leaving Lake Michigan at what is now Benton Harbor, Michigan, and following the St. Joseph River to an easy portage near the Notre Dame campus at South Bend, Indiana. The rest of the trip was down the Kankakee River to the Illinois.

Later in the French period the Maumee River, which enters Lake Erie at Toledo, Ohio, had extensive use because it detoured Lakes Michigan and Huron. In central Indiana, portages could be made at several places in the upper reaches of the Wabash River. It was so busy during the Revolutionary War that the Chicago River had little traffic. By that time the Mississippi River was extensively used to and from the Gulf of Mexico. The upstream trip against the strong current could require from two to four months. Lesser rivers, such as the Kaskaskia, the Rock, and the Muddy, served as avenues to the interior.

Since the midcontinental rivers required a minimum of portaging and heavy loads had to be transported long distances, the canoe gave way to larger craft. The pirogue or dugout essentially was the trunk of a tree, usually sycamore or cottonwood, often

---

[18] Robert Knight and Lucius H. Zeuch, *The Location of the Chicago Portage in the Seventeenth Century.* Support for the belief that major use was made of the Calumet River portage, rather than the Chicago, is given by Henry W. Lee, "The Calumet Portage," *Transactions of the Illinois State Historical Society,* XVII (1912), 24-43.

forty feet or more long, which had been hollowed by fire or an adz. To increase capacity, they could be split lengthwise and fastened together by planks. The bateau, built of planks, was flat-bottomed and sharp-ended. A large bateau could carry forty tons of cargo and needed a crew of eighteen or twenty to propel it with oars or poles. A keelboat, long and narrow, had a plank nailed the length of the bottom to make steering easier. At times upstream propulsion was by sail or by pulling on a rope. Those were the commercial boats, designed to travel against the current as well as to float downstream. When settlers made one-way trips down such rivers as the Ohio, they used cumbersome rectangular craft of light draft, known variously by such names as rafts, flatboats, arks, barks, skiffs, and Kentucky boats.[19]

In its early years Illinois was a wetter state than it is today. Streams ran more slowly and at higher levels, while numerous ponds and sloughs held back the runoff. Especially in the wet seasons, the early boats navigated streams which, as a result of changes in drainage patterns, now carry little water.

INDIANS: THE ILINIWEK VERSUS THE IROQUOIS

The Illinois or Iliniwek Indians were not at all displeased when the white men arrived in their midst. Formerly important, worthy of emulation by a university football team, they had recently been demoted to minor league status and were glad to live near a trading post or mission for whatever protection it afforded. Like most of the other Algonquian tribes spread through Canada and down the Atlantic seaboard, the Illinois had been having trouble with the Iroquois confederation of five eastern tribes. Based in the Mohawk valley of New York, the Iroquois controlled everything around the Great Lakes and looked for more beaver-trapping grounds to dominate. They were aggressive, intelligent, far-ranging, and efficient in the woodland pastime of ambush and scalping. Their flintlocks and rum came from Albany, first from the Dutch and then from the British, and they insisted upon being middlemen in the profitable fur trade.[20]

[19] Alvord, op. cit., pp. 212-215. For a treatise on types of river craft in the presteamboat era, see R. C. Buley, The Old Northwest, I, 411-444.

[20] The best on-the-scenes description of the Illinois Indians is the so-called DeGannes Memoir, which Milo M. Quaife believes was written in 1702 by Pierre Liette, a nephew or cousin of Henri de Tonti. As Tonti's successor, Liette spent several decades in the

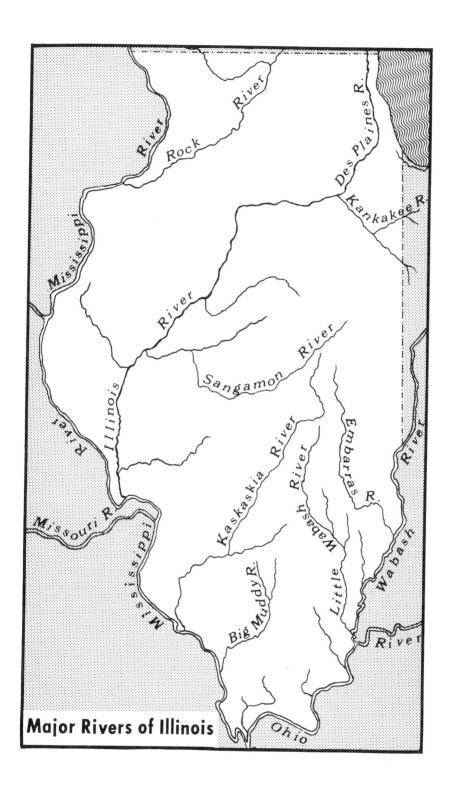

River

Rock

River

Des Plaines R.

Kankakee R.

Mississippi

River

Sangamon River

Illinois

River

Kaskaskia River

Embarras R.

River

Wabash River

Missouri R.

Mississippi

Big Muddy R.

Wabash

Little

River

River

Ohio

Major Rivers of Illinois

The raw power of the Iroquois delayed for decades the exploration and settlement of the region west of the Allegheny Mountains and between the Ohio River and the Great Lakes. To avoid the Iroquois, the original French route westward from Quebec did not use Lakes Ontario and Erie, but kept to the north to follow the Ottawa River toward Lake Nipissing and Georgian Bay. A lot of portaging was required, but most of the time it was safer. Had the Iroquois been tamer, the English might have had the honor of discovering Illinois. As it was, the French did it by making an end run through Canada.

Among the primitive and seminomadic northern Indians, the Iliniwek once had been the equivalent of the country club set. They had been the largest tribe in the Illinois valley region and gave their name not only to the state and the river but to the Lake of the Illinois, the original name of Lake Michigan. A loose and not always cooperative confederation of the Kaskaskia, Cahokia, Tamaroa, Peoria, Michigamea, Moingwena, and several lesser bands, the Illinois lived in towns and constructed mat-covered huts in which six to twelve families might live. All year around, the chief food was maize or Indian corn, but the squaws also cultivated beans, squash, and other vegetables. Breaking the sod was hard work, even for an Indian woman, and only in an emergency would a band move from an established corn field. Twice a year, after the spring planting and in the winter, they migrated as far as one hundred miles to a hunting ground where game abounded. The buffalo meat they smoked and other possessions had to be back-packed, for the dog was the only domesticated animal of the Iliniwek. One missionary described them as handsome, tall, strong, brave, fast, proud, and affable. They also were called idle, revengeful, jealous, dissolute, and thievish. Perhaps all the adjectives were applicable not only to the Illinois but to neighboring tribes.

Warfare, sometimes desultory but often on a large scale, was their natural activity. To prove his manhood, a young brave

upper Mississippi valley. See Quaife's introduction to *The Western Country in the 17th Century*, which contains the *DeGannes Memoir* attributed to Liette. It also can be found, as a document of uncertain authorship, in Louise Phelps Kellogg, *Early Narratives of the Northwest* and *The French Foundations*, edited by Theodore C. Pease and Raymond C. Werner. Another account of Illinois Indians is J. Joe Bauxar, "The Historic Period," *Illinois Archaeology*, a 1959 publication of the Illinois Archaeological Society. See also Alvord, *op. cit.*, pp. 21-55; Moses, *op. cit.*, I, 36-51; Davidson-Stuvé, *A Complete History of Illinois*, pp. 30-52; and Hiram W. Beckwith, *The Illinois and Indiana Indians*. A chapter on the Iroquois is part of Farb, *op. cit.*, pp. 95-111.

needed to go on the warpath in search of a scalp or a captive. Whether alone or with a large party, any foray constituted aggression and invited retaliation. Among Indians, peace and quiet could only be temporary.

In their bow-and-arrow and stone pottery civilization they had been self-sufficient, but with the arrival of the French they made a quick jump from the stone age to the use of gunpowder and iron. The fur traders created a demand for weapons, metal kettles, blankets, and cloth, in addition to trinkets, beads, mirrors, and brandy. These became necessities, and to pay for them the Indian became a professional trapper of beaver and other animals. In a vicious circle, the Indians had to get their supplies from somewhere and the white men had to give them presents to keep them from taking their pelts elsewhere. The gifts could be trinkets, but the red man knew what he wanted most. He would travel far for English rum, which was cheaper, if he could not get French brandy, which was weaker. To alcohol they had no inherited resistance and the result, in the complaint of the Jesuit fathers, was debauchery. With equal misfortune, the white man also spread measles, smallpox, and tuberculosis, which helped to decimate the native peoples. Throughout North America, the arrival of Europeans was consistently followed by a decrease in the Indian population.

The Iroquois invaded the Great Lakes region after 1570 and the Illinois country about 1655 for an economic reason, because the fur supply of the Mohawk valley had been depleted. As fighters and traders they consistently bested the Algonquian tribes. Occasionally the Illinois could wipe out a war party of Iroquois, but generally the tide of battle favored the better-armed invaders. As a result of invasion, disease, and alcohol, the Iliniwek became less and less important. Despite these weaknesses, they occasionally turned Indian style against their white benefactors and at the same time showed a fatal penchant for disunity when the occasion called for strong and decisive action against red enemies.

By the time the Indians realized that the white man was the ruination of the hunting grounds, it was too late. Pontiac and Tecumseh found this out later when they tried to mount multitribal offensives and drive the settlers back across the eastern mountains. By 1832, before the last land cession treaty was signed, the once great Illinois confederacy had dwindled to a little more than one hundred persons who were ejected from their

Courtesy Illinois State Museum

Middle Mississippian burials at Dickson Mounds

homeland and herded to a Kansas reservation.[21] No identifiable descendant of an Illinois tribe is now alive. When the last one died no one knows.

THE NAME ILLINOIS

The Illinois country never had clearly defined boundaries during the periods of French and British occupation. Its name came from the Illinois or Illiniwek Indians, and as a region it referred to the area they occupied when the white men arrived. Generally it was the Illinois River valley and the territory northward and southward, extending into present-day Wisconsin. Later, when Fort de

[21] Grant Foreman, *The Last Trek of the Indians,* pp. 201-206. Frederick W. Hodge, *Handbook of American Indians North of Mexico,* I, 598, 662, and II, 228, 240, 925. Wayne C. Temple, *Indian Villages of the Illinois Country,* pp. 55-56. Charles C. Royce, *Indian Land Cessions in the United States,* pp. 742-745, 794-795, 842-849.

Chartres was the seat of government for the upper Mississippi valley, the Illinois country was understood to mean the areas of French influence, including parts of the Ohio and Missouri rivers. What was back of the rivers was not well known and hence not important. Under French grammar, the definite article was used in referring to the Illinois country or just to the Illinois. As a single noun place name, Illinois came after the Revolution when it was time to fix definite boundaries.

In the Indian tongue, Iliniwek meant "the men." The French dropped the last two syllables and substituted their own ending. That gave the state its name. It is the only major inheritance from either the Indians or the French.

The Chicago River got its name from an Indian word of various spellings and definitions. Its origin has been disputed by several writers without anyone getting a clear decision. Milo M. Quaife, who was one of the better midwestern historians, believes that Chicago (he spelled it Checagou) was an adjective signifying great or powerful, the equivalent of grand in the French language. [22] Others insisted the name was derived from the Indian word for an onionlike plant that grew along the river.

Most of the geographical features and towns of Illinois were named by English-speaking men who came from the southeast and east. That may be a reason why the state does not have more place names of French and Indian origin or has Anglicized them. Consider one of the major downstate cities: Louis Jolliet, who discovered the state, spelled his name with two l's. The city in Will County was named Juliet until 1845, when by act of the legislature it was changed to Joliet. Juliet Campbell's father founded the town, but the next generation decided to honor the Canadian explorer's memory.[23]

[22] See also Mrs. John H. Kinzie, *Wau-Bun* (1932 Lakeside Press edition), p. 219.

[23] William E. Keller, *Illinois Place Names*, p. 404.

2

THE FRENCH AND THE BRITISH

THE SEVENTEENTH-CENTURY FRENCH POSSESSED A SPECTAC-
ular talent for exploring the northern wilderness and striking up
profitable friendships with strange Indian tribes. Before the Pil-
grims landed at Plymouth Rock, they had settled at Quebec,
pushed westward as far as Georgian Bay, and opened a trade in the
furs of beaver and other animals whose pelts were in demand in
Europe. The French, like other explorers, dreamed of a Northwest
Passage to the Orient, but North American ventures cost a lot of
money, European wars demanded first attention, and the Iroquois
already were their enemies. As a result, they lacked the resources
for prompt exploitation of their early discoveries. The French first
took possession of the midcontinent, but their colonists were thin
in numbers, inadequately supported from Versailles, and subjected
to an often erratic colonial policy. Under those circumstances,
failure was foreordained.

In the four decades preceding the discovery of the Illinois
country, occasional Frenchmen roamed westward. By 1622 Etienne Brulé, an emissary of Samuel de Champlain, reached Lake
Superior. Twelve years later Jean Nicolet journeyed through the
Straits of Mackinac into Lake Michigan and Green Bay. Because he
hoped to find a trade route to Asia and wanted to be properly
costumed for audiences with oriental potentates, he took along a
damask robe ornamented with birds and flowers. Nicolet's disappointing exploration was followed by a generation of official

neglect, but Jesuits and fur traders kept pushing westward. Father Claude Allouez found pure copper specimens near a mission he established in 1665 not far from the present city of Ashland, Wisconsin. That encouraged King Louis XIV's advisers to decide that the possessions across the seas should be developed commercially, along paternalistic and monopolistic lines. In 1663 they had made New France a royal colony and sent reinforcements in manpower. Jean Baptiste Colbert, the king's finance minister, wanted emphasis placed on the protection of the St. Lawrence settlements, and he sought to restrict the fur traders by ordering that the Indians be required to bring their pelts to Montreal. That decision did not forbid explorations, since France hoped that a westward passage could be located and that precious metals could replenish the national treasury.[1]

Three classes of Frenchmen, each with its own motive, braved the hardships and perils of life among the Indians. The explorers, imbued with loyalty to their king and country, often were accompanied and sometimes preceded by missionaries. The black-robed priests, dedicated to carrying out the will of God, dismissed all thought of bodily comfort and attempted to convert the red men. Ascetic in their heroism, they risked torture at the hands of the people they were trying to help. The explorers and missionaries made written reports of their adventures in new lands where, for all we know, they may have been preceded by the far-ranging and often illiterate fur trader. Possibly the first white man to beach his canoe on Illinois soil was some lonely *coureur de bois* who was interested only in bargaining for a cargo of pelts and who had no thought of leaving posterity a record of his travels. Picturesque and hardy, the French traders were more willing to accept the Indians as equals than the independent English and the gold-hungry Spanish. The *coureurs de bois* wintered in the villages of the Indians, married their women, and occupied only a small

---

[1] Fuller treatment of the French explorations that reached Lake Superior can be found in Willis F. Dunbar, *Michigan: A History of the Wolverine State*, and Reuben G. Thwaites, *France in America, 1497-1763*.

Because of a proclamation by Columbus, for two centuries Spain technically claimed title to the entire Mississippi valley. Hernando de Soto, who hoped to repeat Spain's conquest of Mexico and Peru, discovered the lower Mississippi River in 1541 on a journey from Florida into Arkansas and Oklahoma. However, no Spanish explorer penetrated as far north as the confluence of the Mississippi and Ohio rivers and the flag of Spain never flew over Illinois soil. Timothy Severin, *Explorers of the Mississippi*, pp. 14-72.

Courtesy Illinois State Historical Library

Father Jacques Marquette

portion of their land. Had the government followed a more consistent policy of encouraging the traders, France might have had a
firmer grip on the wilderness when the English penetrated the
Alleghenies.[2]

DISCOVERY: JOLLIET AND MARQUETTE, 1673-1675

In a dramatic pageant in the wilderness, attended by nineteen
white men and Indians from fourteen widely spaced tribes, the

[2] The statement that it was easier for a Frenchman to learn to live like an Indian than
for an Indian to live like a Frenchman was credited to a nun in Quebec in 1668. Arthur
C. Boggess, *Settlement of Illinois*, p. 11.

French officially claimed title to the yet undiscovered Illinois country June 14, 1671. The scene was a Chippewa village at Sault Ste. Marie, the navigation center connecting the St. Lawrence valley with inland waters. Father Allouez, one of the four Jesuit priests at the civil and religious ceremony, orated about the greatness of Louis XIV. The sieur de St. Lusson, who ranked next to the governor and the bishop in the officialdom of New France, then claimed for his king and country the vast and unknown interior of the continent, with all its countries, rivers, and lakes, discovered and undiscovered. While the Indians watched uncomprehendingly, he displayed the fleur-de-lis and three times warned against trespassing.

The real significance of the Sault Ste. Marie ceremony came in the small talk with the Indians, who told of a great river some distance to the south. Details were vague, but possibly it flowed into the Pacific Ocean. The report stirred the persistent hope that somewhere a trade route would permit silks and spices to be transported through the wilderness by canoe and portage if not by a continuous journey.

An expedition was organized to search for the river. Placed in charge was Louis Jolliet, a young Canadian who had studied in France, had abandoned an ecclesiastical career for a life in the woods, and had been at St. Lusson's gathering. Jolliet was an expert map maker, he had traveled the Great Lakes, and he knew how to get along with the Indians. Obviously he was an ideal choice to lead the search for a westward-flowing river.[3]

Father Jacques Marquette, one of the Jesuit priests whose gentle spirit was resigned to any trouble he might encounter on

[3] The standard work on events leading to Illinois statehood is Clarence W. Alvord, *The Illinois Country, 1673-1818.* The writings of the French missionaries and explorers have been translated and compiled by Reuben G. Thwaites, *The Jesuit Relations.* They were condensed in one volume by Edna Kenton, *The Jesuit Relations and Allied Documents,* with the Sault Ste. Marie ceremony starting on page 326 and Marquette's story completed on page 387. See Paul M Angle, *Prairie State: Impressions of Illinois,* pp 8-12, for Marquette and Jolliet excerpts. For modern accounts of the Jolliet-Marquette expedition, see Severin, *op. cit.,* pp. 73-102, and Virginia S. Eifert, *Louis Jolliet, Explorer of Rivers.*

Full accounts of the French period are contained in John Moses, *Illinois Historical and Statistical,* I, 52-122, and Alexander Davidson and Bernard Stuvé, *A Complete History of Illinois,* pp. 53-137. See also Edward G. Mason, *Chapters from Illinois History,* pp. 1-191; Jean Delanglez, *Life and Voyages of Louis Jolliet, 1645-1700;* Francis B. Steck, *The Jolliet-Marquette Expedition, 1673;* Joseph P. Donnelly, *Jacques Marquette, S.J., 1637-1675;* Raphael N. Hamilton, *Marquette's Explorations: The Narratives Re-examined;* and Bernard De Voto, *The Course of Empire,* pp. 83-156.

earth, arrived from France in 1666 and promptly went into the wilderness to evangelize the savages. After abandoning a mission on Lake Superior, he carried on religious work at St. Ignace, on the north shore of the Mackinac Straits, where some Illinois tribes traded. Marquette, an expert in speaking Algonquian tongues, considered them to be gentle and polite. He wanted to establish a mission among them, and he considered himself fortunate to be assigned to go along with Jolliet.

Jolliet was twenty-seven and Marquette thirty-five when they left St. Ignace May 17, 1673, with five boatmen and a supply of smoked meat and Indian corn in two birchbark canoes. Down Lake Michigan, into Green Bay, and up the Fox River of Wisconsin they had been preceded by other white men. The Indians showed them the portage to the Wisconsin River but warned them not to use it. The Frenchmen insisted on pushing ahead and on June 17 paddled into the broad Mississippi.

Probably three days later Jolliet's expedition saw the rugged hills of the northwestern corner of the present state of Illinois, and on that day the state's recorded history began. Jolliet and Marquette marveled as the scenery changed to a flatter terrain with fewer trees, with buffalo and deer on the river's banks. They floated down the western border of Illinois far enough past the mouth of the Ohio River to know that the great river empties into the Gulf of Mexico and hence is valueless as a route to the Orient. Then they turned back because hostile Spaniards might be ahead. Marquette's journal tells of visiting an Indian village on the Iowa bank, of being frightened by the roar of water at the mouth of the Missouri River, of meeting Indians with firearms of European manufacture, and of going as far as the Arkansas River. Perhaps the strangest sight, some fifty feet up on a rocky bluff below the mouth of the Illinois River, was a multicolored pictograph, awesome to the Indians. Known later as the Piasa Bird, named for a local creek, it presumably was the thunderbird or storm spirit of the Iliniwek.[4]

_____

[4] Marquette described the Piasa Bird as being green, red, and black, with the face of a man, beard of a tiger, horns of a deer, and elongated tail of a fish. Later travelers gave conflicting descriptions of the pictograph, which apparently faded before the rock disintegrated, while the painting was reproduced and restored several times, not necessarily in the same place or with the same colors. Wayne C. Temple, *The Piasa Bird: Fact or Fiction?*, concluded only that whatever Marquette saw was "not the dragon-like figure which has come to be known as the Piasa Bird."

Louis Jolliet

On their return trip the Frenchmen crossed the future state of Illinois. Presumably on the advice of Indians they took the Illinois and Des Plaines rivers to Lake Michigan. On the way they stopped at a Peoria and Kaskaskia village of seventy-four cabins near the present city of Ottawa. Marquette received a friendly welcome and promised to return to establish a mission.

Marquette and Jolliet parted at the De Pere mission at the head of Green Bay. The priest was ill and stayed behind while his companion pushed ahead to Montreal. When almost home, at a place where he should have been traveling by cart, Jolliet lost his maps, records, and two men when his canoe capsized in a rapids. As a result, the only firsthand account of the discovery of Illinois is in Marquette's journal, which has vague details and questionable dates.[5] Presumably because he was on friendly terms with the currently out-of-favor Jesuits, Jolliet was denied permission to return to Illinois and establish a French colony. He did receive further honors as a result of eastern explorations that included a trip to Hudson Bay. Among his descendants were two archbishops.

Marquette convalesced at Green Bay until the autumn of 1674. Then he started for the Illinois to keep his promise to the Indians, but he was seriously ill and hemorrhaging on arrival at the Chicago portage. He spent the winter in a small hut, visited by *coureurs de bois* who already were crossing to the Des Plaines River. In the spring he went to the Kaskaskia village and founded the Mission of the Immaculate Conception of the Blessed Virgin. On Good Friday and Easter Sunday five hundred chiefs and elders sat in a circle while he preached to an assemblage of fifteen hundred savages. Seriously ill, Marquette soon started for St. Ignace, but life ended in the wilderness, as he had wished it to, for this most famous of missionary priests. He died May 18, 1675, on the east side of Lake Michigan, presumably near Ludington at the mouth of a river later named for him.

Because of his dramatic journey into the Illinois country, Marquette's name is better remembered than those of other priests who with equal zeal and fortitude faced hardships and death among the uncivilized tribes, also without thought of glory, riches, or self-advancement. Others toiled longer in filthy Indian villages with the constant knowledge that martyrdom by torture might be their release from earthly woes.

Marquette's place at the Kaskaskia mission was taken by Father Allouez, who in twenty-four years as a missionary was said to have baptized ten thousand Indians and instructed one hundred thousand in the Catholic faith. His successor was Father Jacques Gravier, whose long career ended when he was fatally shot by one

[5] The importance and obscurity of the Jolliet-Marquette expedition has resulted in intensified, research and some controversy, especially as to the authorship of the Marquette journal. Until 1928, with publication of Francis Borgia Steck's *The Jolliet-Marquette Expedition, 1673*, it had been assumed that the priest wrote it in the wilderness during his last illness. Steck was supported by Father Jean Delanglez, who contended in *Life and Voyages of Louis Jolliet, 1645-1700* that the journal actually was the work of Claude Dablon, the superior of the Jesuit missions in New France. Delanglez says that Dablon used oral information given him by Jolliet. That is disputed by a later Jesuit historian, Joseph P. Donnelly, who in *Jacques Marquette, S.J., 1637-1675,* argues that the priest was the author. See also Raphael N. Hamilton, *Marquette's Explorations: The Narratives Re-examined.*

of the Peoria tribesmen he was trying to befriend. An abbreviated honor roll must include Father Pierre Gibault, the "patriot-priest" of the Revolutionary War era, and Father Sebastien Meurin, the last of the Jesuits in early Illinois, who in the enfeeblement of old age served parishes on both sides of the Mississippi River. The Jesuits have records of thirty-two priests who served in the Illinois country.[6] By comparison, only a handful of Seminarian and Recollect missionaries reached the Illinois country during the period of French occupation.

EXPLORATION: LA SALLE AND TONTI, 1679-1690

Robert Cavelier, sieur de la Salle, a fabulous woodsman and international promoter, first envisioned the economic potential of the great Middle West. He roamed many rivers by canoe and had courage to strike out on foot through a strange wilderness. Tyrannical and arrogant, he could dominate the Indians, win the confidence of rulers, and borrow large sums from relatives and acquaintances. One of his greatest feats was to retain the loyalty of Henri de Tonti, an Italian soldier of fortune who had lost his right hand in a Mediterranean naval battle. The hand was replaced with a metal hook, an "iron hand" that made Tonti a man of distinction among the Indians. Together La Salle and Tonti started the settlement of the Illinois. Tonti continued the task after the ambitious and haughty La Salle, who has been called a man of magnificent failures, encountered his final tragedy.[7]

Born in 1643 in Rouen, France, of minor nobility, La Salle at twenty-three followed an older brother to Canada. There he farmed for two years, dreamed of going to China, and launched a career as an explorer. On his first trip, hunting for the Ohio River, he met Jolliet coming back from the Illinois. La Salle was an enemy of the puritanical Jesuits and a protégé and secret business partner of Count Frontenac, the able governor of Canada, who directed him to organize a company to develop the West, a

[6] Sister Mary Borgias Palm, *The Jesuit Missions in the Illinois Country, 1673-1763.*

[7] La Salle is the subject of a historical masterpiece, Francis Parkman's *La Salle and the Discovery of the Great West.* See also Severin, *op. cit.,* pp. 103-184, and De Voto, *op. cit.,* pp. 131-156. For a biography of his associate, Edmund R. Murphy, *Henry de Tonty: Fur Trader of the Mississippi,* is recommended. The narratives of La Salle, Tonti, Hennepin and others, including Marquette, are found in *Collections of the Illinois State Historical Library,* I, edited by H. W. Beckwith.

privilege that had been denied Jolliet. La Salle made two trips to France to get financial backing, obtained at usurious interest, and returned with Tonti. He had a land grant and a monopoly on the fur trade south of the lakes, and in return he promised to explore the lower Mississippi in search of valuable metals and a waterway to the western ocean.

From France La Salle brought anchors, rigging, and tools with which, within sound of Niagara Falls, he built the forty-five-ton *Griffon*, the first sailing vessel on the western lakes. He took it to Green Bay and ordered it back east with a crew of six and a fur cargo that would have ended his immediate money problems. The *Griffon* disappeared without a trace, leaving one of the great mysteries of the stormy lakes. Also lost was the equipment for a second ship planned for the fur trade on the rivers.

La Salle meanwhile made his first trip into the Illinois, leading fourteen men, including three Recollect monks of the Franciscan order, as he pioneered the St. Joseph-Kankakee river route in the dead of winter. At the site of Peoria, where the Illinois River was wide enough to be called a lake, in early 1680 he erected Fort Crèvecoeur.[8] It stood on a low knoll between two ravines two hundred feet from the east bank on a ridge that cannot now be exactly located. Rudely built of logs, with lodgings, a forge, and a magazine, it was the first building erected by white men in Illinois and the first fort built by the French in the West. From there La Salle sent Father Hennepin on an adventuresome and successful exploration of the upper Mississippi.

Worried about the *Griffon* and harassed by creditors who had seized his Canadian property, La Salle in late winter with an Indian guide and four white men started on foot for Fort Frontenac, which he owned, on the north shore of Lake Ontario. In enemy country, through ice, snow, and spring floods, they traveled an estimated one thousand miles in sixty-five arduous days. During his absence the men at Fort Crèvecoeur mutinied, plundering and destroying the three-month-old fort, which was never rebuilt. That misfortune demonstrated that, except for Tonti, La Salle never could rely on his subordinates.

Back he came for a second time, bringing twenty-five men,

8 Samuel Wilson, Jr., "Colonial Fortifications and Military Architecture in the Mississippi Valley," in *The French in the Mississippi Valley,* John Francis McDermott, ed., pp. 104-105.

including some artisans. They found that Iroquois war parties, stirred up by the British, had wiped out the Kaskaskia town, which had been enlarged since Marquette twice stopped there. By this time the Illinois tribesmen were definitely second-raters, unable to unite for their own protection and afraid to challenge the enemy.

Courtesy Illinois State Historical Library

La Salle

Tonti, who had been wounded in a dramatic confrontation with the Iroquois, rejoined La Salle. With twenty-five Frenchmen and eighteen eastern Indians, in the spring of 1682 they made the first journey to the mouth of the Mississippi. There at the climax of his career, La Salle on April 9 erected a column and in a loud voice

claimed possession for his king of all the region watered by the
Mississippi, from the Appalachians to the Rockies. He named it
Louisiana. He envisioned an ice-free port from which, without
interference from Canadian rivals, he could be governor and ex-
ploiter of a great French colony and conqueror of northern
Mexico at the head of an Indian army.

Returning upstream, La Salle built Fort St. Louis on Starved
Rock.[9] On three-quarters of an acre atop the sandstone promon-
tory, which rises 125 feet above the Illinois River, La Salle erected
a blockhouse, a storchouse, and a dwelling. The cliff could not be
scaled on three sides and, on the eastern slope, palisades and two
small cannon guarded the rocky path to the summit. Around the
rock La Salle gathered Indians, bands of Wea, Piankashaw, Shawnee, and Miami, as well as the Iliniwek, in a cluster of towns
having a total population of eighteen thousand. Fort St. Louis
would keep back the Iroquois while friendly natives brought in
their winter catch of furs. The first land patents in Illinois were
signed, a winter wheat crop flourished, and a small post was
established at the Chicago portage.

Prospects seemed bright for a combined military post and trade
center that might have insured permanent control of the West, had
France held resolutely to a policy of protection and development
of the fur trade. However, the vacillating government, which
generally favored the regulation of trading by restricting the issuance of permits, listened to the Jesuits at Versailles and Quebec
who complained continually that brandy sales made it difficult to
convert Indians. When a decision was reached that financial emphasis should be centered on the settlements along the St. Lawrence, Frontenac was replaced by a pro-Jesuit. The new governor
disliked La Salle and the monopoly, and he wished to pacify the
Iroquois. He sided with the Jesuits, canceled the monopoly,
encouraged the Iroquois, and sent in a replacement for La Salle.

Five years after his arrival, La Salle left Illinois for the last time.
He went directly to France and found himself a hero as the result

[9] The French knew it only as the Rock. Sometime in the next century, according to
Indian legend, a band from some Illinois tribe starved on the summit while under siege
by Potawatomi enemies. It could have been other Indians at another time, since the
French missionaries, whose letters and reports provide the most valuable source for
historical research, had gone down the river. For an account of Starved Rock as a
strategic point in the Fox War era, see Eaton G. Osman, *Starved Rock, A Historical
Sketch.*

of a book attributed to Hennepin. France, at war with Spain, needed a strong point on the Gulf of Mexico. La Salle, again displaying his genius as a promoter, promised that thousands of Indian allies could be assembled at the mouth of the Mississippi for an invasion of Mexico. He asked for two ships and got four. In 1684 he sailed from France with two hundred colonists and several girls who were attracted by the prospect of certain matrimony. They were bound for the mouth of the Mississippi, the longitude of which La Salle did not know. Incredibly, during quarrels with his ship captains, he missed it by four hundred miles and landed in what is now Texas. After some of his ships were sent back, the others became disabled. Four times La Salle conducted expeditions to the northeast looking for the Mississippi. On the fourth, in 1687, at the age of forty-three, he was shot and killed from ambush by his own men and left on the spot without burial. A few of his followers made their way to Starved Rock. The final act of the tragedy came two years later when Spaniards captured a handful who had survived at Matagorda Bay.

Tonti, who was more suave and less dictatorial than La Salle, was his equal as an explorer and in the oratorical ritual of Indian diplomacy. He took over La Salle's work and for fifteen years devoted himself to getting a handful of French homes established in the Illinois. He went down the Mississippi to search for La Salle and back again to hunt for his survivors. He went East with sixteen Frenchmen and two hundred Indians to assist in a war against the Iroquois. On his return he escorted settlers. He roamed far, going north of Lake Superior in the interest of the fur trade, and he established a post in Arkansas. The Jesuits, whom La Salle had not allowed to erect a chapel at the Starved Rock settlement, were his friends.

The timber and wildlife resources in the Starved Rock vicinity could not support the large Indian population assembled there by La Salle. Because their environment was being despoiled, the tribesmen scattered and Tonti was forced to abandon the fort. In the winter of 1691-92, he followed part of the Iliniwek some eighty miles downstream and built a larger Fort St. Louis at one of the favorite Kaskaskia wintering grounds, on the right bank of the Illinois River about a mile and a half above the outlet of Lake Peoria. The common name was Fort Pimitoui, after a local Indian village. It had eighteen hundred wooden pickets, two large houses for lodging and storage, and two other houses built of uprights for barracks. It became the second site of Marquette's mission. Indian towns sprang up nearby, and around the fort traders with squaw wives and half-breed children formed a French village.

At a time when they should have been concerned about British competition from the seaboard colonies, the French placed the stifling hand of governmental regulation on the fur traders. In 1696 they required that the distant Indians, now completely dependent upon the white men, bring their furs to the trading posts. As a concession to Tonti, he was permitted to receive two canoe loads of trade merchandise a year, but no more. In contrast to the French, who handicapped themselves with centralized administration, the British provided a classic demonstration of the free enterprise system. Their traders reached the fringes of the Illinois country and threatened to capture the Wabash valley trade. The generally licentious and often lawless *coureurs de bois* for years had lived in Indian villages and scorned the restraints imposed by their government. They began diverting business to the British, who paid more for beaver and charged less for goods. With

Starved Rock

Courtesy Illinois State Historical Library

Tonti's monopoly abolished, independent traders took over the collection of furs. Their cheating and high prices infuriated the Indians, but in the long run the French retained more of their goodwill than the British.

The British threat was countered by Pierre le Moyne, sieur de la Iberville, who had the unusual qualifications of being both a French naval officer and a Canadian-born Indian fighter. He located the mouth of the Mississippi and erected a fort at Biloxi in 1699. The French then had a long and thin line of settlement, in which there were many gaps, from the St. Lawrence to the Gulf of Mexico. Tonti received permission to go south and left a nephew in charge at Peoria. The grand strategy was to protect the interior with strong points, but Tonti was turned down when he offered to erect a fort and trading post just below the mouth of the Ohio. In the lower Mississippi region he gave valuable service as an explorer and Indian expert until 1704, when at the age of fifty-four he died of yellow fever at Mobile.

COLONIZATION: VILLAGES ALONG THE MISSISSIPPI, 1699-1763

Primarily because of pressure from the Fox Indians, the French shifted their weak hold on the Illinois country to a new and final location, the fertile flood plain on the east side of the Mississippi River. The Iliniwek were unstable and the Fox, their stronger enemies to the north, forced the Jesuits after four years to abandon the Mission of the Guardian Angel they had established at Chicago in 1696. For all practical purposes, that closed the portage there until after the Revolutionary War. The Kaskaskia left Pimitoui in 1700, and the traders and missionaries followed them down the river where another Catholic order had established a wilderness outpost.

With a reputation newly won in China, the Seminary of Foreign Missions obtained permission to work at the north end of the American Bottom. Indian villages nearby and along the rivers made the location excellent, and three Seminarian priests founded the Mission of the Holy Family there in March, 1699. By May they built a chapel and a house. Traders gathered and the settlement took the name of Cahokia.[10] It is the oldest settlement in

[10] Cahokia has lost its glamour and now is a workingman's suburb at the edge of the East St. Louis industrial district. The meandering Mississippi is a mile west of Cahokia's

the American interior. The Jesuits, however, claimed the prior and sole right to work among the Illinois tribes and they sent priests to erect a competing mission at Cahokia. In an atmosphere of ecclesiastical friendliness, the matter was sent overseas for arbitration. A commission of bishops ruled that the Seminarians could stay at Cahokia while the Jesuits attended the religious needs of the other Iliniwek tribes.

The Kaskaskia Indians meanwhile spent two and a half years at the future site of St. Louis, and the Jesuits followed them, leaving no one at Peoria to keep a historical record. Under Father Gabriel Marest, the priests again moved when the Indians went to the lower end of the American Bottom. A new settlement there took the name of Kaskaskia in 1703. For more than a century it was the commercial and cultural capital of Illinois, and it was the third site of Marquette's Mission of the Immaculate Conception. The buildings were on low ground, on a peninsula between the Mississippi and Kaskaskia rivers, and nearly two centuries later the Mississippi demonstrated that Father Marest had located unwisely. Floods in 1844 and 1881 broke the narrow tongue of land on which the town stood and, in cutting a new channel, wiped out the only town that was almost as old as Cahokia.[11]

At the new site, on some of the most fertile land in North America, gathered *coureurs de bois* who no longer could carry on a legal fur trade out of Montreal. Outpost villages slowly took form, the priests encouraged agriculture, and men who had traveled smaller rivers in birchbark canoes made pirogues out of tree trunks for trips down the Mississippi. By using the Wabash-Maumee river route, the Illinois settlements kept in contact with New France. Detroit, founded by Cadillac in 1701, became the closest market for the furs the French trapped during the winter months. Because of the Mississippi, however, the Illinois country became an economic dependency of New Orleans.

two priceless possessions, a restored courthouse dating to about 1737 and the Church of the Holy Family, built in 1799.

[11] Peripheral damage in the 1844 flood forced the removal of Randolph County's seat of government from Kaskaskia to Chester, which is safely located on a bluff. The next big flood in 1881 wiped out Kaskaskia. The Mississippi now flows in the old bed of the Kaskaskia, and on the Missouri side is Kaskaskia Island, a twenty-thousand-acre portion of Illinois. A state memorial on the island houses a 650-pound bell, the gift of King Louis XV to the colonists. It was found in the river after the Church of the Immaculate Conception was inundated. See *Illinois Guide and Gazetteer,* pp. 322-324, and John H. Burnham, "The Destruction of Kaskaskia by the Mississippi River," *Transactions of the Illinois State Historical Society,* XX (1914), 95-112.

Missing from the reports of missionaries and other early documents is any account of how and when the first white woman arrived in the Illinois country. Undoubtedly she came from Canada, through the Great Lakes and across the portages. Possibly she was a peasant, shipped from Europe at government expense because of a demand for wives in New France. Most of the French women in the Mississippi villages were Canadians, although some in later years sat in bateaux during the long journey from New Orleans. Household furnishings also came from Canada, as did the horned cattle and hogs owned by French families. There is a record that in 1700, when Tonti reached Biloxi with five canoe loads of furs, most of the nineteen men in his party were married and lived in Cahokia or along the river. Their wives could have been Indians, brought from a trapping ground where white men wintered.

The Europeans who encouraged settlement had strange ideas of the potential wealth of the future corn belt. Malaria forced abandonment of a buffalo hide tannery near the present site of Mound City.[12] Lead and copper samples were sent to Paris by men who hunted for more valuable metals. Antoine Crozat, a wealthy French merchant, was given a fifteen-year monopoly on trade that proved so disappointing that he was released from his contract after three years. One of the world's greatest frenzies of speculation was generated by John Law, a Scotsman, who was granted a twenty-five-year trade monopoly. His assignment was to liquidate the French national debt by exploiting Mississippi valley mines and by establishing cities in which one of the industries would be the weaving of cloth from buffalo wool. Farmers were expected to hitch buffaloes to plows.[13]

By 1717, during the short-lived Law regime, the Illinois, which had been a dependency of Canada, was placed under the government of Louisiana. In search of gold, Philippe Renault, the French director of mines, arrived in 1720 after stopping at Santo Domingo to purchase Negro slaves.[14] The financial bubbles burst, but thereafter the priests and even the less affluent villagers owned

[12] John Fortier and Donald Chaput, "A Historical Re-examination of Juchereau's Illinois Tannery," *Journal of the Illinois State Historical Society,* LXII (Winter, 1969), 385-406.

[13] Alvord, *op. cit.,* pp. 142-152.

[14] *Ibid.,* pp. 154-159, 205-209.

slaves, mostly black but some of them Indians captured from distant tribes. The descendants of the French chattels caused a legal problem that resulted in the existence of de facto slavery in Illinois until the Civil War.[15]

The Mississippi villages began to boom when New Orleans did. Fort de Chartres, fifteen miles upstream from Kaskaskia, in 1720 became the seat of military and civil power. Illogically located on the swampy bank of the Mississippi, it was destroyed by flood in seven years and then rebuilt of stone as the strongest military post away from the Atlantic seaboard. The fort typified the French strategy of passive defense. Its brass cannon never fired a shot to protect French honor and the garrison usually was limited to a few-score men. Their presence, however, helped keep the Indians in line and enabled the weak villages to survive at the far edge of imperial warfare, which was intercontinental in extent.[16]

Prairie du Rocher, a pastoral village named for the bluff behind it, about 1723 became the third most important French settlement. A small village developed outside the fort and another at St. Philippe. Across the Mississippi, a French settlement at Ste. Genevieve duplicated the Illinois mode of life. Here was the only concentration of population, although the French established Vincennes on the Wabash River and a post at Ouiatenon, near what is now Lafayette, Indiana, to guard the upper Wabash portages. For a time a fort but no village existed at Fort Massac, on the Ohio opposite the mouth of the Tennessee River. Far to the northwest, Detroit grew more rapidly. Clarence W. Alvord in his exhaustive study of the French period found that the white population at its peak was probably fifteen hundred to two thousand, including soldiers and temporary residents, and that the slaves, having been found to be economically unprofitable, may have numbered only five hundred to six hundred.[17]

[15] N. Dwight Harris, *The History of Negro Servitude in Illinois*, pp. 1-5.

[16] John F. Snyder, "Captain Jean Baptiste Saucier at Fort Chartres, 1751-1763," *Transactions of the Illinois State Historical Society*, XXVI (1919), 215-263. John Francis Snyder, *Selected Writings*, pp. 27-85. Samuel Wilson, Jr., *op. cit.*, p. 119. Snyder, "The Armament of Fort Chartres," *Transactions of the Illinois State Historical Society*, XI (1906), 219-231.

[17] Alvord, *op. cit.*, p. 202. The literature of the French period in Illinois is extensive. Professor Alvord, who in 1905 discovered the voluminous and supposedly lost 1720-1790 Kaskaskia records in the courthouse at Chester, is editor of *Kaskaskia Records, 1778-1790*. See "The Finding of the Kaskaskia Records," *Transactions of the Illinois State Historical Society*, XI (1906), 27-31. Alvord is also editor of *Cahokia*

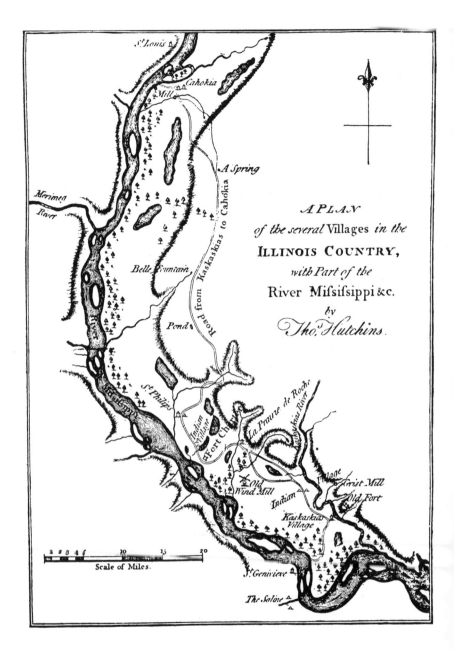

American Bottom

By habit and for protection, the French lived in compact villages. Narrow streets were lined with whitewashed one-story houses with wide verandas. Unlike the cabins of notched horizontal logs which became the standard first habitation on the frontier, the French homes were built of upright timbers, with horizontals only at the top and bottom and the interstices filled with a composition of clay and straw or moss.[18] These were the homes of the *habitants,* but the Mississippi villages also had an upper class of wealthy merchants who lived in better homes and imported some of their furniture. Each *habitant* farmed a narrow ribbon of land, running from the river to the bluff, and pastured his livestock in a common field.

Most men favored the romantic life of the trader or the hard work of the *voyageur.* Their largest boats could carry thirty tons of merchandise and were propelled sometimes by sail but mostly by oars, poles, or ropes on the upstream trip. The French accepted conditions as they found them and for guidance depended upon the priest and the notary when such authorities were present. They were cheerful, patient, and industrious at work, timid and unimaginative under attack, and given to dancing, gossiping, and gambling when at home. Efforts to build an empire were handicapped by the French tradition of centralized administration, and they never challenged the superiority of the men who came later from the English-speaking colonies.

Dr. John Francis Snyder, whose great grandfather designed Fort de Chartres, said that the native French on the American Bottom

> were, with few exceptions, non-progressive, indolent and generally illiterate, giving little thought to the problems of life beyond the gratification of present wants and comfort, trusting the future to Providence and the priest—the priests especially, who were their amanuensis, business adviser, and spiritual guide. They had no incentive to avarice, no inclination to depravity, nor ambition for wealth or distinction. Personal ease and festive amusement were apparently the chief

Records. See also Natalia Maree Belting, *Kaskaskia Under the French Regime;* John Francis McDermott, *Old Cahokia;* Norman W. Caldwell, *The French in the Mississippi Valley;* J. H. Schlarman, *From Quebec to New Orleans;* Stuart Brown, "Old Kaskaskia Days and Ways," *Transactions of the Illinois State Historical Society,* X (1905), 128-144; and Nelson Vance Russell, "The French and British at Play in the Old Northwest, 1760-1796," *Journal of the Illinois State Historical Society,* XXXI (March, 1938), 22-53.

[18] Betty Madden, "Buildings in a Wilderness," *The Living Museum,* XXIX, No. 12 (April, 1968).

objects of their existence. They were merry, friendly and hospitable, and while the broadest freedom of speech and action was tolerated in social intercourse, they were sober, honest, and virtuous . . . . They assimilated readily with inferior races, adopting unhesitatingly inferior methods, but their simple habits, manners and customs were little affected or improved by contact with people of advanced culture.[19]

Spread thinly over a vast area, the French lacked manpower. With a comparative handful of people, the military commandant at Fort de Chartres, who also acted as governor and judge, had jurisdiction over an area from south of the Great Lakes to Arkansas. Keeping the Illinois Indians under control was not a major task, but the Fox tribe operating out of Wisconsin fought a long and troublesome war that ended with their virtual extinction in a battle along the Fox River, probably in what is now Kendall County. English-speaking traders meanwhile circled the southern end of the Appalachians and stirred up tribes which threatened to stop the vital river traffic on the Mississippi. As a result of poor coordination of a retaliatory expedition, one Fort de Chartres commandant, Pierre Dartaguiette, was burned at the stake by Chickasaw Indians in present-day Mississippi.[20]

The Illinois settlements slowly gained in population while submitting to orders from New Orleans and Versailles. Cargoes of flour, bacon, tallow, lumber, and lead were shipped down the Mississippi and some furs went to Detroit and Mackinac. Meanwhile the stronger tribes from the surrounding areas sold part of their furs to the independent traders from the English-speaking colonies.

The Mississippi villages played small roles in the French and Indian War, which involved control of the Ohio region as one

[19] John F. Snyder, *Adam W. Snyder and His Period in Illinois History*, p. 24.

[20] Alvord, *op. cit.*, pp 177-180. See also "Ackia Battleground National Monument," *Southeastern Tour Book*, American Automobile Association (1957-58), p. 157. Sketches of the eleven men of French blood who served, some temporarily, as Fort de Chartres commandants, which made them ex officio governors of the Illinois country, are in Helen W. Mumford, *The French Governors of Illinois*. See Margaret A. Flint, "A Chronology of Illinois History," *Illinois Blue Book, 1961-62*, pp. 3-6. In an effort to ease friction with the northern Indians, a Jesuit in 1724 escorted Chief Chicagou, an eloquent Michigamea, and chiefs of three Missouri tribes to Paris and Versailles. Chicagou begged the French not to drive his people from their hunting grounds. Received in royal court with the highest honors, he returned home laden with presents. Chicagou presumably came from the west side of the Mississippi River, and it is coincidental that his name resembles that of the metropolis.

phase of an international conflict. In the struggle against the English colonists, a convoy of pork and flour was sent to Fort Duquesne and one commandant led a force of twenty-two men up the Ohio River to seek revenge for the death of his brother, killed in a skirmish with George Washington. Fort de Chartres was too isolated to be of help when La Salle's rebuilt fort at Frontenac fell in 1758. That broke the inadequate French line of communication. The next year the fate of New France was settled far to the east with the British capture of Quebec and Montreal. All French possessions east of the Mississippi, except for New Orleans, were ceded to Great Britain in 1763, just ninety years after Jolliet discovered the Illinois.

BRITISH RULE AND FRENCH EXODUS, 1763-1778

At Fort de Chartres the fleur-de-lis last flew over the North American continent. On October 10, 1765, two years after the Treaty of Paris, Captain Thomas Stirling marched through the fort's high arched gateway at the head of one hundred men from the Black Watch or Forty-Second Highlanders regiment. The next day the remnant of the French garrison was relieved and the venerable Louis St. Ange de Bellerive, who had acted as caretaker commandant, retired across the Mississippi to the brand new village of St. Louis.[21]

The two years' delay, during which the Indians turned back several British parties, was due to an uprising known as Pontiac's Conspiracy. The Indians, who long had been courted by the British, were unhappy with a new policy that shut off their presents, attempted to prohibit liquor sales, and decreed punishment for misbehavior. Meanwhile Tennessee and Kentucky hunting grounds were being infiltrated by English-speaking settlers and traders who dispensed watered whiskey and rum along with shoddy goods. Pontiac, chief of the Ottawa in the Detroit area, and other Indians yearned for the restoration to power of the more paternalistic French, who basically were traders rather than settlers and who sought only to exploit the native tribes, not to expel them. In 1763 and 1764 the Indians captured nine British forts, forced abandonment of a tenth, and besieged two more. Pontiac's strategy might have succeeded had he gained time by

21 Moses, *op. cit.*, I, 133.

storming the Detroit fort, but that was not the way the Indians made war.[22] The Mississippi outposts again were too far away to be directly involved in the rebellion, and St. Ange did nothing to support rumors, spread by French traders, that the great father across the sea was sending new armies to help his red children. A tragic figure with an accumulation of enemies, the old chief came to Cahokia in 1769 and got drunk. A Peoria companion hit him on the head and stabbed him to death. Along the Mississippi the assassination caused fear but brought retaliation only against the remnants of the Iliniwek.

Pierre La Clede, one of the forgotten men who made America great, came up the Mississippi in 1763 with a heavy cargo of trade goods, transported in a bateau that required a crew of twenty. A well-educated native of France, La Clede had monopoly privileges to undertake a fur business with the Missouri Indians. Just before his departure word reached New Orleans that the land east of the Mississippi had been ceded to England by France. More than a year would pass, however, before the scattered residents of the great valley learned the other half of the story, that Spain now owned New Orleans and everything west of the river. La Clede spent the winter at St. Anne, using Fort de Chartres as a warehouse. In the spring he sent his young stepson, Auguste Chouteau, and a crew of thirty men to build a village on the west bank, near a sloping bluff where his future establishment would be above high-water danger. He named it St. Louis and, although his eight-year trade monopoly was revoked, La Clede and the city he founded both prospered.[23] On the east bank, alarm spread with word that the Illinois country had been turned over to Protestant England. The French assumed that their slaves would be freed, and some went to Ste. Genevieve or back to New Orleans, but La Clede persuaded many of them to cross over to his town. Some floated their houses to the west side. A general exodus of community leaders continued for several years. They helped St. Louis grow into a great city while the old villages struggled to stay alive. As a creative force, the French blood and culture would be

[22] Francis Parkman's *The Conspiracy of Pontiac* credited the Indian leader with being the strategist of a far-flung uprising. He has been downgraded by Howard Peckham in *Pontiac and the Indian Uprising* to leadership in the attack on the Detroit fort. For a more popular account which restores Pontiac to a major role in the wilderness tragedy, see John Tebbel and Keith Jennison, *The American Indian Wars*, pp. 83-99.

[23] John Francis McDermott, *The French in the Mississippi Valley*, pp. 1-16.

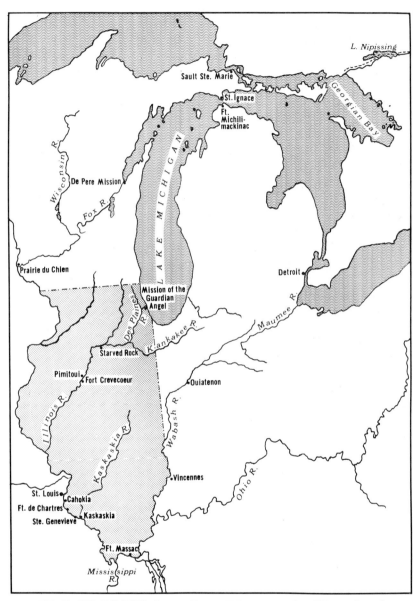

ILLINOIS in the French Period

influential in the development of Missouri, but of minor consequence in Illinois.

Troubles accumulated. The Jesuits were withdrawn when their order was suppressed in France. In a needless panic, the property of the Seminarians at Cahokia was sold at auction. While they never established a civil government, the often corrupt British did nothing to disturb the religion and customs of the French, whose right to hold slaves was recognized. For economy, Fort de Chartres, its eighteen-foot walls already damaged by floods, was abandoned and Captain Hugh Lord, the most sympathetic of the nine British who served as governors, took his small garrison to Kaskaskia and fortified the big house the Jesuits had left. At one time the British considered ordering all the French to move into one village where their own militia would provide self-protection.[24]

Nothing but large-scale Indian raids could block the westward spread of the English, and some of the most influential men on both sides of the Atlantic regarded as temporary the ban on settlement. They went ahead with the organization, mostly on paper, of land companies with get-rich-quick motives. George Washington and his brothers and the Lee family of Virginia were partners in a company aspiring to take title to two and a half million acres which on modern maps would cover much of southern Illinois, western Kentucky, and Tennessee. Benjamin Franklin and his son William invested in a Pennsylvania company that sought possession of 1.2 million acres in the West. The land speculations turned out to be premature.

The exploitation of the interior took a new turn as merchandising firms sent wagon trains over the Alleghenies. They were too enthusiastic in anticipating early profits in sales to settlers and Indians, but they established a permanent trade connection that meant the end of French commercial domination. Most active was the Philadelphia house of Baynton, Wharton, and Morgan, which had a store at Kaskaskia and branches at Vincennes and Cahokia. George Morgan, the junior partner, was the man on the ground in

[24] Three volumes make up the British Series of the Illinois Historical Collections, published by the Illinois State Historical Library. Edited by Clarence W. Alvord and Clarence E. Carter, they are *The Critical Period, 1763-1765, The New Regime, 1765-1767,* and *Trade and Politics, 1767-1769.* See also Clarence E. Carter, *Great Britain and the Illinois Country, 1763-1774;* Theodore C. Pease, *The Story of Illinois,* pp. 16-33; and Robert L. Schuyler, *The Transition from British to American Government.* Also see Alvord, *op. cit.,* pp. 286-307; Moses, *op. cit.,* I, 131-144; and Davidson-Stuvé, *op. cit.,* pp. 162-172.

Illinois.[25] Morgan had competitors and some commandants had their favorite sources of supply. Debts were hard to collect, and one British officer established a civil court which functioned for nearly two years with Morgan as chief judge.

So far as Indian policy was concerned, England under George III was as unsettled as France under Louis XIV. The neglected Mississippi villages were left without a civil government when a proclamation in 1763 fixed the crest of the Alleghenies as a boundary beyond which whites could not settle. The British had decided to adopt the French system of managing Indian relations, and the hunting grounds in the West were to be a vast reservation which only licensed fur traders could enter. The lure of the new land was stronger than the governmental edict, however, and the vanguard of the English-speaking disregarded both the danger from the Indians and the legal effect of the proclamation. They continued to cross the mountains and their encroachments were one of the causes of Pontiac's War. In five years a treaty at Fort Stanwix in New York state relaxed the restriction by opening for settlement an area around Fort Pitt and the territory between the Ohio and Tennessee rivers.

Major General Thomas Gage had plans to evacuate the French from the Mississippi, which could have repeated the removal of the Arcadians and the legend of Evangeline. In 1774, however, Parliament passed the Quebec Act, which, as part of a series of reforms, would have restored the French civil code and Catholic religion to the interior. Lieutenant governors would have charge of districts at Detroit, Vincennes, and Kaskaskia. The Illinois residents never knew whether it would have worked, since the Quebec Act coincided with the Boston Tea Party. With the Revolutionary War under way, Captain Lord and his garrison were ordered to Detroit. The British no longer had a military force in the Illinois country and the weakened French villages were losing population.

[25] Max Savelle, *George Morgan, Colony Builder*. See also the Alvord-Carter introduction to *Trade and Politics*.

3

THE ARRIVAL OF
THE ENGLISH - SPEAKING

THE SPECTER OF AN INDIAN RAID NEVER LEFT THE ISOLATED cabins of the early frontier. A man going about his work could be ambushed and scalped, his wife and children might be butchered in his absence, or the whole family wiped out at night. Groups huddled together for self-protection might be overpowered by a war party. A man who escaped immediate murder faced the prolonged agony of mutilation and roasting, while the lucky ones were taken to Detroit as captives. A British strong point, Detroit had a French and half-breed population of two thousand and a fort commanded by Henry Hamilton, the lieutenant governor. Within the Detroit sphere of influence some eight thousand Indians used the red man's prerogative of taking sides in the war for control of their own wilderness.

The Americans in the new Kentucky settlements hated Hamilton most of all. They called him a "hair buyer," complaining that he encouraged barbarous warfare on women and children and paid for scalps and captives at the same rate. Hamilton's raiding parties, Kentucky-bound, offered no threat to the Illinois villages. There Philippe de Rocheblave, who earlier had fought for the French and for a time served as Spanish commandant at Ste. Genevieve, now was the British agent, ambitiously and efficiently loyal to Hamil-

49

ton. He recommended that troops be returned to Kaskaskia, but Hamilton preferred to depend upon Indians.

Hamilton intended to clear out Kentucky and then turn his attention to Fort Pitt while Iroquois and other pro-British Indians raided in New York's Mohawk valley. That would have confined the revolting colonies to the seaboard. Had he succeeded, the border of the new United States would have been the crest of the Alleghenies and west of it would be British territory, populated by a few French and a multitude of Indians.

CONQUEST: GEORGE ROGERS CLARK, 1778-1779

George Rogers Clark and Thomas Jefferson, who was nine years his senior, had adjoining birthplaces. Clark spend his boyhood on a small plantation and acquired outside of school a knowledge of mathematics and geography. A rugged six-footer, he had red hair and sparkling black eyes, and it pleased his vanity that he looked like another Virginian, George Washington. There were other resemblances; Clark too became a surveyor and his Revolutionary War career combined military brilliance with frustration.

Clark also had a streak of Daniel Boone in his makeup. At an early age he headed for the frontier and as a twenty-two-year-old militia captain helped Lord Dunmore, the last of the royal governors, make war on the Shawnee. At twenty-four he led a company of settlers into Kentucky at an inopportune time. War parties from the Miami and other tribes were slipping across the Ohio River to raid the white families who had taken over their hunting grounds. The toll was frightful, and by the end of 1776 those who had not retreated through the Cumberland Gap were cooped up in three stockaded forts.

Clark, who presumably never saw a military textbook, organized the defense of Kentucky and made a trip to Williamsburg, the Virginia capital, to argue that "if a country was not worth protecting, it was not worth claiming." At his request the county of Kentucky was created and five hundred pounds of powder were provided for its protection. Clark also got the ear of Patrick Henry, the first governor of the new commonwealth, with a plan to stop the Indian raids at their source by capturing Detroit. Now a lieutenant colonel, he was given twelve hundred pounds sterling, badly depreciated, and authorized to raise seven companies of fifty men each for the defense of the frontier. He also

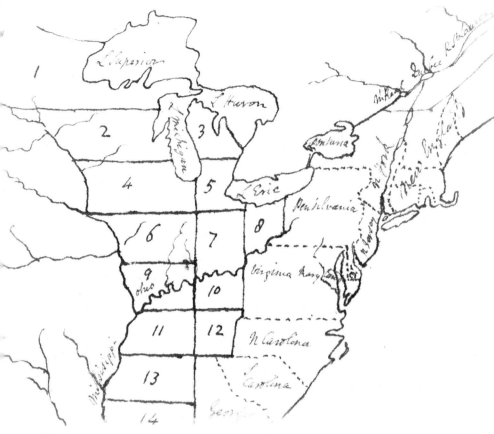

Jefferson's State Names

had secret orders from Henry to attack Kaskaskia. The other half of his master plan called for a second colonial force to march against Detroit from Fort Pitt.[1]

[1] Because of the glamour of his career and the sweep of his strategy, Clark has received close attention from historians and popular writers. Clark's own account of his exploits is found in *Clark's Memoirs, 1773-1779,* and the *George Rogers Clark Papers, 1771-1781,* published by the Illinois State Historical Library. Both books contain introductions by James A. James, who also is author of *The Life of George Rogers Clark.* Milo Milton Quaife edited *The Conquest of the Illinois,* which covers Clark's account of his Kaskaskia and Vincennes triumphs. Extracts are found in H. W. Beckwith (ed.), *Collections of the Illinois State Historical Library,* Vol. I. See also Reuben G. Thwaites, *How George Rogers Clark Won the Northwest,* and Francis M. Woolard, "Route of George Rogers Clark and His Army from Kaskaskia to Vincennes, 1779," *Transactions of the Illinois State Historical Society,* XLI (1934), 48-63; Walter Havighurst, *George Rogers Clark, Soldier of the West;* Theodore Calvin Pease, *George Rogers Clark and the Revolution in Illinois;* and John D. Barnhart, *Henry Hamilton and George Rogers Clark in the American Revolution.*

Difficulties arose at once. Clark could enlist only 175 men for his army. To lessen the desertion rate, he trained them on an island near the falls of the Ohio, the present site of Louisville. During an eclipse of the sun, he started down the river in keelboats. Rocheblave expected an attack by water, so Clark marched his men with inadequate provisions from Fort Massac to Kaskaskia in six days. On the nation's second birthday, July 4, 1778, Rocheblave was in bed when he learned that the "long knives," as the Indians respectfully called the Kentuckians, had captured the town without firing a shot.

Clark now demonstrated that he was also a diplomat and a master of psychology. He allowed the French to become alarmed and then broke the news that France had entered the war on the side of the American colonies. He won the loyalty of Father Gibault by espousing freedom of worship for Catholics.[2] He sent a joint force of Kentuckians and French to rally the other American Bottom villages. He neutralized Indian chiefs who would not swear brotherhood. Father Gibault as an envoy to Vincennes found that the French there were friendly and the town defenseless. Clark sent a small detachment to occupy it.

As winter approached, Hamilton retaliated by bringing 175 troops and miscellaneous Indians on a slow trip in the low water of the Maumee and Wabash rivers. Vincennes promptly capitulated since its French militiamen, who had sworn allegiance to both sides, objected to fighting their countrymen from Detroit. Hamilton dismissed his Indians until spring, confident he then could complete a British triumph in the western war. Clark faced desperate danger. He was cut off from Williamsburg, he had no hope of getting reinforcements, and nothing had been done about a counterpunch on Detroit from the east.

In terms of total manpower it was a small war, but big men supported Clark. One minor hero was Francois Vigo, a Sardinian merchant at St. Louis who owned trading posts at Kaskaskia and Vincennes. Vigo managed to be captured outside Vincennes. After imprisonment for three weeks in Fort Sackville, which was the British name for the post on the Wabash, he hurried to Kaskaskia to inform Clark that Hamilton had released his Indian allies for the

[2] Joseph P. Donnelly, "Pierre Gibault and the Critical Period of the Illinois Country, 1768-78," in *The French in the Mississippi Valley*, J. F. McDermott, ed. J. P. Dunn, "Father Gibault, the Patriot Priest of the Northwest," *Transactions of the Illinois State Historical Society*, X (1905), 15-34.

winter. Furthermore, the French at Vincennes would welcome Americans.

On Vigo's information, Clark did the unexpected under presumably impossible conditions. With approximately 170 men, half of them French volunteers, on February 5, 1779, he marched out of Kaskaskia across country toward Vincennes, 140 air-line miles away, east by northeast. The route was over what Clark called drowned lands, and for miles his men had to wade.

The real difficulties were the last sixty miles and eight days. Vincennes is on the east bank of the Wabash River, a major stream into which several rivers flow from the Illinois side in that area. Mild weather had melted the snow and ice, sending the rivers out of their banks and flooding the bottomland for miles around.

The Little Wabash, with two branches, was five miles wide from bank to bank. The men made a pirogue from a fallen tree so they could be ferried across the deep places, but the rest of the five miles they had to wade in water between two and four feet deep. Out of food and within sound of the fort's morning gun, Clark could not ford the Embarras River but detoured through mud and water to the Wabash. Some days brought driving rain. One deer provided the only food. Two small boats were used in a slow and wet crossing of the Wabash, after which the men camped without fires on a muddy half-acre that wasn't quite under water. From a passing Indian they confiscated a buffalo quarter, ground corn, and kettles, enough to provide broth for the weaker men. At daybreak February 23 a half-inch of ice marked the water's edge. Dry land was three miles away and there was no time to waste. Clark promptly led his nearly exhausted men into water up to their shoulders, with the big men helping support the short and the weak.

By evening they were firing into the portholes of Fort Sackville, using ammunition furnished by villagers who had not alerted the garrison. Hamilton surrendered February 25 and was sent to meditate in a Williamsburg dungeon.

Clark now had a golden opportunity to take Detroit at once, but Kentuckians dissipated a new force of three hundred in an independent and unsuccessful attack on Chillicothe, in present-day Ohio. That erased the last chance to stop the Indian warfare at its source. Without adequate manpower, money, or supplies, for the rest of the war he was unhappily on the defensive, keeping possession of Vincennes and the Mississippi villages and preventing the British from establishing a base south of Detroit.

For Clark, peace was a failure and Virginia an ingrate. At the age of thirty-five, he could not collect two thousand dollars in salary and personal advances. Had he acquired any wealth from the fruits of free enterprise, it would have been seized by the creditors of Virginia. Fortunately he could live with well-to-do relatives. He supervised the allocation of land grants to his men. An unauthorized effort to retaliate against the Wabash Indians collapsed when the Kentucky troops mutinied. An embarrassment to the nation that neglected him, Clark entered into futile French plots to capture Louisiana from Spain. He drank heavily, lost his right leg as the result of an accident, and was partially paralyzed before he died at the age of sixty-nine. This was the man who almost single-handedly saw to it that the Americans won the western phase of the Revolutionary War.

A VIRGINIA COUNTY AND ANARCHY, 1778-1783

As soon as word of the capture of Kaskaskia reached Williamsburg, the young commonwealth of Virginia had a Texas-sized dream of expansion. Acting promptly, on December 9, 1778, it created the county of Illinois, a vast area of indefinite boundaries that extended from the Ohio River to the Mississippi and onward to Canada. The legal basis for the distant claim was that its original royal charter gave Virginia the right to extend from sea to sea.

Virginia asserted that it acted "for the more effectual protection and defense" of an area that was in the almost undisputed possession of Indians. For all practical purposes, however, the government concerned itself only with the Mississippi River villages, Vincennes, and a few outposts as far away as Peoria and Ouiatenon. In this domain were almost two thousand white persons, including soldiers and scattered traders, and possibly one thousand Negro slaves.[3] The settlements on the American Bottom counted almost one thousand French and most of the slaves.

---

[3] In this, as in most phases of the prestatehood history of Illinois, the definitive work is Clarence W. Alvord, *The Illinois Country, 1673-1818*, pp. 329-378. A detailed account also is found in Arthur C. Boggess, *The Settlement of Illinois, 1778-1830*, pp. 9-70. See also the general histories, John Moses, *Illinois Historical and Statistical*, I, 158-173; Alexander Davidson and Bernard Stuvé, *A Complete History of Illinois*, pp. 202-209; and Theodore C. Pease, *The Story of Illinois*, pp. 34-48.

Kaskaskia was the metropolis, with five hundred white persons and almost the same number of slaves. Cahokia had three hundred whites and eighty Negroes. Prairie du Rocher's population was approximately one hundred whites and eighty slaves. The other villages had all but disappeared and were on their way to extinction. A few families resided at St. Philippe, Prairie du Pont, and outside the abandoned Fort de Chartres. Clustered nearby were fewer than five hundred degenerate and debauched Kaskaskia, Peoria, Michigamea, and Cahokia Indians, all that were left of the Iliniwek. Because it was on the route to Canada, which led through Ouiatenon, Vincennes was almost as important as Kaskaskia. At Peoria, the old trading post had recently been revived.

Far outside the sphere of influence of the county of Illinois was a trading post operated at the Chicago portage by Jean Baptiste Point du Sable, a Negro or mulatto who began the permanent settlement of Chicago. Between 1700, when the Jesuit Father Francois Pinet had been transferred to Cahokia from the Mission of the Guardian Angel, and du Sable's arrival about 1779 there is no authentic record of a white man living at the portage, although several may have made use of its commercial opportunities for the

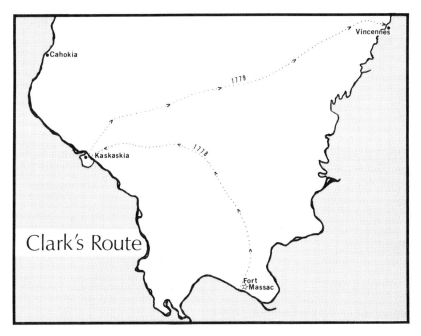

tur business. Du Sable could have been a descendant of Renault's slaves from Santo Domingo, but of his birth and parentage nothing is known. During the Revolution he was arrested by the British and sent to Michilimackinac, the fortified trading center now known as Mackinac Island. Upon his release, he settled at Chicago. Around his establishment gathered the usual small group of traders and Indians.[4]

Du Sable and his Potawatomi wife prospered during the twenty years they lived at Chicago. When he left the portage in 1800, du Sable sold a forty-by-twenty-two-foot house, a horse-powered mill, and outbuildings that sheltered two mules, thirty head of cattle, hogs, hens, farm machinery, and carpenter's tools, all evidence that he had accumulated more property than most frontiersmen. To be successful on the fringes of civilization a man needed to be a jack-of-all-trades, and du Sable in addition to his fur business was a farmer, carpenter, cooper, and miller, and probably also a distiller.

The Virginia law setting up Illinois county government retained the French code, modified by Virginia law, and recognized that legal improvisation might be necessary in meeting wilderness problems. It stipulated that the religion and customs of the inhabitants were to be respected, a provision that would be cited in the future as a perpetual guarantee of the right of the descendants of the French to own slaves.

To be chief executive and commander of the militia, Governor Henry appointed John Todd, giving him the title of county lieutenant.[5] Todd was a little man of twenty eight years, well educated, and a competent Indian fighter. In his official capacity he arrived at Kaskaskia in May, 1779, and in a welcoming ceremony in front of the church announced that an election would be held to choose magistrates of the courts already set up by Clark, his good friend. The magistrates were elected by districts, and the courts, which had both judicial and executive authority, governed the villages. A letter from Henry instructed Todd to befriend the French and Indians and to teach them the value of democracy. Full of wisdom, it was a premature blueprint for a representative government in an area that soon lapsed into anarchy.

[4] Thomas Meehan, "Jean Baptiste Point du Sable, the First Chicagoan," *Journal of the Illinois State Historical Society*, LVI, 3 (Autumn, 1963), 439-453. M. M. Quaife, *Chicago and the Old Northwest*, pp. 79-104.

[5] Edward G. Mason, *Chapters from Illinois History*, pp. 250-279.

Henry did nothing else for Illinois. Almost as soon as the new land claim was staked out, Virginia abandoned Clark and Todd, leaving them a legacy of unpaid bills. The Revolution was going badly in the northern colonies, Virginia's own treasury was depleted, and General Washington also was in dire need of men and supplies. As a result, Virginia was unable to administer its distant county and the Illinois officials had to rely on their own resources. As long as his credit lasted, Clark gave personal security for governmental obligations. For a time the army of occupation was supported on credit extended by merchants and traders. Gabriel Cerré, the richest man in Kaskaskia, and several other French were generous with loans. Oliver Pollock, who was the financial agent at New Orleans for both the colonial government and Virginia, exhausted his private funds in an effort to keep the war going.[6] There was sympathy and some help from St. Louis after Spain entered the war in 1779. Eventually the civilians had to support the army and the French complained that the soldiers were killing oxen, milk cows, and chickens. Clark had no answer, since his men had to eat.

Todd found himself in a continual crisis based on clashes of Gallic and Anglo-Saxon temperament. The easygoing French, Catholic by training and imbued with respect for any authority, lacked a talent for self-government. They disliked the Kentucky riflemen who practiced no religion and had inherited some of the prejudices of their Calvinist forebears. Clark's men had great physical strength, loved individual liberty, and were not noted for tolerance, sobriety, or culture. Woodsmen turned citizen soldiers, they established a base·for the coming hordes who would plant a new civilization in Illinois.

During the period of lawlessness and while the Revolutionary War was still being fought, the English-speaking settlement of the Northwest began at its far western edge. The year was 1779 and the site Bellefontaine, a beautifully located spring midway between Prairie du Rocher and Cahokia, just south of the present city of Waterloo. Courageous Virginians and Marylanders, moving westward to take up Kentucky land, heard from Clark's soldiers of the richness of the Illinois soil. Some decided to see for themselves and, although non-French settlement was forbidden north of the

6 James A. James, "Oliver Pollock and the Winning of the Illinois Country," *Transactions of the Illinois State Historical Society*, XLI (1934), 35-39.

Ohio River, men with Anglo-Saxon names brought their families to the American Bottom. James Moore, who came from Maryland and had been an Indian trader in Kentucky, led the group that made the first permanent settlement of the English-speaking. Fifteen Americans voted there when the first election was held in 1782. Shadrach Bond settled nearer Kaskaskia with a smaller group. The newcomers built blockhouses and small stockades, and started farming land they did not own. In numbers they were small, but Grand Ruisseau, on the road to Cahokia, became a second American settlement.[7] Four miles south of Bellefontaine, Virginians by 1787 started a settlement named New Design.

With the gradual arrival of the English-speaking, the entire area became known as the American Bottom, a name that helped distinguish it from the Spanish territory on the west bank of the Mississippi. Partly open prairie, it extends on modern maps from Alton to Chester. A range of rocky bluffs some four miles from the river marked the eastern boundary. Untrained in archaeology, the settlers were puzzled by the presence of Indian burial and ceremonial mounds ranging from one hundred to four hundred feet in diameter and from fifteen to sixty feet in height. Many farmers built their houses on the mounds because the low, marshy ground was dotted with stagnant pools. Poor drainage gave early Illinois a reputation for being unhealthful, but nowhere in the East did corn grow so tall year after year.

The French complained that the Americans were encroaching on their property and selling liquor to the Indians. Despite their heavy load of troubles, accompanied by a longing for the good old days before the English tongue was heard along the Mississippi, the French were loyal and active in the spasmodic action on the outskirts of the war.[8] A British force from Mackinac, augmented

[7] Names of sixty-five Americans living in Illinois were attached to a French petition sent to Congress in 1787. The list, which apparently contains some errors, shows four Americans as inhabitants in 1779, seven more in 1780, and nine more, including Bond, the following year. The petition also listed the names of thirty-six male children. See Alvord's *Kaskaskia Records*, pp. 421-423. Bond's nephew, namesake, and protégé became the first governor of Illinois. The Bond name does not appear in "The Army Led by Col. George Rogers Clark in His Conquest of the Illinois, 1778-9," *Transactions of the Illinois State Historical Society*, VIII (1903), 150-165. For additional information about Bellefontaine see Alvord, *The Illinois Country*, p. 359; Moses, *op. cit.*, I, 226-229; Davidson-Stuvé, *op. cit.*, pp. 173-183; and John W. Allen, *It Happened in Southern Illinois*, pp. 348.

[8] James Alton James, "Illinois and the Revolution in the West," *Transactions of the Illinois State Historical Society*, XV (1910), 63-71. Theodore Calvin Pease, "The Revolu-

Courtesy Illinois State Historical Library

George Rogers Clark

by Sioux warriors, assembled at Prairie du Chien for a futile drive toward St. Louis and Cahokia. Surprised and repulsed, the British suffered one of their few defeats of 1780. Clark retaliated by sending Colonel John Montgomery to raid a Sauk and Fox village at Rock Island in the westernmost fighting of the Revolution. Three expeditions from St. Louis toward Michigan accomplished little. In 1780 Augustin La Balme, a new arrival with a mysterious background, raised possibly two hundred Frenchmen for a march on Detroit. He was killed by Indians after he plundered a fort on

tion at Crisis in the West," *Journal of the Illinois State Historical Society,* XXIII (Jan., 1931), 664-681.

the site of Fort Wayne, Indiana. Seeking revenge, another French raiding party suffered heavy losses after holding for a day the St. Joseph trading post near what is now Niles, Michigan. French prestige dropped as a result of the two failures. Then Eugenio Pierre, a Spanish militia captain from St. Louis, crossed the Illinois country in early 1781 at the head of an expedition that included Spaniards, Indians, and perhaps twenty men from Cahokia. He easily captured the St. Joseph post and flew the Spanish flag over it for one day.[9] There was some minor alarm in diplomatic circles when Pierre boasted that he claimed the Illinois country for the crown of Spain.

The collapse of civil government began almost at once. Todd did not like his job and stayed as county lieutenant only five months before returning to Kentucky, where he was killed in an Indian raid. Unable to resign his Illinois post, he appointed Richard Winston as his deputy and successor. Unfortunately for the Kaskaskians, John Dodge, an adventurer from Connecticut, showed up in 1780 and began a reign of terror in which he oppressed the isolated French for six years. Dodge, who was backed by the Americans at Bellefontaine, gave himself the title of captain commandant, moved into the fort, and arrested Winston. The Kaskaskia court hesitated to interfere and Winston, when he regained his liberty, dissolved the court by tacking a proclamation on the church door, the universal bulletin board. Winston soon left town after turning his title and weak powers over to a follower of Dodge.

The county of Illinois existed for three years. Realizing that it could not support a government in the far Northwest, Virginia offered to cede its claims north of the Ohio to the impotent Continental Congress and allowed the law which created the county of Illinois to lapse January 5, 1782. The result was eight years of anarchy, until a legal government could be restored to the Illinois country. Dodge finally left, but the French were too exhausted to restore law and order in Kaskaskia and environs. The situation was better at Cahokia, where troops had been quartered only two years.

Petitions to Congress finally resulted in an inspection trip in 1787 by Colonel Josiah Harmar, commander of troops in the Northwest, who fell under the influence of the Dodge faction.

9 Mason, *op. cit.*, pp. 293-311.

Harmar advised the French to obey the magistrates and wait patiently until Congress established a government. The Kaskaskia court meanwhile came under the control of the Americans and accomplished little as a dispenser of justice. Indians of the Miami, Wea, Kickapoo, and Potawatomi tribes, who had taken over the Iliniwek hunting grounds, turned against the impotent French. Two priests from Canada accepted invitations to cross the Mississippi and swear allegiance to Spain. The Kaskaskia French despairingly petitioned for a civil government and twenty soldiers to return law and order. John Edgar, a recently arrived merchant, offered rock bottom prices for supplies and barracks if troops would be stationed at Kaskaskia.[10] That brought official recognition of the problems of the Mississippi villages. Between 1787 and 1790, the greatest period of anarchy and emigration, Kaskaskia suffered a serious loss of population, especially among the leadership class, when such men as Father Gibault and Cerré crossed the river. Cahokia meanwhile kept its court in operation and grew in population and importance, possibly because the English-speaking frontiersmen had not reached that far north.

In the Treaty of Paris that ended the Revolutionary War, Lord Shelburne did not exercise what could have been a strong British claim for the territory north of the Ohio River, which became known as the Old Northwest. Much of it was occupied by British troops and pro-British Indians, but Benjamin Franklin pointed out that generosity in giving up the area could lead to centuries of Anglo-Saxon friendship. The British diplomats did not want Spain to get any territory east of the Mississippi and were willing to let the Americans have the job of preventing it. Consequently the international border was placed along the Great Lakes, which meant that the present states of Illinois, Indiana, Michigan, Ohio, and Wisconsin, and enough of Minnesota to include St. Paul and Duluth henceforth would be American and not British. At the time no one imagined there ever would be another Northwest bounded by the Pacific Ocean.

Clark's capture of Kaskaskia and Vincennes had little direct bearing on the treaty settlement. Indirectly, however, Clark and his men served notice that the Americans wanted the land and that the British and Indians could not keep them from possessing it.

<hr/>

[10] James H. Roberts, "The Life and Times of General John Edgar," *Transactions of the Illinois State Historical Society*, XII (1907), 64-73.

UNDER THE ARTICLES OF CONFEDERATION

The former seaboard colonies that had just won their independence had many problems, only one of which directly involved the newly acquired and distant expanse that made up the Old Northwest. Formation of a centralized government demanded immediate attention, but Maryland refused to ratify the Articles of Confederation unless Virginia and four other states gave up their western land claims. Connecticut contended that as a result of its colonial charter it owned a strip extending into northern Illinois. New York, Pennsylvania, and Massachusetts also claimed areas which were smaller in extent and closer to the Appalachians.

Virginia led the way in solving that problem. In 1781 it kept title to Kentucky but agreed to relinquish its all-inclusive claims north of the Ohio River, with several reservations. Most important, Virginia insisted that the other states must make the same concessions so that the Old Northwest could be nationalized and eventually organized into states of from one hundred to one hundred fifty miles square. Virginia also wanted reimbursement of its expenses of conquest and required that promises to Clark and his men be honored with a 150,000-acre grant. Virginia also asked that the French and Canadian settlers "shall have their possessions and titles confirmed to them and be protected in the enjoyment of their rights and liberties." Specifically, that meant they could continue to own slaves.

Virginia executed a deed of cession in 1784, and the other states followed within two years. Thomas Jefferson drafted an ordinance calling for organization of the West into rectangular states with illogical boundaries and names of Greek and Indian origin. If he had had his way, Chicago would be in Assenisipia, Springfield in Illinoia, and Carbondale in Polypotamia.[11] Jefferson then went to Paris on a diplomatic mission, which permitted his fancy names to be forgotten. James Monroe took his place and made one of history's greatest misjudgments. Like most of the men who struggled to convert the former seaboard colonies into a nation, Monroe had only sketchy information about the interior of the country. He made two brief trips into the region and in 1786 reported that the Old Northwest was a dubious asset. Much

11 F. L. Paxson, *History of the American Frontier,* pp. 61-65. Alvord, *op. cit.,* p. 387. Henry S. Randall, *Life of Thomas Jefferson,* I, 397-401. Jefferson wanted the other states to be named Sylvania, Michigania, Chersonesus, and Metropolitamia.

of the territory was "miserably poor," especially the parts near Lakes Michigan and Erie, he said, adding that extensive plains along the Mississippi River "from all appearances will not have a bush on them for ages." Therefore he concluded that the area "will never contain a sufficient number of inhabitants to entitle them to membership in the confederacy" and recommended that three to five states would be enough for the entire Northwest. [12]

New Englanders who had been officers in Washington's army helped organize the Ohio Company and offered to buy one and a half million acres in the Old Northwest, paying eight or nine cents an acre in unmarketable certificates of indebtedness. For the Continental Congress, it had financial benefits as a reduction of the public debt. The Rev. Manasseh Cutler, a Congregational minister and botanist who was the Ohio Company's lobbyist, made a secret deal with a congressional group that wanted five million acres of its own for a speculation that eventually failed. The New Englanders said potential investors would insist upon an orderly government, so an ordinance organizing the "territory of the United States northwest of the river Ohio" was adopted July 13, 1787. The Northwest Ordinance was the most important action taken under the Confederation and provided a blueprint that was followed as the nation expanded into fifty states.

As appointive officialdom, the Ordinance of 1787 provided for a governor, a secretary, and three judges. The governor and judges had quasi-legislative functions, with power to adopt civil and criminal laws from those of the original states. When the population reached "five thousand free male inhabitants of full age," an element of democracy could be introduced with election of a house of representatives, accompanied by appointment of a legislative council or upper house by Congress. Owners of fifty acres of land could vote. Upon attainment of that second grade of government, the governor had power to establish counties and appoint their officials, and the legislature could elect a delegate to Congress.

Without consulting the scattered residents of the Old Northwest, the ordinance included a compact that could be altered only by mutual consent. Under its terms, from three to five states could be created as soon as an area attained a population of sixty thousand. In all respects a new state would be equal to the original

---

[12] Monroe, *Writings,* I, 117.

thirteen. For future boundaries, a line would be drawn north from Vincennes and from the mouth of the Miami River. That would provide three states. Congress could create one or two additional ones north of an east-west line through the southern tip of Lake Michigan.

A bill of rights included a statement that: "Religion, morality, and knowledge being necessary to good government and the happiness of mankind, schools and the means of education shall forever be encouraged."

The sixth and final article of the compact foreshadowed future controversies by outlawing slavery. "There shall be neither slavery nor involuntary servitude in the said territory, otherwise than for the punishment of crimes, whereof the party shall have been duly convicted," it said, adding a provision for the return of fugitives from any of the original states. The Ohio Company's promoters insisted that, without such a prohibition of slavery, New England residents might hesitate to buy land in the Old Northwest.[13]

ST. CLAIR COUNTY AND THE NORTHWEST TERRITORY, 1787-1799

As part of the agreement with the Ohio Company, the governorship of the Northwest Territory went to Arthur St. Clair, president of the Continental Congress, who received a three-year appointment and a freehold of one thousand acres. Scottish-born, St. Clair had stormed Quebec with Wolfe, became a sizable Pennsylvania landowner, and as a major general in the Revolutionary War evacuated supposedly impregnable Fort Ticonderoga, after which a court martial exonerated him. In the summer of 1788 he installed a rudimentary government at Marietta, far up the Ohio River, where the Ohio Company had made its first settlement a few months earlier.[14]

As a result of prodding by the Congress of the new United States and by President Washington, St. Clair finally reached Kaskaskia March 5, 1790, and within a month inspected Cahokia. Technically that visit ended the period of anarchy. St. Clair began the establishment of a legal government by creating a county

---

[13] The Ordinance of 1787 can be found in T. C. Pease (ed.), *The Laws of the Northwest Territory*, pp. 521-528, and Emil J. Verlie, *Illinois Constitutions*, pp. 1-8.

[14] F. E. Wilson, *Arthur St. Clair: Rugged Ruler of the Old Northwest*, and W. H. Smith, *The St. Clair Papers*.

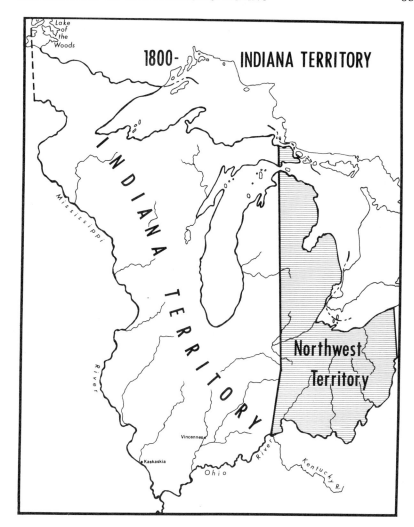

named for himself and giving his cousin, William St. Clair, the job of prothonotary or court clerk. St. Clair County, which became the mother of many Illinois counties, covered almost a third of the present state.

Indian occupation continued to be a major problem. St. Clair, who did not return to Illinois for five years, in 1791 suffered a humiliating defeat while leading an army against the Miami Indians near Fort Wayne. The Illinois settlers again were outside the main theater of warfare when General "Mad Anthony" Wayne three years later broke the back of tribal resistance in the Battle of Fallen Timbers, fought in the wreckage of an Ohio tornado. St. Clair had become increasingly unpopular, and by military ineptitude he forfeited the right to negotiate the first treaty that gave the whites a legal right to develop strategic areas in Illinois.

Wayne's 1795 Treaty of Greenville was a good real estate deal for the whites. The defeated Indians ceded their claims to a six-mile-square tract at the mouth of the Chicago River, where Fort Dearborn would be built to dominate the portage. The treaty had other clauses of importance to Illinois. It granted white settlers title to the land they already occupied. It also extinguished Indian rights to a six-mile square at Peoria, where Fort Clark would be built; a twelve-mile square at the mouth of the Illinois River, a presumably strategic but low-lying location which was never developed militarily or commercially; and the post at Fort Massac.[15] The rest of Illinois, the treaty conceded, belonged to the Indians. Further eastward, it settled the Indian problem for more than a decade by fixing a new boundary line that opened up most of southern and eastern Ohio for settlement. For their part of the bargain, the Potawatomi were promised one thousand dollars in trade goods each year and the Kaskaskia, Piankashaw, and Kickapoo five hundred dollars each.

At Fort Massac, which never saw military action, new pickets were erected by a small garrison sent in by Wayne. For eight years starting in 1799 boats on the Ohio River stopped there to pay duties on their cargo. Brigands and robbers always were a danger on the Ohio, and settlers floating down the river faced a major hazard at Cave-in-Rock, an appropriately named cavern halfway up a bluff. The site had been notorious before 1799, when Sam Mason, a renegade Virginian, lured boatmen ashore with a sign advertising a "Liquor Vault and House of Entertainment." Becoming both rich and infamous from his plundering of the unwary, Mason moved on, but other river pirates and counterfeiters occupied the lair. The bloodthirsty Harpe brothers helped make Cave-in-Rock known for wanton cruelty and brutal executions and

---

15 The history of Fort Massac, never exciting, has been covered by Norman W. Caldwell in three articles in the *Journal of the Illinois State Historical Society*—"Fort Massac During the French and Indian War," XLIII (Summer, 1950), 100-119; "Fort Massac: The American Frontier Post, 1778-1806," XLIII (Winter, 1950), and "Fort Massac Since 1805," XLIV (Spring, 1951), 47-60.

emphasized a need for law and order. For travelers by boat, the best advice was to stay in midstream between the mouth of the Wabash and Fort Massac.[16]

Since the United States, like Virginia, had failed to administer the Illinois country, the dark period for the French had not ended. William St. Clair after three years reported that court sessions were spasmodic and organized government almost nonexistent. Repeated floods, early frosts that killed the corn crop, and loss of Indian trade added to the misery of French, Negroes, and Indians.

The Americans, as the English-speaking arrivals were called, also suffered. Most of them had fought for Virginia or Maryland in the Revolution, and now they found a new enemy in the Kickapoo tribesmen who had moved below the Illinois River and until 1795 frequently raided the white settlements. Because of occasional murders and frequent thefts of horses and other property, families "forted up" inside palisades and kept firearms handy when at work outside. In 1790, James Smith, an itinerant Separate Baptist elder who was the first Protestant to expound the gospel in Illinois, was captured by a Kickapoo party while traveling between settlements. The Indians killed a woman who accompanied him but spared Smith, who within a few months was ransomed for $170, raised by the people of the New Design community.[17]

New Design was hardly a promised land. The original settlement was reinforced in 1797 by a party of 154 Virginians who exhausted themselves traveling 135 miles over hills and through mud and swamps from Fort Massac in twenty-six days. They found that the earlier arrivals had been harassed by Indians and that cabins were overcrowded, food inadequate, salt scarce, and medical help unavailable. Half of the group died of a "putrid and malignant fever."

The leader of that group was the Rev. Daniel Badgley, who organized a Baptist church with twenty-eight members at New Design and was credited with being the first Protestant minister in Illinois. Baptists had been the first preachers in the state, and Smith had reached the region as early as 1787, while the Rev. Josiah Dodge visited the American Bottom in 1794. By 1807 a Baptist association was formed by five churches which had four

[16] Robert M. Coates, *Outlaw Years: The History of the Land Pirates of the Natchez Trace.*

[17] Davidson-Stuvé, *op. cit.,* pp. 217-227, contains an account of the Indian violence that was almost routine on the frontier between 1783 and 1795.

ministers and 111 members. The first Methodist, the Rev. Joseph Lillard, came in 1793. Two others began missionary work three years later, and in 1803 the Rev. Benjamin Young became the first circuit rider.[18]

Catholic churches were abandoned by the time a group of Trappist monks established a monastery on a mound near Cahokia. There for several years the members of the ascetic order erected buildings, performed hard labor, observed their rule of silence, and lived on a diet of vegetables and water. Father Urbain Guillet brought the Trappists to America in 1803 in the hope they could convert the Indians. After stopping in Kentucky, they came to Cahokia under the encouragement of Nicholas Jarrott, one of the newer and wealthier French. Beset by hardships, including plague and crop failures, and turned down by Congress when they tried to obtain four thousand acres by grant or purchase, the Trappists returned east in 1813 and eventually went back to France. The site of their labors is still known as Monks' Mound.

Because of the hardships, more French crossed the Mississippi to Spanish soil, but among new arrivals were men with money and business acumen who recognized the potential of Illinois. They included several able and energetic French-Canadians who played major roles in the development of the region and were by no means typical of the descendants of the *voyageurs* and *coureurs de bois*. Pierre Menard, the most prominent, opened his own store in Kaskaskia in 1791. While acquiring a reputation for private charities, Menard served in the Indiana and Illinois territorial legislatures before he became a naturalized citizen. Jarrott, a contemporary, built what was probably the first brick house in Illinois. Construction began in 1799, and some accounts say the brick was manufactured on the grounds by workmen who fired a local clay. The brick could have been imported from Pittsburgh. Brickmaking on a commercial basis began sometime before 1818 in the Alton area.

Although reluctant to give up any of his authority, St. Clair in 1798 conceded that the Old Northwest had at least one thousand white males among its adult population. Accordingly, he called for the election of representatives to participate in a legislative session at Cincinnati. Of the twenty-three elected, two came from Illi-

18 In addition to Alvord, Moses, Boggess, and Davidson-Stuvé, whose works on early Illinois history have been cited previously, information on early churches can be found in Cecil K. Byrd (ed.), *A Bibliography of Illinois Imprints, 1814-58.*

nois—the elder Shadrach Bond and John Edgar, an Irishman and former British naval officer who came to Kaskaskia in the dark days of 1784 and began accumulating a fortune in land. The territorial laws they helped enact reflected the primitive nature of the problems faced by the first settlers. They established and regulated ferries, but there is no mention of bridges. They stipulated how grain could be ground and prescribed the toll to be taken by millers. Livestock could legally stray in the woods between April and November, when fences protected growing crops. Prairie land could be fired only between December 1 and March 10. Counties were allowed to tax horses not more than fifty cents and bondservants one dollar.[19]

THE TERRITORY OF INDIANA, 1800-1808

From the Mississippi villages and Vincennes complaints were heard that the seat of government was too far to the east,[20] and by 1800 it was time for William Henry Harrison to begin the division of the Old Northwest into territories and states. Harrison, who had been aide-de-camp to Wayne at Fallen Timbers, resigned from the army in 1798 to become the Northwest Territory's secretary and then its first delegate to Congress. As an advocate of a decentralized judiciary and a liberal land policy, he won the nonvoting seat in Congress over Arthur St. Clair, Jr., by one vote.

The election of a delegate, which came with advancement to the second grade of territorial government, was important to the frontier. For the first time petitions and memorials from the Old Northwest could be addressed to an interested official who represented the area. Although he could not vote, Harrison took care of his constituency. As chairman of the house committee on public lands, he maneuvered the passage of an 1800 law creating the territory of Indiana, with Vincennes as its capital, covering the modern states of Illinois, Indiana, Wisconsin, most of Michigan, and part of Minnesota. The portion to the east retained the name of the Northwest Territory until 1802, when the expansionist movement allowed Ohio to be admitted as a state with a population of 43,365, mostly New Englanders. Kentucky, settled earlier

[19] See T. C. Pease's introduction to *Laws of the Northwest Territory.*

[20] Clarence E. Carter (ed.), *Territorial Papers of the United States,* III, 76-78. Beverly Bond, *The Civilization of the Old Northwest.*

because the Cumberland Gap was a natural gateway, had 220,000 residents.

A census in 1800 showed that the Illinois country had only 2,458 residents, approximately the same number as a half-century earlier. The arrival of the first parties of the English-speaking had been canceled by the emigration of the impoverished French across the Mississippi, which had started before the Revolution and continued because of uncertainty surrounding the antislavery article of the Ordinance of 1787. Indian troubles, clouds over French land titles, delays in opening other land for public sale, and the lack of effective government in a largely lawless region were other reasons why Illinois, at the farthest reach of the frontier, was slow to attract settlers.

In the old and shabby villages, Cahokia had 719 residents, Kaskaskia 467, and Prairie du Rocher 212. Close by were 286 Americans at Bellefontaine, some 250 in southern St. Clair County, and 334 scattered in Monroe County. Far away at Peoria an estimated one hundred French carried on a fur trade. About ninety Americans were in the Fort Massac vicinity. Because roads were little more than trails for single horses, the only settlements of consequence were beside or near the navigable streams. Between Kaskaskia and the Ohio and Wabash rivers there is no record of a single home.

The appointment as governor of Indiana went to Harrison, who found that the Illinois residents had not been satisfied to be part of the new territory. The situation was not new on the frontier, and Kentucky had insisted upon separation from Virginia and Tennessee from North Carolina. In each instance the established government to the east lacked the strength to aid the distant settlements. The western element used any available complaint, including in the Illinois case a charge that Harrison was guilty of local favoritism. In 1803 the protest went to the extreme of petitioning for annexation of Illinois to the new territory of Louisiana. Since Indiana was a new territory of the first grade, the frontier had lost its delegate to Congress, and from the American Bottom complaints arose that the legislature and court at Vincennes were too far away.

Harrison meanwhile had trouble with an Illinois faction, men of wealth and influence, who agitated for repeal of the 1787 ordinance's prohibition of slavery.[21] St. Clair had sought to quiet that

21 R. Carlyle Buley, *The Old Northwest, Pioneer Period, 1815-1840*, I, 58-60.

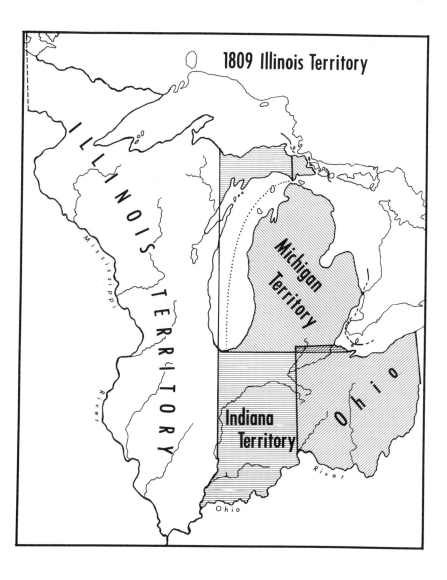

1809 Illinois Territory

situation by holding that the ordinance did not free the slaves owned by the French, but that did not satisfy territorial leaders who had southern backgrounds. They pointed out that labor was scarce in Illinois and slavery legal across the Mississippi. William Morrison, the leading merchant at Kaskaskia, and John Edgar headed the opposition. They advocated advancement to the second grade as a means of reducing Harrison's power and electing a proslavery delegate to Congress.

Harrison, who had no desire to divide his power with an elected legislature, and his judges in 1803 passed a law for an indenture of servants. Slavery in disguise, an indenture was a contract, usually with elements of duress, which bound a Negro to work for a long period for his owner. A question arose whether Harrison and the judges had authority to adopt such a law. A legislative enactment would have a sounder legal basis, and Harrison in 1804 ordered a referendum on the issue of advancement to second-grade government. To be contrary, the Morrison-Edgar faction complained of insufficient notice, changed positions, and opposed the proposition, which nevertheless carried, 269 to 131. Harrison promptly called an election at which his adherents captured the three seats from Illinois.[22]

Illinois sentiment for separation increased and in 1808 a deal was made with Jesse B. Thomas, speaker of the territorial house of representatives, who lived in eastern Indiana.[23] Thomas won election as delegate to Congress with solid Illinois support and not a vote to spare. He had given a written pledge to the separationists and made good on the bargain by getting a law enacted February 3, 1809, establishing the territory of Illinois effective March 1. Ancient Kaskaskia was made the capital. Under terms of the Ordinance of 1787, the eastern boundary ran north from Vincennes to Canada. The other boundaries were the Wabash, Ohio, and Mississippi rivers, and a line running from the Mississippi to the Lake of the Woods, which gave the new territory an area two and a half times that of the present state.

Indiana officials regarded separation of Illinois as a dirty trick. It left their legislature without a quorum and forced Harrison to take extralegal steps for the continuation of government. Also, the Indiana capital had to be moved from Vincennes to a more central location. Thomas showed up at Kaskaskia with an appointment as one of the three federal judges for Illinois and did not care that he had been hung in effigy at Vincennes.[24] He settled at Cahokia and served two terms as United States senator.

22 For a detailed study of this period see Francis S. Philbrick's introduction to the *Laws of Indiana Territory*.

23 Dr. John F. Snyder, "Forgotten Statesmen of Illinois: Hon. Jesse Burgess Thomas," *Transactions of the Illinois State Historical Society*, IX (1904), 514-523. See also Snyder's *Adam W. Snyder in Illinois History, 1817-1842*, pp. 9-18.

24 Davidson-Stuvé, *op. cit.*, p. 242.

Meanwhile, events far beyond its borders involved Illinois during the Indiana territorial period. Napoleon Bonaparte, whose ambitions included restoration of France as an American colonial power, in 1801 acquired from Spain the title to the vast territory west of the Mississippi River. A Spanish official still on duty at New Orleans ordered the lower Mississippi closed to cargoes from the United States, but that market was soon regained. Napoleon, upon the failure of an expedition to the West Indies, abandoned his plans for the western hemisphere and in 1803 sold Louisiana to President Jefferson's emissaries. As a result of the Louisiana Purchase, Illinois no longer was on the western border of the United States. From a new position in the nation's center it was able to trade down and across the Mississippi without restrictions. To find out what was beyond that river, two army officers with a party of twenty-six camped during the winter of 1803-04 at the mouth of the Wood River and, joined by two civilians, left May 14 in three boats for a trip up the Missouri River and over the Rocky Mountains. The Lewis and Clark expedition returned in two years and three months without finding a Northwest Passage but with a clearer conception of the nation's magnitude.[25]

25 Bernard De Voto, *The Course of Empire*, pp. 383-554.

4

THE TERRITORY OF ILLINOIS

THE ENGLISH-SPEAKING PIONEERS WHO BEGAN THE PERMANENT settlement of Illinois came primarily from southern upland stock. Their Anglo-Saxon forefathers had crossed the Atlantic from the British Isles and Germany to reach Virginia and the Carolinas, and in later generations they spread into Kentucky and Tennessee. Then, after more time passed, they moved into southern Indiana, southern Illinois, and eastern Missouri to take up land along the river bottoms. Those from the Middle Atlantic states who came down the Ohio River had basically the same backgrounds, although most of them had not lived as long in the comparative isolation of the wilderness. Even some of the minority Yankees had reached the state after a circuit into the South. As a result, the beliefs and prejudices of the southern uplanders dominated the early decades of Illinois statehood.

The average man who lived in a log cabin, displaced the Indians, and opened the frontier may have been a poorly educated lover of the outdoors with no yearning for close neighbors, but not all fitted that category. Some came directly from the cities. Some sought isolation because they were fugitives or rogues. Some had been exposed to degrees of culture and learning but abandoned them for adventure or seclusion in the West. Usually the first arrivals were the most lawless or unruly.

In the heterogenous society there were volunteers for leadership, especially as settlements became towns. From the start

Illinois attracted ambitious speculators, lawyers, merchants, and mechanics hopeful of finding more opportunity and less competition for riches and honors. The westward movement of the frontier also meant that new governments must be formed and public offices filled. The frontier was democratic, but public salaries were low and the filling of offices put a premium on men who had economic means if not education and administrative experience. Part of St. Clair's delay in setting up a court system for the Old Northwest could be attributed to a shortage of men who were willing to travel long distances for the pay offered.

ARISTOCRATS AND BACKWOODSMEN

Strangers from Kentucky came in to officiate over the new territory of Illinois, to the disappointment of factional leaders engaged in a power struggle at Kaskaskia. To avoid taking sides, President Madison gave the appointment as governor to a man who lived south of the Ohio River, Ninian Edwards, an aristocrat sponsored politically by Henry Clay and Senator John Pope of Kentucky. Edwards required time to transport his Negroes and livestock from Kentucky, and in his absence the proclamation establishing territorial government was issued April 28, 1809, by Nathaniel Pope, who was the territorial secretary, the senator's brother, and the governor's cousin.

Successful both financially and politically, Edwards had a long career in Illinois as governor and senator. He was born in 1775, the son of a Maryland congressman and the nephew of an earlier Kentucky senator. Sent to Kentucky by his father to buy land for the family, he sowed his wild oats. A rather stuffy biography by his son, Ninian Wirt Edwards, whose wife was Abraham Lincoln's sister-in-law, omits details in reciting that "Governor Edwards from the time he was nineteen years of age until he was twenty-one or twenty-two led a dissolute life; he indulged in dissipation and gambling to an extent which alarmed his friends."[1] During this period he was twice elected to the legislature, the second time almost unanimously. Edwards reformed, became a leading lawyer

---

[1] Ninian W. Edwards, *A History of Illinois from 1778 to 1833; and Life and Times of Ninian Edwards,* p. 22. *The Edwards Papers* were edited by Elihu B. Washburne. For short biographical sketches of Edwards, see Cecil K. Byrd, *A Bibliography of Illinois Imprints,* pp. 3-4; John Moses, *Illinois Historical and Statistical,* I, 241; and E. B. Greene and C. W. Alvord (eds.), *The Governors' Letter-Books, 1818-1834,* p. 4n.

in Kentucky and western Tennessee, amassed what his son called a large fortune, and was chief justice of Kentucky before his thirty-second birthday. A large and distinguished-looking man with courtly manners, the governor was regarded as the ablest man in the territory. He was paid two thousand dollars a year and, having the free choice of a thousand acres of land, settled on a farm near Kaskaskia.

Courtesy Illinois State Historical Library

Governor Ninian Edwards

Pope was a college-educated lawyer who spoke fluent French and, after the Louisiana Purchase, had headed for the lead-shipping town of Ste. Genevieve, which had a population of about one thousand and was the largest French community along the

Mississippi. He also practiced law at Kaskaskia, and moved there as soon as he learned that Illinois would be a territory.[2] For six months, at the age of twenty-four, Pope acted as governor in the midst of local quarrels. After Edwards assumed office and astutely steered clear of factionalism, Pope reverted to his appointive status as secretary, for which he received one thousand dollars a year in salary and charged the federal government sixty dollars a year rent for office space in his father-in-law's house. In a day of small government, when officials wrote their own letters and kept their own records, the purchase of writing paper was a major expense. The territorial court held its first session in a private home. Edwards and two of the appointed judges began their work with blanket adoption of pertinent portions of the Indiana territorial code.[3]

Because Illinois had been settled by squatters, the provision of the Ordinance of 1787 that only landowners could vote was inoperative in the new territory. In many cases legal titles to land did not exist because conflicting claims were still being adjudicated and settlers were waiting for the right to buy the farms they occupied. Western sentiment for greater public participation in government was increasing, and Indiana in 1909 had been granted the right to elect its delegate. Edwards had no hesitancy about giving up part of his authority. When Illinois settlers began agitating in early 1812 for the right to elect their officials, the governor called a referendum at which it was established that public sentiment was nearly unanimous for the change. Petitioned by Edwards, Congress promptly passed a law granting second-grade territorial government.[4] Revolutionary in its scope, the law granted the right to vote to all free white males who had lived in Illinois one year and who paid any county or territorial tax, no matter how small. The law let squatters have the right of franchise and gave Illinois a more democratic form of government than any other territory possessed. At the first general election, held during

2 Paul M. Angle, "Nathaniel Pope, 1784-1850: A Memoir," *Transactions of the Illinois State Historical Society*, XLIII (1936), 111-181.

3 Clarence E. Carter (ed.), *The Territorial Papers of the United States*, XVI.

4 Francis S. Philbrick, *Laws of the Illinois Territory*. His lengthy introduction analyzes in detail the legal foundation of territorial government. Alexander Davidson and Bernard Stuvé, *A Complete History of Illinois*, pp. 287-290. John Moses, *op. cit.*, I, 258-259, 287-290. See also Clarence W. Alvord, *Laws of the Territory of Illinois, 1809-1811*.

three days in October, Shadrach Bond, nephew and namesake of one of the first English-speaking arrivals, went to Congress as the first representative of Illinois. Pierre Menard became president of the elected council of five, one from each county, which assisted the governor. The house had six representatives, with two coming from St. Clair County. Most of the new officials had southern backgrounds. To finance the new territory, a tax of seventy-five cents per hundred acres was levied. Counties could tax horses at a fifty-cent rate and cattle at ten cents, and require that merchants pay ten or fifteen dollars as licenses.

The territory had a shortage of lawyers, disputes piled up for years, some of the newcomers were troublemakers, and there was work for judges if they would be diligent. Under the earlier territorial governments complaints had arisen that judges from Marietta and Vincennes did not appear often enough in Illinois. Now the same cry arose concerning the difficulty in getting attention from the Kaskaskia judiciary. To the excuse that travel was difficult, the reply was given that federally appointed judges received one hundred dollars a month, which was a good salary. The St. Clair and Randolph county grand juries at one time took official note of the nonattendance of judges, and in 1814 the legislature sought to remedy the situation by creating a system of circuit courts. Each judge would be assigned two counties and required to hold court at regular intervals, but the judges objected. Judge Thomas, who consistently lined up against Edwards, contended that the territorial law was an infringement on a federal matter. The governor disagreed and submitted the dispute to Congress, which responded by reenacting the territorial law in substance. The judges were required to hold two terms of court at the circuit level in each county and then assemble at Kaskaskia as a Court of Appeals twice a year.

The first book printed in Illinois, a comprehensive collection of territorial laws, was a Pope achievement. Authorized by the legislature and known as *Pope's Digest*,[5] it was printed with coarse paper and clumsy type in 1815 by Matthew Duncan, who a year earlier had founded the *Illinois Herald,* the territory's first newspaper. Duncan, the first printer in Illinois, came from Kentucky as a protégé of the governor. He soon sold the paper and it, like most

---

[5] Originally entitled *Laws of the Territory of Illinois* and reissued as *Pope's Digest, 1815,* by the Illinois State Historical Society in 1906.

others of that time, continued as a political organ. Pope received one hundred dollars for revising the territorial law, but his work was never enacted by the legislature.

The night of December 11, 1811, cabins trembled and John Reynolds' father mistakenly shouted that "the Indians are on the house."[6] A series of intense earthquakes centered at New Madrid, Missouri, shook wide areas of the midcontinent. The earth quivered almost constantly for several weeks, and another major earthquake occurred January 7, 1812. In the largely unsettled Mississippi valley only one death was reported and property damage was slight, because there were few buildings except the sturdy cabins with interlocking notched logs. Over a thirty-thousand-square-mile area, especially in Missouri and Arkansas, topographical features were altered. At some places the ground surface rose or sank ten to fifteen feet and some changes were made in the course of the Mississippi River.

SURVEYS, LAND GRANTS, AND TITLE DISPUTES

For past and present owners of Illinois real estate, a red-letter day was May 20, 1785. The Continental Congress then adopted a land ordinance establishing the neat and orderly system of rectangular surveys now used in thirty states. Thanks to Thomas Jefferson, Congress turned down the Virginia system of "tomahawk claims" under which a settler staked out his own domain, following zigzag boundaries if he pleased, and hoped some surveyor would confirm it later. Kentucky used it, and Abraham Lincoln's father and many others found they did not own the land they farmed.

Under the rectangular or grid system, surveyors work on north-south or east-west lines and property ownership is based on townships six miles square, each having thirty-six sections of 640 acres. The sections are divisible into squares and rectangles and

6 Reynolds, *My Own Times,* p. 79. Daniel Berry, "The Illinois Earthquake of 1811 and 1812," *Transactions of the Illinois State Historical Society,* XII (1907), 74-78.

Southern Illinois has had other earthquakes, although none so severe as the one in 1811. No major damage was done November 9, 1968, by a quake that centered on Broughton, Hamilton County. It had a Richter scale magnitude of 5.5, compared with the 8.5 of the disastrous Alaskan earthquake four years earlier. The far southern counties of Illinois are in a geologically faulted region, subject to fairly frequent quakes, but the stresses built up within the earth are usually released in small shocks, with minor damage.

any field can be exactly located by a universal system of number-
ing and description. Credit for it goes to Thomas Hutchins, who
once served at Fort de Chartres as a British topographical officer.[7]
After the Revolution he had charge of the survey of the Old
Northwest and personally ran the first meridians upon which the
system depended.

Congress required that surveys precede the sale of public lands,
that sales be completed township by township in order to solidify
settlement, and that part of each township be dedicated for the
support of public schools. The ordinance prohibited sales to political favorites and, to discourage speculators, required that half of
the tracts be sold in sections and half in townships at one dollar an
acre. Congressional policy also held up surveying until the land
was purchased from the Indians. From the frontier demands arose
for smaller parcels, lower prices, and liberal credit terms. In
response, William Henry Harrison pushed enactment of an 1800
law which permitted a man with $160 to make a down payment
on a farm. Since 1797, the government had allowed the cash sale
of complete sections at two dollars an acre. The new law reduced
the minimum sale to a half-section of 320 acres under a four-year
credit system requiring only one-fourth to be paid down. It set a
trend toward family-sized farms, stimulated migration, and helped
Ohio become a state in 1803. The Harrison law generally met
frontier needs, although many could not pay two dollars an acre.
It was in effect until 1820 with minor revisions, and it permitted
newly opened land to be sold for the two-dollar minimum price at
a public auction which lasted three weeks. After that, purchases
could be made at private sales. Transactions were handled at
government land offices. Each was staffed by two federally appointed officials, a register who kept ownership records and a
receiver who handled the money.[8] Other politicians envied them.

Congress in 1804 established land offices at Kaskaskia, Vincennes, and Detroit. At Kaskaskia the land sale was delayed ten
years, however, while the register and receiver acted as federal
commissioners in passing on the validity of land grants made in the
French and British periods.

[7] Hutchins' reports are found in *A Topographical Description of Virginia . . .*,
published in London in 1778.

[8] Solon J. Buck, *Illinois in 1818*, pp. 36-55. Also see Thomas Donaldson, *The Public
Domain.*

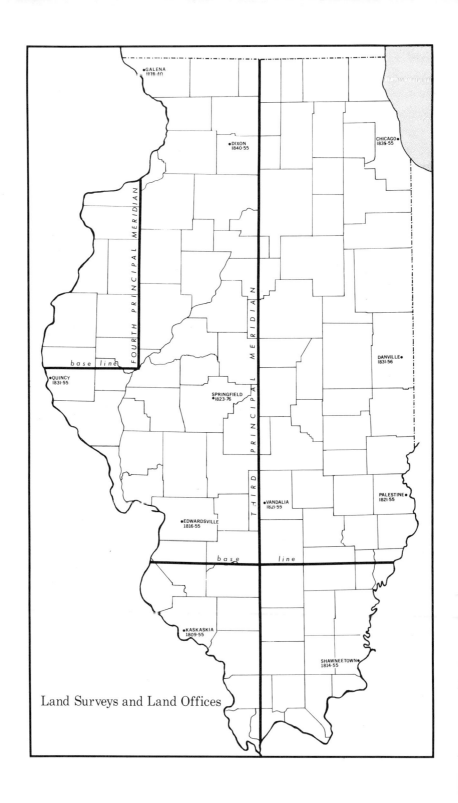

GALENA
1835-60

DIXON
1840-55

CHICAGO
1835-55

FOURTH PRINCIPAL MERIDIAN

base line

QUINCY
1831-55

DANVILLE
1831-56

SPRINGFIELD
1823-76

THIRD PRINCIPAL MERIDIAN

VANDALIA
1821-55

PALESTINE
1821-55

EDWARDSVILLE
1816-55

base line

KASKASKIA
1809-55

SHAWNEETOWN
1814-55

Land Surveys and Land Offices

The dream of riches through large holdings of valuable land began with the French explorers, who recruited settlers and assigned land under a feudal system of rent collections. Fraud flourished in the British period, when some commanders parceled out large tracts in violation of orders. They granted away French property on the assumption that titles had been forfeited, and neglected to preserve records of former ownership. Lieutenant Colonel John Wilkins, the most notorious, was generous to his favorites in Illinois and on the seaboard, apparently requiring only that they reconvey to him an interest in the land they received, To the owners of the Baynton, Wharton, and Morgan stores he granted twenty-four thousand valuable acres between Kaskaskia and Prairie du Rocher. They promptly reassigned part of it to Wilkins.

Virginia had stipulated that French possessions and titles must be confirmed. The Confederation in 1788 acted to legalize their land ownership, but the fur trade dwindled and few of the French, if they still lived in the American Bottom, could pay for a surveyor. As recompense for Revolutionary War hardships, Congress granted a maximum of four hundred acres of land to heads of families which had lived in Illinois during or before 1783. Eventually 244 of the head-right claims were filed in a situation which in modern times would keep a battery of law firms busy. St. Clair confirmed land titles in a questionable manner and in wholesale lots. The thirty-thousand-acre British grant under Wilkins had been assigned to John Edgar, who turned over a one-third interest to John Murray St. Clair, the governor's son. St. Clair confirmed their right to the land.[9]

For generations the French had considered their holdings to be of little worth and sales had been made at bargain basement prices, but when statehood loomed the land claims became valuable. A few speculators, men of prominence and increasing wealth, acquired most of them. Edgar worked closely with William Morrison, one of six brothers who came to Illinois from Philadelphia. Their father had been knighted in Cork County and their uncle was a noted merchant in Philadelphia. Morrison, who reached Kaskaskia in 1790, developed trading operations that extended as far as Pittsburgh, New Orleans, Prairie du Chien, and the Rocky Mountains. In time Edgar had title to 49,200 acres, spread through

[9] Francis S. Philbrick, *Laws of Indiana Territory,* pp. lxv-xcix.

eight counties. Morrison owned 15,040, and Nicholas Jarrott 25,000.

The two commissioners at Kaskaskia, in an 1810 report to the secretary of the treasury, rejected 890 land claims as illegal and fraudulent. They found that forgery and perjury had been common and that Edgar and the Morrisons, among others, had suborned witnesses to swear to whatever was required to make a claim appear legal. The two commissioners upheld some of the claims, with Congress concurring.

No one wanted to invest in unsurveyed land of doubtful title, and not until 1814 was the government ready to offer the public domain for sale. Surveying parties began marking Illinois township and section lines four years earlier. They used chains for measurement, marked section corners with tree notches or stakes, and made notations in their records when they found salt licks or sites for mills that could be powered by water. The surveyors, who gave Illinois a close inspection at one-mile intervals, also had instructions to make a record of the nature of the land. Unlike the Indians or other white men, they had to work on straight lines, regardless of swamps, hills, streams, and tangled growth. They lived a hard life under primitive conditions, sleeping under lean-tos or tents of grass or boughs.

The east-west base line from which the surveyors worked had been started in Ohio and intersected the southwest corner of a tract of land at Vincennes. The Old Northwest had several north-south meridians. Part of Illinois was surveyed from the Second Principal Meridian, which ran through Indiana, but more use was made of the Third Principal Meridian, which started at the mouth of the Ohio River and almost bisected Illinois.[10] Trouble was not limited to the convergence of the lines as they extended northward. As surveyed between 1831 and 1833, the Illinois-Wisconsin border was about three-quarters of a mile too far north at the Mississippi and the same distance too far south by the time it reached Lake Michigan.

The men who had pushed into Illinois without legal permission and taken possession of unsurveyed lands presented a problem before land offices were belatedly opened at Shawneetown in 1812 and Edwardsville in 1816. Some of the squatters feared loss of valuable improvements on which they had worked as long as

[10] Douglas C. Ridgley, *Geography of Illinois,* pp. 1-6.

thirty years. To protect their investments in time and money they petitioned for a preemption law which Shadrach Bond helped pass in 1813. A boon to Illinois, it permitted men who had arrived early to have the first chance to buy the land they occupied and made moving to Illinois less of a gamble. Sales opened slowly, but after the War of 1812 settlers and speculative buyers rushed in. Most tracts went at the minimum of two dollars an acre, which was the uniform price regardless of obvious variations in value. The bulk of the Illinois land was bought on credit. An 1804 amendment authorized quarter-section or 160-acre sales, and the minimum was again halved in 1817 to allow some eighty-acre farms. A 5 percent down payment would hold the land forty days, after which 20 percent more was due. The balance was payable in three equal annual installments, without interest. Land reverted to the government after five years' delinquency.

Congress reserved the big triangle between the Mississippi and Illinois rivers for payment of 160-acre bounties to soldiers of the War of 1812. In 1816 at St. Louis, Edwards, William Clark, and Auguste Chouteau talked the Indians into conceding white ownership. The Military Tract, as it was known for generations, covered three and a half million acres and in time was organized into fourteen counties and parts of four others. It was surveyed from a Fourth Principal Meridian running north from the mouth of the Illinois River and by a base line west from Beardstown. Surveyors worked rapidly and land distribution began in October, 1817. In less than four months some eighteen thousand warrants, each entitling a veteran or his heirs to 160 acres, were exchanged at the general land office at Washington for patents which covered much of the Military Tract. The warrants were nontransferable, but the veteran was not required to settle on the land and the patent could be sold the day it was received. Eastern speculators picked up most of them quickly, sometimes for ten cents an acre.[11]

In the trend toward sale of smaller tracts on easier credit terms, Congress in 1820 lowered the price of government land to $1.25 an acre and the minimum purchase to eighty acres. Speculators lost heavily, but it aided settlement. Now any man who could scrape together one hundred dollars could get a debt-free title to a farm that was big enough for a poor family in the days before

[11] William V. Pooley, *Settlement of Illinois from 1830 to 1850*, pp. 326-327. Edmund Dana, *A Description of the Bounty Lands of the State of Illinois*.

farm machinery was manufactured. The $1.25 price stayed in effect until the last government land was sold in Illinois.

MASSACRE AT FORT DEARBORN, AUGUST 15, 1812

The British were difficult to dislodge from the Old Northwest. The 1783 treaty that ended the Revolutionary War gave their traders access to the United States, and they tried to keep control of the fur harvest from regions still occupied by Indians. The savages accepted their promises and presents but could not understand why, in the 1794 Battle at Fallen Timbers, the redcoats who encouraged them did not assist in the losing fight against Mad Anthony Wayne's Americans. Only after that loss of face did the British give up Detroit and the border forts.

The United States needed additional links in the frontier defense chain, and the Indians in the Treaty of Greenville had ceded strategic areas along the Illinois River and given the whites the right to occupy the Chicago portage.[12] In 1803 a detachment of soldiers spent thirty-five days on the Sauk trail walking from Detroit to Chicago, where they were met by Captain James Whistler, who came by schooner. On unsurveyed land, they felled trees, hauled and notched logs, and by the next year had built Fort Dearborn, named for the secretary of war. There the garrison, which at the start numbered three officers, seven noncoms, and fifty-four privates, spent nine unexciting years.

At the fort the government also maintained an Indian agency and a factory. The Indian agent as a matter of goodwill distributed presents to the Indians and held solemn council sessions with the chiefs. The factory, or trading house, served as a government-operated retail outlet at which the Indians could get the trade goods upon which they long had been dependent. The low prices pleased the red men, who nevertheless had not broken away from British influence. Across the narrow and sluggish river stood the house which du Sable had sold in 1800 when he took his Indian wife to Peoria. In 1804 it had been bought and enlarged by John Kinzie, trader and friend of the Indians. Two other houses stood

12 The defense line included Detroit and Mackinac and extended as far south as Fort Bellefontaine, an almost forgotten name, four miles up the Missouri River from its junction with the Mississippi. It served as military headquarters for the West from 1805 to 1826, and because of its existence the army did not need to station troops at the mouth of the Illinois River.

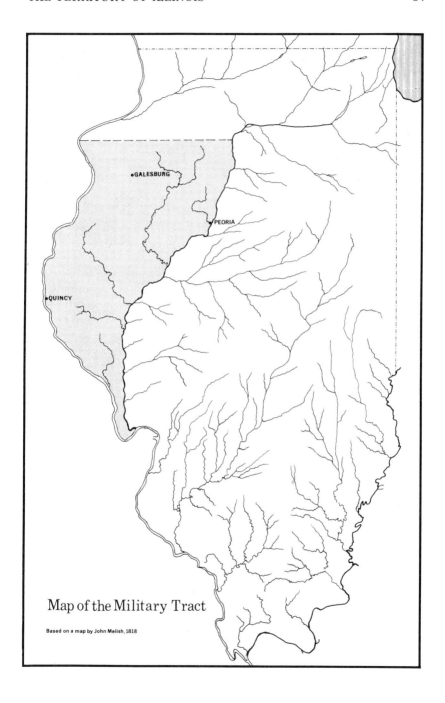

Map of the Military Tract

Based on a map by John Melish, 1818

nearby and others were some distance away. Kinzie and a few private traders competed with the government by sending their own agents into the wilderness. Including half-breeds but not counting the garrison, by 1812 perhaps forty persons lived at the Chicago portage.

The inland phase of the War of 1812, which was provoked more by Great Britain's maritime policy than by her wooing of the northwestern tribes, opened disastrously.[13] Indian hostility had not died down in the year since Harrison routed Tecumseh's warriors at Tippecanoe, 150 miles up the Wabash from Vincennes. Fort Mackinac, at the far end of Lake Michigan, quickly fell to the British and Indians when war was declared June 18. General William Hull, who had been a Revolutionary War colonel and governor of Michigan Territory, panicked and ordered the evacuation of Fort Dearborn.

Ten days out of Detroit, an Indian runner brought the orders to the log fort on the Chicago River. There Captain Nathan Heald considered that he had no choice but to obey. The instructions were specific: "It is with regret that I order the evacuation of your post, owing to want of provisions only, a neglect of the Commandant at Detroit. You will therefore destroy all arms and ammunition; but the goods of the Factory you may give to friendly Indians who may be desirous of escorting you to Fort Wayne, and to the poor and needy of your post."[14] The remaining sentence contained bad news and some hope about the situation elsewhere in Hull's theater of war.

Typical of the frontier, Fort Dearborn's strong points were blockhouses with overhanging second stories at the southeast and northwest corners of the stockaded enclosure. A second line of pickets coverged toward the blockhouses, which held four artillery pieces. The garrison numbered four officers and sixty-six men, of

---

[13] The full scope of the war is covered in Alec R. Gilpin, *The War of 1812 in the Old Northwest,* and J. Mackay Hitsman, *The Incredible War of 1812, A Military History.*

[14] For a detailed account of Fort Dearborn, from its founding to an inventory of the massacre's survivors, see Milo Milton Quaife, *Chicago and the Old Northwest,* pp. 127-261. Quaife's six chapters in this book are condensed in *Checagou, From Indian Wigwam to Modern City,* pp. 63-158. In *Wau-Bun,* Mrs. John H. Kinzie devoted three chapters to the eyewitness story of her mother-in-law. Also see J. Seymour Currey, *The Story of Old Fort Dearborn,* and Harry A. Musham, "Where Did the Battle of Chicago Take Place?", *Journal of the Illinois State Historical Society,* XXXVI (March, 1943), 21-40.

whom twelve were militia and the rest regulars. The supply of guns, ammunition, and provisions could outlast a siege.

Winnemeg, the friendly Potawatomi who brought the orders from Hull, and Kinzie urgently advised that the fort should be held but that, if the captain insisted upon evacuation, it should be done the next day, before the already excited Indians could organize war parties. Four months earlier, Kinzie recalled, a Winnebago band had killed two men on a farm near the river's south branch. Heald, who lacked the imagination to meet frontier emergencies, assumed that Hull had a master plan that must be followed. He would not listen to junior officers, but delayed five vital days before calling a council of Indians and announcing that he would march to Fort Wayne. The Potawatomi, known troublemakers, agreed to furnish an escort. The next day Heald emptied the trading factory, distributing to the Indians the blankets, paints, and other trade goods. Indian tempers rose when they smelled whiskey poured into the river. Most of the ammunition was discarded, leaving each man twenty-five rounds for the dangerous march ahead.

Deliberately sacrificing himself, Captain William Wells rode in from Fort Wayne the next day with thirty mounted Miami Indians. A heroic Indian fighter, Wells was the uncle of Heald's wife. Kidnaped by Indians when he was twelve years old, Wells had lived and fought with them for years, but returned to his white family in time to be a captain of scouts in the Fallen Timbers campaign. Now, he told Heald, it was too late to cancel the march because the food and ammunition had been destroyed.

August 15 was clear, still, and hot. Heald was ready to leave at nine o'clock. Wells, at the head of the column, blackened his face Indian style in recognition of impending doom. The fife and drum played a death march as the soldiers filed out, followed by provision wagons in which nine women and eighteen children rode. Low sand dunes and occasional cottonwoods marked the first desolate mile out of the fort.

Wells gave the alarm as the Potawatomi escort, which had taken a parallel route, turned to attack the column. The Miami Indians fled when the first shot was fired. The soldiers charged but the Indians swept around the flanks, using guns, tomahawks, and scalping knives. In furious fighting Wells was killed by the Indians, who paid tribute to his bravery by eating his heart. Heald surrendered after being wounded. Mrs. Heald and the wife of another officer were saved by friendly Indians. Two junior officers were killed. In all, about sixty white men died, including some wounded who were tomahawked after the surrender and five soldiers who were tortured to death that night. Two women were killed and five carried into captivity. Twelve children were killed outright and few of the others were ever heard from.

The savages completed the carnage by burning the fort. They spared Kinzie, who had placed his family safely on a boat. Also untouched in their home was the family of Antoine Ouilmette, who had part-Indian blood. Heald and his wife eventually reached civilization by different routes. Kinzie returned in 1816 and lived to see Chicago attain commerical importance.

The day after the massacre Hull surrendered Detroit without a battle because of concern for members of his family and other civilians. At a court martial he was sentenced to be shot for cowardice and neglect of duty. The President remanded the execution because of Hull's services in the Revolution, but two years would pass before national morale recovered from the loss of the two forts.

INDIAN LOSERS IN THE WAR OF 1812

Five months before the Fort Dearborn massacre, Governor Edwards in an alarming letter told the secretary of war that Indian depredations had become so serious that he expected to lose half of the white population of Illinois.[15] The Kickapoo, Winnebago, and Potawatomi far outnumbered the whites, and the increased number of killings, robberies, and horse thefts had caused Congress in 1811 to authorize formation of ten companies of mounted rangers, with four of them assigned to Illinois. From his own pocket, Edwards helped pay organization expenses of other mounted militia companies. Each ranger received a dollar a day, but had to furnish his own horse, equipment, and provisions. Future politicians would find that ranger service was a campaign asset, as valuable as Grand Army of the Republic or American Legion memberships after later wars.

Edwards assigned the rangers to patrol the Indian country in advance of the line of settlements. To anchor the defense, he built Fort Russell northwest of Edwardsville and ornamented it with a

15 Edwards to William Eustis, Feb. 10, 1812.

Louis XIV cannon from old Fort de Chartres. The sparsity of settlement was shown by the location of a long chain of block-house forts which helped furnish protection. One of the most exposed was at the present site of Carlyle. Others were further south, and rangers patrolled the lower Wabash River. Usually the blockhouses were sturdy two-story cabins, with portholes through which muskets could be fired downward as well as outward and with the log corners closely trimmed to make it difficult for arsonous Indians to climb to the roof. Stockaded forts had block-houses at the corners, twelve-to-fifteen-foot-high fences, and gates through which wagons and cattle could be driven.

Ambitious for a military career, Edwards took the offensive against the nearest concentration of the enemy, the Indian villages at Peoria.[16] In the new war, the governor mustered two regiments at Fort Russell and assumed personal command of a mounted army of eight hundred men. Near the future site of Springfield they destroyed two Kickapoo villages. Reaching a Miami and Kickapoo village near the head of Lake Peoria, the undisciplined militia turned into a mob. They killed from twenty-two to thirty of the fleeing Indians, burned several towns, and returned home in thirteen days without losing a man. The occasion called for speeches, with the commander extolling the patriotism and valor of his men. An orator of the florid school, Edwards was at his best in such a role. A second expedition up the river to Peoria had elements of disgrace. Led by Captain Thomas E. Craig, it found the town deserted and appropriated the possessions of the missing residents. Most of them were given back on the return of Thomas Forsyth, the Indian agent, but after several days someone fired a shot at Craig's boats. Without further provocation, his men plundered and burned half of the town and carried away forty inhabitants. They were ordered released, and Edwards used Indian funds in his hands to compensate for the losses. To Edwards' chagrin, in 1813 he was bypassed in a military reorganization. Harrison took command of a military district encompassing Illinois, Indiana,

---

[16] French traders abandoned the Peoria post sometime after the Tonti era, but in approximately 1778 they returned under the leadership of John Maillet. In 1781, fearing hostile Indians, the French sought protection in the Mississippi villages, but they returned in two years. By 1812 the settlement was small, with perhaps twelve to twenty families existing on the profits of the fur trade. There was no church or school, and the whites lived little better than their Indian customers. Charles Ballance, *The History of Peoria*, pp. 25-41. Lewis C. Beck, *A Gazetteer of the States of Illinois and Missouri*, pp. 143-149.

Nathaniel Pope

Missouri, and Michigan. Benjamin Howard resigned as governor of Missouri to become brigadier general commanding the Illinois-Missouri subdistrict. Sulking, Edwards left Pope as acting governor and spent the summer in Kentucky.

At Peoria, Howard's rangers rebuilt Fort Clark, which regulars garrisoned. In the absence of British forces, General William Clark and two hundred men occupied Prairie du Chien, which was surrendered the next year by the small force left there. Two later expeditions up the Mississippi the next year ended at Rock Island, where the British had reinforced the Sauk and Fox stronghold. The second, commanded by Zachary Taylor, suffered heavy losses.

Until the end of the war the Americans held a fort, soon to be named for Governor Edwards, opposite the mouth of the Des Moines River at the present site of Warsaw. After the fall of Fort Dearborn, United States influence ended at the Fort Edwards-Peoria-Vincennes line. As in earlier wars, victory was won further east and action in Illinois was of minor significance.

In a demonstration of the frontier's hatred of the Indian, the territorial legislature in late 1814, ten days after the war officially ended, established a system of bounties for the killing of hostile braves. The state obligated itself to pay fifty dollars for the death of an Indian who entered a settlement with murderous intent. Civilians who had official permission to send an expedition into Indian country could qualify for a one-hundred-dollar reward by killing an Indian warrior. For rangers and any others on frontier defense duty the payment would be halved. In each case the same amount was promised for the capture of a squaw or child. Presumably no one collected.[17]

With peace, the British agreed to a treaty that again denied them an Indian buffer state in the Old Northwest. A new Fort Dearborn in 1816 reestablished federal authority at Chicago. Fort Armstrong was placed at Rock Island to signal that British control had ended. The army in 1818 abandoned Fort Clark as no longer needed for the protection of Peoria. Government trading factories reappeared at Chicago, Prairie du Chien and Fort Edwards so that the Indians would not have to trade with the British. Because of water connections, Indian agents at Peoria and Prairie du Chien reported directly to Governor Edwards, who was ex officio superintendent of Indian affairs, while the men at Chicago and Green Bay were under the jurisdiction of Governor Cass of Michigan. There were several subagents, with Pierre Menard holding the job for a time at Kaskaskia. As a partner in a firm headed by Manuel Lisa of St. Louis, Menard had led the first invasion of trappers up the Missouri River to Fort Mandan. Driven out by Indians, he returned to his commercial and public career at Kaskaskia.

Although Canada produced better pelts, chiefly because of climatic differences, the Illinois and Wabash river valleys and the Mississippi between St. Louis and Prairie du Chien were major fur-bearing areas. From the Illinois valley in 1816 traders shipped the hides of ten thousand deer, three hundred bears, ten thousand

17 F. S. Philbrick, *Laws of Illinois Territory,* pp. 177-178.

raccoons, four hundred otter, and beaver, cat, fox, and mink for a total value of $23,700. In one year ten thousand pounds of maple sugar were shipped from the same area. Wilderness bartering also involved lead, beeswax, tallow, and mats.[18]

The fur traders, who for more than a century had demonstrated the merits of the free enterprise system, soon put the government factories out of business. The government would not extend credit to the Indians, and the traders carried their liquor and goods directly to the source of supply. As the cheapest and most effective way of keeping the Indians under control, the government agents passed out presents. Nothing else could wean them from British influence, Edwards believed. The agents also paid annuities promised in land cession treaties. The Kaskaskia tribe received a thousand dollars, with like amounts going to the Ottawa, Chippewa, and Potawatomi along the Illinois River, but for some reason the Kickapoo received only nine hundred dollars a year. During those years the Cahokia, Michigamea, and Tamaroa disappeared as distinct bands. The weakened Kaskaskia, victims of the white man's alcohol, lived on a three-hundred-acre reservation near the capital.

After the war, during which westward migration ceased and land sales slumped, the Indians were relatively peaceful. The British, in an effort to hang on to the fur trade, enticed the red men to Canada with lavish presents and caused minor trouble. Except for the indispensable French-Canadian *voyageurs* and interpreters, the government in 1816 excluded foreigners from the fur trade, and the next year John Jacob Astor's American Fur Company moved into the field as a near monopoly. Half-breed descendants of the original French were crewmen, with trading brigades out of Mackinac each fall. They left merchandise with the Indians, who promised to deliver their fur catch in the spring. In the winter of 1813-15 the fur company had clerks, traders, interpreters, and boatmen on the Illinois, Wabash, Des Plaines, and Kankakee rivers. Astor's system was to send American clerks along with the *voyageurs* and *engages*. One was Gurdon Saltonstall Hubbard, who first visited Fort Dearborn in 1818, a few weeks before Illinois achieved statehood.[19] In addition to the soldiers, only a few fur

18 Buck, *op. cit.*, pp. 1-35.

19 Caroline M. McIlvane (ed.), *The Autobiography of Gurdon Saltonstall Hubbard.* Henry E. Hamilton, *Incidents and Events in the Life of Gurdon Saltonstall Hubbard, . . . by His Nephew.* Clint Clay Tilton, "John W. Vance and the Vermilion Salines," *Transactions of the Illinois State Historical Society,* XXXVIII (1931), 83-178.

traders lived at the Chicago portage. Hubbard, who began his trading career when he was sixteen years old, spent his winters in the wilderness. Hubbard had unusual executive ability, and in 1827 became a partner in the fur company and the next year bought out its Illinois interests. To avoid the laborious boat trip across the Chicago portage, he used pack ponies on the trail south of Chicago. Hubbard's Trace became the State Road and was the only clearly marked route toward the Wabash River country, through Watseka and Danville and into Effingham County.

Although white settlers were a fact of life in the wilderness, the government could not survey and sell the land as long as the legal title rested with the Indian tribes. Wayne's Treaty of Greenville recognized for the first time that white men had property rights in the Old Northwest, but it specified that all land not in their possession belonged to the Indians.[20] St. Clair had attempted to open the way for settlement by direct purchase from the Indians, but had difficulty finding any tribe with a clear title to the hunting grounds. Harrison was an expansionist, determined to open the way for the whites. As Indian superintendent he negotiated a series of treaties with such aggressiveness that Jefferson urged restraint. The first Harrison treaty involving Illinois, signed at Fort Wayne in 1803, obtained title to the salt springs on the Saline River through acquisition of the Vincennes Tract, a seventy-by-forty-two-mile rectangle, for a yearly consideration of 150 bushels of salt. Two months later at Vincennes the Kaskaskia signed away the greater portion of southern Illinois in return for $580 cash, an annuity increased to one thousand dollars, a grant of three hundred dollars toward the cost of a church, and one hundred dollars annually for seven years to support a priest. For all practical purposes that extinguished Indian titles in southern Illinois, but overlapping treaties were signed later with other tribes. To open the way for settlement along the Wabash River, in 1809 Harrison negotiated with the Potawatomi, Kickapoo, and others for a narrow strip along the Indian line as far as the Vermilion River.

Several treaties were needed to extinguish titles to the vague holdings in northern and central Illinois of the tribes that had

[20] Frank R. Grover, "Indian Treaties Affecting Lands in the Present State of Illinois," *Transactions of the Illinois State Historical Society,* XXI (1915), 84-105. John Clayton, *Illinois Fact Book and Historical Almanac,* pp. 10-14. Arthur C. Boggess, *The Settlement of Illinois, 1778-1830,* pp. 71-78.

replaced the Iliniwek. In 1804 the Sauk and Fox at St. Louis signed away a big area extending from the Illinois and Fox rivers westward to the Mississippi and northward into Wisconsin. The Indians caused trouble by claiming that the signers were not the legitimate spokesmen for the tribe. As a result, the treaty was renegotiated in 1816 as Edwards and Menard, among others, became experienced in the ritual that went with agreement on an interracial contract. In the 1816 treaty the whites retroceded a large part of northern Illinois, for which they had no immediate use, but took title to a broad strip needed for a canal to Chicago.

The white leaders were never scrupulous about making certain they were dealing with a tribe's actual chiefs and payments were not generous, even by the standards of the frontier. Although the last treaty involving Illinois would not be negotiated until 1833 at Chicago, by the end of the territorial period in 1818 the federal government had legal title to most of Illinois. The Indians still owned the bulk of the northern quarter of the state and a strip along the eastern side, but those areas were not yet in demand for settlement. Enough treaties had been negotiated to guarantee that the white men would take over Illinois whenever they were ready.

5

NEW STATE ON THE FRONTIER

THE NEWLY ESTABLISHED IMPORTANCE OF THE MIDCONTINENT became obvious when Indiana achieved statehood in 1816 and, in a little more than four years, Mississippi, Illinois, Alabama, and Missouri in that sequence also became states. The rapid and successful occupation of the Mississippi not only was a triumph for individual initiative but it ranks as one of the foremost accomplishments of the English-speaking people. Clarence W. Alvord, writing a half-century ago, called it "the most important event in the history of the United States and one of the most momentous in the history of humanity."[1]

Nevertheless, statehood for Illinois came prematurely by a short period of time, since sufficient population and public demand were both lacking in 1818. Migration to the West had been resumed after the War of 1812, and between 1816 and 1818 one of the great periods of American land speculation stirred up interest in the future of Illinois and its neighbors. Only the advance wave of settlement had reached Illinois, however, even though the steamboat was revolutionizing inland transportation and making it easier to reach the inhabited areas along the Ohio, the Mississippi, and their tributaries. The cycle of prosperity ended in 1818, and a national depression that lasted until 1825 put a

---

[1] *The Illinois Country, 1673-1818,* p. 414. See also Theodore Roosevelt, *The Spread of the English-Speaking Peoples,* pp. 17-47, and Fred A. Shannon, *The Farmer's Last Frontier,* p. 37.

check on westward migration. Despite the sparsity of population and the coming setback, however, it was inevitable that the rich and strategically located prairie land soon would become one of the United States. A sickly twenty-two-year-old who started the agitation for statehood was a few years ahead of his time, and on a population basis Illinois has the distinction of being the smallest state ever admitted into the Union.[2]

INSTANT STATEHOOD: COOK, POPE, AND KANE

Had young Daniel Pope Cook found glamorous employment in the federal service, statehood for Illinois might have arrived at a later date and under other circumstances. Small, thin, and pale, he had gone to Washington for a brief visit in early 1817 and, in hope that a sea voyage might improve his health, had been sent to London by President Monroe with diplomatic mail for John Quincy Adams. The precocious Cook aspired to be secretary of Alabama Territory and refused to settle for a state department clerkship that paid a good salary. "I am not yet well," he wrote to Governor Edwards, his future father-in-law. So he disappointedly came back to Kaskaskia, where at least he was someone and from where his uncle, Nathaniel Pope, the newly elected delegate to Congress, had just left for Washington. A Kentuckian, Cook at the age of twenty had first arrived in Illinois in 1815 to practice law. Edwards appointed him the territory's first auditor of public accounts and Cook purchased an interest in the *Illinois Herald,* the territory's first newspaper. Nominally the editor, Cook let others run the politically subsidized paper while its name was changed first to the *Western Intelligencer* and then to the *Illinois Intelligencer.*[3]

Cook became influential around the capitol, a rough building of stone that had housed governmental offices since the British abandoned Fort de Chartres. Two days after his return from Washington, the *Intelligencer* on November 20, 1817, editorially advocated statehood. By noting "so many of the grievances of a territorial or semi-monarchial government," it sympathized with

---

2 John Moses, *Illinois Historical and Statistical,* I, 282-286n.

3 The best account of the admission of Illinois into the Union is found in the last five chapters of Solon J. Buck, *Illinois in 1818.* See also R. Carlyle Buley, *The Old Northwest,* I, 82-93. Good biographies of Edwards and Cook have not been written.

legislators who objected to the governor's power of absolute veto and who wanted the right to distribute part of the political patronage. Statehood was inevitable, the editorial continued, and the burden of supporting a government locally was preferable to continued submission to "degradations." Cook's paper opened its columns for a continued discussion of the topic. Over the signature of "A republican," Cook in the next issue conceded that the state would have to pay official salaries totaling $6,200 a year. Then he asserted that the cost, high for a frontier civilization, would be counterbalanced by the advantages of statehood. He enumerated these as including the end of the absolute veto, the need for a law to control the judiciary, and a belief that advancement beyond the territorial stage would attract more settlers. Cook expressed doubt that Illinois would ever become a slave state but urged that the issue be faced.

Cook meanwhile became clerk of the house of representatives, a position from which legislation could be influenced. The governor, addressing the two houses when their session opened December 2, proposed a census so that the statehood issue could be acted upon at the 1818 session. Four days later, with Cook's approval if not instigation, the house petitioned Congress that "this territory be admitted as a state, with all the rights and privileges of a state government." The senate and the governor added their approval. The petition estimated the population of Illinois at forty thousand and suggested that Congress give financial aid to the proposed state in the form of a percentage of the proceeds from land sales.

At Washington, Delegate Pope privately doubted that Illinois was large enough to be a state but went ahead to get congressional approval of his nephew's project. Then thirty-four years old, Pope was a short, round man who had a facial resemblance to George Washington. In his one term at Washington, Pope was both a wise statesman and an adept politician. Few men have accomplished as much for Illinois as Pope, who later had a long and distinguished career as a federal judge, did in the next three months.

The statehood bill, reported on January 23 by a select committee headed by Pope, largely duplicated the law under which Indiana became a state in 1816. Indiana had disregarded the 1787 ordinance's provision that its northern border must be a line drawn through the southern tip of Lake Michigan. Indiana's boundary had been moved ten miles northward to give it some forty-five miles of Lake Michigan shore line. Pope's bill took the same step, placing the Illinois border ten miles northward and specifying that a state convention must ratify the boundaries. In a concession to growing western sentiment that immigrants should be allowed to vote as soon as possible, the bill provided that delegates to a state convention should be elected by white males of twenty-one who had lived in Illinois at least six months.

Courtesy Illinois State Historical Library

Daniel Pope Cook

When Congress acted on the bill April 4, Pope offered an amendment that enlarged the area of Illinois and changed the course of history. It moved the northern boundary approximately forty-one miles north of the lake's end, to the line of 42° 30′ north latitude. On the Indiana precedent, the change was made without difficulty. Wisconsin was mostly a wilderness and would not complain about a land grab until 1842. Pope had written to the *Intelligencer* that he wanted Illinois to have a "coast" on Lake Michigan that included the port of Chicago and would allow the state to control the route of a proposed canal from the lake to the Illinois River. He noted that the union of states would increase the ultimate prospect that Illinois would be a free state, which in the long view of history perhaps was the major factor. Pope's amendment added to Illinois its most important eight thousand square miles, covering the bulk of fourteen now populous and prosperous counties. Without it, Chicago, Rockford, and other major cities would be in Wisconsin, and Rock Island and Joliet would be the northernmost cities of Illinois. Had that happened, Illinois would have voted Democratic in 1860 and Abraham Lincoln could not have been elected President.

By a second amendment, Pope earmarked for education 3 percent of the money to be received from the future sale of public lands in Illinois. As an early form of federal aid, the precedent had been set that 5 percent of land proceeds should go to newly formed states, and in Indiana the money was dedicated for roads and canals. On his own initiative, Pope's amendment specified that 2 percent would be used by Congress "in making roads leading to the state" and that 3 percent would be turned over to the legislature "for the encouragement of learning, of which one-sixth part shall be exclusively bestowed on a college or university." This early declaration that in Illinois education should be of prime importance was coupled with a statement by Pope that "nature has left little to be done in the proposed state of Illinois in order to have the finest roads in the world." Most people disagreed with this statement in the century that would pass before paved highways became common.

The enabling act also required that the Illinois constitution, "whenever formed, shall be republican, and not repugnant to the ordinance." In each township, Section 16 was reserved for the use of schools, along with the salt springs in the state. A proposal that the Galena lead mines also be given to Illinois for school support was stricken from the bill. Another amendment required that military bounty lands be tax-exempt for three years and that nonresident landowners must be taxed at the same rate as residents.

Pope had hoped that Congress would omit the minimum population requirement, but to his disappointment the house ordered that Illinois could not achieve statehood until it had forty thousand inhabitants, two-thirds of the minimum required by the Ordinance of 1787. The Illinois delegate did succeed in striking a provision that the required census must be directed by a federal marshal. That would have been fatal.

Doubt about population and the propriety of using federal money for local education caused a brief delay in the senate, which passed the bill April 14. President Monroe signed it four days later.

Edwards already had appointed commissioners to take a census starting April 1. In a supplementary law, the legislature had the foresight to continue the counting from June 1, the original termination date, until December 1 on the ground that a great increase would occur late in the year. Illinois was far short of the required forty thousand and the census was a series of frauds. In mid-June the reported total was 34,620, with all counties reporting but Franklin, which could not possibly make up the difference. As the supplemental census continued, the *Intelligencer* printed a hint that overzealous commissioners were counting some settlers two or three times and even listing families repeatedly as they crossed the state on the way to Missouri. Two counties reported more people than they had when the federal census was taken two years later. Round-figure estimates based "on good information" were entered for distant forts and the Madison County census included an estimate of six hundred residents at Prairie du Chien, far outside the boundaries of the proposed state. Eventually the count reached 40,258 and was reported at face value. Later, when it didn't make any difference, a federal report said Illinois had 34,620 when it was admitted as a state.

Elias Kent Kane, a delegate from Randolph County, dominated the convention which met at Kaskaskia the first Monday in August and adopted a constitution in twenty-one days.[4] The thirty-three delegates, almost double the membership of the legislature, more than filled Bennett's Tavern, the only stopping place. They had been elected from fifteen counties during a debate over the propriety and necessity of legalized slavery. The Edwards faction was in the minority and Judge Jesse Thomas presided over the conven-

---

[4] Henry Barrett Chamberlain, "Elias Kent Kane," *Transactions of the Illinois State Historical Society,* XIII (1908), 162-170. John F. Snyder, *Adam W. Snyder and His Period in Illinois History, 1817-1842,* p. 69.

tion, but the man who counted most was Kane. Young, vigorous, and talented, a member of a prominent New York City family and a Yale graduate, he had practiced law in Tennessee before coming to Kaskaskia in 1814. A few months before the convention he had been appointed judge. As chief architect of the new state's government, Kane served on important committees, hunted up precedents, smoothed out phraseology, and did most of the writing in his law office. The delegates agreed on a brief document of eight articles, mostly taken from the constitutions of New York, Kentucky, and Ohio. It was not submitted to the voters for ratification, but was to be automatically operative when approved by Congress. Popular voting on state constitutions began in 1820 with the admission of Maine.[5]

The biggest headache involved slavery. Ohio's constitution had obeyed the Ordinance of 1787 and included an outright prohibition of slavery. Indiana became a state while ignoring the subject of indentured servants. In the Illinois convention, speeches in opposition to slavery in any form brought answers that its exclusion would put the salines out of business and dry up a lucrative source of public revenue. The final compromise maintained the status quo for the French slaves and indentured servants brought in during the territorial period. For the future, introduction of slavery was prohibited, with the exception that slaves could be used at the salt springs near Shawneetown until 1825. Persons working out valid indentures would be held to their contracts, but renewals would be prohibited. Children born of indentured slaves would be free when males became twenty-one and females eighteen. On its face, the constitution seemed to mean that Illinois ultimately would wipe out the indenture system without disturbing property rights in slaves and indentured servants. The final draft of the Compromise of 1818 was interpreted as a victory for the antislavery forces,[6] a conclusion open to challenge because proslavery delegates frequently voted on the winning side in agreement with their normal opponents. An unstated reason of vital importance was that if the constitution contained stronger inden-

[5] Janet Cornelius, *A History of Constitution Making in Illinois*, pp. 1-12. The journal of the convention is reprinted in the *Journal of the Illinois State Historical Society*, VI, 3 (1913), 355-424.

[6] Buck, *op. cit.*, p. 282, takes the traditional view of the historian whose academic background was not attuned to political motives. The suspicions of a later generation are voiced by Cornelius, *op. cit.*, p. 9.

ture provisions Congress probably would block statehood. Kane, himself a slaveholder, would know that instinctively and not take chances.

Adoption of the constitution called for a celebration. The governor, the delegates, and other officials gathered in front of the capitol for speeches. Twenty rounds were fired from a cannon.

While the new constitution was being printed, the first state election was held September 17 to 19. Shadrach Bond changed his mind about going back to Congress and ran for governor without opposition. Menard, leader of the French, became lieutenant governor, winning handily over two opponents. Both were independents and logical compromise choices. The election had one surprise. John McLean of Shawneetown, another young and brilliant southerner who had sided with Kane in opposing the Edwards faction, became the first full-fledged congressman from Illinois. He defeated Cook, the man most responsible for statehood, by fourteen votes.

New men held most of the seats in the First General Assembly, which convened October 5 and witnessed the inauguration of Bond the next day. The new governor, a farmer who needed a literary man at his side, nominated Kane for secretary of state. The two United States senatorships went to Edwards and Thomas. When they drew straws for the long term, Thomas won. Its organizational work completed, the legislature adjourned without attempting to pass laws. It lacked the power until Congress approved statehood.

Speaker Henry Clay of Kentucky presented the new Illinois constitution to the house of representatives November 16. Four days later a select committee recommended admission of Illinois. The resolution was set for action November 23, when a brisk debate foreshadowed the controversy that arose two years later over admission of Missouri as a slave state. Some Yankee congressmen questioned whether the Illinois constitution contained adequate guarantees against slavery. Conciliatory answers were given and the vote was 117 to 34 for admission, with the opposition coming from New England, New York, New Jersey, and Pennsylvania. Here the wisdom of the Kaskaskia compromise was obvious, since a stronger stand for slavery no doubt would have resulted in rejection of the Illinois constitution and application for statehood.

The senate adopted the resolution without a division December

1. President Monroe's signature December 3 was the final step. Illinois now was a sovereign state, the twenty-first in the Union and on an equal footing with all others. Thomas, Edwards, and McLean were sworn in as members of Congress. The news reached Illinois in less than two weeks, and on December 16 Governor Bond by proclamation called the legislature into session the third Monday of January. Illinois was operating as a state and beginning to face its responsibilities and opportunities.

EMPTY SPACES IN A FRONTIER CIVILIZATION

Statehood for Illinois coincided with the opening of steamboat travel on midcontinental rivers. In 1811, four years after its invention by Robert Fulton, a steamboat built at Pittsburgh ran the falls at Louisville and went on to New Orleans. Upstream travel became practicable in 1816 with the adoption of a shallow draft model that placed the engines on the deck instead of in a deep hold. By 1818 the downstream journey from Louisville to New Orleans could be made in seven days and the upstream trip in fourteen. St. Louis saw its first steamboat in 1817, and farmers along the banks of rivers had a steady market for cordwood needed to fuel the boilers.[7]

Steamboats provided faster contact with the outside world, but they were too expensive for most immigrants, who usually floated down the Ohio to reach Illinois. The keelboats, which required comparatively big crews and were much slower on upstream journeys, were not replaced. For years they carried the bulk of the heavy freight on the big rivers, and in the high-water season they navigated such lesser streams as the Embarras, Little Wabash, and Big Muddy rivers, as well as some creeks.

While they provided a more modern method of navigation, the steamboats did not immediately change the established pattern of settlement concentrated in the South and along major streams. Steam navigation on Lake Michigan came much later, although it officially began on the Great Lakes in 1818 when *Walk-in-the-Water,* which used an engine to supplement sails, began service between Buffalo and Detroit. By the time steamboat trade reached Chicago fourteen years later, St. Louis was the nation's third

---

[7] Buley, *op. cit.,* I, 416-435. Milo M. Quaife (ed.), *Growing Up in Southern Illinois,* pp. xiii-xvi. Leland D. Baldwin, *The Keelboat Age on Western Waters.*

busiest port, ranking below New York and New Orleans in the number of boats stopping there. It was on the Ohio and Mississippi that inland steamboating achieved its early peak.

The slow-moving frontier, which marked the advanced limits of western settlement, had passed through less than half of Illinois when statehood arrived.[8] Irregular in outline, the frontier in Illinois faced northward but only at a few places had it entered the central region. Behind it were sizable areas which had been bypassed by the early arrivals and as yet had no white civilization. A big state with few people, Illinois stretched 385 miles on a north-south axis. White men traveled the navigable waters that formed all but 305 miles of the state's 1,160-mile boundary, but almost no one had any conception of the diversified resources and opportunities of northern Illinois or of the central region where the westernmost bend of the Mississippi was 216 miles from the Indiana border. Lewis Caleb Beck, author of a scholarly gazetteer published in 1823, knew there was a Grand Prairie stretching from the Chicago area southward into midstate. He erroneously described it as being generally high and undulating, with a sandy soil, and added that "it is very questionable whether it will ever be thickly settled."[9] As to the interior of the northern area, Beck frankly stated that little was known of its geography. In 1818 only Georgia covered more land area than the 56,043 square miles that made Illinois almost half as large as Great Britain. The Kinzie trading post at the Chicago portage had almost no connection with the two main areas of settlement radiating from Kaskaskia, with its tradition of comparative wealth and culture, and Shawneetown, the fairly new port of entry on the Ohio River.

Indians had dwindled in number and ferocity, but the tribes that had replaced the Iliniwek could still throw a scare into the

---

[8] Much of this section is based on Buck's *Illinois in 1818* and Buley's *The Old Northwest,* a two-volume study of pioneer life from 1815 to 1840 in the region that included Illinois. See Buck's third chapter on "The Extent of Settlement," and Malcolm J. Rohrbough, *The Land Office Business: The Settlement and Administration of American Public Lands, 1788-1837.*

[9] *A Gazetteer of the States of Illinois and Missouri,* pp. 44, 81. Beck regarded the monotonous and treeless prairie as "little more than a dreary uninhabited waste" and, in describing Fayette County, said that the "great predominance of prairie land is a serious objection to this country." Those views were not unusual among early travelers. Gershom Flagg in 1817 disagreed with those who believed the prairie would have to be turned back to the General Land Office as unfit for cultivation. "Pioneer Letters of Gershom Flagg," edited by Buck, *Transactions of the Illinois State Historical Society,* XV (1910), 153.

settled regions. The secretary of war in 1815 estimated at 12,260 the total population of the tribes living in Illinois and surrounding territories, but there was no exact count of the Kickapoo Indians who had villages in the central region, the Sauk and Fox beyond the Illinois River, and the Winnebago and Potawatomi bands further north. They were in the process of being dislodged by the adventuresome and self-reliant woodsmen, who resembled Indians to the extent that they too cultivated small patches in a rudimentary fashion and were capable of living off the wild game they killed.

Shawneetown, which was Illinois' closest approach to a commercial center, bustled with activity. Named for an Indian tribe that had gone away a half-century earlier, it had been laid out a decade previously by the federal government, which had a proprietary interest in the salt springs twelve miles inland. For more than a century Shawneetown could boast that Washington, D.C., was the only other city plotted by the national government. In addition to the federal land office, it had thirty cabins, several taverns, a bakehouse, a log bank, and annual spring floods. Outsiders wondered why the townspeople insisted on enduring the high water, but until 1937 nothing came of petitions to relocate Shawneetown on higher ground. One traveler reported in 1809 that Shawneetown had "more appearance of business than I have seen this side of Pittsburgh."[10] The prosperity depended in part on the salt trade, but Shawneetown primarily was the first stopping place for many immigrants, especially those destined for homesteads along the Wabash River. Many made down payments at the land office there, and others struck out on overland trails for western Illinois and Missouri.

Shawneetown was the anchor of a strip of settlement extending approximately one hundred miles along the Wabash River from Saline Creek northward. In an analysis of the 1818 population, Solon J. Buck estimated that some twelve thousand persons lived in that area, which averaged fifteen miles in width. On the opposite side of the state, fanned northward from Kaskaskia, some fifteen thousand persons lived in less than two thousand square miles. Kaskaskia was the apex of a triangle bounded by the Kaskaskia and Mississippi rivers, with the northern border reaching almost to present Hillsboro and then curving into Jersey, Greene,

10 Buck, *op. cit.*, pp. 68, 70.

and Calhoun counties before reaching the Mississippi upstream from St. Louis. Buck located another twelve thousand persons scattered between the two areas and north of the one on the Mississippi. The regions of sparse settlement included the rugged Shawnee Hills in the south.

Kaskaskia had regained some of its earlier prestige when it became a land-office town in 1804 and the territorial capital in 1809. It boasted of some stone mansions, but most of its 160 houses were of the typical French inland architecture, aged and inclined to be shabby. Half of the inhabitants were French or French-Indian mixtures who raised cattle, horses, hogs, and poultry and cultivated gardens surrounded by picket fences. Kaskaskia had a post office, and the *Illinois Herald* printed advertisements of nine general stores, a hat shop, and three tailor shops. State officials, military men, land speculators, and adventurers overcrowded the only tavern and urged that the state delay no longer the construction of a bridge over the Kaskaskia River.

Because of its inland site isolated from a main travel route, Prairie du Rocher to this day retains some of the French influence in visible form. A pastoral village with a chapel and a commons, it numbered thirty to forty families. Cahokia, which would suffer severe flood damage in 1844, had lost some of its bloom, partly because Belleville became the county seat in 1814 and partly because it could not compete commercially with St. Louis. At the time of statehood Belleville had possibly five hundred residents, a courthouse, a jail, and such unusual attractions as an academy and a library.

Twenty years earlier Captain James Piggott, an adventurer who boasted of a career in the Revolutionary War, had laid the foundations of East St. Louis by building a bridge across Cahokia Creek and opening a road to the bank of the Mississippi. There he erected two rude cabins for the convenience of travelers bound for Louisiana Territory. In 1797 he made it easier to trade with St. Louis by establishing the first ferry across the river. For a half-century Piggott's small settlement went under the name of Illinois-town and the ferry service continued as a lucrative monopoly under new ownership.

Some settlements sprang up inevitably at the intersection of trade routes or at places where a river could be crossed with a minimum of trouble. Others depended upon promotion by speculators. Edwardsville, founded in 1815, reflected the prosperity of the territorial governor for whom it was named. Edwards moved there in 1818 to oversee his widespread stores, mills, and land speculations after he gave up farming. The town had seventy houses, a courthouse and jail, a land office, and a brick market-house. Upper Alton had more than one hundred homes two years after its founding in 1816. Alton, laid out two years later at a prime site for a steamboat landing, grew rapidly. Nearby out-croppings of coal and a superior quality of limestone helped attract investment capital.

In each of fifteen counties, three elected commissioners trans-acted official business. In a few cases counties preceded the founding of a seat of government. Politicians and other speculators staked out town sites at likely spots, and sometimes a new county seat had a log courthouse, a jail, a store, and a tavern, but not much else. One even lacked a courthouse. Men and women worked long hours, reared families, and dreamed of the future in such towns as Palmyra, Brownsville, Covington, and Perryville, all of which vanished from the map after the county offices moved elsewhere. New in 1818 were the future cities of Carmi, Fairfield, Golconda, Lawrenceville, and Vienna. Further north, Springfield, Decatur, and Quincy had not been founded, although the year before the first log cabin was erected in Sangamon County. Peoria received a new start a mile and a half from Fort Clark, which Indians burned after the troops left. The first group of American settlers, a colony from Clinton County, arrived in 1819. Henry R. Schoolcraft, who came up the Illinois River in 1821, found the huts of a few settlers below Peoria, but between Peoria and Chicago did not see a single white habitation.

Illinois offered freedom, and of it the first arrivals enjoyed a surplus. Far in advance of the county seats, hating the Indians and pushing back the frontier, were the hunters, expert woodsmen who lived in half-faced shelters or small cabins that could be erected without the help of a companion. For protection and a meat supply they depended upon deadeye marksmanship. By girdling trees they killed a small patch of timber and under the leafless branches raised corn and perhaps a truck garden in which squash, cabbages, beans, and cucumbers would eventually grow, possibly under new husbandry. The unsurveyed land was free, and no one collected rent or taxes. Love of the wild was ingrained in the mostly illiterate men, who could abandon their holdings, or under a preemption law dispose of them to a new arrival, and then move on, perhaps across the Mississippi, before acquiring the semipermanence of being classed as settlers.

More permanent, the first real settlers were half-hunters and half-farmers. Their wives also cooked venison in shanties, but they owned more tools and utensils, and like their predecessors had little hesitation about selling out and moving on. The first farmers made their homes in or at least at the edge of timber. In addition to the superstition that something must be wrong with soil that did not grow trees, good reason existed for shunning the prairie. For buildings, for fuel, and later for fences, wood was essential, and the light chopping ax was well worth a long trip to a black-smith and the three or four dollars it cost. Hand-forged, it enabled a lone pioneer to fell and dismantle tall trees that in the climax forest ranged up to ten feet in diameter. The ax was the only tool needed for cabin building and for the splitting of logs to make bunks, tables, and benches. In carving a civilization it played a role as important as the long-barreled, small-bore rifle and the sod-breaking plow. In the cities broadcloths and silks mingled demo-cratically with coonskin caps and hunting shirts, but a major handicap to Illinois was the absence of a laboring class. Most Illinois families lived by subsistence farming. Split rail fences protected the small fields and garden patches while the farmer let his cow and razorback-type hogs roam the nearby forest, hoping that they would not be killed by wolves. Working around the stumps of cleared timber was easier than breaking thick and tough prairie sod. From two to eight yoke of oxen were required to pull a cumbersome plow with a ten-foot wooden beam and moldboard crudely fitted with wrought iron. Easy to cultivate and adaptable to the prairie, corn soon became the staple crop. The root mat of the newly turned turf did not disintegrate for two or three years, but "sod" corn without cultivation could produce from ten to thirty bushels an acre the first year. It was planted by dropping the seed into a hole made with an ax or a pointed stick and then covering it with a bootheel. In established fields, Beck reported yields from fifty to eighty bushels, and asserted that they ran as high as 120 to 130 bushels in the fabulously rich American Bottom.[11] Corn could be ground into food or fed by ear to animals. One bushel made two gallons of marketable whiskey.

[11] Beck, *op. cit.*, pp. 36-40. Ferdinand Ernst, "Travels in Illinois in 1819," *Transactions of the Illinois State Historical Society*, VIII (1903), 150-165.

A dough of salted cornmeal scalded with boiling water could be cooked in ashes or on a hoe blade to provide the basic supplement for the meat of wild animals that dominated the diets of Indians and their immediate successors. Many farmers owned stills which converted sprouted corn mash into a clear but potent whiskey which could be transported easily by pack horse or flatboat. More compact than corn, the final product could be stored or sent to a city market. Much was consumed at home. Corn whiskey was the popular western drink; home consumption ran high, and in many cabins all members of the family drank it at every meal. Whiskey cost from fifteen to twenty-five cents a gallon at groceries, where candidates for office made a free supply available for several weeks before elections. The jug circulated freely at social events such as cabin raisings and militia assemblies, and travelers commented that the people of the West liked whiskey and indulged in it excessively.[12]

Illinois produced a surplus of wheat, the secondary crop, which could be converted into flour only at a mill. The most common type of mill ground meal and flour, with the miller taking his pay by keeping a portion of the final product. For grinding wheat, rye, or malt, the legal withholding was one-eighth, which the settler usually thought was too much. A one-sixth portion could be taken for ground corn, oats, barley, or buckwheat. The mills followed settlement and brought the mechanical age to the prairie. Where dam sites could not be found, horses and oxen provided the power to revolve the grinding stones. Other types of mills sawed logs, carded wool, and performed other specialized tasks at which machinery could be substituted for manual labor. Skilled operators were in demand, and a blacksmith shop and general store in a mill's vicinity provided the nucleus for a village which gave the frontiersmen contact with the outside world.

The self-reliant settler tanned the hides of deer and cattle to make shoes, while his wife with a spinning wheel and loom produced cloth for trousers, shirts, and dresses. At the store the settler could trade small surpluses of eggs, butter, meat, whiskey, and maple sugar for coffee, salt, and sugar. The stores also carried small stocks of tools, powder, glass, dyes, iron utensils, crockery, cloth, and additional foodstuffs. Almost no one had money. Trade

---

[12] The public did not regard moderate drinking as objectionable or abstinence as a virtue. Snyder, *op. cit.*, p. 91.

was commonly carried on by barter, and the settler depended upon himself and the members of his family for the bulk of life's necessities.

New Orleans offered an unsatisfactory market for Illinois flour, pork, beef, venison hams, and some hides produced along the watercourses. The shippers were merchants, local buyers, and some farmers who built flatboats and collected produce to be floated downstream in the spring freshets. The holds leaked, meat and flour spoiled, and prices dropped in the seasonal market at New Orleans, where the boats were sold for lumber. A final danger was the possibility of being robbed while walking back to Illinois.

Early settlement stayed near the streams, but as people moved inland trails became roads which an easterner had difficulty following through tall grass and marshes. Over the original French routes, along paths cut by the hooves of buffalo, men could travel by land from the American Bottom to Peoria and on to Galena or Detroit.[13] The overland trail from Fort Massac to Kaskaskia, on which Clark almost lost his way in 1778, was largely replaced by routes starting at Shawneetown and Golconda. Under congressional authorization, a contract in 1820 provided that the road from Shawneetown should be "cut thirty-three feet wide, with stumps to be very low." Many newcomers took the Goshen Road connecting Shawneetown, Carlyle, Edwardsville, and Alton, with a branch to Kaskaskia. For some miles it coincided with the Vincennes-St. Louis route. The roads were poor, muddy in the wet season and after rains, and dangerous when river torrents had to be forded or at nightfall when a traveler had to seek lodging in a cabin that might be the home of a brigand. Those who escaped that peril often complained of rude inns, unclean accommodations, and discourteous hosts.

Mail service from the East reached Vincennes in 1800 and Cahokia in 1805. The routes spread rapidly but by 1818 had not penetrated further north than Belleville. A stage line between St. Louis and Kaskaskia opened in 1819

Level and low, Illinois was a poorly drained state in the pioneer era. Ponds, sloughs, and other wet places were common, especially along watercourses. Clogged with leaves, trees, and other accumulations, the smaller streams ran slowly until decades later when

[13] The main roads are listed in Buley, *op. cit.*, I, 454-456. See Josephine Boylan, "Illinois Highways, 1700-1848," *Journal of the Illinois State Historical Society*, XXVI, 1-2 (1933), 5-59.

men speeded the runoff by digging ditches, straightening channels, and laying expensive drain tile so that corn could be grown in rich lowland soil. In the wet places, swarms of mosquitoes thrived, although no one recognized them as a health menace.

Life on the frontier may have been desolate and lonely, but worst of all Illinois had a reputation for being unhealthy.[14] For the prevalence of a form of malaria, a severe and widespread affliction commonly known as fever and ague, or "the ager," the early resident had an explanation. Beck, a physician and chemist who did not know that bacteria caused diseases, accepted the belief that the trouble was due to a "miasma" or "noxious effluvia" arising from swamps. Rapidly decomposing vegetable matter, especially on low ground, was believed responsible for "putrid exhalations" that caused agues, bilious fevers, liver complaints, and other ailments. Little quinine was available and the few physicians were as helpless as the Indian doctors and the medicine men who specialized in herb recipes. "The old timers advise that emigrants not plant corn in the immediate vicinity of their dwellings, as its rich and mossy foliage prevents the sun from dispelling the noxious vapors," Beck wrote.

Fever and ague was regarded as inevitable, to be dismissed with the remark that "he ain't sick; he's only got the ager." The attacks began with a series of chills, faster and faster, that reached teeth-chattering intensity so that the victim shook like a leaf. After an hour or so, the chills were slowly replaced with warm flushes that became burning heat accompanied by racking pain in the head and along the back. In time profuse sweating marked a slow return to a more normal condition. Few died, but the patients were subject to periodic relapses. Gershom Flagg wrote from Edwardsville in 1819 that "August and September are generally quite sickly." During that season, Edward Coles preferred Edwardsville to Vandalia.

More deadly in many regions was milk sickness, which took the life of Abraham Lincoln's mother. Discovered in the West in the early 1800's, probably caused by the poisoning of thirsty animals which ate white snakeroot in the dry season, it afflicted both humans and cattle. Medical men confused milk sickness with malaria, arsenic poisoning, typhus, and other fevers.

14 *Ibid.,* I, 240-394. Buley has a long chapter on "Ills, Cures, and Doctors" in the Old Northwest, but the best account of public health on the frontier is Paul M. Angle's "The Hardy Pioneer: How He Lived in the Early Middle West," chapter III in David J. Davis, M.D. (ed.), *History of Medical Practice in Illinois, 1850-1900,* II.

Visitors complained about disregard of personal cleanliness. In the oppressive heat of summer, the housefly came with the settlers, who had no screens on doors and windows and who lived in ignorance of the principles of sanitation. Little soap was available, baths were rare, and water often contaminated. Quincy in 1834 adopted an ordinance prohibiting the abandonment of dead animals inside the town. Chicago the year before made it illegal to throw carcasses into the river. Springfield for years debated the merits of letting hogs run at large as scavengers.

In winter the residents of Illinois endured extreme cold without felt boots and underwear. Diets were heavy with meat and hot breads. Children's diseases, typhoid, tuberculosis, and smallpox were common. In the log cabins with chimney ventilation, pneumonia occurred in a milder form. The country doctors, who doubled as pharmacists, had comparatively few cases involving cancer, heart diseases, and other troubles of the aged. On the rugged frontier, those who survived were a hardy breed.

WEAK GOVERNOR AND STRONG LEGISLATURE

Under the first constitution, the legislature dominated the government of Illinois. The frontier had rebelled against the colonial and territorial system under which an appointed executive wielded an absolute veto and possessed other powers of monarchial derivation. As a result, the state constitution made one-man rule impossible. The lawmakers, who were in session a few months in alternate winters, selected not only the United States senators but also the Supreme Court justices, secondary state officials, and most local officers. Shadrach Bond, who drew a one-thousand-dollar annual salary, could express his disapproval of legislation only through committee action. A council of revision consisting of the "judges of the Supreme Court or a major part of them with the governor" could revise bills and return them with objections to the originating body, but the governor could not act on his own. Furthermore, the council veto could be overridden by a bare majority of the two houses. New York had a similar system but required a two-thirds vote to override. Unfortunately, in Illinois the judiciary became directly involved in the legislative process; having reviewed legislation, the judges found themselves embarrassed when legal questions were raised on appeal.

Other constitutional restrictions weakened the power of the

executive for the next thirty years. The governor had a four-year term but could not seek reelection until he had been out of office another four years. A limitation on the appointive power gave the legislature a firm grip on patronage. The people, who had not been allowed to vote for or against the new constitution, could elect

Courtesy Illinois State Historical Library

Governor Shadrach Bond

only the governor, lieutenant governor, sheriff, coroner, and county commissioners, in addition to the congressman.[15]

Badly organized, the constitution in separate sections required

[15] The political and social development of Illinois through the Civil War period is covered by John Moses' two-volume *Illinois Historical and Statistical* and by Alexander Davidson and Bernard Stuvé in *A Complete History of Illinois from 1673 to 1878,* among other works. Special attention should be given to Theodore Calvin Pease's introduction to *Illinois Election Returns, 1818-1848,* and to the introduction and notes to *The Governors' Letter-Books, 1818-1834,* by Evarts Boutell Greene and Clarence W. Alvord. Both are part of a series of volumes issued by the Illinois State Historical Library. Another valuable book on early Illinois politics is John Francis Snyder, M.D., *Adam W. Snyder in Illinois History, 1817-1842.*

that the governor's appointment of the secretary of state be sent to the senate for confirmation, that the legislature in joint session every two years name the state treasurer and at least one public printer, and that the governor with the advice and consent of the senate appoint all other officers, whether established by the constitution or by law. The legislature had the right to determine the manner of selection of secondary county officers such as inspectors, collectors and their deputies, highway surveyors, and jailers.

The delegates provided great mischief for the future by letting the legislature appoint the auditor of public accounts, the attorney general, and "such other officers for the state as may be necessary." That was because the delegates wanted Elijah C. Berry to continue as auditor but feared that Bond would not appoint him. Bond named state's attorneys and other officials with little interference, but in the years that followed the lawmakers repeatedly found themselves in political disagreement with his successors. Each incident provided opportunity to expand the patronage of the legislature. Continual logrolling and lobbying resulted.

Bond, a gregarious farmer, cared little that his authority had been hobbled.[16] A big man with a military bearing, he had what the writers of his day called a "plain English education," meaning that he had not gone to school long enough to master much more than the rudiments of spelling, grammar, and penmanship. Home for Bond was a large, two-story brick house with broad verandas on a farm outside Kaskaskia. As the first congressional delegate of the territory of Illinois, Bond had increased his political popularity by sponsoring the 1813 redemption law and getting authorization to raise ranger companies. In the War of 1812 he had the rank of captain.

The constitution's political involvement extended to the office of lieutenant governor. Menard, the obvious choice for that office, had been a citizen only two years, so the residency requirement for lieutenant governor was omitted. The constitution, however, required that the governor be a citizen of the United States for thirty years.

Bond's brief and clearly written message to the First General Assembly obviously was the work of Kane, who was the power

<hr />

[16] Kinnie A. Ostewig, "Life of Shadrach Bond, The First Governor of Illinois," *Transactions of the Illinois State Historical Society,* XXXVI (1929), 187-234. Moses, *op. cit.,* I, 287. Snyder, *op. cit.,* p. 36.

behind the throne and relieved the governor of the detail of state business. The message set a precedent for many of Bond's successors by reporting that the state treasury was depleted. As a means of replenishment he suggested a temporary loan. The legislature enacted a code of laws, mostly copied from Virginia and Kentucky statutes. As a basis for taxation, the chief burden of supporting the state was placed on nonresident owners of land, contrary to provisions of the enabling act. The law set three classifications of land, and arbitrarily valued them at two, three, and four dollars an acre, with the bottomlands along the Mississippi, Ohio, and Wabash rivers being taxed at the top rate. Taxes on the property of nonresidents went to the state, while counties taxed locally owned land and personal property. The troublesome system of revenue administration underwent frequent changes during the early years of statehood.

In a state which lacked a penitentiary, the criminal code reenacted the penalties of the territorial period, despite Bond's recommendations for modification. Legal punishment included whipping and confinement in stocks and pillories. Death by hanging was the penalty for murder, rape, arson, and horse stealing. Bond wanted to substitute imprisonment and proposed the building of jails and a penitentiary.

For four dollars a day, the state rented a stucco-and-brick house from Dr. George Fisher for use as its first capitol. The twenty-nine members of the house of representatives and fourteen senators transacted their business in low-ceilinged rooms which also were used by Cook as his law office. Bond considered the seat of government less attractive than his farm.

The legislature's election of the first four Supreme Court justices brought some strange results. Joseph Phillips, who had succeeded Pope as territorial secretary, had a good reputation and became chief justice. Four years later he left the state in disgust after running unsuccessfully for governor. The other places went to Thomas Browne, William P. Foster, and John Reynolds. Browne also ran and lost for governor. Foster was a newcomer whose smooth personality impressed the legislators. Assigned to hear cases on the Wabash circuit, he collected his salary of one thousand dollars and then resigned rather than demonstrate incompetence by holding court.[17] Reynolds, who also became gov-

17 Thomas Ford, *History of Illinois*, p. 29.

ernor and wrote a history and biographies, professed that he had no thought of entering public life but happened to be in Kaskaskia and was importuned to take a seat on the state's highest court.

A futile experiment in lotteries as a means of financing public works improvements was attempted by the First General Assembly. To make the Wabash River navigable near Palmyra, a canal was necessary, and ponds on the American Bottom needed to be drained. A law authorizing a lottery to raise money also specified with considerable optimism how surplus funds could be used on additional projects. When the tickets were placed on sale, few men had enough money to buy them.

THE MOVE TO VANDALIA

A mania for land speculation caused Illinois officials to relocate the seat of government in an unpopulated wilderness. They did not realize that Kaskaskia, doomed because of its low site between two rivers, would be mortally damaged by a flood in less than a quarter of a century. No one really wanted to leave Kaskaskia, but a more central location would have future advantages and on paper the profits looked big, both for the state and the speculating politicians. Government itself seemed to be infected with the early settler's urge to move to some location closer to the edge of civilization.[18]

The capital relocation question came up unexpectedly in the 1818 convention, where only the slavery issue caused more trouble. In the enabling act for statehood, Congress failed to grant the customary four sections of land for a seat of government. Agitation for a move northward and inland came from three groups of speculators with political influence. Their holdings were all upstream on the Kaskaskia River and north of the area then being surveyed. Of the rival sites, only the now vanished town of Covington, then the seat of newly organized Washington County, had any population. At Hill's Ferry, where the Vincennes road crossed the river, the ferry operator occupied the only cabin. The location was superb, and a few months after the convention its owners advertised lots under the new name of Carlyle. Further upstream, attention centered on Pope's Bluff, owned and promoted unsuccessfully by Nathaniel Pope and two associates in the

18 Buck, *op. cit.*, pp. 286-291. Moses, *op. cit.*, I, 298.

Edwards faction. Rivals blocked a move there, and the delegates could not decide whether to relocate or decree that the capital should stay at Kaskaskia for twenty years.

Kane negotiated a compromise and the constitution's schedule contained a section saying that the seat of government would continue in Kaskaskia until the legislature provided otherwise. The First General Assembly was instructed to petition Congress for land—from one to four sections—to be situated on the Kaskaskia River as near as possible to the Third Principal Meridian. If successful, the assembly then would appoint five commissioners to select a site and lay out a town which would be the seat of government for twenty years. Should Congress refuse, the legislature was empowered to work out its own solution.

Senators Thomas and Edwards obtained four sections in early 1819 by convincing their Washington colleagues that a new capital would increase the value of unsurveyed public lands. Legislators serving as commissioners rode eighty-two miles along the Kaskaskia to Reeves Bluff, misnamed for Charles Reavis, the only settler for miles around. They selected a beautiful spot in the timber fifty feet above the river's west bank and named it Vandalia.[19]

Before the virgin forest could be cut down, surveyors plotted a spacious town of big squares and eighty-foot streets. Vandalia was divided into sixty-four squares, with two in the center reserved for public use and the rest divided into eight lots each. Officials and surveyors joined in the brisk bidding at an August auction when 150 of the stump-dotted lots brought inflated prices ranging from a hundred to seven hundred eighty dollars. The gross exceeded thirty-five thousand dollars, enough to operate the new state government for two years had the sales been for cash. Unfortunately most were on credit and prices soon sagged drastically. Few of the contracts were fulfilled and the state realized only a tenth of the original bids. Meanwhile Vandalia received a boost in population when Ferdinand Ernst, a wealthy German liberal, brought in thirty families from Hanover. They had escaped political prosecution in Europe, but in the West they encountered

---

[19] The beginnings of Vandalia and its brief reign as the capital of Illinois are covered in two of the many books inspired by the life of Abraham Lincoln. The Abraham Lincoln Association published William E. Baringer, *Lincoln's Vandalia: A Pioneer Portrait.* See also Mary Burtschi, *Vandalia: Wilderness Capital.*

tragedy and within a few years Ernst and most of his colonists were dead.[20]

For less than five thousand dollars, the commissioners contracted for a two-story state house, with low ceilings and the plainest of exteriors. Sidney Breese, a twenty-year-old stripling from an aristocratic New York family, earned twenty-five dollars by bringing the state archives from Kaskaskia in a small wagon. Breese, who was Kane's friend and one-man office staff, spent a week on the journey. Trees and underbrush in many places had to be chopped away so that the trail to Vandalia could be widened into a road. Although the fireplaces smoked, the auditor moved his family into the state house until the legislature arrived. Governor Bond boarded at a house in which the state treasurer housed his family and kept his office.

On December 4, 1820, the Second General Assembly convened at Vandalia, with legislators crowding into boarding houses and four clerks sleeping in the capitol. Upon adjournment in February, Bond joined the general exodus from the seat of government. The trustees of the newly incorporated town of Vandalia, who had been authorized to look after the state house between sessions, were awakened by a fire that destroyed the building the night of December 9, 1823. Its replacement, a two-story brick structure, also failed to provide adequate space and comfort. Complaints about poor construction soon were heard.

STATE BANKING: THE FIRST MISTAKE

Twice in its early years—in 1821 and again in 1835—the government of Illinois unwisely and disastrously entered the banking business with a stubborn refusal to comprehend the realities of finance. The new state was economically poor, trade was just beginning to develop, and in some parts of the frontier deer hides and raccoon skins still served as a medium of exchange. The settlers who arrived in a boom after the War of 1812 brought some currency, but not enough to satisfy the demand for land-office transactions or to finance a rage of speculation that existed from 1814 to 1818. The barter system operated for a while after mills and stores opened for business. Agricultural products brought

---

[20] Ferdinand Ernst, "Travels in Illinois in 1819," *Transactions of the Illinois State Historical Society*, VIII (1903), 150-165.

little on the New Orleans market, bank notes were subject to a variety of discounts, and merchants had difficulty paying for manufactured goods obtainable from Philadelphia and Pittsburgh. A man who had eighty dollars in sound money usually turned it in at the land office as the down payment on a quarter-section. The land office promptly added to the shortage by shipping the good money back East. The people complained about the shortage of money, but few understood that the basic trouble came from a lack of investment capital. The difficulty, common in new states, continued until the national government, among other reforms, took over the issuance of bank notes. Meanwhile, the next third of a century would demonstrate that financial stability never would come from state-chartered banks which attempted to create credit without surplus funds to back it. Inexperience and unregulated competition were other factors which doomed the western states to repeated banking failures.[21]

Under pressure to follow Ohio and Kentucky examples, the territorial legislature chartered four private banks. A group of Shawneetown men with political connections, who wanted to speculate in land but lacked the capital to make large purchases, obtained a charter for the Bank of Illinois. They had power to sell stock to the public, issue paper currency, and perform limited banking functions. Capitalized at three hundred thousand dollars, chartered for twenty years under a provision that the territory and later the state could purchase one-third of the stock, the bank opened January 1, 1817, and stayed in business seven years. It received additional help from the legislature in the form of a law staying executions for one year unless the party desiring judgment would accept payment in the notes of designated western banks. The primary purpose of that law was to make it unnecessary for settlers to pay their debts in scarce specie, the gold and silver coins whose value did not fluctuate.

The right to issue notes in large quantities and without solid financial support impressed Governor Edwards, who in early 1818 obtained a similar charter for the Bank of Edwardsville. The Shawneetown and Edwardsville banks were made government de-

[21] The definitive work on pre-Civil War banking is George W. Dowrie, *The Development of Banking in Illinois, 1817-1863*, pp. 608, 22-57. For a general view of frontier banking see Buley, *op. cit.*, I, 573-574, 598-601. Also Fred B. Marchkoff, "Currency and Banking in Illinois Before 1865," *Journal of the Illinois State Historical Society*, LII (Autumn, 1959), 365-418.

positories, which allowed them to take temporary custody of money paid at the land offices. They competed with the older and larger Bank of Missouri at St. Louis, which indulged in a common type of harassment by accumulating their notes and presenting a large number with a demand for prompt payment in specie. The Bank of Illinois maintained specie payments until 1821, although the Bank of the United States declined to accept notes not redeemable in specie. The Shawneetown bank finally closed in 1823 but retained its charter. Failure of the Bank of Missouri in 1821 caused a fatal run on the Bank of Edwardsville, in which Edwards was involved although he had resigned as president two years earlier. The government lost forty-six thousand dollars in federal deposits, and Edwards could not prove that he had notified authorities at Washington that the bank was in precarious condition.

Meanwhile, Bond and other incorporators of the Bank and City of Cairo envisioned quick profits without an investment through a financial scheme that was not uncommon for the time. Cairo's location at the confluence of the Mississippi and Ohio rivers was superb, but the site was periodically flooded. The

Kaskaskia

Courtesy Illinois State Historical Library

get-rich-painlessly promotion proposed the sale of two thousand city lots for $150 each. Fifty dollars from each lot would help pay for a levee to hold back the floods, and the other hundred dollars would capitalize the bank. In trouble, the bank never opened at Cairo, but for a while transacted business at Kaskaskia under an unusual charter provision. Because its backers were unable to sell stock in 1818, a bank chartered at Kaskaskia never opened.

The failures left Illinois as well as Indiana without banking service. The shaky notes of the Illinois banks had replaced hard money, a shortage of small change handicapped business, and the few Spanish dollars still in circulation were cut into quarters, bits, and other fractions.[22] Bank notes were often counterfeit, and newspapers printed lists of the amount each should be discounted. Variations from day to day and place to place caused a particular handicap to immigrants. Meanwhile a belief arose that the trouble was due to private banks and that it should be corrected by having the state take over the issuance of notes.

Under pressure from the debtor electorate, early legislators sought to correct the situation by putting the state in the banking business. A State Bank capitalized at four million dollars by the First General Assembly never opened because the initial requirement of fifteen thousand dollars in specie could not be raised. In its determination that the state should have money, the legislature in 1821 chartered a State Bank of Illinois without capital of any kind and without provision for regulation of the security of its loans and note issues. The action, excusable only as a philanthropic measure for the relief of a citizenry beset by depression, muddled state finances for years. The main bank in a brick building at Vandalia had branch offices at Edwardsville, Shawneetown, Brownsville in Jefferson County, and Palmyra in Wabash County. To guarantee that the management would be political, the legislature elected the bank officers and directors biennially. Without invested capital, the bank was authorized to issue three hundred thousand dollars in 2 percent notes and embark on a program of quickly distributing the money on a first-come, first-served basis, with each county getting its share. Without security, any man could apply for a loan of one hundred dollars. Larger amounts, up to a thousand-dollar maximum, required the posting of real estate as security.

[22] Ford, *op. cit.*, p. 47.

The legislators disregarded warnings that the plan was fiscal insanity. Objections by the council of revision were overridden. John McLean, who had been elected to the legislature after losing his congressional seat to Cook, resigned as speaker of the house so that he could denounce the bank scheme.

Distributed among the counties in proportion to their population, the money did not last long after the bank went into operation in the summer of 1821. Any man who could get an endorser could borrow one hundred dollars, and bank officials paid little attention to security and prospects for repayment. The new money rapidly dropped in value and soon was worth only thirty cents on the dollar. Bad money drove out the good, and small change disappeared from circulation. Thomas Ford reports that to make change new bills were cut in half and that for four years only State Bank notes circulated in Illinois. Meanwhile, few persons made any pretense of paying their debts to the bank. A replevin law in effect forced creditors to accept the bank money. The law made no provision for redemption of the bank notes, and many debtors either regarded the money as a gift from the state or contended that repayment was unnecessary because the law was unconstitutional.

By 1825 the legislature determined that the notes were worth only a third of face value and that the bank situation was hopeless. So that state officials and employees would be fairly treated, their salaries were tripled, which added to the tax burden. Investigations of jumbled reports showed that loans had been made to political friends on insufficient security and that some influential men had received more than the thousand-dollar maximum. The findings were ignored by the legislature, which authorized the state auditor to meet the deficit by issuing warrants bearing 6 percent interest. Like the bank notes, they depreciated in value.

Liquidation could not be avoided by 1830. The legislature confessed its error by authorizing the state to borrow one hundred thousand dollars to redeem the depreciated currency. In the absence of an accurate record of the bank's operation, Ford estimated the total loss at four hundred thousand dollars. The reaction of the public was to hold the banks at fault, and the frontiersman considered that he had another reason, based on personal experience, for following Andrew Jackson's antibank policies. As agrarians, the early settlers had no interest in a protective tariff, and when the time would come for the new state to adopt national political party alignments, Illinois would be Democratic.

ENGLISH COLONY ON THE PRAIRIE

On both sides of the Atlantic Ocean, the Illinois prairie received invaluable advertising from literate and idealistic Englishmen who invested and lost money in the Birkbeck-Flower colony in Edwards County. The enthusiastic pen of Morris Birkbeck encouraged thousands to take up a new life on the fertile soil on which trees did not grow and which most settlers shunned.

Birkbeck, son of an influential Quaker, had prospered as the leaseholder of a fifteen-hundred-acre estate on which he raised the first Merino sheep in England. A liberal in politics and religion, he could not vote because he did not own his land, and he could not avoid paying tithes to a church he would not join. In 1814 he toured France with George Flower, a younger man who also was anxious to leave England. Flower managed the large estate of his father, who had invested in land after selling a profitable brewery as a protest against malt and beer taxes. In the wake of the Napoleonic wars, the agricultural future of France did not impress them, but on the tour Birkbeck revealed a talent as a pamphleteer.

Flower in 1816 visited the United States, traveling as far as Illinois and Tennessee and spending part of the winter at Monticello with Jefferson, to whom he brought a letter of introduction from Lafayette. Birkbeck joined him the next spring with a party that included his children and Miss Eliza Julia Andrews, the daughter of a family friend. They planned a transplanted colony in America. Abhorrence of slavery ruled out the South. Flower acted as guide on a westward trip in which they found land prices too high in the eastern states and Ohio. In southern Illinois they discovered that land had been entered only in the timbered sections. At the time the prairies were largely vacant.

Flower especially admired the treeless regions, and of Boltenhouse prairie, in Edwards County, he wrote:

A few steps more, and a beautiful prairie suddenly opened to our view. At first we only received the impressions of its general beauty. With longer gaze, all its distinctive features were revealed, lying in profound repose under the warm light of an afternoon's summer sun. In its dented and irregular outline of wood, its varied surface interspersed with clumps of oaks of centuries' growth, its tall grass, with seed stalks from six to ten feet high, like tall and slender reeds waving in a gentle breeze, the whole presenting a magnificence of park scenery, complete from the hand of Nature, and unrivalled by the same sort of scenery in European art. For once the reality came up to the picture of imagination.[23]

On Boltenhouse prairie they settled. Birkbeck became the best customer of the Shawneetown land office, entering 26,400 acres for himself and others. Flower made a trip back to England and returned with money for more land purchases and the first of a series of parties of English farmers, artisans, and laborers. For an eighteen-by-sixteen-foot log cabin, both labor and materials, Flower paid twenty dollars, plus another ten dollars for the luxuries of a wood floor and ceiling.

The newcomers found that life in England had been easier and more comfortable than on the prairie. "Thunderstorms of daily occurrence sent mosquitoes into swarms," Flower wrote. "My cabin, recently built of course of green logs, with rank vegetation growing around it and up to its very sides, was in its situation and in itself a sufficient cause for disease." The colonists fell ill of fever and ague. Water supplies were distant, and well-digging tools had to be sent thirty miles to Carmi for sharpening. The prairie was difficult to break and the frontiersmen scorned British manners, customs, and accents. The imported agricultural laborers meanwhile decided to buy farms for themselves, and forced Birkbeck and Flower to abandon their plan for a cluster of English-type manors on the prairie.

Romance marred the colony. When the party first arrived at Vincennes, Flower, who was twenty-nine, and Miss Andrews were married. Although he took the role of father of the bride at the wedding, Birkbeck, who at fifty-three was the widower father of seven, presumably had intended that his young ward should be his second wife. Birkbeck later refused to speak to Flower and business dealings were carried on through third parties. The two men had separate villages. Birkbeck sold prairie land for farms and

23 George Flower, *History of the English Settlement in Edwards County, Illinois*, quoted in Charles Boewe, *Prairie Albion: An English Settlement in Pioneer Illinois*, pp. 43-44. Boewe's book is largely based on the works of Birkbeck and Flower and such other firsthand accounts as John Woods, *Two Years Residence on the English Prairie in Illinois*.

gathered tradespeople and mechanics at long-vanished Wanborough, named for the Surrey village of which he had been master. Three miles away Flower founded Albion and on it built the finest residence west of the Alleghenies for his father, Richard Flower. A fifty-by-forty-foot, two-story log building with a hipped roof, it had plastered and papered walls. Elegant furniture filled the rooms of Park House, which was appropriately named for its spacious landscaping. The elder Flower served plum pudding to visitors from Europe and the eastern states, and English-style fox hunts startled the natives.

Birkbeck's great contribution to Illinois was as a writer. To a trans-Atlantic audience he extolled the glories of the prairie and the opportunities of Illinois possibly too glamorously but certainly effectively. *Notes on a Journey from the Coast of Virginia to the Territory of Illinois,* written in 1817, was printed in Philadelphia, London, Dublin, and Cork, and ran through eleven English editions in two years. It also appeared in German. *Letters from Illinois,* written in 1818, was published at Boston, Philadelphia, and London and went through seven English editions, plus French and German translations. Richard Flower also had great influence. A letter describing the prairie, written for the Lowell, Massachusetts, *Courier,* was translated into Norwegian, and encouraged Scandinavian migration to the West.

Not all immigrants received encouraging advice, but most accepted the word of John Mason Peck, who helped advertise the state by telling immigrants in his gazetteer that "in no part of the United States can uncultivated land be made into farms with less labor than in Illinois."

The English colonizers were the first scientific farmers in Illinois, importing improved breeds of livestock and writing tracts to advise settlers of ways to improve yields. Birkbeck was president of the state's first agricultural society. The elder Flower established a public library at a time when not many could read and only lawyers owned book collections.

In 1825, Birkbeck drowned while trying to swim his horse across a flooded river. A true Englishman, he still clutched his umbrella when his body was found. The senior Flower died in 1829 at Park House. George Flower went broke, saving only his household furniture as he moved from Albion to live with his children. His last years were serene, and Flower and his wife died on the same day in a daughter's home.

The English colony and Ferdinand Ernst's unfortunate Germans at Vandalia were the first of a series of group migrations from abroad. During the next three decades the eastern states also furnished numerous examples of a company of settlers being organized to move en masse from the East to the frontier and establish, so far as possible, a duplicate of the community they had left. The group migrations were not always popular with the earlier arrivals from the southern states, who distrusted Yankees in any event and held it was preferable to arrive separately and quietly take on the coloration of the new neighborhood.

6

ALMOST A SLAVE STATE

INDENTURES, BLACK CODES, AND SALINES

IN ITS FIRST YEARS, ILLINOIS WAS HARDLY A NORTHERN STATE. Cairo is further south than Richmond, Virginia, and most of the people came from or through the South. They imported southern customs and traditions, including a prejudice against Negroes and a belief in the desirability of slavery.

The holding of Negroes in lifetime bondage, instituted during the French regime when most of the world accepted slavery, had attractions for many in the West. Slavery could alleviate the shortage of labor and thus speed industrialization. Men of wealth had no other way of providing household servants for their wives. Educated men argued that the 1787 ordinance's prohibition of slavery in the Old Northwest could not stand, since Illinois, now admitted to the Union as the equal of the other states, must have the same rights as those below the Mason and Dixon line. The less sophisticated could not understand why only a Frenchman could own a Negro. Men who needed field hands they could not afford watched enviously as slaveowners took their human chattels across Illinois on the way to Missouri. In Congress Illinois votes helped pass the Compromise of 1820, and Senator Thomas introduced the bill that admitted Missouri as a slave state.

A double standard operated in Illinois. The French owned slaves, and many other Illinois residents, including three of the first four governors, possessed registered servants, a theoretical distinction that made little difference to the Negroes involved. Registration was legal under an indenture law adopted by the Indiana territorial legislature in 1805 and reenacted in Illinois four years later. Its inspiration came from an apprentice system under which many a white youngster bound himself to serve a period of years under a two-way contract or indenture. The white apprentice served the appointed time, often seven years, and in return was taught a trade or perhaps was given transportation to a new colony. The contract specified that the apprentice must receive food, clothing, and shelter in at least minimal amounts.

The registered-servant system differed substantially. The long-term contract, promising a coat or a blanket in exchange for labor, in many cases exceeded the life expectancy of the Negro. The contract had to be registered at the county seat and the Negro had the right to reject it, in which case the owner could return him to a southern state within sixty days. In all probability, the black man dared not refuse or did not understand the situation. A major difference was that while an apprenticeship could not be assigned, an indentured Negro could be sold and resold in Illinois, since the territory and the state accepted the southern legal concept that slaves were property rather than persons with human rights. Children born of indentured servants were automatically bound to serve the mother's master, males until they reached thirty and females twenty-eight. A white man could import Negroes under fifteen and register them to serve until the males were thirty-five and females thirty-two. Should a contract expire, it could be renewed with the servant's theoretical consent or he could be taken South into official slavery.[1]

A long series of official rulings and court decisions helped prolong the slave system, but its support was not universal. Indiana repealed its indenture law, and in 1817 the last session of the Illinois territorial legislature took the same step. Governor Edwards then used his absolute power to veto the repealer with a

[1] N. Dwight Harris, *A History of Negro Servitude in Illinois.* John P. Hand, "Negro Slavery in Illinois," *Transactions of the Illinois State Historical Society,* XV (1910), 42-49. John W. Allen, "Slavery and Negro Servitude in Pope County, Illinois," *Journal of the Illinois State Historical Society,* XLII (Dec., 1949), 411-423. Solon J. Buck, *Illinois in 1818,* pp. 138ff., 187, 214-215. Alexander Davidson and Bernard Stuvé, *A Complete History of Illinois,* pp. 316-319.

message of masterful double-talk. He agreed that the indenture law violated the 1787 ordinance and conceded that the legislature had the right to repeal it. He based the veto on the inviolability of the Virginia deed of cession, expressed the personal belief that the indenture terms should be reduced to one year, and argued that such contracts were "reasonable within themselves, beneficial as to the slaves, and not repugnant to the public interest." In exercising the veto, Edwards, who owned Negroes, said slavery was evil and that he personally would have voted to bar it from the territory.[2]

The constitutional compromise of 1818 put a meaningless one-year limit on new indenture contracts; among its many loopholes it made them renewable and required enforcement of existing contracts for their full term.

The year after it joined the Union, Illinois enacted a slave code that was harsher and wider in scope than some of those in the South. Actually, the slave population of Illinois did not constitute a threat to white domination. The 1800 census showed 133 slaves in Indiana, which included Illinois. By 1819 Illinois separately had 168. The totals of 917 in 1820 and 746 in 1830 presumably included indentured servants. The black code made life uncertain for and gave minimum protection to free Negroes and mulattoes in Illinois. A certificate of freedom and a description of every member of the family had to be recorded at the county seat, but the overseers of the poor nevertheless could expel them. Freedom did not bring equality before the law and a Negro's word had no standing in court. Runaways, the disobedient, and the lazy could be whipped. Whites also were regulated by the code. A fine of $1.50 a day faced anyone who hired a Negro without a certificate of freedom. To harbor a Negro was a felony punishable by a fine or a thirty-five-stripe flogging. The law also discouraged the bringing of slaves into Illinois for the purpose of emancipation. It required a one-thousand-dollar bond that the freed person would not become a public charge. The penalty for noncompliance was a two-hundred-dollar fine. Nothing in the law discouraged the common practice of kidnaping free Negroes. It provided only a civil remedy, and prosecutors seldom interfered with gangs of men who seized Negroes at river towns and ran them South for sale at auction.[3]

---

[2] Davidson-Stuvé, *op. cit.*, p. 316.

[3] Elmer Gertz, "The Black Laws of Illinois," *Journal of the Illinois State Historical Society*, LVI (Autumn, 1963), 454-473.

Heavy demand for Negroes came from the salines west of Shawneetown, which were a major source of salt. Acres of shallow clay pans, used by earlier Indian civilizations for evaporation of brine, helped government surveyors locate two potent springs near the Saline River not far from present-day Equality. Congress authorized the secretary of the treasury to lease them for the benefit of the government and set up a ten-by-thirteen-mile rectangular reservation so that fuel supplies could be protected. Leasing began in 1803, and the federal government collected $28,160 between 1807 and 1818, when ownership was transferred to Illinois. Early governors gave close attention to collecting the rent and protecting the public interest.[4]

From one to two thousand Negroes, many of them leased from Kentucky and Tennessee owners, worked at the salt wells. They cut trees and hauled wood used in heating the spring water as it moved along a row of twenty to thirty cast-iron kettles. At the end of the line other Negroes scooped salt into barrels, which also were made at the scene. From 125 to 280 gallons of water produced a fifty-pound bushel of salt and the daily yield ran from eighty to one hundred bushels. Hauled by oxen to Shawneetown and reloaded into keelboats, the salt found a ready market in Indiana, Tennessee, Kentucky, and Missouri. Illinois men rode more than a hundred miles for a packsaddle load. As the nearby trees were consumed, slaves moved the kettles to a new wood supply and with hand tools drilled holes through logs so that the brine could be piped there. The hundred-gallon kettles straddled a ditch, with the fire stoked at one end and the smokestack at the other.

The Gallatin County salt springs in 1819 produced from two hundred to three hundred thousand bushels of salt, which sold for fifty to seventy-five cents a bushel and was marketed in the Ohio valley for home use and as a preservative for meats shipped to New Orleans. Five salt works operated there in 1828, but in the steamboat era Illinois had difficulty in competing with a better-quality product made from stronger brine at Kanawha, near the present city of Charleston, West Virginia. With congressional approval, the sale of the state reservations was completed in 1847. Private enterprise built a new plant near Equality which used

4 George W. Smith, "The Salines of Southern Illinois," *Transactions of the Illinois State Historical Society*, IX (1904), 245-258. Evarts B. Greene and Clarence W. Alvord (eds.), *The Governors' Letter-Books, 1818-1834*, p. 3n. R. C. Buley, *The Old Northwest*, I, 543-546. John Moses, *Illinois Historical and Statistical*, I, 265-266.

sheet-iron vats over stone fire chambers. When the wood supplies ran out, a nearby coal mine provided fuel. The salines near Shawneetown finally closed in 1873.

Illinois had other salt springs. Danville got its start in 1819 when several families settled near a salt lick which long had attracted animals and Indians. The Vermilion County salines returned a profit for a dozen years. Little state revenue came from two wells operated by Conrad Will at the Big Muddy saline three miles west of present Murphysboro. Will, who also operated a tanyard with Negro labor, first showed up at Kaskaskia in 1811 to buy cattle and drive them back to Pennsylvania. Bond County also had a saline which the state sold in 1833, four years after the legislature authorized disposal of the salt well near Danville.

THE IMPROBABLE EDWARD COLES

Fortuitously, an early-day abolitionist became the second governor of Illinois. A former slaveowner, an idealistic aristocrat, and the confidant of presidents, Edward Coles seemed strangely out of place during the thirteen years he lived in Illinois. No other governor spent so brief a time in the state, and few did so much to influence the tide of events.

At the age of twenty-three, Coles inherited a Virginia plantation and its black work force. Oddly, considering his environment, it troubled his conscience. The son of a Revolutionary War colonel, Coles knew the leading Virginia statesmen socially and his relatives and friends also owned slaves. As private secretary to President Madison, Coles spent six years in the White House. He avidly sought information about the Old Northwest and urged Jefferson to devise and take leadership in some plan for gradual emancipation. Quitting his post, he made a trip to Shawneetown and Kaskaskia. Illinois impressed him, but Madison called Coles back for a diplomatic mission to Russia on the first American warship to enter the Baltic Sea. He restored international goodwill by smoothing out a misunderstanding with Czar Alexander I, after which he toured western Europe.[5]

[5] E. B. Washburne, *Sketch of Edward Coles, Second Governor of Illinois, and of the Slavery Struggle of 1823-4*, edited by Clarence W. Alvord and reissued as *Governor Edward Coles* by the Illinois State Historical Library. Eudora R. Richardson, "The Virginian Who Made Illinois a Free State," *Journal of the Illinois State Historical Society*, XLV (Spring, 1952), 5-22. Donald S. Spencer, "Edward Coles: Virginia Gentleman in Frontier Politics," *Journal of the Illinois State Historical Society*, LXI (Spring, 1968), 150-163. Arthur C. Boggess, *The Settlement of Illinois, 1778-1830*, pp. 176-190.

Back home, Coles made a second trip to Kaskaskia and attended the constitutional convention until he was certain that Illinois would be a free state. Coles then sold his plantation in the spring of 1819 and started his Negroes westward. On an Ohio River flatboat he called his people together and told them that from that moment they were free men and women, at liberty to stay with him or go their own way. If they stayed, he would pay wages and see each family settled on a farm.

In advance, Monroe had appointed him register of the Edwardsville land office. Young, dignified, and courteous, Coles soon became well known in Illinois. Three years after arriving, he ran for governor as the choice of most opponents of slavery. Organized parties had not replaced personal factions, and as candidates to succeed Bond the divided advocates of legal slavery entered two Supreme Court justices. Bond supporters backed the chief justice, Joseph Phillips. Most Edwards men favored Justice Thomas C. Browne. A fourth candidate entered the field late and generally was antislavery.

Coles became a minority governor, getting a third of the vote and finishing fifty votes ahead of Phillips. Proslavery men won the lieutenant governorship and controlled the legislature. Coles, who objected to being addressed by such titles as "Your Excellency," lacked the charm and finesse to be a successful politician. His blunt speech alienated some associates, and he antagonized legislators by announcing programs without prior consultation. His inaugural message reviewed the banking situation and in the name of humanity asked for emancipation of the French slaves. The speech, which also took an unpopular stand on banking, stirred up a storm.

The legislators countered with a drive to legalize slavery through a constitutional amendment. The movement had strong support as a carry-over from the 1818 compromise on indentures. Had it succeeded, undreamed of turmoil would have followed. Slavery north of the Ohio River would have set off action and reaction that could have slowed the development of the northern regions and caused Chicago to be outstripped by some Indiana or Michigan city. The conflict between North and South would have developed on different lines and perhaps ended with a different result. Lincoln would not have been supported for the presidency by a slave state, and he probably would have gone to some state to the east to launch his political career.

Courtesy Illinois State Historical Library

Governor Edward Coles

A special committee dominated by anti-Coles men insisted that Virginia's guarantee to the French took precedence over the 1787 ordinance. Nothing had been or could be done, the legislators averred, to alter that fact. Furthermore, they asserted that Illinois had the same right as any other state to amend its constitution. The committee recommended a referendum for a constitutional convention. The proposition required a two-thirds majority in each legislative house and a majority vote of the people at the 1824 general election. With heavy pressure, a convention resolution was adopted only after a delay of nine weeks enabled the house of representatives to reopen an election contest and seat John Shaw, a known slavery man. He replaced Nicholas Hansen of Pike County, who had been counted upon as a convention supporter but voted against it. In a nocturnal celebration, two Supreme Court justices, a future governor of Missouri, a future lieutenant governor, and most of the legislators blew on horns, beat tin pans, and yowled their disrespect outside the residence of the governor and the boarding houses of convention opponents.

Coles promptly organized an antislavery society and issued an address to the people which exposed the intentions of the convention backers. It closed by saying that if they triumphed "we should write the epitaph of free government." The document, which stressed the immoral aspects of slavery, was signed by fifteen legislators but undoubtedly was written by the governor. Coles recruited anonymous help from prominent Philadelphians, including President Nicholas Biddle of the Bank of the United States. Three pamphlets argued that slavery was both wrong in principle and unprofitable. They told of the cruelty of the slave trade and used arguments taken from the published opinions of prominent Southerners. With others, the governor bought the *Intelligencer,* now published at Vandalia, and switched its editorial position. Of the state's five weekly newspapers, three supported the side of slavery. The governor donated his four-year salary to the cause and spent heavily from his own funds while writing extensively and working long hours.

Birkbeck, at Coles' urging, contributed letters and articles widely distributed under the signature of Jonathan Freeman. His pamphlets accused the legislators of dishonesty and attacked the institution of slavery with vigor and sophistication. In a letter to Coles, Birkbeck expressed regret that he could not pay the printing bill. Also active and influential was John Mason Peck, a Baptist missionary who organized antislavery societies in fifteen counties. Edwards left no record that he took sides in the fight. Cook, now his son-in-law, actively supported the governor.

Arrogant and ardent, the slavery advocates included such well-known men as Thomas, McLean, Kane, and Bond. Working in their favor was the strong racial prejudice against both Negroes and Indians which existed in Illinois during the first half of the nineteenth century. The convention campaign continued nearly a year and a half and the public became intensely involved, perhaps as much as in any election since then. The high-handed seating of Shaw over Hansen had alienated many, and the returns indicated that men on the frontier's edge had little sympathy for the slavery cause. When the lame, aged, and ill joined the able-bodied at the polling places, Coles and the anticonvention cause triumphed, 6,640 to 4,972. Unlike Indiana and Ohio, which had taken earlier stands on the side of the free states, Illinois continued to harbor pseudoslavery, and two decades would pass before the courts finally ruled that the indenture system was illegal.[6]

To the incoming legislature, Coles repeated his request for more humane laws for Negroes. Harassment continued. Madison County officials brought suit because Coles, in freeing his slaves before reaching Illinois, had been ignorant of the law requiring him to post bond guaranteeing that they never would become public charges. The Supreme Court, however, released him from a two-thousand-dollar penalty. To fill a vacancy as secretary of state, Coles appointed Birkbeck, who served three months before a spiteful senate refused confirmation.

The 1824 referendum was Coles' last political victory. After completing his term, he made a poor showing as an anti-Jackson candidate for Congress. Few of his antislavery colleagues won another election of any importance. Meanwhile the proslavery losers scored a succession of triumphs in seeking high office. That situation amazed generations of historians and is explained as the electorate's desire to keep prominent men in office and a willingness to forgive their errors.

Cannon boomed, martial music was played, and Coles made the welcoming speech at Kaskaskia when General Lafayette visited Illinois during an 1825 tour. Kaskaskia's society honored the French hero of the Revolution with a reception in John Edgar's big house, a dinner at Colonel Sweet's tavern, and a ball in William Morrison's stone mansion. The next day the governor escorted the marquis to Nashville in a boat chartered by the state. On the way East, Lafayette made a shorter stop at Shawneetown. John Moses, a historian specializing in statistics, says the entertainment cost the state $6,473, about one-third of the year's tax revenues.[7]

[6] Admittedly with little documentation, a belief that many of those who migrated to Illinois from the South were opponents of slavery is advanced by Carrie Prudence Kofoid in "Puritan Influences in the Formative Years of Illinois History," *Transactions of the Illinois State Historical Society,* X (1905), 308-310. She contends that many early Scotch-Presbyterians came from North Carolina primarily for reasons of conscience and holds that the settlers at New Design and elsewhere crossed the Ohio River to get away from the bondage system.

[7] Moses, *op. cit.,* I, 329.

When his term ended, Coles retired to a bachelor life on his Edwardsville farm. He traveled extensively, made money from St. Louis real estate investments, and in 1832 left Illinois for a happier life in Philadelphia.

A DECADE OF JACKSONIAN POLITICS, 1826-1836

With the slavery issue quieted, reverence for Andrew Jackson became a dominating force in Illinois. Daniel Pope Cook, the state's congressman, gave unwitting help when the 1824 presidential election, for lack of a majority in the electoral college, was thrown into the house of representatives. John Quincy Adams, the Massachusetts statesman, and Jackson, the hero of New Orleans, divided the vote in the three election districts into which the twenty-nine counties had been divided. The results were debatable; Cook had pledged to support whoever carried the state and in the end he helped swing the election to Adams.[8] The Thomas-McLean-Kane element reacted by siding with Jackson, and among the men who lived in log cabins it became gospel that the West had been insulted when Old Hickory was cheated out of the presidency. The trend toward democratic government had long been developing, and Jackson became its symbol and the chief advocate of the popular causes of removal of the Indians and more liberal land laws.

The political career of Cook ended at the next election. After four consecutive congressional election triumphs over the state's best-known men—McLean twice, Kane, and Bond—Cook tarried at Washington and lost to Joseph Duncan, who campaigned energetically as a Jackson supporter.

The Federalist party never functioned in Illinois, and in the first years of statehood political leaders regarded themselves as Jeffersonian Republicans. They split not on party lines but over national or state legislative issues or, more often, over which factional leader to follow. Henry Clay's "American system" promised internal improvements and home manufactures, but it could not compete with the popularity of Jackson's land and Indian causes. As a

8 *Illinois Election Returns, 1818-1848,* Theodore C. Pease, ed., pp. 30-35. Pease's introduction to this volume of the Collections of the State Historical Library surveys the political issues of the period. See also Pease's *The Frontier State, 1818-1848,* the standard histories by Moses and Davidson-Stuvé, and R. C. Buley's *The Old Northwest, Pioneer Period, 1815-1840,* II, 28-29.

result, Illinois rejected the easterners and New Englanders, who let a congressional caucus decide whether Adams or Clay would be supported. Illinois formed an alliance with the South which lasted several decades while the present Democratic party arose on deep foundations. Political chaos continued for several years, but men who agreed with at least part of Jackson's controversial policies or whose loyalty to Old Hickory could never be shaken cast a landslide two-thirds majority in 1828 and again in 1832. Starting in 1826 they elected the congressman, controlled the legislature, and carried most of the major contests, but Illinois would be twenty years old before an all-out Jackson man would sit in the governor's office.

Aristocratic Ninian Edwards could never be a Jacksonite. In 1826, when Coles' term was ending, Edwards was near the end of the road politically. Before his second term in the United States senate expired, he resigned to become minister to Mexico but gave up that honor in an unwise quarrel with William H. Crawford, the secretary of the treasury who wanted to be President and had the backing of Thomas. Edwards denounced Crawford's handling of government deposits in the Edwardsville bank, claiming political motivation. Crawford fought back and forced Edwards to return to Washington for an investigation in which the Illinois leader could not prove his case.[9] Damaged politically, Edwards came home and campaigned for governor by charging that prominent legislators were corruptly involved in the bank at Edwardsville. The immediate result was that he alienated most of the leaders, who ordered an investigation that failed to produce a clear verdict at the end of an era when public men were identified as being for or against Edwards. He was elected governor by a narrow margin over a weak candidate with Jackson backing.

Edwards was a holdover from the colonial times when important men wore powdered wigs. Disdaining the common touch, he dressed in a broadcloth coat, ruffled shirts, and high boots while campaigning in a carriage driven by a Negro servant. Edwards was stately, pompous, overbearing, and verbose in explaining his shifting views. He was rich, having abandoned a law practice to become a land speculator and owner of stores and mills at Kaskaskia, Belleville, Carlyle, Alton, Springfield, and in Missouri. At the same

[9] Ninian W. Edwards, *A History of Illinois*, pp. 135-154, and Pease, *op. cit.*, pp. 93, 99-103.

time he was kindly and charitable. Trained in medicine as well as
the law, Edwards died of Asiatic cholera in an 1833 epidemic.
Refusing to flee, he stayed in Belleville, his final home, to help
stricken neighbors.

Like Coles, Governor Edwards had been elected by a minority
vote and faced an unfriendly legislature. In long speeches he
advocated that the Indians be moved beyond the Mississippi and
that the government adopt a more liberal land policy. Both causes
were popular on the frontier, but in the interest of a constant
labor supply the congressional delegates from seaboard states
wanted to slow down the westward expansion. Edwards contended that the federal government could constitutionally own only
the land on which forts stood. He advocated that the public
domain be acquired by the states and parceled out to newcomers
at minimum prices and on easy credit, arguing that the development of the West would more than counterbalance the immediate
loss to the national treasury. Despite Edwards' sagging popularity,
the legislature supported him by adoption of resolutions. Donation of land to poor settlers was only one of the demands made
upon the federal government by Illinois congressmen. They wanted lower land prices, preemption rights for squatters, more land
offices and post roads, and grants for internal improvements.
Those causes enjoyed western popularity, and no congressman
from a frontier state could oppose them.

Striving to stay alive politically, Edwards in the 1830 election
humiliated himself by supporting John Reynolds, whom he had
scorned in the past, for governor. The voters had a poor choice,
for the other candidate also was a political hack, Lieutenant
Governor William Kinney, a "hard-shell" Baptist preacher who was
a good stump speaker and had been taught to read by his wife.
They represented the two degrees of Jacksonism. Kinney rated
as "whole hog," meaning that his loyalty could never be questioned. Reynolds' "milk and cider" views were sufficiently diluted
to get the votes of Clay and Adams supporters who formed the
nucleus of the new Whig party.

Calling himself the "Old Ranger," Reynolds appealed to the
veterans of 1812. The tall and slender son of Irish Protestants who
had settled on the American Bottom in 1800, he had never seen a
carpet, a papered wall, or a winged chair, or lived in a house with a
shingled roof or glass windows until he was twenty. Then his
comparatively well-to-do parents gave him a homespun suit and a

horse for a trip to Knoxville, where an uncle lived. Reynolds attended an academy long enough to be able to claim a classical education. The depth of his learning is questionable, in view of the disorganized contests of the prolific writings of his later years, [10] but Reynolds had a far-ranging if prejudiced mind and he excelled in the political art of collecting friends. Any superiority he carefully concealed, as Thomas Ford explains:

> ... no one would suppose from hearing his conversation and public addresses that he ever learned more than to read and write and cypher to the rule of three .... He had been a farmer, a lawyer, and a soldier, a judge, and a member of the legislature. He had passed his life on the frontiers among a frontier people; he had learned all the bye-words, catchwords, old sayings and figures of speech invented by the vulgar ingenuity and common among a backwoods people; to these he had added a copious supply of his own, and had diligently compounded them into a language peculiar unto himself, which he used on all occasions, both public and private. He was a man of remarkably good sense and shrewdness for the sphere in which he chose to move, and he possessed a fertile imagination, a ready eloquence, and a continual mirthfulness while mingling with the people. [11]

Reynolds won the governorship with a majority vote and got along with the legislature better than Coles and Edwards. As a monument he left the state's first penitentiary, a limestone building at Alton with twenty-four cells into which the first prisoners moved in 1833. The prison operated on the Auburn Plan, with convicts laboring in silence by day and spending the night in separate confinement. Criminologists regarded that as superior to the old system under which the punishment for non-hanging offenses was public flogging or confinement to stocks or the pillory. Money for the prison construction came from the sale of the Gallatin and Vermilion county saline lands. For the first five years, the state managed the prison through a warden elected biennially. After that, a commission supervised a contractor who furnished supplies, employed guards, and acted as warden.

[10] *The Pioneer History of Illinois* (1852) and *My Own Times* (1855) were reissued by the Fergus Printing Company of Chicago in 1887 and 1879, respectively. Among Reynolds' other works are *Sketches of the Country, on the Northern Route from Belleville, Illinois, to the City of New York* (Belleville, 1854).

[11] Thomas Ford, *A History of Illinois*, p. 106 (Lakeside Classics edition), I, 147-148. Also see Jessie McHarry, "John Reynolds," *Journal of the Illinois State Historical Society*, VI (April, 1913), 7-57.

William Lee Davidson Ewing, a state senator who also had an Irish background, served as governor for fifteen days in 1834. As president pro tem of the senate, he had been next in line when both Reynolds and Lieutenant Governor Zadoc Casey resigned to start congressional careers. Ewing set some kind of a record in going up and down the political ladder. He started in 1826 as clerk of the house of representatives and became state representative, speaker of the house, state senator, governor, and United States senator for a two-year term. Then he served as state representative and speaker, clerk of the house, and finished his days as state auditor. Ewing also was receiver of the Vandalia land office and a Black Hawk War colonel. Twice he defeated Abraham Lincoln for speaker.

Chaos in state politics continued in 1834, when the Whig party appeared as an anti-Jackson coalition. That year Jackson conventions at Belleville and Vandalia entered rival "whole hog" candidates for governor, but Joseph Duncan, in his third term as congressman, won the office with a clear majority without making a speech. He stayed in Washington while his rivals campaigned at home. The Whigs found him acceptable on election day, and in the inaugural speech the Democrats discovered that Duncan had turned against Jackson, whose popularity had reached its peak two years earlier. Jackson had strained the loyalty of many supporters in 1830 by vetoing a federal appropriation to build a road in Kentucky, but he found a new source for western enthusiasm by attacking the Bank of the United States. Duncan blamed the President for shifting views on banking and internal improvements, especially the vetoing of appropriations to improve the Wabash River and the Chicago harbor. Duncan undoubtedly would have been defeated had the voters known of his defection, for Jackson still had the loyalty of the Illinois majority.

Duncan, who had been voted a sword by Congress for services in the War of 1812, thereafter was a Whig, a party slowly emerging without too much success in Illinois. In 1836, when William Henry Harrison made his first try for the presidency, Illinois was the only state in the Old Northwest carried by Martin Van Buren, to whom Jackson had passed his crown.

Secret balloting, in force since statehood, was abandoned in 1831 on the ground that it led to intrigue and double-crossing. The legislators believed it was more straightforward for a voter to call out, within the hearing of hangers-on, the names of the candidates he favored. The Jackson Democrats in 1837 adopted the state convention system of making nominations and enforcing loyalty. Their party had the support of farmers and small businessmen and it offered the best chance for advancement by politicians seeking office at the national level. To the convention procedure the Whigs objected in an unbroken string of failures.

7

YANKEES IN THE NORTH

AT SOME UNRECORDED TIME AROUND 1830, THE SETTLERS OF Illinois began to comprehend a great truth—that Birkbeck had been right and that prairie farming was both possible and desirable. Until that time migration had largely been into or through the southern part of the state and virtually all occupied the woodlands if they did not live in a town. The hunter-pioneers advanced first along the timbered watercourses, chiefly the Illinois and Mississippi rivers, and by 1830 their habitations were found as far northward as Marshall and Putnam counties. The process of settlement necessarily had been slow, since small game cannot be hunted by a crowd and decades could be spent chopping away the giant trees. When the 1830 census was taken, in fifty counties Illinois had a head count of 157,445, which meant that since statehood the population had increased only ten thousand a year. While most had Kentucky, Virginia, and Tennessee backgrounds, some came from Ohio, Pennsylvania, New York, and New England. As a result of new momentum, within four years the center of population would be somewhere north of Vandalia,[1] since the

---

[1] John Moses, *Illinois Historical and Statistical*, I, 387. In tracing the arrival of the families who took over central and northern Illinois, much reliance is placed on William V. Pooley, *The Settlement of Illinois from 1830 to 1850*. See also Douglas C. Ridgley, *Geography of Illinois*, pp. 144-145; Roy M. Robbins, *Our Landed Heritage: The Public Domain*, pp. 48-63; and R. C. Buley, *The Old Northwest*, II, 53-57, 99-121.

Courtesy Illinois State Historical Library

Black Hawk.

edges of the Military Tract had been occupied and immigrants were spreading into the Sangamon valley.

The Sangamon country had many streams and therefore an intermixture of timber and prairie. Men who had been there did not understand why, but they reported that the midstate soil was much richer than in the unglaciated, far southern counties, where comparatively few had attempted to make homes. In midstate the first farmers were just beginning to realize that it was not true that where the oaks grew tallest the soil was richest. In their grandchildren's generation, soil scientists would explain why the best soil was on the prairie, where the fibrous roots of the wild blue-stem grass for centuries had produced humus of great natural fertility. Another reason was that the matted prairie sod helped check the leaching of calcium and other minerals which were valuable plant foods. The upland timber soil had only 25 to 50 percent as much organic matter as the brown silt loam of the more undulating prairies or the black gumbo of the flatlands. Timber and prairie alike had been leveled and enriched by the glaciers, but since then the trees had done little to add to the inherited fertility.[2]

In the Sangamon country tentative experiments in prairie farming were made by men who came into Illinois over the National Road and then turned northward into midstate. As they edged onto the grass, at first they kept close to the timber, because the sod wasn't so thick in the semishady spots and a supply of wood was nearby. Quickly they dismissed one of the original objections to prairie settlement, since well diggers usually found a good supply of water not far below the surface. If anything, a large part of the prairie was too wet for farming until the time came for ditching and tiling. The only valid objection was that a much better plow was needed for prairie breaking.

As a portent of the future, Indiana was twice as populous as Illinois. The white man crowded the East, as Black Hawk learned after his retreat and defeat when, as a prisoner of war and an object of curiosity, he was taken on a tour of the seaboard. "Our young men are as numerous as the leaves in the woods," Andrew Jackson told the elderly Indian, who could see that it was so.[3] With or without resistance, it was inevitable that white settlers would expel the comparative handful of Indians who remained in Illinois, a state of such fertility that none of it could be spared for a reservation.

THE UNNECESSARY WAR ON BLACK HAWK

Out of the frontiersman's hatred of the Indian and the savage's inability to comprehend land treaties grew the last warfare in Illinois and the last Indian trouble in the Old Northwest. Overrated, expensive, and avoidable, it lasted only fifteen weeks and

[2] Edith Muriel Poggi, *The Prairie Province of Illinois, A Study of Human Adjustment to the Natural Environment*, pp. 54-69. This work, regretfully out of print, appeared in Vol. 19, No. 3 of the *Illinois Studies in the Social Sciences*. While her focus is on an area from Champaign County northward, taking in the bulk of the Grand Prairie, much of the book applies to the entire state.

[3] Donald Jackson (ed.), *Black Hawk, An Autobiography*, pp. 1-5.

brought death to only seventy settlers and soldiers, a small toll as wars are measured.

The so-called Winnebago War of 1827 was a prelude. Nothing more than the first bad scare since 1812, it brought action. A Chicago militia company mobilized. Gurdon S. Hubbard, noted as a fast walker, rushed to Danville and returned to Chicago with fifty men. Galena miners turned out under arms. Governor Edwards dispatched a regiment of mounted volunteers, and Colonel Henry Atkinson led five hundred regulars to Fort Crawford at Prairie du Chien. The trouble began when the Winnebago killed two white men on a boat near the fort. There had been provocation, and the Indians feared they were being crowded out of another hunting ground, but Chief Red Bird sacrificed valor for prudence by surrendering six braves wanted for the river killings. Red Bird died in prison, the army restored the garrison at Chicago, and in the customary treaty the Winnebago traded away their rights in southern Wisconsin and northern Illinois for a tract in eastern Iowa.

Hollow-cheeked and hook-nosed, Black Sparrow Hawk did not hold the title of chief. The elderly head man of his ancestral village where the Rock River flows into the Illinois, he led a "British band" of Sauk Indians who frequently traveled past Detroit to Fort Malden, Ontario. Black Hawk complained continually about the 1804 treaty at St. Louis where some Sauk and Fox chiefs signed away fifty million acres roughly bounded by the Mississippi, Fox, and Wisconsin rivers in return for a thousand-dollar annuity. It had been a typical treaty, with the Indians not understanding the concept of private ownership of land and some younger tribesmen repudiating the action of secondary chiefs who were the signers. Black Hawk considered the treaty illegal but no white man would listen to him.

So long as the land remained in the public domain the Indians retained the right to live and hunt east of the Mississippi, but white men were pushing northward from the Sangamon valley, a favorite stopping place for settlers who had taken the National Road. The area near Rock Island attracted squatters who traveled more than fifty miles to reach Black Hawk's town. There they destroyed corn fields, burned lodges, and committed other breaches of the peace. The Indians showed restraint by crossing into present Iowa in hope that someone would restore their treaty rights.[4]

In the spring of 1831 the Indians needed a corn crop. Black Hawk impatiently ordered the squatters to leave and his braves burned isolated cabins. Alarm spread, action was demanded at Vandalia, and it was agreed that Edwards had been right in 1828 when he wanted the Indians expelled from Illinois. Governor Reynolds called out a volunteer army of seven hundred men who marched from Beardstown to Fort Armstrong, where they joined regulars under General Edmund P. Gaines. Against 300 to 2,500 odds, Black Hawk withdrew his people across the river just before the white army shelled his village with grapeshot.

In a new treaty Black Hawk promised not to return to Illinois without permission, but the winter hunt failed and the Iowa prairie had not been broken for corn planting. So with five hundred braves and a thousand squaws and children, he crossed the Mississippi near Oquawka, known then as Yellow Banks. His plan, he related later in an autobiography, was to raise corn with the Winnebago at Prophet's Town nearly fifty miles up the Rock River. Women and children do not go on war parties, but the men were armed and surly. Black Hawk, who ranked with Pontiac and Tecumseh as a leader of lost causes, hoped for an alliance with the Winnebago and Potawatomi and perhaps even with the British.

Promptly notified, Reynolds again called out a militia army whose numbers included Abraham Lincoln, captain of the New Salem company. Reynolds, the "Old Ranger," went along and was allowed the federal pay of a major general. From Fort Armstrong, built on Rock Island in 1816-17 with two blockhouses backed against a limestone cliff, 1,000 regulars and 1,935 militiamen advanced up the river.

---

[4] Jackson's edition of the Black Hawk autobiography (*op. cit.*) is well annotated. While the emphasis is on the preliminaries, the war itself is covered by the newest study of the subject, Anthony F. C. Wallace's *Prelude to Disaster: The Course of Indian-White Relations Which Led to the Black Hawk War of 1832*, issued by the Illinois State Historical Library as the introduction to the *Black Hawk War, 1831-1832*. For comprehensive accounts, standard works are Milo M. Quaife (ed.), *The Life of Ma-Ka-Tai-Me-She-Kia-Kiak or Black Hawk . . . Dictated by Himself*, and Frank E. Stevens, *The Black Hawk War* (Chicago, 1903). The conflict also receives full attention in Theodore C. Pease, *The Frontier State, 1818-1848;* Moses, *op. cit.,* I, 346-348 and 357-378; Alexander Davidson and Bernard Stuvé, *A Complete History of Illinois;* and John Francis Snyder, *Adam W. Snyder and His Period in Illinois History, 1817-1842*, pp. 109-147. The senior Snyder was a captain in the war.

The turning point came in Ogle County, where the tragedy of war had a trace of slapstick comedy. Black Hawk had failed to arouse the other tribes to his cause and was reconciled to returning to Iowa. To troops in the vicinity he sent a flag of truce on the assumption that he could talk to Atkinson, who now was a general. Unfortunately his contact was with 275 newly arrived militiamen under Major Isaiah Stillman. The undisciplined and disorderly whites killed some of the envoys and began a headlong rush toward a handful of Indians in the distance. Black Hawk, who had only forty men with him in ambush, ordered a suicide charge, whereupon most of the whites turned around and stampeded to Dixon's Ferry, twenty-five miles to the rear. Some stopped only when they reached their homes, forty or fifty miles away from what is now the village of Stillman Valley.[5]

The panic led to exaggerated reports of Indian strength and made war inevitable. Far away at Pekin the schoolhouse was converted into a fort. The Indians added to the alarm by killing sixteen whites and capturing two girls, later ransomed, in the Indian Creek massacre in La Salle County. Black Hawk personally led a brief assault on an Apple River fort fourteen miles east of Galena. The damage there included the slaughtering of fifty horses and the emptying of featherbeds in the June breeze. The militiamen had bungled the war and in the emergency some of them refused to reenlist, but Captain Lincoln signed up as a private in a new company. Replacements in the form of a thousand regulars under General Winfield Scott failed to get into action because they brought along a cholera epidemic when they arrived on the first steamers to reach the port of Chicago. The cholera spread to civilian populations at Detroit, Chicago, Fort Armstrong, Galena, and down the Mississippi with a three-year toll far exceeding that of battlefields and camps.[6]

In the war, which could have been avoided, the whites reorganized four thousand regulars and militia before leaving Dixon June 27 to pursue the outnumbered, fatigued, and hungry Indian families into Wisconsin. Tired of the chase, Reynolds and his staff went home. In the Battle of Wisconsin Heights, twenty-five miles north-

[5] Frank E. Stevens, "Stillman's Defeat," *Transactions of the Illinois State Historical Society*, VII (1902), 170-179.

[6] Charles E. Rosenberg, *The Cholera Years: The United States in 1832, 1849, and 1866*. Milo M. Quaife, *Chicago and the Old Northwest*, pp. 310-339.

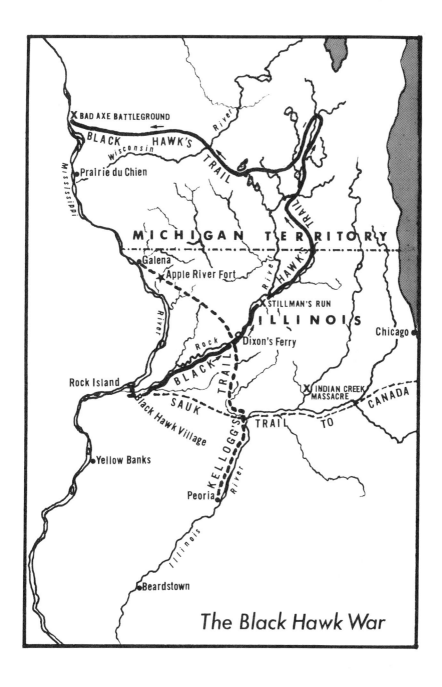

The Black Hawk War

west of what is now Madison, Black Hawk held off the whites while the Indian women and children crossed the Wisconsin River. Then he led his fugitives over unfamiliar ground toward the Mississippi. The end came in the Battle of Bad Axe, on the river midway between Prairie du Chien and La Crosse. General James D. Henry restored part of the militia's prestige by catching the Indians August 2 and summoning an armed steamer.[7] In a heavy slaughter that almost extinguished the Sauk tribe, the warriors, old people, women, and children were driven into the water and then ambushed as they tried to reach the west bank. Black Hawk, who had loved and fought for the beautiful Rock River country, escaped but was soon captured.

Black Hawk received a sword and a medal from President Jackson while on a great circle tour that included imprisonment in Fortress Monroe and ended on a reservation in Iowa. There he suffered the final indignity of being a subordinate to Chief Keokuk, his rival for Sauk and Fox supremacy.

The fur-trading era had ended with the Black Hawk War, and the decade of the 1830's saw a major change in the settlement pattern. The Indian scare had rolled back the outposts of the original settlers, who never recovered momentum for a new northward push. Instead, northern Illinois would be occupied primarily by Yankees who made up a new breed. Unlike Daniel Boone, they had never existed with gun and ax in the woods. In violation of the pioneer tradition, they moved directly onto the prairies and became permanent settlers of the land they first occupied. One of the important results of the Black Hawk War was the selection of attractive sites for farms and towns by soldiers who had erased the last danger of Indian trouble. They preferred to settle on upland prairie not too far from woods and they hoped that later a road would connect their property with a river or a town.[8] Vast numbers of New Yorkers, New Englanders, and in time foreigners were ready to flood into the northern counties and challenge the supremacy of the southerners who had first reached Illinois. Occupation would come quickly because construction of the Erie Canal

[7] Frank E. Stevens, "A Forgotten Hero: General James Dougherty Henry," *Transactions of the Illinois State Historical Society*, XLI (1934), 77-120.

[8] Pooley, *op. cit.*, pp. 421-459. Roy B. Way, *The Rock River Valley*. John L. Conger, *History of the Illinois River Valley*. M. M. Quaife (ed.), *The Early Day of Rock Island and Davenport*.

and the opening of steamboat navigation on the Great Lakes provided a new avenue of immigration into the North.

First, the future of Chicago, northern Illinois, and southern Wisconsin required that the Indians sign away their rights to the land they had taken from other Indians in earlier tribal wars. At a council at Fort Armstrong, the Winnebago chiefs had given up their Wisconsin hunting grounds, but one last treaty was needed to extinguish the title of the Potawatomi, Chippewa, and Ottawa to a tract of more than five million acres.

Summoned to a council at Chicago in the autumn of 1833, the tribes, long dependent on the white men, were unable to resist. Some five thousand set up their camps for five miles around the village. The chiefs insisted they did not want to sell, but the white men provided whiskey and food in quantity. The town was in an around-the-clock uproar as the Indians, painted for war, performed their blood dance. Charles J. Latrobe, an English visitor, wrote that the red men "howled, sang, wept, yelled and whooped" in confusion, mud, and rubbish.[9] Speculators meanwhile rushed the building of new houses and the unscrupulous arranged to cheat the Indians out of the money and blankets they would receive. Horse races and gambling were common. During the Indian carousel, which John D. Caton described as a carnival of condemned souls, treaty negotiations were delayed a week. On September 23 a fire was kindled in an open shed across the river from the fort. The next day seventy-seven chiefs signed a treaty that promised them some money and a tract of land as large as the one from which they were being evicted. That gave the white man absolute control of the future of Illinois, and the dissolution of Indian power led to the organization of the territories of Wisconsin in 1836 and Iowa in 1838.

A few Indians stayed in the state. One was Shabbona, a friendly Ottawa who had warned the whites when Black Hawk threatened. In his old age he died on a twenty-acre farm near Morris.

One more Indian tragedy stained the soil of Illinois. Late in 1838, on a route from Golconda to the Mississippi River near Cape Girardeau, Missouri, troops herded fifteen thousand Cherokee, the unhappy remnants of a prosperous and civilized tribe that had

---

[9] *The Rambler in North America,* II, 152-153. Quaife, *op. cit.,* pp. 340-370. Anselm J. Gerwing, "The Chicago Indian Treaty of 1833," *Journal of the Illinois State Historical Society,* LVII (Summer, 1964), 117-142. John D. Caton, *The Last of the Illinois and a Sketch of the Pottawatomies.*

been forced to surrender its homeland in Georgia. The southern
Indians, unused to snow and cold, suffered pitifully, and probably
10 percent died before they reached a reservation in the Indian
territory. The route across Illinois touched Dixon Springs, Vienna,
and Jonesboro. It is known as the Cherokee Trail of Tears.[10]

THE ERIE CANAL POINTS TOWARD CHICAGO

Appropriately Illinois has two counties and Chicago two streets
named for Governor De Witt Clinton of New York, the man responsible for the Erie Canal. Completed in 1825 at a cost of seven
million dollars, soon repaid in tolls, it stretched 363 miles from
the Hudson River at Albany to Lake Erie at Buffalo. Forty feet
wide at the towpath line and four feet deep, it pointed directly
toward Chicago and helped mightily in the settlement of the Old
Northwest. The canal encouraged Yankees and foreigners to emi-
grate westward and thus helped reduce the population of the
thin-soiled regions of the older states. At the same time it enabled
New York City to achieve economic domination of the Atlantic
seaboard at the expense of Philadelphia and Baltimore. Freight
rates between New York and Buffalo dropped from one hundred
to three dollars a ton and the time of shipment from twenty days
to six. New York became a market for grain that previously had
gone from Great Lakes ports to the St. Lawrence River. Cleveland
prospered. Southern Illinois benefited as settlers and merchandise
fanned out across Ohio and Indiana to reach the Ohio River. Even
more, the canal helped Chicago and northern Illinois, which were
in the direct line of western settlement when one of America's
great land rushes followed the Black Hawk War.

The Erie Canal provided a superior emigrant and trade route. At
Buffalo it connected with schooners and steamers over the circui-
tous and at times hazardous lakes, but wagon roads were optional.
The canal made Illinois much closer to eastern and foreign markets
than the all-water route down the Mississippi to New Orleans, the
landing place for many arrivals from European countries. The
older parts of Illinois still depended chiefly on the Ohio River
thoroughfare, but that also meant bucking the current on the
upstream trip and, in either direction, required a difficult crossing

---

[10] Mable Thompson Rauch, "Along the Trail of Tears," *Journal of the Illinois State
Historical Society*, XLIII (Winter, 1950), 298-301.

of the Pennsylvania mountains. Neither of these routes was as efficient as the canal and the lakes.[11]

In the second decade of Illinois statehood, the Erie Canal helped Chicago stir from its trading post somnambulance. A second Fort Dearborn had arisen in 1816 and been garrisoned for seven years. Henry R. Schoolcraft found only four or five families at the portage in 1820. Two years later the aggressiveness of John Jacob Astor's American Fur Company forced the government to close its trading factory. Except for the Indian scares, Chicago was a quiet village, giving no hint of the boom that would arrive in 1833.

Men in far cities had confidence that Chicago would become important because of its location. At Vandalia members of the legislature talked encouragingly about a canal from the Illinois River. In the eastern cities a new generation of land speculators saw possibilities for making money by getting ownership of property soon to be in demand. Due in large part to the Erie Canal, young and ambitious New Englanders and New Yorkers began to arrive by boat and on foot. They were taking the town over from the French and the half-breeds.[12]

Dissatisfaction with economic conditions in eastern states provided most of the motivation for the western expansion from which Illinois benefited. In the more desirable sections of the older states land prices were considerably higher than the $1.25 an acre the government charged for the public domain. The establishment, to prevent its labor force from being drained away, sought to restrict the rapid sale of government lands, but it could not control the desire to migrate. Middle Atlantic laborers complained of hard times, lost markets, and wage cuts even before a depression in 1837 added to the unrest. Not all came directly from the East. Some stopped first in Ohio and Indiana.

Many arrived by land rather than subject themselves to the storms on Lakes Huron and Michigan. Many single men walked most of the distance as they turned their backs on the East. Families bound for a new homestead often traveled in a Yankee wagon, long-coupled, low-boxed, and drawn by two horses. The

---

[11] The migrations from overseas and the East are traced by Pooley, *op. cit.*, pp. 352-374. See Madeline S. Waggoner, *The Long Haul West: The Great Canal Era, 1817-1850.*

[12] John D. Haeger, "The American Fur Company and the Chicago of 1812-1835," *Journal of the Illinois State Historical Society,* LXI (Summer, 1968), 117-139.

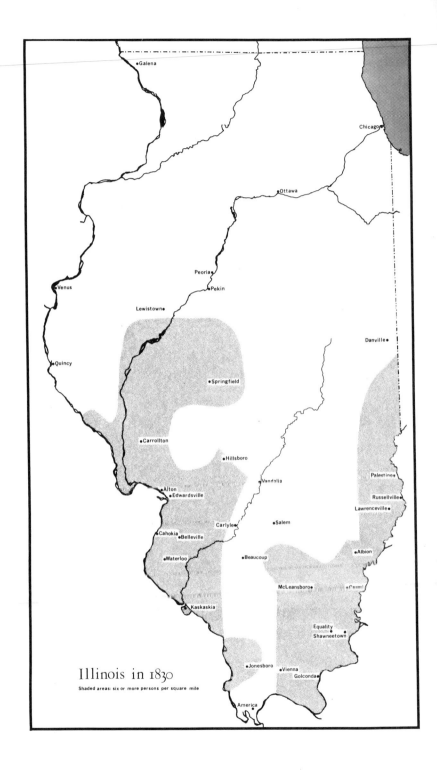

Illinois in 1830

Shaded areas: six or more persons per square mile

land route around the south side of Lake Erie crossed the infamous Black Swamp that covered much of northwestern Ohio
and wasn't the only place where travel was next to impossible in
wet seasons. Some came by water as far as Detroit and then took
the Chicago Road, a more straight-lined version of the Sauk Trail,
which the government had laid out as a defense highway after the
War of 1812. By 1833 Chicago had stagecoach service from
Detroit on a route littered with broken vehicles. It hugged the
south of Lake Michigan and if possible used wave-packed sand. By
1837 the stagecoaches crossed a bridge, sixty rods long, over the
Calumet River.[13]

Chicago, which is closer to the Mississippi River north-south
trade axis than any other point on the Great Lakes, grew because
it was reachable by both water and land. The era of steam
navigation on the lakes coincided with the opening of the Erie
Canal, but for several decades sailing vessels continued to carry
most of the freight and part of the passengers on the lakes, which
form the world's greatest inland waterway system. During the
1820's only a few steamers ventured past Detroit, where most
immigrants were forced to begin land journeys westward. The
adventuresome journey by sail from the Welland Canal to Chicago
required a full month, but 255 schooners made the trip in 1835.

Because Chicago lacked a natural harbor for vessels of that size,
the ships, including those in which General Scott's cholera-infested
troops arrived for the Black Hawk War, had to anchor at least a
half-mile in the lake while their captains worried about storms.
Sandbars blocked the river's mouth and caused the stream to make
a sharp turn southward, just east of the fort, and flow sluggishly a
few hundred yards before entering the lake. A lighthouse, set near
the fort, went up in 1832, and the next year Lieutenant Jefferson
Davis reported there was no other suitable place for a Lake
Michigan harbor. Congress then began a series of appropriations
for river improvements. Despite new sandbars, the first small
schooner entered the river in 1835.

[13] Milo Milton Quaife was one of the most prolific as well as scholarly historians of
the frontier era. See *Chicago's Highways Old and New,* p. 46. This period of Chicago's
development is covered by Bessie Louise Pierce in the first volume of her three-volume *A
History of Chicago.* There are other multivolumes of merit—A. T. Andreas, *History of
Chicago from the Earliest Period to the Present Time,* and John Moses and Joseph
Kirkland, *History of Chicago.* More popular single-volume accounts include Lloyd Lewis
and Henry Justin Smith, *Chicago: The History of Its Reputation,* and Edgar Lee Masters,
The Tale of Chicago.

James Thompson, a surveyor for the state canal commissioners, in 1830 plotted forty-eight prairie blocks and issued the first map of Chicago. He gave permanent names to the streets in the northern loop area and located a square where the City Hall-County Building stands. Thompson limited his map to the area bounded by Madison, State, Kinzie, and Des Plaines streets. The Kinzies lived beyond the northern boundary and the Fort Dearborn reservation was on the east. To the south was a school section, one of those set aside by Nathaniel Pope for the support of education, and it brought $6.72 an acre when auctioned three years later during a land boom. When squatters received the right to enter their holdings at the Danville land office, Robert Kinzie, son of the trader, took title to only 102 acres between the north branch and the lake. His mother urged him to enter an additional corn field, near where the river forks, but he could not see that the title was necessary or the land valuable.

Thompson's plot of Chicago preceded the arrival of civil government at the portage. The next year the legislature created Cook County, which also encompassed the present counties of Lake, McHenry, Du Page, and Will. Three elected commissioners levied a tax of one-half percent on the value of town lots, carriages, distilleries, horses, mules, neat cattle, clocks, and watches. The village of Chicago came into official existence August 10, 1833, after twenty-eight men, out of a population of 150, participated in an election. By that time some beef was being shipped out of the settlement, and the next year the government established a land office, which made it unnecessary for Chicagoans to go to Danville for real estate transactions. The next year a special law extended the village's powers of self-government and enlarged its area. The population was 4,071 on March 4, 1837, when the legislature incorporated Chicago as a city. Two months later the first city officials were elected.

Many speculators cashed in on a land boom that spread through the western country and reached its climax at Chicago in 1836. Downtown lots sold for $250, an increase of 500 percent in four years, while the riverfront lots brought $3,500. Property changed hands frequently, with business done on credit. Charles Butler, a businessman from New York, predicted that the Chicago plains would support millions of people and that Chicago was destined to become the "largest commercial emporium of the United States." In the spring of 1835 Butler paid one hundred thousand dollars for a Chicago tract which a friend had purchased for twenty thousand dollars the preceding autumn. The property was under water when William B. Ogden, Butler's brother-in-law and agent, arrived to inspect it. At first he regarded the situation as impossible, but Ogden waited until hot weather dried out the land and then subdivided and sold one-third of it for enough to realize the purchase price. Thus convinced of Chicago's opportunities, Ogden stayed to become the city's first mayor and early railroad magnate.

"I never saw a busier place than Chicago was at the time of our arrival," wrote Harriet Martineau, a well-traveled Englishwoman, in 1835.[14] "The streets were crowded with land speculators, hurrying from one sale to another. A Negro, dressed up in scarlet, bearing a scarlet flag, and riding a horse with housings of scarlet, announced the time of sale. At every street corner where he stopped, the crowd flocked around him; and it seemed as if some prevalent mania infected the whole people. The rage for speculation might fairly be so regarded. As the gentlemen of our party walked the streets, store-keepers hailed them from their doors, with offers of farms, and all manner of land-lots, advising them to speculate before the price of land rose higher. A young lawyer, of my acquaintance, had realized five hundred dollars per day the five preceding days, by merely making out titles to land."

The land mania was by no means confined to Chicago. Around Lake Michigan and in the inland country, speculators and some legitimate settlers plotted town sites and sold lots at spiraling prices. One observer commented that, at one time or another, virtually all of northeastern Illinois had been promoted for sale as city lots. Typical of inflated hopes was a site at the confluence of the Des Plaines and Kankakee rivers. Its promoters called it Kankakee City and staked out ten public squares and enough parks and avenues for New York City. Kankakee City was never settled.

A census of 1835 showed that Chicago had one hundred merchants, thirty-five lawyers, and twenty-five physicians. In the inflation of wages, carpenters and masons worked for two to three dollars a day and common laborers demanded $1.50 to two dollars, while paying four dollars a week for board. Food supplies became short, the price of flour jumped to twenty dollars a barrel, and from the Wabash River country in Indiana, two hundred miles

14 *Society in America*, I, 259-261.

away, white-topped Conestoga wagons drawn by oxen hauled flour, potatoes, salt pork, bacon, and fruit to Chicago. They returned with such necessities as coffee, salt, and cloth. The lake schooners brought clothing, blasting powder, hardware, dry goods, drugs, medicines, oils, paints, fancy groceries, and choice liquors on their westward passages. Some were freighted on to Galena and other inland settlements, but for years Chicago had an adverse trade balance.

Mail from Niles, Michigan, arrived twice a week. The Rev. Stephen R. Beggs, a Methodist, conducted the first Protestant church service in 1831, two years before Catholic mass was celebrated in Mark Beaubein's cabin. Judge Richard M. Young arrived in 1832 to hold court, but little legal business required his attention. Statistics on the number of houses and total population were quickly made out of date by new arrivals. Beaubein, who was remembered for his fiddle playing, operated the Sauganash Tavern at Lake and Market streets, but Chicago had become a Yankee town. John D. Caton, a lawyer from New York who became chief justice of the Illinois Supreme Court, arrived while Indians were still a problem. John Wentworth, a twenty-one-year-old Dartmouth graduate, came in 1836 and was achieving prominence among townspeople who would elect him mayor and congressman in future years. Ogden sent to New York for John M. Van Osdel, who became Chicago's first architect and built a palatial home for Archibald Clybourn, a meat packer on the river's north bank.

Chicago's suburbs took root in the 1830's. Jefferson, which was annexed years later, became a settlement in 1830, to be followed by the erection of habitations in Oak Park (1835), Norwood Park (1834), Blue Island (1835), and Evanston (1836). Cook County in 1845 had 43,385 inhabitants, and there were a dozen places with a population of more than five hundred.

At Danville, Hubbard kept pace with progress in 1831 by converting his Indian trading post into a white goods store catering to the needs of settlers. In 1834 he moved to Chicago and, making the transition from fur trader to business executive, became one of the larger meat packers in the West and owner of a fleet of lake boats. During a career that began in the wilderness, Hubbard branched into real estate promotions, railroad management, and support of Abraham Lincoln's 1860 campaign.

John Dixon, who had spent fifteen years in New York City as a clothing merchant, was the most influential as well as one of the

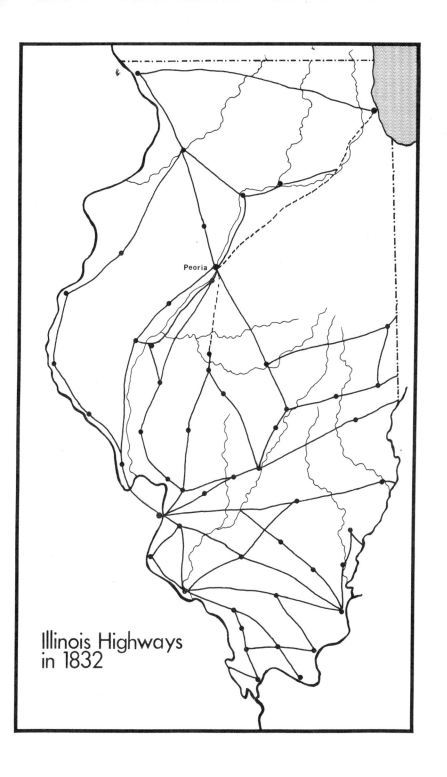

Illinois Highways
in 1832

earliest white men in the northern Illinois interior. In 1820 he brought his family through Shawneetown, stopped five years in Sangamon County, moved on to Fort Clark, and in time obtained a contract to carry mail on the new Peoria-Galena route. Where the trail crossed the Rock River, Dixon established a ferry and appointed Ogee, an unreliable half-breed, as ferryman. The route was prosperous and the ferry demanded better management. As a result, Dixon in 1830 moved his family to the river crossing and founded a city which bears his name. Esteemed by both whites and Indians, he gave valuable service in the Black Hawk War.[15]

Land sales in the southern counties slumped in the first years of statehood, but in the summer of 1825 Vandalians in three weeks counted 250 wagons, all going northward. Word spread that the Sangamon valley offered clear streams and an even balance between friendly timber and comparatively small prairie openings. Farmers quickly replaced the hunters, and seldom has a frontier period been so brief. By 1835 both Chicago and Galena became land-office towns.[16]

Typical of many villages was New Salem. The hunters and the squatters had moved onward before twenty-five families, a majority with southern backgrounds, erected log cabins around the nucleus of a mill, a store, and a saloon. The surrounding farm country was prosperous, but the town declined when it became evident that the Sangamon River wasn't navigable. By 1843, eleven years after New Salem was founded, all its residents had scattered, some to nearby settlements.[17] During his early manhood at New Salem, Abraham Lincoln survived disappointments,

---

[15] Bateman-Selby, *Historical Encyclopedia of Illinois,* I, 134.

[16] Government land offices were opened for business in Illinois in these years: Kaskaskia, 1809; Shawneetown, 1814; Edwardsville, 1816; Palestine and Vandalia, 1821; Springfield, 1823; Danville and Quincy, 1831; Chicago and Galena, 1835; and Dixon, 1840. In some cases there was a delay between congressional authorization and the opening of the office. The Galena office was closed in 1840 when headquarters of the northwestern district were transferred to Dixon. The others were closed in 1855, except that the Springfield office remained open until 1876 to take care of the remnants of federally owned land left in Illinois.

[17] Benjamin P. Thomas, *Lincoln's New Salem.* Also see his "Lincoln and New Salem," *Transactions of the Illinois State Historical Society,* XLI (1934), 61-75. The successful promotions of Mount Carmel and Springfield are recounted in Arthur C. Boggess, *Settlement of Illinois, 1778-1830,* pp. 196-211. For an example of the promotion of a town that flourished briefly and then vanished, Adam W. Snyder and James Semple, two of the most influential public men of their day, invested in Tamarwah, in southeastern St. Clair County. John F. Snyder, *op. cit.,* pp. 204-207.

read law, learned surveying, earned possibly twenty-five or thirty dollars a year as a part-time postmaster, won election to the legislature, and then moved to Springfield, where there was more action.

Until a preemption law was enacted in 1842, claim or squatter associations protected the early settlers by preventing speculators and loan sharks from bidding on their farms. With threat of vigilante action, the associations resolved differences involving the early arrivals.

Hardships were severe, especially in the winter of the deep snow, which began in September, 1830, with a killing frost. Unexpectedly in November a cold rain froze to a crust of snow, which was followed by more snow and cold winds for two weeks. In the annals of early Illinois, that winter was remembered as the one in which the suffering was greatest.[18] It also was undoubtedly responsible for the nickname of Egypt that long has been attached to southern Illinois. Corn was scarce in the newly settled region, and supplies of meal and feed were transported from the older and milder southern counties. The people remembered the account in Genesis of a Mediterranean famine in which the people of the North received help from Pharaoh's court in Egypt. No other explanation for the Egyptian nickname is accepted by such Illinois historians as Paul M. Angle. As applied to southern Illinois, the term Egypt appeared in print as early as 1843. Therefore, "Egypt" could not take its name from the coincidence that Cairo, Thebes, and Karnak are within its borders, since the latter two were founded too late. To dispose of another theory, the delta of the Nile has no resemblance to the geography of southern Illinois. [19]

As in preceding generations, settlers disregarded the hardships when they heard of the richness of the new land. A guidebook for settlers told people in the East, where economic upheavals had led to strikes in several cities, that in Illinois "the produce of the farmer springs up almost spontaneously, not more than one third of the labor being necessary here than is required in the East." [20]

18 Eleanor Atkinson, "The Winter of the Deep Snow," *Transactions of the Illinois State Historical Society*, XIV (1909), 47-62.

19 Paul M. Angle, "Egypt in Illinois," *Chicago History*, VII, 9 (Fall, 1965), 266-270. See also Katherine and Will Griffith, *Spotlight on Egypt*. Will Griffith, "Egypt, Illinois," *Illinois Blue Book, 1945-46*, p. 421. M. M. Quaife (ed.), *Growing Up in Southern Illinois*.

20 S. Augustus Mitchell, *Illinois in 1837*. A compiler of immigrant handbooks, Mitchell borrowed heavily from Peck's gazetteer. With John Grigg, a Philadelphia

Many agreed, and an 1836 letter from a man who had lived several years in the central part of the state said: "Farms are made the quickest here of any place I ever read or heard of. No trees to cut down or stones to pick up. The only thing to do in making a farm is to fence, plough and plant, and the first year's crop will go a long way toward paying the price of the land and the fencing." [21] Illinois had little manufacturing, aside from the mills, but there was a demand for mechanics and skilled workmen. Letters to relatives back East said that, while groceries and clothing might cost more, other expenses of living were less than on the seaboard and they could be reduced even more by raising a garden and feeding a few hogs for home butchering.

Emigration could not be undertaken lightly, however. Money for a down payment on government land had to be hoarded and possessions accumulated or sorted for the long journey that began with the breaking of ties with family and neighbors, who might not be seen again for years, if ever. J. S. Buckingham, an Englishman, in 1840 described the scene on the National Road: "Of these emigrant families, there are often 12 to 15 persons in each, many of them young children; a covered wagon, drawn sometimes by two horses, though frequently by one only, containing all their household furniture, and provisions for the way; and the women and children were piled on these. The men and the older boys walked beside the wagon—and they made a journey of from 12 to 15 miles a day." They followed the advice of Caleb Atwater, who had been in Illinois to negotiate an Indian treaty: "No poor man in the eastern states, who has feet and legs, and can use them has any excuse for remaining poor where he is." [22]

Nevertheless, Illinois had its critics. The journey from the seacoast to the interior "is often as costly and tedious, for a man with a family, as the sea passage," said a German traveler who reached Illinois in the first year of statehood. [23] "Any father of a family, unless he is well-to-do, can certainly count on being impoverished upon his arrival in Illinois," he added. The critics included Charles Dickens, who after an 1842 American tour described Cairo as a

publisher, he speculated in the purchase of 124,000 near the Sangamon River, which they sold at moderate prices.

[21] Richard H. Beach, quoted by Paul M. Angle (ed.), *Prairie State: Impressions of Illinois*, p. 171.

[22] *Sangamo Journal*, September 8, 1832, quoted by Buley, *op. cit.*, II, 45.

[23] Boggess, *op. cit.*, p. 126.

"detestable morass" and said that Belleville was "a small collection of wooden houses, huddled together in the very heart of brush and swamp." The poor opinion expressed in his *American Notes* could have been a case of sour grapes. Dickens had invested and lost money in the Cairo City and Canal Company, one of the projects for building a metropolis at the southern tip of the state. Elaborately detailed and widely circulated maps in the 1836 land boom had shown Cairo as a great city, with miles of graded streets lined with lots already laid out. They did not tell about the spring floods that dampened the promotion.

GALENA: LEAD MINES AND STEAMBOATS

Galena at one time was more important, better known, and considerably larger than any other settlement above St. Louis. During Chicago's last days as a trading post, upwards of ten

Galena: Wells Western Scenery, 1851

Courtesy Illinois State Historical Library

thousand men dug and smelted lead in an isolated district of which Galena was the shipping point and commercial center. Some of the diggings were in Dubuque County, Iowa, and the ore deposits, among the most productive found in the United States, extended into the three southwestern counties of Wisconsin. Inside a triangle connecting Galena, Dubuque, and Schullsburg, Wisconsin, occurred the nation's first mining boom.

The Indians, who hammered ornaments and knives from copper found near Lake Superior, knew about lead but considered it worthless until they learned of guns and bullets. Their French tutors had orders to hunt for more priceless metals, preferably gold and silver, and Father Hennepin on a 1687 map located a lead mine in the Galena region. Nicholas Perrot mined ore there in 1690, ten years before another supply of lead was discovered in Missouri, thirty miles back of Ste. Genevieve. Under Crozat and Renault, the Missouri mines were developed first and Kaskaskia was their shipping point until 1735. In that era only sporadic operations were carried on along the upper Mississippi. The Indians, protecting a monopoly under which a peck of ore could be traded for a peck of corn, discouraged white settlers and worked the mines just enough to satisfy bartering requirements.

During the Revolutionary War lead was in chronically short supply, and not until 1788 did Julien Dubuque, who became Iowa's first settler, obtain permission of the Fox Indians to mine the ore on both sides of the Mississippi. Squaws did the actual digging and Dubuque sent lead and furs in pirogues to St. Louis. Other French-Canadian prospectors and Dubuque's creditors were unable to get the same mining rights.

In the 1804 Sauk treaty, Harrison obtained a fifteen-mile-square concession at the mouth of the Fever River. A short and tortuous stream, it flowed from an area of rounded hills in which rich deposits of lead sulphide (galena) ore cropped to the surface. For years the diggings were comparatively quiet, but after 1818 miners from Missouri were among the adventurers who poled, pushed, and pulled their keelboats up the Mississippi. Others came overland from lower Illinois and south of the Ohio River. Many made the trip annually rather than spend the frozen months in log huts near their mine shafts. Of several theories seeking to explain why Illinois became known as the Sucker State, perhaps the best is that the annual migration of the lead miners resembled the habits of a species of fish known as the sucker. Its proponents held that

Wisconsin got its nickname because some miners holed up all winter like badgers.

Miners found some ore at the surface, but most of it was hauled up a shaft by a windlass or dragged out of a drift tunnel. The white man used black powder for blasting, which was superior to the Indian method of breaking up the rock by building a hot fire under the stone and then dashing cold water on it. In the first smelting operations, the ore was placed on a bed of logs, fire burned out most of the sulphur, and the molten lead flowed into a basin. The wasteful and inefficient process, which depended upon a large supply of trees, could be repeated once every twenty-four hours. The government owned the land and, until three years before the organization of Jo Daviess County in 1827, the only law in the boom camps scattered through the hills was an army lieutenant on duty as superintendent of the Fever River lead distinct.[24]

Large-scale exploitation was attempted unsuccessfully in 1819 by Richard M. Johnson, who became Vice President under Van Buren. He brought a work force of slaves as part of a crew of one hundred men in six or eight boats. Under a leasing system started in 1822, the federal government required that miners pay a 10 percent tax on their production. In practice, the smelter operators paid the tax for several years, but only rich men could afford a big investment in smelter equipment and a ten-thousand-dollar federal license. Moses Meeker, a Cincinnati merchant who obtained one of the first leases, brought the first large party of settlers in 1823, the year the first store opened in Galena. Meeker, with a seven-thousand-dollar outfit, in the first year smelted 425,000 pounds of lead. That started a boom, and in four years the annual lead production passed 13.3 million pounds. Foreigners, including Cornish miners, came to Galena as the lead mines became famous abroad. Southerners, Irishmen, and French predominated in the

---

[24] The literature on the lead-mining region is voluminous. Pooley, *op. cit.*, pp. 461-473, contains a detailed citation of authorities. Also valuable are Reuben Gold Thwaites, "Notes on Early Lead Mining in the Fever River Region," *Wisconsin Historical Collections*, XIII (1895). Joseph Schafer, "The Wisconsin Lead Region," *Wisconsin Domesday Book*, III (1952). James E. Wright, *The Galena Lead Mining District: Federal Policy and Practice, 1824-1847*. Florence Gratoit Bale, "Galena's Century Milestone," *Illinois Blue Book, 1927-28*, pp. 657-668. B. H. Schockel, "Settlement and Development of the Lead and Zinc Mining Region of the Driftless Area with Special Emphasis Upon Jo Daviess County, Illinois," *Mississippi Valley Historical Review*, IV (Sept., 1917), 172-191.

mixed population. Galena never acquired a reputation for rowdiness and claim jumping that made later mining camps notorious in the West.

The Fever River's name, which supposedly traced back to a smallpox epidemic in an Indian village, was considered bad advertising, and after 1827 both the river and the boom town at its head of navigation were called Galena. Isolated far in advance of the frontier, the Galena residents sent petitions for relief to Vandalia. They complained of difficulties with Indians, monthly mail service, inability to secure lands, and inadequate facilities for commerce. Provisions were costly when the river was frozen, but a proposed road from Peoria, the nearest neighbor 170 miles away, was vetoed on the ground that it would pass through federal and Indian lands. Government from Detroit was impossible, and at one time Galena residents hoped to become part of the proposed state of Wisconsin. Galena population figures show a considerable variance and some apparently were inflated by counting temporary workers throughout the area. The town reportedly had one hundred houses and stores in 1827, when from six to seven thousand persons were in the district. A presumably reliable source in 1832 gave the population as 669, living and working in two hundred dwellings, warehouses, and shops. That year other reports credited the town—perhaps the entire area was meant—with five to seven thousand inhabitants.

Galena's business district sat on a narrow alluvial terrace but its houses clung to a limestone bluff. A visitor who watched the wharf from an upper street in 1835 wrote: "The stir and bustle of business, the influx of market and farm wagons, the ponderous ox teams drawing the lead to its place of shipment, the rattling of carts, drays, hackney coaches and carriages . . . announce the present and growing importance of Galena."[25] The mining center seemed destined to hold permanent rank as the most important city of the upper region. By 1839, when it was incorporated as a city, Galena had a fire department, a branch of the State Bank, a temperance society, a library of eight hundred volumes, three new brick-and-stone churches, and a theater. Stone warehouses and stores lined the lower street. The *Miner's Journal* began publication five years before Chicago had a newspaper.

[25] William J. Peterson, *Steamboating on the Upper Mississippi*, does not restrict itself to river transportation in its treatment of Galena. See pp. 90-99, 175-183, 204-297, and 451-454.

An unfavorable tariff law in 1829 caused trouble for mine owners and steamboat captains, but digging continued and some of the new arrivals took up farming and milling. Surplus production brought hard times, and after 1829 the smelter owners balked at paying the 10 percent rental to the government. Miners began evading the law that permitted them to dig only on leased land. After 1834 Congress opened agricultural land to settlement, which brought in New Yorkers and New Englanders, but speculators and others purchased ore-bearing acreage and began illegal mining operations on it. The United States Supreme Court twice upheld the legality of the law, which was not being enforced, and Senator Sidney Breese in 1846 prevailed upon Congress to drop the matter of taxes and authorize the sale of mineral lands. Between 1821 and 1845, the average annual rent collection was $3,196. The district sent to market 472 million pounds of lead valued at 14.178 million dollars, enough to allow the nation to go on an exporting basis. In 1840, 28 percent of the nation's lead production came from Illinois and 48 percent from Wisconsin Territory.

Transportation down the Mississippi was easiest, but an eastern connection was needed. Readers of the *Galena Advertiser* learned September 14, 1829, that "Mr. Soulard's wagon and mule team returned a few days since, from Chicago . . . to which it had been taken across the country with a load of lead. This was the first wagon that has ever passed from the Mississippi River to Chicago." With a load of a ton and a half, the eastbound trip via Ogee's ferry on the Rock River required eleven days and the return journey eight. From Chicago the cargo was sent to Detroit by boat. The editor wished that the "road be marked and surveyed on the best ground and shortest distance." He also regretted that Soulard had not brought back a load of salt.

Some lead reached the Great Lakes over the Wisconsin portage route, but most went downstream to Alton and St. Louis and gave steamboating on the upper Mississippi its greatest impetus. Palatial boats operated on the lower river, but at St. Louis all water traffic stopped for a reloading of passengers and cargo to and from the smaller boats used on the shallower upper Mississippi, Illinois, and Missouri rivers. Rapids at Warsaw, opposite the mouth of the Des Moines River, and at Rock Island provided hazards, especially in the low-water season, and only a small steamer could squirm its way up the Galena River to the busy docks. Lead cargoes provided big profits, with food and manufactured goods carried on the

Chicago in 1831

upstream trip. Measured by the number of arrivals at St. Louis and not by tonnage, until 1848 steamboat activity on the upper Mississippi surpassed that on the lower river and the Ohio. Soldiers and supplies for the Black Hawk War and settlers also arrived by riverboat. In time the trip from New Orleans to Galena could be made in slightly more than seven days. By contrast, at the start of the steamboating era, Meeker's keelboat crew required thirty-one days for the four-hundred-mile trip from St. Louis to Galena. Where possible, Meeker's men pushed the boat with poles. At other times they pulled on brush along the shore or warped the boat with a rope anchored to a tree or rock. The laborious upstream journey averaged a mile an hour. In the 1831-40 decade, farming became as important as mining in Jo Daviess County. Later a decline set in as the richer and shallower deposits were worked out and miners were lured to the California gold fields or jobs with railroad construction crews. By 1850, agriculture was the dominant industry in the driftless area.

Reachable only by steep and winding roads or by the small and inefficient steamers, Galena was poorly located as a commercial center, and the downstream cities were its natural outlet. Dreams of commercial eminence brightened when the railroad arrived, but they faded as it pushed on to the Mississippi. The farm products which had been collected at Galena were soon siphoned to Chicago by the railroad. That left Galena with scenery and picturesque buildings as its chief assets.

Galena had been the busiest steamboat center in Illinois. By 1837, when lake steamers were beginning to serve Chicago on a regular basis, several hundred steamboats carried passengers and freight on the western rivers. Boats navigated the secondary streams, including the Wabash as far as Terre Haute, Indiana, in 1823. On the Illinois River in 1831, Naples watched the arrival of 186 steamers of which seventeen reached Peoria. Each year more boats pushed further up the stream. Springfield had a vision of being a port in 1832 when Abraham Lincoln helped the Talisman make a single trip on the Sangamon River. Beardstown counted 450 arrivals and departures in 1836. One river captain in 1839 told of making fifty-eight trips between St. Louis and Peru with a total of ten thousand passengers. As it grew in population and importance, Peoria counted 1,286 steamers in 1850. No governmental agency kept a record of steamers, but by 1834 tonnage on the Ohio and Mississippi was reported to be larger than that of the Atlantic seaboard cities, where ocean navigation by steam got a later start. Boat owners in the West found that they were in a hazardous and not always profitable business. Shifting channels, snags, ice, sandbars, falling banks, islands, and sunken vessels made navigation difficult for large and small steamers. Fire added to the dangers, with the result that expensive boats were often out of service in five years. Nevertheless, as in the decades of exploration and French settlement, a large share of the travel was by river, and steam provided the first benefits of the machine age. Steam power soon spread to the river banks. By 1826 a Shawneetown grist mill was operated by an engine from a wrecked boat, and two years later a Belleville miller replaced an ox-powered treadmill with a steam engine. The problem of a fuel supply encouraged development of coal mining as the native forests dwindled.

Galena was primarily a lead-mining town and did little to exploit the zinc deposits that also were found there. Discovery of lead in Hardin County, at the far side of the state, resulted in some mining operations in 1842, but production did not become important until after 1900, when lead was produced jointly with fluorspar. In recent years the southern district has produced more lead than Galena. World War II brought increased demand for lead, and Illinois production in 1955 reached a recent high of 4,544 tons. Small quantities of several other metals, including silver, have been found in the southeastern corner of the state.[26] For a time Hardin County residents produced one thousand to four thousand ounces of silver each year as a by-product of lead and fluorspar mining.

[26] For an overly optimistic early account of mineral potentialities, see John M. Peck, *A Gazetteer of Illinois,* pp. 18-19.

8

PREACHERS, PRESSES, AND ABOLITIONISTS

PUBLIC EDUCATION CAME SLOWLY, ALMOST HESITANTLY, TO Illinois. The Ordinance of 1787 and the enabling act of 1818 both attested to its importance, but of the states in the Old Northwest only Illinois adopted a constitution that omitted mention of a school system. Government-supported educational systems had not fully developed on the seaboard, and schools of any kind were luxuries on the frontier. Costs were high, teachers were scarce, the emigrants brought few books, and many men regarded themselves as temporary residents who had nothing to gain from a school system they would not use. As a result, anti-intellectualism was a major force in early Illinois.[1] The deep-rooted prejudice against book-learning was expressed by James Hall, one of the brightest lights on the cultural scene of early Illinois. He put it this way: "A human being may know how to read, and yet be a very stupid fellow . . . . Reading and writing are not magic arts; of themselves, they are of little value . . . and thousands of individuals with diplomas in their pockets are far inferior, in point of common sense and information, to the common run of backwoodsmen."[2]

---

[1] Donald F. Tingley, "Anti-Intellectualism on the Illinois Frontier," *Essays in Illinois History in Honor of Glenn Huron Seymour* (Tingley, ed.), pp. 3-17.

[2] *Western Monthly Magazine,* I (1833), 51.

As a result of such thinking, Illinois lagged behind other western states in the development of an educational system. For the beginnings, much of the credit goes to Protestant preachers and missionaries who worked for literacy as well as morality and the salvation of souls. Anti-intellectualism extended into the clergy, which had its own conflicts as New England missionaries, not all of them abolitionists, came to Illinois to spread the word of God according to their own denominational beliefs. The ministers founded schools as well as churches and established colleges which had a monopoly on higher education until just before the Civil War.

PRIVATE SCHOOLS AND COLLEGES

The first widely scattered schools, beginning with classes taught by one John Seeley in an abandoned log cabin in Monroe County in 1783, operated on a subscription basis. The teacher collected whatever he could from parents willing to pay cash or contribute produce to have their children exposed briefly to the three R's. Records exist of only a few such schools before statehood and, especially at the margin of the frontier, most children and many adults were illiterate by necessity.[3] State government had little concern about the primitive nature of the instruction until State Senator Joseph Duncan, whose own schooling ended at an early age when he became the senior member of an orphaned family in Kentucky, attempted to provide financial support for schools during the Coles administration.[4]

Duncan's law provided that each county should have at least one school district "open and free to every class of white citizens between the age of five and twenty-one." District trustees had authority to employ teachers, and voters could levy a five-mill tax to pay teachers and finance buildings. Also, 2 percent of the state's net taxes would be distributed to the schools, which also were eligible for five sixths of the interest due on the school funds that the state had borrowed from Section 16 rentals and sales. The

[3] Charles B. Johnson, "The Subscription School and the Seminary in Pioneer Days," *Transactions of the Illinois State Historical Society*, XXXII (1925), 54-59.

[4] Elizabeth Duncan Putnam, "The Life and Services of Joseph Duncan, Governor of Illinois, 1834-1838," *Transactions of the Illinois State Historical Society*, XXVI (1919), 107-187. E. W. Blatchford, *Biographical Sketch of Hon. Joseph Duncan*. Theodore C. Pease, *The Frontier State, 1818-1848*, pp. 66-67. Charles D. Jay, *150 Years of Education in Illinois*. R. C. Buley, *The Old Northwest*, II, 363-365.

law's fatal weakness was that the tax was not mandatory, and few wanted to levy it. Furthermore, 2 percent of the state's revenue would yield not much more than one thousand dollars a year for all schools. Four years later the legislature recognized the unpopularity of taxes by repealing the law, and public education again depended upon the subscription system.[5]

Duncan, who also wanted the legislature to establish a state university, became governor and saw a second school law enacted in 1836. It specified how school funds would be handled and teachers examined and employed, and that funds be paid on the basis of attendance. The law was forward-looking except that the tax again was made optional. Not until 1855 did Illinois have a free school system covering the state.

Congress had been generous in granting Section 16 of every township, a total of 998,448 acres, for the support of schools, but few settlers wanted to rent school land when farms could be purchased at small cost.[6] Because of public indifference, official incompetency, and pressure from squatters and speculators, the state in 1831 authorized sale of the reserved property. Two years later the bulk of Chicago's sixteenth section, which now takes in part of the loop district, sold for thirty-nine thousand dollars. Up to 1882, when most of the land had passed to private ownership, the average price received for school land was $3.78 an acre and the lowest seventy cents. The proceeds went into an investment fund that over the years was largely dissipated by bank failures, bad loans, and defaulted bonds. In hard times the state government meanwhile borrowed from the school funds.

Upper Alton in 1821 received authority to establish a free school, but whether it did is doubtful. Newton Bateman, who was state superintendent of schools in the Civil War era and later served as president of Knox College, credited Chicago with opening the first free school in 1834, followed by Alton in 1837 and Springfield and Jacksonville in 1840.[7] Illiteracy was more preva-

[5] That legislature "was one of the worst that has ever afflicted the state," said Alexander Davidson and Bernard Stuvé in *A Complete History of Illinois,* p. 612, published in 1874.

[6] Francis G. Blair, "Development and Growth of the Public Schools," *Illinois Blue Book, 1917-18,* pp. 40-44. "Centennial of the First Free School Law in Illinois," *Illinois Blue Book, 1925-26,* pp. 415-423.

[7] Newton Bateman and Paul Selby, *Historical Encyclopedia of Illinois,* I, 148. Paul E. Belting, "Development of the Free Public High School in Illinois to 1860," *Journal of the Illinois State Historical Society,* XI (1918), 269-369, 467-561. Buley, *op. cit.,* II, 340, 363-364.

Alton

lent in the southern counties where many families had spent at least one generation on the frontier.

Private schools were all that Illinois had at the secondary level. John Russell at Vandalia in 1830 charged $2.50 a quarter for instruction in what he called a high school. Boys under six years were admitted, an additional fifty cents was charged for teaching writing and arithmetic, and another fifty cents for grammar and geography. Russell offered a "female department" under a woman teacher. The Rev. Peter Cartwright the same year advertised a school at Pleasant Plains offering elementary subjects, Latin, Greek, and moral philosophy. Other schools, some for girls, opened in downstate communities and in Chicago during the 1830's.

A series of school conventions, at which friends of education met with legislators and other officials, opened in 1835 at Vandalia. A state teachers association, organized in 1836, collapsed in a few years. By 1844, when the school convention met at Peoria, professional teachers and school officers dominated the meetings and exerted continuous pressure for publicly supported education.

The Convent of the Ladies of Visitation opened at Kaskaskia in 1833 but was removed to St. Louis after flood damage in 1844. Catholics operated day schools at Cahokia, La Salle, and elsewhere. Among Protestant ministers who held services in settlers' cabins, John Mason Peck, the first Baptist missionary in the West, traveled tirelessly in Illinois, Missouri, and Indiana to establish Bible societies and Sunday schools, and tried to place qualified teachers in them. Peck, a native of Connecticut who arrived in the West in 1817, saw the need of training teachers and ministers. In 1827 he helped establish Rock Spring Seminary on a farm he owned near Shiloh, in St. Clair County. Within four years his school was moved to Alton, and in 1836 it became Shurtleff College, named for an Easterner who donated half of a twenty-thousand-dollar trust fund solicited by Peck.[8]

In a Dartmouth College case made famous by Daniel Webster, the United States Supreme Court ruled that a state could not control church schools. Although the legislature had been reluctant to approve denominational colleges, three of them—Shurtleff, McKendree at Lebanon, and Illinois at Jacksonville—combined lobbying pressure and received charters in 1837. Among Methodist ministers, Cartwright and Peter Akers helped Bishop William McKendree give impetus to a college named for the latter. By 1838 McKendree had four professors and 116 students.[9] The state had twelve colleges in 1840, but only Illinois College granted degrees.

At the Yale Divinity School seven young theologians in 1829 organized the Illinois Association, pledged to go to Illinois to establish a seminary at which some would teach while the others preached in the surrounding country. Known as the "Yale Band," they played a distinctive role in their adopted state. Theron Baldwin and Julian M. Sturtevant arrived first, coming by way of the Erie Canal, overland across Ohio, and the Ohio and Mississippi rivers. Sturtevant became the first instructor and later president of

[8] Rufus Babcock (ed.), *Memoirs of John Mason Peck.* Judge J. Otis Humphrey, "Dr. John Mason Peck and Shurtleff College," *Transactions of the Illinois State Historical Society,* XII (1907), 145-163.

[9] M. H. Chamberlin, "Historical Sketch of McKendree College," *Transactions of the Illinois State Historical Society,* IX (1904), 328-364. A. F. Ewert, "Early History of Education in Illinois—The Three Oldest Colleges," *Illinois Blue Book, 1929-30,* pp. 301-334.

Illinois College, which had been started on an eighty-acre tract bought by the Rev. John M. Ellis, a missionary who arrived in 1828.[10] Baldwin went to Vandalia as a home missionary and later helped Benjamin Godfrey found Monticello Seminary for Girls at Godfrey.[11] Baldwin later returned East and was the driving force in enabling eight midwestern colleges to survive financially. With those who followed—John F. Brooks, Mason Grosvenor, Elisha Jenner, William Kirby, and Asa Turner—they taught, preached, established an academy at Springfield, encouraged public schools, raised money, and uplifted the spiritual and intellectual climate.

A depression in 1837 complicated money-raising problems, but an unusual solution was offered by Rev. George Washington Gale, a Princeton graduate and Presbyterian minister who had founded Oneida Institute in upstate New York as a radical experiment in social and religious thinking. He organized a company of New Yorkers, purchased a township of fertile land with their joint funds, and reserved a townsite and a farm for use by a college to train ministers. Selling the rest of the land with tuition rights at five dollars an acre, he endowed the college with the surplus in confidence that settlement of the area by sober, industrious farmers would raise land prices. The result was the founding of Galesburg and Knox Manual Labor College, opened in 1843.[12] The concept of student labor on the campus and of endowment from profits in land was used elsewhere. The Rev. Gideon Blackburn, a Virginian and eloquent Presbyterian, raised money by buying large tracts at the government price of $1.25 an acre and selling them at two dollars to his friends. Of the balance, he kept twenty-five cents for himself and spent fifty cents in buying land to endow a school at Carlinville. The financing proved difficult, and the delayed opening of a primary school in 1857 was followed by classes at Blackburn Theological Seminary.[13]

[10] C. H. Rammelkamp, *Illinois College: A Centennial History*. For an account of New England influence on education and religion see Carrie Prudence Kofoid, "Puritan Influences in the Formative Years of Illinois History," *Transactions of the Illinois State Historical Society*, X (1905), 264-338. See also Clarence P. McClelland, "The Education of Females in Early Illinois," *Journal of the Illinois State Historical Society*, XXXVI (Winter, 1943), 378-407.

[11] Harriet Rice Congdon, "The Early History of Monticello College," *Transactions of the Illinois State Historical Society*, XXXI (1924), 58-63.

[12] Ernest E. Calkins, *They Broke the Prairie*.

[13] Thomas Rinaker, *Gideon Blackburn, the Founder of Blackburn University*.

In contrast to the intellectual Easterners, the early Baptists and Methodists were indigenous to the frontier and often had little more education than the settlers. Their marathon sermons emphasized the simple beliefs that salvation could come only from conversion and that eternal damnation was the consequence of unbelief, drinking, gambling, and other sins. Cartwright converted hundreds at camp meetings where his ability to keep order with his fists was almost as much of an asset as his eloquence. Like several other preachers, Cartwright also was a politician. He twice was elected to the legislature, but lost to Abraham Lincoln when he ran for Congress. His enemies included Baptists, Presbyterians, and other sects. Near the end of his career he found difficulty in adjusting to the intellectual interests of younger Methodists.[14]

Like the Methodists, the early Baptists gave little thought to the training and financial support of the missionaries they entrusted with spreading religion in Illinois. They had numerical success, however, and counted six churches, four ministers, and 113 laymen as early as 1807 when a state association was formed. James Lemen, who like the Methodist circuit riders spent much of his time in the saddle, two years later raised the issue that slaveholding was incompatible with church membership. Majority sentiment was against him, so Lemen withdrew from the association and formed a new church which sometimes went under the name of Friends of Humanity. It made comparatively little progress, but its members helped Lemen support Governor Coles, himself a Baptist, in his fight against a proslavery convention. Some frontier Baptists adopted a "holy whine" form of delivery which Easterners found objectionable.

Baptists pioneered with the use of the printing press.[15] Peck, who was a part-time farmer because his income from his church could not support his family, persuaded a part-time minister to bring a hand press and type from Cape Girardeau, Missouri. The first issue of a semimonthly paper appeared in 1828. Peck took the lead in organizing the Illinois Sunday School Union, which held its first meeting at Vandalia in 1830. The Sunday schools

---

[14] *Autobiography of Peter Cartwright, the Backwoods Preacher.* A. C. Boggess, *Settlement of Illinois from 1778 to 1830,* pp. 191-192.

[15] Cecil K. Byrd, *A Bibliography of Illinois Imprints, 1814-58,* contains a vast amount of detailed information on many subjects, including the organization and activities of the early churches. See also William Oliver, *Eight Months in Illinois,* pp. 69-71.

appealed to all denominations and the youngsters who attended them had the opportunity to get some instruction in the three R's and to commit to memory portions of the Scriptures. In many communities the Sunday school library held the only reading matter. A Northern Baptist association, which first met in 1835, soon stood on its own feet without support of Wisconsin and Indiana congregations.

James Hall in 1831 voiced a not uncommon complaint about the arrival of "young, inefficient, inexperienced men as agents— men just from their books—or rather boys just out of college— without any knowledge of human nature, deficient in common sense and some of them lamentably ignorant of everything but their Bibles."[16] The Easterners found themselves competing with amateur preachers, uneducated farmers and craftsmen who conducted noisy services with loud and tuneless singing and preaching that subordinated intellectual ideas.

Western Protestants in the first half of the nineteenth century frequently splintered on issues of dogma and church organization. Presbyterians in 1831 split between the "Old School" that emphasized traditional doctrines and a "New School" group whose members cooperated with Congregationalists and were on the verge of becoming abolitionists. The Old Schoolers had more success in Illinois than in some western states, and as a result New Schoolers broke away from the Illinois synod, which had been formed in 1831. Heresy charges were pressed inconclusively against Edward Beecher, president of Illinois College, and two of his professors, Sturtevant and Kirby. In 1835 Asa Turner and Carter of the Yale Band helped form a Congregational Association of Illinois.

Roman Catholic priests all but disappeared from the Old Northwest after the Revolution. The church was reestablished through migration from the East of English-speaking Catholics, and after 1808 all of the West became part of the diocese of Bardstown, Kentucky. In 1833 a petition bearing thirty-seven names, mostly French-Canadian or Indian, reported that about one hundred Catholics lived in Chicago and asked that a priest be sent there. The bishop of St. Louis assigned a newly ordained French priest,

---

[16] Buley, op. cit., II, 437. Buley's chapter on religion, from which this is taken, contains an exhaustive account of the progress, amid splintering, of the Protestant churches in early Illinois.

Irenaeus St. Cyr, who said mass in a cabin. A thirty-six-by-twenty-four-foot frame chapel, unplastered and unpainted, was opened on the south side of Lake Street in October. Simon Bruté, the first bishop of Vincennes, visited Chicago in 1838, and five years later Chicago was made the see for all of Illinois.[17] William Quarter, a native of Ireland who was personally popular with canal work crews, was consecrated bishop of Chicago in 1844. In the four years before his death he established parochial schools, built churches, brought in forty priests, and obtained a legislative enactment making the bishop of Chicago a corporation with exclusive rights to all diocesan property.

Illinois Episcopalians organized in 1835 with the election as bishop of Philander Chase, who had founded Kenyon College while serving as bishop of Ohio. Chase brought his family from Michigan, where he had retired on a farm, and at a timbered site fourteen miles west of Peoria built his home, "Robin's Nest," named because it was made of mud and sticks and filled with young ones. Alarmed at the speculative fever in Illinois, he warned Episcopalians of the sin of covetousness. By 1839 he laid the cornerstone for Jubilee College, and four years later was chosen presiding bishop of his church. The raising of money required that he make trips to Europe and to eastern and southern cities. His school, always in financial trouble, finally closed during the Civil War.[18]

The Disciples of Christ, founded by Alexander Campbell, had a few scattered churches in Illinois before 1830, but expanded in the next decade with more than sixty congregations and twenty-seven ministers. Lutherans became important after the German and Scandinavian emigration of the 1840's but, like the Episcopalians, did not reach the numerical importance of the Methodists, Baptists, and Presbyterians. Among the smaller denominations, members of the United Brethren Church reached McLean and neighboring counties as early as 1830. The first Amish, from Alsace and Lorraine, settled in the timbered sections along the Illinois River in Woodford, Tazewell, and Bureau counties in 1831

---

[17] Gilbert J. Carraghan, *The Catholic Church in Chicago,* pp. 45-136.

[18] Lorene Martin, "Old Jubilee College and Its Founder, Bishop Chase," *Transactions of the Illinois State Historical Society,* XLI (1934), 121-152. Roma Louise Shively, *Jubilee—A Prairie College.* Rev. C. W. Leffingwell, "Bishop Chase and Jubilee College," *Transactions of the Illinois State Historical Society,* X (1905), 82-100.

and a few years later moved eastward onto prairie lands. Mennon-
ites came in 1833 from Ohio, Pennsylvania, and Bavaria. Like
many other sects, both groups split on doctrinal grounds.

A few Negro churches, principally Methodist and Baptist, also
organized. A Colored Baptist association, the first in Illinois, began
in 1839 with members from St. Clair and Madison counties. It
later expanded to take in churches as far away as Salem and
Decatur.[19]

THE PRINTED WORD ON THE PRAIRIE

In early Illinois, James Hall became the dominant literary figure
by establishing at Vandalia in 1830 the *Illinois Monthly Magazine*,
the first literary periodical west of Ohio. A voluminous writer of
both prose and poetry, Hall contributed half of the contents of his
magazine and also turned out popular books published in many
editions. He could be controversial, but he excelled in descriptions
of the scenery, soil, climate, and people of the new country, given
in such works as *Legends of the West* (1832) and *Sketches of the
History, Life and Manners of the West* (1834 and 1835). They
were popular with distant readers. *Notes on Western States* (1838)
was a guidebook of pioneer farming.[20]

Hall was a man of many talents. Restored to rank after a court
martial in the War of 1812, he came to Shawneetown in 1820,
became editor and part owner of the *Illinois Gazette,* and served as
prosecuting attorney and judge of a nine-county circuit. He also
reorganized the state's finances, edited the *Illinois Intelligencer,*
and was a leader in agricultural and Bible societies and a trustee of
Illinois College. Hall was president of a short-lived state historical
society organized in 1827 with the help of Coles and others. After
several meetings, the group disbanded and its records disappeared.
Hall's last speech in Illinois was a main event at the first state

19 Sylvestre C. Watkins, "Some of Early Illinois' Free Negroes," *Journal of the
Illinois State Historical Society,* LVI (Autumn, 1963), 495-507, and in the same issue
Miles Mark Fisher, "Negro Churches in Illinois: A Fragmentary History with Emphasis on
Chicago," pp. 552-569.

20 Randolph C. Randall, *James Hall: Spokesman of the New West,* includes a
bibliography of Hall's writings while in Illinois. John T. Flanagan, *James Hall, Literary
Pioneer of the Ohio Valley,* and "James Hall and the Antiquarian and Historical Society
of Illinois," *Journal of the Illinois State Historical Society,* XXXIV (Dec., 1941),
439-452. Isabel Jamison, "Literature and Literary People of Early Illinois," *Transactions
of the Illinois State Historical Society,* XIII (1908), 123-139.

school convention. Illinois could not support a literary magazine and in 1833 Hall moved his publication to greener fields at Cincinnati. Renamed the *Western Monthly,* it lost circulation in a vigorous defense of Catholicism.

John Mason Peck rivaled Hall and Birkbeck, his associate with Coles in the campaign against slavery, as an authoritative writer on the western country.[21] He compiled a *Guide for Emigrants,* which appeared in three editions starting in 1831. Peck's *Gazetteer of Illinois* was issued twice. With John Messinger, a surveyor and early legislator, he prepared a sectional map of the state. He issued a *Traveler's Directory,* wrote a *Life of Daniel Boone,* and edited an enlarged and revised version of the *Annals of the West.* Meanwhile he founded Baptist periodicals and contributed regularly to others.

Continuing the tradition of Pope, Sidney Breese as the first official reporter for the Illinois Supreme Court published its opinions for eleven years.

Dr. Lewis Caleb Beck, a New Yorker, in 1823 issued his *Gazetteer of the States of Illinois and Missouri,* the first reliable description of the state. It was filled with information collected on horseback before he decided not to practice medicine at St. Louis.

Jonathan Baldwin Turner contributed significantly to the betterment of Illinois in many fields. Six years younger than his brother Asa, a Yale Band member, he came West in 1833 as instructor in Latin and Greek at Illinois College. He made Jacksonville his home as he lectured in central Illinois for the public schools, alienated southern students by editing an antislavery magazine, and resigned his professorship in 1847 in a dispute over slavery and denominational questions. An early exponent of the conservation of wildlife and natural resources, he invented implements and developed techniques to help farmers and fruit growers.[22]

Hall edited the state's first two newspapers. His *Illinois Gazette* at Shawneetown was a continuation of the *Illinois Emigrant,* opened two years earlier. The *Intelligencer,* a typical fold-over sheet with four-column pages and a large typeface with a prominent long S, was moved from Kaskaskia to Vandalia when the state government made the transfer. Early papers appeared and disappeared at Edwardsville, Springfield, Alton, Jacksonville, Dan-

21 Rufus Babcock, *Forty Years of Pioneer Life: Memoirs of John Mason Peck.*
22 Mary Turner Carriel, *The Life of Jonathan Baldwin Turner.*

ville, and Beardstown. The first outside the southern counties was the Galena *Miner's Journal,* founded in 1828. John Calhoun published Chicago's first newspaper, the *Chicago Democrat,* in 1833, and turned it over to John Wentworth two years later. Chicago's first daily, the *American,* was founded in 1835. The *Alton Telegraph* in 1839 listed thirty-six Illinois newspapers. The typical editor had trouble getting payment for subscriptions, in cash or produce, and many were forced to accept a subsidy and become partisan organs.[23]

Edwardsville had a library with books on history, biography, poetry, fiction, and essays in 1819. It probably was the state's first library, but apathy and lack of financial support brought its dissolution in six years. During the 1830's, Chicago, Vandalia, and several other towns organized lyceums, dedicated to the diffusion of useful knowledge. The 1837 legislature appropriated funds to establish a library for the Supreme Court. The year before the Galena Library Association ordered books worth three hundred dollars.

ELIJAH LOVEJOY, ABOLITIONIST AND MARTYR

Most Illinois people regarded abolitionists as a fanatical and unpopular minority, a Yankee importation in a state which had not brought itself to erase the last vestiges of pseudoslavery. Some showed symptoms of a guilt complex about Negroes still being held in bondage as French slaves and indentured servants, but a general acceptance of slavery had its roots in the state's economic and historic ties with the South. As cotton prosperity increased the value of Negroes, their owners aggressively insisted upon property rights. In southern and central Illinois, which had not been reached by the new influx of Yankee immigrants, the average man had no desire to permit extremists from New England to upset the status quo and attack an institution that was legal in neighboring Missouri and Kentucky.

Indicative of majority sentiment, the legislature in 1837 adopted resolutions denouncing abolitionism. Senate action was

[23] Buley, *op. cit.,* II, 489-523. A. L. Bowen, "The Press of Illinois," *Illinois Blue Book, 1907-08,* pp. 549-582. Edmund J. James and Milo J. Loveless, *A Bibliography of Newspapers Published in Illinois Prior to 1860.* Douglas C. McMurtrie, "The Contribution of the Pioneer Printers to Illinois History," *Transactions of the Illinois State Historical Society,* XLV (1938), 20-38.

unanimous. Among six dissenting state representatives, Abraham Lincoln and Daniel Stone later recorded a protest in the official journal. They raised a moral point by condemning slavery as both unjust and bad policy, but they agreed with the majority that the "promulgation of abolition doctrines tends rather to increase than abate the evils." Despite the delay and the qualification, their protest showed political courage.

There were other exceptions. Many in the southern counties were descendants of men who had left the South because of a dislike for slavery, either on philosophical grounds or because they could not compete economically with the planter class. They had crossed the Ohio River because Illinois after 1824 was the only free state with cheap land. Outnumbered and unorganized, they constituted a silent minority that had some reinforcements from New England, including such home missionaries as Peck the Baptist and the Yale Band.[24] The American Colonization Society, mildly antislavery, had a few branches in northern and central counties. Its members advocated that Negroes be freed and returned to a colony in Africa. Opponents of slavery as a moral wrong seldom took the drastic step of advocating that it be abolished. Elijah Parish Lovejoy considered that distinction during his first month in Alton as a Presbyterian editor and preacher.

Born in Maine of puritanical heritage, Lovejoy came West as part of a New England movement to uplift the morality and culture of the newly settled states. At St. Louis, a dynamic city of about five thousand, he successfully established a classical high school and then edited a political newspaper in which he gave attention to other reform causes but ignored slavery. After five years he experienced a religious conversion, entered Princeton Theological Seminary, and obtained a license to preach. In 1833 he came back to St. Louis as editor of the *St. Louis Observer,* a Presbyterian journal for the Far West. In it he opposed Catholics, Campbellites, Baptists, and liquor with fanaticism and intolerance. A member of the New School or liberal wing of his denomination, Lovejoy preached against slavery to Missouri settlers who were too poor or too scattered to support a minister and who in the past had heard sermons dealing only with worldliness and immorality. Slowly he adopted an abolitionist belief that slavery was a sin and

[24] Merton L. Dillon, "Abolitionism Comes to Illinois," *Journal of the Illinois State Historical Society,* LIII (Winter, 1960), 389-403.

"must cease to exist." Zealous and stubborn, often in physical danger, Lovejoy refused to stop his antislavery preachings and editorials in a paper that never became self-supporting. A St. Louis synod meeting refused to adopt resolutions he submitted, but prominent men backed Lovejoy in his constitutional right to discuss slavery. Amid growing hostility, he became the unpopular champion of broad civil rights, including the right to publish, to speak, to petition, and to assemble. Editorials denouncing the burning at the stake in St. Louis of a free Negro resulted in mob threats and vandalism in his printing plant. To protect his wife and infant son, Lovejoy moved to Alton, the largest and most progressive city of Illinois. When it arrived on a Sunday, his unguarded and previously damaged press was dumped into the river.[25]

Dominated by businessmen from New England, Alton was a progressive and comparatively enlightened city which tried to compete commercially with St. Louis. During the 1830's it grew steadily and aspired to be the point at which the National Road reached the Mississippi. Alton was a steamboat and packing center, and its commission houses dealt in beef, pork, lard, whiskey, furs,

[25] Edward Beecher, *Narrative of the Riots at Alton.* Paul Simon, *Lovejoy, Martyr to Freedom.* Merton L. Dillon, *Elijah P. Lovejoy, Abolitionist Editor.*

The martyrdom of Elijah Lovejoy

Courtesy Illinois State Historical Library

flour, and lead. Much of their business was with southern states, and new laborers who arrived in a boom displayed a not uncommon hostility to Negroes. Nevertheless the Alton leaders gave financial and moral support to Lovejoy, who at their first meeting ambiguously led them to believe he would edit the *Alton Observer* with less emphasis on freeing slaves. "Now having come to a free state where the evil does not exist, I feel myself less called upon to discuss the subject than when I was in St. Louis," he said. At the same time he espoused freedom of the press, saying: "But, gentlemen, as long as I am an American citizen, and as long as American blood runs in these veins, I shall hold myself at liberty to speak, to write, and to publish whatever I please on any subject."

In the first issue of the *Alton Observer,* printed in September, 1836, on a new press shipped from Cincinnati, Lovejoy wrote that "the system of Negro slavery is an awful evil and sin" and that he would not give up "the rights of conscience, the freedom of opinion, and of the press." By the next Fourth of July his editorials were more and more antislavery. Amid general antipathy, some of his backers complained that Lovejoy had broken a pledge to avoid controversy, and preachers of the more indigenous denominations, including Peck, refused to support him. To many he was guilty of intolerance and was regarded as more than a public nuisance, but all respected the raw courage of the man who several times faced down mobs which had planned to tar and feather him or commit other violence. The night of August 21, 1837, a mob broke into the *Observer* office and destroyed Lovejoy's press and type. Eastern contributions helped pay for a third press, which arrived one month later and was immediately taken from a warehouse and dumped into the Mississippi.

Lovejoy, who believed that 80 percent of the people of Alton approved the destruction of his property, determined to make the city a testing ground for freedom. Edward Beecher, another New England reformer who was president of Illinois College, helped with plans to organize a state antislavery society. Lovejoy issued a call, signed by 255 persons, including twenty-five from Alton, for a convention. Beecher unwisely broadened the call by inviting "friends of free discussion." Sympathetic delegates came from as far as Jacksonville, Quincy, and Galesburg, but the proceedings were taken over by a group of slavery supporters that included Usher F. Linder, the young and brilliant attorney general of the state. Compromises failed and Linder and Cyrus Edwards won majority support for a rejection of Lovejoy's constitutional right to publish the *Observer*. Asked to leave Alton, he replied: "Mr. Chairman, I do not admit that it is the business of this assembly to decide whether I shall or shall not publish a newspaper in this city . . . . I know that I have the right freely to speak and publish my sentiments, subject only to the laws of the land for the abuse of that right . . . . You can crush me if you will; but I shall die at my post, for I cannot and will not forsake it . . . . The contest was commenced here; and here it must be finished. Before God and you all, I here pledge myself to continue it, if need be, till death. If I fail, my grave shall be made in Alton."

His backers included Winthrop S. Gilman, owner of a massive stone warehouse on the riverfront, and Lovejoy decided that his fourth press should be protected there by an armed force of home guards. It arrived by steamer at 3 a.m. November 7. The next night a mob gathered and gunfire broke out. A man in the crowd fell mortally wounded. Someone carried a flaming torch up a ladder to ignite the roof. Lovejoy ran out of the warehouse to fire at him. In return he was shot five times and died almost immediately. His companions fled. The mob put out the fire and destroyed the press.

In a wave of indignation, northern antislavery societies gained members, but the mob leaders went unpunished and Linder went to the extreme of trying to prosecute Gilman on a charge of starting a riot. Lovejoy, a failure as a reformer, had proved that moral suasion would not end slavery. Another decade would pass before the bloodshed of a fratricidal war finally brought abolition.

Until the Civil War, the free Negroes in Illinois existed in a legal and political no-man's-land. They were not allowed to vote, sue or testify in court, or serve in the militia. The law did not provide for their education and it obstructed their ownership of property. A two-way traffic in slaves continued for years. Free Negroes were kidnaped and shipped South in bondage, especially from Shawnee-town and Illinoistown (East St. Louis), while others followed the "underground railway" northward toward freedom. The record of that nocturnal passageway is necessarily vague, but presumably it had terminals at such river towns as Quincy, Alton, and Chester. The procedure called for white sympathizers to hide fleeing Negroes by day and to spirit them to the next "station" in darkness. The goal was to reach Canada by way of the upper Illinois River and Chicago, where public sentiment refused to permit blacks to be taken into custody and shipped back to the South.[26]

Helping Negroes involved danger. In 1841, Alanson Work, James E. Burr, and George Thompson, arrested in Missouri for attempting to aid escaping slaves, were sentenced to twelve years in prison for grand larceny. Other evidence of the underground road exists in court records of such scattered incidents as the indictment of Owen Lovejoy, brother of the martyr, in Bureau County for helping two women in 1843 and the arrest of Dr. Richard Eells of Quincy for aiding a fugitive. Judge Stephen A. Douglas fined him four hundred dollars, and Eells later became president of the Illinois Anti-Slavery Society and in 1844 the candidate for governor of the Liberty party. In 1846 a Chicago mob freed two Negroes. After the assassination of his brother, Owen Lovejoy devoted his life to a crusade against slavery. He became a Congregational pastor at Princeton and as a state legislator and congressman supported Lincoln in a series of events that led to the Emancipation Proclamation in 1862.[27]

The black laws were not repealed until the Civil War, but court rulings gradually established the rights of Negroes.[28] In a slow beginning, the state Supreme Court in 1825 voided indentures not signed by the master. Three years later Justice Samuel D. Lockwood, who served on the high court twenty-four years, ruled that registered servants could be sold in Illinois, since they were property. With involved reasoning in another case, he voided the Indiana law which first established indentures, held that the 1787 ordinance's prohibition had been abrogated by common consent, and ruled that the 1818 constitutional convention had power to legalize indentures. But Lockwood held that Negroes could not be bequeathed but must pass through the hands of legatees, executors, or administrators. A small step taken in 1836 insisted that indentures must be technically correct. The same year the court freed children of servants registered in territorial days. The selling

[26] Wilbur Henry Siebert, *The Underground Rail Road from Slavery to Freedom.* Kofoid, *op. cit.,* pp. 513-551. Larry Gara, "The Underground Railroad in Illinois," *Journal of the Illinois State Historical Society,* LVI (Autumn, 1963), 508-556.

[27] Edward Magdol, *Owen Lovejoy, Abolitionist in Congress.*

[28] N. Dwight Harris, *The History of Negro Servitude in Illinois,* pp. 68-145. Mark M. Krug, *Lyman Trumbull, Conservative Radical,* pp. 61-65. Mason M. Fishback, "Illinois Legislation on Slavery and Free Negroes, 1818-1865," *Transactions of the Illinois State Historical Society,* IX (1904), 414-432.

of indentured servants was outlawed in 1841. In 1845, after a 4 to 3 decision, the court ruled that descendants of French slaves could no longer be held in bondage. That case, which virtually ended the indenture system, came to the court's attention when Pete Jarrott, whose grandmother was the slave of a Frenchman, sued his mistress for wages. Not until 1842 did the court invalidate an 1829 law under which a Negro without freedom papers could be arrested and hired out by the sheriff on a monthly basis. In the case involving Owen Lovejoy, an opinion in 1843 held that a slave brought into Illinois was automatically freed. It was the first Illinois ruling that residence in a free territory entitled a slave to freedom, but the United States Supreme Court disregarded it in the Dred Scott case. The same year Julius A. Willard, a Jacksonville abolitionist, was fined twenty-five dollars and costs for hiding a runaway. In fining Eells, Douglas held that to hide a Negro was to interfere with a property right. By 1852 the court voided contracts for the sale of Negroes. The state law providing for the return of fugitive slaves was invalidated by the Illinois Supreme Court in 1849. The ruling by Justice Samuel Hubbel Treat was a victory for a Negro from Missouri who claimed that his arrest in Sangamon County was unconstitutional. The law had held that a Negro coming into Illinois without a certificate of freedom could be jailed on the presumption that he was a runaway. Treat said that the state could not legislate on a matter within the exclusive jurdisdiction of Congress.

Especially in the northern counties, some of the cases stirred up intense feeling locally in behalf of the blacks, but race prejudice had not been eliminated and free Negroes were not welcome in Illinois. The legislature in 1853 passed a law forbidding free Negroes to enter the state, under penalty of a fifty-dollar fine or sale by the sheriff to whoever would pay the fine. That law was not invalidated until 1864, toward the end of the Civil War. Repeal of the forty-six-year-old black laws came in 1865.

The court rulings came on cases brought by a small group of lawyers who on their own initiative and without any prospect for pay started unpopular litigation on behalf of the Negroes. Most prominent was Lyman Trumbull, a Connecticut native who later served three terms in the United States senate. His associates also were New Englanders, with the exception of Gustave Koerner, a German who fled to America after getting involved in an 1833 revolutionary movement. Koerner was the most prominent of the early Germans in Illinois and, like others from his homeland, stood solidly on the side of freedom.[29]

An effort to divorce the churches from slavery persisted, and delegates from thirteen northern states held a Christian Anti-Slavery Convention in Chicago in 1851. President Jonathan Blanchard of Knox College was elected president of the group, which included representatives from Canada and England. A convention of Colored Citizens of Illinois in Chicago in 1853 was attended by thirty-eight delegates from Peoria, Morgan, Will, Madison, Jo Daviess, Sangamon, Edgar, Cook, and McLean counties. Resolutions opposed black codes and agitation for colonization in Africa.

---

[29] Gustave Koerner, *Memoirs of Gustave Koerner, 1809-1896: Life Sketches Written at the Suggestion of His Children.*

9

INTERNAL IMPROVEMENTS: A FIASCO

As soon as he could produce more food than he needed for survival, and especially as he moved inland from navigable streams, the pioneer became an advocate of internal improvements, a term synonymous with better transportation. He had reached his home by boat in the high-water season and by wagon after the spring rains stopped, and soon he needed a relatively cheap and convenient means of moving bulky agricultural products to a town from which they could be transported to distant markets. There, in increasing volume, the settler needed to make purchases of staples and manufactured articles whose cost would depend to a considerable degree upon transportation expenses. The economic problem was not limited to Illinois, and it still existed nearly a century later when a demand arose on the prairies for farm-to-market roads.

AN EXPENSIVE CANAL TO CHICAGO

Before and after statehood no one disputed Jolliet's idea that Lake Michigan and the Illinois River could be connected without great difficulty and with great benefit. Eventually the Illinois and Michigan Canal became one of the nation's most successful in-

193

ternal improvements, but its construction was long delayed by engineering and financial difficulties.

The Indians, hoodwinked by Ninian Edwards into believing that a canal would be advantageous to them, in 1816 ceded a one-hundred-mile strip of land for a trifle. Major Stephen Long of the army engineers reported the next year that a canal there would be "the first in importance" in the West and could be constructed "with very little expense compared with the magnitude of the object." Secretary of War John C. Calhoun agreed, but President Monroe like most Easterners and Southerners held that the federal government could not constitutionally finance such a project. As a result, nothing was done about a canal before Illinois statehood. By that time it was realized that the short portage between the Chicago and Des Plaines rivers would require a long canal. Because of rocks and shallow water, steamboats could not go above Peru in La Salle County. Suggestions for an intermittent canal that could use part of the upper reaches of the river were abandoned for engineering reasons. In its final form the waterway started at Bridgeport, just west of Chicago, and ran ninety-six miles south-westerly to La Salle, where a turning basin for riverboats was constructed.

In response to a petition from the legislature, Congress in 1822 authorized construction of an Illinois and Michigan Canal. Instead of a major grant of public lands that could be sold to meet construction costs, the state received only the right-of-way plus a ninety-foot strip on each side, enough for towpaths. The Bond administration nevertheless went ahead with the project, and two civil engineers estimated the cost at from $639,000 to $713,000. A private corporation received a legislative charter but accomplished nothing. In the East canals were becoming common when Congress in 1827 granted Illinois alternate sections of land for five miles on each side of the proposed canal, a total of 290,915 acres. Congress stipulated that the work must be started within five years and completed within twenty, and that tolls must forever be free to the federal government.[1]

---

[1] The difficulties with the canal and the failure of the experiment with state ownership of railroads are covered in detail by John H. Krenkel in *Illinois Internal Improvements, 1818-1848,* one of the many excellent books dealing with specialized phases of Illinois history. It has been the main source of information in the first two sections of this chapter. Major treatment also is given in Theodore C. Pease, *The Frontier State, 1818-1848,* chapters X and XI; John Moses, *Illinois Historical and Statistical,* I, 404-416; Alexander Davidson and Bernard Stuvé, *A Complete History of Illinois,* chapter XXXVII; and R. Carlyle Buley, *The Old Northwest,* I, 504-518. See also Leslie C. Swanson, *Canals of Mid-America.*

A board of three commissioners laid out the towns of Chicago and Ottawa in 1830 but received less than eighteen thousand dollars from the first sale of lots. As a result, some men began to doubt the wisdom of a canal. John Reynolds, who had been elected governor that year as a canal advocate, swung to the view that a state railroad might be preferable. Joseph Duncan, his successor, optimistically wanted a canal wide enough for steamboats. The southern counties lacked enthusiasm for a project in the North, but the cause of inland transportation had been helped when the federal government improved the Chicago harbor, widening the river's mouth to eighty feet, dredging it to a depth of seven or eight feet, and constructing a pier into the lake on the river's north side. As a result more lake vessels called at Chicago. The legislature decided that a canal should be constructed by the state, rather than by a private company, but former Governor Coles, who from his Philadelphia home assisted the canal commissioners with financing negotiations, found that eastern capitalists could be difficult. They insisted that Illinois, like other states, pledge its faith for the payment of principal and interest on funds borrowed.

Cost estimates arose steadily and alarmingly, but Duncan borrowed five hundred thousand dollars in time for construction to start July 4, 1836. In a big celebration at Bridgeport, Gurdon S. Hubbard and others spoke glowingly of the future of Chicago and Illinois. That the canal was built at all was an engineering miracle. Hand tools, horses, and black powder were used, and much of the route passed through marshes that were virtual lakes in the spring and early winter. Roads had to be built to the right-of-way, and tools and equipment shipped from the seaboard. Shortages inflated the cost of food, supplies, and wages. Needing manpower, the contractors made a major contribution to the state by importing Irish laborers. They worked in wet ground for twenty to twenty-six dollars a month and, with a steady stream of their countrymen, helped build Chicago and the new towns that sprang up along the canal. There the Irish influence has been strong.[2]

[2] W. V. Pooley, *The Settlement of Illinois, 1830 to 1850,* pp. 383-391. A cement industry developed in time to be used in construction of canal locks. A deposit of natural cement rock, a limestone containing clay and a small amount of magnesium, was found near Utica. When burned, ground to a powder, and mixed with water, it dried to form a concrete material. That technique had been discovered in 1817 by engineers working on the Erie Canal. In 1838 the natural cement came into regular production at Utica. It expanded until the first portland cement plants in Illinois were built in the 1890's.

The speculative boom collapsed with the Panic of 1837, which started in the East and brought five lean years. Causes of the economic disaster included land speculation, which had been national in scope, and the enormous state debts piled up for public improvements and the chartering of banks, in which Illinois fortunately had lagged behind some other states. Land values plunged from the inflated 1836 high, prices of grain and meat dropped, skilled mechanics found themselves out of work, and businessmen were ruined. The blow was softened because canal contracts and payrolls allowed local businessmen to carry on for a while. Before the crash Chicago and Ottawa lots had sold at premium prices, but canal commissioners experienced difficulty in collecting second installment payments. Financial worries increased when canal cost estimates reached $13,253,875. The state then abandoned a deep-cut plan which would have enabled water from Lake Michigan to maintain a six-foot depth during the entire length of a canal that was sixty feet wide. Engineers insisted that the big canal was needed in the future, but economy dictated new specifications calling for a shallow cut with the water level maintained by feeder canals from the Calumet, Fox, and Kankakee rivers.

In the period of national economic stagnation, a financial solution eluded the state during the administration of Governor Thomas Carlin, a frontiersman with little education and no capacity for handling complex matters. For a time contractors paid wages and met other obligations by issuing scrip in denominations from one dollar to a hundred dollars. The scrip, noninterest bearing, was generally accepted at par out of confidence that the state would redeem it. By 1840 the legislature authorized issuance of contractors' checks bearing 6 percent interest and payable sometime. Another emergency law put canal lands on sale at a time when there were few buyers. In 1842 construction stopped. The chief engineer reported nearly five million dollars had been spent on the canal and that three million dollars more were needed. By that time Illinois had compounded its debts by attempting to build a state-owned railroad system.

PIPE DREAMS ABOUT RAILROADS

For talent in depth, the Tenth General Assembly, elected in 1836, has never been equaled. State Representative Abraham Lincoln's colleagues included Stephen A. Douglas and six others who became United States senators. Others served as governor, went to Congress, and held secondary state offices. Yet they voted overwhelmingly for a reckless and imprudent system of internal improvements that ruined the state's credit for years. True, the need existed. Bulk commodities were difficult to market, the people demanded transportation outlays, and the level prairie was admirably suited for rail lines.

Illinois feared it would be penalized economically if it failed to follow the example of states to the east. Private companies in the East collected tolls on turnpikes they widened and bridged. The federal government had decided to pay the cost of extending the old Cumberland Road westward from Wheeling, Virginia, through Vandalia until it reached the Mississippi River. Jealous of New York's success with the Erie Canal, Pennsylvania in 1826 started to construct between Philadelphia and Pittsburgh a great transportation route that used two stretches of rails as a portage over mountains but primarily was a canal system. Building of railroads began the preceding year in Maryland and South Carolina. With overenthusiasm, Pennsylvania next adopted a plan for auxiliary canals and also built railroads. To soothe local jealousies, Ohio began work on three canals linking Lake Erie with the Ohio River. The first, between Cleveland and Portsmouth, opened in 1832. Michigan started two state-owned railroads toward Lake Michigan. Indiana in 1832 began a canal to connect the Wabash River with Lake Erie, and in 1836 reached a peak of optimism by adopting a thirteen-million-dollar system for more canals, a state railroad, and some turnpikes.[3] The proposed expenditures represented one-sixth of Indiana's wealth, but in the speculative boom the projects did not seem to be inflated. Internal improvements had the support of some Democrats, and the Whigs backed Henry Clay's "American system" which proposed that canals and roads be linked with a protective tariff and the Bank of the United States. President Jackson, who in 1830 had strained the loyalty of the West by vetoing a federal appropriation for an intrastate road in Kentucky, had added to the feeling of optimism by signing a bill to distribute the treasury surplus to the states, starting in 1837. Under it Illinois received $640,000.

The case for internal improvements had been emphasized by Governor Duncan in his inaugural November 3, 1834. "Our state is

[3] Buley, *op. cit.*, I, 409-508. Swanson, *op. cit.*

comparatively in its infancy, and if roads, trackways, railroads, and canals, are now laid out, they can be made straight between most of the important points, with very little expense and difficulty, compared with what will result, if their location is postponed until lands increase in value, and settlements are formed on the roads which are now in use or daily making."

At the start the Illinois legislature did not favor state ownership. Sixteen private companies in 1836 received charters to build railroads, including one between Galena and Chicago, but despite the inflation they could not raise the capital. Only then did the state step into the situation, prodded by a well-attended internal improvements convention at Vandalia just before the 1836-37 legislative session. The delegates estimated that river improvements and railroads would cost ten million dollars and recommended that the state finance them with a bond issue. Governor Duncan, who had lost some of the enthusiasm of his inaugural address, opposed state construction but suggested a general law under which the state could buy stock in private companies. As the session opened Douglas submitted the first internal improvements plan, which was revised, expanded, and finally passed February 27, 1837. The council of revision vetoed it on the ground that only private corporations should undertake the financing and construction of projects aggregating ten million dollars, an immense sum at that time. Repassage over the veto came easily.

The law to "establish and maintain a general system of internal improvements" created two boards. Three fund commissioners, elected by the legislature, would raise money from the profits of a new state bank. Seven members of a board of public works, politicians also, would let contracts for simultaneous construction of eight railroads and improvements in five rivers. All settled portions of the state would be treated equally and none would have cause to complain that it had been barred from the pork barrel.

Lincoln and the other tall Whigs who composed the "Long Nine" from Sangamon County voted for the omnibus bill, but recent historical research challenges the long-accepted belief that they traded votes, helping other cities get railroads in return for support for moving the capital from Vandalia to Springfield. Thomas Ford, who died before Lincoln became famous, first implied that logrolling approached the scandalous stage, saying that "the whole state was bought up and bribed."[4] He gave the "Long Nine" credit for political logrolling. After the Civil War the story was embellished by writers who wished to show that young Lincoln had exceptional political talent. Lincoln historians came to accept it. The debunking process began when John H. Krenkel in an exhaustive study of the internal improvements phase of Illinois history found no conclusive evidence of logrolling and vote trading. Under 1837 standards, Krenkel said, the location of the proposed railroads was not illogical. Paul Simon, the only writer who analyzed every internal improvements roll call, flatly denies that the "Long Nine" voted as a bloc and says the record gives no hint of a master strategy being followed by Lincoln.[5]

The biggest project, for which three and a half million dollars were allocated, was an Illinois Central railroad from Cairo to the Illinois River at the southern end of the canal and then northwest to Galena and the lead mines. No other railroad was planned for the northern third of the state, then sparsely settled. Because the canal was already under construction, Chicago did not get a railroad. The legislature provided for two major east-west lines: a Northern Cross road from Quincy through Springfield and Danville to the Indiana state line, to cost 1.85 million dollars, and a Southern Cross from Alton to Mount Carmel, with a branch at Edwardsville to Equality, near Shawneetown, for all of which 1.6 million dollars were appropriated. There were other lines: from Peoria to Warsaw on the Mississippi, seven hundred thousand dollars; a branch from the Central toward Shelbyville and Terre Haute, Indiana, $650,000; a railroad from lower Alton via Hillsboro to the Central, six hundred thousand dollars; a road from Belleville and Lebanon to intersect with the Alton and Mount Carmel, $150,000; and a line from Bloomington to Mackinaw with forks to Pekin and Peoria, $350,000. The law required a sign— "Railroad Crossing—Look out for the engine while the bell

[4] Thomas Ford, *A History of Illinois*, pp. 186-187 (Lakeside Classics edition, 1945, pp. 288-289).

[5] Krenkel, *op. cit.*, p. 72. Paul Simon, *Lincoln's Preparation for Greatness: The Illinois Legislative Years*, pp. 76-105. The "Long Nine" legend has been so widely accepted for so long a time that Krenkel's conclusions and Simon's research have been largely ignored by historians and Illinois agencies dealing with tourism. Douglas repeatedly attempted to make Jacksonville the capital. Simon credits Senator Orville H. Browning of Quincy with the leading role in moving the capital to Springfield. See Maurice Baxter, *Orville H. Browning, Lincoln's Friend and Critic*, p. 22. Baxter's book was published one year before Krenkel's and eight before Simon's.

rings"—in nine-inch capital letters at every highway. For river improvements, the legislature allocated expenditures of a hundred thousand dollars each on the Wabash, the Illinois, and the Rock, and for fifty thousand dollars each on the Little Wabash and the Kaskaskia. On the Great Western mail route connecting St. Louis with Vincennes, $250,000 were to be spent. Other counties would divide a two-hundred-thousand-dollar consolation prize which could be spent on roads.

As the largest Illinois city on the Mississippi and an aspiring rival of St. Louis, Alton received terminals of three railroads. Illinois policy at the time called for diverting trade from St. Louis, which suffered loss of river traffic when an Illinois Central railroad finally connected Cairo and Galena. Those factors were overlooked by men who accepted the "Long Nine" legend that Alton received the railroads because it did not get the seat of government. Springfield's place on the Northern Cross was all that its importance deserved, and it got both the capital and the railroad. In the public improvements fiasco, Krenkel found no ground for criticizing the allocation of railroads by the legislature. As to the commissioners who had charge of finances and construction, he reported mistakes of judgment but no hint of dishonesty. In contrast, the Indiana public improvements system became involved in gross incompetency, mismanagement, and fraud.

The plan called for simultaneous construction of the entire system, but no one realized that Illinois in its pioneering days lacked engineering talent, money, manpower, and materials to do the job. Private groups optimistically began promoting a canal from Beardstown to Springfield, while the state board of public works let initial contracts for 294 miles of railroads and for the dams and locks where rapids blocked traffic on the Rock and Wabash rivers. Laying of rail began in the spring of 1838 at Meredosia, a Northern Cross point on the Illinois River. Contractors advertised for one thousand laborers, offering twenty dollars a month and board. In the primitive construction, cross ties rested on cedar sills placed in dirt without ballasting. English-made wrought-iron rails, about two and a half inches wide and five-eighths of an inch thick, were nailed to oak stringers. Top management rejected heavier rails as too expensive. In November a locomotive was unloaded from a steamship at Meredosia. The first train reached Springfield, fifty-nine miles away, February 14, 1842, to pick up a consignment of flour and pork for New

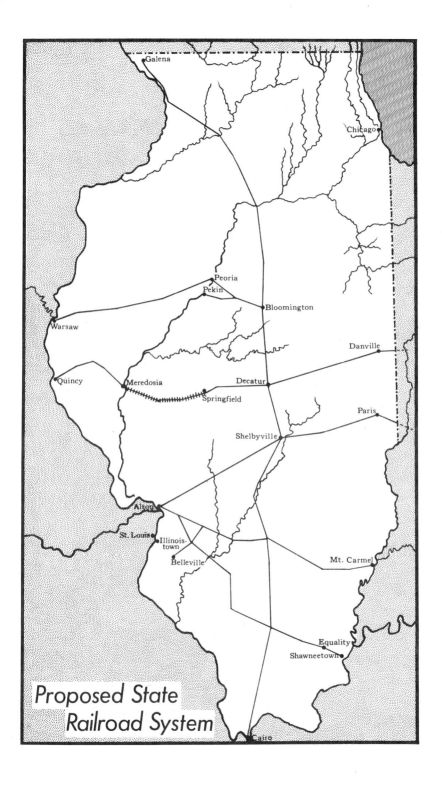

Galena

Chicago

Peoria
Pekin
Bloomington

Warsaw

Danville

Quincy
Meredosia
Decatur
Springfield

Paris

Shelbyville

Altona
St. Louis
Illinois-
town
Belleville
Mt. Carmel

Equality
Shawneetown

Cairo

Proposed State
Railroad System

Orleans. The timetable called for three round trips a week, with a steamer making connections, but travel was slow and erratic, and one of the hazards was that a rail might catch on a carriage wheel and pierce the floor of a car. The Northern Cross was a financial flop. It never earned enough to pay operating and repair costs, and experiments with private operation on a lease basis failed. Mules were substituted for the worn-out locomotive in 1844, and three years later the state sold the Northern Cross at auction for $21,100, one-fortieth of its original cost.[6]

Only the one section of the Northern Cross reached the completion stage. Elsewhere some embankments, bridges, and culverts were finished. Management was inexperienced and simultaneous construction one of the mistakes, but no town would wait for its railroad and the 1838-39 legislature authorized additional lines to cost nearly one million dollars. Already the Panic of 1837 had washed away any chance that Illinois could finance a rail network, and by the end of 1839 virtually all work was suspended. Sentiment swung in favor of repeal of the system, and officials reported they had spent $2,625,803 and needed $6,269,813 more. Abandonment of the system became official during the 1840-41 legislative session as the result of a financial muddle that seemed impossible to solve.

ANOTHER STATE BANK AND MORE DEBT

The uproar that accompanied the liquidation of the first state banking experiment should have taught Illinois a lesson. The disastrous 1821 issue of State Bank notes had been retired ten years later with one hundred thousand dollars borrowed from Samuel Wiggins, a Cincinnati capitalist, on a pledge that it would be redeemed from taxes on land owned by nonresidents. "The honor of the state was saved," Governor Ford wrote, "but the legislature was damned for all time to come."[7] In his colorful history, which lacks total accuracy, the governor said that demagogues claimed that Illinois had been sold out to Wiggins, that legislators made abject excuses instead of valid explanations, and that election-day casualties were high. Most of the state debt of

---

[6] George M. McConnel, "Recollections of the Northern Cross Railroad," *Transactions of the Illinois State Historical Society,* XIII (1908), 145-152.

[7] Ford, *op. cit.,* pp. 107-108 (Lakeside Classics edition, 1945, pp. 149-150).

four hundred thousand dollars was chargeable to the unfortunate bank, and for years the Wiggins loan was a campaign issue.

Some bank notes appeared in local trade, but the bulk of the money circulating in Illinois consisted of silver coins, mostly Spanish, French, and Mexican. The nation's economy needed paper money, but President Jackson had closed the second Bank of the United States on the grounds that it was a monopoly and had interfered with the 1832 election. In that situation state bank systems came into vogue, and a new generation of legislators forgot what had happened under the 1821 law. In anticipation of a great era of expansion, the belief spread that a state bank would be so profitable that it could pay for railroads and other permanent improvements.[8]

Under that delusion and over the opposition of Governor Duncan, Whigs who believed in a federal banking system combined with some Democrats to charter a second State Bank of Illinois with a capital of one and a half million dollars, of which one hundred thousand dollars were reserved for purchase by the state. In addition, the state had the right to increase its bank holdings by another million dollars. Springfield, not yet the capital, was made the bank's main office. Branches were located at Vandalia, Chicago, Alton, Jacksonville, and Galena, and later at Mount Carmel, Danville, Belleville, and Quincy. The bank was authorized to issue notes, discount bills and notes, and buy and sell bullion, but was forbidden to speculate in real estate except for its own buildings. It was a state bank in name only, without regulation by any official and with control soon going to a group of moneyed speculators. The stock, quickly oversubscribed, supposedly could be bought only by Illinois residents. Wiggins, however, employed Illinois men to subscribe for stock which he secretly owned. As a result, bank control was in the hands of Wiggins, Thomas Mather, a Springfield businessman and state senator, and the influential Alton commission house of Godfrey, Gilman, and Company.

In the land speculation mania that spread across the state from Chicago, the State Bank encountered difficulties. At times specie payments were difficult, and the Whig management suffered heavy losses trying to monopolize the Galena lead output and establish

[8] George W. Dowrie, *The Development of Banking in Illinois, 1817-1863,* pp. 59-130. Krenkel, *op. cit.,* pp. 126-176. Pease, *op. cit.,* pp. 303-315. Buley, *op. cit.,* II, 288-299. Davidson-Stuvé, *op. cit.,* pp. 417-427. John F. Snyder, *Adam W. Snyder in Illinois History,* pp. 342-345. Gustave Koerner, *Memoirs,* I, 435-437.

Alton as a more important commercial center than St. Louis. No one could check on secret operations, and when Wiggins needed to put up collateral to support the bank he violated ethical standards by borrowing the money from the institution. The stock meanwhile rose to 113 and became more speculative as a result of the 1837 pipe dream that banking profits could pay for railroads. In the overexpansion, the Bank of Illinois at Shawneetown, which had closed in 1823, reopened in 1834 under its unexpired charter so as to participate in the period of prosperity.[9] Illinois had a third bank in this period. The Bank of Cairo opened in 1834 under a territorial charter and issued smaller notes which became a leading medium of exchange in a region tributary to St. Louis. Controlled by London investors, it avoided political entanglements but went out of business in 1843 when its notes depreciated and the cashier disappeared with the specie in the vault.

The State Bank's high financing started immediately after enactment of the internal improvements law, when the legislature empowered the fund commissioners to issue three million dollars of their own 6 percent notes. Simultaneously the bank's capitalization was increased by two million dollars, to be subscribed by the state, and stock in the Shawneetown bank was increased by 1.4 million dollars, of which one million dollars were to be subscribed by the state. In neither case did the state have money to invest in

[9] The deflation of a delightful legend is always distasteful, but there is no historical basis for a widely circulated legend that Shawneetown bankers refused to loan money to Chicagoans on the ground that Chicago could never be important because it was too far away from Shawneetown. Except possibly to recall that Beck's gazetteer identified Chicago as a village of twelve to fifteen houses in Pike County, the circulators of the legend avoid trouble by omitting details. Who in Chicago asked for such a loan? Was it during the first or second period of state banking? It couldn't have been in the first phase, which lasted from 1817 to 1823, when only a handful of fur traders lived beside Fort Dearborn. Those men transacted business by barter, had no need for bank notes, and certainly would not have made a canoe trip on the Chicago, Des Plaines, Illinois, Mississippi, and Ohio rivers to apply for a loan at the Bank of Illinois. Banks at Edwardsville and St. Louis were much closer to Chicago, but any trader who needed credit could have arranged it with one of John J. Astor's agents. In any event the early banks existed primarily to make money by issuing bank notes rather than making commercial loans in an era when Illinois commerce was still in its infancy.

The Bank of Illinois at Shawneetown reopened in 1834 with enough prestige and capital to erect an imposing building, with Doric columns and other Grecian architectural features, that is still standing. Chicago was just beginning to boom, but again there was no reason why a Chicagoan would apply to Shawneetown for a loan. Shawneetown was—and still is—too far away to be accessible to Chicagoans, and the two communities have never been in the same economic orbit. Chicago's trading and financial connections always were with the East, and any businessman at Chicago who needed credit could have arranged it with Gurdon Saltonstall Hubbard, who had close connections with businessmen at Buffalo.

bank stock. Meanwhile the bank's currency competed with scrip issued by corporations, cities, counties, and others. Small traders made change with scrip, usually in denominations between five cents and a dollar, which was redeemable in groceries or other merchandise.

The Panic of 1837 spread economic ruin across the country, and banks, including the Illinois institutions, suspended specie payments when they were unable to redeem their notes with gold or silver. That presented problems, since eight hundred thousand dollars of state funds were tied up and, under the law, the State Bank's charter would be forfeited if suspension lasted more than sixty days. Meanwhile the federal government refused to make the banks depositories for public moneys or to allow their notes to be accepted in payment for public lands. Governor Duncan recommended that the state repeal the internal improvements system and not buy the three million dollars additional stock in the two banks. The legislature, however, refused to curtail the construction system but suspended the forfeiture provision until the next session.

Into the governor's office in late 1838 moved Thomas Carlin, whose formal education came in his adult years. A typical frontiersman, he admired Jackson and adopted his antibank policies. The new governor, whose biographers list honesty and courage as his best qualities, lacked comprehension of economics. His inaugural message criticized the state's banking system and asserted that the internal improvements system must go forward, but he offered no financial solution. The rest of the Carlin administration was marked by a series of major and minor steps, many of them desperate and unfortunate, in efforts to continue railroad construction and then to pay interest on the mounting debt.[10] An official investigation produced divergent conclusions. Wiggins,

[10] Abraham Lincoln was personally involved in some of the widespread ramifications of the banking situation. Because the bank had suspended specie payments, under terms of the law its charter would be forfeited upon adjournment of a special legislative session in 1840. Lincoln as the Whig leader in the house of representatives tried to prevent adjournment in hope that the charter could be kept alive during the regular legislative session that would immediately follow. In a futile effort to prevent a quorum, Lincoln sacrificed his dignity by jumping from a window of the Second Presbyterian Church, in which the house was meeting. A series of "Dear Rebecca" letters which almost resulted in a duel between Lincoln and State Auditor James Shields also grew out of the bank controversy. Shields, a Democrat, favored forfeiture of the charter and the anonymous letters ridiculed his position. Harry E. Pratt, "Abraham Lincoln, A Chronology," *Illinois Blue Book, 1955-56,* p. 78.

among other improper practices, was found to have drawn dividends on stock he had not paid for. The Alton house of Godfrey, Gilman, and Company and other firms had received liberal advances in an effort to corner the Galena lead market. Those transactions cost the bank one million dollars and resulted in a business setback for Alton. Private banking, unsanctioned by law, made Chicago firms less dependent upon the State Bank branch there. Gurdon Saltonstall Hubbard and other Chicago businessmen received what credit they needed from Buffalo and New York connections.

To negotiate loans in New York and Europe, Carlin with bad judgment appointed John Reynolds and United States Senator Richard M. Young, who as a state representative had introduced the bills that brought about the first state banking fiasco.[11] They were equally unqualified to deal with bankers and in New York borrowed 1.3 million dollars on terms that displeased Carlin. In Europe, Reynolds went touring while Young, joined by two state fund commissioners, arranged on controversial terms to get one and a half million dollars from a London house that went bankrupt before the deal was completed. At home small borrowings gave only temporary relief. Congress refused a land grant for railroads, and the board of public works stopped most construction.

As the bad situation became worse, the two old boards were replaced by a three-man ex officio board empowered to settle all internal improvements liabilities and give drafts to contractors for amounts due. That ended the system, but the debt remained and the annual interest exceeded the treasury's income. As an alternative to repudiation, the Carlin administration in 1841 sold bonds under par to pay interest. John D. Whiteside, the fund commissioner, turned over bonds with a face value of $804,000 to the New York firm of Macalister and Stebbins, which paid the state $261,000. The price of bonds dropped, Macalister and Stebbins sold additional securities to satisfy advances to the state, and the officials at Springfield complained that Whiteside had not followed instructions. For years Illinois was involved in a costly dispute about redemption of bonds which without its approval had passed into the hands of third parties.

11 John F. Snyder, "Forgotten Statesmen of Illinois: Richard M. Young," *Transactions of the Illinois State Historical Society,* XI (1906), 302-327.

The state defaulted on interest in July, 1841, and bonds fell to fifteen cents on the dollar. Counting two banks, the unfinished canal, and the abandoned railroads, the state's debt exceeded fifteen million dollars. Paying it off seemed impossible. Interest charges were nearly eight hundred thousand dollars a year, compared with $98,546 collected in taxes for support of the state government. In the gloom of hard times, some men talked of steps that would amount to bankruptcy and debt repudiation by the state. They had no consolation that other states—Ohio, Indiana, Michigan, Arkansas, and Louisiana—also were in critical financial dilemmas. Carlin in his farewell message offered no solution, but a stronger man succeeded him as governor.

EXPERIMENTS WITH PLANK ROADS

In summer and in the frozen winter, land travel presented only minor problems, but the rich black prairie soil turned to deep clinging mud when saturated by the rains of spring and late autumn. Travel in wheeled vehicles then was often next to impossible as horses "sank literally to their girths" and only light loads could be hauled. Robert Dale Owen in a treatise on plank-road construction told of a wet winter when the people of McLeansboro ran out of coffee, sugar, and other necessities. A farmer who boasted of his four-horse team volunteered to get supplies. He reached Shawneetown, some forty miles away, with great exertion and took on half a load. After a ten-day absence he returned home with an empty wagon. Two of his horses had died and the purchases had been abandoned at one of the seemingly bottomless mudholes.[12]

Such hardships were not uncommon. Stagecoaches operated by the Frink and Walker line with a mail subsidy had trouble negotiating many obstacles, including a "nine mile swamp" immediately southwest of Chicago. Complaints led to the raising of $2,480 by popular subscription so that the road could be graded two and a half feet above the level of the prairie and ditches dug alongside. "The turnpike was never a success," recalled Edwin O. Gale in a book of reminiscences. "The mud, when in its normal plastic condition always seemed to be several feet deeper than the prairie. The clay of which it was composed appeared to have a grudge

[12] Milo M. Quaife, *Chicago's Highways Old and New*, pp. 123-124.

against every living thing, horse, ox, or man, and threw its tenacious tentacles around all things, to draw them to its infernal level."[13]

Plank roads, a Russian invention used successfully in Canada and experimentally in New York, briefly promised to get the prairie out of the mud. First among the states, the Illinois legislature in 1847 authorized incorporation of plank-road companies. By September, 1848, traffic opened on ten miles of eight-foot planks, three inches thick, laid on the prairie between Chicago and Duffy's Tavern at Riverside. The road had been graded and ditched and the planks placed on stringers bedded in the ground. The total cost was sixteen thousand dollars, and in the first month tolls of fifteen hundred dollars were collected on the basis of thirty-seven and a half cents for a four-horse vehicle, twenty-five cents for a single team, and twelve and a half cents for a horse and rider. Other companies were attracted by dividends of from 30 to 40 percent, and within a few years plank roads extended as far as Naperville, Sycamore, Oswego, Elgin, and Genoa. South of Chicago, the approach of the Illinois Central railroad discouraged construction. Almost every steamboat landing on the Illinois River had its plank road to the interior. By the middle of 1851, possibly a million dollars had been invested in six hundred miles of highways. They soon disappeared, having proved to be unsatisfactory, expensive, and actually dangerous. Despite the grading, water accumulated and caused cavities under the oak and walnut planks, which warped in the sun since they were not spiked to the stringers. The companies had failed to set aside reserves for maintenance, the planks decayed, and the roadways became uncomfortably rough. Before long traffic returned to the open prairie, which in its natural state was an excellent roadway in dry seasons.

Many immigrants preferred Ohio River boats to a slow wagon journey over the deep ruts and low stumps of the National Road.[14] It was an extension of the Cumberland Road and competed with the Erie Canal by providing a government-financed highway westward from Wheeling, Virginia. As authorized by Congress in 1820, it extended on a straight line through Ohio and Indiana and was supposed to cross Illinois to a point on the

13 *Ibid.*, p. 129.

14 Buley, *op. cit.,* I, 449-454. Thomas L. Hardin, "The National Road in Illinois," *Journal of the Illinois State Historical Society,* LX (Spring, 1967), 5-22. Robert Bruce, *The National Road.* Philip D. Jordan, *The National Road.*

Mississippi River between St. Louis and the mouth of the Illinois River. The road reached Columbus, Ohio, in 1833, five years after contracts were let for surveying and grubbing the eighty-nine miles between the Indiana line and Vandalia.

Prospects for a toll-free highway encouraged settlement, and by 1831 some three hundred persons lived in previously vacant Effingham County. During the summer of 1839 the nearly completed road was opened for travel in Illinois and coaches pulled by four horses brought mail to Vandalia three times a week. Congress quit supporting the National Road the next year, and no work was done west of Vandalia, although Illinois wanted an extension to Jefferson City, Missouri, that would cross the Mississippi at Alton. To the east, but not in Illinois, the road had been macadamized by the use of crushed rock bound with clay and water. Illinois officials complained first about construction delays and then about the stoppage, but the importance of the National Road was that in Ohio it diverted considerable traffic from the river. Thousands of emigrant wagons followed it as far as Vandalia, and over it Illinois stockmen drove cattle and hogs to eastern markets. In 1843 the legislature authorized local districts to do repair work on the federal road, which became state property in 1856. For the rest of the century, construction and maintenance of roads would be left to the townships.

As the capital, Vandalia became the center of a network authorized by the state but not improved for spring and early winter travel. The road system, poor as it was, expanded partly under the influence of free enterprise as ferry operators and tavern owners spread word that they offered superior facilities.

THE MOVE TO SPRINGFIELD

Inadequate state houses and the northward spread of population doomed Vandalia as the seat of government. After the first capitol burned in 1823, the townspeople replaced it with a two-story brick structure whose walls soon bulged and sagged while the senate floor began to assume the shape of a bowl. The first legislature had provided for reopening the capital location question in twenty years and a referendum in 1834 proved inconclusive. In light balloting, Alton received a third of the vote, finishing barely ahead of Vandalia and Springfield, while scattering returns favored the state's unpopulated geographical center (now Illiopolis in eastern Sangamon County), Peoria, and Jacksonville. Meanwhile, plaster fell in the state house, walls cracked, and Methodists refused to hold church services there. Governor Duncan approved a five-thousand-dollar expenditure on a new building, and townspeople furnished additional money, trusting that the state would repay them.

Brick from a local kiln formed the walls of Vandalia's third and last capitol. During the 1836-37 session, carpenters trying to finish interior work got in the way of legislators and wet plaster was blamed for respiratory ailments. Outside, the public square had a ramshackle aspect. In those surroundings, Vandalia fought a losing battle to retain the seat of state government. Roll calls on the relocation issue began as soon as the permanent improvements law was passed. Most men from the newly settled northern areas made Springfield their first or second choice. On the fourth ballot, Springfield won with opposition only from Vandalia.

After adjournment, Abraham Lincoln, who had been beaten for the speakership, moved from the log cabin village of New Salem to Springfield, which had reached the frame house stage and had a population of about 1,100.[15] Licensed to practice law, young Lincoln wanted to live in the state's governmental and political center. Had the state house been awarded to another town, Lincoln would have moved there.

To get the capitol, Springfield contributed the town square and pledged a fifty-thousand-dollar contribution. No state in the West had a more imposing seat of government than the two-story Greek Renaissance building, with dome, porticos, and rotunda, designed by an amateur architect, J. F. Rague, who was the president of the Mechanics Institute, a school in Springfield. Ox teams hauled the stone blocks from a quarry eight miles south of town. Edward D. Baker, one of the great orators of the region, spoke at the cornerstone-laying July 4, 1837, and two years later the state's movable property arrived by wagons after Vandalia lost a final effort to reverse the decision. For a time the Supreme Court sat in the Episcopal church and the two legislative houses met in other churches.

The move to Springfield found the Democrats more solidly

[15] Paul M. Angle, *"Here I Have Lived."* Henry A. Converse, "The House of the House Divided," *Linco! Centennial Assn. Papers,* 1924. Howard F. Rissler, "The State Capitol, 1837-1876," *Journal of the Illinois State Historical Society,* LXI (Winter, 1968), 397-430. "The Capitals and Capitols of Illinois," *Illinois Blue Book, 1900,* pp. 172-173.

entrenched in Illinois, thanks in part to the political genius of Stephen A. Douglas. Joseph Duncan, who ranked with Coles as an advocate of public education and could not be held responsible for the public improvements fiasco, had been as strong a governor as the constitution permitted, but he was an apostate from the Democrats and in 1838 the Whigs failed to name his successor. Douglas, a short-legged former cabinetmaker's apprentice from Vermont, had wandered into Illinois in 1833. Boundless in his political ambitions, Douglas preached party loyalty and discipline and insisted that the Democrats adopt the new practice of making nominations at conventions where delegates represented local party members. He had been active in 1836, when Harrison carried every state in the Old Northwest but Illinois. That year casualties had been heavy among legislators who had voted for a "little bull" law. Based on sound but undiscovered principles of genetics, it sought to improve the breed of cattle by prohibiting bulls from running at large.[16] Pioneer farmers regarded the law as an undemocratic effort to favor rich men who could afford to buy larger breeding stock. The law created more disfavor than the misunderstood Wiggins loan and was repealed in eleven months.

Carlin in 1838 won the governorship by less than one thousand votes over Cyrus Edwards, who was the former governor's younger brother and had declared for internal improvements. The Democrats, who had held their first convention the preceding year, wanted a candidate from the North. They nominated James W. Stephenson, receiver of the land office at Galena, but learned just in time that his accounts with the federal government were short by more than forty thousand dollars. Carlin, who took his place on the ticket, embroiled the Supreme Court in politics by attempting to remove from office Secretary of State Alexander P. Field, a Whig whose lifetime appointment dated back to the Edwards administration. The senate refused to affirm Carlin's appointment of John A. McClernand, an active Democrat for several decades. The Whig majority of the Supreme Court held that the governor could appoint only when a vacancy existed. Democrats made the court an issue in a campaign in which they gained control of the legislature. Field then resigned, and Douglas became secretary of state briefly as he moved quickly up the political ladder.[17]

16 Snyder, *op. cit.*, pp. 192-193.

17 Walter A. Townsend, *Illinois Democracy*, I, 58-59.

Illinois had been generous in granting the right to vote. Some newly organized counties were populated only by squatters, and special laws for Sangamon and Morgan counties met the situation by providing that householders could perform the duties and receive the privileges of freeholders. As early as 1829 the newly arrived Irish had been given the right of franchise in all elections. During the Carlin administration Whig lawyers challenged the system under which aliens, including Germans as well as Irish canal laborers, had been allowed to vote. An estimated ten thousand aliens, mostly Democrats, could turn the 1840 elections, and the Whigs in a test case won a favorable ruling from Circuit Judge Daniel Stone, who had been a Lincoln associate on the "Long Nine." Douglas spotted a flaw in the appeal record which enabled the Democrats to delay a ruling until the aliens helped score another election-day triumph. For future safety, the Democratic legislature in 1841 packed the Supreme Court with a reorganization that created five additional judgeships. The posts went to such Democrats as Douglas, Ford, and Breese. To give them something to do, the legislature abolished circuit judgeships and required that the Supreme Court justices preside over trials as well as hear cases on appeal.

To climax their "log cabin and hard cider" campaign of 1840, enthusiastic Whigs held a gigantic three-day rally in Springfield that probably has never been equaled in Illinois. An estimated twenty thousand persons, nearly 5 percent of the state's population, came from all parts of Illinois. They camped on the prairie, drank hard cider, rode in log cabins on wheels, and sang campaign songs. The Chicago delegation, which was a week on the road, brought a band, a six-pounder to fire salutes, and a thirty-foot model of a brig drawn by six white horses. Fayette County Whigs dragged a log cabin from Vandalia.[18] Nevertheless, Illinois again went Democratic.

[18] Isabel Jamison, "The Young Men's Convention and Old Soldiers' Meeting at Springfield, June 3-4, 1840," *Transactions of the Illinois State Historical Society*, XX (1914), 160-171. Moses, *op. cit.*, I, 438.

10

THE MORMON YEARS

Most of the illinois residents arrived singly or in family groups, but there were exceptions, such as the English at Albion, Ernst's Germans at Vandalia, and later the Swedes at Bishop Hill. In some cases the people of an eastern community would optimistically seek to transplant their culture and friendships into new surroundings in the West. The mass migrations were usually for ethnic or religious reasons, and of all the people who came to Illinois the impermanent Mormons were the most spectacular. They came in large numbers, first from Missouri as outcasts in retreat and then from England and the East as converts to a new religion. Their tragic departure after a few years was a dramatic reminder that Illinois was both gaining and losing population. Many who emigrated into the state stayed for a comparatively brief span of months or years before moving on to some other part of the American mixing-pot. For Illinois, however, the immigration gains always exceeded the losses.

NAUVOO: JOSEPH SMITH'S CITY-STATE, 1839-1846

For the Mormons eight years of expansion, conflict, and tragedy in Illinois began early in 1839 at the Quincy ferry, where Brigham Young shepherded five thousand refugees from Missouri.

Nine years had passed since Joseph Smith, youthful prophet of a new religion, told of angelic visitations and published the Book

213

of Mormon in New York state, a breeding ground of unorthodox sects and experimental societies. During that period his Latter-Day Saints found themselves in almost continual controversy. They had moved to Kirtland, Ohio, and became involved in town lot speculation and wildcat banking. Smith then regathered his converts in Missouri, where anti-Mormon sentiment erupted for the first time. Political and social pressures forced the Latter-Day Saints to leave Independence, and at Far West, in the sparsely settled northwestern corner of that state, they founded a new town and a new county. The pious Yankee sect grew in numbers, and Missourians, who were southern by inheritance, feared that the Mormons would become more powerful. Meanwhile a secret Mormon vigilante organization became controversial during violence in which friends and enemies participated. After a polling place riot, Governor Lillburn W. Boggs mobilized the militia to "expel or exterminate" the Mormons. Smith and some other leaders were jailed. Welcoming immigrants, Illinois offered asylum and the Mormons made a major contribution to the state.

Smith escaped and resumed his charismatic leadership of Mormons who had existed through the winter on the charity of Quincy people. Seventy miles upstream, at a bend in the Mississippi River, they bought land on contract and Smith founded Nauvoo on the site of Commerce, a town of swamps, underbrush, and a few houses. "The place was literally a wilderness," Smith wrote. "The land was mostly covered with trees and bushes, and much of it was so wet that it was with the utmost difficulty that a footman could get through, and totally impossible for teams. Commerce was so unhealthful, very few could live there." But many did in time. For a new City of Zion, a city-state that violated the American tradition of separation of church and state, the Mormon leader plotted four-acre blocks divided into four lots so that each family could have space for gardens, fruit trees, and domesticated animals. There his destitute followers gathered and soon were joined by a steady stream of converts. Most of the original Nauvoo residents were of New England origin or ancestry, and many had been Methodists, Baptists, and Campbellites. Reinforcements came from Europe and especially England, where nine of the church's Twelve Apostles had great success as missionaries among distressed factory workers. Almost miraculously, by 1842 Hancock County had a Mormon population of sixteen thousand, with more living in nearby Illinois counties and across the river in Iowa.[1]

A tall, muscular man with blond hair and a simple eloquence abounding in scriptural illustrations, Smith was the leading citizen and promoter of Nauvoo as well as the prophet of an unorthodox religion. In a state closely divided politically, both parties courted the bloc-voting Mormons, and the Whigs helped Secretary of State Stephen A. Douglas round up legislative support for a charter which in 1840 granted Nauvoo almost complete home rule. Under it officials of the unique city had authority to do anything not inconsistent with the federal and state constitutions. They presided over a court system that had extraordinary powers and they selected a site for a university which never was built. The Nauvoo Legion as an independent part of the state militia received cannon and small arms from Springfield. Commanded by Smith, it constituted in effect a well-trained Mormon army. As a military force, it was second in size only to the United States army. The prophet became mayor and chief magistrate as well as lieutenant general, newspaper editor, real estate promoter, and bankrupt businessman. Although he was inspirational as a leader, persuasive as an orator, and prolific as a writer, Smith's visions did not bring business success, and Nauvoo had a hollow prosperity. The town

---

[1] Robert Bruce Flanders, *Nauvoo: Kingdom on the Mississippi*, p. 38. The Mormons were fairly widespread in Illinois. Some of the Missouri refugees spent their first winter at Pittsfield. During Smith's time the church organized stakes in Adams, Morgan, Vermilion, and Bureau counties, and sizable land purchases were made in Iowa across the Mississippi from Nauvoo. Stanley B. Kimball, "The Mormons in Illinois, 1838-1846: A Special Introduction," *Journal of the Illinois State Historical Society*, LXIV (Spring, 1971), 4-21. Kimball's essay contains complete references to recent historical research during the Mormon years in Illinois. This issue of the *Journal* is devoted exclusively to Illinois Mormonism and includes James L. Kimball, "The Nauvoo Charter: A Re-interpretation," pp. 181-197. Flanders' *Nauvoo: Kingdom on the Mississippi* is a recent book emphasizing the temporal phase of the Mormon years in Illinois. A contemporary work giving major attention to the theological beliefs of the Latter-Day Saints is B. H. Roberts, *The Rise and Fall of Nauvoo*.

Literature on the Mormon years in Illinois is extensive. Thomas Ford, a participant, gave it two chapters in his *History of Illinois*. Among early writings, see also Harry R. Beardsley, *Joseph Smith and His Mormon Empire* (New York, 1931); M. R. Werner, *Brigham Young* (New York, 1925); William A. Linn, *The Story of the Mormons* (New York, 1902). Thomas Rees, "Nauvoo, Illinois, Under Mormon and Icarian Occupations," *Journal of the Illinois State Historical Society*, XXI (Jan., 1929), 506-524.

See also William V. Pooley, *The Settlement of Illinois, 1830-1850*, pp. 508-525. T. C. Pease, *The Frontier State*, pp. 340-362. John Moses, *Illinois Historical and Statistical*, I, 469-489. Alexander Davidson and Bernard Stuvé, *A Complete History of Illinois*, pp. 489-521. Thomas F. O'Dea, *The Mormons*.

never was a trading center for the surrounding territory, and the people primarily worked at crafts. Real estate sales were the chief business, most of the leaders became speculators, and the town's wealth came chiefly from money and jewelry contributed by new converts. Had Illinois been more friendly, Smith's city could have suffered an economic collapse before many years. With little investment capital and no industrial payrolls, it became the largest city in Illinois, and by 1845 its population was at least twelve thousand. A beautiful city, trim and clean, Nauvoo escaped the umkempt aspect of many early settlements. Many homes were built of red brick with Federalist-type architecture.

The Nauvoo years witnessed major extensions in the doctrines of the Latter-Day Saints as the result of a series of revelations by the prophet. Atop the city's imposing hill, artisans who otherwise would have been unemployed contributed labor on a stone temple, tall and boxlike, one of the largest and most imposing buildings west of the Alleghenies. Completed in five years, it cost an estimated one million dollars. A new doctrine of the baptism of the dead required use of the temple for its rites. Baptisms which had been performed in the river were transferred to a temporary font, resting on twelve carved oxen, in the basement of the unfinished structure. The Mormon practice of polygamy began, possibly in 1841, after Smith told close associates that an earlier revelation called for a system of plural marriages. It drew objections from some church leaders.

Because of their rapid growth and majority status in the area around Nauvoo, avoidance of controversy would have been difficult for the Mormons. To the exclusion of others they practiced economic, political, and social solidarity, and unwisely they became involved in partisan politics in western Illinois. Their vote, steadily increasing in size, supported Whig candidates in 1838 and 1840. Then, on Smith's orders, they backed Governor Thomas Ford and other Democrats.[2] While a Supreme Court justice, Douglas had won Mormon gratitude by blocking an effort to extradite Smith to Missouri. The frontier had always been inclined to tolerate strange religious beliefs, but Smith's followers were more than a sect. As a monolithic organization they dominated Nauvoo and spread its influence beyond its borders. There they

[2] George R. Gayler, "The Mormons and Politics in Illinois, 1839-1844," *Journal of the Illinois State Historical Society*, IL (Spring, 1956), 48-66.

Joseph Smith, Mormon prophet

encountered gentile elements which in much of Illinois included the lawless. Antagonisms became inevitable. Smith meanwhile found that some of his converts were of questionable character. Dr. John C. Bennett, who had been quartermaster-general of the Illinois militia and the first mayor of Nauvoo, was expelled from the church and spread stories that discredited its leaders and generated fear that the Mormons planned to take over the state by force of arms. Missouri officials persisted in attempts to extradite Smith on charges of treason, murder, and arson. His legal battles in several courts were intensified after an assassination attempt on Boggs in Missouri.

Hopeful for federal protection and for restitution of property losses in Missouri, Smith went to Washington for an unsatisfactory call on President Van Buren. Other appeals failed, and a month before his death Smith announced that he was a candidate for President of the United States. Across the nation he dispatched the church's Twelve Apostles on joint religious and campaign missions. The Mormon candidate for Vice President was Sidney Rigdon, who in the early days played a leading role in translating some of the church's basic documents but who, with others, had recently rebelled against polygamy. Smith's Reform party platform proposed use of the army to suppress mobs, government purchase of the slaves, and a national bank with state branches whose profits would defray the expense of government. Intemperately he attacked other presidential aspirants.

Some Mormon converts had become apostates. Among gentiles, fear of the church's power led to rumors of counterfeiting and other crimes in Nauvoo. In the Military Tract sectarian bitterness intensified as each side accused the other of plots, threats, and violence. When he was arrested at Dixon on a warrant charging treason against Missouri, Smith obtained a writ of habeas corpus and insisted on going to Nauvoo for a hearing. There his own Municipal Court quickly released him for want of evidence. The prophet again shocked the state by having himself freed on a charge that he had used the Nauvoo Legion to destroy an opposition newspaper that, on its first press day, had made a direct attack upon the authority of his church. The situation demanded action and the governor called out the militia, in which anti-Mormons predominated, to keep the peace. Many feared that a religious war was imminent.

"I am going like a lamb to the slaughter," Smith said on June 27, 1844, as he left for Carthage, the county seat eighteen miles away, to meet the strict governor and an unfriendly justice of the peace concerning a destruction of the press charge. There Missourians revived the treason warrant. Ford postponed a decision on the validity of the Missouri warrant and for safekeeping placed Smith and his brother Hyrum in a two-story stone jail. The brothers visited with two Mormon elders in a second-story room. The governor dismissed most of the militia and erred by assigning the Carthage Grays, an unfriendly company, to protect the Smiths. Ford then went to Nauvoo and, speaking to the townspeople, insisted upon law and order. The Mormons in the audience protested when he recited the complaints that had been brought against them.

At about 5 o'clock, approximately the same hour the governor was speaking, the Carthage Grays furnished token resistance when a mob rushed the jail. The first volley killed Hyrum Smith and wounded one of the elders. Joseph Smith's pistol misfired. Fatally shot from the hall doorway, he fell through a window to the ground. The prophet, a man of wide talents who stirred up controversy, became the martyr as well as the founder of a religion that survived and prospered.

The governor, who had personally guaranteed the Smiths' safety, retreated to Quincy, where he established headquarters and stayed for a month. He ordered troops left in Carthage to defend its property against small numbers but to retreat if menaced by a superior force. Preparations for the town's defense proved unnecessary as the Mormons, who feared an attack from Missouri, kept the peace and buried the brothers in unmarked graves in Nauvoo. Ford issued a broadside asking the gentiles to stop threats to exterminate the Mormons. In the long controversy, both sides complained about the governor's actions.

Again the Mormons found themselves incompatible with their neighbors as a murder trial ended in acquittals and the legislature repealed the Nauvoo charter, which left the city without a government. Ford twice visited Nauvoo in 1845 to insist upon law and order, but hostility developed into mob violence. Lawlessness continued for two years in what became known as the Mormon War. During that time the Mormons complained of murders and burnings, while sentiment simultaneously grew that they should be expelled from Illinois. Until they left for Utah, the Mormons had an affinity for trouble, and until recently most accounts of the Nauvoo years stressed the belief of those who remained behind that the fault rested chiefly with the Mormons in general and Smith in particular. On the other hand, charges such as those made by Bennett are questionable in retrospect. At least in the final years in Illinois the Mormons were the victims of persecution. Some of the opposition was motivated by distrust of a strange religion, but strong evidence points to harassment by gentile elements who wanted to rid the Military Tract of a politically powerful group and in doing so have a chance to acquire their land and buildings at bargain prices.

Bitter editorials in the *Warsaw Signal* kept the gentiles stirred up, and delegates from nine counties met at Carthage in the autumn of 1845 to make plans to set up a military organization if

The Mormon temple at Nauvoo

the Mormons stayed. John J. Hardin, a former congressman who commanded troops sent to keep order in Hancock County, worked out an agreement that the Mormons would leave for some remote place. By proclamation Hardin unsuccessfully ordered an end of the violence that tore the countryside. Brigham Young, who had brought the Mormons to Illinois, bested Rigdon in a contest for leadership of the largest faction and again became a colonizer, the greatest of his century. Mormon activities turned to the manufacture of 2,500 wagons. "We want teams, and we want money and merchandise," said the *Nauvoo Neighbor*. Some Mormons abandoned their real estate and possessions, but most sold them to strangers at ridiculously low prices to get equipment for the long journey across Iowa that would end in the Salt Lake basin, then Mexican territory. On February 11, 1846, Young led the first four hundred families over the icy Mississippi. Most were gone before more sporadic violence broke out in July, and in mid-September a Battle of Nauvoo lasted several days before the city surrendered to a seven-hundred-man posse. The remaining Mormons were guaranteed protection until they could move across the river.

Not all left. Among those who stayed behind were members of Smith's family, including Joseph Smith III, who became leader of a separate Mormon denomination calling itself the Reorganized Church of Jesus Christ of Latter-Day Saints. Their headquarters were at Amboy and Plano before they moved to Iowa and then to Independence, Missouri.[3]

New residents of Nauvoo continued to have trouble with Smith's old enemies. An Icarian society, a group of utopian communists from France by way of Texas, moved into Nauvoo in 1849 and introduced a grape culture. From Nauvoo printing presses highly literate Icarians distributed proselyting literature in French, German, and English. Their colony also failed. The leader, Etienne Cabet, surrendered dictatorial powers and the legislature granted the Icarians a charter with broad provisions, but the community had financial difficulties. It split into factions and in 1856 expelled Cabet.[4]

The Nauvoo temple, a symbol of Mormon faith in Smith's prophecies, was dedicated after Young's departure but soon succumbed to a fire and a tornado. Nauvoo, almost a ghost town, became one of the many German settlements in Illinois.

FOREIGNERS AND EASTERNERS

Emigration from overseas to Illinois, which had a spectacular phase in the flocking of English converts to Nauvoo, first became significant during the 1830's. From northern Europe and the British Isles, new settlers came for a variety of reasons. Chiefly

[3] Both Mormon denominations are actively engaged in the preservation and restoration of Nauvoo. Leadership and finances from Salt Lake City have helped organize Nauvoo Restorations, Inc., which erected a visitors' center and plans to reproduce the Mormon Temple. It has preserved and opened to the public the homes of Brigham Young and some other Mormon leaders. The Reorganized branch of the Latter-Day Saints has its own Nauvoo shrines, including the home of Joseph Smith and the cemetery in which the graves of the Smith brothers have been relocated. The two churches, which have theological differences, do not cooperate in the restoration work that has made Nauvoo a major attraction for tourists.

[4] Much of the remaining portion of this chapter is taken from William V. Pooley, *op. cit.*, the definitive work on why foreigners and Easterners decided to migrate, which routes they took to Illinois, and where and how they settled.

they sought to escape famines that followed crop failures, the unemployment and overpopulation that went with the industrial revolution, and religious and political differences. In increasing thousands they crossed the Atlantic and many, especially those with limited finances, came directly to Illinois because good land in almost unlimited quantities could be obtained cheaply. As a result, the state became an amalgamation of three population elements, with the Europeans intermingling with the Yankees and the Southerners.[5]

The New Englanders and New Yorkers came in self-defense. Their agriculture could not compete with the western states once a transportation system for bulk commodities began operating. To stay on the thin and stony soil meant poverty; the alternatives were to become city workmen or to accept the challenge and go westward. Many had emigrated earlier, and the flow to new homes on rich soil would increase perceptibly in the 1850's. Most of the Europeans also took the northern route into Illinois, and in midstate they collided and intermingled with the people of southern blood who had first settled Illinois. The Yankees did not meld into the scene with complete harmony. Their down-eastern background made them more reserved, acquisitive, and formal, and they placed more emphasis on education. Their Protestantism lacked the camp-meeting fervor of the native preachers, and their morality would not accept slavery. Linguistic and religious differences, however, helped focus more attention on the foreigners, especially the numerous Germans and Irish.

The virtually unlimited opportunities for land ownership attracted Germans at a time when crops were poor along the Rhine valley and jobs hard to get. A wave of German settlement following an attempted uprising in 1830 had resulted in a concentration of Germans across the river from St. Louis. Gustave Koerner, who became lieutenant governor in 1852, was their political and literary leader.[6] On the National Road, Teutopolis and Effingham were founded by Germans from Cincinnati and reinforced by others who came directly from overseas. In the northern counties

5 See Pooley, *op. cit.,* pp. 526-537, for more obscure colonies, more or less communistic, which failed in Illinois. They included a group of Fourierists who briefly formed an Integral Phalanx in Sangamon County.

6 Koerner wrote prolifically, in German and English. A study of German settlement should begin with his *Memoirs.* See also Pooley, *op. cit.,* pp. 493-498, and John F. Snyder, *Adam W. Snyder,* pp. 158-159, 209-210.

the Germans also spread rapidly, and Chicago was heavily German, although not to the same extent as Cincinnati, St. Louis, and Milwaukee. The early Jews came mostly from Germany and in 1841 established their first Chicago synagogue. The *Staats-Zeitung* at Chicago became a daily paper in 1851, when it was three years old. Alton, Belleville, Galena, Peoria, and Quincy were among the larger downstate cities with German Lutheran churches. German schools, fraternal and cultural groups, and gymnastic companies were common. Many of the German immigrants were well-to-do farmers and tradesmen, and they took construction jobs until they could make the transition to the land. Others followed their old country trades in the cities of Illinois. When a second revolution failed in 1852, Friedrich Hecker, who led the opposition in Baden, brought many of his followers to Illinois. Hecker established a home in St. Clair County where he participated in antislavery politics and through the turnverein movement propagated an interest in the music and sports of the homeland. In Chicago both the Germans and the Irish organized societies to protect new arrivals and help them find roofs.

Predominantly laborers, the Irish mostly went to work in the East, but contractors sent for them to help build the West.[7] They were willing to move from job to job, but some settled in Will and La Salle counties, where canal workers who were paid with depreciated scrip used it to buy farms. Others followed the paymasters into other states or went into the towns where manufacturing plants were beginning to spring up. By 1860 there were four times as many Irish in Chicago as in the rest of the state. Uprooted by the economic distress of their homeland, the Irish in their American absorption aroused anti-Catholic and nativism prejudices.

The Scandinavians tended to bypass the cities and push on toward frontier farms. Along the Fox River some twelve miles northeast of Ottawa, Cleng Peerson in 1834 founded the first Norwegian settlement in the Midwest and the second in the nation. Near the present town of Norway he brought six families to make homes on land he had purchased the year before. Peerson escorted larger Norwegian groups there in 1838 and 1842. A former sailor, he still had the wanderlust, but his community

---

[7] Pooley, *op. cit.*, pp. 499-501.

prospered and from it radiated other permanent settlements of his countrymen.

The first Swedes came to Illinois as a result of religious persecution. Starting in 1846, they began an exodus under the leadership of Eric Janson, an ecclesiastical leader who insisted that the Bible must be used to the exclusion of all other books.[8] He abandoned the Lutheran Church and brought some fifteen hundred adherents to the Bishop Hill colony in Henry County. Their communal existence began with privation, sickness, and suffering in dugouts and log houses. In the food shortage of the first winter, fasting became mandatory. Whether the Swedes were happy at Bishop Hill is not clear, but by 1850 Janson had established his dynamic leadership by acquiring land, building homes and a church, and setting up a sawmill. The murder of Janson, who was attempting to prevent a woman follower from leaving Bishop Hill with her husband, preceded the incorporation of the colony in 1853 and the internal quarrels that led to its dissolution in 1860. The Jansonists, who in time became Methodists, spread into Knox County, and other Swedes came into northern Illinois or stopped at Chicago. Lars Paul Esbjorn, leader of a group of 146 emigrants in 1849, founded the Swedish Lutheran Church in the United States. Tuve Nilsson Hasselquist, who in 1852 became pastor of a Galesburg church, three years later founded a religious and political newpaper there, and in 1863 began a long career as professor of theology and manager of Augustana College, which he moved from Paxton to Chicago to Rock Island.

Among the foreign groups which prospered through hard work were two colonies of Portuguese, Protestant exiles from the island of Maderia, who settled at Springfield and Jacksonville starting in 1849.

Father Charles Chiniquy, a priest who quarreled with his Roman Catholic superiors, after 1851 wrote articles to Canadian newpapers about the attractions of the Kankakee River country where François Bourbonnais, a partner of Hubbard, had founded a trading post. French-Canadians began a migration of such volume that their government spread stories about health hazards in Illinois. Kankakee County thus took on a French flavor around

---

8 Olov Isaksson and Soren Hallgren, *Bishop Hill: Svensk Koloni pa Prairien/Bishop Hill, Illinois: A Utopia on the Prairie.* Theodore J. Anderson (compiler), *100 Years: A History of Bishop Hill, Illinois.* Kendric C. Babcock, *The Scandinavian Element in the United States.*

Bourbonnais, Kankakee, St. Anne, Momence, and Manteno. Chiniquy, involved in a new challenge to the Catholic hierarchy, led one thousand communicants from a French parish and set up a Presbyterian congregation at St. Anne. Immigrants from France opened stores and a hotel in Chicago and formed communities downstate, including the post-Mormon colony at Nauvoo. E. E. Malhoit, a Louisiana sugar planter, went broke when he overextended his finances backing a French-Canadian settlement at Assumption after the Illinois Central railroad began service.[9]

Despite the Birkbeck-Flowers example, British emigrants had difficulty in adapting to the Illinois prairies; the Scotch, however, were more successful. A Polish group received a land grant on the Fox River near Rockford but did not settle there.[10]

Not all of the newcomers stayed in Illinois. Single men and families who had lived in the state helped settle Kansas and Nebraska, joined the gold rush to California, followed the wagon ruts of the Oregon Trail, and sought land on the Iowa prairies. In 1854, on a trail near Peoria, 1,743 wagons headed for Iowa were reported in one month, and the *Rock Islander* the next year said hundreds of wagons were crossing the Mississippi. Since the 1830's thousands left Illinois at Andalusia, downstream from Rock Island, where Clark's Ferry had been one of the best-known river crossings above St. Louis.

Sometimes the western migrations ended tragically. In the spring of 1846, George Donner assembled a California-bound wagon party at the Springfield square. Attempting to find a new trail through the Sierras, they were trapped in heavy snow. Some forty-two died in an ordeal during which some of the forty-eight survivors resorted to cannibalism.

[9] Charles B. Campbell, "Bourbonnais, or the Early French Settlements in Kankakee County," *Transactions of the Illinois State Historical Society*, XI (1906), 65-72.

[10] Grant Foreman, "English Settlers in Illinois," *Journal of the Illinois State Historical Society*, XXXIV (Sept., 1941), 303-333.

11

FISCAL HONOR

Incongruously cast for a strong role in the shaping of Illinois, Thomas Ford became governor by accident. Born in poverty, limited in education, a failure in business, but finally a success as a lawyer, he bore some resemblance to Abraham Lincoln. By contrast he was scarcely five and a half feet tall, and an indifferent speaker. Obscurely born in Pennsylvania of Irish parentage, Ford spent years advancing in Democratic recognition. As a jurist he showed superior talent; had he stayed on the bench he might have had a career as long and honored as those of Pope and Breese.

The Whigs in 1842 made one last hard try for the governorship by running Joseph Duncan a second time. Adam W. Snyder, who had been nominated by a Democratic convention, died less than three months before the election. Drafted to fill the vacancy, Ford resigned from the Supreme Court. As chief qualifications, he came from the North and had kept out of controversies, including the gathering storm over Mormonism. The disunited Whigs lacked time to mount a campaign against a new opponent, and Ford won the election by 7,487 votes, at the time a record for Illinois.

Ford's great contribution was the preservation of the fiscal honor of Illinois. He is best known, however, for a history of Illinois covering the period from statehood to 1847. Ford wrote it

227

shortly before his death in an effort to provide funds for his family.[1]

ILLINOIS PAYS ITS DEBTS

Governor Ford, who was destined to die penniless, understood both the enormity of the state's debt, which he computed at $15,187,348, and the necessity of preserving the honor of Illinois. As a first step, he cut the state's ties to the two banks, and twice in the late winter of 1843 the members of the legislature gathered in front of the state house to watch the governor burn bonds and certificates aggregating $2,575,246. As one of a series of debt-reducing measures, they had been obtained from the State Bank and the Bank of Illinois in a trade for the stock bought by the state eight years earlier. Divorced from the state, the banks were soon liquidated.

Under the circumstances, the state had no immediate means of meeting the interest payments, let alone paying the debt that had accumulated since the first bank experiment. Many believed that repudiation was inevitable. Under Ford's leadership, however, the legislature by resolution recognized that the state had a moral and legal obligation to pay every cent contracted by its authorized agents. Officials pledged that Illinois would use its revenue and resources as soon as they could be made available without oppressing the people. Among retrenchment steps, the governor became ex officio fund commissioner with authority to accept depreciated state bonds in payment of lands and property.

Ford considered it essential to complete the Illinois and Michigan Canal and, over the objections of southern counties, made it a Democratic program. The legislature authorized the governor to borrow 1.6 million dollars by putting up the canal property—230,476 acres along the right-of-way and 3,493 lots in Chicago, Lockport, La Salle, and Ottawa— as collateral.

---

[1] Like Edward Coles and some other governors, Thomas Ford is deserving of full-length biographical treatment. Milo M. Quaife emphasized his ancestry, personal background, and familial tragedy in his introduction to the 1945 Lakeside Classics edition of Ford's *A History of Illinois*. Paul M. Angle combined a book review with sympathetic treatment of the governor in the *Journal of the Illinois State Historical Society*, XXXVIII (March, 1945), 99-104. Charles Manfred Thompson dealt with the political and governmental issues in a special introduction to the *Governors' Letter-Books, 1840-1853*, pp. xxix-cxviii.

Courtesy Illinois State Historical Library

Governor Thomas Ford

British bondholders refused to make further loans unless the state would tax itself to pay part of the accruing interest. The governor promoted the cause with a letter, widely reprinted in newspapers, saying that the only alternative to repudiation was taxation, starting at a low rate and progressively increasing as the people could bear the load. The solution, worked out during the 1845 legislative session, required a one-mill tax on each dollar valuation of property. It was achieved by canceling a similar levy which the state since 1827 had distributed to the counties for their debt reduction and for construction of courthouses and jails. The canal tax was increased to one and a half mills in 1846, with proceeds going into an interest fund from which the governor made semiannual pro rata payments on all canal and internal

improvements bonds. Illinois meanwhile surrendered temporarily
its control over the canal property. A new board of trustees, with
two of the three members appointed by the bondholders, then
finished the construction, while Ford raised money by selling the
Northern Cross line and four hundred tons of iron rail shipped
from England for never completed railroads. The policy of non-
repudiation was followed by the next governor, Augustus C.
French, who pushed debt-refunding steps through the legislature,
and by delegates to an 1847 constitutional convention, who provided for a mandatory two-mill levy to be applied to the debt.
The greatest financial help, however, resulted from the general
prosperity that arrived with an era of privately operated railroads
during the decade before the Civil War.[2]

A financial scandal in 1859 involved Joel A. Matteson, who
succeeded French as governor in 1853, and $223,000 of the
unused twenty-year-old canal scrip.[3] Uninventoried and un-
canceled as a result of slipshod business practices, the scrip had
been shipped to Springfield by Matteson when he was governor.
Later it was exchanged for new state bonds as part of the re-
funding operations. When the transaction was discovered, Matteson, a rich contractor, claimed he had innocently bought the
bonds, but he never attempted to prove it. A senate committee
dropped an investigation when the former governor voluntarily
made restitution for the state's loss. Another political uproar in
1859 grew out of an attempt to refund at face value $114,000 of
the controversial 1847 bonds, which came into the possession of
the Macalister and Stebbins financial house in New York. At the
last minute, the transaction was blocked. The state computed at
twenty-six cents on the dollar its liability in the bond involvement
and paid off on that percentage.

Full interest payments began by 1857. After 1859, the growing
and comparatively prosperous state had no difficulty in meeting
its debts. In 1880, more than four decades after repudiation
seemed inevitable, a later governor called in the last bonds. By
comparison with some other states, the record of Illinois was
commendable. Ohio with a comparable debt did not make its final

---

[2] John H. Krenkel, *Illinois Internal Improvements*, pp. 177, 199. Ford, *op. cit.*, pp.
370-402. Arthur C. Cole, *The Era of the Civil War*, p. 91. Gustave Koerner, *Memoirs*, I,
477-478. Alexander Davidson and Bernard Stuvé, *A Complete History of Illinois*, pp.
466-473. Theodore C. Pease, *The Frontier State*, pp. 316-326.

[3] Davidson-Stuvé, *op. cit.*, pp. 668-678.

payment until 1902. Indiana, Michigan, and Pennsylvania repudiated part of their internal improvements obligations.

WAR WITH MEXICO AND NEW HEROES

The adventure of war with Mexico diverted the attention of the West from hard times. Joining in the expansionist mood, the Illinois legislature sided with the slave states and memorialized Congress for the annexation of Texas. Abraham Lincoln, the only Whig elected to Congress in 1846, took an antiwar stand and suffered politically.

In a warm-up for the larger war fifteen years later, Governor Ford found that volunteers exceeded the call for troops. When President Polk asked that Illinois provide three regiments, enough companies responded for nine. Edward D. Baker, Lincoln's friend and predecessor in Congress, became a colonel by getting authorization for a fourth regiment. At Alton the men mobilized, elected captains and colonels, and drilled while waiting to be loaded into steamboats for a trip down the Mississippi and into the Gulf of Mexico.

In two major battles, Illinois troops performed with honor. At Buena Vista, in northern Mexico, two regiments were among 4,500 men under Zachary Taylor who fought a bloody two-day defensive battle against Santa Anna's twenty thousand Mexicans. Colonel John J. Hardin, who with Lincoln and Baker provided Whig leadership at Springfield, was killed just before the enemy withdrew.[4] James Shields of Springfield, who had resigned as commissioner of the general land office at Washington to become a brigadier general of the volunteers, with the other two regiments helped capture the Cerro Gordo mountain pass. Before the fall of the Mexican capital, the four regiments had completed their year's enlistment and been sent home. Two more Illinois regiments missed battlefield action.

New political careers began when the men returned, and many used military service as a springboard for seeking public office. Colonel William H. Bissell of Belleville, who commanded a regiment at Buena Vista, easily won Democratic election to Congress.

[4] David Lavender, *Climax at Buena Vista: The American Campaigns in Northeastern Mexico, 1846-47*. John Moses, *Illinois Historical and Statistical*, I, 489-501. Pease, *op. cit.*, pp. 400-406. Davidson-Stuvé, *op. cit.*, pp. 522-542.

A severe wound at Cerro Gordo made Shields an even greater hero and Senator Sidney Breese a political casualty. When Shields' election to the senate was voided because he had not been a citizen the required number of years, he resigned, waited a year for unquestioned eligibility, and was elected again.[5]

Stephen A. Douglas, an ambitious and audacious pioneer in the field of political organization, reached the United States senate in 1847 and defended the war. In less than three decades, eleven Illinois men had preceded him in the senate, but only Jesse B. Thomas completed two full terms. Death, ineptitude, or political misfortune had cut short the careers of others. Now for the first time Illinois had a man of national stature in the senate.

Consistent losers in state elections, the Whigs preferred to let party leaders select candidates and were slow to adopt the Democratic practice of nominations by party conventions, which Joseph Duncan considered despotic.

A SECOND CONSTITUTION

The frontier-era constitution of 1818, unsatisfactory chiefly because of a concentration of power in the hands of the legislature, lasted three decades. Demand for its replacement came from many quarters: Jacksonian Democrats were anxious to end the life terms of Supreme Court justices, they opposed banks, and they wanted the governor to have an effective veto power. The Whigs desired to stop voting by aliens, and the belief became widespread that the rapid development of Illinois made a revision advisable. After a failure by a narrow margin in 1842, a convention proposal carried with 72 percent of the vote in 1846, the year a Yankee for the first time occupied the governor's office. The next summer an unwieldy assemblage of 162 delegates sat from June 7 to August 31 and produced a bulky set of compromises three times the length of the original document.[6]

The new constitution corrected some of the faults of its predecessor, but it also proved to be imperfect. Sweeping in its

[5] Later he served short terms as United States senator from Minnesota and Missouri. Francis O'Shaughnessy, "General James Shields of Illinois," *Transactions of the Illinois State Historical Society,* XXI (1915), 113-122.

[6] Janet Cornelius, *A History of Constitution Making in Illinois,* pp. 19-31. Emil J. Verlie, *Illinois Constitutions,* pp. 51-99. Willard L. King, *Lincoln's Manager, David Davis,* pp. 55-56. Arthur C. Cole (ed.), *The Constitutional Debates of 1847.*

reorganization and acceptance of new concepts, it made many changes. Not all were to the liking of the majority, since Whigs had elected a strong minority of seventy-one and carried important roll calls in a coalition with conservative Democrats. As the chief difference, the power of the legislature was curbed and provision made for election of all state and county officials. To prevent the legislature from packing the Supreme Court again, the delegates said that the justices, reduced in number to three, must be elected for nine-year terms from geographical divisions or districts. Popular election of Supreme Court clerks also dates from the 1848 constitution. The council of revision was abolished in an elimination of another court function, but the governor received only a limited veto power, which could be overridden by a bare majority of the legislative houses.

The length of legislative sessions was curtailed by a provision that after forty-two days legislators' pay would be reduced from two dollars a day to one dollar. No longer could the lawmakers plunge the state into debt through grandiose public works and banking schemes; only by referendum approval of a specific law could the legislature contract debts in excess of fifty thousand dollars. Another provision made it impossible to grant the state's credit to any corporation or association. An effort was made to prevent the legislature from establishing corporations, but the new constitution said special charters could be granted when in the judgment of the assembly a general law would not apply. That loophole was used hundreds of times in the next two decades.

The biggest arguments involved banking. Whigs wanted to incorporate provisions which would be favorable to the organization of banks, and Democratic opposition had softened. The final compromise prohibited state banks but permitted the legislature to establish corporations with banking powers, provided that the law was approved by the voters at the next election.

The Whig-conservative coalition insisted that only citizens could vote, and triumphed over a Democratic effort to continue the 1818 provision under which white male inhabitants of twenty-one and over could vote. The proposal of a northern Illinois delegate who wanted to extend the right of suffrage to Negroes was defeated, 137 to 7. The new constitution again provided that a property tax should support the state government, but Whigs added a requirement for a poll tax, from fifty cents to a dollar, to be paid by all between the ages of twenty-one and sixty who were eligible to vote. Its intent was to require that nonproperty owners bear part of the tax burden. In a time of big debt and strict economy, the new constitution fixed official salaries at parsimonious levels. The salary scale ranged downward from fifteen hundred dollars a year for the governor and twelve hundred dollars for Supreme Court justices and provided only eight hundred dollars for the secretary of state and state treasurer.

The amending process was relaxed to allow proposed changes to be submitted to the electorate by the legislature without calling a convention. Township government, favored by new settlers with Yankee backgrounds, was authorized as an alternative to the southern system of county commissioner control of local affairs.

Democrats were unhappy because the Whig-conservative coalition had carried most of the disputed points, but they did not try to campaign against the new constitution, which had strong newspaper support. More than three-fourths of the voters ratified it March 6, 1848.

Almost simultaneously, Wisconsin adopted its first state constitution, and upon admission to the Union in 1848 conceded at last that the northern boundary of Illinois would remain where Nathaniel Pope had set it thirty years earlier.[7] In the far northern and northwestern counties, residents had long complained of official neglect and more recently of the immense public debt facing the people of Illinois. A solution would be to transfer allegiance and join the Territory of Wisconsin, which lacked sufficient population of its own, in forming a new state. As early as 1838 Wisconsin officials in a petition to Congress claimed without success that Pope's amendment to the 1818 statehood law, which put fourteen counties in Illinois, was a violation of the Ordinance of 1787. At a suggestion from Wisconsin officials, delegates from nine counties—Jo Daviess, Stephenson, Winnebago, Boone, Mc-Henry, Carroll, Ogle, Whiteside, and Rock Island—held a convention in Rockford and asserted that they legally and rightfully belonged in Wisconsin. In a referendum that followed, Cook County refused to participate, but elsewhere the vote was surprisingly one-sided in favor of leaving Illinois. Governor Carlin

7 Moses M. Strong, *History of the Territory of Wisconsin*, pp. 312-314. Milo M Quaife, *The Movement for Statehood, 1845-46*. William Radebaugh, *The Boundary Dispute Between Illinois and Wisconsin*. Moses, *op. cit.*, I, 278-282. John F. Snyder, *Adam W. Snyder in Illinois History*, pp. 414-417. Cecil K. Byrd, *Bibliography of Illinois Imprints*, p. 119.

ignored an official notice that the territorial governor of Wisconsin considered the fourteen counties to be under the "accidental and temporary" jurisdiction of Illinois. The effort to get support included an unofficial offer of a United States senatorship to one of Chicago's prominent citizens. Wisconsin voters meanwhile lined up on the side of those who believed they couldn't afford statehood until more settlers arrived. By the time the canal had been built to Chicago and telegraph service inaugurated, northern Illinois residents were satisfied to keep the northern boundary at the 42° 30′ line.

Augustus C. French, a new Hampshire-born lawyer of moderate abilities, was picked for governor by the 1846 Democratic state convention when better-known candidates dropped out to keep the nomination from going to Lyman Trumbull. Ford says that French had been a member of an unofficial company of "regulators" who enforced law and order in Edgar County by whipping and expelling horse thieves and other brigands. Lawlessness was common in the new country, and similar citizen action against rural gangsters became necessary in several other parts of the state in the 1840's. While Governor Ford was preoccupied with anti-Mormon violence in Hancock County in 1846, he considered use of the militia in Massac County where regulators, who considered that they had adequate provocation, had driven out the sheriff and other officials. At the other end of the state, in Ogle and DeKalb counties settlers took the law in their own hands to get rid of a criminal gang that had killed the captain of a vigilante group. Other regulators then rounded up and shot two members of the gang.[8]

French consented that the new constitution should end his term of office at two years so that state elections could coincide with presidential balloting. In 1848 he won a second term, for a full four years, without real opposition from the badly split Whigs. He became the first Illinois governor to be reelected and the only Democrat to win that honor in the first century of statehood.

Joel A. Matteson, a Yankee with a moneymaking talent, succeeded French, built a large woolen mill, and became president of the railroad from Chicago to Alton, as the Democrats in 1852

[8] Robert H. Jones, "Three Days of Violence: The Regulators of the Rock River Valley," *Journal of the Illinois State Historical Society*, LIX (Summer, 1966), 131-142. Moses, *op. cit.*, I, 512-514. James A. Rose, "The Regulators and Flatheads in Southern Illinois," *Transactions of the Illinois State Historical Society*, XI (1906), 108-121.

elected their last governor in forty years. He had not been a partisan, and his nomination showed the growing strength of the northern Illinois men who held moderate views on the slavery and banking controversies.

12

THE ARRIVAL OF THE RAILROADS

A PROVINCIAL STATE POLICY WHICH ADVOCATED THAT ILlinois do nothing to build up cities outside its borders caused trouble at the opening of the railroad era. Its proponents preached that it would be wise for the state to concentrate on opening up its own unsettled areas and especially to show favoritism to its cities. Anything that did not promote those ends was to be opposed. State policy theorists approved the Illinois and Michigan Canal, since it was entirely within the state, but frowned on suggestions for a joint canal project with Indiana. They did not want railroads to help such cities as Terre Haute and Vincennes, on the Indiana side of the Wabash River, and most of all they wanted to build up Alton as a rival of St. Louis. The businessmen of Alton conspired to have all railroads from the East converge on their city so that it could become a great metropolis and overshadow St. Louis, which was some twenty-three miles downstream by Mississippi River packet boat. Over the objection of Governors French and Matteson and other important men, including Stephen A. Douglas, state policy prevailed in the legislature five years, long enough to handicap St. Louis while Chicago achieved economic supremacy in the western region.[1]

---

[1] Theodore C. Pease, *The Story of Illinois,* p. 134. John Moses, *Illinois Historical and Statistical,* II, 566-567. Alexander Davidson and Bernard Stuvé, *A Complete History of Illinois,* pp. 562-570.

St. Louis mistakenly assumed that midcontinental commerce would continue to run on north-south lines and that the new railroads would automatically converge upon it.[2] Much of Illinois was in its economic orbit; more than half of the agricultural trade of St. Louis was drawn from Illinois, and Illinois merchants bought nearly three-fourths of the merchandise from St. Louis wholesale houses. The city's position seemed so strong that in 1849 the Missouri legislature levied a tax of $4.50 on every thousand dollars' worth of merchandise grown, produced, or manufactured elsewhere. The intent was to have other states— Iowa and Minnesota as well as Illinois—pay the expenses of Missouri's state government. The tax, which soon was held unconstitutional, boomeranged by helping stir up Illinois opposition to the chartering of railroads to St. Louis.

Chicago ignored economic fallacies about trade stopping at state lines. Its business leaders welcomed the arrival of railroads from the East and promoted their own lines into Iowa and Wisconsin. As a result of the east-west axis developed by the Erie Canal, Chicago had an economic partner in New York City, which reached westward for the profits that went with the settlement of the Old Northwest. As a result, New York outdistanced its rivals of Boston, Philadelphia, and Baltimore. Equally important to Chicago was Lake Michigan. It served not only as a water route to and from Chicago, but it was a 320-mile barrier that forced railroads and wagons to go around its southern end. Chicago had the only good harbor at the end of the lake and inevitably became the rail center for lines from the East. When the time came to develop Wisconsin, Iowa, and the regions beyond, many of the settlers came through Chicago and much of their produce returned to it. Milwaukee and other competitors never overcame the early advantage that Chicago achieved through geography and an aggressive economic policy.

A WATER ROUTE ACROSS THE CHICAGO PORTAGE

The Illinois and Michigan Canal, connecting the Great Lakes with a major tributary of the Mississippi River, opened April 23, 1848, with a boom along its towpath that justified the optimism

---

[2] W. W. Belcher, *The Economic Rivalry Between St. Louis and Chicago, 1850-1880*, pp. 18-50, 72-89, 125-127.

of Louis Jolliet nearly two centuries earlier. By July seventy boats hauled cargo and passengers between La Salle and Bridgeport. More were needed, and by the end of the first 180-day navigation season 162 boats paid $87,890 in tolls. The canal, for which the federal government had donated nearly a half-million acres of

Courtesy Illinois State Historical Library

Illinois and Michigan canal barges in La Salle basin awaiting opening of 1865 navigation season

land, had cost nearly six and a half million dollars and taken twelve years to build with crude tools and black powder, but it was worth it to northern and central Illinois in the brief interval before the railroads arrived.[3] So great was the canal's help in developing northern Illinois that, of all man-made waterways in North America, only the Erie Canal surpassed it in importance.

[3] James W. Putnam, *The Illinois and Michigan Canal, A Study in Economic History.* John G. Clark, *The Grain Trade in the Old Northwest,* pp. 22-29, 81-101, 145-156. Leslie C. Swanson, *Canals of Mid-America,* pp. 36-40. Louis B. Schmidt, "The Internal Grain Trade of the United States," *Iowa Journal of History and Politics,* I (Jan., 1928), pp. 94-124. Walter A. Howe, *Documentary History of the Illinois and Michigan Canal.*

Chicago now was more than a lake port. It had an inland water route and anyone with access to a river could ship to and buy from Chicagoans. Grain grown along the Illinois and upper Mississippi rivers could be shipped to market by way of the canal and Great Lakes at less cost than by way of New Orleans. Merchandise from the East appeared on the shelves of stores along the Illinois River. Lumber from Michigan and Wisconsin came down the canal to replace log cabins and build new towns. Chicago received pork from such packing centers as Beardstown as well as goods from New Orleans.

The canal, sixty feet wide at the water line, went through seventeen locks and under twenty-five bridges. Its boats exchanged cargoes with river steamers at La Salle. Peru also prospered, as did Ottawa, Du Page, Joliet, and Lockport, which had special basins for discharging and taking on freight. The first horse-drawn canal boats—narrow, rounded, and long—resembled keelboats, but wider, flatter, and blunt-ended craft replaced them. The regular or line boats offered narrow shelves for bunks and also sold deck space to immigrating families, but supplied neither food nor bedding. Established lines traveled about two and a half miles an hour, but the time was a mile or so faster for the luxury or packet boats. The "Queen of the Prairies" made the trip to La Salle in the unusually fast time of twenty hours while ninety passengers lived, ate, and slept in a fifty-by-nine-foot cabin with a seven-foot ceiling.[4] Especially in the deep mud of the rainy season, canal packets and the connecting river steamers proved more reliable and comfortable than stagecoaches, which had no competition in winter. In the drought of 1853, shallow water proved a handicap, but toll revenues increased steadily each year as more boats went into service.

The opening of the canal coincided with a row between Illinois and St. Louis. The trouble started when the Missouri city, which sought to protect its harbor from sandbars, neglected to obtain Illinois consent for a dike across the Mississippi's eastern channel at Bloody Island, which now is part of the East St. Louis mainland. Complaints arose that cities as far away as Quincy would be flooded, and Governor French joined in the bellicose mood by threatening to call out the militia. The 1848 legislature agreed to a peace formula, and the dike, as it turned out, benefited all parties,

4 M. M. Quaife, *Chicago's Highways Old and New*, pp. 85-86.

but the controversy demonstrated that important Illinois interests were jealous of St. Louis.[5]

On his first visit to Chicago, Congressman Abraham Lincoln mingled with more than six thousand persons from eighteen of the twenty-nine states at a three-day harbor and rivers convention opening July 4, 1847.[6] Horace Greeley, Thurlow Weed, and Millard Fillmore were among eastern delegates who protested that President Polk had vetoed an appropriation for navigational improvements. Speakers insisted that, regardless of Jackson's old teachings, Congress had constitutional authority to improve the Great Lakes and river routes of national importance. Resolutions asserted that the interior of the nation had not received its share of appropriations to improve harbors and navigable rivers. Four years later delegates from northwestern Illinois at a Peoria convention asked for federal aid in removing obstacles in the Illinois River.

The telegraph reached Illinois ahead of the railroads, and by 1850 many Illinois towns received erratic service on wires strung from tree to tree.[7] The first telegram in Chicago was received in 1848, four years after the first line was opened between Washington and Baltimore. The telegraph was immediately popular, and extension of lines went ahead despite primitive equipment, fierce competition, and difficult financing. On the spur of the moment stockholders of the Illinois and Mississippi Telegraph Company asked John Dean Caton, an Illinois Supreme Court justice, to preside at a meeting in Ottawa, where he was holding court. Caton, while still on the bench, became the line's largest stockholder and president. He learned the Morse code and built more lines, which became a major part of the Western Union system. The telegraph speeded up market reports and business transactions while enabling newspapers to print dispatches from the outside world several days earlier than before.

AT LAST, A TRANSPORTATION SYSTEM

The era of railroads built and operated by private corporations rather than by a state agency reached Illinois in 1848. Almost in

[5] Moses, *op. cit.*, II, 565-566. Davidson-Stuvé, *op. cit.*, pp. 558-561.

[6] John Moses and Joseph Kirkland, *History of Chicago*, I, 109-111. A. T. Andreas, *History of Chicago*. Donald W. Riddle, *Lincoln Runs for Congress*, p. 172.

[7] R. L. Thompson, *Wiring a Continent*, pp. 91-134, 203-293. Arthur C. Cole, *Era of the Civil War*, p. 31.

epidemic fashion, rail promotions spread across the prairie, and by the end of 1855 Illinois had 2,005 miles of track, more than any other western state. No longer a frontier town, Chicago became the railroad center and eventually the commercial giant of the West. By 1857 eleven main lines of track radiated from the city. Their 3,953 miles of direct connections brought to the city immense quantities of pork, beef, and grain and hauled from it trainloads of merchandise and lumber. The railroads from the East brought immigrants; some stayed in Chicago, but lines through Illinois took the others to the hinterland to build up the city's expanding trade territory.[8]

Geography made it inevitable that Chicago would be a transportation center, but the city's aggressive and far-sighted business leaders made the most of the natural advantages. Many men helped finance, construct, and operate the rail lines, but a big share of credit for Chicago's growth goes to William B. Ogden, whose real estate investments had recouped the fortune he lost in the 1837 panic. An imposing man, Ogden insisted that Chicagoans honor their business obligations so as to insure the continued goodwill of the outcountry traders and the credit sources in New York. Ogden and his colleagues believed in getting rich quickly, and many of them accomplished it while their city and state benefited. Their careers set the pattern for the corporate giants who would come under muckraking attack in another generation, and simultaneously they established the tradition of civic enthusiasm and progressiveness which became the city's boast.

Railroads were promoted and constructed almost simultaneously. The first successful railroad in Illinois ran westward from Chicago under the guidance of Ogden. He acquired the dormant 1836 charter for a railroad to the lead mines, the Galena and Chicago Union, whose name showed the comparative early importance of the two towns. Eastern lines were stretching toward Illinois, especially the Michigan Central and the Michigan Southern, which had been sold to eastern capitalists after a failure of state ownership. The new owners refused to help Ogden finance his line, explaining frankly that they expected to pick it up at a bargain rate after the local promotion failed. Ogden circumvented them by selling stock to farmers who were anxious for access to a grain and livestock market. In the autumn of 1848 the *Pioneer,* a

8 Harold M. Mayer, *The Railway Pattern of Metropolitan Chicago.*

secondhand locomotive which had arrived on a lake steamer, made its first five-mile run on strap-iron rails. The tracks reached Elgin in 1850, Belvidere in 1852, and Freeport in 1853. There the Galena and Chicago Union stopped at a connection with the Illinois Central, which already had reached Galena. Ogden's railroad quickly returned big dividends, averaging 16 percent between 1850 and 1855. Soon moneyed men on the seaboard volunteered to help finance other lines in Illinois.[9]

Senator Douglas moved to Chicago in 1847 and invested heavily in strategically located real estate. As part of his efforts to push the frontier westward, the senator wanted a railroad to the Pacific coast, but he wanted it located so that traffic would be brought to Chicago. No one expected that there would be more than one transcontinental line, and at Washington Douglas blocked the southern dream of a Pacific road connecting with New Orleans or Memphis. After his death, when the Civil War canceled southern opposition, Congress subsidized the Union Pacific line westward from Omaha, which was what Douglas wanted. The Union Pacific's route ended the hopes of St. Louis for midwestern economic domination.

Of more importance, Douglas revived the projected Illinois Central railroad northward from Cairo, which had been a key part of the 1837 system. Trains would be faster than steamers, at least on the northbound trips, and would permit all-year transportation without suspension of service in the frozen months. Also a rail line from Cairo to Galena, which the early promoters regarded as the main line, would bypass St. Louis. Senator Sidney Breese and other politicians had invested in the Cairo City and Canal Company. Darius B. Holbrook of Boston, its promoter, lobbied at Springfield and Washington for a land grant for a road to Cairo, and Breese urged unsuccessfully that the Illinois Central be given the right to preempt the land it needed.[10]

When he reached the senate, Douglas took over the campaign in

[9] Belcher, *op. cit.*, pp. 56-58, 128-129, 258-274.

[10] Carlton J. Corliss, *Main Line to Mid-America: The Story of the Illinois Central.* Cole, *op. cit.*, pp. 36-42. Howard G. Bronson, "Early Illinois Railroads: The Place of the Illinois Central in Illinois History Prior to the Civil War," *Transactions of the Illinois State Historical Society*, XIII (1908), 171-183. Moses, *op. cit.*, II, 574-581. Davidson-Stuvé, *op. cit.*, pp. 571-584. Paul W. Gates, "The Struggle Over the Charter of the Illinois Central Railroad," *Transactions of the Illinois State Historical Society*, XL (1933), 55-66. W. H. Perrin, *History of Alexander, Union and Pulaski Counties*, pp. 82-110. John M. Lansden, *A History of the City of Cairo.*

revised form. Disinterested in Cairo, he stressed that a terminal at Chicago would be more important than a line to Galena. No railroad had ever received a federal grant, however, and Douglas faced strong opposition. After one failure, he broadened his bill to provide land grants in Mississippi and Alabama so that the central railroad could be extended to the Gulf of Mexico at Mobile. That brought in southern support, and he appeased states' righters by providing that the land would be granted directly to the states, which then could transfer it to railroad companies. Enacted in 1850, it gave 2.595 million acres to Illinois to be used in financing a road from Cairo to Dunleith (East Dubuque), with a branch to Chicago. The grant covered alternate even-numbered sections on each side of the road for six miles. The odd-numbered sections would be held by the government for double the usual $1.25 price which, Douglas contended, meant that the government actually would not lose any money. To avoid a forfeit, the work had to be completed in ten years.

The 1851 legislature encountered competitive bidding for charters for railroads, ferries, plank roads, insurance companies, and mines. Holbrook wanted the land grant for his Cairo company. Spokesmen for holders of state bonds proposed that they be allowed to build the railroad. Towns in midstate lobbied for places on the right-of-way. The big prize finally went to an eastern group which owned the Michigan Central and was seeking a charter for a road in northern Illinois. In their behalf Robert Rantoul of Massachusetts promised to give the state 7 percent of the gross receipts from the main line and the branch, which would be a major source of state tax revenue.

Decisions as to the route had been left to the company, and the so-called branch line to Chicago started at a new town named Centralia. The branch became all-important as Colonel Roswell B. Mason, one of the nation's best-known railroad builders, brought a staff from New York and sent surveying parties into areas which had been avoided by settlers.

Building the 705.5-mile railroad, the world's longest, was a bigger public works project than digging the Erie Canal. In a time of labor shortage Illinois Central contractors hired more than ten thousand men. Some were recruited by labor and immigration agents in New York, and part of the work force came directly from Ireland. The railroad shipped iron from England, opened quarries, and cut into the forests of Michigan, Wisconsin, and southern Illinois. Under a program of rapid and simultaneous construction, the first train from Calumet (Kensington) reached Chicago in 1852 by way of a wooden trestle. Chicago, a city of unpaved streets, plank sidewalks, and a population of forty thousand, lacked money to pay for a breakwater to provide storm protection for lakefront homes. The city council granted a three-hundred-foot right-of-way at the lake's edge, which forced the Illinois Central to build a trestle, and the city with foresight prohibited the erection of buildings between Twelfth and Randolph streets. At the other end of the state, Holbrook's company forced the railroad to build embankments and levees on which trains would run and to pay one hundred thousand dollars for land needed for a station and railroad yards. That money was invested in a large hotel, several mills, and other industrial buildings which failed to bring prosperity to Cairo.

Up and down the state crews laid track, farmers moved onto land which the Illinois Central widely advertised in English and German, and locomotives with sixty-inch drive wheels jerked passenger coaches that lacked vestibules. By September, 1856, the work was finished, and the Illinois Central, twice as long as any other road, became the marvel of the transportation industry, in Europe as well as the United States.

Train service from the East also reached Chicago in 1852. The Michigan Central and Michigan Southern during a great struggle that extended from courtrooms to fisticuffs at trackside crossed Indiana by buying into local companies. The Michigan Central entered Chicago on Illinois Central trackage, since the two roads had interlocking directorates. The Michigan Southern followed as a result of its friendship with the owners of the new Rock Island. The eastern roads then turned their attention to extending their lines, standardizing gauges, and bridging rivers, with the result that Chicago soon had direct connections with seaboard cities. The two roads competed with each other and with lake boats, which enabled northern Illinois to profit from low fares and freight charges. A third eastern line, which in time became the Pennsylvania, began service in 1858 from Pittsburgh.

Twice Chicago's position as the midcontinental freight interchange center was threatened. Richard P. Morgan, who surveyed the Galena and Chicago Union, proposed that it intercept the Michigan Central at New Buffalo, Michigan.[11] Had it been done,

11 Mayer, *op. cit.*, p. 8n.

freight could have been shipped around Chicago, and New Buffalo well could have attracted additional railways and developed as the point of interchange. Fortunately for Chicago, Morgan and his backers failed to acquire an Indiana charter. Later a Joliet Cutoff, which would have saved sixty miles by making it unnecessary for Michigan Central trains to enter Chicago, raised a possibility that some of the city's facilities might be shifted elsewhere. Chicagoans might not practice state policy, but they believed in protecting their own interests, and the cutoff proposal was blocked.

Additional lines spread across northern Illinois. The Rock Island, built at the same time as the Galena and Chicago Union, provided competition along much of the route of the Illinois and Michigan Canal. By 1852 it had the first continuous service to the Mississippi River, 181 miles away. There it established steamer connections with St. Louis and St. Paul and four years later built the first bridge across the river at a narrow point where currents were dangerous. Steamship interests at St. Louis contended that the bridge not only obstructed traffic but was illegal, since it had been authorized by the state but not the federal government. Within a few months a steamer wrecked a pier and the bridge company sued. Abraham Lincoln participated in an inconclusive courtroom contest between railroad and river transportation interests. The Rock Island enlarged Chicago's trade territory by building to the Missouri River in 1869, three years before the federal government replaced the controversial bridge.[12]

Over much of the state and with varying success, local interests raised money to finance railroads of limited mileage. In some cases the promotions preceded the actual need for trains, and in others lack of capital as well as competition for manpower blocked efforts to put together a rail system. Only the Illinois Central had help from the state, but cities and counties were induced to buy bonds from rail promoters and in many cases went into debt to keep projected lines from going to rival communities. Many farmers and other landowners were persuaded to trade mortgages for company bonds. Eastern capitalists, who were not interested in the bonds, then would buy the mortgages.

Some of the locally promoted roads became branch lines. Some became important as a result of consolidations as big city capitalists provided additional financing. An end-to-end amalgamation

---

12 William E. Hayes, *Iron Road to Empire: The Rock Island Lines.*

masterminded by Michigan Central backers helped open western Illinois to settlement. They took over the Military Tract road and other local lines, and filled in the gaps to organize the Chicago, Burlington, and Quincy in 1855. It reached the Mississippi at Quincy and Burlington, Iowa, the next year.[13]

While extending his own lines, Ogden encouraged other railroads and took over management of some of them. Under his presidency the Galena and Chicago Union completed the Dixon Air Line, which in 1855 reached Fulton, 136 miles westward on the Mississippi.[14] The road continued into Iowa, helping with the settlement of that new state, and was the first to reach Council Bluffs and the Missouri River. To divert commerce from Minnesota and part of Wisconsin from Milwaukee, Ogden built the Chicago, St. Paul, and Fond du Lac, which became the nucleus of the Chicago and North Western, the name adopted in 1859. Chicago business firms recovered quickly from the 1857 panic by following Ogden's policy of accepting at par the bills of country banks in Illinois and Wisconsin. As a result the merchants of the smaller towns were able to settle old obligations and open new transactions with their business friends in Chicago.

Other lines tapped Wisconsin. The Chicago and Milwaukee helped develop the north shore with train service, starting in 1856, that encouraged the growth of Evanston and Lake Forest as university communities. Chicago's first suburban service began that year when a real estate developer at Hyde Park, seven miles southward, induced the Illinois Central to operate daily trains to his property by agreeing to pay any deficit.

The first railroad southwest of Chicago dates from 1847 and started from Alton. Captain Benjamin Godfrey, who had sailed the Atlantic as master of a merchantman, built a road to Springfield. At its completion, in the customary celebration Springfield entertained its new customers from Alton and St. Louis with a gala dinner. With a new charter and more capital, the road continued on a straight line, locating stations every ten miles so that new towns could spring up on the prairie. By late 1853 the railroad

[13] R. C. Overton, the railroad's historian, has written three books—*The First 90 Years, An Historical Sketch of the Burlington Railroad; Burlington West: A Colonization History of the Burlington Railroad;* and *Burlington Route: A History of the Burlington Lines.*

[14] Robert J. Casey and W. A. S. Douglas, *Pioneer Railroad: The Story of the Chicago and North Western System.*

reached Bloomington, and for the first time it was possible to travel by rail from the Mississippi to New York, by taking the Chicago and Alton to Bloomington, the Illinois Central to La Salle, and the Chicago and Rock Island to Chicago. On January 1, 1858, the Chicago and Alton ran the first trains on the old Chicago portage route. The line also helped open new farming country and the coal fields south of Joliet and, like other roads, it became a major carrier of grain and livestock.[15] To handle business at the other end of the line, an extra packet boat ran between Alton and St. Louis. Also helping open up the midstate were two east-west lines—the old Great Western, which became the Wabash, and the Peoria and Oquawka, which in time was taken over by the Burlington.

The rail line to Chicago represented a state policy victory for Alton, but a long battle to keep trains away from St. Louis already had been lost. The constitution contained a mandate for a general law that would permit a railroad to incorporate without a special charter, but Alton interests for some time prevailed upon the lawmakers to insist upon the right to dictate terminals and routes. Protests meanwhile came from the southern counties, which wanted rail lines terminating at the Illinoistown ferry station. The opposing factions sponsored railroad conventions and, under pressure, the legislature granted a charter for the Ohio and Mississippi railroad, the important Vincennes-St. Louis route that had connections with Cincinnati and eventually became the Baltimore and Ohio. Alton interests meanwhile rushed construction of their favorite railroad, the Terre Haute and Alton, and until 1854 blocked the Atlantic and Mississippi, which ran from Terre Haute directly to Illinoistown and eventually became part of the Pennsylvania system. Its chartering marked the collapse of the state policy movement. Meanwhile a joker inserted in a bill by Lieutenant Governor Gustave Koerner had chartered a road between Alton and the ferry, which meant that after 1856 Alton was only a way stop on the railroads it promoted. The line from Vincennes to St. Louis was completed in 1857 but had financial and operating troubles. The Terre Haute and Alton had been finished a year earlier, but trains did not run on the Atlantic and Mississippi until the next decade. The result was that, except for the Illinois

15 D. W. Yungmeyer, "An Excursion Into the Early History of the Chicago and Alton Railroad," *Journal of the Illinois State Historical Society*, XXXVIII (March, 1945), 7-37.

Central, railroad development lagged in southern Illinois. St. Louis interests were even slower in getting railroads started in Missouri.

With eleven trunk lines, Chicago by 1860 was the American railroad center. In a decade Illinois mileage increased from 110 to 2,867, more than any other state except Ohio. New branches and extensions connected Chicago with distant states. The effects were widespread. Steamboats and the canal lost business but provided competition that kept rail fares at reasonable levels. Stage lines shut down, since the trip between Springfield and Chicago had been shortened from three days and nights to twelve hours. Passenger fares were mostly three cents a mile or less. Livestock straying onto tracks caused accidents, and other complaints involved crowded and often dirty coaches that were lighted by candles and warmed only by box stoves. In 1858 George M. Pullman rebuilt two Chicago and Alton coaches into sleeping cars. The first dining car service also began on the Chicago-St. Louis line during the Civil War. Railway mail service was inaugurated with immediate success on a run between Chicago and Clinton, Iowa, in 1864.

EARLY COAL MINING

When the time came to build railroads, most of the original timber had been chopped away and the state needed a new supply of fuel. Wisconsin and Michigan had seemingly limitless forests, but wood was not suitable for boilers and, besides, it was needed for the construction of houses, stores, and other buildings that must be erected if Illinois outgrew the log cabin years. To make possible the development of railroads and factories, the state turned to the thick beds of bituminous coal under most of its surface.[16]

Some of the first rail shipments of coal were from Ottawa and Utica, where Jolliet and Marquette reported seeing "charbon de terre" in 1673 and Hennepin in 1682 "found in Several Places Some Pit-Coal." Those were the first discoveries of bituminous on the North American continent. Commercial mining began about 1810 in Jackson County when several barges of coal were shipped from the Big Muddy River to New Orleans. Stone coal, used by blacksmiths and for domestic heating, was welcomed when timber

[16] J. P. Goode, *The Geographic Background of Chicago*, pp. 9-15.

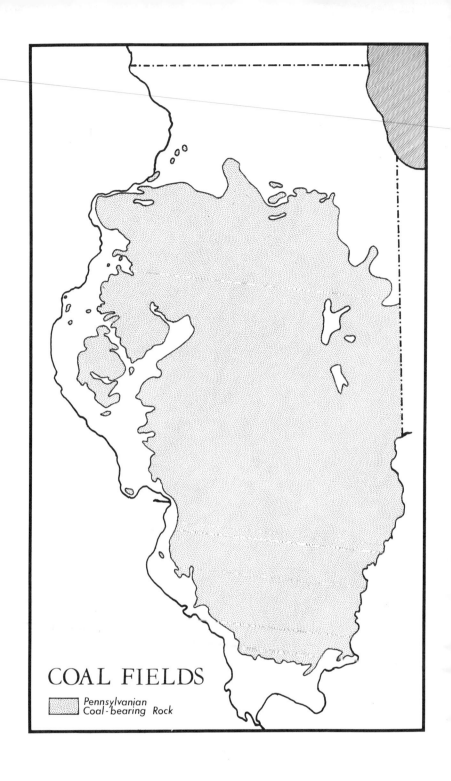

COAL FIELDS

Pennsylvanian
Coal-bearing Rock

supplies around settlements were depleted. Coal was found near the salines in Gallatin and Vermilion counties and by a government surveyor working west of Peoria in 1817. Boatloads of coal from the Peoria vicinity were floated to New Orleans as early as 1822.

Like settlement, the first mines bordered the rivers. Starting in 1823 St. Louis used coal from the bluffs back of the American Bottom. John Reynolds helped promote one of the first crude railroads west of the Alleghenies when horse-draw cars were used to pull coal on wooden rails six miles to the Illinoistown ferry. Coal wagons comprised most of the traffic on a macadam road, the first in the state, from Belleville to the ferry. In 1840 Illinois produced 424,000 bushels of coal. Measurement by the ton was years in the future.[17]

Most of the first coal came from drift or slope mines cut into seams exposed on bluffs or hillsides, but to reach greater depths shafts were sunk to subterranean veins. Shaft mining was reported near Belleville as early as 1842. A year earlier coal went to Chicago by wagon from the upper Illinois River country. Mines on the right bank of the river in time were equally accessible to boats and trains, which could deliver fuel to Chicago cheaper than it could be shipped from Erie, Pennsylvania. Three uplifted strata, the middle one six feet thick and the upper one nearly four, were worked both by vertical shafts and drift tunnels from the bank of the canal and contiguous ravines. Even before it was discovered that coal was cheaper and more efficient than wood as a locomotive fuel, the Illinois Central leased coal lands in the Du Quoin area on a royalty basis. Geologists did not yet comprehend the vast supplies of coal, but mines were sunk adjacent to the Rock Island right-of-way in Grundy, Bureau, and Rock Island counties and along the Burlington road in Stark and Knox counties. Fred Gerhard in *Illinois As It Is* said that the Great Western crossed a coal bed in Vermilion County and also located mines at Kingston in Peoria County. In southern Illinois he reported good coal at Du Quoin and De Soto.

The railroads, coal mining, and manufacturing grew in lockstep, while farmers became independent of woodlots. At the start of the Civil War, domestic iron production was unimportant, compared

[17] Howard N. Eavenson, *The First Century and a Quarter of the American Coal Industry.*

with Great Britain, but in the next quarter-century the United States took first place, with Chicago and its environs playing a leading role in that accomplishment. Thanks to Lake Michigan, iron ore from newly developed deposits in the Lake Superior country could be floated to harbors that were strategically located near coal reserves. They included Chicago, where mills and foundries began to supply a market for metal products.

GEORGE SMITH'S NONLEGAL MONEY

The expansion of population and business required a mammoth supply of paper money, more than the shaky notes of far-off banks could provide. Fortunately for northern Illinois, where the need was greatest, a form of deposit banking developed outside the law and under the auspices of insurance companies. The Chicago Marine and Fire Insurance Company, chartered in 1836, had power to receive deposits and lend money but was forbidden to circulate paper "in the similitude of bank notes." In the emergency of the 1837 depression the company, headed by J. Young Scammon, went into the banking business nevertheless and gave depositors certificates, in denominations from one to five hundred dollars, which were redeemable on demand. Physically they did not resemble bank notes, but they performed all their functions. In varying supply they circulated at par for years.

George Smith, who had visited Chicago in 1834, told his friends back in Aberdeen, Scotland, that the Old Northwest had great possibilities for moneymaking. So long as the boom lasted, he invested their money in real estate and at one time owned most of the present site of Milwaukee. During the 1837 panic, he admired Scammon's insurance company and obtained an almost identical charter from the Wisconsin legislature. Soon his Wisconsin Marine and Fire Insurance Company was issuing great amounts of nonlegal certificates of deposit, payable to the bearer on demand and redeemable in specie at his Milwaukee office or Chicago branch agency. Smith never suspended specie payments. His certificates were preferred over the heavily discounted notes of the old state banks and the wildcat currency from other states. By 1851 Smith had paper aggregating 1.47 million dollars circulating in six states, most heavily in northern Illinois. Additional redemption centers were opened at Galena, St. Louis, Detroit, and Cincinnati.[18]

Even the legitimate banks which had a solid financial structure sought to avoid the responsibility of having to redeem their notes with hard money. A favorite strategy was to put notes in circulation in a distant state and to make redemption possible only in some obscure community which a noteholder would have difficulty in locating and reaching. Meanwhile, especially in the southern and western counties, private scrip circulated as a substitute for money. Some towns had private banks, which had the option of issuing their own paper without sanction of the law or of handling only paper from distant places.

Businessmen, especially in Chicago, wanted a better system, but Democrats continued to be an antibank party and much of the public distrusted all corporations. Surprisingly, the 1847 constitutional convention elected a probank president. The delegates in a compromise gave the legislature authority to pass general laws on banking, subject to a referendum, and make stockholders doubly liable if their bank failed. In 1851 a "free bank" law received overwhelming referendum approval in the North. As a result, Illinois for the first time had a system of incorporated banks that could issue notes under state supervision, with redemption in specie guaranteed by law. Applicants with fifty thousand dollars capital could get twenty-five-year charters and circulate notes obtained from the state auditor in exchange for the deposit of the bonds of the federal government or any of the states. The first charter went to the Marine Bank of Chicago, which took over the operations of Scammon's insurance company. Some private banks acquired legal status, and seventeen banks were organized within a year. Smith, who had storage, commission, and railroad interests in Chicago, withstood continual attacks from his rivals until 1853, when the Illinois and Wisconsin legislatures outlawed the issuance of paper money of any kind other than bank notes. Then he sold out and bought a castle in Scotland with part of the money he made in Chicago.

As the value of currency fluctuated and counterfeiting con-

[18] Alice E. Smith, *George Smith's Money*. George W. Dowrie, *The Development of Banking in Illinois, 1817-1863*, pp. 128-155. Fred B. Marchkoff, "Currency and Banking in Illinois Before 1865," *Journal of the Illinois State Historical Society*, LII (Autumn, 1959), 383-418. Cole, *op. cit.*, pp. 91-100. Davidson-Stuvé, *op. cit.*, pp. 585-598.

tinued, newspaper editorials voiced a common wish that Smith's certificates, always redeemable at par, were still circulating. In 1857, most of the banks rode out a depression by retiring part of their notes to compensate for declining bond valuations. The legislature tightened the law by prohibiting branch banking and by forbidding the location of banks in inaccessible spots. The state's free banking system still had a major defect, the deposit of state bonds to secure note issues, which would cause trouble in the Civil War.

13

THE FOURTH LARGEST STATE

THANKS TO THE NEW RAILROADS AND TO THE CROWDED WATER and overland routes from the East, sometime in the early 1850's Illinois passed the one million mark in population. Before it was forty years old, the state that had been admitted to the Union without meeting minimum population requirements became the fourth largest in the nation. The 1850 census showed that Illinois with 851,470 residents had passed Indiana, its earlier settled neighbor. During the next ten years Illinois doubled in size and jumped from eleventh to fourth place with an 1860 population of 1,711,951. Flood stage had not yet been reached, however, and three more decades would pass before Illinois would overtake Ohio and rank third in population behind New York and Pennsylvania.

As the northern port of entry for throngs arriving from eastern states and Europe, Chicago also experienced a dramatic and prolonged boom. The 1850 census showed that the Indian trading center of 1812 had expanded to a population of 29,963 and was the nation's twentieth largest city. By 1860, Chicago ranked ninth with 112,172 residents, a majority of them foreign-born. Away from the eastern seaboard, only New Orleans, Cincinnati, and St. Louis were larger. The growth of Illinois had not been confined to Chicago, which increased by 274.4 percent during the decade. That was approximately the same rate as Freeport, but less than that of Bloomington.

Illinois would have decades of greater expansion after the Civil War, but the 1850's marked a turning point. The frontier had disappeared to the west, and industrialization had begun to move in from the East. Some families still lived in log cabins, but that primitive habitation was largely replaced by frame houses made of boards cut from trees which had grown in Michigan and Wisconsin. Most towns still had dirt streets and travelers agreed they were dismal in appearance, with housing scarce and frequent complaints about high rents. Each family had its own backyard sanitary facility, but the larger communities illuminated their stores and better homes with gas. Water piped through mains began to replace the well and pump. Illinois was laying the foundations for industrial greatness, and in Chicago the foreign-born outnumbered the native-born. Meanwhile the Prairie State established itself as the center of the greatest agricultural region of the nation.[1]

LANDOWNERS: SPECULATORS AND SETTLERS

Slightly more than fourteen million acres, which was nearly 40 percent of the land area of Illinois, remained in the possession of the federal government in 1849, just before the state's second great real estate boom.[2] The bulk of it was prairie located miles from navigable streams and the biggest portion was in the comparatively isolated central and east-central counties through which the Illinois Central soon would be built. In the next six momentous years practically all of the government land passed into private ownership. Some was sold directly to settlers, both immigrants and Easterners, for the standard price of $1.25 an acre at government land offices. Probably more than half of the land, however, was acquired first by speculators, who sought a profit before reselling to the men who eventually would break the prairie sod. Part of Illinois remained unoccupied, the property of speculators, until after the Civil War.

The boom of the 1850's arrived with the railroad builders, who

[1] Illinois grew in population for many reasons. One was that until the 1850's much land in central and northern Indiana was held by speculators for prices beyond the reach of many people. Unable to buy in Indiana, they pushed westward. Ray A. Billington, "The Frontier in Illinois History," *Journal of the Illinois State Historical Society*, XLIII (Spring, 1950), 28-45.

[2] Paul W. Gates, "Disposal of the Public Domain in Illinois," *Journal of Economic and Business History*, III, 2 (Feb., 1931), 216-240.

made the upper Mississippi valley easily reachable in any season. By that time more men understood that farming the tall grass areas did not require proximity to a woodlot. A technological breakthrough in the manufacture of machinery for plowing and harvesting came at a time when new banks increased the supply of available credit and Chicago business leaders encouraged the development of their trade territory. Until the Panic of 1857, good crops brought high prices. Those factors encouraged a new wave of immigration from Germany and Scandinavia, and families from the East joined them in the desire to establish new homes on the prairies of Illinois and eastern Iowa, the areas most in demand. Liberal land laws passed by Congress encouraged the boom, although they usually helped the speculators more than the settlers. As the prairies filled up, Chicago inevitably and dramatically became a commercial center rather than a frontier town.

A belief that more than a quarter of the entire area of Illinois passed into private hands through the medium of military warrants is held by Paul Wallace Gates of Cornell University, a leading agricultural historian.[3] The Military Tract, the triangle west of the Illinois River, had been set aside for veterans of the War of 1812, but the warrants entitling them to 160 acres each fell mostly into the hands of individual speculators, partnerships, and land companies. They paid between fifty cents and $1.15 per acre for the warrants in eastern cities. A system of tenancy developed, with some squatters being allowed to stay on their farms for payment of taxes and perhaps a little rent, but land titles became involved in tax liens and the litigation that resulted made the Military Tract a paradise for lawyers.[4]

On the Military Tract precedent, Congress between 1847 and 1855 authorized issuance of warrants, each good for 160 acres, to soldiers who had participated in the Mexican War and Indian engagements. They were legally assignable and could be bought at county seats, often at a rate of a dollar an acre, from land agents who offered ready credit at interest rates that ran as high as 50 percent. As a result, the government received nothing and speculators invested less than $1.25 in their land-warrant holdings. Gates

[3] *Ibid.,* p. 218.

[4] Paul W. Gates, *The Farmer's Age: Agriculture, 1815-1860,* pp. 94-95. Theodore L. Carlson, *The Illinois Military Tract: A Study in Land Occupation, Utilization and Tenure.*

found that after 1850 more Illinois land was exchanged for military warrants than was sold for cash.

The wetter prairies and areas subject to stream overflow had a white elephant status. Congress in 1850 granted one and a half million acres to Illinois. The legislature donated the swamplands to the counties with a requirement that they be sold for not less than ten cents an acre and that the proceeds be used first for levees and drainage systems. Most went for the minimum price. With the passage of years, the swamplands became immensely valuable, but only after expenditure of much more money for drainage and levee protection than had been envisioned in midcentury.[5]

As a debt-reduction measure, the state pushed disposal of the eighty-four thousand acres remaining from the 1841 federal land grant for canal construction and took payment in the depreciated bonds and scrip it had issued during the construction difficulties. These discounted securities enabled the purchase of land, mostly in the Chicago, Dixon, and Danville districts, at 18 to 47 percent of valuation.

Illinois did not follow the precedent set in 1845 when Michigan stationed an immigration agent in New York City and distributed thousands of pamphlets in the East and Germany.[6] Wisconsin and some other states also advertised heavily, as did railroad contractors and land companies with Illinois acreage to sell. The Illinois Central railroad introduced giant-sized and multifaceted corporate management to the West. While it laid rails and ran trains, the Illinois Central also was in the real estate business, offering land tracts for sale at prices up to twenty-four dollars an acre, with the bulk going for ten dollars or less. The railroad's agents met boats at eastern ports, traveled through rural sections of the East and South, and carried on domestic and foreign advertising campaigns. Virtually all of the western settlers came through Chicago, where trains were met by runners for railroads and land companies. Prior to the Union Pacific, probably no railroad received as much publicity as the Illinois Central. There was a rush to buy, and almost a third of the Illinois Central

[5] Margaret Beattie Bogue, "The Swamp Land Act and Wet Land Utilization in Illinois, 1850-1890," *Agricultural History*, XXV (Oct., 1951), 169-180.

[6] Paul W. Gates, *The Illinois Central and Its Colonization Work*, pp. 169-218. In the tradition of the Boggess and Pooley works on earlier phases of the settlement of Illinois, this book by Gates contains information about the founding of many towns, especially in territory served by the Illinois Central.

holdings were sold on credit. Especially after arrival of the Panic of 1857 the prices seemed high to critics, who pointed out that the same land could have been had for $1.25 an acre a few years earlier, but that was before the railroad made it practical to live on those prairies. The railroad gave concessions to land purchasers when the panic made it difficult to meet installment payments.

Congress with an 1852 price graduation law sought to dispose of the less desirable areas, including part of southern Illinois, for which settlers had refused to pay $1.25. The result was a scramble, especially in the Kaskaskia and Shawneetown districts. Most land sold for twelve and a half cents an acre, the new minimum. Collusion was common. Speculators frequently were accused of agreeing in advance to avoid bidding competition. At the same time, settlers banded together for mutual protection, especially before the preemption law. Members of claim associations discouraged new arrivals from bidding against squatters, and they agreed not to bid against each other.

Land speculation was rampant in the 1850's. Some settlers entered the inflationary spirit and borrowed money to get a second quarter-section, which was more than one farm family could handle, at interest rates that turned out to be too high. Lawyers, politicians, and businessmen invested in land on the side. Senator Stephen A. Douglas bought nearly one hundred acres of choice lakefront lots in Chicago and later purchased 2,872 acres around Lake Calumet at $2.50. Governor French used land warrants to acquire 3,840 acres in the Danville district. Men of that class were inclined to sell promptly to substantial foreigners or Easterners.

The professional speculators operated mostly from Chicago and eastern cities, with the aid of land agents in the smaller towns who were ready to handle transactions, arrange loans, supervise tenants, or buy a farm. One of the biggest speculators was Solomon Sturges of New York, who acquired one hundred thousand acres of land in the West, including forty thousand acres selected in advance along the Illinois Central route through the Danville district. Instances of individual speculators holding fifty thousand acres of Illinois land were not uncommon. Expenses were high; taxes and financing charges had to be met, sales promoted, and tenants supervised. Advertising attracted the potential buyers, but long-term credit closed the deals with men who lacked the capital to buy government land and pay operating costs until a crop could be sold. Interest rates of 10 to 15 percent were common.

In 1859, after the Grand Prairie had been bisected by the Illinois Central, laws creating Ford and Douglas counties completed the organization of the state into 102 counties, the final number. The existence of two types of counties—those with commission and township government—reflects the two streams of immigration that, from different directions and at different times, brought diverse cultures to Illinois. Settlers who had southern backgrounds made the county the local administrative agency under the commission form, and the 1818 constitution prescribed no other type of local government. By 1848 enough Yankees and New Englanders had arrived so that the second constitution provided for township government as an alternate system. As settlement grew the early legislatures devoted part of their time to dividing the larger counties. In the early years people complained that it was too difficult to travel miles to a seat of government, but often there was no settlement worthy of county seat status if the territory were divided. The coming of the railroads resulted in the development of new towns, and most of them wanted the prestige of having a courthouse and jail and the payroll that went with the official jobs. The result was the creation of additional counties of a size suitable for primitive transportation. In the automobile era consolidation efforts have failed because local sentiment has been stronger than agitation for economy and efficiency.

The county organization problem was almost settled by 1843.[7] Saline County, in a slowly developing southern area, was formed in 1847 by splitting off the western part of Gallatin County. Kankakee County, another late bloomer, represented parts of Will and Iroquois. Of the last two formed, Ford had been an unorganized territory attached to Vermilion County, and Douglas was formed by splitting off the northern part of Coles County. The last boundary adjustments were made in 1869. Rivalries between aspirants for county seats often led to agitation for or against a new county.

The 1848 constitution's optional procedure permitted counties to change by majority vote to the township form. Of the state's 102 counties, 85 have formed 1,433 townships, with elected

[7] Clyde F. Snider and Irving Howards, *County Government in Illinois*.

supervisors performing both township and county functions. Six-teen counties, mostly in the southern portion, stayed with the more simplified system under which the governing power is cen-tralized in a three-man board of commissioners. Cook County went on a township basis, but the 1870 constitution permitted it to modify its government to combine features of both systems.

DEERE'S PLOW AND McCORMICK'S REAPER

The wheat and livestock that fed the cities and were carried to market by the new railroads could not have been produced under the primitive farming methods used in the first decades of Illinois statehood. With the scythe and flail an energetic frontiersman could harvest enough grain for his family and a small surplus to sell, but only with long hours of back-breaking and inefficient labor. The agricultural development of the fertile midcontinent required machine methods, and when the need became critical it

Courtesy Illinois State Historical Library

John Deere plow, 1838

was met by inventors and manufacturers who mass-produced im-plements with interchangeable parts.

John Deere, a Vermont-born blacksmith who had a shop at Grand Detour, Ogle County, in 1837 became a major benefactor of prairie farming by perfecting the steel plow. Previously the cast-iron plow, which Jethro Wood had placed on sale in the East in 1817, was little better than the ancient wooden plow improved by covering the moldboard with iron strips. In either form, the plow was heavy and cumbersome, requiring several yoke of oxen and frequent sharpening. The problem of breakage caused less trouble than the persistency with which the heavy, sticky prairie soil clung to the pitted iron surface, changing the intended knife-like cutting edge to a ball of dirt. The only remedy was to rest the oxen frequently and scrape the soil from the plow. Prairie-breaking proceeded slowly, at a rate of one or two acres a day and a cost of $1.50 to two dollars an acre, more than the government charged for the land itself. Because of its fertility, farmers kept nibbling at the prairie, sometimes with furrows a mile long, and the inventive-minded searched for a better method. Deere used a large circular sawblade, which had been broken and discarded, to make the first steel plow. Tried out on a field across the Rock River from Grand Detour, the plow cut cleanly, scoured brightly, and required less animal power.[8]

The next year Deere made three steel plows, and in 1839 production jumped to ten. By 1842 he averaged two a week. A decade after inventing the steel plow he moved his plant to Moline, chiefly because it had better transportation facilities. The family-controlled firm of Deere and Company, organized in 1858, soon was the world's largest plow manufacturer. Deere and his competitors sold ten thousand plows a year and draft horses replaced oxen as the chief motive power. The plated surface gave way to the use of cast steel, imported from England, and while the plows were brittle and expensive the Bessemer process of producing the steel reduced the cost. Illinois men took out twenty-five plow patents in 1860 as part of a series of improvements that included a wheeled plow on which the farmer could ride, a gang plow with multiple shares, and experiments with a steam-powered plow.

In the new science of factory production of machinery, Cyrus Hall McCormick did as much for the farmer as John Deere. A man with a scythe and cradle, the best previously known method, could cut three acres of wheat a day in 1840. Within a few years

8 Darragh Aldrich, *The Story of John Deere, A Saga of American Industry.* Neil M. Clark, *John Deere: He Gave the World the Steel Plow.* Also see Richard Bardolph, "Illinois Agriculture in Transition, 1820-1870," *Journal of the Illinois State Historical Society,* XLI (Sept., 1948), 244-264; (Dec., 1948), 415-437.

the first grain reapers could cover fifteen acres a day in the same time. As a result they were immediately popular. Others were a step ahead in inventing the reaper, the basic parts of which had been patented in 1834 and first placed on the market in 1838. McCormick, however, excelled as an industrialist and sales promoter during the long process of perfecting the machine so that it could be produced in quantity.[9]

To get closer to the big midwestern market, McCormick in 1847 moved from Virginia to Chicago. That helped put Chicago on the road to industrial greatness at a time when Cincinnati and St. Louis were larger cities. To the farmer, the efficient reaper meant that labor costs could be reduced and the danger of weather loss lessened. Without the reaper, the increased production that came with the steel plow would have rotted in the field. Rival manufacturers, including Obed Hussey of Chicago, J. H. Manny of Freeport, and Jerome Atkins of Will County, had patented improvements which were more effective in rank prairie wheat and superior as grass cutters. The result was competition which kept the price around one hundred to one hundred fifty dollars, and a succession of patent infringement suits which usually went against McCormick. He advertised aggressively and pioneered in field trials, guarantees, testimonials, deferred payments, and mass production with labor-saving machinery.

In the agricultural revolution, inventors turned out a long list of horse-drawn machines which helped increase crop production while saving manpower. The cultivator appeared in the 1840's, and before the Civil War the straddle type had been marketed. Threshers powered by horses produced three hundred bushels of wheat a day. Several brands of reapers, along with threshers, mowers, hay tedders, cultivators, and seed drills, were on exhibit at the first Illinois state fair.

Among early benefactors of the farmer, high rank goes to Jonathan Baldwin Turner, who came to Jacksonville in the footsteps of his brother, Asa, a member of the "Yale Band." Farming required fences, rails were practicable only near timber, and the shortage of wood almost as much as anything else delayed the

[9] William T. Hutchinson, *Cyrus Hall McCormick,* a two-volume biography that covers the invention of the reaper and the industrial and public career of a leading Chicagoan. Fred A. Shannon, *The Farmer's Last Frontier: Agriculture, 1860-1897,* pp. 128-148. Cyrus McCormick, *The Century of the Reaper.* J. F. Steward, *The Reaper: A History of the Efforts of Those Who Justly May Be Said to Have Made Bread Cheap.*

settlement of the prairies. Turner experimented first with bar-
berry, box, and hawthorn in hope of duplicating the hedge fences
of England. Then he brought the spiny Osage orange to Illinois
from its native Arkansas and Kansas. As a hedge tree it withstood
drought and was "horse high, hog tight, and bull strong." Turner
in 1847 offered hedge plants for sale. Large quantities of Osage
orange seed were shipped to Illinois, with speculative prices running as high as fifty dollars a bushel. Sometimes the trees winter-
killed, leaving gaps, but it was the best available fencing. Prairie
farmers used it extensively until barbed wire was invented after
the Civil War.[10]

In the era of subsistence farming, few cared about the work of
Birkbeck and others in behalf of scientific agriculture, but the
cause was not entirely abandoned. A state agricultural society
donated premiums for the first state fair, held at Springfield in
mid-October, 1853. That society was the outgrowth of a demand
for a state university which, among other activities, would train
teachers to tell farmers how to improve their methods and profits.
In its early years the fair rotated annually from city to city.[11] The
state society encouraged local fairs, and by the end of the decade
eight county societies promoted better agriculture.

[10] Walter P. Webb, *The Great Plains,* pp. 290-294. Mary T. Carriel, *The Life of
Jonathan Baldwin Turner.*

[11] Homer J. Tice, "The Illinois State Fair," *Illinois Blue Book, 1931-32,* pp.
436-439.

McCormick self-rake reaper, 1858

Courtesy Illinois State Historical Library

"The lands are already cleared for the plough, the timber is ready for the axe," the *Illinois State Register,* a weekly at Springfield, said in 1849. "A few rails, a cabin, frugality and industry, and the poor man is independent." In a guide for immigrants, Fred Gerhard eight years later advised that forty to eighty acres should be enough for a man of small means. "A pair of horses, a wagon, one cow, a couple of hogs, several domestic fowls, two ploughs (one for breaking up the prairie, and the other for tillage), together with a few other tools and implements, are all that is necessary," he wrote. "A log house can soon be erected." He recommended that the farm be located not more than five or so miles from a timber supply. Gerhard also said that a man who bought at a reasonable price could obtain 75 percent long-term credit and be independent, free of debt, within a few years. "Of such success, innumerable instances may be found in the state of Illinois," he added in *Illinois As It Is.* Gerhard did not limit his success story to farmers. The guidebooks understandably leaned toward optimism as they encouraged settlement.[12]

The greater success story involved Isaac Funk and other cattle kings who accumulated acres by the tens of thousands on which they fed wild and raw-boned bullocks and drove them to city markets for slaughter as three- or four-year-olds. Their bonanza farms, dependent upon cheap land and an abundance of succulent native grasses, were forerunners of the vast ranches which spread across the western plains in the 1880's.[13]

Illinois specialized in feeding rather than raising livestock. Every farmer had cows for milking and hogs for home butchering, and most sold the surplus stock to buyers who drove them to feedlots. Prominent among the feeders was Funk, a day-laborer when he reached McLean County before the land offices were opened. He saved fourteen hundred dollars in five years, invested heavily in prairie and cattle, and in time owned twenty-six thousand acres, purchased at a ratio of two acres of prairie to one acre of timber. At first Funk raised his own corn with hired labor, but when it became unreliable and costs increased, he divided his land into small farms which he leased on a crop-share basis. That spread the profits and losses, and provided a more dependable labor supply.

[12] Fred Gerhard, *Illinois As It Is,* pp. 444-447.

[13] Helen M. Cavanagh, *Funk of Funk's Grove.* L. H. Kerrick, "Life and Character of Hon. Isaac Funk," *Transactions of the Illinois State Historical Society,* VII (1902), 159-170.

There were other livestock kings. John T. Alexander, a big
landowner east of Jacksonville, was credited with shipping fifteen
thousand head of cattle to New York between 1857 and 1860.
Jacob Strawn, who also lived in Morgan County, accumulated a
million dollars in the livestock business and at times controlled the
St. Louis market. On the unfenced prairie, James McConnell of
Springfield pastured seventeen thousand sheep, probably more
than anyone else in the nation. Most of the big ranches were found
in central Illinois and along the Kankakee River, extending into
Indiana. Including speculators and the livestock specialists, 112
groups and individuals acquired more than two million acres from
the land offices in Illinois, an average of eighteen thousand
each.[14]

The biggest of the big operators, Michael L. Sullivant, sold his
inherited land in Ohio and bought eighty thousand acres, chiefly
in Champaign, Ford, Piatt, and Livingston counties. Many immigrants from Germany and Scandinavia worked for Sullivant, learning prairie methods until they had experience and savings to
become tenants or buy cheaper land further west. In time Sullivant overextended himself and had to sell his main operation to
Alexander, but he still owned forty thousand acres in the Paxton
vicinity.

For the individual farmer, wheat became the great cash crop of
the Northwest. "It pays debts, buys groceries, and answers most
emphatically the purposes of trade among the farmers," said the
Prairie Farmer in 1850.[15] The center of production shifted from
the thinner soil to northern Illinois and southern Wisconsin, which
had not yet become infested with parasites and plant diseases. By
1859 Illinois was the leading wheat state, producing 23.837 million bushels and sending most of it to the Chicago market.
Farmers in the eleven highest wheat-producing counties in northern Illinois bought one-fourth of the McCormick reapers sold
between 1849 and 1857.

Corn, the gift of the Indians to the white man, remained the
universal and permanently important crop, however. Hardy and
virile, it produced fabulous yields on the black or brown soil

---

[14] Clarence P. McClelland, "Jacob Strawn and John T. Alexander—Central Illinois
Stockmen," *Journal of the Illinois State Historical Society*, XXXIV (March, 1941),
177-208. Margaret Beattie Bogue, *Patterns from the Sod: Land Use and Tenure in the
Grand Prairie, 1850-1900*, pp. 35-78, 259-261. Gates, *Farmer's Age*, pp. 197-214.

[15] *Ibid.*, pp. 166-169.

exposed by the prairie-breaking plow. Harvest could be delayed until after frost, and when the ears had been removed the tall stalks made fodder. Wheat was superior as a cash crop and as food, but the farm families and the city poor ate corn at their tables in several forms. Much of the crop was consumed as animal feed.

URBANIZATION'S FIRST STAGES

Illinois was still a rural state, with large stretches of unturned prairie, but during the 1850's the downstate cities also grew, many of them at amazing rates, although none in size or importance would ever aspire to be a rival of Chicago. By midcentury the population pattern of the state established itself. At the Chicago portage had arisen a major city that would have an even more spectacular growth and would dominate the interior of the continent. Important to southern Illinois was St. Louis, just across the Mississippi and exerting a strong influence over a sizable portion of the state. Chicago was becoming industrialized and soon would be larger than St. Louis, but the Missouri city would continue to be bigger than any municipality in the downstate counties. The only future rivalry would be for the honor of being the second largest city in Illinois.

The 1860 census showed that Peoria had increased 175.7 percent in population in ten years and overtaken Quincy and Galena to establish itself in second place, a position it would hold for a century. But Peoria with 14,045 residents was only 12 percent of the size of Chicago and would proportionately lose ground in the future. Already a distilling center, Peoria had a superb location for trade territory, railroads had connected with steamboat lines, and it was one of the towns where capital was being invested in shops that employed workmen to convert raw materials into manufactured products. Peoria was one of the twenty-three urban centers in which 1860 census officials found that 14.3 percent of the people of Illinois lived. Ten years earlier there had been 7.6 percent living in nine urban centers.

Quincy, which manufactured stoves and had a railroad as well as steamboat landings, had doubled in size during the decade but dropped to third ranking with 13,718 residents. No other city in Illinois had a population of ten thousand in 1860. Springfield ranked fourth with 9,320, and Galena at 8,196 had slipped to fifth

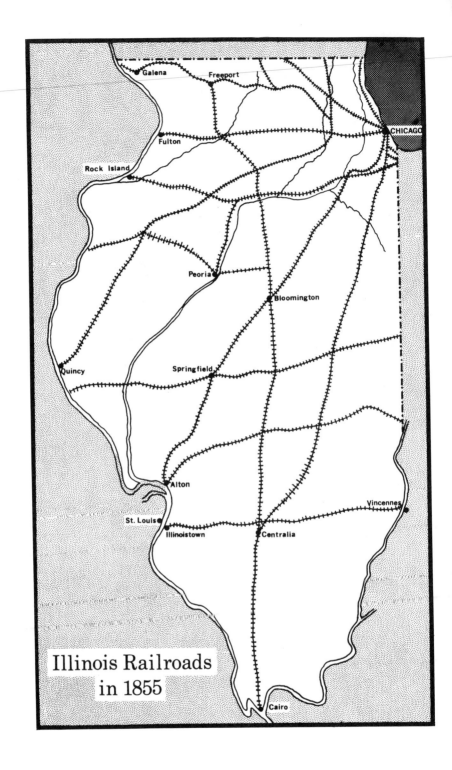

Illinois Railroads
in 1855

place. Nine other cities—Belleville, Bloomington, Joliet, Rockford, Alton, Aurora, Jacksonville, Freeport, and Rock Island, in that order—had more than five thousand residents. Nauvoo in its post-Mormon doldrums had dropped out of the individual census listings. Shawneetown, without a railroad, became a second-rate steamboat stop. Kaskaskia had fallen behind even before it suffered flood damage.

Like Belleville and Jacksonville, Bloomington grew without having the advantage of a site on a navigable river. In a rich area, it was a sizable town before the arrival of two railroads made it a transhipment center. Other railroad junction points also boomed. La Salle had the benefit of the canal and nearby coal mines, in addition to two rail lines. Galesburg, Mendota, Decatur, and Mattoon also prospered from trade where railroads crossed. Along the Illinois Central, new towns were started. Centralia, at the junction of the branch to Chicago, was moved a mile southward because local speculators put exorbitant prices on their holdings. A year after a depot was built at West Urbana, the new town of Champaign had a hundred houses. Because of the railroad, Kankakee became more important than Bourbonnais, Anna outstripped Jonesboro, and La Salle outgrew Peru. Carbondale was not on the map until surveyors marked a station site. Cairo's population increased tenfold in the 1850's. Effingham, Harvey, Homewood, Normal, Pana, and many other towns began as Illinois Central stations. In other areas, on other railroads, new towns began their growth, and the Military Tract counted Galesburg, Monmouth, and Macomb as major centers.

Chicago was rough and sprawling, bursting at the seams as it almost tripled in population in ten years.[16] Along with grain elevators, stockyards, and a Board of Trade, Chicago acquired a reputation of being a wide-open city where visitors could get any entertainment they wanted. The more respectable residents called it the "garden city," since the cottages of newcomers as well as the mansions of the rich were centered on lots big enough to have some grass and vegetable plots. Downtown walls of brick and stone were replacing the haphazard wooden construction of the previous decades. The building boom reached its peak in 1856 when Chicagoans built 145 stores, several hundred houses, seven churches, and a high school.

[16] A. T. Andreas, *History of Cook County, Illinois,* I, 384-393.

Eastern and European publications marveled at Chicago's solution of its worst handicap, the fact that its streets were only four to six feet higher than the surface of the lake. As could be expected of a city built on a low, flat plain, Chicago was wet. Drainage difficulties caused high death rates. With a bootstrap operation, Chicago lifted itself out of the mud by raising the grade of the streets four to seven feet, which in the downtown section was done in two stages, in 1855 and again in 1857. Mud and sand dredged from the bottom and banks of the river filled in the courthouse square and the streets adjacent and at the same time improved navigation. Excavations for basements and building foundations were placed on other streets to raise the grade. The job was expensive and traffic was badly disrupted but as the streets filled up, pipes for sewage, water, and gas were placed on the surface.

That left the sidewalks higher than the front doors, but young George M. Pullman raised big buildings, including those of brick and stone, with jackscrews placed under beams in the basements. He assigned one man to four jacks; when the foreman blew a whistle each man gave his jacks a half-turn. Pullman in 1861 raised the Tremont Hotel, the best in the city, five feet without cracking the plaster or disturbing the guests.

Originally Chicago streets were dirt graded to the center, with open ditches like country lanes. After a twenty-seven-mile experiment, planked streets were abandoned in 1854. Bridewell prisoners broke up stones for macadam paving. Tooth-shaking cobblestones had the merit of permanence, but the best surfacing seemed to be wooden blocks, a Chicago invention known as Nicholson pavement, which proved to be comparatively durable. Omnibuses provided the only local transportation until 1859, when the first city rail line started horsecar service.

Water had to be peddled by the bucket until 1840 when a company capitalized at two hundred thousand dollars extended an iron pipe to a crib 150 feet out in the lake.[17]

The railroads made Chicago the nation's leading livestock market. In the trading post days of Clybourn and Hubbard, the packing industry had started on a country slaughterhouse basis and, before rails and refrigeration, was largely a cold weather operation. Trains put the long-distance drovers out of business and

[17] John Moses and Joseph Kirkland, *History of Chicago*, I, 119-133.

commission firms handled consignments of live cattle to packers in eastern cities. Except for the local trade, fresh pork was not available, but mess pork, preserved in salt, was shipped in barrels. By the advent of the Civil War, Chicago had achieved supremacy over Cincinnati, St. Louis, and other out-of-state cities. Its growth also was at the expense of several river towns, Beardstown among them. Six separately operated stockyards, each owned by a railroad, required a complex interchange system and brought a demand for centralization. The legislature in 1865 incorporated the Union Stock Yards and Transit Company, authorized to manage stockyards and operate branch railroads, a bank, and a hotel. The leading western roads subscribed most of the million-dollar capital, and around the yards at Thirty-ninth and Halsted streets, on the city's southern edge, great packing plants were built as evidence of the foresight and enterprise of the city's businessmen.

The Board of Trade, which began as a voluntary association of wheat buyers, in 1849 received a charter from the legislature as a means of standardizing the market with a rigid system of grain inspection and grading. By 1858 only members had access to the trading floor and price quotations were transmitted by telegraph. Farmers who long had wanted a city market began to complain about the prices they received, but the Board of Trade achieved its major goal of uniformity. Solid stone elevators more than one hundred feet high rose on pier foundations on the banks of the Chicago and Calumet rivers. Trainloads of grain were unloaded on the land side of the elevators, with the grain hoisted into bins to await shipment during the navigation season. Steam engines provided the power for the elevators and the factories, which were linked with freight houses and team tracks. In the transformed city, the north branch of the river became one of the business sections.

Chicago also became the leading market for lumber. For six miles along the river, lumberyards were filled with boards, planks, and beams shipped from the pine forests of Wisconsin and Michigan. Part was used in the expansion of Chicago, but the settlement of the prairie regions, which was accompanied by the cutting down of the timber along the streams and in groves, resulted in a heavy downstate demand for lumber. Chicago also shipped lumber to the southern states.

14

TAX-SUPPORTED EDUCATION

In the middle of the nineteenth century, Illinois all but exhausted its intellectual resources in a struggle to establish a public school system worthy of the name. The immense strides in settling farms, building railroads, and enlarging cities occupied the populace, and cultural programs did not keep pace. The state was not an intellectual wasteland: lyceums helped adult education, denominational colleges came into being and in some cases survived, the first theaters provided entertainment, and each town had at least one printing press. Joseph Medill's *Chicago Tribune* competed for the mass audience with Horace Greeley's New York newspaper of the same name. No writer, however, had influence comparable to that of Hall and Birkbeck of the earlier generation. A few literary publications fell by the wayside, and the writers of that era are largely forgotten, with the exception that the English language was mastered superbly by Lincoln, who rose above the all-too-common environment of semi-illiteracy.

Stock companies, itinerant actors, and circuses provided occasional entertainment in the larger cities. In Chicago John B. Rice built a theater where works of Shakespeare and lesser dramatists were performed. Chicago had a season of orchestral concerts in 1858, two years after the Chicago Historical Society organized. In 1859 an art exhibition was attended by twelve thousand persons, who looked at 369 works of painters and sculptors.

Among men of culture, two names are remembered. G. P. A.

Healy, a Bostonian, after 1855 painted portraits of the prominent businessmen who had begun to buy works of art. Leonard Volk, a marble cutter, came to Chicago in 1857 as an artistic protégé of Stephen A. Douglas. Volk made a life mask of Lincoln and designed the Douglas monument at Thirty-First Street.

SCHOOLS AND TEACHERS

Until 1855, when state and local educational tax laws at last were enacted, not more than one-third of the children of school age came under any form of pedagogical instruction and for all practical purposes Illinois did not have a public school system. The legislature had passed a series of largely futile school laws, with none facing the financial reality that only with money could teachers be hired and buildings constructed.

Some money was available. By 1851 a property tax could be levied by a majority vote in a school township, the governmental agency originally created to manage the public lands which the government had dedicated for the support of local education. By that method, however, only fifty-one thousand dollars were raised in the entire state. Comparatively few townships had any investment income left from the sale or rental of school sections. The state school fund had suffered during the internal improvements debacle, and officials at Washington withheld the 3 percent due on land sales in Illinois because the state had stopped paying interest on bonds held in trust by the federal government. Nevertheless with increased population and better times the state fund had been built up considerably with fines and swampland sales, but by 1855 the interest approximated only $42,300, which had to be distributed through all counties.

In a series of school conventions, a few teachers provided leadership during a long campaign to combat parental ignorance, taxpayer objections, and a belief that economy was more essential than education. Occasionally public-spirited citizens joined the cause. One was John S. Wright, who celebrated his first fortune by building at his own expense the first public school building in Chicago.[1] "We believe that at least three-fourths of the teachers in the common schools of Illinois could not pass an examination in

[1] Lloyd Lewis, *John S. Wright, Prophet of the Prairies*. F. James Evans, *Prairie Farmer and WLS: America's Oldest Farm Paper Since 1841*.

the rudiments of the English language, and most of them have taken to teaching because they hadn't anything in particular to do," Wright said in 1842 in his *Union Agriculturalist,* which soon would be renamed the *Prairie Farmer.* A perpetual booster, Wright at an 1844 school convention in Peoria helped draft a memorial asking the legislature to recognize the problem by creating a new office, that of state superintendent of public instruction.

The lawmakers compromised by giving the title on an ex officio basis to the secretary of state, who in succeeding administrations was too busy to bother much about collecting educational information. That 1845 law had many good features, including a requirement that teachers be knowledgeable in reading, writing, arithmetic, geography, grammar, and history. Two years later the qualification was lowered so that a person versed in any one of those fields could get a teaching certificate.

The school law might have remained a dead letter except for two well-attended conventions in 1853, one on a regional basis at Jerseyville and the other a statewide gathering at Bloomington. There the Illinois State Teachers Association was organized with Charles E. Hovey, a Peoria principal, as president. Newton Bateman of Jacksonville, whom Lincoln later referred to as the "little schoolmaster," became corresponding secretary and traveling agent. The next year the legislature yielded to their pleas by making the state superintendent an elected officer, paid fifteen hundred dollars a year and concerned only with the betterment of schools. To fill the post until the next election, Governor Matteson appointed Ninian W. Edwards, son of the old governor and a friend of Lincoln. Edwards, who had the benefit of an expensive private education, surveyed the state, consulted with school people, and submitted the draft of a law, enacted in 1855, which established the principle that the state should use its taxing power to support local schools.[2]

Edwards' law levied a two-mill tax to support the state school fund. The counties received two-thirds of the revenue, distributed in proportion to the number of residents under twenty-one years. To help the new and sparsely settled regions, one-third went directly to the townships on an area basis. With modifications, the

[2] Newton Bateman and Paul Selby, *Historical Encyclopedia of Illinois,* I, 148-150. Charles D. Jay, *150 Years of Education in Illinois.* Alexander Davidson and Bernard Stuvé, *A Complete History of Illinois,* pp. 610-616. John Moses, *Illinois Historical and Statistical,* II, 989-991.

principle of the double formula has been used ever since in distributing state school aid. To qualify for aid, the townships had to levy their own tax, enough to pay the remainder of the cost of operating a free school at least six months a year. As a result of the two-mill tax, the school distribution increased from $37,155 in 1854 to $606,809 the next year. The legislature refused to change the basic system when Cook, Sangamon, and other large counties protested that they paid the state more than they received in the distribution.

The superintendent's report for 1860 showed that, out of 549,604 persons of school age, 472,247 were enrolled in 8,958 districts that maintained 9,162 public schools. As attendance went up, the wages of teachers doubled until men received forty-five dollars a month and women twenty-five dollars on the average. Virtually all of the schools were of the one-room variety, with the lone teacher trying to cope with a wide range of ages. In 1860, only 294 schools, all in sizable cities, were graded as to levels of instruction. The districts were usually two miles square, big enough to support one teacher and small enough for the children to walk from home.

Except in some of the cities, instruction did not go beyond the eighth grade. Public high schools were just beginning to supplant the private academies that had been the nation's chief means of secondary education for several decades, and only a city could have enough population and financial resources to superimpose a high school on a system of grammar schools.[3] The West Jacksonville district in 1851 organized the state's first free public high school. Chicago's first superintendent of schools, William H. Wells, arrived in 1856 from Massachusetts. Wells promptly organized the city's first high school, which admitted girls as well as boys. He put the board of education under centralized control and as early as 1861 introduced a graded system in all schools. The legislature in 1857 passed a law encouraging the organization of high school districts, but a decade went by before any downstate community took advantage of the authority it offered.

Jonathan B. Turner, who understood that better schools would require more teachers with better education, in 1851 showed up at

---

[3] Paul E. Belting, "The Development of the Free Public High School in Illinois to 1860," *Journal of the Illinois State Historical Society,* XI (Oct., 1918), 269-369, and XII (Jan., 1919), 467-561.

a farmers' convention at Granville and unfolded a plan for federal land grants to enable each state to establish an industrial university. Turner wanted the university to have a teacher-training department, as well as classes for the training of farmers and various types of mechanics and craftsmen. The state could not wait for action at Washington, and the denominational colleges wanted to share in the state seminary fund, which had been established when the federal government donated two townships in 1818. There were perhaps twenty colleges in the state, but only President Julian M. Sturtevant of Illinois College supported Turner's dream of a single state institution supported by land grants. Eventually Turner prevailed, but opposition of the private colleges delayed the opening of a state university.[4]

Hovey and Bateman demonstrated the power of their association by pushing a bill, which Governor Bissell signed in 1857, creating a Normal school controlled by a state board of education and endowed with about ten thousand dollars annual interest from the state seminary fund.[5] Afraid of opposition, the sponsors did not ask for a direct appropriation from the state. Influential in setting classroom policies, it was the first teachers' college in the Mississippi valley and the first state-supported institution of higher learning in Illinois. Jesse Fell of Bloomington, a land speculator, raised seventy-one thousand dollars by popular subscription and influenced McLean County to pledge an additional seventy thousand dollars, which bettered Peoria's bid of $80,032 in competition for the site. A three-man faculty started teaching nineteen students in a rented hall while waiting for the Normal school's three-story, domed building, which stood alone and majestic in open country two miles north of Bloomington, to be completed in 1861.

A group of Chicago businessmen with Methodist affiliations and

[4] Ernest G. Hildner, "Higher Education in Transition, 1850-1870," *Journal of the Illinois State Historical Society*, LVI (Spring, 1963), 61-87. Paul Selby, "The Part of Illinoisans in the National Education Movement, 1851-1862," *Transactions of the Illinois State Historical Society*, IX (1904), 214-229, gives full details of the plan. Mary Turner Carriel, *The Life of Jonathan Baldwin Turner*, chapters XI-XXIV. D. M. Inman, "Professor Jonathan Baldwin Turner and the Granville Convention," *Journal of the Illinois State Historical Society*, XVII (1924), 144-150.

[5] Charles A. Harper, *Development of the Teachers College in the United States with Special Reference to the Illinois State Normal University*. Helen E. Marshall, *Grandest of Enterprises—Illinois State Normal University*. *Illinois Blue Book, 1907*, pp. 419, 422-423. F. M. I. Morehouse, *The Life of Jesse W. Fell*.

New England backgrounds obtained a charter for a private liberal
arts college which they named Northwestern University.[6] Orring-
ton Lunt, who became the father of Evanston, waded through a
swamp to reach lakefront ridges and hardwood groves which
became the campus site. The school opened in 1855 with ten
students. A charter amendment stipulated that no liquor could be
sold within five miles and granted tax exemption to the university's property.

Stephen A. Douglas in 1854 offered to donate two acres of his
estate at Chicago's south edge if others would contribute one
hundred thousand dollars for buildings for a university. Cornerstone-laying coincided with the Panic of 1857, and the senator
finally deeded the land without reservation to Baptists. Known
first as Douglas University and then as the University of Chicago,
it struggled under a heavy debt and finally collapsed in 1885. The
Douglas school had no connection with a later University of
Chicago, a few miles southward, which had better financing.[7]

A START AT WELFARE

Welfare preceded education in Illinois. Before the legislature
levied a tax for schools, it created three charitable institutions,
largely because of the influence of a group of Jacksonville men
and of Dorothea Dix, a reformer from Massachusetts who roamed
the nation in behalf of better custodial care of the unfortunate.
All three of the institutions were located at Jacksonville, then one
of the major cities of the state.

Illinois entered the welfare field almost by chance and after
other states had started to assume some responsibility for the
handicapped. The first charitable institution, the State Asylum for
the Deaf and Dumb, grew out of an accidental encounter in 1838
of Orville H. Browning, the state senator from Quincy, and a man
who had learned lip-reading at a school in another state. Within a
year Browning had pushed to enactment a bill for a similar
institution, but the state's financial troubles delayed until 1846
the opening of the school with two pupils in a small building.
Although larger than Jacksonville, Quincy was too far from the

[6] Estelle Francis Ward, *The Story of Northwestern University.*
[7] Thomas Wakefield Goodspeed, *A History of the University of Chicago*, pp. 12-14.

center of the state to have the new institution located within its limits.

Samuel Bacon, who had been educated at the Ohio School for the Blind, came to Jacksonville and opened a private school for blind children. In 1848 he had his four pupils demonstrate finger-tip reading to members of the legislature. William Thomas, an early legislator and Jacksonville attorney, immediately drafted a bill to have the state take over Bacon's school. Because Jacksonville men had financed for Bacon a survey showing there were sixty blind children of school age in Illinois, no other city attempted to get the Institution for the Education of the Blind, which was the official name. The school opened in 1848 on a twenty-two-acre site a half-mile east of the city square. For the second year there were eighteen pupils, but Bacon quit as superintendent to move westward and open blind schools in Iowa and Nebraska. A new superintendent boasted that all but two of his charges could "read the inspired word with pleasure and profit." One of the early teachers, Frank H. Hall, invented the Braille writer.

Dorothea Dix, a feminine whirlwind, reached Illinois in 1846, seven years after she became incensed at the condition of Massachusetts prisons and jails and, during an investigation, learned that the insane had equally pitiable care and housing. En route by steamboat to St. Louis, where she planned to set up headquarters for an investigation of conditions in western states, she encountered a Jacksonville merchant who invited her to come to his city instead. He then accompanied her on a tour of Illinois jails, almshouses, and private institutions.[8] In 1847 with one speech she convinced the legislature that Illinois needed a "well-established, skillfully conducted hospital" as the only means of treating its mentally afflicted. She told of "scenes of misery" in almshouses and jails, and "distressing circumstances" when private families attempted to care for relatives.

A bill to create an Illinois institution at Peoria met Miss Dix's disapproval because it lacked an appropriation. A substitute provided money for the Illinois State Hospital for the Insane at Jacksonville, and a board of trustees purchased a quarter-section of land at twenty-one dollars an acre south of Jacksonville. The first patient arrived in early 1851, followed by 137 others the first

---

[8] *Illinois Blue Book, 1927-28,* pp. 378-382. See also *Blue Book, 1915-16,* pp. 307-309, 319. Helen E. Marshall, *Dorothea Dix, Forgotten Samaritan.*

year. The one building, designed to hold 250 patients, soon proved inadequate and many were turned away as an effort was made to restrict admissions to those who might be cured. Because of serious overcrowding, the legislature in 1869 ordered additional asylums built at Elgin and Anna.

Miss Dix also started agitation for abandonment of the original stone penitentiary at Alton, with the result that between 1857 and 1860 its hard-worked inmates were transferred to a new northern penitentiary at Joliet, which also operated on the Auburn plan of silence. The massive structure, planned for one thousand cells, typified institutional architecture at midcentury. Prison overcrowding forced the transfer in 1878 of two hundred men to a new southern penitentiary at Chester, which also was built in part by inmate labor.

Some competent men were among the physicians who joined the migration to Illinois and tried to cope with the high incidence of serious epidemics and other diseases at a time when inadequate sanitation multiplied public health problems. The continued presence of ague and other fevers made it necessary for Illinois boosters to deny that diseases were more prevalent on the prairies than in other states. Dr. T. A. Huffman of Beardstown came close to a diagnosis of the trouble when he urged the draining of bottomlands, and some others knew that miasmatic fevers prevailed in the summer, particularly after a moist spring. No one yet suspected that mosquitoes were responsible, but the ague was more common on low land with a poor runoff than on high rolling prairie. Some attributed the fever to improper foods, such as fruit, lard, eggs, and fish, as well as stagnant water.

The medical talent included quacks and various types of amateurs who lacked scientific training and knowledge, but some of the doctors founded medical schools, started scientific publications, and established the first hospitals. In a history of Illinois medical practice, Dr. David J. Davis wrote that at one time the state was reported to have fourteen medical schools, but some of them died in infancy.[9] The first to survive was Rush Medical College, founded in Chicago by a group of doctors headed by Daniel Brainerd. He aided in starting the *Illinois Medical and Surgical Journal,* which became the *Chicago Medical Journal,* and helped establish the city's first general hospital. One of his Rush

[9] *History of Medical Practice in Illinois,* II, 413-417.

associates was Dr. John Evans, who gave his name to Evanston, helped found Northwestern University, and then switched to railroad building and became territorial governor of Colorado by appointment of Lincoln. Dr. Nathan Smith Davis, who lived long enough to help put the American Medical Association on its feet, campaigned for a sewage system and a pure water supply. When a schism developed in the Rush staff, Davis led a group which founded the Lind University College of Medicine. In time it became part of Northwestern University.

A few months older than Rush was the medical college at Illinois College, which closed without explanation in 1848. Public distrust of the medical profession and a lack of sympathy for medical education reached a peak when a mob searched for a faculty member and a group of helpers who were accused of exhuming the body of a prominent man for secret anatomical research. The law made grave robbing a misdemeanor, subject to a maximum fine of five hundred dollars, but instructors had no legal way of obtaining cadavers for anatomy students. In 1849 a student at the St. Charles school was killed and a teacher permanently crippled by rioters who claimed that a new grave had been desecrated.

CONFLICTS OVER LIQUOR

Illinois experimented with prohibition during the early 1850's when a campaign to restrict the availability of alcoholic liquors rolled westward from Maine. Reaching Illinois, taken up by evangelical Protestants and then by part of the business community, it became a subject of political and social controversy and twice scored victories in the legislature. Hard drinking had been common in early Illinois, where whiskey was in widespread use. In the cities the German and Irish immigrants retained a fondness for beer and more potent beverages and a tradition for unrestricted personal liberty. Belleville had forty establishments licensed to sell liquor, and probably an equal number which lacked legal sanction. A touring lecturer who reached Chicago in 1849 said he had never seen a city or town where liquor was so universally obtainable. [10]

[10] Davidson-Stuvé, *op. cit.,* pp. 606-608. Arthur C. Cole, *The Era of the Civil War,* pp. 204-210. Moses, *op. cit.,* II, 883-893. Bateman-Selby, *op. cit.,* pp. 339-340. Herbert Wiltsee, "The Temperance Movement, 1848-1871," *Transactions of the Illinois State Historical Society,* XLIV (1937), 82-92.

For the first twenty years of statehood, county commissioners could license taverns, alehouses, and dram shops at not more than twelve dollars a year. Starting in 1838, the subject of intemperance received increasing attention and a petition from fourteen counties asked the legislature to repeal all laws permitting the sale of ardent spirits. John J. Hardin, as chairman of the house judiciary committee, asserted the state's right to legislate regarding liquor in the same way it passed laws on concealed weapons, poisons, interest rates, and charges made by ferries and mills. The result was the first Illinois local option law, which enabled a majority of the voters in a community to petition county officials to forbid the licensing of groceries, the common name for the establishments where liquor and wine were sold in quantities of less than a quart. The law also fixed a twenty-five-dollar to three-hundred-dollar range for licenses and made them revocable. The local option portion of the new law proved too revolutionary and it was repealed in 1841.

The Sons of Temperance, a secret ritualistic group, organized in Illinois in 1847 and joined church congregations and lecturers in demanding regulation of the liquor trade. By 1850 Quincy, Rockford, and Springfield adopted ordinances forbidding licensing, and the cause narrowly lost at Ottawa. Four years earlier Maine had passed a law forbidding the statewide sale of intoxicants, and other states were beginning to follow its example. In that atmosphere the legislature in 1851 passed a quart law, forbidding the sale of spirituous or mixed liquor in quantities of less than a quart. All license laws were repealed, and a twenty-five-dollar penalty set for violations. In a wave of popular indignation, the quart law was widely violated and then repealed as a nullity in two years. A licensing system replaced it.

With strong church support, the temperance people made a counterattack by presenting petitions with twenty-six thousand signatures to the 1853 legislature. The next year the Illinois Supreme Court upheld the principle of local option by ruling in favor of a Jacksonville ordinance which declared that the sale of liquor was a nuisance, punishable by a fine. The defense argued that liquor was property and that the constitutional right to acquire, hold, use, and dispose of it could not be restricted by the state. The court made a distinction in the kind of property. The growing sentiment for prohibition gained the support of many businessmen, and the Illinois Central railroad refused to transport spirituous liquor. Springfield, Ottawa, Rockford, Joliet, Canton,

Macomb, and Princeton were among the cities which adopted dry ordinances.

The Democrats were the liquor party, and when the legislature came under the control of a coalition of Whigs and anti-Nebraska Democrats in 1855, Illinois passed a Maine law for total prohibition. The law called for a popular referendum in three months, and the dry forces worked hard, with the support of most newspapers, to get out their vote. The liquor forces decried compulsion, argued that real temperance could not be legislated, and told farmers that prohibition would ruin the corn market. In the heaviest vote that had been cast in Illinois, the drys carried most of the northern counties, except Cook and Rock Island, but the southern counties provided the vote that kept the Maine law from going into effect. Since the chief attention of reformers had centered on the slavery issue, Illinois for another two decades depended upon licensing to control the liquor trade.

The Maine law controversy had brought beer rioting to Chicago, which early in its municipal career became a liberal town. The water transportation lines brought in a rough element, customers of saloons and disreputable establishments which offered gambling and prostitution. As it grew, Chicago attracted gamblers, pickpockets, strong-arm men, and other criminals who sought victims, official leniency, or an opportunity to hide.

The official problems of "Long John" Wentworth, a man of action who became mayor in 1857, were compounded by a financial panic which brought more of the criminal element to the city but reduced the amount of money that could be fleeced from their victims. With unemployment as well as crime increasing, and "1,000 prostitutes working in 110 houses," the mayor took action. With thirty policeman, he raided the most disreputable area, known as the Sands, on the north side of the river near the lake.[11] They tore down five disreputable houses and four shanties, scattering the inmates into other areas. As a reform measure, Wentworth's raid accomplished little except to give the displaced thieves and burglars a wider base of operations.

As Illinois grew, the Catholic Church also expanded in membership.[12] By 1843 it had fifty thousand communicants served by twenty-four priests under the jurisdiction of the Vincennes and St.

[11] Bessie Louise Pierce, *A History of Chicago*, II, 433-440.

[12] Cathedral of the Holy Name, *100 Years: History of the Holy Name/ The Church That Became a Cathedral and the Story of Catholicism in Chicago*. Theodore C. Pease, *The Frontier State*, p. 422.

Louis dioceses. Much of its growth was due to Irish immigration, but one-third of Chicago's three thousand Catholics were German-speaking. In 1843 Chicago became a diocese for the entire state, and Bishop William Quarter in 1845 consecrated a Cathedral of St. Mary, a one-hundred-by-fifty-foot chuch at Madison and Wabash streets. The first cross in Chicago topped its steeple. St. Mary's stood for twenty-eight years, until the Chicago fire, with five bishops having served as pastors. Although Rush Medical College had been incorporated in 1837, the first institute of higher learning to open its doors in Chicago was the University of St. Mary of the Lake, a three-story structure at Chicago and State streets, which was dedicated in 1846. The first downstate diocese was formed at Quincy in 1853 and transferred to Alton four years later.

Methodists retained their first rank as the largest religious denomination. A compilation in 1855 showed that they had 405 of the 1,223 churches in Illinois and 178,450 of the 486,576 members. The Baptists had 282 churches and 94,130 members, followed by Presbyterians with 206 churches and 83,129 members. For fourth place, the Christian Church with 69 congregations and 30,864 members was ahead of the Catholics with 59 parishes and 29,100 communicants. Lutherans, Congregationalists, and Episcopalians followed in order, each with at least fourteen thousand members.

15

DOUGLAS, LINCOLN, AND SLAVERY

D EMOCRATS AND WHIGS BOTH REGARDED STEPHEN A. DOUG-
las, the "Little Giant," as the biggest man in Illinois, one of the
biggest in the nation, and a possible President. Endowed with
immense ability and ambition, he advanced rapidly after reaching
Illinois, friendless and impoverished, in 1833 at the age of twenty.
In the next five years he taught a subscription school at Winches-
ter for a three-month term, read law from borrowed books, was
elected state's attorney and state representative at Jacksonville,
won appointment as register of the land office at Springfield, and
by thirty-five votes missed Democratic election to Congress in a
Whig district. Physically small, he stood a foot shorter than Abraham Lincoln, his contemporary at Springfield. To Douglas, politics
was more important than the law, and during his boyhood in New
York he had observed the Albany Regency, the first American
political machine, and learned from it that party discipline was
vital to success and could be promoted through the convention
system. Soon he became secretary of state, Supreme Court justice,
Democratic state chairman, and manager of winning campaigns. A
political genius, at the age of thirty he was elected to Congress. In
1847, during his third term, he advanced to the senate and
promptly became chairman of the committee on territories, a
sensitive assignment. The same year he moved to Chicago, whose
commercial greatness he foresaw, and assisted in the promotion of
railroads. There real estate investments brought independent

wealth to the large-headed, barrel-chested, short-legged extrovert who could sway audiences.

Douglas consistently stood for the Union and its expansion. On slavery, a moral issue which troubled the consciences of most other New Englanders, he was steadfastly neutral, a position he had taken before his first wife in 1848 inherited 150 slaves upon the death of her father, a Mississippi plantation owner. Successive generations of historians have disagreed about his motivation, with one school holding that his railroad projects were part of a far-sighted and statesmanlike effort to achieve a compromise that would enable both North and South to forget their differences. Rather than condemn slavery, Douglas sought to subordinate it through adjustment and compromise as he went about the glamorous task of enlarging the United States. In Congress he wrote the laws that organized five territories and admitted five states. He made possible the Illinois Central railroad and then turned his political talents to promoting a railroad to the Pacific, where gold had been discovered in 1848, on a route that would favor Chicago and his real estate investments. Such a career might take him to the White House if a neutral policy could be maintained on the sectional issue of slavery.[1]

THE LITTLE GIANT: EXPANSIONIST AND COMPROMISER

The exact status of public opinion is often difficult to gauge, even for an experienced politician, and Senator Douglas misjudged the amount of antislavery sentiment in the North. During the 1850's it grew steadily in volume while the South insisted that slavery must not be barred from the territories lest the national balance of power pass into northern hands.[2]

The North lacked unity. Although it was a national failure in 1848, a new Free Soil party and its allies won control of the legislature and by resolution compelled Senators Douglas and Shields to vote for the Wilmot Proviso, which tried to keep slavery out of the territory acquired in the Mexican War. Among the

[1] Allan Nevins, "Stephen A. Douglas: His Weaknesses and His Greatness," *Journal of the Illinois State Historical Society,* XLII (Dec., 1949), 385-410.

[2] The sectional differences that led to the Civil War are summarized in Paul M. Angle's introduction to *Created Equal? The Complete Lincoln-Douglas Debates of 1858.* See also George F. Milton, *The Eve of Conflict.*

Illinois congressmen, only John Wentworth,[3] a Chicago Democrat, and Edward D. Baker, a Whig, would vote for it.

By 1849 sectionalism threatened the nation with dissolution, but Henry Clay calmed the storm with a compromise which Douglas put through the senate as a series of individual bills. On his return to Chicago the senator in a three-and-a-half-hour speech talked a hostile meeting into approving the compromise as a step essential to the preservation of the Union.

Douglas then turned his attention to a railroad to the Pacific Ocean. He wanted it to cross Nebraska, in which Indian titles had been extinguished. A railroad would need settlers to provide traffic and a government, but Southerners for sectional reasons blocked action. Early in 1854 he introduced a bill to organize Nebraska as a territory which could come into the Union with or without slavery, as its constitution might prescribe at the time of admission. The bill seemed safe enough, since Utah and New Mexico became territories in 1850 under identical provisions. Also, the 1853 legislature had implemented the constitution by making it a crime to bring a free Negro into Illinois.[4] Sure of his political ground, Douglas went ahead to set up two territories, with the southern half of Nebraska to be known as Kansas. At southern insistence he provided for the outright repeal of the Missouri Compromise, which in 1820 sought to keep slavery below the 36° 30' line. Kansas was north of it. With backing of the Pierce administration, the bill became law while antislavery men stormed.

Under unexpectedly strong attack, Douglas defended his program as popular sovereignty, the right of the people of a territory to make their own decisions in any way that did not conflict with the Constitution. This time, when he returned from Chicago, hecklers kept him from speaking for four hours. Later he spoke at Geneva only after Ichabod Codding, an abolitionist leader, had quieted the crowd.

[3] Don E. Fehrenbacher, *Chicago Giant: A Biography of "Long John" Wentworth.* Ann Windle, "John Wentworth—His Contributions to Chicago," *Transactions of the Illinois State Historical Society,* XLIV (1937), 1-17.

[4] Racial prejudice among settlers with southern backgrounds was a factor in the opposition to the western spread of slavery. They wanted Negroes, freedmen as well as slaves, confined to the South and thus were temporary allies of the slaveholders. Eugene H. Berwanger, *The Frontier Against Slavery: Western Anti-Negro Prejudice and the Slavery Extension Controversy.*

Stephen A. Douglas

The controversy brought out of retirement Abraham Lincoln, the former Whig congressman who, discouraged by political reverses, had been giving full time to his law practice. When Douglas spoke at Springfield, Lincoln gave the anti-Nebraska answer the next day. Such prominent Democrats as Lyman Trumbull and Sidney Breese took Lincoln's side in speeches that followed.

As an unexpected result of the repeal of the compromise, the 1854 election reduced the Democrats to a legislative minority. With Shields' term expiring, Lincoln became a candidate for United States senator. When the legislature met in joint session he led for nine ballots, but five anti-Nebraska Democrats could not bring themselves to vote for a Whig. It became apparent that the Douglas forces would desert Shields and support Governor Matteson, who had not taken a pronounced stand on slavery. Lincoln then released the Whigs and swung the election to Trumbull, an anti-Nebraska Democrat.[5]

Lincoln had lost the big prize but Douglas had failed to elect a senator. Philosophically, Trumbull and Lincoln stood side by side, then and in the future. The sacrifice of ambition to principle earned Lincoln the friendship of the anti-Nebraskans. Henceforth he would be the Illinois leader of those who opposed the expansion of slavery.

A NEW PARTY WINS ITS FIRST ELECTION, 1856

In a time of political fragmentation, the Republican party emerged as an amalgamation of diverse elements united only on the antislavery issue. In Illinois the evolution came slowly and was possible because of the infusion of new attitudes in newly settled areas. A Liberty party, which served as an abolitionist political arm, in 1848 held the balance of power in thirteen northern counties but soon disappeared. A Free Soil convention at Ottawa that year opposed the extension of slavery, but its members typically refused to coalesce with other groups. Antislavery elements reorganized and in 1851 held meetings at Sparta, Rockford, Princeton, and Chicago. The next year the weakened and apathetic Whigs, unable to take a stand on the Kansas-Nebraska issue, lost their last presidential election. Some drifted back into political fellowship with the Democrats, but the "conscience" Whigs of the North had no choice but to join the new coalition whose name recalled Jefferson's Democratic-Republican party and the banning of slavery in the Old Northwest.

The first use of the Republican name in Illinois came in 1854 when a group of abolitionists from northern counties held a Springfield convention. Lincoln, who as a senate aspirant did not want to be classed as an extremist, avoided public association with the group and refused to serve on its central committee. That year

[5] Like Lincoln, Trumbull came out of political retirement when Douglas introduced his Nebraska bill. Mark M. Krug, *Lyman Trumbull, Conservative Radical*, pp. 77-161. Also see Horace White, *The Life of Lyman Trumbull*.

the Republicans held statewide meetings at Ripon, Wisconsin, and Jackson, Michigan, but the only activity in Illinois was at the congressional district level. The Republicans elected their candidate in the Chicago district and endorsed anti-Nebraska Whigs who won in two other districts.

Lincoln by 1856 cast his lot with the Republicans. The times called for diplomacy, and the astute prairie lawyer recognized that leadership must come from dissident Democrats and that the new coalition would be jeopardized if abolitionist and Know-Nothing extremists were not handled carefully. He went to Decatur but stayed in the background while helping shape resolutions adopted by a group of editors with Free Soil sympathies. The editorial convention, presided over by Paul Selby of Jacksonville, protested the extension of slavery, appointed a state central committee, and issued a call for all like-minded persons to gather in Bloomington May 29.

In response, some 270 delegates from seventy counties met in a third-floor room of Major's Hall, a brick structure that had temporarily housed the Normal school.[6] The gathering was sectional, with almost no representation of the southern counties. The convention, more accurately a mass meeting, marked the birth of the Republican party in Illinois, although the name was not used. Senator John M. Palmer of Carlinville, who had insisted upon the election of Trumbull two years earlier, presided during a long afternoon of oratory. Orville H. Browning, a Whig who also had been slow to abandon his old party, with Lincoln's help drafted resolutions which gave the new movement a conservative base.[7] Owen Lovejoy brought abolitionists into Republican ranks and accepted the Lincoln strategy that they should work outside the limelight.[8] Lincoln closed the meeting with a "lost speech"

[6] A detailed account of the Bloomington meeting is contained in Ezra M. Prince (ed.), "Convention of May 29, 1857, That Organized the Republican Party in Illinois," *Transactions of the McLean County Historical Society,* III (1900). Paul M. Selby wrote the "Genesis of the Republican Party in Illinois," *Transactions of the Illinois State Historical Society,* XI (1906), 270-283. See also Joseph O. Cunningham, "The Bloomington Convention of 1856 and Those Who Participated in It," *Transactions of the Illinois State Historical Society,* X (1905), 101-110. Alexander Davidson and Bernard Stuvé, *A Complete History of Illinois,* pp. 635-655. Charles A. Church, *History of the Republican Party in Illinois.* D. W. Lusk, *Politics and Politicians: A Succinct History of the Politics of Illinois from 1856 to 1884.* Green B. Raum, *History of Illinois Republicanism.*

[7] Maurice Baxter, *Orville H. Browning: Lincoln's Friend and Critic,* pp. 80-94.

[8] Edward Magdol, *Owen Lovejoy: Abolitionist in Congress.*

that took an advanced stand against slavery but was not distributed after the convention.

By acclamation, the first Republican nomination for governor went to William H. Bissell, a Democratic lawyer and former physician who had served three terms in Congress as a Mexican War hero. Bissell had been a celebrity since 1850 when he answered on the house floor a Southerner's declaration that Mississippi troops commanded by Jefferson Davis had saved the day at Buena Vista. Bissell, who had been in the heaviest fighting as a colonel, told the congressmen it wasn't true and denounced Southerners for glorifying themselves and belittling Northerners.[9] Challenged to a duel by Davis, Bissell accepted and stipulated that the weapons would be army muskets loaded with ball and buckshot. President Taylor aided the shocked Southerners by arranging a settlement.

Bissell, who had retired from Congress as an invalid, with overoptimism sent word to Bloomington that he was recovering the use of his legs. He stayed at home, made one campaign speech, and was elected over William A. Richardson of Quincy, a Douglas stalwart. Republicans elected all their state candidates and four of the nine congressmen. Of major importance, Bissell's election gave Lincoln the necessary Republican home base for his national campaign four years later. Yankees and Europeans who disliked slavery had changed the political balance of power. Among the new elements in Illinois, the Democrats henceforth could count only on the support of the Irish.[10]

Democrats controlled the legislature and continually heckled Bissell, who was the first Catholic and only invalid to be elected governor. Because of his paralysis, he took the oath of office in the executive mansion which had first been occupied when Matteson was governor. Led by John A. Logan, a fire-eater from Jackson County, Democrats insisted that Bissell's acceptance of the challenge to a duel had made him constitutionally ineligible to be governor.

Ten months before the end of his term Bissell died of pneumonia. His successor, bearded John Wood, in 1822 had built the first log cabin at Quincy.

9 Davidson-Stuvé, *op. cit.,* pp. 656-678.
10 Raum, *op. cit.,* pp. 35-40.

NATIONAL SPOTLIGHT: LINCOLN DEBATES DOUGLAS

Kansas had been settled largely by Northerners—mostly from Illinois, Indiana, and Ohio—but it was the last remaining federal territory where conditions were favorable for slavery. Consequently it was of vital importance to the South, and the pressure of sectional rivalries provided the issues of 1858 when Douglas ran for a third term. Concerned about the outcome, he defied President Buchanan and refused to support the Lecompton proslavery constitution, which he called a travesty on popular sovereignty. Most Illinois Democrats accepted his stand, although the senator received abuse from the Democratic press and his friends were turned out of postmasterships.

Eastern Republicans admired Douglas' courage and urged that the party in Illinois permit his reelection without opposition, but to Lincoln and his associates their rival had been and was still wrong on the main issue of the extension of slavery. Endorsed for senator as the first and only choice of the Republicans, Lincoln used a biblical theme in one of his most historic speeches, delivered before his party's state convention in the house chamber at Springfield. "A house divided against itself cannot stand," he began. "I believe this government cannot endure permanently half slave and half free. I do not expect the Union to be dissolved. I do not expect the house to fall, but I do expect it will cease to be divided." David Davis, the judge of Lincoln's circuit-riding years, and some other close advisers were alarmed that those opening sentences had an abolitionist taint. As expected, Douglas referred to the speech repeatedly in the campaign.

The campaign opened in Chicago with the better-known Douglas drawing a big crowd as he spoke from the Tremont House balcony. Lincoln listened, and replied the next night. The Republican was at a disadvantage as Douglas spent his own money freely and traveled on a special train. Alarmed at the situation, Lincoln's managers asked that the Democrat spend the rest of the campaign debating. Douglas yielded his advantage by agreeing to one debate in each of the seven congressional districts in which he had not yet spoken.

The issues they expounded were national and monumental. In the first debate at Ottawa Douglas insisted that Republicans advocated sectional strife and contended that Negroes were inferior. Lincoln did not argue political and social equality but he

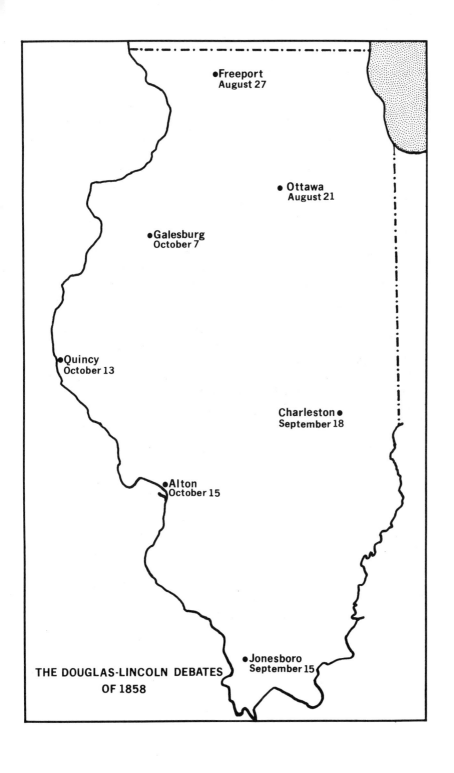

•Freeport
August 27

• Ottawa
August 21

•Galesburg
October 7

•Quincy
October 13

Charleston•
September 18

•Alton
October 15

•Jonesboro
September 15

THE DOUGLAS-LINCOLN DEBATES
OF 1858

said that Negroes have the same natural rights as white men. He contended that repeal of the 1820 compromise had broken a contract and that popular sovereignty had been nullified by the Dred Scott decision. At Freeport, the second appearance, Lincoln presented Douglas with a dilemma.[11] He insisted that Douglas answer a key question: Could the people of a territory, in any lawful way, against the wish of any citizen, exclude slavery from its limits prior to the formation of a state constitution? He asked that Douglas either concede that slavery could go anywhere or else cease urging the sanctity of Supreme Court decisions. The question was not new, and Douglas had a ready answer: "Slavery cannot exist for a day or an hour, anywhere, unless it is supported by local police regulations." The reply was politically effective in the Illinois campaign, but both principals knew that it cost Douglas ground in the South, which wanted a direct statement upholding the slave power.[12]

The other debates were anticlimactic. At Charleston, where the crowd was evenly divided, Douglas kept attacking the House Divided speech and accused Lincoln of favoring Negro equality. When the Republican modified earlier statements Douglas accused him of being "jet black in the North, a decent mulatto in the center, and almost white in the South." The other debates were at Jonesboro, Galesburg, Quincy, and Alton. In the final arguments Lincoln repeated his charge that Douglas "looks to no end of the institution of slavery," and Douglas replied that "I care more for the great principle of self-government, the right of the people to rule, than I do for all the Negroes in Christendom. I would not endanger the perpetuity of this Union."

Much of the debates was little more than political sparring, and neither of the antagonists lived up to the reputation of Webster, Hayne, and Calhoun. Their great significance was that Douglas was forced into a position that made him unacceptable to the South and cost him his chance to become President in 1860. Lincoln benefited from crowd exposure and acquired a nationwide reputation as a worthy opponent of the famed Douglas. The debates also

[11] Avery Craven, *The Coming of the Civil War*, pp. 381-382. Willard L. King, *Lincoln's Manager, David Davis*, pp. 116-117.

[12] In addition to Angle's introduction, *op. cit.*, see Edwin Erle Sparks (ed.), *The Lincoln-Douglas Debates of 1858*. Sparks begins his introduction with the 1858 campaign. Both books contain the texts of the debates. Harry E. Pratt, "The Great Debates," *Illinois Blue Book, 1953-54*, pp. 2-29.

made journalism history when newspaper correspondents for the first time telegraphed daily stories of the campaign.

Both candidates made solo appearances before other audiences, and Republicans followed the Democratic example of organizing to make certain that the aged, infirm, and forgetful went to the polls. A confidential memorandum from Republican headquarters at Chicago recommended vigilance in challenging new arrivals from Ireland. The popular vote favored Lincoln, 125,430 to 121,609, with 5,071 for the Buchanan ticket. The Republicans also carried the two state offices. The legislature had been gerrymandered in favor of the Democrats, however, and in January Douglas was reelected, 54 to 46.[13]

A PRESIDENT FROM ILLINOIS

On a national scale, the two men again were rivals in 1860. The country lawyer who now tried cases for corporations, the homely giant whose early years had been spent in frontier proverty, the orator who had mastered the English tongue from borrowed books, began to get serious consideration for the presidency. Lincoln went to New York and displayed his intellectual prowess with a carefully reasoned speech at Cooper Union. At the first Republican national convention in 1856, Lincoln had received a handful of votes as a vice presidential possibility, but now he had national stature and a home state rival. A pledge of solid and continuous support of Illinois Republicans was given in a state convention at Decatur, where press agentry gave Lincoln the common touch of being a "rail-splitter" candidate.[14]

Chicago's convention career had been launched at the 1847 harbor and rivers gathering, but that session received far less attention than the nomination of a presidential ticket in an hour of crisis. The site was the Wigwam, a sprawling two-story hall of pine. Lincoln had stiff competition. William H. Seward of New York rated as the favorite, but Salmon P. Chase and others split the field. Lincoln had astute managers as well as the advantage of a noisy, friendly crowd in the galleries. David Davis, who weighed

---

13 Moses, *Illinois Historical and Statistical*, II, 621, says Republican counties had a population of 646,748 and thirty-four representatives, while Democratic counties had a population of 477,678 and forty-one representatives.

14 Many specialized books deal with one place or one event in the life of Lincoln. One of the best is Otto R. Kyle, *Lincoln in Decatur*.

three hundred pounds and excelled in campaign management, took charge of headquarters in the Tremont Hotel. The chief argument was that only Lincoln could carry Illinois and other pivotal states against Douglas.[15] At the Springfield telegraph station Lincoln received word that they succeeded on the third ballot.

Because of his comparative youth, Douglas had been passed over for the 1852 and 1856 Democratic presidential nomination. Now he had acquired enemies and, since the Freeport speech, had been stripped of the chairmanship of the territories committee. At Charleston, South Carolina, Democrats met amid great excitement, bitterness, and a deadlock. Fighting desperately, Douglas led for fifty-seven ballots but lacked the required two-thirds majority. After a recess, in two segments the convention reassembled at Baltimore, where Douglas finally received the nomination of his party's northern wing. Southern Democrats and Whig remnants split the field by entering their own presidential tickets.

In the custom of the time, Lincoln stayed in Springfield.[16] Douglas while touring the nation gradually lost confidence that he could carry most of the South and enough free states to either win the presidency or throw the election into the house of representatives. Recognizing the possibility that Lincoln could win, he turned his efforts to reorganizing the Democratic party and quelling the southern movement for secession. Meanwhile the Republican ticket attracted the support of farmers and industrial workers, since the new party's foundations included advocacy of a homestead law and a protective tariff.

Douglas carried only Missouri and New Jersey, but in the split popular vote Lincoln went to Washington as a minority choice. He had 50.7 percent of the vote in Illinois, where Republicans carried their state ticket again and for the first time won majorities in both legislative houses.

[15] King, *op. cit.*, pp. 134-141. Harry E. Pratt, "David Davis, 1815-1886," *Transactions of the Illinois State Historical Society*, XXXVII (1930), 157-183.

[16] William E. Baringer, "Campaign Techniques in Illinois—1860," *Transactions of the Illinois State Historical Society*, XXXIX (1932), 202-281.

16

THE CIVIL WAR

THE PRESIDENT-ELECT SPOKE HIS FAREWELL TO SPRINGFIELD and moved cautiously to reduce the possibility that the South would secede. While working for a compromise, Douglas gave full support to Lincoln and at the inauguration ceremony symbolically held his former rival's hat. After Fort Sumter the senator went promptly to the White House to assure the President that in the developing war he stood steadfastly with the Union. Frequently the two men conferred.

In the national split, there was doubt about the loyalty of parts of the Northwest, for which Douglas long had been the spokesman. Lincoln asked the senator to go back to Illinois, to arouse the people to the seriousness of the crisis and to speak to his Democratic followers in behalf of unity. En route he twice urged Ohio audiences to support the government without reservation. Reaching Springfield, he went before the legislature April 25 to deliver a remarkably eloquent plea for preservation of the Union. The sonorous voice stirred a frenzy of excitement in the house chamber as Douglas condemned the secessionists and asked that partisanship be set aside. The man who had promoted railroads gave the northern cause a special economic basis by pointing out that unobstructed use of the Mississippi River steamboat route was essential to the prosperity of the upper valley.[1] As word of the

[1] Shelby M. Cullom, who was speaker of the house, was so impressed with the

loyalty speech spread among the Democrats, Douglas went to Chicago and faced his final audience in the Wigwam May 1. Again he accused the South of a conspiracy and asked that all Illinois rally around the flag.

"Every man must be for the United States or against it," he said. "There can be no neutrals in this war, only patriots and traitors."

Then, when his nation most needed his counsel and his oratory, the Little Giant died June 3 of typhoid fever, asking with his last words that his sons obey the laws and support the Constitution. At the start of the war the North had suffered a major loss.

THE BOYS IN BLUE START SOUTHWARD

President Lincoln's state responded promptly to repeated calls for men who would fight and die to preserve the Union. In the four years between Fort Sumter and Appomattox, the roster would show the names of 259,092 Illinois men in the army and navy. Of these nearly thirty-five thousand died in the excitement of battle, the agony of hospitals, the boredom of camps, and the malnutrition of prisons.

The volunteers were mostly young, the bulk being between eighteen and twenty-five years, and generally untrained. Including uniformed drill teams, when Fort Sumter fell the state had possibly thirty militia companies good for little but holiday parading. The men were woefully unequipped and totally ignorant of the amount of blood and sweat that would be spilled on the other sides of the Ohio and Mississippi rivers. They volunteered early, when the need was greatest, and as farm boys were expert in the use of firearms. Generally they fought well and, although an occasional outfit had to be disciplined, the men from Illinois showed in scores of campaigns, battles, and skirmishes that they could be as brave and rugged as their forebears who had exterminated the Indians.[2]

Douglas speech that a half-century later he included the text in his autobiography, *Fifty Years of Public Service*, pp. 64-72. Excerpts of the Chicago speech are found in Clark E. Carr, *Stephen A. Douglas, His Life, Public Service, Speeches and Patriotism*, p. 138. James P. Jones, *"Black Jack": John A. Logan and Southern Illinois in the Civil War*.

[2] The exploits and difficulties of Illinois soldiers and regiments are covered in Victor Hicken, *Illinois in the Civil War*. Detailed information about troops, battles, and casualties can be found in John Moses, *Illinois Historical and Statistical*, II, 1213-1240;

Semidormant Cairo, which pointed at the heart of the confederacy, was vitally important. Washington asked that four regiments occupy the strategic town, and Governor Richard Yates sent 595 men, members of zouave drill teams and militia companies, with all the rifles and shotguns Chicago stores had in stock. At Cairo the first troops moved into fairground sheds that were converted into temporary barracks. The war stopped the triweekly steamer service to New Orleans and paralyzed the economy of Cairo until army paymasters arrived as part of a vast concentration of armies, munitions, and gunboats, as well as camp followers, tent theaters, and dives.[3]

Immediately after Fort Sumter, Lincoln called on the states for seventy-five thousand militiamen, supposedly to serve only three months, of which Illinois' share was to be six regiments. Supply exceeded demand, and the response almost was a race to Springfield. Men left their farms and jobs, and in five days more than sixty hurriedly recruited companies were offered for service. The nation had no other procedure for raising an army, and prominent men, many of them politicians, were asked by Springfield to recruit regiments of volunteers. In a democratic fashion, the men elected captains and colonels. Anyone who had been in the Mexican War was in demand.

A great early wave of patriotism swept through Illinois. The legislature, convened the day Governor Yates received the militia call, unanimously resolved "that the faith, credit and resources of the state of Illinois, both in men and money are pledged, to any amount, and to every extent, which the federal government may demand." The special session appropriated for war purposes three and a half million dollars which the state did not have, but Chicago and Springfield bankers kept the treasury solvent with unsecured loans. The legislature also authorized ten additional regiments and the war department soon accepted them, in part because the surplus volunteers insisted upon assignment to active duty. In July, when Bull Run ended in a rout outside Washington, the state had more men ready and Yates telegraphed that "Illinois demands the right to do her full share in the work of preserving

Alexander Davidson and Bernard Stuvé, *A Complete History of Illinois,* pp. 746-865; and Newton Bateman and Paul Selby, *Historical Encyclopedia of Illinois,* Cook County edition, II, 551-576.

[3] Wm. Henry Perrin (ed.), *History of Alexander, Union and Pulaski Counties,* pp. 161ff. John M. Lansden, *A History of the City of Cairo, Illinois.*

our glorious Union from the assaults of high-handed rebellion." By October, Illinois had more regiments in the field than New York, and some of its impatient men avoided delays by enlisting in Missouri and Kentucky.

Someone had to be quartermaster general, responsible for obtaining food, uniforms, tents, and other equipment for the Illinois regiments and batteries. Yates gave the job to former Governor Wood, who also had the duty of obtaining arms and ammunition. Wood, who was left-handed and did not like to write, let his second assistant worry about keeping records.[4] They showed that the quartermaster's office made purchases totaling $3,714,122 to clothe and equip the first sixty thousand men who went to war. By 1862, federal officers took over the procurement duties. At the age of 65, Wood then recruited an infantry regiment and went to Memphis as its colonel.

Many counties exceeded manpower quotas, and in the close scrutiny that has been given all phases of the Civil War no one has asserted that any geographical region or population segment of Illinois failed to send its full share of men into northern armies. The southern counties, despite early concern, exceeded their quotas, and volunteering ran at high levels in areas soon to be tainted with Copperheadism. By the first December of the war Chicago had an Irish brigade. Regiments formed on nationalistic, occupational, and educational lines. All had official numbers, but many, such as the Rock River Rifles, were also known for their place of origin. Two regiments were known as German and two as Scotch. A Lead Mine regiment formed in the Galena hills. Two regiments got their names because preachers were in their ranks. Schoolteachers and students predominated in a "brains" regiment commanded by Charles E. Hovey, who resigned as president of the Normal school and began recruiting on the campus.

Ulysses S. Grant, a West Pointer who had been in the Mexican War, had drilled the volunteer company at Galena and escorted it to Springfield. Because Grant understood military paper work, the governor gave him a two-dollar-a-day job as assistant quartermaster

[4] Edward Everett, "Operation of the Quarter-Master's Department of the State of Illinois, 1861-2," *Transactions of the Illinois State Historical Society,* X (1905), 230-236, and Cora Agnes Benneson, "The Work of Edward Everett of Quincy in the Quarter-Master's Department in Illinois During the First Years of the Civil War," *Transactions of the Illinois State Historical Society,* XIV (1909), 147-153.

general. Later he was made commander of a troublesome regiment. Congressman Elihu B. Washburne of Galena was his friend, and soon Grant wore brigadier's stars and as commander at Cairo sent troops from Illinois and neighboring states into battle at Belmont and Fort Donelson. The casualties were heavy, but he scored the first Union successes of important magnitude.

Almost every building of adequate size became a temporary barracks. Most Illinois troops were sent to Camp Douglas at Chicago's southern edge or to Camp Butler six miles east of Springfield. Both had railroad connections and space for drill grounds. Carpenters erected rows of wooden barracks and stables, and soon added log stockades and more barracks to serve as prison camps.[5] Union soldiers remembered Camp Butler for vermin and lack of recreational facilities. Typhoid, primitive sanitation, and the cold winters caused a high mortality at Camp Douglas, where at various times some thirty thousand Confederates were confined.

[5] Joseph L. Eisendrath, Jr., "Chicago's Camp Douglas, 1861-1865," *Journal of the Illinois State Historical Society,* LIII, 1 (Spring, 1960), 37-63.

Cairo: federal troops transferring from Illinois Central station to riverboats

Courtesy Illinois State Historical Library

As many as three thousand prisoners were crowded into Camp Butler. Other captured Confederates were guarded at Rock Island and in the old penitentiary at Alton.

Mound City, eight miles above Cairo on the Ohio River, became the chief naval depot for the "fresh-water fleet" which helped break the Confederacy. In 1857, Mound City had an iron foundry, an immense warehouse, and a marine ways from which boats were launched for the Memphis-New Orleans cotton trade. There steamboats were converted into gunboats and unprotected mortars were floated on boats made of layers of log rafts. Cairo was overloaded as an army supply center, and the government leased the Mound City shipbuilding plant for forty thousand dollars a year. Quickly expanded, it turned out craft that were manned by steamboatmen whose jobs had been wiped out by the war. Wounded from the early battles of Belmont and Shiloh were brought to a hastily improvised riverfront hospital. By necessity Mound City became the site of a national cemetery with 5,555 Civil War graves. The naval station survived rivalry from Cairo and Carondelet, Missouri, and was maintained by the federal government until 1874.[6]

REAPERS AND RAILROADS: THE ECONOMIC FRONT

Before the shooting started, Illinois had a railroad network and the beginnings of an industrial system, in addition to its fertile soil. Fortunately for the North, the combination of transportation, factories, and farms aided mightily in overcoming the slave labor and cotton economy of the South. In 1861, the Old Northwest was on the verge of its full development; Michigan and Wisconsin also underwent rapid population growth in the 1850's, and of the loyalist states the five organized under the 1787 ordinance ranked among the first eight in population. Illinois led as a wheat and corn state and ranked second in the value of its livestock. The total improved acreage increased from five hundred thousand to 13.291 million in the decade, but 7.8 million acres of prairie were still classed as unimproved. The aggregate wealth of the state had multiplied five times and the value of its farms four and a half times. At a slower pace, industry was following popula-

6 Perrin, op. cit., pp. 539-552. John W. Allen, It Happened in Southern Illinois, pp. 328-329. Fletcher Pratt, The Civil War on Western Waters—The Story of the Union and Confederate River Navies.

tion into Illinois. The 1860 census showed that the state had
approximately three thousand manufacturing establishments, a
thousand less than Indiana and far behind the number in New
York, Pennsylvania, and Ohio.[7]

The younger men went to war, but those left at home produced
enough to feed their families, the cities, and the northern armies,
and to meet a new export demand from Europe. Factories at
Chicago, Moline, and other cities used mass production methods
to make possible the miracle as the plow and the reaper revolu-
tionized agriculture.

Small shops became factories and, in imitation of the McCormick and Deere plants, used metals both as raw materials and as
production tools. At Canton, William Parlin expanded the shop in
which he turned out the first steel-bottomed plow and did away
with the wooden moldboard. William Worth Burson invented a
grain binder that featured machine-tied knots, but he had not yet
perfected the automatic knitting machine that made Rockford
famous for its socks. Edward Hegeler and Frederick W. Matthies-
sen, recent arrivals from Germany, decided that because of its coal
supplies La Salle County would be an ideal site for the nation's
first zinc smelter. The zinc ore, shipped by the Illinois Central, was
a by-product of the Galena lead mines. Richard T. Crane, who had
worked in a New England cotton mill when he was nine, began a
brass foundry in a corner of his uncle's lumberyard in Chicago.
Philetus W. Gates, who had gone bankrupt as a canal subcontrac-
tor, reached Chicago earlier and started a blacksmith shop and
foundry that, combined with his inventive talents, in later years
expanded into a series of corporations.

Because railroads and farm machinery required immense
amounts of iron, Chicago began development as a heavy metals
center before the Civil War. Eber Brock Ward, who in 1855, at
Wyandotte, Michigan, built the first iron works west of Pittsburgh,
two years later built a plant on the north branch of the Chicago
River. He used ore from the newly opened Lake Superior ranges.
He specialized in rails and in 1865 was credited with rolling the

---

[7] Statistics on the agricultural and industrial growth of Illinois and the upper Middle
West can be found in Moses, *op. cit.*, II, 869-870; Bruce Catton, *The Coming Fury,* p.
470; Fred A. Shannon, *The Farmer's Last Frontier,* pp. 163, 182-183. Paul W. Gates,
Agriculture and the Civil War, pp. 136-141, 150-152, 171-180, 233-246, 276-284, 308,
346-353: and Eugene Davenport, "A Century of Agricultural Progress," *Illinois Blue
Book, 1917-18,* pp. 27-29.

first steel produced in the United States. Ward's plant in 1869 made about one-third of the iron and steel produced in the country.

For the farmers and many people in towns, the war opened badly. Corn, wheat, barreled pork, and whiskey normally sold in the South piled up in warehouses, and a depression worse than that of 1857 settled over the North in 1861. Unemployment increased and business houses closed. Farmers suffered when hog quotations at Chicago were halved, and a hundred miles away corn sold as low as six cents a bushel. The 1851 free banking system did not survive the war. Many banks were in trouble at the start because bonds of southern states backed two-thirds of the Illinois note issues. When the state auditor called for more securities, most of the banks were forced to the wall and the bondholders suffered large losses. Among some politicians the concept of a statewide banking system still had appeal and in 1861 the legislature authorized a union bank, with semi-independent branches and a central board of directors, but the voters rejected it overwhelmingly at a referendum. In the emergency, the federal government filled the gap with greenbacks and national bank notes, which began flooding the state in 1862 and met the need for a circulating medium with legal tender status. Businessmen welcomed the system of national banks first authorized in 1863. At the end of the war the state banks were reduced to the same status when their notes were driven out of circulation by a federal tax. The greenbacks depreciated in value, which brought on a paper money inflation during which the cost of living skyrocketed.[8]

Military buying in the North and three years of bad weather and crop failures in Europe helped trigger economic recovery for Illinois, and the loss of the southern markets temporarily became unimportant. Trade turned eastward, and many small-town packers moved to Chicago, which also became a warehouse center.

The Illinois Central under the presidency of William H. Osborn helped in the recovery. The railroad took a loss at the start of the war by accepting corn at Chicago prices, minus transportation charges, so that farmers could meet payments on their land contracts. As a result they unloaded the surplus from the abundant 1860 and 1861 crops. With free transportation and special trains,

[8] George W. Dowrie, *The Development of Banking in Illinois, 1817-1863*, pp. 15-173.

the Illinois Central had helped promote state fairs at Chicago in 1855 and at Centralia in 1858. A pioneer in agricultural promotion, it turned to the new cause of crop diversification during the war by urging farmers to plant cotton, sugar beets, and flax. The railroad coupled fruit cars with passenger trains and in 1862 ran the first special fruit train to the Chicago market.

During the war Chicago solidified its position as the rail center of the interior. Although construction of new lines slowed down, due to shortages of manpower and materials, nevertheless some twelve hundred miles were added to the tributary lines during the war years. Complaints about rail fares and service began to be heard and the wartime emergency turned attention back to the Illinois and Michigan Canal. Congressman Isaac N. Arnold tried to get it enlarged so that ships could pass from the Mississippi into the Great Lakes, but the railroads blocked the effort to increase competition from water routes.

FAILURE OF A WARTIME CON-CON

As a political distraction, a constitutional convention dominated by his Democratic opponents faced Governor Yates in early 1862. The state's population had doubled since adoption of the 1848 constitution and proponents of another revision objected especially to the low salaries fixed for state officials and to loopholes which led to the flooding of the legislature with bills for private and special laws. In 1860 a convention proposal carried as a side issue in the Lincoln campaign.

The election of delegates a year later is explained by Alexander Davidson and Bernard Stuvé in their history of Illinois as a successful Democratic strategy to enter fusion candidates in Republican districts but to run their own men elsewhere.[9] "Indeed, for party organization and alertness, democratic leaders have ever outmaneuvered their opponents, probably because the rank and file of their party have ever been tractable," their 1874 history said. With one delegate allotted to each of the seventy-five representative districts, the Democrats elected forty-five men and Republi-

[9] Davidson-Stuvé, *op. cit.*, pp. 872-877. Janet Cornelius, *A History of Constitution Making in Illinois*, pp. 33-41. Emil Joseph Verlie, *Illinois Constitutions*, pp. xxvi-xxviii. Oliver M. Dickerson, *The Illinois Constitutional Convention of 1862*. Stanley L. Jones, "Agrarian Radicalism in Illinois' Constitutional Convention of 1862," *Journal of the Illinois State Historical Society*, XLVIII (Autumn, 1955), 271-282.

cans twenty-one. The seven fusionists and the two classified as doubtful supported the Democrats most of the time.

The delegates, who included some of the state's most prominent men, asserted that they had supreme authority limited only by the federal Constitution. On that theory, they refused to take the oath prescribed by the legislature. They voted to ratify an amendment to the federal Constitution which had been submitted to the legislature and for a time they considered appointing a United States senator. In its omnipotent mood, the convention tried to dictate to the executives and the courts and to take over control of military affairs. Major attention centered on expenditure of state funds to feed, clothe, equip, and organize the Illinois regiments. The governor for a time complied with the convention's requests for a wide variety of information, but after a month in a curt letter said he "did not acknowledge the right of the convention to instruct him in the performance of his duty." Several troop commanders refused to answer communications from the convention. When a sour public reaction became apparent, the delegates sought to improve their image by voting to raise five hundred thousand dollars for the care of sick and wounded soldiers. The money was to come from a financially impossible bond issue.

The document finally drafted contained some constructive changes, but they were canceled by political blunders, including a reapportionment that was gerrymandered to favor Democrats and a provision that incumbent state officers, all Republicans, be turned out of office in midterm while circuit and county clerks, mostly Democrats, finished their full four-year terms. The final delegate vote March 22 was 44 to 4 for adoption, but most of the Republicans refused to sign the document. The revision was denounced by the predominantly Republican newspapers, and business interests objected to a provision that corporation charters could be amended or repealed by later legislatures. The proposed constitution was rejected by 24,515 votes at a special June election, with articles that would have prohibited free banking and set up congressional districts being defeated also.

While a debate over emancipation of slaves occupied the North, Illinois voted overwhelmingly for three anti-Negro propositions which also were separately submitted to the electorate.[10] Majorities were as high as 154,524 for proposals to write into the

[10] Arthur C. Cole, *The Era of the Civil War, 1848-1870*, pp. 333-338. V. Jacque Voegeli, *Free but Not Equal: The Midwest and the Negro During the Civil War.*

Richard Yates, Civil War Governor

constitution the black laws of 1853 which prohibited Negroes from migrating into Illinois and denied them the right to vote and to hold office. The drafters of the unsuccessful constitution contended that former slaves, who were coming North as contraband of war, endangered white employment. The refugee Negroes who had been liberated by northern armies poured into Cairo, Quincy, Rock Island, and other river ports. Trains then spread them over the state.

DISSENSION ON THE HOME FRONT

No governor worked harder in behalf of the war effort than Richard Yates of Illinois. An antislavery Kentuckian, strikingly handsome, an orator of the spread-eagle school and somewhat temperamental, Yates divided his loyalties between Lincoln, with whom he was at times impatient, and the men in blue from Illinois, whom he had urged to enlist with promises that they would not be forgotten.[11]

Yates was the "soldiers' friend." Illinois had mobilized the regiments and the governor felt that, although they had passed to the jurisdiction of the war department, the state still had responsibilities for their care and comfort. Repeatedly he visited camps and hospitals to give encouragement and solace to the men from Illinois. A political partisan, he equated patriotism with support of the Republican national and state administrations, and he called upon the legislature to appropriate additional funds for the soldiers. As the fighting dragged on, bloodily, expensively, and often discouragingly, many throughout Illinois and the Northwest lacked the fervor and determination of the governor of Lincoln's state. Acrimony spread as the early patriotic enthusiasm ebbed. On the home front it was not a happy war.

Political differences became evident a month and a half before Lincoln's inauguration, when a statewide mass meeting of Democrats at Springfield adopted resolutions urging that the slavery issue be compromised and the war avoided by means of a national convention. To such a meeting, held at Washington without accomplishment, Yates after consultation with Lincoln sent five prominent Republicans.

When the war broke out, sentiment for joining the Confederacy existed in some of the southern parts of Illinois, Indiana, and Ohio. A meeting in Pope County endorsed the idea, and some public officials were suspected of being secessionists at heart. Douglas' two speeches, Logan's decision to wear the army blue, and the early wave of patriotism drowned out the discord for a few months only. By 1862, when significant victories failed to materialize, a sharp difference of opinion split the Northwest and a peace faction of Democrats criticized Lincoln's policies.

The death of Douglas left Illinois Democrats without strong

---

[11] Jack Nortrup, "Richard Yates: A Personal Glimpse of the Illinois Soldiers' Friend," *Journal of the Illinois State Historical Society,* LVI (Summer, 1963), 121-133. John H. Krenkel is editor of *Richard Yates, Civil War Governor,* by Richard Yates and Catherine Yates Pickering, based on a biography by the governor's son and namesake. See also Davidson-Stuvé, *op. cit.,* pp. 718-719. E. L. Kimball, "Richard Yates: His Record as Civil War Governor," *Journal of the Illinois State Historical Society,"* XXIII (April, 1930), 1-83.

leadership. Logan and McClernand had resigned from Congress to become generals and, as leading War Democrats, their political roles were largely confined to trips back home for patriotic speeches. The Democrats were aloof and the Douglas vacancy went to Orville H. Browning, a former Whig. For a time the Little Giant's followers heeded his advice to be loyal. Congressman William A. Richardson, who had been a Mexican War major, turned down Lincoln's offer of an appointment as a brigadier general.[12] In Congress he lined up with a conservative faction determined to restore the Democratic party to power. The Peace Democrats included a sizable proportion of the men who held party positions and influenced decisions, and their support came from both the city Irish and the southern-oriented farmers. The peace slogan—"The Constitution as it is, and the Union as it was"—demonstrated a conservative desire to return to prewar conditions economically, socially, and politically. As partisans, some wanted to check Republican ascendancy. Anti-abolitionism was a major influence among the traditional Democrats and the city laborers, who feared job competition from Negroes. In the economic upsets early in the war, some believed that the sectional interests of Illinois were closer to the South than to the East. They talked of setting up a Northwest Confederacy to match that headed by Jefferson Davis. As secessionists scored the first victories, Peace Democrats objected to the President's assumption of strong executive powers in mobilizing the nation's potential strength. To cope with the disloyalty in the North while fighting the South, Lincoln considered that a national emergency existed. He fed the flames in late 1862 by suspending the writ of habeas corpus and allowing some civilian critics, all Democrats, to be arrested and held for military trial. The opposition, both political and philosophical, multiplied as Lincoln took the first steps toward emancipation of the slaves. By that time the antiwar Democrats were popularly known as Copperheads, named for a snake that strikes without warning. They criticized Lincoln and Yates almost continually, and some were guilty of obstructing the war effort.[13]

[12] Maurice Baxter, *Orville H. Browning: Lincoln's Friend and Critic,* pp. 121ff. Theodore C. Pease and James G. Randall (eds.), *The Diary of Orville Hickman Browning.* Robert D. Holt, "The Political Career of William A. Richardson," *Journal of the Illinois State Historical Society,* XXVI (Oct., 1933), 255.

[13] In the home-front controversy, each faction has its historian. The Peace Democrats are depicted by Frank W. Klement in *The Copperheads in the Middle West* as an

In his home state many Republicans also criticized Lincoln, who faced immense diplomatic problems involving border state loyalty and European neutrality. Early in the war, many grumbled when the President overruled General John C. Fremont, a popular hero who attempted to confiscate the property of Missouri rebels. The *Chicago Tribune* joined in the criticism when Lincoln postponed steps that would lead to freedom of the Negroes. Like Yates, Senator Lyman Trumbull held the radical Republican view that Lincoln should display more zeal in pushing the antislavery cause. Trumbull believed that the rebellion could be suppressed with proper interpretation of constitutional powers. He disapproved the extraordinary steps taken by Lincoln between sessions, but held that Congress nevertheless should give the administration the necessary power to put down the rebellion.

With some moderation, the Democratic state convention of 1862 criticized extremists on both sides but tabled resolutions, submitted by a member of McClernand's staff, which quoted Douglas on loyalty and asked all Americans to rally around the flag. During the autumn months, the arbitrary arrests caused concern that the administration was intent on stifling all dissent. Talk of emancipation and the scarcity of good news from the battlefields were other factors, and the November election turned out to be a major victory for the Democrats in much of the North. In the first Illinois balloting for a congressman-at-large, a War Democrat nominated by Republicans in a fusion effort lost to a Peace Democrat from southern Illinois.

Consequently, Democrats controlled the 1863 legislature, 13 to 12 in the senate and 54 to 32 in the house of representatives. The session opened with a Democratic mass meeting at which criticism

early agrarian movement with philosophical and constitutional objections to the war program that fell far short of disloyalty and treason. He dissents from Wood Gray's *The Hidden Civil War: The Story of the Copperheads,* which places the onus for obstructionism and some violence on the Peace Democrats. Both authors go into great detail. Gray presents a mass of evidence about Copperhead efforts to thwart the war effort. Klement challenges the veracity of some of the reports and in others contends that the evidence presented does not prove a conspiracy. On many major events and disputes they are close to general agreement and are the source of a major part of this portion of the home-front story. Klement's defense of the Peace Democrats has some parallels with objections to participation in the Vietnamese war more than a century later. Klement contends that militant Copperhead secret orders late in the war never existed but were the product of inflammatory fiction by a Springfield correspondent for Chicago and St. Louis newspapers. See also Edgar Bernhard, *et al., Pursuit of Freedom: A History of Civil Liberty in Illinois, 1787-1942,* pp. 131-132.

centered on Lincoln's newly issued Emancipation Proclamation. Other resolutions condemned military arrests of civilians, advocated that the South be allowed to return to the Union with slave state status, blamed New Englanders for a partisan war, and asked that no more money be spent or men recruited in its behalf. To replace Browning, the legislature elected Richardson, who lined up with Clement L. Vallandigham, a former Ohio congressman who contended that prolonging the war would only force the Northwest to join the South and permanently break up the Union. From Ohio to Iowa, Vallandigham had a sizable following.

At Springfield the house of representatives proposed that appointment of officers and all war spending in Illinois be turned over to a three-man commission. It adopted resolutions listing fifteen grievances against Lincoln and Yates and designating leading Peace Democrats as five of the six Illinois commissioners to a proposed armistice convention at Louisville. Upper house action was blocked by the death of a Democratic senator.

Senator Isaac Funk, the McLean County cattle king, lost his patience. In a fiery speech widely reprinted in the North, he called the Democrats "traitors and secessionists at heart" and said "they should have asses' ears to set off their heads." Funk volunteered to donate his fortune to the Union cause and at the age of sixty-five offered to fight with his fists the men across the aisle. In a political coup, Yates got rid of the legislature by issuing, for the first time in Illinois, a proroguing resolution that dissolved the two houses because they were in technical disagreement about adjournment.

Two weeks before the Battle of Gettysburg, Democrats who believed that the war should be ended without military victory held a giant mass meeting at Camp Yates, the fairgrounds a mile west of the capitol. Davidson and Stuvé wrote that the crowd was impressive not only for its size, which they estimated at more than forty thousand, but also as a serious-minded and orderly cross section of the citizenry's better element. Some of the state's most prominent men spoke, and the guests on the platform included civilians who had been released from military prisons. They stated the Democratic position in twenty-four long paragraphs which pledged loyalty in peace and war to the federal Constitution and expressed a willingness to obey all laws. Quoting from the Bill of Rights, they asserted that nearly every constitutional guarantee had been violated by the Lincoln administration. They demanded the return of Vallandigham, who had been arrested and banished

John A. Logan

to the South, and they condemned the arrest of such persons as William H. Carlin, son of a former governor. As believers in state sovereignty, they denounced martial law and said that Yates had violated the Constitution by proroguing the legislature. At the same time they condemned secession as a heresy and offered to cooperate in enabling the southern states to be returned to their former position. In calling for a national convention to restore the Union, one resolution said that "the further offensive prosecution of this war tends to subvert the constitution and the government, and entail upon this nation all the disastrous consequences of misrule and anarchy." The final resolution asserted support for the soldiers and pride in their accomplishments. To prove that point, a collection of forty-seven thousand dollars was taken for the Illinois sick and wounded.

Vicksburg and Gettysburg turned the course of the war before Republicans answered with their own immense gathering September 3. Yates, Generals McClernand and Richard J. Oglesby, and speakers from other states urged that the war effort be continued. Lincoln sent to Chairman James C. Conkling a letter, as carefully reasoned as his Cooper Union address, which stated his thesis that compromise was impossible.[14]

Lincoln's suspension in 1862 of the writ of habeas corpus so that civilians could be tried in military courts brought protests from northern lawyers.[15] Not until the next year, under pressure of military necessity, did Congress grant him right of suspension. After the war, the use of military courts in districts where civil courts were open was held unconstitutional in an opinion written by David Davis, whom Lincoln had appointed to the United States Supreme Court. Meanwhile, in Illinois cases federal and state judges ruled against the President's stand and Circuit Judge Charles H. Constable of Mount Carmel became a Democratic hero. Colonel Henry H. Carrington, who had charge of the Indiana military district, rode into Marshall in March, 1863, at the head of a cavalry detachment and arrested Constable while he was trying two army sergeants on kidnaping charges. The judge previously had released four deserters whom the sergeants had arrested on Carrington's orders. On the legal point that Carrington's men lacked authority to hunt deserters outside Indiana, a federal judge released Constable.

Some newspapers were suppressed by officials and by mob action. On orders from General Ambrose E. Burnside, a squad of soldiers in 1863 stopped the press of the *Chicago Times* because of "repeated expression of disloyal and incendiary statements." Under the editorship of Wilbur F. Storey, the *Times* had consistently and bitterly assailed Lincoln, especially after the Emancipation Proclamation.[16] Prominent men, including Trumbull, protested in the name of freedom of the press and in two days the *Times* resumed publication, while other Republicans criticized Lincoln for revers-

[14] Paul Selby, "The Lincoln-Conkling Letter, September 3, 1863," *Transactions of the Illinois State Historical Society*, XIII (1908), 240-250.

[15] King, *op. cit.*, pp. 209-213, 245-249.

[16] Justin E. Walsh, *To Print the News and Raise Hell! A Biography of Wilbur F. Storey.* Edward F. Dunne, *Illinois, The Heart of the Nation*, I, 50-63. George W. Smith, *History of Illinois and Her People*, III, 32-42.

314   ILLINOIS: A HISTORY OF THE PRAIRIE STATE

ing Burnside's order. Some downstate editors also spread unpopular doctrines. Soldiers on leave wrecked the office of the *Bloomington Times* and showed their displeasure with the *Chester Picket Guard* by throwing its type into the street. The *Jonesboro Gazette* was closed for six weeks while a detachment from Iowa rounded up deserters in the vicinity.

On the home front, both sides engaged in bushwhacking, murder, arson, and pillage in efforts to discourage minority sentiment. Several times troops were used to disperse Copperhead mobs. In a few instances, Illinois soldiers were on the verge of mutiny.[17] Deserters caused much of the trouble, while moderate Democrats sought to quiet resistance to the draft. Two guerrilla bands operating in Williamson County reportedly were in touch with Confederate partisans in Missouri. Cavalrymen chased deserters and partisans in the Fulton County lowlands. Wood Gray in a study of Copperheadism said that in five months eight hundred deserters were arrested in Perry, Saline, Jackson, and Williamson counties.[18] He gave the statewide total as two thousand.

Both sides had secret societies. Union Leagues, modeled after an organization in Tennessee, spread throughout the North as a propaganda agency to bolster home-front morale and support Republican candidates. They played an important behind-the-scenes role in a period of despair during which battlefield news contained more casualty lists than reports of victories.[19] Copperhead secret orders meanwhile fought the draft, caused violence, and embarrassed leading Democratic politicians and editors, who denied that underground groups were important or had any connection with their party. Gray's *Hidden Civil War* produces evidence of a long series of incidents, most of them comparatively minor in nature but troublesome nevertheless, on the part of dissenters. A different view is given in a recent study by Frank L. Klement, who contends that disloyal activities were unimportant and in many cases were distorted reports in Republican newspapers. He regarded the Democratic dissenters as spokesmen for

[17] One regiment, largely from southern Illinois, was arrested and placed under guard in March, 1963, at Holly Springs, Mississippi, because of desertions and fraternalization with the enemy. Another regiment at Cairo was reduced by desertions to an effective strength of thirty-five men. Cole, *op. cit.*, p. 306n.

[18] Gray, *op. cit.*, p. 135.

[19] Bentley Hamilton, "The Union League: Its Origin and Achievements in the Civil War," *Transactions of the Illinois State Historical Society*, XXVIII (1921), 110-115.

northwestern sectionalism and the forerunners of the agrarian discontent that swept through Illinois after the war. Under the Klement definition, Copperheads included the broad rank and file of the Democratic party, not just the hidden membership of the secret societies.

Sympathizers with the Confederacy made up the membership of the Knights of the Golden Circle, a secret society imported from the South. It spread into Copperhead regions and in 1863 reorganized under the name of the Order of the American Knights. S. Corning Judd, a minor Democratic figure from Lewistown, became state commander of the society, which in 1864 changed its name to the Sons of Liberty because it had Revolutionary War connotations.

On the divided home front, furloughed soldiers, imbued with a regimental esprit de corps and unsympathetic with anyone who sided with the enemy, caused trouble with their fists and sometimes with guns, especially if they had been drinking. In 1864 Congressman John R. Eden canceled a Democratic speech at Paris because soldiers on leave had been involved in rowdyism. A fight started nevertheless and three men were wounded. A few days later, six soldiers and three civilians were killed and four soldiers and eight civilians wounded in a gun battle on the courthouse square at Charleston, a Copperhead center. The riot ended with the arrival by train from Mattoon of a troop detachment which arrested fifteen Copperheads. Lincoln ordered them released to civil authorities. Two men went to trial and were acquitted.[20]

Some of the Sons of Liberty plotted with Confederate agents in 1864 to start an armed insurrection in Illinois, Indiana, Ohio, Kentucky, and Missouri. The Northwest Conspiracy's immediate objectives were to free Confederate prisoners of war and, by burning cities and seizing rail lines, to relieve military pressure on the South. At its ultimate, the plot envisioned a duplication of the Confederate government in the Northwest, which would reduce the United States to a dozen northeastern states at most. Jacob Thompson, who had been secretary of the interior under President Buchanan, from Canada negotiated with Vallandigham, the national commander of the Sons of Liberty, and other leaders. Confederate raiders hid near Mattoon and Marshall waiting for a

[20] Charles H. Coleman, *Abraham Lincoln and Coles County, Illinois*, pp. 226-233. Coleman and Paul H. Spence, "The Charleston Riot, March 28, 1864," *Journal of the Illinois State Historical Society*, XXXIII (March, 1940), 7-56.

delayed signal to attack Camp Douglas, where nearly five thousand prisoners from the South were guarded by invalids. The timetable called for men in prison camps at Rock Island and Camp Butler to reinforce them and then turn attention to seizure of the state house.

Such an uprising could succeed only with guerrilla support from the Sons of Liberty, which never materialized. The largely disorganized rural Copperheads had neither training nor desire to storm a military post, and after a series of postponements the Camp Douglas garrison was reinforced. Meanwhile the tide of northern sentiment turned with Union victories and Copperhead political errors. The Democratic national convention at Chicago gave the presidential nomination to General McClellan, who was loyal to the North, but let Vallandigham dictate a platform saying the war was a failure. Home-front opposition melted away in the weeks after Atlanta fell. Buckner S. Morris, a circuit judge who had been Chicago's second mayor, and several other men were arrested on charges that they were leaders of the Northwest Conspiracy. A military trial acquitted Morris and only one man went to prison. A judge advocate general's investigation reported that Vallandigham had commanded a subversive society which had from 100,000 to 140,000 members in Illinois, but submitted no documentation of the charges. The Sons of Liberty disintegrated as an organization, leaving no records. Under the circumstances, Klement contends that the entire Camp Douglas conspiracy was a myth.

Some leading Copperheads received public honors after the war. Melville W. Fuller, a Democratic partisan in the 1862 constitutional convention, became chief justice of the United States. [21] William Joshua Allen, who had been held in prisons at Cairo and Washington, after two decades started a long career as a federal judge at Springfield. Several served in Congress. Another became mayor of Galena. Under Storey, the *Chicago Times* prospered. Twenty years after the war, S. Corning Judd was postmaster of Chicago.

THE LONG, SLOW ROAD TO VICTORY

Illinois troops had a proud military record in the Civil War. Most fought or did occupation duty in the West and Southwest,

[21] Willard L. King, *Melville Weston Fuller, Chief Justice of the United States, 1888-1910.*

Courtesy University of Illinois

University Hall: the original building on the University of Illinois campus

but some helped in the East. An Illinois cavalry unit opened the shooting at Gettysburg and occasional infantry outfits fought from the Peninsula to Appomattox. In the western armies men from the Prairie State played major roles in engagements that began in Missouri and Kentucky and dragged into the fifth year of combat. Fort Donelson and Pea Ridge were initiations for the bloodshed at Shiloh, where seven Illinois regiments were among the ten that suffered the highest casualties. Some Illinois men guarded supply lines or served as garrisons in quiet sectors, but Illinois regiments and batteries did their share of the fighting in sharp skirmishes and prolonged battles, which in some cases ended with calamitous results. Those who survived the gunfire and the perils of camp life developed into professional fighters who were bored with the routine of drilling but were capable of long marches and desired only that competent officers lead them into battle. Loyal to Lincoln and Yates, with few exceptions they had no sympathy for disharmony back home. Often defeated, frequently inflicted with heavy casualties, they needed two full years to open the Mississippi at Vicksburg, where Illinois provided twice as many regiments as any other state. Then they made faster time on the hard-fought road to Atlanta.

The official records show that Illinois sent 259,092 men into the war, exceeding manpower quotas and contributing 15.1 percent of its population to the army and navy. John Moses, a historian who was Yates' private secretary, said that only Kansas did better proportionately.[22] Negro regiments were organized beginning in 1863, and 1,811 men from Illinois enlisted directly into them. The records are inexact because some soldiers, black and white, went across state lines to sign up. For white troops, Illinois contributed 150 infantry regiments, seventeen regiments of cavalry, two regiments of light artillery, eight independent artillery batteries, several special units, and 2,224 sailors and marines. Among its policy mistakes the state recruited fresh regiments when it should have assigned new men to fill casualty gaps in battle-tested outfits. As a result, the survivors of veteran regiments sometimes were at skeleton strength and new men missed their steadying influence, especially at the officer level.

Casualty lists showed 34,834 dead, which was 13.65 percent of the men in uniform. No one counted those who came home with crutches, empty sleeves, or less obvious wounds. The large number of deaths from disease reflected the comparatively primitive sanitary facilities of the Civil War. They totaled 22,786, compared with 5,874 killed in battle, 4,020 dead of wounds, and 2,154 who succumbed from other causes.

The home front helped. As the inexperienced recruits left for training camps, women formed aid societies. They rolled bandages, made shirts and socks, assembled hospital supplies, solicited money, and saw to it that soldiers' families suffered a minimum of deprivation. The aid societies were merged into sanitary commissions which were formed on a state and local basis because, twenty years before the organization of the Red Cross, the government had no other facilities for caring for the nonmilitary needs of the soldiers and their dependent families. Church women took the lead in renting and renovating an old hotel for use as a shelter for

22 Moses, *op. cit.*, II, 734.

soldiers passing through Chicago. Opened in the summer of 1863, it soon was filled with recruits, paroled prisoners, and wounded from Chickamauga. Before the war ended a more permanent Soldiers' Rest, a two-hundred-by-fifty-foot building, had been erected at the lake shore near Dearborn Park, and Chicago residents supported another soldiers' home at Cairo. The Chicago home fed returning regiments at the war's end.

A Chicago Sanitary Commission, organized in 1861 and supported largely by private contributions, did its first work in camps at Chicago and Springfield. Medical men branched out to inspect camps and hospitals at Cairo, Mound City, and elsewhere. The commission continually forwarded supplies as the men reported suffering, poor facilities, and disease.[23]

Throughout the state festivals were held to raise money for war work. At Chicago a Northwestern Sanitary Fair in July, 1863, raised eighty-six thousand dollars, triple the amount expected, from the sale of donated articles. A grand bazaar for the sale of fancy and useful articles, the fair included a display of battle-torn banners and other war relics and trophies. At a second fair in 1865, the original draft of the Emancipation Proclamation, donated by President Lincoln, sold for three thousand dollars at auction and was soon acquired by the Chicago Historical Society. That fair raised $240,000. Decatur in 1864 was the scene of a sanitary fair at the state level.

The war cracked some of the prejudices against women in medicine. The Chicago Hospital for Women and Children opened in 1863 with Dr. Mary H. Thompson as director and a staff from the sanitary commission. Mrs. Mary Bickerdyke, a Galesburg widow with nursing experience, volunteered to help in regimental hospitals at Cairo and stayed with western armies during nineteen major battles. One of the most famous of the women who served in the war, she gave first aid in the field, assisted at operating tables, ran diet kitchens, foraged for supplies, superintended hospitals, and cut red tape with the approval of Grant and Sherman. A big woman, she took charge wherever she happened to be. One of her accomplishments was to establish the first army laundries and make it unnecessary to burn clothing and bedding of wounded soldiers.

Generals were in demand and Illinois furnished 177, including

23 A. T. Andreas, *History of Chicago*, III, 310-323. Cole, *op. cit.*, pp. 282-284.

the unassuming Grant, who captured the public's imagination by demanding the unconditional surrender of Fort Donelson and who ended the war by refusing to turn back on the Wilderness Road to Richmond. Volunteers were among the eleven from Illinois who became full generals and among the twenty-four brigadier generals. The records show more than 120 were recognized with brevet commissions as generals.

John A. Logan, regarded as the best of the citizen soldiers, as a major general commanded an army corps near Atlanta. The walrus-moustached Logan was magnificent in battle but impatient of logistics, with the result that Sherman would not give him a higher command. To his credit, Logan did not complain. Logan's advance credentials duplicated those of John A. McClernand, the other former congressman, who was too much of a politician in uniform. McClernand kept one eye on his political fences back home as he plotted for advancement and talked Lincoln into letting him make an independent try at capturing Vicksburg. Eventually he overplayed his hand and finished the war in obscure theaters. John M. Palmer, another of the successful political generals, fought gallantly in Tennessee and won command of an army corps but refused the honor because he would not take orders from John M. Schofield, a West Pointer whom he considered his junior in rank. Some politicians failed as troop commanders and had to be replaced. Some West Point graduates did well with their first commands but suffered defeat when promoted. The most prominent example was General John Pope, son of the old territorial secretary and federal judge, who when called East was no match for Lee at Second Bull Run.

Nine generals, including two named John Smith, came from Galena. Two of them wore generals' stars because Grant trusted them in private life. John A. Rawlins served as the commander's staff chief, closest aide, and private adviser. He became army chief of staff and later secretary of war. Ely S. Parker, a full-blooded Seneca Indian with brilliant talent, went to Galena as government engineer in charge of building the post office and a hospital. As Grant's military secretary, he wrote the surrender terms at Appomattox.

Benjamin H. Grierson, a music teacher from Jacksonville who disliked horses, became a general by commanding two Illinois cavalry regiments on a spectacular six-hundred-mile, sixteen-day raid across Mississippi that disrupted Confederate aplomb while

Grant maneuvered before Vicksburg.[24] The last survivor among the generals who had top commands under Grant was James H. Wilson, a West Pointer who was born outside Shawneetown. An engineer turned cavalryman, as the war ended he commanded a sweep through the South that exceeded Grierson's exploit. As its conclusion, Wilson's men arrested Jefferson Davis.

Fifty Illinois regiments under Sherman foraged their way through Georgia, from Atlanta to the coast, and then turned northward, intent on helping Grant and the eastern armies take Richmond, had time permitted.

In the big victory celebration at Washington, the western armies, proud of their long arc of conquest through the Confederacy, paraded down Pennsylvania Avenue to the applause of thousands May 24, 1865. The eastern armies had preceded them a day earlier, but the climax fittingly was reserved for the survivors of the northwestern regiments that had made famous the names of Grant and Logan and many others.

Then they turned homeward, less than three weeks after Abraham Lincoln had been buried at Springfield. Illinois had contributed more than its share to the preservation of the Union.

[24] D. Alexander Brown, *Grierson's Raid.*

17

THE CONSTITUTION OF 1870

THE WARTIME CRITICISM OF LINCOLN DIED DOWN AND WAS barely audible the night of his fatal trip to Ford's Theater. With the shock of the assassination, a wave of grief and admiration swept across Illinois and the nation. Lincoln, who had told William H. Herndon he would come back to Springfield to resume law practice, arrived at the end of a funeral train's slow journey. Oak Ridge cemetery became a national shrine and lesser men took over the leadership of the Republican party.

THE G.A.R. GOES G.O.P.

A bullet in the left lung at Corinth, a year after he resigned as state senator from the Decatur district, ended the battlefield career of Richard J. Oglesby, a brigadier general who had fought gallantly and seemed destined for larger commands. He recovered and as a major general served in noncombatant areas while ardently supporting Lincoln's war policies. Just before the 1864 election he resigned from the army to become one of the earliest and most successful of the hundreds of former soldiers who ran for public office.

Illinois Republicans, seeking to end two years of frustration, needed a candidate for governor with popular appeal. Orphaned in Kentucky and reared in Illinois by an uncle, Oglesby was an indifferent lawyer who before the war was best known as a

323

politician. For the governorship he was easily nominated over Allen C. Fuller, the state adjutant general who had served efficiently as a home-front administrator. The attitude of the public was emphatically demonstrated at the state convention when the platform committee submitted a document that was lukewarm about the national administration and gave Lincoln a quasi endorsement. The delegates rejected it vociferously and insisted upon a platform that pledged complete support of the President, thanked Yates and the Illinois regiments for their services, and declared that the war would be fought through until victory.[1] Democrats in the legislature had prevented enactment of a law, which other states had passed at the urging of Joseph Medill of the *Chicago Tribune,* to permit soldiers to vote in the field. Republicans wanted the soldier vote, and General Sherman complained that too many regiments were being furloughed home at election time.

The badly split Democrats adopted a platform that declared the war both a failure and unconstitutional. It proposed peace on any terms with the South and simultaneously pledged to support a war candidate for the presidency. The partisan theme in wartime provided Republicans with a campaign issue that was used for a quarter of a century. Against a state ticket that had deep taints of Copperheadism, Lincoln and Oglesby carried the state by thirty-thousand votes. Taken into office with them was a Republican legislature that, as a replacement for Richardson, rewarded Yates with election to the senate. For the man who had led Illinois through the worst years of the war, the future would be anticlimactic.

Like Lincoln, Oglesby had always been an opponent of slavery, and under the governor's leadership Illinois became the first state to ratify the Thirteenth Amendment, which abolished it. The legislature, which had instructed the Illinois delegation in Congress to vote for a resolution drafted by Senator Trumbull, on February 1, 1865, received from him a telegram telling of its adoption. Oglesby urged immediate ratification. "It is just, it is constitutional, it is right to do so," he said. Before the day was over, with token opposition from some Democrats, both houses solemnly voted approval.[2] Later in the session the legislature repealed the

---

[1] George W. Smith, *History of Illinois,* III, 50-51.

[2] William Bross, "Illinois and the Thirteenth Amendment to the Constitution of the

restrictive black laws which, in varying form, had been in force since statehood.

Sentiment had swung away from Copperhead sympathy for the now-defeated South, and a large sector of Illinois opinion supported the position of the radical Republicans who controlled Congress and believed that the secessionists deserved punishment. Andrew Johnson, the new occupant of the White House, became unpopular by adopting the moderate reconstruction views originally espoused by Lincoln. Orville H. Browning, who had stayed in Washington as a lawyer after his two-year senate term ended, sympathized with the new President and was appointed secretary of the interior, becoming the first Illinois man to hold a cabinet position. Browning controlled federal patronage in the state, but Johnson would not listen to his advice on policy matters.[3]

Before the 1866 election, the President during a trip into Illinois demonstrated a penchant for saying the wrong thing in an undignified manner. Seeking reflected glory, Johnson ordered General Grant, Admiral Farragut, and Secretaries Seward and Welles to accompany him during the dedication of the Douglas monument at Chicago and a visit to Lincoln's grave at Springfield. The Springfield city council extended a formal welcome to Grant and Farragut but refused to hold a public reception for the President.

The 1866 balloting made it clear that Illinois was a Republican state. Democrats nominated a general and two colonels for their midterm ticket, but General Logan had turned Republican and ranked next to Grant as the hero of the former soldiers. Democrats sought to question his prewar loyalty, but as a candidate for congressman-at-large Logan won over a moderate.

The 1867 legislature had no reason for not giving a third term to Senator Trumbull, a straight-laced intellectual who had little popular appeal but was one of the most influential men in Washington.

Trumbull took the side of the radicals during the early innings of their fight with Johnson. He drafted a freedman's bureau bill, intended to provide food, clothing, and shelter for the former

United States," paper read before the Chicago Historical Society, Dec. 15, 1884 (Chicago, 1884).

[3] Maurice Baxter, *Orville H. Browning, Lincoln's Friend and Critic*, pp. 181-212. Browning became a benefactor of Civil War-era historians by keeping a detailed diary. *The Diary of Orville Hickman Browning*, 2 vols., Theodore C. Pease and James G. Randall, eds.

Courtesy University of Illinois

Assembly Hall, University of Illinois, Champaign

slaves, and a civil rights bill which implemented the Thirteenth Amendment. Johnson vetoed both and lost virtually all of his remaining support in Illinois. Oglesby in his official capacity made a special trip to Washington to demand that action be taken against the President.

In a crisis precipitated by the President's suspension of Secretary of War Stanton, Logan took a leading role in drafting articles of impeachment which the house of representatives adopted. The two senators split. Yates voted for impeachment but Trumbull now considered that the President had a sounder legal position than his congressional enemies. The senior senator had the courage of his convictions and gave Johnson one of the seven Republican votes which kept him from being turned out of office. Trumbull with that vote lost his Republican following and sacrificed his prospects for a fourth term.

After the welcoming speeches, early returning soldiers encountered unemployment and disillusionment. In some local elections they joined with Democrats to enter fusion tickets, with occasional success, against Republicans who had stayed at home during the fighting. Then in the American tradition they began to organize for fraternal, charitable, and patriotic purposes throughout the North. Perhaps also inevitably, Republican generals provided the early leadership for the Grand Army of the Republic, which by 1890 had some 7,500 posts with more than four hundred thousand members, in addition to auxiliary organizations for their wives and children. Repeatedly the G.A.R. turned out its members to support Republican candidates who "waved the bloody shirt" with speeches that fanned the enmity of the war years. Republicans claimed a monopoly on patriotism, recited with embellishments the story of Copperhead obstructionism on the home front, and shouted that no self-respecting veteran would vote for a Democrat. That demagoguery, overlooking the loyalty of the War Democrats, helped Republicans keep control of the state house for a quarter of a century.

The G.A.R. was born in Illinois. Official records credit the original inspiration to Dr. B. F. Stephenson of Springfield and the Rev. William J. Rutledge, a Methodist who preached at Jacksonville and elsewhere. They had been surgeon and chaplain, respectively, of the regiment first commanded by John M. Palmer. The evidence, however, indicates that Governor Oglesby, as much as anyone, was responsible for the organization that enabled Republican politicians to merge their forces with the former soldiers. Oglesby's private secretary, a colonel, helped work out a ritual and other details in Springfield, and the charter for the first post was issued April 6, 1866, to Decatur, which was the governor's home town.[4]

Palmer, who had just retired as a major general, became the first state commander. For five years Illinois generals had a monopoly on the national commandership.

In the 1868 campaign, Democrats advocated greenbacks and opposed the tariff in an effort to emphasize the economic situation and keep reconstruction from being the only issue. Meanwhile Republicans and veterans made Grant their hero and insisted that

[4] Mary R. Dearing, *Veterans in Politics: The Story of the G.A.R.*, pp. 56, 80-112, 571-572. Newton Bateman and Paul Selby, *Historical Encyclopedia of Illinois*, I, 205-206.

he must be the second President elected from Illinois. On the ground that the governorship also should go to a soldier, Oglesby and Logan supported Palmer, who refused to indicate any interest in the office until the convention nominated him. Competition came chiefly from Robert G. Ingersoll, a former cavalry colonel from Peoria. Ingersoll, the "great agnostic," ranked foremost among the orators of his day and might have become governor had he not in lectures, sensational at the time, challenged the integrity of the Christian religion.[5]

Grant had little time to settle down in his sixteen-thousand-dollar house at Galena, the gift of his home-town neighbors. Chicago's second national convention, held in Crosby's Opera House, was preceded by a mass meeting at which Boys in Blue, the Republican arm of the G.A.R., demanded Grant's nomination for the presidency. The delegates complied as a matter of general consent. Illinois Democrats wanted George H. Pendleton of Ohio for President on the greenback issue, but their nomination went to Horatio Seymour of New York, who had been a Copperhead. The Democratic nominee for governor, John R. Eden, had been a wartime congressman whose followers participated in the Charleston riot. Under the circumstances, the Republicans "waved the bloody shirt" successfully.

Logan as national commander started the G.A.R. on its career as a pressure organization that demanded pensions for all veterans who had suffered a disability of any nature. He also was responsible for observance of Memorial Day as a holiday. Logan encouraged the practice, which had started in the South, of decorating the graves of the war dead with springtime flowers. At Carbondale April 4, 1867, he spoke at a Decoration Day celebration at which a brass band led a parade from the public square to the cemetery east of town. The next year as G.A.R. national commander he asked that all posts arrange "fitting services and memorials" on May 30.

---

[5] The son of a clergyman, Ingersoll enjoyed debating church leaders and lecturing on such subjects as "Some Mistakes of Moses" and "What Must We Do to Be Saved?" He also drew crowds with talks on noncontroversial literary topics. Ingersoll was never elected to public office. In his later years, he practiced law at Washington and New York. Orvin Larson, *American Infidel: Robert G. Ingersoll;* Eva Ingersoll Wakefield, *Letters of Robert G. Ingersoll;* Clarence H. Cramer, *Royal Bob: The Life of Robert G. Ingersoll;* and "Robert Green Ingersoll," *Transactions of the Illinois State Historical Society,* XLVII (1940), 59-68.

SPECIAL INTERESTS IN THE LEGISLATURE

Before the end of the Civil War the Illinois legislature was notorious for enacting, in increasing numbers, a biennial flood of private bills requested by corporations and municipalities. Corruption was freely charged as lobbyists obtained passage of special interest laws, and complaints were heard that matters of public interest did not get adequate attention. Governors found it impossible to analyze the mass of legislation, and the veto messages they were able to prepare were usually overridden by majority votes of the two houses. For the 1867 session, the public laws filled 205 printed pages, while 2,500 pages were needed for the private laws, chiefly incorporations.[6]

The detailed provisions of the Constitution of 1848 caused part of the trouble. Not only were they inadequate to cope with the rapid expansion of Illinois but they contained loopholes. In seeking to prevent private bills, the constitution provided that only general laws could deal with divorces and townships, but it permitted special bills on municipalities. A section on nonbanking corporations said they could not be formed by special acts except "where, in the judgment of the General Assembly, the objects of the corporation cannot be attained under general laws." That loophole became bigger and bigger as the floods of bills led to scandalous situations to which Governor Palmer added his protests.

Lobbyists seeking special interest bills for corporations began attending legislative sessions as early as 1855 and became increasingly active until 1870, reports John Moses, who served in the house of representatives in 1875 before he took up a career as historian.[7] He wrote that tangible proof was impossible but that enactment or defeat of bills was unquestionably influenced by the shameless expediture of money and by promises of political support. Adoption of the 1848 constitution, which curtailed the power of the legislature, resulted in diminished attendance at legislative sessions until a demand arose for special corporation charters. The low tide of official morality in that era was indicated by the canal scrip scandal which involved Governor Matteson.

[6] Edward F. Dunne, *Illinois, The Heart of the Nation,* pp. 67-75.

[7] John Moses, *Illinois Historical and Statistical,* II, 955-960, 774-787. See also Janet Cornelius, *A History of Illinois Constitution Making,* p. 45.

Criticism of lawmakers began as early as the Third General Assembly, which used high-handed tactics in the Shaw-Hansen election contest.

The moral climate at Springfield also was damaged by the provisions of the pre-Civil War constitution which froze official salaries at economy-era levels. Subterfuges became common, and the fifteen-hundred-dollar-a-year salary of the governor was supplemented by expense money to operate the executive mansion. Judges received additional pay for minor "services rendered," and in some cases their clerks received large salaries under a tacit understanding that they would be shared with the judges. The public became agitated at reports that perquisites were circumventing the low salary scale.

Abuses of legislative power in other states were not uncommon after the Civil War when commercial and financial interests were expanding. By 1870, however, a nationwide reaction had set in, and during the rest of the nineteenth century the trend was toward restriction of the legislative power. A century later, some constitutional historians hold that pressures for limitation of the legislative branch were more extreme elsewhere than in Illinois.

In an 1867 emergency, when the lessees of the Joliet penitentiary served notice that they would abandon their contract at the end of the month, Oglesby recommended abandonment of the lease system. He regarded it as un-Christian and he believed that the prison could be made self-sustaining. Three state prison commissioners were appointed and the state took over the payroll of the warden, guards, and other staff members and the cost of feeding and clothing the inmates. Heavy expenses included a starting appropriation of five hundred thousand dollars to buy machinery, stock, and tools, but Illinois was proud of the walls, six feet thick and twenty-five feet high, which made Joliet the equal of any prison in the nation. The commissioners, elected by statewide vote in 1868, quarreled so much that the next legislature gave the power of appointment and discharge to the governor. The hope that the prison would pay its way was never realized, and it became obvious that one thousand cells would not be adequate for the rest of the century.[8]

Meanwhile men from distant counties questioned the necessity of building a new state house at Springfield, as well as the honesty

[8] Alexander Davidson and Bernard Stuvé, *A Complete History of Illinois*, pp. 924-928.

of its advocates. Complaints also were made about designating Champaign as the site of an industrial university and establishing a new penitentiary in southern Illinois. Almost any appropriation was suspect.

The special interest bill situation became more disgraceful after Governor Palmer took office in 1869. Lobbyists in large numbers rounded up votes for the incorporation of private manufacturing companies, hotels, banks, land companies, and dozens of other types of enterprises, all intended to create profitable monopolies. Meanwhile county officials formed statewide associations while they got votes to raise the fees they collected for their work. The special laws passed filled three books, but only one was needed for general legislation. The governor vetoed more than eighty and saw most of them repassed. Palmer was overridden when he vetoed a "tax grab" bill under which state levies on property could be reduced for ten years to compensate counties and municipalities which had issued bonds to help finance privately owned railroads. The bond issues exceeded fifteen million dollars. Palmer did not think the state should be obligated for the debts of local governments.[9]

BASIC LAW FOR A CENTURY

The constitutional convention in 1869-70, which wrote the state's basic law for the next hundred years, almost never met. Governor Oglesby hoped that the end of the war had dissolved the antipathies that wrecked the work of the delegates in 1862 and, on his recommendation, the legislature in 1867 ordered another referendum. Newspapers gave editorial support, but the public displayed little interest in another effort at domestic reform. In the face of apathy, at the 1868 election the proposition carried by only 704 votes.[10]

By contrast to the turmoil eight years earlier, the eighty-five delegates convened at Springfield December 13, 1869, in an at-

[9] John M. Palmer, *Personal Recollections: The Story of an Earnest Life*, pp. 290-322. George T. Palmer, *A Conscientious Turncoat: The Story of John M. Palmer, 1817-1900*.

[10] Cornelius, *op. cit.*, pp. 44-65. Baxter, *op. cit.*, pp. 213-240. Emil Joseph Verlie (ed.), *Illinois Constitutions*, pp. xxvi-xxxii. Davidson-Stuvé, *op. cit.*, pp. 911-914. A. L. Bowen, "The Background of the Constitution of Illinois—The Constitution of 1870," *Illinois Blue Book, 1927-28*, pp. 22-57. Theodore C. Pease, *The Story of Illinois*, pp. 219-220. Arthur C. Cole, *The Era of the Civil War*, p. 418.

Courtesy Illinois State Historical Library

Richard J. Oglesby

mosphere that approached nonpartisanship. Republicans held a nominal edge, 44 to 41, but fifteen had been elected on independent tickets in Republican districts. That group held the balance of power and few delegates seemed inclined to revive political squabbles. Democrats helped the independent group elect Charles Hitchcock of Chicago, an attorney who never held another office of importance, as president over Joseph Medill, who had not yet returned to majority control of the *Chicago Tribune*. For the first time, there were more lawyers than farmers among the delegates, and the changes brought by the population growth were shown when men with New York and New England backgrounds outnumbered those from Kentucky, Tennessee, and Virginia. A few of the delegates were of statewide prominence. Orville H. Browning, the best known, sat as a Democrat from the Quincy district. Reuben Benjamin of Bloomington rated as an authority on constitutional law and played the leading role in revising the bill of rights and convincing his colleagues that restrictions could be placed on railroad corporations. Elliott Anthony of Chicago later wrote a constitutional history.

In five months of deliberations, the delegates cured most of the faults of the 1848 constitution. They drafted a new basic law that was voluminous in detail and in time would be criticized as being a straitjacket on progress. Nevertheless the new constitution endured for a century as Illinois kept abreast of its sister states while advancing from a predominantly rural civilization into the atomic age.

To end complaints that the 1848 delegates were penurious in fixing the salaries of public officials, the convention left that question, along with many others, to be determined by future legislatures. To expand the power of the executive, a two-thirds majority, difficult to obtain, was required to override a veto. In a major change, reelection of the governor was allowed. The offices of attorney general and state superintendent of public instruction were made elective. Strong curbs were placed on the legislature. The time limit on General Assembly sessions was removed, for all practical purposes, by allowing sessions to continue until June 30, and safeguards were placed against the hurried passage of bills. The new constitution forbade special laws if a general law could be made applicable. For emphasis, it specifically barred special laws involving twenty-three topics, beginning with the granting of divorces and the changing of names of persons and places. The list ended by prohibiting the legislature from granting any special or exclusive privilege, immunity, or franchise to any corporation, association, or individual. That ended the abuses that went with passage of private bills under which in the preceding year charters had been granted to sixty-seven banks, fourteen loan and trust companies, and thirty-six insurance companies. None of them were placed under the jurisdiction of the state. Moses, who regretted that the people no longer were electing their best men to the legislature, said the tables were reversed and that corporations, unable to seek special privileges, were made the target of restrictive bills and amendments. Previously leading lawyers, wealthy businessmen, and large farmers considered it an honor to serve in Congress and the legislature, but at this period their number was diminished by the increasing demands of their occupations as the state expanded. The result was that their place was taken, especially in city districts, by men identified by Moses as "ward politicians, small officeholders, and saloon keepers, who seek political preferment either for themselves or their friends."

Of national importance at a time when Grangers and other farm groups demanded that something be done about rates charged by railroads and warehouses, the convention took a pioneering stand by placing them under state regulation. In early deliberations, the delegates believed that more competition was the only remedy for excessive and discriminatory charges. Under the current conservative interpretation, railroad charters were regarded as perpetual contracts which the state must always recognize. Congressman Shelby M. Cullom of the Springfield district accepted that theory when he asked that a second railroad be built between Washington and New York because he regarded as atrocious the service on the Baltimore and Ohio, which then had a monopoly. As the debates became prolonged, Benjamin contended that, since railroads had been created for the public good and had been granted the power of eminent domain, they could be controlled by the state. In addition, he took an advanced stand by arguing that the rights of private corporations should not be allowed to interfere with the rights of the public. Under his influence, the new constitution declared that railroads are "public highways, and shall be free to all persons." The legislature was mandated to pass laws establishing maximum charges in freight and passenger tariffs. As the direct result of those provisions, the 1871 legislature passed a regulatory law that was upheld by the Supreme Court of the United States.

Remembering the internal improvements fiasco of 1837, the delegates fixed a debt limit of not more than 5 percent on the valuation of the state's taxable property, and required referendum approval for any borrowing in excess of $250,000. They also prohibited any local government from subscribing to the capital stock of a railroad or other private enterprise.

Political sectionalism, among the delegates as well as in the legislature, concerned many. As evidence of it, only two Republican delegates sat among the former Copperheads from southern Illinois. In general, Democrats traditionally drew their political strength from the lower and western portions of the state, while Republicans built up heavy majorities in the central and northern regions. Medill had support in believing that this disenfranchised northern Democrats and southern Republicans. He contended that smaller majorities would be in the public interest and offered an innovation designed to diminish sectionalism. For the house of representatives he set up a minority representation system, based on cumulative voting and designed so that the weaker party almost always gets one of the three house seats in each district. That was accomplished by providing for the election of three representatives from each district and letting a party member, if he wished, cast all three of his votes for a single candidate.

Opponents of Negro suffrage were overruled and the convention granted the right to vote to all male citizens above twenty-one years who had resided in the state a year. The question of racial discrimination was finally solved by omitting all mention of it. During the convention the Fifteenth Amendment had extended suffrage to Negroes, and giving them the right to vote was the chief partisan issue before the delegates. Elijah M. Haines of Lake County failed repeatedly when he tried to strike the word "male" from the suffrage article which would have given women the right to vote.

The convention solved a statewide problem that was especially acute in Cook County by reorganizing the judiciary. Disputes over land sales and Board of Trade transactions had congested the civil courts, and Chicago needed a criminal court for the robbery, theft, and murder cases on the docket. The delegates increased the Supreme Court from three to seven justices, elected by districts, and authorized the creation of appellate courts. The number of secondary courts was expanded and the number of judges increased, especially in Cook County. Provision was made for the election of justices of the peace and police magistrates.

The revenue article reaffirmed the property tax as the most fair and equitable way of supporting government. The two-mill tax, no longer needed for retirement of canal bonds, and permission for a poll tax were deleted from the constitution. The list of articles which could be specially taxed was increased greatly, and limits were placed on tax rates for county purposes and local debt.

Despite the great length required for its mass of details, the new constitution represented a marked improvement in the basic law. The delegates completed their work May 13, 1870, and submitted the basic document and eight supplemental propositions to the voters July 2. The strategy of the separate submissions was to obviate any chance that the whole constitution might be defeated

by opposition to a single controversial subject, such as requirements that the Illinois Central railroad could never be released
from its charter line tax, that the Illinois and Michigan Canal could
never be sold or leased, or that contracts for convict labor would
be prohibited. All were ratified without difficulty and the new
constitution became effective August 8, 1870. The closest vote,
99,022 to 70,080, was for minority representation in the legislature. The northern counties, especially Cook, gave it strong support.

A restrictive clause provided that the legislature by a two-thirds
majority could submit only one amendment at a time to a referendum at which a majority of the total vote cast at the general

Judge David Davis

Courtesy Illinois State Historical Library

election was required. Five amendments were adopted without difficulty during the following two decades, when political parties furnished ballots and usually marked them for constitutional propositions. After 1891, when county clerks and election commissions began printing official ballots, the voter had to mark specifically for or against each amendment and it became more difficult to get the required majority. Complaints that the amendment process was too difficult continued into the following century and helped generate sentiment for another constitutional convention.

THE EXPANSION OF GOVERNMENT

In considerably less than three decades, Illinois' expanding government outgrew the stone state house on Springfield's downtown square. Its early admirers, who stood on plank sidewalks while staring across muddy streets at porticos and dome, had expected the building to last forever, but during the war everyone felt crowded and Governor Yates needed more than a single room. The superintendent of public instruction contributed to the war effort by moving out of the adjacent office.

A legislator from Peoria in 1865 sought to solve the problem by introducing a bill to move the seat of government to his city. Chicago, Jacksonville, and Decatur also entered bids, and the *Chicago Tribune* and several other newspapers endorsed the idea of leaving Springfield. They criticized the capital city's hotels for poor accommodations and high charges, but Springfield fought back with a grand ball and supper at which lawmakers and officials were guests. Work was rushed on a new hotel, the Leland, which was praised as being one of the best in the state, and James C. Conkling, one of the town's leading citizens, ran for state representative so that he could have inside influence.

Springfield's offer, accepted in 1867, involved two hundred thousand dollars and a land trade in which the state received a seven-acre plot, with a knoll in the center, as the site for a new state house, the fifth owned by Illinois. It was five blocks southwest of the 1837-era capitol which Sangamon County took over because it too was expanding and needed a larger courthouse. In 1899 the county met its next expansion problem by jacking up the old building eleven feet and inserting a new first floor. By that time the interior had been altered considerably and the Circuit

Court used the chamber in which Lincoln and Douglas had delivered some of their greatest speeches. When Sangamon County again had to seek larger quarters, the state in 1961 purchased the historic Old Capitol for restoration as it was in Lincoln's years.

Agitation to remove the seat of government from Springfield did not die down until 1871, after eight hundred thousand dollars had been spent on the new state house. Preparation of bills needed to implement the new constitution required that the legislature recess from May until November. A formal invitation to hold the adjourned session in Chicago was received from the mayor and city council, who offered to furnish ample accommodations, for the governor as well as the legislators, without expense to the state. Both houses voted to accept the offer. Peoria meanwhile offered to reimburse the state for the eight hundred thousand dollars already spent, to donate a ten-acre capitol site, and to give the General Assembly free accommodations for five years. Governor Palmer believed that the public opposed any move and, under his influence, a special session in June appropriated funds to resume construction at Springfield. Because of the Chicago fire in October, the legislature was forced to hold the recessed session in its usual quarters.[11] Had it not been for the fire, however, the effort to move the seat of government to Chicago might have succeeded.

For the new capitol, workmen dug twenty-five feet to bedrock for the foundations of a massive building of mongrel architecture featuring columned porticoes, mansard roofs, and a dome which measured 405 feet to the flagstaff tip. Far into the next century it would be the tallest building in midstate. Financing caused great difficulty. Builders estimated that the job would cost 2.65 million dollars, but the skeptical constitution convention stipulated that any expenditure over three and a half million dollars would have to be approved by the people. Niggardly appropriations coincided with rumors of graft, which no one verified, and work stopped for long periods. In 1877 and again in 1882 the voters disapproved further spending on the new capitol, but in 1884 they voted to finish the work. Meanwhile enough construction had been finished so that occupation of new offices began in 1874, but not until 1884 would the 4.5-million-dollar building be declared completed.

[11] *Illinois Blue Book, 1900,* p. 175. *Biographies of the State Officers and Thirty-Third General Assembly of Illinois,* pp. 5-8. Davidson-Stuvé, *op. cit.,* pp. 914-924. Moses, *op. cit.,* II, 802-804.

The launching of the state-supported Normal school did not deter Jonathan Baldwin Turner from his dream of an industrial university. He contended that a practical education of the type needed by farmers and city men could best be obtained at an entirely new type of institution, a state university. The *Prairie Farmer* helped promote a series of meetings which kept the proposal before the legislature; and the movement spread to other states. When the state's first university finally opened, it had federal financial help and belonged to the same generation as the new state house.

President Lincoln in 1862 signed a bill by Senator Justin S. Morrill of Vermont which granted to each loyal state thirty thousand acres for each senator and representative in Congress. The General Assembly the next year accepted a grant of 480,000 acres of land in western states. They could be sold to get funds for a college of agriculture and mechanic arts which also could teach classical and scientific studies. Most of the land scrip was promptly sold at the market price. The total income reached $613,026, but approximately half of that amount came from twenty-five thousand acres in Minnesota and Nebraska. They were not sold until prices increased after several decades.

The other states in the Old Northwest established their land-grant universities while Illinois quarreled over the location of its institution. The denominational private colleges wanted to take over the federal endowment, dividing it as necessary, and at least fifteen communities and agencies entered the competition for either the site or control of the funds. McLean, Logan, and Morgan counties offered to contribute money or buildings, but the award in 1867 went to an unsettled tract between the hamlets of Urbana and Champaign, while disappointed men elsewhere complained that the winners had lobbied unfairly. Among the competing sectional interests, southern Illinois gave its chief attention to a new penitentiary, Chicago wanted legislation for parks and boulevards, Springfield and Peoria considered the state house to be the big prize, Jacksonville already had three institutions, and Bloomington the Normal school.

Slow growth marked the university's first two decades. The field of higher education had been largely usurped by the private colleges, and the endowment income of some twenty-five thousand dollars a year, supplemented by niggardly appropriations by the legislature, was inadequate. Michigan's state university had been operating for thirty-one years and Wisconsin's for nineteen

Courtesy Illinois State Historical Library

Senator Lyman Trumbull

when a new board of trustees in 1867 picked John Milton Gregory to head the industrial university, with the title of regent.[12] Gregory, a former Baptist minister, had twice been elected state superintendent of public instruction in Michigan. In a five-story structure that was the only building on the campus, fifty men enrolled in the first classes, taught by a faculty of three that included

[12] Allan Nevins, *Illinois*. Fred H. Turner, "Misconceptions Concerning the Early History of the University of Illinois," *Transactions of the Illinois State Historical Society*, XXXIX (1932), 63-90. Ernest G. Hildner, "Higher Education in Transition, 1850-1870," *Journal of the Illinois State Historical Society*, LVI (Spring, 1963), 61-73. Harry A. Kersey, Jr., *John Milton Gregory and the University of Illinois*. Donald R. Brown, "Jonathan B. Turner and the Land Grant Idea," *Journal of the Illinois State Historical Society*, LV (Winter, 1962), 370-384.

Gregory and a head farmer. Gregory had some trustee help in resisting western sentiment for primarily vocational education, but in 1870 Illinois was the first American university to offer shop instruction. Women students were admitted the next year. Revenues were inadequate, the public often indifferent, and the faculty and students at times troublesome, but the university managed to survive. In 1885 the name was changed from Illinois Industrial University to the University of Illinois.

Under an 1869 law, a Normal school for southern Illinois was located at Carbondale, which won the competitive bidding by offering land and bonds valued at $229,000, later depreciated to seventy-five thousand dollars. It had classical and scientific courses and a preparatory department, and gave free tuition to students who promised to teach in the state.

Rural education was available only in one-room schools. Districts usually were two miles square and any pretense of education usually ended before the eighth grade. The children had to walk to school, and an area of that size supposedly was large enough to finance a teacher's salary at whatever rate the people wanted to pay within revenues available from taxes. The 1855 free school law had the effect of putting the private academies out of business, and several public high schools were established before the Civil War, some on a special charter basis. Usually, however, only a municipality could support a four-year high school on top of a grade-school system. Princeton had a successful high school covering an entire township, the courts had upheld a Michigan law permitting property to be taxed to support high schools, and the new constitution gave the legislature a mandate to provide a "good common school education" for all Illinois children. Consequently an 1872 law gave the voters the right to set up township high schools if they wished.

THE LIBERAL REPUBLICAN FAILURE OF 1872

Except that he was a military hero, Illinois had little reason to be proud of its second President. Grant's only training had been for an army career, and in the White House he became a politician who was naive in his outlook, vacillating in facing complex problems, petty in making appointments, and unfortunate in his associates. Damaging scandals were yet to be exposed, but after he had been in office two years the President's critics accused him of nepotism and inadequacy. They questioned the wisdom of the iron-fisted rule of the South imposed by the radical Republicans who controlled Congress with Grant's acquiescence.

Farmers and city workers had been dissatisfied since the war, and the platforms of both parties contained references to if not promises of a monetary system that would put more money in circulation, a tariff that might reduce machinery prices, more reasonable freight rates, and "an honest day's pay for a faithful day's work," as the Republican state platform phrased it in 1868. A revolt began in Missouri, where Republican dissenters had help from Democrats in electing a governor in 1870. Led by Senator Carl Schurz, who considered civil service reform the big issue, the Missourians called a convention of Liberal Republicans in Cincinnati May 1, 1872, to nominate a presidential ticket.[13]

Charles Sumner and Charles Francis Adams were among the eastern leaders of the movement, which developed such an important top-level following in Illinois that the state had too many presidential aspirants. Four men from the state hoped to run against Grant as a large sector of the top Republican leadership split away from the party which Lincoln had helped found.

Governor Palmer did not protest when some Illinois delegates suggested that he be the presidential candidate of the Liberal Republicans. Palmer had signed Oglesby's petition for the impeachment of Andrew Johnson and in 1868 he had campaigned for governor as an extremist who favored subjugation of the South. In his inaugural address, the spade-bearded Palmer surprised old-line Republicans by taking a states' rights stand, and he later quarreled with the President about unrequested use of troops at the scene of the Chicago fire of 1871. A stubborn man who refused to yield on any point of principle, Palmer during his term as governor felt that the state needed a civil service system. Alienated from other Republicans who were thinking of returning Oglesby to the governor's office, Palmer turned down a second-term nomination and signed the call of the Cincinnati convention.

Gustave Koerner, who had been elected Democratic lieutenant governor twenty years earlier and was leader of the Germans who

---

[13] E. L. Bogart and C. M. Thompson, *The Industrial State, 1870-1893*, pp. 54-80. Solon J. Buck, *The Agrarian Crusade*, pp. 11-21. Gustave Koerner, *Memoirs*, II, 535-578. Willard L. King, *Lincoln's Manager, David Davis*, pp. 277-282.

had followed him into the Republican fold on the slavery issue, considered himself available for the presidency. He had no open support, however, because the Illinois delegation was badly split between David Davis and Senator Lyman Trumbull, both of whom had some backing from other states. Trumbull had broken with Grant and been cast out by the radical Republican element for blocking the impeachment of Johnson. Davis, who sought the nomination while holding the seat on the Supreme Court to which he had been appointed by Lincoln, had been commended by Democrats in 1866 for holding unconstitutional the arbitrary arrests of civilians outside the theater of war.

Also in Cincinnati, in addition to the governor, were the lieutenant governor, secretary of state, attorney general, and superintendent of public instruction, along with a group of former state officeholders. The Liberal Republicans had influential newspaper support from Horace White, editor of the *Chicago Tribune* from 1865 until 1874.[14]

During six ballots, the Illinois delegation deadlocked between Davis and Trumbull, and the convention picked its weakest man, Horace Greeley, the New York editor, over Adams. Greeley had made a career of criticizing the Democrats whose support he now needed.

In midsummer Democrats and Liberal Republicans held simultaneous state conventions on opposite sides of the capitol square at Springfield, dividing the nominations in a coalition headed by Koerner for governor. To make certain that the G.A.R. would stay loyal, Republicans for the second time nominated Oglesby for governor. They believed he was the only man sure to carry the state.

The liberals, interested chiefly in governmental reform, did nothing to attract the votes of farmers who were bitterly dissatisfied with railroad rates. The public cared little about reconstruction and civil service, Grant remained the popular hero, and Greeley lost more Democratic votes than the liberals produced. Had either Trumbull or Davis headed the protesting national ticket, the result could have been closer, at least in Illinois, which was easily carried by Grant and Oglesby. The Liberal Republican movement promptly collapsed, to be followed by a succession of

14 Harris L. Dante, "The Chicago Tribune's Lost Years, 1865-74," *Journal of the Illinois State Historical Society*, LVIII, 2 (Summer, 1965), 139-164.

third parties which largely represented agrarian and labor protests. Conservative in its economics and radical in its attitude toward the conquered South, the Republican party held firm control at Washington and Springfield. The postwar period, however, saw a great shifting of political allegiances. Many followed Palmer, Trumbull, Koerner, and Davis in leaving the ranks of the Republicans, who no longer had opposition to the extension of slavery as a unifying issue. The only alternative for the dissenters, if they were to be politically influential, was to return to the Democratic party, which after the war lacked a leader with the popular appeal of Douglas and whose own reconstruction was being hampered by the partisan mistakes of the Copperhead years.

Oglesby served ten days of his second term as governor and resigned so that he could be elected United States senator to succeed Trumbull. Two years earlier Logan had replaced Yates, so Illinois now had two former generals in the senate. Lieutenant Governor John L. Beveridge, a former Cook County sheriff and congressman-at-large, filled out Oglesby's term as chief executive. Beveridge, who had commanded a cavalry unit at Gettysburg, also was a former general.

18

CHICAGO BURNS AND GROWS

A CITY OF BALLOON-FRAME HOUSES

GEORGE WASHINGTON SNOW, A VERMONT MAN WHO ARRIVED
in time to vote in the first Chicago election in 1833, soon thereafter qualified to be the patron saint of residential subdividers by
inventing the balloon-frame method of building construction.[1]
The first of several architectural innovations credited to Chicagoans, it made obsolete the expensive and laborious use of heavy
beams in walls. Snow substituted the two-by-four, which was
ripped from logs and used as studding, plates, and rafters to form
the skeleton of buildings of lumber. Snow's method required
bracing techniques and, instead of wooden pegs, the copious use
of machine-cut iron nails, but both materials and labor cost less.
Except where brick and stone were used, balloon framing became
universal and was as important in houses, barns, and small stores as
the caisson and skyscraper, later Chicago products, have been to
downtown skylines. Snow became an alderman and the owner of a
lumberyard, and he prospered because his clapboard-covered cottages answered the needs of the newcomers, who usually reached
Illinois short of time and money. As Chicago's population

[1] Frank A. Randall, *History of the Development of Building Construction in Chicago,* p. 6. John Moses and Joseph Kirkland, *History of Chicago,* I, 91. William Bross,
History of Chicago.

CHICAGO, IN 1812.

From "MASSACRE OF CHICAGO," by Mrs. JOHN H. KINZIE. "Ellis & Fergus, Chicago, 1844."

boomed, many of its residential lots were crowded with two balloon-frame houses and their coterie of outbuildings.

Especially in the residential districts, home builders had to anticipate that the grade level would be changed, with the result that some sidewalks were built several feet above the streets and the tiny front yards. In those cases, front steps led to second-story doors. The levels of the pine plank sidewalks frequently changed and an approaching man might disappear or seem to sink into the ground to his hips, only because he was using steps to lower levels. In some Chicago neighborhoods, miniature front yards still are several feet below the sidewalk level and second-floor entrances can be seen on ancient homes. Downtown East St. Louis, where the streets were raised in a later generation because of Mississippi River floods, still has sunken blocks which show the original level of the town.

Chicago had a retailing district along Lake Street where some men prospered with new merchandising methods. Potter Palmer, who opened a dry-goods store in 1862 with his father's help, astonished his competitors by letting his customers take goods home for inspection and by making cash refunds without question if they returned purchases. Palmer, who had poor health and in any event preferred real estate speculation, retired in 1867 after turning the business over to Marshall Field and Levi S. Leiter, two young clerks he had enticed from another store. Field, who had come from New York state in 1856, got his start by saving half of his four-hundred-dollar yearly salary, even though it meant sleeping in the store. By the time he was thirty he headed the firm of Field, Palmer, and Leiter, in which he had a $260,000 interest. With Palmer's help it became Field and Leiter. Field, the master merchant, expanded on Palmer's one-price sales methods, while Leiter set a credit policy that decreased losses and made friends.[2]

Houses alternated with pastures as far as Fullerton Avenue on the north, Crawford (Pulaski) on the west, and Thirty-Ninth Street on the south. For expensive homes the area near Lincoln Park was in demand, and lots on Michigan, Calumet, Prairie, and Indiana avenues were purchased by the well-to-do. Downtown business buildings were from four to six stories tall, which was the top limit for structural safety, but they also were constructed largely of pine. Some had one-layer facings of brick or thin veneers of metal or stone. The downtown structures of that type included magnificent hotels and Crosby's Opera House, which opened in 1865 with a four-week season of grand opera. Approximately half of the population was foreign-born, and most people lived in buildings roofed with wood shingles or tar and felt. No ward heeler, the mayor was Roswell B. Mason, the man who built the Illinois Central railroad. For more than a decade, the police and fire departments had been staffed with paid professionals, but in the rush of expansion few took time to worry about the possibility of a bad fire when the wind was from the southwest.

THE GREAT CHICAGO FIRE, OCTOBER 9-10, 1871

In the drought year of 1871, since early July almost no rain had fallen on tinder-dry Chicago and the hazard of fire increased. On the Saturday night of September 30, a warehouse burned on the south side with a loss of six hundred thousand dollars. A week later, also before midnight, a $750,000 fire hit a planing mill on the west side. The entire fire department managed to confine it to a four-block area, but many of the men were left unfit for duty

[2] Lloyd Wendt and Herman Kogan, *Give the Lady What She Wants! The Story of Marshall Field & Co.* Robert W. Twyman, *History of Marshall Field & Co., 1852-1906.*

and several pieces of fire equipment were destroyed or disabled. Those conflagrations were but preliminaries to the great Chicago fire that began October 9, the following night.[3]

On the unusually warm Sunday, the Patrick O'Leary family went to bed in their five-hundred-dollar cottage at 137 DeKoven Street on the west side before 8:45 p.m., the time when fire broke out in the cowbarn at the rear of the lot. The cause is unknown, and evidence does not support a legend that a cow kicked over a lantern. The O'Leary house was left standing because a steady wind, which never exceeded thirty miles an hour, blew the flames toward the heart of the city.

Soon out of control, the fire within two hours jumped the South Branch of the Chicago River, a supposedly natural barrier. By 1:30 a.m. Monday it reached the Courthouse, where Mayor Mason had established a command post. An hour after Mason ordered the jail prisoners released the fire blew across the river into the north side, and in another hour it forced abandonment of the waterworks building, a landmark still standing at Chicago Avenue.

Witnesses told of a gale or tornado accompanying the conflagration, resembling the fire storms that resulted from the World War II bombing of European cities. Colonel Harry A. Musham, in a definitive study of the fire, attributed the phenomenon to convention whirls or "fire devils" which sent superheated air in advance of the flames to start new fires. Sparks and burning boards helped, and the elevated sidewalks served as flues. In supposedly fireproof buildings, beams burned in brick walls, while facings of limestone veneer and iron proved valueless for protection from the intense heat.

For most of Monday, the fire raged over the north side as far as the city limits and completed the destruction of the business district. The mayor supervised demolition of buildings on Wabash Avenue and Harrison Street, which with the wind direction helped

[3] A book about the great Chicago fire would have an obvious title. Several have been published. Paul M. Angle wrote the introduction and notes for *The Great Chicago Fire: The Human Account,* issued by the Chicago Historical Society in 1946, and for an enlarged centennial edition, *The Great Chicago Fire,* in 1971. Robert Cromie in 1958 wrote a popular account entitled *The Great Chicago Fire.* Harry A. Musham, a historian and naval architect, amassed scientific and technical information for "The Great Fire, October 8-10, 1871," *Transactions of the Illinois State Historical Society,* XLVII (1940), 69-189. For a centennial book, Kogan and Cromie varied the title slightly to *The Great Fire, Chicago, 1871.*

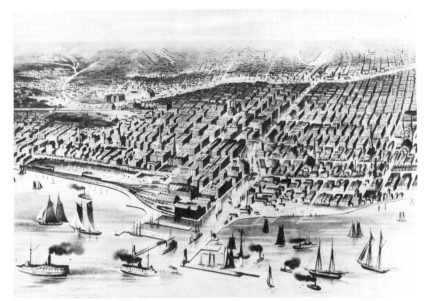

Courtesy Illinois State Historical Library

Chicago before the Fire

prevent the southward spread of the flames. The fire had almost burned out at midnight when a cold rain started falling on refugees huddled on the lakefront, in a cemetery south of Lincoln Park, and on the bleak prairie.[4]

An estimated three hundred persons perished, although only 120 bodies were found. The fire destroyed some eighteen thousand buildings, turning into rubble property valued at nearly two hundred million dollars. In an area of three and a third square miles or 2,124 acres, only the water towers and four buildings stood. The business district, mansions and cottages, the McCormick reaper plant and the Tremont Hotel, the Chicago Historical Society with its original of the Emancipation Proclamation, and the slum dens of the criminal element were in ashes and rubble. Thirty percent of all the Chicago property valued for taxation had been consumed in the most spectacular event in the city's history.

Western Union informed the world, and help was on the way before the flames died down. Fire engines from Milwaukee and

---

[4] Simultaneous fires killed 750 at Pestigo, Wisconsin, destroyed three-fourths of Manistee, Michigan, and caused extensive damage at Holland, Michigan.

more distant cities helped contain the destruction. Special trains brought food, provisions, blankets, and clothing as word spread that Chicago needed cooked food. Schools and churches, tents and temporary barracks provided makeshift housing. Cash contributions, some from Europe, approximated five million dollars. The Chicago Relief and Aid Society, already in existence for smaller jobs, helped with emergency distribution of supplies. Medical aid included vaccination of sixty-four thousand for smallpox.

The legislature, immediately called into session by Governor Palmer, under the new constitution could not give direct aid to a city, but it passed laws to relieve Chicago from payment of its share of the cost of canal improvements and it appropriated $2,955,340, the amount already paid by Chicago, for reconstruction of bridges and public buildings and for maintenance of the police and fire departments.

Sixty thousand persons who fled the scene of disaster by train helped spread rumors, largely exaggerated, that looting was prevalent and out-of-town criminals arriving. Mayor Mason issued a martial law proclamation entrusting the preservation of good order and peace to General Philip H. Sheridan, the dashing Civil War cavalryman who was stationed at Chicago. Sheridan brought in several companies of regular infantrymen at the same time that Palmer dispatched his adjutant general with state militiamen. Palmer, who had heard the rumors of lawlessness, acted in response to a telegram which he considered official but about which Mason knew nothing. The governor himself went to Chicago on Thursday and conferred with Mason and Sheridan, but was not told that martial law was in effect.[5]

After the state troops withdrew and Palmer learned of the real situation, he told the mayor in a blistering letter that the dignity and authority of Illinois had been insulted and that the state was competent to protect its citizens. Mason replied that during the fire he had not had time to consider policy questions and that in any event Sheridan's troops would be withdrawn in two days.

At the request of prominent Chicagoans and with approval from Washington, Sheridan later called in four companies of regulars to guard Chicago relief depots. Palmer protested to President Grant that the state could and should furnish the protection. Grant

[5] John M. Palmer, *Personal Recollections,* pp. 343-377. George T. Palmer, *Conscientious Turncoat,* pp. 229-233.

politely replied that he had no intention of distrusting the state's obligations and ability, and he asked Sheridan to rescind any orders in conflict with the Illinois constitution and laws. Palmer fired back a complaint that such decisions should not be left to the military.

Sheridan ordered the enlistment of a twenty-day regiment to act as property guards. One cadet, an inexperienced University of Chicago student, fatally shot a prominent citizen, a cavalry general, who refused to halt and give the password as he was returning after midnight from a party. The governor asked the state's attorney to have the cadet, Mason, and Sheridan indicted for murder. A grand jury, in obvious accord with public sentiment, commended the mayor for calling in Sheridan and refused to hold the cadet. Palmer, never a quitter, asked the legislature to take a hand. An investigating committee gave him a 4 to 3 split decision, and the senate took no action on a resolution, adopted by the house, which sustained the governor and censured Sheridan for an "illegal and dangerous" example.

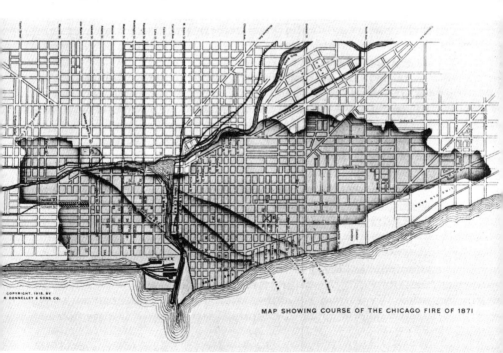

COPYRIGHT, 1915, BY
R. DONNELLEY & SONS CO.

MAP SHOWING COURSE OF THE CHICAGO FIRE OF 1871

LIKE A PHOENIX, FROM THE ASHES

Location, topography, financial ties with New York City, and the aggressiveness of Chicago businessmen guaranteed that a great city would rise again around the harbor at Lake Michigan's southwestern corner. The central business district and the north side had been wiped out, but the west and south sides were mostly intact and the people who lived there were ready to start the task of rebuilding while they helped give relief to the homeless. The stockyards, most of the grain elevators, and many of the lumberyards were untouched. Some railroad property had been damaged, but the tracks still led to far places and trains still unloaded at Chicago. The enterprising men who had given Chicago its reputation as a grain, livestock, lumber, and merchandising center were determined to rebuild and resume the making of money before St. Louis or other competitors grabbed their customers. In this they had the full cooperation of New York banks and suppliers who had developed an alliance with Chicago based on the east-west trade route. If some other city should achieve midwestern domination, its seaboard ties might have been with Philadelphia or Baltimore. As a result, New York for its own selfish reasons helped Chicago rebuild.[6]

Chicago's revival and speedy growth, perhaps without parallel, became widely advertised. Despite the fire and a bad setback from a panic in 1873, the city almost doubled in population during the 1870's. At the time of the fire an estimated 335,000 lived there, compared with 298,977 at the 1870 census. After the conflagration, many left the city, but many more saw Chicago's opportunities and succumbed to its lure. By 1880, the population had passed the half-million mark and Chicago was the nation's fourth largest city, now larger than St. Louis.

Before the ashes cooled, stronghearted men resumed their careers. Burned out Monday morning, the *Tribune* two days later in rented quarters and with misfit type published a "Cheer Up" editorial. W. D. Kerfoot tacked an "all gone but wife, children, and energy" sign on the small shack that was his new real estate office. Cyrus Hall McCormick told his employees that the reaper plant would be rebuilt promptly. Destruction of bridges proved a

[6] W. W. Belcher, *The Economic Rivalry Between St. Louis and Chicago*, pp. 183-185, 201-203.

handicap, but jobs awaited workmen. East of Michigan Avenue the city temporarily leased space in which businessmen, operating mostly on credit, erected shanties for offices and stores. In a step that restored confidence, the banks opened in a week, although currency in some vaults was charred. Some insurance companies went broke and payments to policyholders were less than half of the eighty-eight-million-dollar claims submitted. By the end of 1871, permanent brick and stone buildings were going up and a rubble-covered lot was valuable property.[7]

In one major way, the fire turned out to be a blessing. With the downtown slate wiped clean, architects built more permanently and at higher levels than before, and tall buildings arose in the rubble of slum shacks. Architects used fire clay for protection, since brick and stone walls were inadequate. In the new Chicago, buildings of six stories, the previous maximum, became common, and some complained that the new seven- and eight-story buildings were too high. John Mills Van Osdel, now an alderman as well as an architect, established a new city grade and drafted the first Chicago building code.[8]

As the 1873 panic subsided, Chicago had to construct replacement buildings and simultaneously provide for expansion. The boom continued through the 1880's, a golden decade for Chicago construction, and between the fire and 1890 new construction cost 257 million dollars. Potter Palmer, who lost heavily in the fire, recouped by building larger and more permanent buildings. On a new site on State Street, which had been little more than a country lane, he erected a second Palmer House which became internationally famous. Palmer developed State Street into the main merchandising area, and Lake Street became of secondary importance. He also spent heavily to transform the lake area north of the river into drives and beautiful building sites.

For meat as well as grain, Chicago was the great distribution point upon which much of the nation depended for basic foodstuffs. Around the stockyards developed a Packingtown that had banks, hotels, a board of trade, post offices, and other essentials of a separate city. Livestock men who had accompanied their own

[7] Randall, *op. cit.,* p. 11. Angle, *op. cit.,* 2nd edition, pp. 3-5.

[8] Van Osdel built many notable Chicago buildings before and after the fire. He also designed the governor's mansion at Springfield and University Hall, the first large building at the University of Illinois, where he served on the first board of trustees.

Courtesy Illinois State Historical Library

John M. Palmer

shipments there needed to go downtown only to catch a train for the return trip home.

Civil War contracts enabled Nelson Morris, a German who was an unorthodox trader, to build one of the first big packing plants at the stockyards. He was the first of the Chicago packers who combined efficiency with volume. Philip D. Armour, an Easterner who made his first stake building sluices in the California gold fields, and Gustavus F. Swift, partner of a Boston meat dealer, reached Chicago after the fire.[9] Armour and several relatives had a

[9] Harper Leech and John C. Carroll, *Armour and His Times*. Louis F. Swift, *The Yankee of the Yards: The Biography of Gustavus Franklin Swift, The National Provisioner*, Jan. 26, 1952.

grain commission and meat-packing business in Milwaukee that gradually shifted its base of operations to Chicago. Swift came west to reach the source of supply for the beef, which was shipped live and slaughtered locally, an expensive and wasteful process. As competitors, Armour and Swift put maximum efficiency and by-product utilization in the slaughtering business. The real packing boom came with refrigeration, which used natural ice and became practicable around 1880. Never agreeing on who made the biggest contribution to the new science, they bought their own refrigerator cars to send fresh beef to the eastern markets. Pushing for advantage, they sold abroad and began large-scale preparation of canned meats. The public demanded beef, and the Chicago packers, including the Chicago firm established by John Cudahy, started to establish branch plants in such distant cities as Kansas City, Omaha, and East St. Louis, where a major stockyard developed in the adjacent community of National City.

A traditional opposition to blue laws was demonstrated by Chicago after the fire. Drafted to head a Fire-proof ticket, Medill became mayor but had difficulty with the Germans, the most populous foreign-born element. They protested when the reform-minded city officials insisted upon enforcing a Sunday closing law for saloons. The result was that Medill served only one term. Under his successor, the council repealed the Sunday closing ordinance and set an example for law nonenforcement that was followed by several downstate cities. Elected county commissioner on the same ticket with Medill was Carter Harrison, a Yale graduate and former Kentucky plantation owner who had latent political talents.[10] Harrison held liberal views that made him popular with the increasing number of immigrant Chicagoans and did not conflict with the frontier morality that characterized the city. Only a minority sought enforcement of blue laws, while most residents gave at least passive acquiescence to a policy of minimum regulation of drinking, gambling, and prostitution.

Professional gambling in Chicago began at least two decades before the Civil War, and before the fire illegal activities included prostitution in widely advertised houses. Inevitably ambitious men sought centralized control of at least part of the lawlessness, and the first alliance between crime and politics has been traced to the 1873 city election. Michael Cassius McDonald, who at fifteen was

10 Claudius O. Johnson, *Carter Henry Harrison I.*

a candy butcher on railroad trains, adva1 ced to the operation of gambling houses in the downtown area and the collection of tribute for the financing of political activities. Within a few years McDonald was known as the big boss among Chicago Democrats.[11]

[11] Herbert Asbury, *Gem of the Prairie, An Informal History of the Chicago Underworld.* John H. Lyle, *The Dry and Lawless Years,* pp. 26-27.

19

GRANGERS AND GREENBACKERS

In the years after the civil war, a persistent rural depression spawned an agrarian discontent that gave impetus to third-party movements—Grangers, Greenbackers, and Populists among others. The farmer protesters objected that Republican leaders were too closely involved with the big businessmen who helped finance political campaigns and expected favors in return. Political amateurs, the agrarians had indifferent success at the ballot box, but the dominant Republicans made some adjustment to popular demand while depending on the election-day loyalty of the ex-soldier vote. On economic policy and other issues, the pre-Populist Democrats offered few important alternatives and consequently had difficulty in getting rural sympathy and support. The Grangers, who were stronger in other farm states, dropped out of sight in a few years largely because Republicans in Illinois had unusual success in solving the railroad regulation issue.

The opportunity for pioneering had ended and there was really no place further west where a man could be independent of the marketplace or escape the unemployment that went with a business panic. Nevertheless, over the years there was a great stirring of the native population that attracted less attention than the arrival of the immigrants. Many Illinois families yielded to their grandfathers' instinct to pull out and cross the Mississippi. Some villages, unfortunately located, acquired a surplus of empty houses and in time disappeared. Of those who left the small towns and farms, more went to the cities than to the new lands. Many struck out for the metropolitan centers, where the immigrant hordes also were seeking the jobs created by expanding industries. Chicago especially offered the prospect of employment and excitement for the ambitious and adventurous young.

PROTESTS FROM FARMERS

During the three decades beginning with 1860, Illinois raised more corn and wheat than any other state. Before the century ended, however, wheat became of secondary importance because the western plains took over the growing of the staple crops. Increasingly the emphasis in Illinois centered on corn, and a rivalry with Iowa developed to see which state could produce the largest crop, much of which was marketed on the hoof after being fed to cattle and hogs. Fertility did not insure prosperity for the men who tilled the soil, since the economic law of supply and demand operated, and the glaciated midwestern soil produced more foodstuffs than city and foreign markets needed. Demobilization of the armies had coincided with a slackening of European demand. Immigration increased and the homestead law helped settlement of western lands which competed with Illinois. Manufacturers made almost yearly improvements in farm machinery, and the spreading railroads brought grain from the new states to the Chicago market. The result was overproduction, with lower prices at a time when costs were increasing.[1]

In anticipating that the greenback prosperity and sellers' market of the Civil War would be permanent, many on the farms had expanded their operations with mortgage financing. The price deflation and a diminished supply of money that followed made it difficult to pay debts and fixed interest charges. At the same time the farmers complained of currency fluctuations and argued that it was unfair for them as producers to sell staples at world competitive prices when as consumers they bought manufactured goods at costs increased by a tariff. The expanding cities meanwhile enjoyed a high level of prosperity until 1873. Then the economic

[1] Allan G. Bogue, *Money at Interest: The Farm Mortgage on the Middle Border* and *From Prairie to Corn Belt: Farming on the Illinois and Iowa Prairies in the Nineteenth Century*. Margaret B. Bogue, *Patterns from the Sod*, pp. 138-146. Richard B. Bardolph, "Agriculture in Transition, 1820-1870," *Journal of the Illinois State Historical Society*, XLI (Dec., 1948), 415-437.

conditions returned to panic conditions, which lasted a decade and were the severest the nation had experienced.

Rural life, even in intervals of prosperity, hardly could be described by other adjectives than drab and dreary.[2] Roads were poor, trips to town were infrequent, and the few neighbors seldom lived close at hand. Hired girls were difficult to employ, and the wife of the farmer labored long hours in drudgery that was relieved chiefly by weekly church services that were somber in character. Household conveniences were rare and, except for occasional heirlooms, furnishings were roughly hand-crafted. Sinks were unnecessary because there was no running water, and baths were taken in wooden tubs or tin basins. Privies could contaminate wells. Wood and coal stoves did the cooking and space heating. Before 1860, lamps that burned whale or lard oil replaced candles until kerosene came on the market when the petroleum industry was developed after the Civil War. Until late in the century, windows were screened with cloth mosquito bars. Typical frame houses had spartan designs, with two rooms on each floor and usually no halls or closets, but about 1875 improvements became noticeable in construction, architecture, and conveniences. Then some of the better houses had ten-foot ceilings.

Continued improvements in farm machinery helped increase production, and Joseph F. Glidden, who in 1852 was the last Democratic sheriff of DeKalb County, helped settle the West by becoming the most successful of a number of men who invented barbed wire. Timber was scarce, smooth wire could not turn back animals, the widely used Osage orange had drawbacks, and an increase in the number of farms created a demand for better fencing. Glidden in 1874 began the sale of a twisted fence wire armed with sharp spurs. Hundreds of other fence patents were issued, and a debate over priorities continued until the United States Supreme Court in 1892 upheld Glidden's claims and eliminated the possibility that a farmer who bought fencing might be sued for royalties. Glidden's new industry, based at DeKalb, let the midwestern farmer fence his pastures and crops and, further west, handicapped cattle ranchers by converting open ranges into pastures. Barbed wire was credited with doing more for the West than the long rifle and covered wagon.[3]

2 Fred A. Shannon, *The Farmer's Last Frontier, 1860-1897*, pp. 362-371.
3 Walter P. Webb, *The Great Plains*, pp. 295-310.

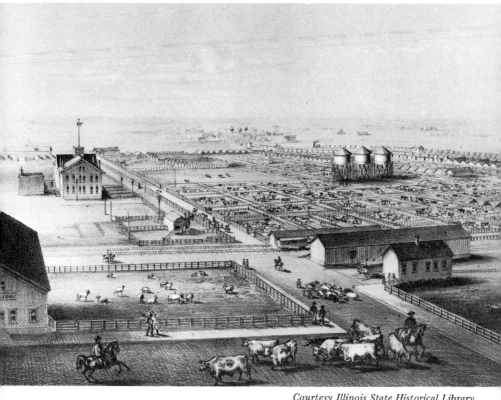

Chicago Stockyards after 1865 opening

Because the efficiency of the steel plows, reapers, and mowers increased both crop yields and land values, economics required that the immense pastures of the big estates be broken up into family-sized tracts. By 1880 Illinois still had 649 superfarms, of which twenty-seven were in Champaign County, but the cattle business was being shifted to the plains. That year the census showed that the average Illinois farmer worked 124 acres.[4] The small farmers experimented, none too successfully, with bulk purchasing and cooperative selling. Attempts at cooperative selling made more headway in Iowa than in Illinois.

With major tracks radiating from Chicago and St. Louis and branches serving the farming towns and tapping the coal fields, Illinois had more miles of railroad than any other state. By 1870

[4] Shannon, *op. cit.*, pp. 155-156.

the rail mileage was 4,707, compared with 2,790 a decade before. Track crews in 1872 laid another 1,197 miles, the most since the rush work on the Illinois Central. Not until 1874 could trains from the East cross the Mississippi River. Then James B. Eads, a St. Louis man who turned to engineering after making a fortune salvaging wrecked steamboats, built a bridge bearing his name.[5] Too late to permit St. Louis to offer real economic competition to Chicago, the bridge opened July 4, 1874, with a celebration in which East St. Louis transfer houses and ferryboat operators did not join. By 1880 the Illinois rail mileage had jumped to 7,851, despite a slowdown from the 1873 panic. Roadbeds were still primitive and accidents frequent, but passenger accommodations improved and almost every town had at least a branch line which led to a junction where trains carried sleeping and dining cars. Stagecoach and river traffic became a memory as the nation took a big step forward in mobility.

Farmers throughout the Middle West complained in 1866 that a "livestock ring" of commission men at the Chicago stockyards refused to reveal the prices paid for cattle and hogs. The daily newspapers soon ended the secrecy by printing information on market fluctuations. Speculation was rampant, and attempts to corner the grain market were another source of rural discontent. For a time warehousemen refused to announce the amount of grain in storage, which facilitated speculative raiding. The fourteen giant grain elevators at Chicago, controlled by nine firms, constituted a monopoly through which nearly all of the grain marketed in seven or eight states was funneled by the railroads. The Chicago elevators by 1865 could store 10.055 million bushels of wheat and corn and, despite standards set by the Board of Trade, they acquired a reputation for cheating on weights and paying for a lower quality of grain than that delivered by the farmer. Arbitrary and extortionate storage and handling charges were made by the elevator owners, with the result that Chicago would have lost its grain market primacy had facilities been available elsewhere.[6]

Most of all the farmers complained about the railroads they had helped finance in the 1850's. A few of the original short lines prospered, but many had been absorbed through consolidations or

[5] W. W. Belcher, *The Economic Rivalry Between St. Louis and Chicago, 1850-1880,* p. 181. Rosemary Yager, *James Buchanan Eads: Master of the Great River.*

[6] *Ibid.,* pp. 166-172, 186-192. Shannon, *op. cit.,* pp. 179-182. Charles H. Taylor, *History of the Board of Trade of the City of Chicago.*

wrecked by mismanagement or fraud, with the result that the farmers who had purchased stock lost their investments and in some cases their farms through mortgage foreclosures. Meanwhile taxes, which often were burdensome, had to be paid to retire the bonds which had been issued by counties and cities to attract the railroads. As the cost-prize squeeze tightened, farmers protested that the railroads, which watered their stock and issued passes to get the goodwill of public officials, were charging too much for hauling people and freight and were in league with the Chicago grain handlers.[7]

THE GRANGERS WIN THEIR POINT

Clubs of farmers organized spontaneously during the 1860's and in a pooling of political and economic influence won enactment of a law to compel the railroads to handle grain from independent elevators. They also were the motivating force behind a law which declared that railroad rates should be just, reasonable, and uniform, but it turned out to be a dead letter because there was no yardstick for compliance.

A department of agriculture clerk at Washington in 1867 meanwhile founded the Patrons of Husbandry, whose local granges had a secret ritual, admitted women as well as men to membership, and sought to improve both the culture and the prosperity of rural people. Other states, chiefly Iowa, Wisconsin, and Minnesota, had more grange members than Illinois, and during the big Panic of 1873 the Granger protest reached a political peak in Wisconsin by electing a governor.[8]

The 1870 constitutional convention recognized the problem with a mandate for laws to correct abuses and to prevent unjust discrimination in freight and passenger tariffs. The legislature promptly complied by enacting a series of laws seeking to regulate the tariffs of the railroad companies it had incorporated. One established maximum passenger fares ranging from two and a half

---

[7] Arthur C. Cole, *The Era of the Civil War*, pp. 359-361. Maurice G. Baxter, *Orville H. Browning, Lincoln's Friend and Critic*, p. 261.

[8] Solon J. Buck, *The Agrarian Crusade: A Chronicle of the Farmer in Politics*, pp. 21-56. See also his *The Granger Movement: A Study of Agricultural Organization and Its Political, Economic, and Social Manifestation*. Also E. L. Bogart and C. M. Thompson, *The Industrial State, 1870-1893*, pp. 82-90. Roy V. Scott, *The Agrarian Movement in Illinois, 1880-1896*.

to five and a half cents a mile, graduated according to a classification of railroads. Another provided in effect that freight rates should be based entirely on the distance traveled. It also prohibited fare increases in an effort to force all charges to the level of the lowest competitive fares in effect in 1870. Another established a supervisory board of railroad and warehouse commissioners, appointed by the governor and empowered to examine carrier and storage companies and investigate charges of discrimination.[9]

In response, the railroads ignored the inexperienced commissioners, and most refused to file the required reports. They ejected passengers who refused to pay more than the legal fare, and once a passenger car loaded with farmers was left on a Rantoul sidetrack. In the litigation that followed, the Supreme Court held unconstitutional the attempt to regulate freight rates on the ground that it sought to prevent all discrimination, whether justified or not.

Other states were abandoning their Granger laws on constitutional grounds, but in 1873 the Illinois legislature, guided by Speaker Shelby M. Cullom and inspired by a farmers' convention at Springfield, passed a new law which gave the commission power to prescribe reasonable rates. It avoided a constitutional pitfall by saying that discrimination would be prima facie but not absolute evidence of unjust rate schedules. The burden of proof was on the railroads, but they had the right to show that cost of service factors, such as light traffic on a branch line, justified higher charges.

In Illinois the political arm in the Granger era was an Independent Farmers Organization headed by Willard C. Flagg, whose followers had a spectacular success in the 1873 judicial election by defeating Chief Justice Charles B. Lawrence of the Illinois Supreme Court, an eminent Republican from Galesburg who had held the first rate law unconstitutional.[10] Flagg and his followers in their wrath elected their choices to two vacancies on the high court and carried some circuit judgeships.

High tide for the Granger movement came the next year, with limited success in Illinois. John M. Palmer within a few months formally returned to the Democratic party by presiding over its state convention while an antimonopoly platform with a green-

[9] Buck, *Agrarian Crusade*, pp. 19-72. Shannon, *op. cit.*, pp. 309-311. John Moses, *Illinois Historical and Statistical*, II, 801-824, 1059-1062.

[10] Edward F. Dunne, *Illinois, The Heart of the Nation*, II, 130.

back plank was adopted.[11] The antimonopolists had great strength in a majority of the downstate counties and in a coalition with Democrats elected the state superintendent of public instruction, which gave Republicans their first statewide defeat since 1862. Miscellaneous independents, chiefly farm protesters, won nine seats in the state senate and forty-one in the house of representatives. A fusion Democrat became president pro tem of the senate. Democrats helped give Elijah M. Haines of Waukegan, a cantankerous independent, the house speakership at the start of a turbulent and disorderly session marked by economy and the throwing of books. The senate rejected Governor Beveridge's nominations to the railroad and warehouse commission and forced him to name a second board that included two farmers, one a Democrat.

In the litigation, which proceeded slowly through the courts, the key case involved the Chicago elevator firm of Munn and Scott, which the commission sued for failing to take out a grain storage license. The firm's appeal brought national attention to the elderly Sidney Breese, chief justice of the state's Supreme Court, who wrote a landmark opinion upholding the validity of the rate law by asserting that, regardless of charter provisions, a business could be regulated if it was in the public interest. His doctrine of the regulatory power of the state over public service corporations was sustained at every point by the United States Supreme Court in the *Munn vs. Illinois* opinion of 1877. Illinois had done an intelligent and effective job of regulation, and in 1881 the railroads cooperated in revising the rate and fare schedule and then complied with its provisions. Other states enacted duplicates of the 1873 law, which preceded by three decades Theodore Roosevelt's war on the trusts. Later court decisions put limitations on the powers of the states, but Breese's interpretation of the Granger law furnished the legal basis for continuing governmental regulation of railroads.[12]

By the time the *Munn vs. Illinois* doctrine had been promulgated, the Granger movement, experiencing internal difficulties as a result of its rapid growth, was collapsing as a political force.

---

[11] Moses, *op. cit.*, II, 823-828.

[12] 94 U. S. 113 (1877). James W. Neilson, *Shelby M. Cullom, Prairie State Republican*, pp. 79-113. Buck, *op. cit.*, pp. 56-76. For a biographical sketch of Breese, see the memoir by Melville W. Fuller in Breese's *Early History of Illinois*, pp. 3-62.

Courtesy Illinois State Historical Library

Sidney Breese

A SURPLUS OF THIRD PARTIES

Greenbackers quickly replaced Grangers as the third-party protest movement. The name came from the currency inflation in
which four hundred million dollars in treasury notes were issued
to help finance the Civil War, at the end of which a paper dollar
was worth about half its face value in gold. The farmers, troubled
to meet mortgage payments, received greenbacks for everything
they sold and complained that holders of government bonds, paid
in gold, were making a handsome profit. Greenbackers asked for
an increase in the supply of money and were critical of the new
notes, which since 1863 had been issued by national banks and
which were used until the Federal Reserve System was established
in 1913. The volume of national bank currency in circulation

tended to fluctuate with the price of government bonds and did not fully meet the needs of business.[13]

Advocates of more dependence on greenbacks existed in both parties, especially in rural areas. For a decade, Greenback candidates ran in Illinois with some success in congressional and local races, but the party's single-minded leadership seldom achieved fusion with the basically conservative Democrats. Both major parties recognized the inflationary sentiment in their ranks and did not hesitate to adopt platforms and run candidates favoring easy money. This made the issue sectional and helped keep potential Greenbackers in their original parties. In 1876 the independents had just enough strength in legislative races to make certain that Republican Rutherford B. Hayes would become President in the election contested by Democrat Samuel J. Tilden, who had almost carried the state. Agreement had been reached in Washington that the dispute over southern state returns would be turned over to a commission of fifteen men from Congress and the Supreme Court. A Supreme Court justice, picked by other justices, would be the fifteenth man on an otherwise evenly divided commission. Presumably the position would go to Davis, whom the Democrats trusted. Back in Springfield, however, the situation got out of control during the legislative session. "Black Jack" Logan, leader of Illinois Republicans, wanted a second term. Democrats supported Palmer, but the fifteen independents refused to cooperate. After forty ballots of continual switching, the Democrats finally accepted Davis as better than an organization Republican, but there was consternation in Washington. Davis resigned to accept the senate seat and his replacement on the presidential commission voted for Hayes.[14] In the senate Davis gave increasing support to the Arthur administration and was elected president pro tem.

At the state level, the Greenbackers never again approached their 1876 showing. Two years later the Republicans elected their state ticket, although by a minority vote, and for the first time in six years won a majority in both houses of the legislature. The Greenbackers continued to enter tickets through 1884. Among isolated successes, Adlai E. Stevenson of Bloomington, who later became Vice President, was elected to Congress as a Greenback

[13] Buck, *op. cit.*, pp. 77-90. Shannon, *op. cit.*, pp. 184-188. Neilson, *op. cit.*, pp. 34-41.

[14] Willard L. King, *Lincoln's Manager, David Davis*, pp. 290-293. Davis was the best hope of the Democrats, but King does not believe he would have voted for Tilden.

candidate in 1874 and as a Democrat in 1878, but lost three other races. During the Civil War, Stevenson was master-in-chancery and state's attorney of Woodford County.

After a temporary eclipse during the Civil War, the temperance issue again stirred up controversy. A major element in the Republican party pushed for legal steps to stop the sale of intoxicants and had the backing of Governors Palmer and Beveridge, but the biggest impetus came from women. Four times starting in 1882 Prohibition party tickets ran for state office without success, but organized women persisted in efforts to close the drinking places whose patrons included Germans and others who refused to give up Old World customs.[15]

When the 1884 Republican state convention took up the nomination of a candidate for state superintendent of public instruction, the leader on the first ballot was Frances E. Willard of Evanston, who with other members of her sex was ineligible to vote. That was the year Miss Willard quit as president of the Evanston College for Ladies to become president of the brand new Chicago Women's Temperance Union. Within five years Miss Willard was national W.C.T.U. president, a position she held until 1898. Meanwhile she worked for women's suffrage, helped organize the Prohibition party, served as president of the National Council of Women, crusaded abroad, and objected to taking a salary. After her death the state of Illinois honored her with one of two statues placed in the national capitol.

Men granted women the right to hold school offices and become notaries public, and in 1870 Mrs. Amelia Hobbs, a justice of the peace in Jersey County, apparently became the first of her sex to be elected to an office in Illinois.[16] Governor Palmer earlier rejected an application of Mrs. Myra Colby Bradwell, editor of the *Chicago Legal News,* for appointment as a notary public. She passed the state bar examination in 1871, but on the sole ground of her sex the Illinois Supreme Court refused to let her become a lawyer. She persevered and in 1892 became the first woman member of the state bar association. The first woman to be nominated for a statewide office was Elizabeth Brown, who in 1882 was the Prohibition party choice for state superintendent of public instruction.

[15] Moses, *op. cit.,* II, 882-897. Bogart-Thompson, *op. cit.,* pp. 42-48.
[16] Cole, *op. cit.,* pp. 427-428.

Women gave chief support to antiliquor agitation which twice scored successes in the legislature. An 1872 law required a tavern keeper to post a three-thousand-dollar bond for payment of damages to an intoxicated person or his family. The family also could sue the owner of saloon property, and insurance companies found a new source of business in the writing of dram-shop policies. Miss Willard led a long campaign which resulted in enactment in 1883 of the Harper high-license law. Named for a Chicago Republican, it required a minimum license of $500 for the sale of alcohol and $150 for malt liquor. Nine other states had similar laws. Some saloons went out of business and Chicago collected an additional million dollars in fees as opposition to high licenses became a Democratic campaign issue. The character of the saloons in many cases was improved, but no reduction was noted in the number of drinkers.

Meanwhile a few Negroes received public recognition. Governor Beveridge appointed John J. Bird, the elected police magistrate at Cairo, to the board of trustees of the state industrial university.[17] J. W. E. Thomas of Chicago in 1877 became the first Negro to sit in the state house of representatives. John Jones, who accumulated property and actively urged repeal of the black laws, died in 1879 after twice being elected Cook County commissioner. Another exceptional case was Augustine Tolton, who became the first Negro priest in the United States. Born of Catholic parents and tutored by priests at Quincy, he was ordained at Rome in 1880 and served all-Negro parishes at Quincy and Chicago.[18]

SHELBY M. CULLOM, SENATOR FOR THIRTY YEARS

During the decades when elections were swung by the Grand Army of the Republic, a man who never wore the army blue had a distinguished political career that lasted a half-century. Shelby Moore Cullom, a Tazewell County farm boy who had been born in Kentucky, was a thirty-one-year-old Springfield lawyer when his friend Lincoln first called for troops. Older men carried muskets and won commands while Cullom became speaker of the house of representatives and lost a race for Congress. His health was poor,

[17] D. W. Lusk, *Politics and Politicians,* p. 341.

[18] *Illinois Intelligencer,* April 18, 1968.

Courtesy Illinois State Historical Library

Senator Shelby M. Cullom

the result of an early exposure, but Cullom scarcely mentioned it in his biography.[19]

Cullom looked something like Lincoln and preferred political office to legal fees. He served three terms in Congress and, after losing to a Democrat, filled in by returning to his old post as speaker in 1873, where he played an active role in putting railroads under state regulation. Three years later at the Republican state convention he proved himself a better politician than Governor Beveridge, one of the generals in public life, who succeeded Oglesby and wanted a full term. Then Cullom became governor by

[19] *Fifty Years of Public Service.* Cullom is the subject of a biography that surveys the economic and political trends of his half-century in state and national office, James W. Neilson's *Shelby M. Cullom, Prairie State Republican.* It has been invaluable in the preparation of several chapters of this book.

"waving the bloody shirt" before G.A.R. audiences in running against a fusionist.

Cullom was a United States senator thirty years, a record for Illinois. First he won a second term as governor, defeating Trumbull without difficulty in 1880, and then he resigned in 1882 to succeed Davis as senator. Throughout his career Cullom combined a rural background, conservative instincts, an ability to keep even or slightly ahead of public sentiment, sympathy with both sides of a question, a knack of putting federal patronage in loyal hands, and an unusual ability to get reelected without active participation in the campaign. During his final term, under the seniority system he took over the chairmanship of the senate committee on foreign relations.

His greatest achievement put interstate commerce under the control of the federal government. It was a major project for Cullom, who as speaker and governor had worked for an effective state railroad and warehouse commission. The federal courts in a succession of cases had established the principle of state regulation, but when the Wabash, St. Louis, and Pacific road sued the Illinois commission the United States Supreme Court ruled in 1886 that only the federal government could have jurisdiction over interstate commerce. Cullom earlier became convinced that federal control was necessary. As chairman of the senate committee on interstate commerce he adopted the major premise that the evil was in unjust discrimination, but he conceded that some variation in rates could be proper. His solution was to win enactment in 1887 of the law creating the Interstate Commerce Commission, composed of experts with power to deal with transportation problems on their merits as they arose. Cullom's law had defects, since the commission lacked power to fix rates and the burden of proof rested on the injured shipper, but the loopholes gradually were plugged.[20]

Only at the end of his first term in 1888 did Cullom win renomination and reelection without a fight. During an era when Republicans lacked strong leadership in Illinois, the senator from a distance built up a reputation for trustworthiness and an ability to get things done. Colorless but abler than other Illinois politicians, Cullom in 1888 and again in 1892 aspired to be the Republican presidential candidate but failed to get the solid support of his

[20] Shannon, *op. cit.*, pp. 178-179.

home state delegation.[21] One of his minor achievements, at the 1872 convention, was to put Grant in second-term nomination with the shortest speech on record—a single sentence of seventy-nine words.[22]

REPUBLICANS KEEP CONTROL

The passing decades became politically complex as labor began to enter its own candidates in emulation of the agrarians. Republicans maintained domination until 1892, but Illinois developed its character as a two-party state in which the swinging pendulum usually gave the victors some cause for concern and the losers hope that setbacks would end before long. Simultaneously parties developed factions, which led to struggles for control that in the last half of the nineteenth century often were settled on the floors of conventions or in the legislature when United States senators were elected.

Former President Grant occupied a controversial position in 1880. Back from a world tour, he returned to Galena without too much to do. Many Republicans regarded James G. Blaine of Maine as their logical presidential choice, but the Old Guard split the party in Illinois with a third-term drive for Grant. At the state convention the Grant forces, led by Senator Logan, won control. In a break from precedent they refused to allow Blaine Republicans, who had carried some districts, to name their own delegates to the national convention that met in the Exposition Building in Chicago.[23] The national convention debated two days before seating the contesting Blaine delegates, and in a deadlock the presidential nomination went to James A. Garfield, who was elected handily.

The 1882 off-year voting showed a Democratic tide in other states, but the only Illinois Republican defeated was the nominee for superintendent of public instruction, who lost chiefly because he favored a referendum on prohibition.

Because his party was in trouble, Richard J. Oglesby won his third nonconsecutive election as governor twenty years after he

[21] William A. Pitkin, "Shelby M. Cullom, Presidential Prospect," *Journal of the Illinois State Historical Society,* XLIX (Winter, 1956), 375-386.

[22] Neilson, *op. cit.,* p. 26n.

[23] *Ibid.,* pp. 55-58.

had first carried the state in the closing years of the war. In his first term Oglesby's administrative record had been good and, after a four-year layoff, he won again in 1872. Then he resigned immediately to go to the senate where, as in the earlier case of Richard Yates, his verbose oratory seemed out of place. Logan, the most popular politician in the state, after six years ousted Oglesby without difficulty. In 1884 Democrats seemed to be on the move, pushing Grover Cleveland of New York for President and Carter Harrison, the colorful mayor of Chicago, for governor. John M. Hamilton, who had replaced Cullom, lacked color, and Republicans by acclamation gave the nomination to Oglesby.

Factional troubles popped up among Democrats. Harrison, a rough-and-tumble campaigner who wore a black hat at a rakish angle while riding a Kentucky mare through Chicago streets, ran better than his party, but under Oglesby and Logan Republicans managed to carry the state.

Logan had Illinois backing for the Republican presidential nomination. At the convention, again held in Chicago's Exposition Building, he finished fourth in the balloting and then ran for Vice President on a ticket headed by Blaine. Cleveland carried the nation but not Illinois in the first national Democratic victory since 1856.

Logan's senate term had ended, and the legislature in 1885 divided so evenly that, after a month, a deadlock over the speakership ended in the selection of Elijah M. Haines, the lone independent. Balloting for a United States senator then dragged on for months. When a Democratic state representative died in a downstate district which Cleveland had carried by two thousand votes, Republicans did not enter a candidate for the vacancy at a special election. Men disguised as cattle buyers and lightning rod salesmen left secretly printed ballots at the homes of trusted Republicans and instructed them to stay away from the polls until late in the day. The complacent Democrats discovered the plot too late to prevent a Republican victory that sent Logan to the senate a third time. Within two years he died.[24]

The vacancy went to Congressman Charles B. Farwell, one of the rich men in Republican politics. Farwell piled up wealth in real estate and as a partner in his brother's wholesale dry-goods firm, which ranked second only to Field and Leiter. Farwell had been

[24] Moses, *op. cit.*, II, 905-907.

state chairman and had been under attack for leading a "Chicago Tammany." With the exception of Douglas and Trumbull, who had moved to Chicago while holding office, Farwell was the first United States senator from Cook County.

To help Democrats celebrate their national triumph, President Cleveland gave Adlai E. Stevenson, the former Bloomington congressman, the job of firing forty thousand Republican postmasters. A pleasant and tactful man who gave the minimum amount of offense to the opposition party, Stevenson held the title of first assistant postmaster general.

The question of whether the government had been overly generous in pensioning Civil War veterans came up in the 1884 campaign and, soon after his inauguration, Cleveland turned the matter over to John C. Black of Danville, an attorney and former general. As commissioner of pensions, Black charged that his predecessors had favored Republicans and cited State Senator Joseph W. Fifer of Bloomington as an example. Fifer had enlisted early in the war, had been shot in the lung and liver after Vicksburg, and the next year, still a private, had returned to his company. For the wound he received twenty-four dollars a month, the same pension paid for a missing leg or hand. As self-appointed spokesman for the common soldier, Fifer promptly denounced the general, charged that Black drew a pension of one hundred dollars by act of Congress, and offered to compare wounds.[25]

As a direct result, Fifer became governor. At the 1888 Republican state convention he won the nomination over several generals of political prominence. The Democratic nominee was Palmer, which enabled "Private Joe" to continue his campaign against men of high rank.

[25] A. L. Bowen, "Personal Reminiscences of Joseph W. Fifer, An Interview with the Former Governor and a Description of His Times," *Illinois Blue Book, 1925-26,* pp. 279-310.

20

THE WORKINGMAN ORGANIZES

INDUSTRY EXPANDED AND DIVERSIFIED IN ILLINOIS BECAUSE the state had several advantages—the availability of agricultural products for processing, the network of rail lines, the delivery of iron ore by lake steamers, the coal from nearby mines, and the stream of job applicants from Europe and the hinterland. An oversupply of manpower meant complications as extremes of wealth and poverty became more pronounced in the larger cities, factories became bigger and more impersonal, and labor trouble developed. As the labor market became glutted, newcomers who had crossed the ocean to find a better life could not argue about wages. Overtime pay, paid vacations, and fringe benefits were unheard of. Overcrowding in the new cities resulted in tenements and slums, poverty and discontent. The immigrant who settled on a prairie farm could have a measure of independence in his dawn-to-dusk tasks, but the city workers found it difficult to accumulate any property at the wages paid for long hours. At times they were short of grocery money.

In the cutthroat era, men of ability and ambition invested money and energy in shops and factories that provided jobs for the immigrants, in downstate cities as well as Chicago. The capitalist had his own problems, since the manufacturing plants faced price competition from firms in eastern cities. Bond interest had to be paid and other fixed charges met, and to maintain solvency in times of economic slowdown he cut prices and expenses, including payrolls. If necessary, the cuts were repeated.

In a protest against low wages and the twelve-hour or longer day, the workingman staged strikes that were at first disorganized, often spontaneous, and for a time usually unsuccessful. The odds were against him, because the two major parties were equally conservative on most economic matters. Labor had yet to establish its legal rights, and judicial precedents and public opinion both backed the sanctity of property and contracts. As a result, the power of the government and most of the newspapers usually lined up against the workingman. In the developing struggle, the military and the courts became antistrike weapons.

UNIONS, STRIKES, AND THE MILITIA

The Panic of 1873, precipitated by failure of a Philadelphia financial house, ended the industrial prosperity of the Civil War era and provided the nation's first major confrontation between capital and labor. For a decade labor had been restless, and during the war a few groups in Chicago had formed unions, but a wage strike of railroad workers fizzled. Strikes also occurred at Springfield and some other downstate cities as workingmen rebelled against long hours of low-paid drudgery at factory jobs that at best were semiskilled. They organized in an effort to retaliate against an 1863 statute known as the La Salle Black Law, the first of a long series of repressive legislation. It grew out of a strike of coal miners in La Salle County, and the laboring class considered it as onerous as the anti-Negro black code which had been enacted long before the war. Never enforced, the law prohibited strikes and picketing by making it unlawful to prevent by threat or intimidation any person from working at a lawful business. In some cases the legislature passed bills which factory owners opposed. In 1867, when agitation was heard for a new labor party, the lawmakers placated the worker with a law stipulating that, except on farms, eight hours would be considered a normal day's work. Employers ignored that statute. The first safety legislation was an 1869 tumbling rod law, governing operation of threshing machines and corn shellers which had exposed machinery.[1]

---

[1] Two books published at the start of the depression as part of the University of Chicago's *Social Science Studies* are the basic works concerning the early struggle to

In the hard times of the 1873 panic, an early survey by the Chicago Relief and Aid Society concluded that 37 percent of the workingmen were jobless at a time when many had scarcely recovered from losses of the fire two years earlier. The threat and actuality of business failures resulted in layoffs and in some cases wages were halved, but four years passed before mobs took to the streets in a mass protest. Many railroads had gone into receivership before the Baltimore and Ohio announced a 10 percent cut of all wages over one dollar a day. The railroad men, who had strong brotherhoods and were accustomed to good wages, blamed watered stocks and financial racketeering for their troubles and began striking. Baltimore and Pittsburgh became centers of major disorders that helped turn public sentiment against the protesters. Workers at East St. Louis joined the walkout and Chicago became a strike center. In the face of mobs, the Chicago and Alton suspended service and only the Wabash and the Illinois Central carried passenger trains. During a succession of riots the next day, mobs attacked the Chicago, Burlington, and Quincy roundhouse and battled police. Strikers also shut down the Braidwood mines and blocked railroad yards at East St. Louis, Peoria, Galesburg, and Decatur.[2]

To Governor Shelby M. Cullom, who believed that government had a duty to protect private property, it was unthinkable that rioters would dictate to owners of railroads, mines, and factories. In the face of what he regarded as a domestic insurrection, he took the side of law and order, proclaimed the right to peaceful assembly, and warned that troops would be summoned if violence did not cease. The governor then asked for help from President Hayes, who sent six companies of regular troops from the Indian country. At the same time the frugal governor used contingent funds to help equip the state's three brigades of militia, untried as a result of an unfinished reorganization. Striker morale broke at the sight

form unions in Illinois. They are Earl R. Beckner's *A History of Labor Legislation in Illinois* and Eugene Staley's *History of the Illinois State Federation of Labor.* See also Dorothy Culp, "The Radical Labor Movement, 1873-1895," *Transactions of the Illinois State Historical Society,* XLIV (1937), 92-99.

2 James W. Neilson, *Shelby M. Cullom, Prairie State Republican,* pp. 45-49. Harry Barnard, *Eagle Forgotten: The Life of John Peter Altgeld,* pp. 52-54. Edgar Bernhard, *et al., Pursuit of Freedom: A History of Civil Liberty in Illinois, 1787-1942,* pp. 172-173. John Moses, *Illinois Historical and Statistical,* II, 851-852. Herbert G. Gutman, "The Braidwood Lockout of 1874," *Journal of the Illinois State Historical Society,* LIII (Spring, 1960), 5-28.

of the blue-uniformed regulars, and the crowds melted away. A militia battalion restored order at Braidwood. When trouble erupted at East St. Louis, Cullom went there to take personal command of two militia regiments, which were joined, without a formal request, by three hundred regulars from Jefferson Barracks, Missouri. Trains soon ran on all Illinois lines, and the strikers and their sympathizers, who had gained nothing, counted at least nineteen dead. The governors of Maryland, Pennsylvania, and West Virginia also received the help of federal troops that year. The courts assisted in breaking the strike, and judges freely used a stringent 1873 injunction law providing a five-hundred-dollar fine for preventing a person from working. Criminal contempt citations were issued where roads were under receivership.

Chicago socialists hoped to become a major political force, but by 1879 the return of prosperity intervened. They were important, with four newspapers, but didn't always agree among themselves. Part of the group wanted to work with the Greenbackers, but a ticket entered by the Socialist Labor party polled enough votes to elect four state representatives in 1877 and three aldermen two years later, when it ran a well-to-do physician for mayor. The chief socialist accomplishment was a law establishing a state bureau of labor statistics, the first agency charged with taking an interest in the workingman.

Despite the setbacks, the labor movement forged ahead and Chicago became a militant union center.[3] Brotherhoods were strengthened, new unions and central bodies were formed, and in 1884 the Illinois State Federation of Labor held its first state convention in a Chicago labor hall. The chief business was organization of a boycott against boots and shoes made by convict labor, and two years later a constitutional amendment outlawed that source of competition. For fifteen years the state had operated the penitentiaries but leased the convicts as day-laborers to outside firms. The state federation received support from a Chicago council of trade unions formed in 1877. The council, in which German leadership was prominent, rejected amalgamation with the Knights of Labor.

Other governors also called out troops, who restored order, if necessary, by firing into the ranks of strikers and sympathizers. In 1883 militiamen mobilized by Governor John M. Hamilton at the

[3] Staley, *op. cit.*, pp. 6-58.

sheriff's request dispersed coal miners at Collinsville and followed them across the boundary into St. Clair County at Marissa. Rioters fired on troops, and in an exchange of volleys one striker was killed and twenty-six arrested. Governor Richard J. Oglesby used troops in 1885 against striking quarry workers at Lemont and the following year against striking railroad switchmen at East St. Louis, where four men were killed by deputy sheriffs before order was restored. Oglesby, who insisted that the sheriff must first try to handle the situation, also sent troops to preserve the peace and protect property at the Chicago stockyards.

Before his death in 1894, Allan Pinkerton, the Civil War secret service head who developed a dislike for the early unions, went into the business of furnishing men who would guard plants and perform other protective services. The Pinkerton agency not only provided detectives for espionage work but had an industrial department with sixteen hundred armed men, many of them barracked in Chicago, and a private jail.[4]

The Knights of Labor had spectacular growth in the early 1880's as it sought to organize all workingmen into a common brotherhood. In Illinois their dream of a single disciplined army counted at its peak fifty-two thousand members in 306 local assemblies. Trade unionists, who claimed sixty-two thousand members in 328 locals, joined them for an 1884 organization convention. Approximately two-thirds of the membership came from Chicago.

Chiefly as a result of local friction, the Knights of Labor broke away from the state federation by 1888 and soon disintegrated. The trade unionists, under the leadership of the cigarmakers' union, then affiliated with the American Federation of Labor on an autonomous basis. Some of the state federation's early leaders were incompetents, oddballs or worse, but the organization stayed alive and made some gains, although significant legislative accomplishments had to wait until the turn of the century.

HAYMARKET: A LABOR TRAGEDY

As part of labor's drive for an eight-hour day, industrial disturbances became common in 1886. More than a thousand strikes

---

[4] James D. Horan, *The Pinkertons: The Detective Dynasty That Made History.* Allan Pinkerton, *Strikers, Communists, Tramps, and Detectives.*

were called in Illinois, some of them by unskilled and virtually
unorganized men, and approximately half ended with a reduction
in hours. Swedes, Bohemians, Norwegians, and Welshmen participated in walkouts of quarrymen at Lemont and Joliet. Banking
house employees, miners, metal workers, building tradesmen, and
others also left their jobs. To a degree labor ranks were split
between the native-born and the immigrants, and in the latter
group a comparatively small number of anarchists were noisily
prominent.

Some five years earlier Chicago had become a center for an
anarchist movement founded in London. Its fanatical spokesmen,
some of them unnaturalized Germans, argued that the miserable
condition of the working classes justified the use of force. They
urged that free workers unite to form independent and autonomous groups to combat the state. Anarchist newspapers, printed in
German and English, distributed inflammatory propaganda advocating revolution and political assassination.

They found a natural enemy in the big McCormick harvester
plant, which had been moved to Chicago's west side. Since 1868
frequent wage reductions had forced men to speed up production.
Strikes and lockouts became intermixed, and the employers hired
Pinkerton operatives and strikebreakers. The militant workers collected arms and organized, but the company refused to yield to
their demands, and in February, 1886, a general lockout became
effective. As violence spread, some fifty thousand men found their
jobs involved.

At Haymarket Square, where Randolph Street widened into an
open-air produce market, anarchists called a meeting the night of
May 4 to protest that two persons had been shot to death the
night before in a demonstration in front of the reaper plant.
Speakers included such professed anarchists as August Spies,
editor of the *Arbeiter-Zeitung*, and Albert R. Parsons, a former
Confederate soldier who was editor of the *Alarm*.

The highest estimate placed the crowd at three thousand, but
possibly only a third of that number heard the speeches. Mayor
Harrison walked through the assemblage and at the nearby Des
Plaines Street police station advised Inspector John Bonfield, who
hated union militance, that all seemed quiet. Before he went
home, the mayor did not object when Bonfield suggested that the
police reserves should not be dismissed immediately. During the
closing minutes of the meeting, when the crowd had dwindled to

somewhere around two hundred, almost that many uniformed police marched into the square and a captain ordered the group to disperse. Someone, never identified, threw a bomb that killed seven officers and wounded seventy-six others. The surviving police opened fire on the fleeing men, with one fatality. The Haymarket tragedy was hardly a riot. Only one bomb exploded and the resultant gunfire came only from the police. Rioting was not attempted by the men who ran from Haymarket Square.[5]

The bomber's major achievement was to inflame public sentiment against labor and, through guilt by association, to brand as anarchistic sympathizers any exponent of collective bargaining. Newspapers boosted circulation by sensationally warning that Chicago was endangered by alien anarchists. Pinkerton detectives helped with a general roundup of suspects after which thirty-one persons were indicted for murder and conspiracy. In a trial that attracted national attention and lasted nearly two months, it was not disputed that the defendants were anarchists. The prosecution did not know who threw the bomb but contended it had only to show, by direct or circumstantial evidence, that the unidentified man was a member of a conspiracy. Near the end of a tumultuous summer, Judge Joseph E. Gary sentenced seven men to death by hanging and another man to fifteen years in prison. Some of them had not attended the Haymarket meeting, and Parsons, the only native American among the defendants, had left before the violence.

The Haymarket verdict was widely acclaimed, but some conservative men in important positions had doubts about it and signed widely circulated petitions for clemency. The Illinois Supreme Court affirmed the sentences and the United States Supreme Court refused to take jurisdiction on the ground that it did not involve a federal constitutional question.[6] Governor Oglesby commuted to life imprisonment the sentences of Samuel Fielden and Michael Schwab, who with Spies signed a statement of contri-

[5] One scholarly book has been written about the so-called riot: Henry David, *The History of the Haymarket Affair: A Study on the American Social, Revolutionary and Labor Movements.* It also received major attention in Barnard's excellent biography of Altgeld, *op. cit.* Moses, *op. cit.,* II, 910-913.

[6] Francis X. Busch, who was Chicago corporation counsel in a Democratic administration and later president of the Chicago Bar Association, conceals his own sympathies in a study of the judge, the lawyers, and the evidence. "The Haymarket Riot and the Trial of the Anarchists," *Journal of the Illinois State Historical Society,* XLVIII (Autumn, 1955), 247-270.

tion. Had he requested it, Parsons also would have received clemency from Oglesby. On November 11, 1887, Spies, Parsons, George Engel, and Adolph Fischer were hanged by the sheriff. Four days earlier Louis Lingg, a manufacturer of bombs who had been miles away from the Haymarket violence, cheated the gallows by exploding a percussion cap with his teeth. To Judge Gary it was enough that evidence had been received that Lingg and the others had advocated violence. The legislature accepted his ruling and passed a law decreeing that any co-conspirator would be legally liable for any offense of another.

The Chicago establishment felt more comfortable with troops nearby and arranged in Springfield for passage of a law allowing the federal government to build Fort Sheridan twenty-seven miles away on the north shore of Lake Michigan. The inflamed public made no distinction between anarchists, the Knights of Labor, and the trade unionists, with the result that all suffered and the labor movement underwent a ten-year setback.

GOVERNOR JOHN PETER ALTGELD

The first foreign-born governor of Illinois in 1892 became the first Democrat to win the office in four decades. John Peter Altgeld, who was three months old when his wagon-maker father emigrated from Germany, won the idolatry of liberals by pardoning the three Haymarket anarchists still in prison. It was one facet of a complex political career that ranged from Grangerism to a briefly fulfilled desire to associate with millionaires on financial equality. The political leadership of the state had included conservatives of courage and independence, but the stubborn Altgeld was both a liberal, the first to attain the governorship, and a politician who aspired to control and remold the Democratic party.[7]

Altgeld spent his boyhood of hard work and limited education on an Ohio farm. Like Governor Fifer, his predecessor, he served as a young volunteer private in a Union regiment. After teaching school, at the age of twenty-two he tramped across southern

[7] Barnard's *Eagle Forgotten* is the basic work on the Altgeld era. For a shorter sketch, see Henry M. Christman's preface to *The Mind and Spirit of John Peter Altgeld: Selected Writings and Addresses*. It contains the text of the executive order pardoning the three anarchists. See also Harvey Wish, "Governor Altgeld Pardons the Anarchists," *Journal of the Illinois State Historical Society*, XXXI (Dec., 1938), 424-448.

Courtesy Illinois State Historical Library

Governor John Peter Altgeld

Illinois and finally stopped in a rural Missouri town where he read law and was elected prosecuting attorney on a Granger ticket. Four years after the Chicago fire, still deficient in his use of the English language, Altgeld went to the metropolis, made new friends, and became important politically. As a struggling lawyer who could hardly afford a downtown office, he received helping hands from corporation attorneys. He saved pennies, married his childhood sweetheart, invested in real estate, and became rich. Active among the German population, Altgeld in 1884 as a Democratic candidate for Congress made a better showing than Judge Lambert Tree, a leading citizen, had two years earlier. The next year he went to Springfield and plotted to be the Democratic choice for United States senator in the long deadlock at the end of which Logan eventually won reelection. In these years Altgeld had friends among gamblers with political connections but made no alliances with labor. He began a part-time literary career with *Our Penal Machinery and Its Victims,* which contended that the man at the bottom of the economic heap was not getting a fair deal. Autographed copies went to important men, and in 1886 Altgeld gave up his corporation law practice to run successfully for election as a judge of the Superior Court. He had the support of labor, which scored a local success in Cook County by electing some legislative and judicial candidates.

In the 1890 off-year election, Illinois went Democratic, chiefly because of dissatisfaction with the Harrison administration in Washington and a new tariff law. Some local tickets had been entered by the Farmers' Alliance, a precursor of populism which helped increase the number of cooperative creameries in the state. The alliance program had Granger and Greenback planks, including government ownership of railroads, and also advocated a graduated income tax. When the legislature met, the balance of power was held by three Farmers' Alliance representatives who in the balloting for senator insisted upon supporting Alson J. Streeter, a confirmed radical. Republicans dropped Senator Charles B. Farwell, whose term had expired, to back the old-reliable Oglesby. Democrats supported John M. Palmer, who had the status of a perennial candidate. With Clarence S. Darrow as his agent, Altgeld again tried to get the support of the Democrats, but the deadlock was finally broken, on the 154th ballot, with the election of Palmer.

As a judge, Altgeld was accused of arbitrary rulings and was better known for his wealth than for liberalism. With bad financial judgment, he organized a million-dollar corporation and erected an imposing office building, the Unity Block, at 127 North Dearborn Street, which was intended to be his monument. In 1891 he resigned as judge and the next year became the first Cook County man to be nominated for governor.

Altgeld's campaign was indefatigable and, on the compulsory education issue, two-faced. He had supported a bill, passed with bipartisan support and signed by Fifer, which required children to attend school until twelve. As a candidate, however, he turned against the law, to which Lutherans objected because it required that basic classes be taught in English, and Catholics on the ground that it let truant officers inspect parochial schools.[8] On election day Cleveland was returned to the White House after a four-year absence with an Illinois man, Adlai E. Stevenson, as his Vice President. Altgeld defeated Fifer by twenty-three thousand votes. In large part the Democratic victory was due to support of labor and rural populist elements who backed Altgeld. His inauguration was marred by illness, and the new governor, trying to salvage his investment in the Unity Block, borrowed heavily from a factional opponent.

Altgeld, a short man with a brown beard, had never signed a clemency petition for the Haymarket defendants or spoken up in support of those who believed the convictions unfair. After taking office he read the trial and appeal records and collected new evidence. On June 26, without advance notice, he pardoned the three imprisoned men with a ringing eighteen-thousand-word statement. In great detail and with vituperative rhetoric he declared that the men had been unfairly convicted by a packed jury before a prejudiced judge. Scathingly he criticized the police, the prosecution, the evidence, and Judge Gary, whom he accused of "malicious ferocity." Altgeld analyzed the case at length, emphasized that the thrower of the bomb had never been identified, and asserted that no connection had been shown between the bombing and the anarchists. The governor refused when associates urged that he at least soften his personal condemnation of the judge and Inspector Bonfield.

Altgeld had expected a storm and remained calm during a public uproar that was greater than had been anticipated. Under modern jurisprudence, appeals courts would have ruled with the governor on all counts, but in the last decade of the nineteenth century public opinion was shocked that the legal system had been criticized and anarchists freed. Republican newspapers and Republican speakers fanned the flames, calling the governor an anarchist, a socialist, and a fomenter of lawlessness, and asserting that he had allied the Democratic party with revolution. The assassination of Mayor Carter H. Harrison of Chicago in October provided the public with a new reason for dreading anarchy, and when a mob lynched two men at Danville the excuse was given

[8] Barnard, *op. cit.,* p. 160.

that, had their fate been left to the courts, the governor undoubtedly would have pardoned them also.

At least outwardly, Altgeld ignored the storm and acted as
spokesman for liberal causes during an administration that gave
Chicago better police courts, provided for indeterminate prison
sentences, and raised corporation and inheritance taxes. He also
gave major impetus to passage of important labor legislation. An
earlier law to prohibit factory and sweatshop employment of
children under thirteen years had been ignored for two years, but
at Altgeld's first legislative session Illinois, following the lead of
Massachusetts, passed a strong factory inspection statute. It set up
a state agency to regulate conditions, which were especially bad in
the garment trades, regarding employment of children under fourteen and women. The sweating system depended upon cheap labor
and an adaptability to homework or the small workshop, and its
evils, in addition to child labor, included long hours, low wages,
unsanitary conditions, and the speedup. Mrs. Florence Kelley,
whom Altgeld appointed to head the factory inspection service,
reported that nearly 10 percent of the sweatshop employees were
between fourteen and sixteen years. To meet a demand for governmental help in composing disputes between labor and employers,
the state in 1895 created a state board of arbitration that accomplished little. Because of a general belief that the 1870 constitution restricted enactment of labor legislation, Altgeld in 1893
sponsored an amendment which would give the legislature the
right to regulate and control relations between corporations and
their workers, but at a referendum the proposition fell short of the
necessary majority. Governor Fifer, who was less conservative than
his predecessors, in 1879 had signed a law creating a bureau of
labor statistics at the request of unions. The bureau, composed of
three manual laborers and two men from industry, issued biennial
reports on commercial, industrial, social, and educational conditions but also was instructed to look out for the permanent
prosperity of the manufacturing and productive industries.

Along with its liberalism, the Altgeld administration played
Democratic politics. Ambitious for more power, he expanded a
following among the economically deprived.[9] From welfare institutions he fired career executives and psychiatrists who had been
appointed by Republican governors. To Altgeld's embarrassment,

9 *Ibid.*, pp. 169-178.

some of his men became the centers of financial scandals. One was a University of Illinois treasurer, appointed on orders from the governor, who misapplied endowment funds and went to the penitentiary.

THE PULLMAN STRIKE

Hardhearted George M. Pullman never understood why his employees did not appreciate the model town he built and controlled on the prairie south of Chicago, alongside the railroads running on the west side of Lake Calumet. A paternalistic experiment in city planning, the town of Pullman resembled a feudalistic English village in that it lacked both home ownership and local self-government. It had brick apartment buildings, tree-lined macadamized streets, and facilities for the wholesome entertainment as well as the cultural and religious needs of the twelve thousand residents. In new and modern shops, the men built sleeping and dining cars which the Pullman Corporation operated over the bulk of the nation's railroads. Even though rentals were 25 percent higher than in Chicago, Pullman benevolently assumed that good homes in a model town would solve his labor problems. He also insisted upon a profit of at least 6 percent on all of his investments, including the town.[10]

In a long depression that started in 1893, he refused to revise rental schedules and utility charges downward when he cut the pay of his tenant-employees as much as 25 percent. The panic, which lasted until 1898, reached Chicago when two national banks, each capitalized at one million dollars, crashed in May. Factory and mine production fell off, rail traffic declined, and new construction stopped. The inevitable unemployment caused great suffering, especially in Chicago, where the world fair boom had attracted a large number of workers. Despite pressure from other important men in the business world, Pullman declined to arbitrate, and after an employee committee called on him some of its members were fired. Strikes against wage cuts were common in

[10] Almont Lindsey, *The Pullman Strike: The Story of a Unique Experiment and a Great Labor Upheaval.* Stanley Buder, *Pullman: An Experiment in Industrial Order and Community Planning, 1880-1930.* Joseph Husband, *The Story of the Pullman Car.* See also Barnard, *op. cit.,* and Harvey Wish, "The Pullman Strike: A Study in Industrial Warfare," *Journal of the Illinois State Historical Society,* XXXII (Sept., 1939), 288-312.

1894, and the Pullman workers, desperate and destitute, quit work May 11.

The American Railway Union, to which some of the Pullman workers belonged, at a convention in Chicago celebrated its achievement of forcing James J. Hill's Great Northern railroad to restore most of a wage cut. The aggressive union, which encompassed all classes of rail employees, was headed by Eugene V. Debs, an eloquent speaker and fluent writer from Terre Haute, Indiana, who had abandoned a political career after one term in the Indiana legislature. Debs' union had nothing to gain by taking the side of the Pullman workers, but in an altruistic spirit the delegates voted that they would refuse to handle Pullman cars. A boycott was ordered in effect June 26. Debs issued instructions to avoid any semblance of disorder and not to interfere with mail cars.

From Ohio to California, the strike spread to twenty-seven states and territories. A General Managers Association, which from Chicago headquarters coordinated a blacklist and other employment practices for western railroads, evolved the strategy of adding mail cars to Pullman trains. Management had an ally in Richard Olney, a Boston lawyer who was President Cleveland's attorney general. Olney appointed Edwin Walker, a Chicagoan who was general counsel for the Chicago, Milwaukee, and St. Paul road, as his special assistant attorney general on the strike scene. Thousands of deputy federal marshals were sworn in and, for the first time in the struggle between capital and labor, major use was made of an omnibus injunction against a union and its officers.

Walker advised Olney that the injunction could be enforced only by the regular army. Trouble in suburban Blue Island was used as the excuse and, on orders from the President, troops from Fort Sheridan arrived July 4. Crowds gathered to express sympathy for the Pullman strikers and the Debs boycott. During the following week the presence of the soldiers helped foment rioting, especially along the Rock Island tracks, and Chicago was on the verge of a general strike. Altgeld, who was ready to send militia if Mayor John P. Hopkins requested help, believed that most of the rioters were not former railroad employees.

Against the unrequested presence of federal troops, Governor Altgeld protested more vigorously and vehemently than Palmer had spoken up to Grant in a similar situation after the Chicago fire. Although sympathetic to labor, Altgeld considered it was his duty to use the state militia whenever necessary to keep the peace in labor disputes. In a half-dozen cases he sent militiamen to strike scenes, changing the policy of his predecessors only to require that actual emergencies must exist and that the soldiers could not be used as guards or custodians of private property. Several weeks earlier at Olney's request he had sent troops to Mount Olive when striking coal miners, in spite of an injunction, interfered with the movement of trains carrying nonunion coal.

In a long telegram to the President July 5, the governor on constitutional grounds protested the presence of troops. He cited the Mount Olive precedent, insisted that the state militia could handle the Pullman situation, and promised to ask for federal help in case of failure. Cleveland in a short reply that evening said that the presence of troops in Chicago was necessary and constitutional. Altgeld fired back a longer and more vigorous telegram in which he refused to accept Cleveland's statement of the facts of the strike situation and insisted that the American system of government does not permit the President to send troops into a community at his pleasure and to keep them there as long as he chooses. The reply from the White House was unyielding and abrupt. Meanwhile omnibus injunctions were issued in other states, and five other governors backed Altgeld by protesting the use of federal troops in Chicago.

Debs, who believed he could have won the strike had it not been for the restraints imposed by the federal court, gave up after he was arrested July 10 on charges of conspiring to violate the injunction. Clarence S. Darrow and Lyman Trumbull acted as defense attorneys, but Debs was sentenced to six months and three associates to three months for contempt of court.[11] While serving time in the Woodstock jail Debs adopted the socialist doctrines on which he repeatedly and unsuccessfully ran for Presi-

[11] Darrow, an ally of Altgeld and Democratic worker who had been recognized with appointment as Chicago corporation counsel, was launched on a new career as a result of his defense of Debs. For the next two decades most of his practice was in the field of labor, and many of the major courtroom cases he handled took him outside Illinois. In 1911 he defended the McNamara brothers who pleaded guilty while being tried for bombing the *Los Angeles Times.* After that, Darrow lost his standing with labor. He returned to Chicago and began a new practice as a criminal lawyer which reached its climax in the Loeb-Leopold murder trial of 1924. In it Darrow, long an opponent of capital punishment, insisted that his young clients plead guilty but saved them from the electric chair. Clarence Darrow, *The Story of My Life* (New York, 1932), and Irving Stone, *Clarence Darrow for the Defense* (Garden City, 1941).

dent. Altgeld's enemies denounced him as furiously for challenging the President as they had called him an anarchist and fomenter of disorder after the Haymarket pardons the previous year. The destitute Pullman residents received a flood of contributions after Altgeld issued a proclamation condemning Pullman for ignoring their plight. The state Supreme Court later ordered the Pullman Company to sell all land in the town not needed for industrial purposes.

The strike wrecked the American Railway Union with the result that rail employees abandoned the one-big-union format and later organized as several brotherhoods. One of the winners was Samuel Gompers, president of the American Federation of Labor, who disliked Debs' militancy and disapproved of a general strike. The defeat of the Pullman strikers brought a shift to the more conservative AFL, which was a boon for craft unionism.

Robert Todd Lincoln, who had been the corporation's attorney, became its president after Pullman died in 1897. The son of the Civil War President, he had prospered as a railroad and corporation lawyer in Chicago while secluding himself from public attention. He served uneventfully for a time as secretary of war under Grant and capably as minister to Great Britain under Harrison, but only occasionally took a discreet part in helping shape the course of Republican politics in Illinois.[12]

The 1893 panic soon became critical in Chicago, where some unemployment was normal. The city was flooded with transients and, before the Pullman strike, cuts in pay had forced a series of major strikes. In the crisis labor undertook political action, but the conservative trade unionists failed to work with an incongruous and inharmonious group that included populists with both farm and city backgrounds. Attempts to enter a labor ticket in the 1894 election saw a split in which the trade unionists supported Democrats at the state level and the populist group in Chicago. As a result, Republicans carried the state by more than 120,000 votes, the union-backed candidates failed locally, and the effort to establish an independent labor party collapsed. Meanwhile the national leadership insisted upon a merger that resulted in the formation in 1896 of a central body that became the Chicago Federation of Labor.

[12] John S. Goff, *Robert Todd Lincoln: A Man in His Own Right,* pp. 217-218.

21

THIRD STATE AND SECOND CITY

M OST OF ILLINOIS GREW SPECTACULARLY IN THE LAST
years of the nineteenth century. The 1890 census showed that the
Prairie State had 3,826,352 residents, an increase of almost 25
percent in ten years. As a result, it was larger than Ohio and
growing faster than New York and Pennsylvania, which it would
never overtake. For that showing, which continued at a slightly
faster rate during the next ten years, the bulk of the credit went to
Chicago, which had begun to benefit from a new wave of immigration from eastern and southern Europe. By 1890 Chicago was the
nation's second city with a population of 1,099,850. A secondary
reason for the city's increase of 118 percent was that by annexation its area had expanded from 35 to 178 square miles.[1]

Starting about 1880, immigrant trains brought increasing hordes
who were fleeing European oppression. Unlike the earlier arrivals,
they could not be absorbed by the land. The foreign-born therefore concentrated in the cities to get their start in America, and
Chicago became the new home of multitudes from Poland,
Austria-Hungary, the Balkans, and Italy. The Poles, who had
numbered more than fifty thousand by 1890, were the largest of
the nationality groups. To a large extent they concentrated in
their own neighborhoods and retained some of the Old World

[1] For details on the growth of Chicago especially, see John Moses, *Illinois Historical and Statistical*, II, 938-944.

flavor. The heavy flow from Europe was the major factor in the equally rapid growth that continued during the first third of the twentieth century. Illinois added 995,198 residents between 1890 and 1900, while Chicago increased by 598,725 and had 35 percent of the state's population.

Most but not all of the downstate counties also grew. The 1890 census showed that a total of thirty-one counties had lost population in ten years. Only a few of them were in the originally settled southern part of the state, and the bulk were in prime agricultural regions. Mechanization enabled a man to cultivate and harvest a larger acreage, while factories and wholesalers had taken away the jobs of shoemakers and other craftsmen who had been the mainstay of numerous villages. In search of better opportunities, some families pursued the frontier westward, but more took up city life and manufacturing, retailing, and railroad employment. That trend had started twenty years earlier, and the 1890 census classified 55.1 percent of the Illinois population as rural, compared with 69.4 percent in 1880. Agriculture continued to slip in overall importance, and by 1900 only 45.7 percent of the people led rural lives. In the next century census after census showed that some western and southern counties were still losing population.

Meat packing was the state's biggest industry, with distilling second. Following were foundry and machine products, iron and steel, men's clothing, agricultural products, and lumber and carpentry.

Some downstate cities also grew in population and in commercial and industrial importance. Peoria with 41,024 residents passed Quincy for the honor of being the largest downstate center. In 1890 the state had twenty cities with a population of more than ten thousand, the others in order being Springfield, Rockford, Joliet, Bloomington, Aurora, Elgin, Decatur, Belleville, Galesburg, East St. Louis, Rock Island, Jacksonville, Moline, Danville, Cairo, Alton, and Freeport.

THE WORLD'S COLUMBIAN EXPOSITION, 1893

In 1893, a milestone year, Chicago had the deserved good fortune to be the site of a world's fair commemorating, one year late, the four hundredth anniversary of the discovery of America. At least in the Western Hemisphere, no city has had a greater exposition. The World's Columbian Exposition did more than put

Illinois Building, World's Columbian Exposition

Chicago in the center of global attention. It gave the nation a vision of an improved world in which such inventions as the incandescent electric lamp would lighten labor and enable mankind to appreciate the wonders of near and distant lands.

Chicago had produced smaller fairs, starting with the rivers convention in 1847. The state fair exhibited on the lakefront eight times between 1853 and 1894, when Springfield became its permanent home. Two years after the great fire, Chicago erected a convention hall, a marble Exposition Building with an elliptical glass dome rising over a giant fountain. Primarily used for sales exhibits and an annual industrial exposition, it also served as an entertainment and cultural center until it was torn down in 1891 to permit erection of the Art Institute.

Almost miraculously, Chicago got ready for the Columbian Exposition in three hectic years. President Harrison signed a bill, passage of which was an accomplishment of Senator Cullom, that awarded to the city beside Lake Michigan the fair that also had been sought by New York, Washington, and St. Louis. National and Illinois commissions worked on arrangements, and Chicagoans contributed millions. The legislature authorized a five-million-dollar city bond issue and legalized the use of Jackson Park as an unlikely site. The 633 acre tract was marshy and flat, distinguished chiefly by stunted scrub pines and low sand ridges, but railroads ran close by.

Daniel H. Burnham as chief of construction produced a fair which one writer says was "very likely the most beautiful thing ever created on the western hemisphere."[2] When President Cleveland arrived for the opening speech, the raw land had been transformed into expanses of sod, long driveways and wide boardwalks, fountains, artificial pools and lagoons, and a mooring place for reproductions of Christopher Columbus' three caravels. Seventeen major buildings and scores of smaller structures, massed as a dominantly classical white city, were crowded with exhibits of forty-six foreign nations and most of the American states, and had an aggregate floor space of two hundred acres. Chicagoans boasted that the Manufacturers and Liberal Arts Building could seat three hundred thousand persons and was the largest in the world. A stone replica of the Fine Arts Building later became the Museum of Science and Industry.

The fair gave the Midwest massive injections of culture. Theodore Thomas directed a series of programs at which the foremost orchestra and soloists performed. Downtown the theaters had their greatest season. In the new Art Institute, at a notable series of congresses and conferences, 5,978 addresses were delivered. The 27.539 million persons who attended during six months saw not only the newest products of American manufacture but prized and significant possessions brought by strange people from far-off continents. Exhibits left behind became the nucleus of a great museum endowed by Marshall Field. The Midway contributed to American folklore the memory of a belly dancer known as Little Egypt. Carnivals to this day feature smaller editions of a giant wheel which could carry forty persons in each of thirty-six cars as it revolved 250 feet above the ground. George W. G. Ferris, who was born at Galesburg, invented it because Burnham wanted something as startling as the Eiffel Tower, the sensation of the Paris exhibition four years earlier. Only six decades away from its Indian post beginning, Chicago came within five hundred thousand of equaling the attendance at the Parisian fair.

2 Edward Wagenknecht, *Chicago*, p. 6. Newton Bateman and Paul Selby, *Historical Encyclopedia of Illinois*, II, 600-601.

The Art Institute by early winter began the display of its first collections of paintings and statuary, which were increased by donations of private collections of Chicago millionaires. Lorado Taft, son of a geology professor at the University of Illinois, already was a sculptor of note at the start of his twenty-two-year career as a teacher at the institute's school.

Chicago gave birth to the skyscraper, and the twenty-one-story Masonic Temple, erected in 1892 and for thirteen years the tallest building in the world, impressed visitors as much as the Columbian Exposition. Passenger elevators and the genius of Chicago architects a decade earlier had made possible the first ten-story buildings, which caused some men to express alarm about the trend toward height. The first skyscraper was the Montauk Building, erected in 1882, a year before William Le Baron Jenney pioneered the original skeleton construction for the Home Insurance Building. Replacement of fire losses and the rapid growth of population stimulated the golden age of Chicago building. The practical use of iron and steel frameworks carrying exterior and interior walls originated in Chicago, and 1894 saw the first use of Chicago caissons, cylindrical concrete piers extending to hardpan or bedrock. Chicago architects in that generation developed steel girders, fireproofing, wind-bracing, and reinforced concrete construction. In 1914, with the erection of the sixty-story Woolworth Building, New York finally had skyscrapers taller than those in Chicago.[3]

Henry Louis Sullivan, who preached that ornament should be tied to function, and Dankmar Adler created the Auditorium Theater, an architectural jewel dedicated in 1889. Theodore Thomas considered it too big for his Chicago Symphony, which he moved to Orchestra Hall. In another generation, Samuel Insull built an operatic theater with a larger seating capacity west of the loop.

Of the same era is the Chicago sanitary district, an engineering marvel and occasional civic scandal which traces its beginnings to the summer of 1885 when a six-inch, two-day rain flushed the sewer system into the river and then into the lake. The solution to the old problem, as worked out by a city commission and approved by the 1889 legislature, protected the lake by reversing the flow of the river. Nine elected trustees received authority to spend

[3] Frank A. Randall, *History of the Development of Building Construction in Chicago.*

fifteen million dollars on locks at the river's mouth and a twenty-eight-mile sanitary and ship canal connecting with the Des Plaines River at Lockport. The project had an added attraction in that the new canal was the first major step in a deep waterway connecting the Great Lakes and the Gulf of Mexico, a goal of men who wanted to give Chicago better transportation facilities. Downstream on the Illinois River two dams at Henry in Marshall County and Copperas Creek in Fulton County had been only of limited aid to navigation, and the legislature petitioned Congress for financial help with a channel that would be twenty-two feet deep from Chicago to Joliet and at least fourteen feet between Joliet and La Salle.

Isham Randolph, the district's chief engineer, bossed a force of 8,500 men who labored eight years digging thirty million cubic yards of earth and removing twelve million cubic yards of rock. Until the Panama Canal was built, it was second only to the Suez Canal as the largest artificial waterway in the world. When the control gates were lowered in January, 1900, water from Lake Michigan flowed backward through the Chicago River. The infant death rate in Chicago soon dropped, but complaints arose from towns along the Illinois River that their water supply was being polluted.

The day of rapid railroad building had ended. In the decade of the 1880's, an additional 2,362 miles of track had been laid, bringing the state's total to 10,213. Of the new trackage, the most important was the line that the Santa Fe built eastward in time for its trains to reach Chicago in 1886.[4] Future construction, laid at a maximum of eight hundred miles a decade, would be devoted chiefly to freight bypasses, interchange routes in the Chicago area, the tapping of coal fields in southern counties, and the electric interurbans that became important after 1900. The Illinois Central extended to the Gulf of Mexico by acquiring local roads in the South and bridging the Ohio River at Cairo in 1889. The new bridge, 104 feet above low water, received its first test when a train of ten of the line's heaviest locomotives inched its way onto the span.

Agriculture underwent more changes and, while populist causes lost at elections, farmers were on the verge of higher prices that came with a general revival of prosperity beginning in 1900.

4 James Marshall, *Santa Fe: The Railroad That Built an Empire.*

Landowners had legal authority to organize drainage districts which by assessments could pay for construction of levees and ditches.[5] Individual farmers dug ditches and laid drain tile in wet fields, which enabled more of the prairie to be cultivated. In search of a new cash crop, University of Illinois scientists experimented with cereals and legumes. On his Tazewell County farm James L. Reid developed a highly productive yellow dent variety of corn that was widely grown in the Middle West and in time became the source of the inbred lines used as the parent stock of modern hybrid seed. Livestock men still preferred to feed their steers until they were two or three years old, although Professor George E. Morrow of the University of Illinois demonstrated there was more profit in fattening them earlier. Purebred lines received more attention, and manufacturers made more improvements in machinery. Tenants operated more than a third of the farms.

One of the biggest controversies of the 1880's revolved around the leasing practices of William Scully, an Irishman who paid 1.35 million dollars for a midcontinental empire of 220,000 acres. Riding across the prairie, spading up the rich soil to see where it was deepest, he made his first purchase in 1850 at the Springfield land office. Scully invested heavily in low-lying tracts that had been shunned by earlier arrivals. His largest Illinois holdings were Logan County, but Scully also bought heavily in Grundy and Livingston counties and to a smaller extent in Sangamon. He also acquired mammoth holdings in Nebraska, Kansas, Missouri, and Louisiana.[6]

Other big landlords helped their tenants get started by financing improvements, but Scully spent money only for land. In some places, settlement was delayed ten years because of difficulty in finding men to work his farms. They were required to pay for barns, fences, and houses, and in addition their cash rent was always increased by the amount of the tax bill. Nevertheless, because the leases were renewable and improvements could be sold if a family moved, the Illinois renters were more secure than the Irish peasants who lived on Scully's county Tipperary estate. When Parliament acted to reform the leasing system, Scully sold out, which gave him more money to invest in American land.

[5] Margaret B. Bogue, *Patterns from the Sod,* pp. 146-147, 152-153.

[6] Paul W. Gates, "Frontier Landlords and Pioneer Tenants," *Journal of the Illinois State Historical Society,* XXXVIII (June, 1945), 143-206. See also E. L. Bogart and C. M. Thompson, *The Industrial State,* pp. 220-221.

Regardless of whether yields were poor or prices low, other landlords divided the harvested crop with their tenants, but Scully insisted upon an inflexible cash-rent system. At a time when British cattle interests were acquiring big ranches in western states, editorial writers and politicians joined the tenants in complaining that Scully was able to get rich without paying taxes. Logan County unsuccessfully attempted to tax his rent rolls and the legislatures of nine states passed anti-Scully laws. Those in Illinois, enacted in 1887, prohibited land ownership by nonresidents and prevented alien landlords from requiring that tenants pay the taxes. Congress joined the cause by restricting land ownership in territories to American citizens. Scully nullified the effect of the laws by taking out United States citizenship and revising the tax payment clause in his leases. In later years the policies of the Scully estate have been regarded as enlightened.

Without waiting for inauguration of rural free delivery mail service in 1896, competing Chicago mail-order houses helped ease some of the shopping difficulties of isolated farm families. A. Montgomery Ward, who made rural friends by supplying dry goods to grange cooperative stores, in 1872 began a new merchandising system. From a loft over a livery stable he bought in large quantities for cash direct from the manufacturer and sold for cash direct to the farmer. By 1900 Ward had expanded to a tower building at Michigan Avenue and Madison Street and was ready to do battle to protect Grant Park and its lakefront from commercialization. Richard Warren Sears in 1893 moved to Chicago a mail-order business that started when, as a railroad agent in Minnesota, he took over a shipment of watches rejected by a local jeweler. Sears, a genius at promotion, lost a partner when A. C. Roebuck, his jeweler, sold out, but Julius Rosenwald, a native of Springfield who had headed his own business, bought an interest in the firm and became vice president in charge of financing. The growth of the company allowed Rosenwald, who was board chairman when he died, to become a civic crusader and to contribute millions to philanthropies.

After the Civil War, until the coming of quicker communications and inventions such as the linotype, almost every town supported at least one newspaper and many had at least two in competition. Joseph Medill had as powerful a voice as that of Horace Greeley in New York. Medill dominated the *Chicago Tribune* until his death in 1899 and received his strongest competition from Victor Lawson, who had inherited a Scandinavian newspaper that happened to be printed in the same building as the *Chicago Daily News,* the first penny paper in the West.[7] Lawson took over the *News* and developed a foreign service. Like William F. Storey's *Times,* the *Chicago Inter-Ocean* struggled to survive under several ownerships and eventually stepped aside when William Randolph Hearst began operating in Chicago.[8]

JANE ADDAMS, SMALL-TOWN GIRL IN THE SLUMS

Jane Addams moved into the slums on the west side of Chicago in 1889 to open a settlement house dedicated to helping the

[7] Charles H. Dennis, *Victor Lawson: His Time and His Work.*

[8] A. L. Bowen, "The Press of Illinois," *Illinois Blue Book, 1907-08,* pp. 549-582. W. A. Swanberg, *Citizen Hearst: Biography of William Randolph Hearst.* Edward Wagenknecht, *op. cit.,* pp. 125-136. Moses, *op. cit.,* II, 944-948.

Jane Addams

Courtesy Illinois State Historical Library

impoverished and the unschooled, especially the immigrant families, during their struggle to find a better life in a new world. Until
then Chicago had preferred not to notice that many of its people
lived hopelessly in the squalor of tenements, surrounded by criminal elements, earning a pittance and saving nothing, the victims of
an urban poverty that existed in all cities and from which only the
fortunate and gifted could escape.

Miss Addams stayed in Chicago for an idealistic career that
made famous her name and that of Hull House.[9] The protected
daughter of a country bank president in Stephenson County, she
became interested in social reform while convalescing during a
European trip. Determined to help the immigrant needy, she
rented part of a Halsted Street mansion whose owner had moved
to a suburb. Enlisting help and raising money, she developed Hull
House into a complex of thirteen buildings which performed a
myriad of services to its neighbors. Hull House began as a kindergarten that grew into a day nursery and infant care center. Eventually its educational work reached the level of college extension
classes. It had social and cooperative living clubs, playgrounds, and
gymnasiums, part of an effort to draw youngsters from the streets.
At Hull House immigrant wives and mothers found a social life
and learned how to battle city hall about impure milk and infrequent garbage collections. Neighborhood improvement did not
end there. Hull House attracted other dedicated women whose
influence and determination received respectful attention at
Springfield and Washington as they attacked the evils of urban life,
political corruption, and lethargy.

Julia C. Lathrop, a Vassar graduate whose father had served a
term in Congress from the Rockford district, moved into Hull
House in 1890. Altgeld made her the first woman member of the
state board of public charities, and in 1912, when President Taft
appointed her chief of the new children's bureau, she was the first
of her sex to hold a federal position that required senate confirmation. She helped draft the Illinois juvenile court law, which in
1899 was the first in the world. Grace Abbott, who came to Hull

9 Her *Twenty Years at Hull House* and *The Second Twenty Years at Hull House*
combined are an autobiography and a history of the social settlement movement. See
also *Jane Addams: A Centennial Reader* and her "Social Settlements in Illinois,"
Transactions of the Illinois State Historical Society, XI (1906), 162-171. James Weber
Linn, *Jane Addams: A Biography*. Wagenknecht, *op. cit.*, pp. 105-122. Louise C. Wade,
"The Heritage from Chicago's Early Settlement Houses," *Journal of the Illinois State
Historical Society*, LX (Winter, 1967), 411-441.

House in 1908, worked nine years to prevent exploitation of immigrants and later succeeded Miss Lathrop at Washington. During nine years with the Hull House group, Florence Kelley helped stir up sentiment that resulted in an 1893 law designed to stop employment of children in sweatshops.[10] By appointment of Altgeld, she became the first factory inspector in Illinois. Miss Addams had the help of other women, among them Sophonisba Breckenridge, Dr. Alice Hamilton, Mary McDowell,[11] and Mrs. Louise DeKoven Bowen,[12] in aiding the poor and underprivileged.

The settlement house movement received male leadership when Graham Taylor in 1894 began Chicago Commons by moving his family into a changing neighborhood where Germans, Scandinavians, and Irish were being replaced by Poles, Hungarians, Greeks, Russians, Armenians, and Turks.[13]

Also active in philanthropic work was Bertha Honore Palmer, who was Chicago's social queen and one of the nation's most influential women. The widow of Potter Palmer, she had the business acumen to double the value of his estate. As president of the Board of Lady Managers of the Columbian Exposition, she made social contacts in Europe and persuaded royal women to participate in the fair. She contributed to charity and, before women had the right to vote, talked labor and management into cooperating for the good of her city.

Miss Addams, a vigorous speaker and prolific writer, did much to call the nation's attention to slum problems. Her first published work in 1895 described the living conditions of the nineteen nationalities then living in one ward. Her seventh book in 1910 was the classical *Twenty Years at Hull House*. By that time she had turned her talents to fighting militarism, a cause which received much of her attention after the outbreak of the First World War. Continuing to live at Hull House, she became national chairman of the Woman's Peace party and headed American delegations to international peace conferences held by women in Europe. In 1931, four years before her death at the age of 74, she was

[10] Dorothy R. Blumberg, *Florence Kelley: The Making of a Social Pioneer.*

[11] Mary E. McDowell, "A Quarter of a Century in the Stockyards District," *Transactions of the Illinois State Historical Society,* XXVII (1920), 72-83. Howard E. Wilson, *Mary McDowell, Neighbor.*

[12] Louise DeKoven Bowen, *Growing Up with a City.*

[13] Louise C. Wade, *Graham Taylor, Pioneer for Social Justice, 1851-1938.*

co-recipient with Dr. Nicholas Murray Butler of the Nobel Peace Prize.

William T. Stead, an Englishman who spent six months in Chicago at the start of the Panic of 1893, also helped stir the city's social consciousness with a book entitled *If Christ Came to Chicago*. Stead, who was editor of the *Review of Reviews*, told not only of brothels and corrupt police but also of slums and the exploitation of labor by millionaires.

ALTGELD, FREE SILVER, AND EDUCATION

In Illinois and nationally, the silver issue split the Democratic party. Inflation advocates, recalling the Civil War experience with greenbacks, contended that more money should be in circulation and that bimetallism would increase the supply. A belief arose in the West that demonetization of silver was a British-American plot to put the United States on a gold standard. Its proponents took the side of western silver interests who wanted a government-supported market for their new mines.

Governor Altgeld, who was a populist at heart, in preparing for a second-term campaign refused to compromise with the conservative eastern group, led by President Cleveland, whose monetary policies had the approval of many Republicans and the men who controlled the Democratic party machinery in Illinois. Altgeld in 1895 jumped the gun on the Chicagoans by calling a Democratic state convention in Springfield that adopted a sixteen-to-one plank. Uninvited, William Jennings Bryan showed up and was permitted to make a speech advocating free coinage of silver. Bryan had been born at Salem and educated at Illinois College, but he had little interest in practicing law at Chicago or Jacksonville. He had gone to Nebraska, become a convert to the silver cause, and developed the golden tongue that was his great resource.

Altgeld, who felt that he could have been the Democratic presidential nominee had not his foreign birth made him constitutionally ineligible, and other westerners dominated the 1896 convention in the Coliseum.[14] The platform, a personal triumph for

---

[14] Harry Barnard, *Eagle Forgotten*, pp. 345-373. James A. Barnes, "Illinois and the Gold-Silver Controversy, 1890-1896," *Transactions of the Illinois State Historical Society*, XXXVIII (1931), 35-59. Solon J. Buck, *The Agrarian Crusade*, pp. 150-191. Fred A. Shannon, *The Farmer's Last Frontier*, pp. 315-316.

the Illinois governor, for the first time took a liberal stand. It pledged observance of constitutional limitations and thus took the side of Altgeld in his quarrel with the President over the use of troops in the Pullman strike. As Altgeld wished, it opposed injunctions in strikes, disapproved government intervention in local affairs, favored an income tax, and contained a free silver plank that repudiated the Cleveland monetary policies.

For the presidential nomination, Altgeld favored Richard P. Bland of Missouri, a free silver man with an established reputation, but the thirty-six-year-old Bryan could not be prevented from taking the floor at a climactic moment. His speech, well rehearsed before obscure audiences in the preceding months, swept the delegates and galleries into a frenzy. Mankind, he said, must not be crucified on a cross of gold. On the fifth ballot, when Altgeld finally cast the vote of the Illinois delegation for him, Bryan won the nomination.

Republicans at St. Louis nominated William McKinley of Ohio on a platform declaring for the gold standard until bimetallism could come by international agreement, which no one thought possible. Senator John M. Palmer, who in a long career had been a Democrat, a Free Soiler, a Republican, a Liberal Republican, and again a Democrat, split his party by making another switch and accepting the presidential nomination of a Gold Democratic party. Palmer did not seek votes for himself but told his friends not to vote for Bryan. In McKinley's expensive campaign, workingmen were told that their jobs could be jeopardized by Bryan's economic policies. A "flying squadron" of five former governors toured Illinois to speak for the Republican ticket. Populists, who had made a weak showing in 1892, and other reformers returned to the Democratic party, but Bryan lost the election with 43 percent of the vote. Altgeld also lost, but he received ten thousand more votes than Bryan. Illinois had returned to Republicanism after four years. The new governor, John R. Tanner, was a conservative and a genius at political organization.

At the long-neglected university level, forward steps in education coincided with the Columbian Exposition. Governor Altgeld befriended the University of Illinois by going before the legislature to ask for increased appropriations and by providing leadership that helped transform what primarily had been an agricultural college into a comprehensive university.[15] Andrew Sloan Draper, who had been superintendent of public instruction in New York state, became president and set a keynote for two decades by arguing that it was wrong for Illinois to spend less on its university than Ohio, Michigan, Wisconsin, and other smaller states. The Democratic governor, whose formal education had been minimal, and Draper, a Republican experienced in dealing with legislators, worked closely together. The professional schools in Chicago date from the Altgeld administration, when existing medical and pharmacy schools were taken over. The liberal arts program was strengthened, the agricultural college improved, graduate and law schools founded, and other steps taken in an effort to bring the university generally up to the level of the engineering and science curriculums.[16] Dr. Edmund J. James, a historian who had been president of Northwestern University, in 1904 replaced Draper and carried forward the development of an institution that had outgrown its earlier emphasis on vocational education. Between 1889 and 1905, the number of buildings on the campus increased from four to twenty-three and the faculty from thirty-five to more than four hundred. There was an equivalent increase in the student body, which in 1889 numbered less than three hundred outside the preparatory school, where instruction at the high-school level was given.

Athletics became a by-product of higher education when George Huff in 1895 returned to the University of Illinois from Dartmouth to be football and baseball coach. With Northwestern, Lake Forest, and the University of Chicago, Illinois formed an athletic conference that reached outside the state to take in Wisconsin, Purdue, and Minnesota. The next year Michigan replaced Lake Forest.

Several state superintendents of public instruction had reported that more teachers were needed and almost every county wanted to be the site of a new state institution. As a result, with Altgeld's approval the legislature authorized more Normal schools, patterned after the one at Normal, and distributed them on a geo-

[15] Neil Thornburn, "John P. Altgeld: Promoter of Higher Education in Illinois," *Essays in Illinois History* (Donald F. Tingley, ed.), pp. 37-51.

[16] Allan Nevins, *Illinois*. Winton U. Solberg, *The University of Illinois, 1867-1894, An Intellectual and Cultural History*. Jerome L. Rodnitzky, "President James and His Campaigns for University of Illinois Funds," *Journal of the Illinois State Historical Society*, LXIII (Spring, 1970), 69-90.

graphical basis. Charleston, less than sixty miles from Champaign, won the Normal school for eastern Illinois since the course of study did not conflict with that of the university. Partly because Joseph F. Glidden, the barbed-wire king, donated the campus, DeKalb became the site of the northern Illinois institution, which opened in 1899 before its building was completed. The same year the legislature awarded the western school to Macomb, which was in the center of the Military Tract.[17] A graduate of a reputable college could qualify as a trained teacher in one year and graduates of approved high schools in two years. Many aspiring teachers had gone only to an ungraded country school, and for them three- and four-year courses were offered. By custom the classrooms, offices, and social halls were crowded into one building, usually box-shaped and multi-storied. The $265,000 donated building at Carbondale burned in 1883, nine years after the southern school opened with an enrollment of 396.[18]

While fair visitors swarmed through the Midway, the first Gothic towers of the second University of Chicago rose alongside. Chicago millionaires helped with the financing after John D. Rockefeller announced the first of a series of major contributions to construction and endowment. Dr. William Rainey Harper recruited a faculty by offering salaries of six to seven thousand dollars to the top men of other schools.[19] Nine college presidents joined his teaching staff.

Frank W. Gunsaulus, one of the most powerful of the Protestant ministers in Chicago, preached a Central Church sermon on "What I Would Do If I Had a Million Dollars," a popular topic at the time. That day his answer was that Chicago needed a technical institute where poor boys could have educational advantages. After the service, Philip D. Armour, the packer, offered to give the money if Gunsaulus would head the institution. Together they opened Armour Institute of Technology, with Gunsaulus as president.[20]

As the century turned, more than fifty privately supported universities, colleges, institutes, academies, seminaries, and busi-

---

[17] Victor Hicken, *The Purple and the Gold: The Story of Western Illinois University.*

[18] George K. Plochmann, *The Ordeal of Southern Illinois University.*

[19] Richard J. Storr, *Harper's University: The Beginnings, a History of the University of Chicago.*

[20] Wagenknecht, *op. cit.,* pp. 86-90. Harper Leech and John C. Carroll, *Armour and His Times.*

ness colleges operated under state charter. The bulk had state sponsorship, and many have long since disappeared. Some new institutions of higher learning appeared with solid backing. Mrs. Lydia Bradley in 1897 donated a two-million-dollar endowment for a polytechnic institute that had flourished at Peoria. James Millikin, who was Decatur's most prominent banker, provided most of the funds for a school which took his name and became a university in 1903. Lewis Institute in Chicago, which dates from 1896, received major bequests from Allen C. and John Lewis.

Two major universities, Loyola and DePaul, took root in Chi-cago during the 1880 to 1902 regime of Patrick Feehan, the city's first archbishop. For more than three decades, Roman Catholics had outnumbered the combined Protestant denominations and the church grew with the city. Feehan saw the parishes increase from 194 to 298, while the number of priests, schools, and the total Catholic population more than doubled.

The new Normal schools and the growth of the University of Illinois helped the public school system recover from the setback of Altgeld's veto of the compulsory education law. One-third of the pupils walked to ungraded one-room schools where the term averaged ninety-four days and many of the underpaid teachers had fewer than fifteen pupils. In some southern districts the pupils sat on split-log benches. The state superintendent in 1890 reported that the average school year had been extended to 7.4 months and that men teachers were paid $54.63 and women $44.41 monthly. Some townships used the 1872 law to establish high schools. Officials denied that high schools were available only to the children of the well-to-do, and a 1903 law created nonhigh dis-tricts which were obligated to pay tuition of rural youngsters who wanted to go to high school in town. Meanwhile complaints were heard that education was costing too much and that only the welfare institutions were a bigger expense to the state.

The Altgeld administration acted to relieve overcrowding at welfare institutions. The activist governor went to Watertown, outside Moline, in 1896 to lay the cornerstone for the Western Hospital for the Insane, which was filled beyond rated capacity two weeks after its delayed opening in 1898. Because of unfor-tunate experiences with fire at other institutions, especially at the southern asylum at Anna where most of the single building was destroyed in 1895, the ward buildings were built of stone. Club women at Peoria furnished the impetus for an 1895 law establishing the Asylum for the Incurable Insane at Bartonville, which opened on the cottage plan, without window bars or mechanical restraints. Illinois in 1877 pioneered in the detached cottage plan at the Kankakee asylum. Under Altgeld, work also was started on the industrial home for the blind, a trade school in Chicago, and a school for wayward girls at Geneva. The 1901 legislature authorized a training school for boys after Chicagoans contributed one thousand acres of farmland outside St. Charles. Because of overcrowding at the Asylum for Feeble-Minded Children at Lincoln, an 1890 building for custodial care proved inadequate and two cottages were added a decade later. A second institution for epileptics at Dixon was authorized in 1913. The state hospital at Manteno dates from the 1905 legislature.[21]

To relieve pressure on the prisons at Joliet and Chester, the 1891 legislature raised to twenty-one years the age limit for the reform school at Pontiac, which had opened in 1871 for boys under sixteen. The higher age limit required enlargement of the Pontiac institution, where inmates were required to attend school a half-day and participate in military drill.

Welfare administration was decentralized, and each institution had its own board of trustees. Since 1869 a state board of charities had power to inspect and give advice, but it could not interfere with the management.

UTILITIES, BOODLERS, AND REFORM

The bribery, shakedowns, and vote-buying that made Tammany Hall notorious extended into other cities, and the legislatures of many large states became involved in the graft that went with the issuance or denial of franchises for streetcar lines and for gas and electric service. For a growing city, mass transportation and utilities were necessities, and their owners became either prey or partners of political machines that manipulated voting blocs and counted upon campaign contributions from business executives who wanted legislation or service. For a time the Chicago City Hall's reputation for well-organized corruption and disregard of the public interest equaled that of Tammany. Graft in earlier years had mostly been petty, but during the 1890's the city council

[21] A. L. Bowen, "State Charities of Illinois," *Illinois Blue Book, 1917-18*, pp. 34-35. See also *Blue Book, 1900*, pp. 151ff.; *1905*, pp. 471-488; and *1927-28*, p. 425.

developed a technique for the extraction of funds from unwilling corporations.

The bulk of the aldermen, known as Gray Wolves, came to expect pay for their votes on a graduated scale, requiring more for the passage of a franchise ordinance than for permission for some incidental use of a street. They scoffed at reformers who complained about inadequate compensation for use of public property and whose protest movements usually collapsed in futility. Under an especially blatant form of boodling, city officials organized dummy utility companies and granted them favorable franchises. The companies, although without financial assets and operating equipment, usually were then sold at big prices to existing firms, which had to pay up or face competition because, if necessary, a dummy company could start service. As a notorious example, a new and mysteriously organized Ogden Gas Company received a franchise that would allow it to undersell the Peoples Gas Light and Coke Company, which already was serving Chicagoans. As expected, Peoples Gas bought it out for several million dollars. The biggest Ogden Gas stockholder turned out to be Roger C. Sullivan, the Democratic power behind John P. Hopkins, who was mayor when the franchise was voted. Hopkins and key aldermen were among other stockholders. No one accused Sullivan of dipping into the public till, but under the ethical code of the day it was fair game to profit from utilities, coal, building supplies, and junk.

Occasionally the boodlers erred, especially when they granted a fifty-year franchise to Commonwealth Electric Company, a dummy which portended trouble for Chicago Edison Company's service in the downtown area. Samuel Insull, a slender thirty-two-year-old who spoke with the accent of his native London, had come to Chicago in 1892 to be president of Chicago Edison and had borrowed $250,000 from Marshall Field to invest in its stock.[22] No one knew more about the economics and technology of generating electricity, a new field, and he had been smart enough to get exclusive rights to buy generating equipment from every American manufacturer. As a result Commonwealth Electric had no way of competing with Insull, who eventually bought the company for fifty thousand dollars because it had the only fifty-year franchise in the state.

Local transit service began under a system of small monopolies,

22 Forrest McDonald, *Insull,* pp. 55-73.

based on franchises granted by city councils at a time when no other city or state agency had authority to regulate utilities. When a new part of town had enough homes to justify a horsecar line, a promoter would seek a franchise, asking that competition be kept out and offering, if it couldn't be avoided, a minimum payment to the city. Sometimes, as a real estate promotion, a car line would start first. Between 1860 and 1890 the number of companies increased from ten to thirty-eight. As early as the Civil War they had sought special privileges.

Intent on getting rich and consolidating the traction lines into a big monopoly, Charles Tyson Yerkes moved to Chicago in 1882. Backed by eastern money, Yerkes soon controlled the lines on the north and west sides. He modernized horsecar lines by substituting cars hauled by clanking cables. He expanded his lines by five hundred miles and began electrification, replacing cables with overhead trolleys. He built the first elevated tracks, on which miniature steam locomotives ran to Jackson Park in time for world fair traffic. He erected the elevated loop, completed in 1897, which increased the value of downtown property. The Yerkes technique involved repeated reorganizations, watered stock, court injunctions, lots of straphangers, and a deaf ear to complaints. Despite the complaints, however, Yerkes' unified system undoubtedly gave better service than its small-fry predecessors.

For further expansion, Yerkes needed long-term financing, which was impossible to get under the existing twenty-year limit on franchises. No other procedure was possible, so in 1895 he paid for enough legislators to obtain enactment of a ninety-nine-year franchise, only to have it vetoed by Governor Altgeld. Two years later he maneuvered passage of a bill which would extend streetcar and elevated franchises for fifty years, give the city from 3 to 7 percent of the gross receipts, and set up a city regulatory agency that would take franchise control out of the city council. Reformers, who wanted municipal ownership or nothing, and other enemies of Yerkes objected to any long-term franchise, and as a result they turned down the compensation and let the Gray Wolves keep control of traction matters. All Yerkes received from the 1897 legislature was a substitute, known as the Allen Bill, which would permit cities to negotiate franchises for as long as fifty years.[23] Governor Tanner signed it and encountered virulent

[23] Carter Harrison, *Stormy Years,* pp. 136-182. James W. Neilson, *Shelby M. Cullom, Prairie State Republican,* p. 176, takes the minority view by holding that Tanner was

criticism, which was intensified by a new reform wave that constituted Chicago's most successful although temporary mobilization of civic virtue.

With the presumably futile objective of electing more than a handful of honest aldermen, prominent Chicagoans in early 1896 organized the Municipal Voters League.[24] No one wanted to be its president, but George E. Cole, who was five feet tall and owned a stationery and printing shop, took the job under a promise that the men who paid the bills would not challenge his decisions. Energetic and stubborn, Cole announced before the primary that twenty-four of the thirty-four aldermen whose terms were expiring were unfit for renomination. The league investigated, denounced, and recruited volunteer workers, ran independent candidates, stirred up public interest, and elected its own men in thirty wards. Since each ward had two aldermen and half were holdovers, the Gray Wolves still had a council majority, but the Municipal Voters League repeated its triumph in the next three elections. By 1900 honest men had an overwhelming majority in the council.

In a three-sided mayoral election in 1897, the cause of reform was led by John M. Harlan, an alderman whose father sat on the United States Supreme Court. He placed second. The winner, elected to the first of five terms, was young Carter Harrison, whose father also served five terms and had been assassinated by an anarchist at the end of the Columbian Exposition. Both Harrisons were social liberals who did not care if saloons stayed open seven days a week. The younger Harrison built a personal political machine by making an alliance with ward leaders who wanted immunity from prosecution for gambling, prostitution, and other vocations. Maneuvering a course between grafters and reformers, he used opposition to Yerkes as his big issue.

When the traction forces confidently presented the Allen Bill to the city council, the mayor used pressure generated at neighborhood mass meetings to keep in line a majority of the aldermen. The ordinance was defeated and a new legislature repealed the Allen law.

justified in signing the Allen bill. A utility company had to expand in order to serve a growing city, and Yerkes needed long-term financing, which could not be obtained if his franchising situation was uncertain. In the Yerkes era, corporate trusts were under attack from muckrakers and utilities were unregulated. Harrison capitalized on the issue and painted Yerkes as a villain.

24 Sidney I. Roberts, "The Municipal Voters League and Chicago's Boodlers," *Journal of the Illinois State Historical Society*, LIII (Summer, 1960), 117-148.

Unable to get financing, Yerkes sold out his Chicago interests and became head of a syndicate building subways in London. After a few years, the reform element found that most voters had lost interest in electing honest aldermen.

GROWTH AND TROUBLE IN THE COAL FIELDS

Both the coal-mining industry, which had begun to develop on a large scale twenty years earlier, and the new United Mine Workers union, which made a weak start in 1890, gained strength while fighting each other in the 1890's, a time of bloody rivalry. In the decade the tonnage of Illinois-mined coal doubled; by 1898, a tumultuous year that brought a major union victory, 889 mines located in 52 counties employed 36,976 men who dug 23,434,445 tons of bituminous coal. The northern fields were beginning to wear out and the thick veins in Franklin and Williamson counties were just coming into production. As a result most of the biggest-producing mines were in the central part of the state and the leading counties were Vermilion, Sangamon, La Salle, Bureau, Clinton, Christian, Grundy, Macoupin, Marshall, and Williamson.

In a time of labor surplus, recently arrived Slavic and Italian coal diggers provided job competition for the Welsh, Irish, English and Scotch who gave the union its original membership. The work was back-breaking, boys in their early teens and their fathers saw daylight only on Sundays, and mining towns offered little but drab homes and abundant saloons. Braidwood in Will County had a population of fifteen thousand, which exceeded that of Joliet, but it was a one-industry town dominated by the Chicago and Wilmington Coal Company. Wages of its Irish and Bohemian workers averaged $1.50 daily in the thin veins. Mining was dangerous and tedious, even though a system of state safety inspection had been set up after sixty-nine men drowned in the Diamond mine at Braidwood in 1883. Six years later troops were sent to Braidwood to keep order and a strike at La Salle ended with a concession to the workers. At that time young Anton Cermak, who had spent seven of his sixteen years working in Braidwood mines and was regarded by management as an agitator, climbed into a boxcar to see if things were better in Chicago.[25]

---

[25] Alex Gottfried, *Boss Cermak of Chicago*, pp. 1-14, describes a boyhood of hard work in a rough mining town.

The chief grievance was low pay, and the men revolted when the operators, in an effort to hold down wages, imported Negro strikebreakers who had been receiving even less money in Alabama mines. At Spring Valley one man was killed and several injured in an 1895 riot involving Italians and Negroes. In desperation, some men risked their jobs by listening to organizers for the struggling union. John Mitchell, who was born in Braidwood, became the United Mine Workers national president the year the union received national attention by winning a strike settlement that included recognition of the eight-hour day and six-day week. The new scale paid forty cents a ton for mine-run coal, which meant a one-third increase in earnings. The strike, which began July 4, 1897, at Mount Olive, produced a colorful leader in "General" Alexander Bradley, who wore a Prince Albert coat and top hat and displayed great oratorical talent in exhorting central and southern Illinois miners to quit their jobs and join a law-abiding march to the next town. Bradley was not an executive and did not rise in the union hierarchy. In the following years Mitchell and John H. Walker,[26] who was born in Scotland and at the age of twenty organized a miners' local at Braceville, Grundy County, worked closely together as officials of a union that grew steadily in membership and influence.

The precedent-setting agreement with the Illinois Coal Operators association was rejected by about twenty mines whose officials contended they were being priced out of the Chicago fuel market. The Chicago-Virden Coal Company discharged its workers, brought in armed guards from St. Louis, and sent agents to Birmingham to recruit experienced Negro miners. Some thirty miles eastward the Pana Coal Company adopted the same policy after threatening to import Chinese. Black strikebreakers at Pana were closely guarded in a stockade beside the mine tipple.

Governor John R. Tanner had much the same background as Shelby M. Cullom, but the passage of two decades made a difference in the handling of strike situations. Cullom had considered it his sworn duty to call out troops when property rights and public safety were in danger. Although equally conservative, Tanner in 1898, a campaign year, saw the long shadow of Altgeld over his shoulder and departed from established Republican doctrine. He

26 John H. Keiser, "John H. Walker: Labor Leader from Illinois," *Essays in Illinois History* (Donald F. Tingley, ed.), pp. 75-100.

took the side of the miners and refused when the Chicago-Virden company asked for protection for its imported cheap labor. Company officials arranged for a St. Louis detective agency to provide guards for a train which arrived with thoroughly frightened Negroes who had just learned of the trouble ahead. In the past miners with Slavic backgrounds, badly needing jobs for themselves or newly arrived relatives, had scabbed on the miners who had arrived earlier, but now all stood shoulder-to-shoulder to fight the company. Both sides opened fire, and seven miners and four guards were killed. More than two score were wounded. The train finally unloaded at Springfield and its passengers drifted back to Alabama or increased the black populations of Chicago and East St. Louis.[27]

Tanner denounced the coal company, saying that militia would have met the train at the state line if he had known that a private army was on board. The next day he sent troops to Virden and Pana with orders to keep out strikebreakers. Within weeks the mines there began paying the forty-cent wage to white miners, and thereafter Negroes who happened to stop in the towns were advised to be gone by sundown. The governor lost status with some rural and small-town Republicans who had no sympathy for labor and could not understand the departure from Cullom's policy. For the United Mine Workers, the winning of the strike meant that henceforth coal diggers would be less reluctant to join its embattled forces. The cemetery at Mount Olive where the miners were buried became a shrine of unionism and scene of annual memorial services.[28] The main job had yet to be done and in 1900 several thousand building tradesmen in Chicago went on strike for a eight-hour day.

THE SPANISH-AMERICAN WAR

Two days after the battleship *Maine* sank in Havana harbor, victim of an unexplained bombing, Governor Tanner in early 1898 responded to a nationwide protest by asking the legislature for all authority necessary to put the resources of Illinois at President

[27] Victor Hicken, "The Virden and Pana Mine Wars of 1898," *Journal of the Illinois State Historical Society*, LII (Summer, 1959), 263-278.

[28] John H. Keiser, "The Union Miners Cemetery at Mt. Olive, Illinois: A Spirit-Thread of Labor History," *Journal of the Illinois State Historical Society*, LXII (Autumn, 1969), 229-266.

McKinley's disposal. By joint resolution, he promptly received permission to raise men, munitions, and money.

In the short and decisive war with Spain that followed, Illinois contributed ten regiments and one military hero. In the first call for troops, the state quickly mobilized, with most of the infantry units coming from the National Guard. Tanner used his influence to have an artillery battery added, and later two more regiments were assigned to Illinois. Only the First Regiment, a Chicago outfit, saw active service during the period of hostilities. After several days in trenches, its men witnessed the surrender of Santiago and then spent a month on guard duty. Meanwhile they suffered heavily from yellow fever.[29]

General Wesley Merritt, a native of Salem who had stayed in the army after the Civil War, commanded the forces that captured Manila after Admiral Dewey's fleet controlled the harbor.

On the home front, William E. Mason, a rotund and jovial Chicagoan who had replaced Palmer in the senate, became a leader of lost causes at Washington. With speeches and occasional filibusters, he denounced McKinley for executive inaction when the Cuban people needed help. Later he deplored a trend toward imperialism which did not seem to concern the people of his home state. By protesting the acquisition of the Philippines and then working for their self-government, Mason established a reputation as an insurgent and, like other colleagues of Cullom, served only one senate term.

The aftermath of the war involved Chicago packers, whose business was expanding and starting to decentralize, in an "embalmed beef" investigation. They had signed contracts to furnish the army with fresh meat, but General Nelson A. Miles complained that chemically treated meat had been served to the troops, resulting in sickness and distress. The packers answered that canned meat had spoiled because it was mishandled in the field. A presidential commission looked into bribery and other charges and reported that nothing could be proved.

A state food commission, empowered to inspect foodstuffs in an effort to prevent impurities and adulterations, was created by the legislature in 1899. Much of its attention centered on the dairy industry which was a prominent feature of the countryside around cities. Passage of a federal meat inspection law came in 1906

29 Bateman-Selby, *op. cit.,* II, 571-576. *Illinois Intelligencer,* October 5, 1968.

primarily as the result of a muckraking novel, *The Jungle,* written by Sinclair Lewis for serialization in a socialist paper. It told of the troubles of a Lithuanian immigrant who worked in the stockyards and lived in poverty nearby. The packers became noted for work specialization and by-product utilization and, more than anything else, their giant plants epitomized the magnitude of the industrialization that made Chicago famous. By 1891 Swift and Armour had perfected railroad cars which were mechanically refrigerated, a major development in meat marketing. Large packing plants were being built west of the Mississippi, and in 1893 both Armour and Swift built plants at the National City yards, outside East St. Louis. Whenever strikes became troublesome, Negro labor was brought in. The big companies required a large amount of capital and, at a time when corporations were rapidly combining into trusts, the major firms in 1902 organized the National Packing Company in an effort to get control of the slaughterhouses at East St. Louis, Kansas City, and Omaha. Under attack as a beef trust, the Armour, Swift, Morris, and Cudahy companies were prosecuted for accepting rebates and for restraint of trade in refraining from bidding against each other. The National Packing consolidation was dissolved in 1912.

22

THE PROGRESSIVE MOVEMENT

D ISSATISFACTION WITH SOCIAL, ECONOMIC, AND POLITICAL
conditions increased during the 1890's and reached a climax in the
first dozen years of the twentieth century. Known as the Progressive movement, a rising tide of insurgency and reform swept
over the nation with some success of a permanent nature in
Illinois, but nevertheless it fell short of its major goals.

Instances of political corruption had drawn protests before the
Civil War, and in 1865 the first voter registration law, intended to
prevent ballot box frauds, was enacted. Logan would have been
denied his last senate election had not Governor Hamilton, arbitrarily ruling that fraud had been committed, changed the result of
a state senate election in Chicago. Charges that election frauds
were rampant, especially in the cities, helped generate sentiment
for enactment of the 1891 law providing that the state would
furnish the ballots and guarantee their authenticity. When Samuel
W. Allerton lost for mayor of Chicago in 1893, a special Union
League Club committee claimed that four thousand men had been
colonized in tenement wards to vote for Carter Harrison.[1]

By 1890, half of the states had enacted primary laws, with
Illinois one of the holdouts. In an era of muckraking journalism,
Illinois political machines and corporate trusts received less atten-

[1] William T. Hutchinson, *Lowden of Illinois,* I, 79.

tion than those in the East, with the exception of the meat packers.

NOMINATIONS BY BOSS DICTATION

The nomination of state candidates by convention, a procedure dating back to the early days of Stephen A. Douglas, came into disrepute as a result of adventures in factionalism by both parties. The chief blame rested with Republicans, who managed to win another series of elections in spite of themselves.[2]

If policy differences existed in Republican ranks, it seemed to make little difference to the party leaders. Instead, the outcome of elections depended upon shifting rivalries and alliances, made at the top level without consultation with or consideration of the rank and file. In the continuing struggles, no factional leader was strong enough to win without help from others and part of the game was that friends and foes changed roles frequently. The astute Senator Cullom masterminded a "federal crowd" patronage machine that could shift quickly into high gear when a convention neared. A "state crowd" generally took leadership from the governor, who knew that, regardless of surface harmony, ambitious men waited for opportunity to shove him aside. In Chicago, the rivalries were more complex and apt to be more self-centered and impermanent. Consequently nominating conventions usually witnessed a series of bargains and trades in which factions pooled their assets to form slates of candidates. Jealousies, bitterness, and misunderstandings were inevitable at the leadership level. Lower down, the belief increased that individual voters should have something to say about who ran for office.

John R. Tanner, who had been influential in Cullom's machine, did not ask for reelection in 1900. Without warning, he tried for the senate seat held by Cullom, who was seventy-two years and at the end of his third term. It provided the senator with one of his toughest fights, but Tanner withdrew when the delegates assembled at Peoria.[3]

---

[2] *Ibid.,* pp. 79-80, 94, 259-260, summarizes the divisions and power centers of the Republican party. Hutchinson's biography and James W. Neilson's *Shelby M. Cullom, Prairie State Republican,* provide detailed accounts of several decades of Republican politics in Illinois.

[3] Neilson, *op. cit.,* pp. 176-191. Hutchinson, *op. cit.,* I, 97-98. *Illinois Blue Book, 1901,* pp. 137-142.

Courtesy Illinois State Historical Library

Vice President Adlai E. Stevenson

Charles Gates Dawes, a political whirlwind who moved from Lincoln, Nebraska, to Evanston as a promoter of gas companies, in 1896 saw to it that Illinois delegates were instructed for William McKinley.[4] It rated as a major accomplishment, since Cullom with the aid of Tanner had dreamed of being the presidential nominee. The roles were reversed in 1900, when Dawes rode to the rescue of Cullom. Dawes, who had been made comptroller of the currency, wanted to replace Senator William E. Mason in 1902, but his influence evaporated when McKinley was assassinated and the

4 Paul R. Leach, *That Man Dawes.* Hutchinson, *op. cit.,* I, 104-105. John E. Pixton, Jr., "Charles G. Dawes and the McKinley Campaign," *Journal of the Illinois State Historical Society,* XLVIII (Autumn, 1955), 283-306.

senate seat went to Congressman Albert J. Hopkins of Aurora. Cullom's ability to stay in the senate five terms was impressive when contrasted to the careers of other leaders of his era. None of the five senators who were his colleagues could win a second term, and in the first four decades after the Civil War only Oglesby and Cullom were reelected governor.

The 1900 state convention brought into prominence William Lorimer, a Chicago manipulator who for years was the evil genius of Illinois Republicanism.⁵ Just when the nomination seemed certain, Lorimer organized a noisy and prolonged demonstration that in the confusion brought out a fourth candidate, Richard Yates of Jacksonville, the namesake son of the Civil War governor. Party leaders accepted Yates as preferable to a division that might permit a Democrat to be elected.

The faults of the convention system became more obvious in 1904. As governor, Yates made a patronage alliance with Lorimer and aspired to a second term. Lorimer, however, lined up with Frank O. Lowden, who sought the governorship in the dual role of a rich Chicagoan with a personal interest in good government and a downstater who lived on a model farm in Ogle County. Born on the Minnesota frontier, Lowden had achieved wealth as a corporation lawyer in Chicago before marrying George M. Pullman's daughter, Florence. Sinissippi Farm, where Lowden built a mansion and demonstrated methods of improving agricultural production, became his campaign base. Yates, however, controlled the most downstate delegates. In Cook County a majority favored Charles S. Deneen, the state's attorney who had made a brilliant record as a prosecutor. The convention opened May 12 in the castellated state armory at Springfield and promptly settled into a deadlock. The delegates answered fifty-eight roll calls during eight days, recessed for eight days of maneuvering during which the Leland Hotel burned, and on the seventy-ninth ballot nominated Deneen June 3. The outcome was the culmination of a deal made with Yates.⁶

Democrats also had factional troubles and long conventions. In Chicago, Mayor Carter Harrison, who like his father was a cosmopolitan, kept getting reelected by combining personal appeal with

⁵ Carroll H. Wooddy, *The Case of Frank L. Smith,* pp. 147-155. Hutchinson, *op. cit.,* I, 8-82. Neilson, *op. cit.,* pp. 239-240.

⁶ Hutchinson, *op. cit.,* pp. 110-145. J. McCan Davis, *The Breaking of the Deadlock.* John H. Krenkel (ed.), *Serving the Republic: Richard Yates.*

patronage. He succeeded locally without the backing of Roger C. Sullivan, a factional leader who had left his native Belvidere at the age of eighteen to take a $1.25 a day job in the streetcar shops. While losing to Harrison, Sullivan managed to keep control of the Democratic state central committee, although he had little in common ideologically with Altgeld, Bryan, and the downstate populist adherents.

Bryan, who would not permit the Democrats to make McKinley imperialism the dominant issue, took the presidential nomination again in 1900, and on the silver issue lost more heavily than he had four years earlier. Harrison refused to run for Vice President but helped Adlai E. Stevenson get the nomination. In 1904 Deneen and Theodore Roosevelt set new records by carrying Illinois by more than three hundred thousand votes. That year neither Stevenson nor Bryan was on the opposing ticket.[7]

PRIMARIES AND CIVIL SERVICE

Charles S. Deneen served two terms as governor without satisfying either the standpat conservatives, who had prospered for a half-century in the image of Cullom, or Progressive adherents who believed that, since Theodore Roosevelt was in the White House, the reformation of the world was overdue. A clean-cut figure, he came into office in 1905 when the President asked for action against trusts and a new breed of muckraking journalists filled magazines with exposés of municipal and corporate wrongdoing. The new governor, who had made an eight-year record as an energetic and impartial state's attorney, headed a Republican faction based on his residence in the Englewood district on Chicago's southwest side. He lacked rabble-rousing talent. Harold L. Ickes, whose primary allegiance in that era was to Theodore Roosevelt, thought him cautious, selfish, and too conservative.[8] Old-line Republicans believed the governor was too liberal.

[7] Election returns for major offices have been compiled by Samuel K. Gove in *Illinois Votes, 1900-1958, A Compilation of Illinois Election Statistics.* More detailed returns, including those for legislative and congressional primaries and elections, can be found for most but not all elections in the biennial *Illinois Blue Book.* During the 1920's the secretary of state began publishing them biennially as *Official Vote of the State of Illinois.*

[8] Harold L. Ickes, *Autobiography of a Curmudgeon,* p. 116. See also Wooddy, *op. cit.,* pp. 184-197.

Deneen worked for years to get the legislature to pass a primary law that the Supreme Court would hold valid.[9] Increasing public support was demonstrated in a 1904 referendum which favored abolition of the convention nomination system. Deneen-backed laws passed in 1905, 1906, and 1908 were ruled unconstitutional, but nevertheless primaries were held under the latter two and the courts recognized the winners as the legal nominees. In 1910 Deneen and the legislature finally satisfied the judges. Since then modifications of the primary system have been minor in nature, and state political conventions nominate only trustees of the University of Illinois. As the original sponsors wished, the primaries have increased the number of candidates and improved the chances of independents.

Nationwide complaints about the spoils system brought agitation for Illinois to adopt civil service. The loudest demands came from Chicago, and at the end of Mayor Hopkins' term an optional civil service law was ratified by Chicago voters, but the Municipal Voters League soon complained of violations. Basically unchanged since then, the law provided for a three-man city commission, the exemption of certain provisions, and the right to make temporary sixty-day appointments in emergencies. The latter provision has had the effect of nullifying the law, since mayors soon hit upon the device of giving thousands of political workers sixty-day appointments which were renewed every two months as long as their party stayed in office.[10]

In 1898, after a legislative commission found that the Chicago civil service law had been abused in the appointment of policemen, Governor Tanner tried to have the Chicago police department placed under the control of a board to be appointed by the governor. A Cook County civil service law also fell into disrepute, and in 1901 members of the county commission were convicted of malfeasance. The Supreme Court held unconstitutional a 1903 law to provide civil service for police and firemen in downstate cities with a population of seven thousand.

The state government operated under a spoils system until 1905 when a comprehensive law covered the seventeen welfare institutions where the worst abuses existed. It placed 2,200 existing

9 Charles E. Merriam and Louise Overacker, *Primary Elections,* pp. 3-27, 62-65, 113-114, 142. Hutchinson, *op. cit.,* I, 84-85.

10 E. L. Bogart and J. M. Mathews, *The Modern Commonwealth, 1893-1918,* pp. 271-286.

employees under blanket coverage, permitted permanent employees to be discharged for incompetency or good cause, and provided for examination of applicants. The legislature omitted an appropriation and the governor paid the commission's expenses from an emergency fund. The 1911 session extended the system to cover 80 percent of the state service. The unclassified positions were sizable and exemptions allowed, but Illinois government was more completely covered than any other state.

In his first term the governor ordered the payrolls pruned of incompetents. Promptly and indignantly he demanded that a grand jury indict men arrested in a Springfield race riot. He charged that the Illinois Central railroad had improperly reported its taxable gross receipts, with the result that Attorney General William H. Stead won major points for the state in a suit for an accounting that dragged on for years.[11]

At a time when the state needed money and the governor wanted to make a record for economy, he helped the University of Illinois double its budget. The university, adding new schools and colleges, achieved a measure of financial independence when the legislature gave it the proceeds of a one-mill tax. The common school system also received increased support. Upon adoption of the 1870 constitution, the state appropriated one million dollars a year for school aid, which was one hundred thousand dollars more than had been raised previously by a special two-mill tax on property. Despite increasing enrollments and costs, the amount of state aid remained stationary until 1911, when an educational commission prevailed upon legislators to vote a series of one-million-dollar yearly increases so as to provide a better balance of state and local financing.

Winning some strikes and losing others, the labor movement also made progress. The Mine Workers union, the most powerful in Illinois, affiliated with the state federation of labor, which as a result became more powerful than its counterparts in other states. John H. Mitchell of the miners and other leaders accepted responsibility for living up to trade agreements, in line with progressive traditions, but union after union became involved in strikes and lockouts.[12] In 1905, which was the year a group of

[11] A. L. Bowen, "The Illinois Central Case," *Illinois Blue Book, 1927-28,* pp. 526-536.

[12] John H. Keiser, "John H. Walker, Labor Leader from Illinois," in *Essays in Illinois History* (Donald F. Tingley, ed.), pp. 75-100.

gregarious businessmen in Chicago founded Rotary International as a luncheon club, one of the most violent strikes pitted five thousand teamsters against the Chicago Employers Association and was marked by almost daily street battles that blocked downtown traffic. The powerful Teamsters brotherhood had arbitrated labor disputes in other industries, and some of its leaders had been suspected of profiting from private deals to guarantee peace. The employers forced the issue by refusing to renew closed shop agreements, and the teamsters surrendered after nearly four months of conflict. Because of a blacklist, more than half of the strikers had to hunt for other jobs. The courts consistently upheld the common law right of the workers to organize, but they also supported the right of employers to refuse to recognize the unions.

Despite the failures and strong resistance by employers, the unions with major assistance from a group of social reformers obtained enactment between 1900 and 1915 of many of the basic laws for the protection of workers.[13] With the persistent help of Jane Addams, a stronger law to restrict factory and sweatshop jobs for fourteen-year-olds was passed in 1903, and a year later child labor in mines was prohibited. Florence Kelley then credited Illinois with having surpassed Massachusetts as the leader in that field. A ten-hour day for women required a longer struggle. In the preceding decade an eight-hour law for women was held unconstitutional as a discriminatory and unwarranted restriction on the fundamental right of a person to control his or her own time. Miss Addams and other members of a Women's Trade Union League in 1909 won passage of a ten-hour law covering work in factories, mechanical establishments, and laundries. To hold it constitutional, the state Supreme Court reversed the Circuit Court. A disastrous fire which killed 259 men in a mine at Cherry, Bureau County, in 1909 gave impetus to safety legislation and a workmen's compensation system.[14] Illinois in 1911 had the nation's first mother's pension law in the form of an appropriation for care of dependent and neglected children. Governor Dunne in 1913 succeeded in broadening the compensation system to increase payments and put administration under a nonpolitical board. He also reorganized the free employment service and gave more power to the state factory inspector.

[13] Bogart-Mathews, *op. cit.*, pp. 179-184.
[14] F. P. Buck, *The Cherry Mine Disaster.*

THE TRIUMPH AND FALL OF WILLIAM LORIMER

United States senators were elected by the two houses of the legislature, balloting in joint session and often engaging in political deals of a nature that had not been anticipated by the founding fathers. Complaints about the system had been heard as early as Douglas' 1858 election, which had reflected a gerrymandering of the legislature rather than the vote received by Lincoln supporters. The deadlocks that eventually resulted in the election of Logan in 1885 and Palmer in 1891 had interfered with lawmaking duties. The choice of Hopkins in 1903, the result of manipulations by Governor Yates and Lorimer, came as a surprise to the citizenry. The year before, on a public policy referendum, a proposal for direct election of senators carried overwhelmingly. Critics of the lawmakers also ardently favored a system of direct legislation by initiative and referendum which was in effect in Oregon. It twice carried Illinois by smaller majorities when submitted to the voters as a public policy question, but was rejected by the legislature and in 1920 by a constitutional convention. On other public policy questions, the people voted for limitation of governmental expenditures, taxation reform, and a short ballot. The advisory results in most cases were ignored by lawmakers.

Governor Deneen, who had won by a landslide in 1904, survived efforts by Yates and Lorimer to block his renomination. At the election he almost missed a second term, although Taft carried the state handily over Bryan's third attempt to win the presidency. Adlai E. Stevenson, who was the Democratic nominee for governor, finished only 23,164 votes behind Deneen. Lorimer backed him, and some Democrats claimed that the former Vice President had lost due to vote frauds in the wards controlled by Fred A. Busse, who at the time was serving as Chicago's first four-year mayor. James W. Neilson, a biographer of Cullom, concludes that perhaps Deneen was weaker than the Republican party and Stevenson stronger than the Democrats.[15]

During Deneen's second term, many of the Republicans the governor wished to purge had no hesitancy about dealing with the Democrats at a time when the liquor traffic furnished an issue that crossed party lines. The progressives, who refused to compromise

[15] Neilson, *op. cit.,* p. 241. Also see Charles E. Merriam, *Chicago: A More Intimate View of Urban Politics,* pp. 181-182.

Courtesy Illinois State Historical Library

Charles S. Deneen

on questions of what they saw as right and wrong, in effect were a separate political entity. Differences of opinion led to bitter attacks of a personal nature in which anyone who disagreed with them was assumed to have base motives.[16] The 1909 legislature, faced with the necessity of reelecting or replacing Senator Hopkins, was safely Republican, but factional and ideological differences split the majority. While Deneen expressed disapproval of the reported use of jackpots to pay legislators for votes, the Old Guard made a bipartisan deal and reelected Speaker Edward D.

[16] In the 1903 legislative session, Speaker John Henry Miller of Hamilton County and his followers were physically driven from the house chamber by representatives who objected to an arbitrary ruling against a bill to give home rule to Chicago. Enough stayed to transact business under a temporary speaker, L. Y. Sherman of Macomb. After the home rule action had been reconsidered, Miller was allowed to return to the rostrum. Denison B. Hull, *The Legislative Life of Morton Denison Hull,* pp. 30-31.

Shurtleff of Marengo with the votes of twenty-five Republicans and sixty Democrats. In return, Shurtleff let Sullivan's Democrats have eleven committee chairmanships. Deneen's young turks meanwhile controlled the senate.

In the legislative chambers, Lorimer maneuvered on familiar ground. Then serving his eighth term in Congress, the blond boss had the appearance and personal habits of a Sunday school superintendent. The orphaned, English-born son of a minister, he had lived on Chicago's west side since his ninth year. He prospered in years of bargaining with friend and foe in a kaleidoscopic succession of deals. Lorimer gave Illinois government a bad name. To the civic-minded, he epitomized Tammany at its worst.

In the advisory primary, Hopkins failed to get a majority of the popular vote. Lorimer blocked his election and precipitated an eighteen-week deadlock during which a score of names received consideration. When public clamor reached its peak, with the votes of fifty-five Republicans and fifty-three Democrats Lorimer was elected senator.[17]

The fall of the new senator began eleven months later. The *Chicago Tribune* printed a confession by Representative Charles A. White of O'Fallon, a Democrat, that he and some others had been paid one thousand dollars each to vote for Lorimer and also had received nine hundred dollars as individual shares of a general slush fund or jackpot for votes on miscellaneous bills. The repercussions began with wholesale denials, confessions, repudiations, explanations, and refusals to talk. The state's attorneys of Cook and Sangamon counties investigated. Lee O'Neil Browne of Ottawa, a Democrat who had a long career as a house leader, won acquittal at a second trial at Chicago on a charge that he paid the bribe. In all the long and sensational case, the primary sources never agreed on the basic point of whether Lorimer owed his senate seat to bribery.

Lorimerism became a national issue, contributing to the rising tide of progressivism and splitting the Republican party. Theodore Roosevelt refused to address the Hamilton Club in Chicago in 1910 until an invitation to the junior senator was withdrawn.[18]

[17] The involved situation that led to the election of Lorimer is traced in Hutchinson, *op. cit.,* I, 177-188, and Neilson, *op. cit.,* pp. 241-250.

[18] Joel A. Tarr, "President Theodore Roosevelt and Illinois Politics, 1901-1904," *Journal of the Illinois State Historical Society,* LVIII (Autumn, 1965), 245-264.

The majority of a United States senate subcommittee found that the evidence did not show that Lorimer participated in the paying of any bribe, and the senate voted, 47 to 40, that Lorimer should retain his seat. On the ground that reasonable doubt existed, Cullom voted for his colleague. The *Chicago Record-Herald* then charged that a one-hundred-thousand-dollar fund had been raised in advance of Lorimer's election, and a state senate committee investigated and concluded that Lorimer could not have been elected but for bribery and corruption. The state senate then asked the United States senate to reopen the case. A second committee from Washington after extensive hearings found for Lorimer, again on a split vote, but the full membership of the senate, on July 13, 1911, voted 55 to 28 that Lorimer had been illegally elected and was not entitled to his seat. Cullom joined the majority in favoring expulsion.

Cullom's chance for reelection had been terminated by his first vote for Lorimer. Cullom, who was eighty-two years old at the time, during the investigations entered a preferential primary for a sixth term but was beaten by Lawrence Y. Sherman, a former lieutenant governor.

Speaker Joseph G. Cannon also became a casualty of the reform movement in 1910 when he was stripped of his dictatorial power over legislation as the result of an insurgent revolt led by George W. Norris of Nebraska.[19] Cannon, who had a sophisticated knowledge of governmental machinery and congressional ambitions, believed that most proposed legislation was useless if not dangerous. The symbol of the conservatism against which progressives protested, Cannon was a poker-playing Quaker who affected a rustic appearance. His representation of the Danville district covered a half-century, from 1872 to 1922, broken only by defeats in 1890 and 1912.

A year after Lorimer's expulsion, the senate finally agreed to a constitutional amendment, which became effective in 1913, for the direct election of senators.[20] By that time Woodrow Wilson

[19] Blair Bolles, *Tyrant from Illinois.* L. White Busbey, *Uncle Joe Cannon, The Story of a Pioneer American.* William Rae Gwinn, *Uncle Joe Cannon, Arch Foe of Insurgency: A History of the Rise and Fall of Cannonism.*

[20] In the 1912 election Illinois voted at least 4 to 1 in favor of three public policy questions which were key tenets of the Progressive philosophy. They proposed a constitutional amendment for classification of property, intended to relieve the comparatively heavier burden on the poor; a revised primary law which would abolish scandals and disorder in the filing of petitions, and also simplify the system, reduce

was President and the movement for reform simultaneously brought ratification of an amendment permitting a federal income tax.

THE SHORT LIFE OF THE BULL MOOSE

During 1911 the Progressive movement developed rapidly in Illinois and Theodore Roosevelt's war on trusts and monopolies enjoyed great popularity among rank-and-file Republicans. Their popular enthusiasm, however, did not penetrate far among the conservative leaders. By tradition they regarded President Taft as their leader so long as he was in office, and they sided with the campaign contributors who smarted at Teddy's denunciation of "wealthy malefactors."

Lorimer's disrepute and Cullom's approaching retirement had weakened the standpatters, but the Progressives also were split. In the 1911 Chicago mayoral campaign Mayor Busse gave up without a fight and the Republican nomination went to a University of Chicago political science professor, Charles E. Merriam, who had been elected alderman from the Hyde Park ward. In the primary, without too much trouble, Merriam beat Busse-Lorimer and Deneen candidates. In the election he had undercover encouragement from Sullivan-Brennan Democrats. They gave only token support to Carter Harrison, who came out of retirement to win his fifth term. Ickes blamed Deneen, Busse, and Lorimer, among others, for Merriam's defeat.

As soon as Roosevelt revealed that he would enter primaries to fight Taft for 1912 delegates, presidential preferential balloting became the key part of the primary movement and Illinois became contested ground. Deneen called a special session when the *Tribune* lined up support of legislators in favor of extending the Illinois primary law.[21]

For Roosevelt, the Illinois balloting was a massive victory. He received 61 percent of the vote in running against Taft, who carried only five of the smaller counties. Better yet, delegates who ran on his coattails were elected in all but the Lorimer district in Chicago. The Ickes candidates for nomination as senator and

expenses, and encourage greater participation in elections; and creation of a legislative commission to study the short ballot.

[21] G. E. Mowry, *Theodore Roosevelt and the Progressive Movement*, pp. 211-303. Hutchinson, *op. cit.*, I, 243-246.

governor ran poorly, however. Some Progressives did not want to run a candidate against Deneen, but Ickes insisted that the governor be punished for helping defeat Merriam.

Roosevelt broke tradition by coming to Chicago for the highly emotional national convention in the Coliseum. On its eve his speech about battling at Armageddon stirred up a crowd of five thousand which sang "Onward Christian Soldiers" with evangelistic fervor. Specifically he accused party leaders of theft because, at the culmination of a ten-day wrangle, credentials had been denied seventy-two delegates who had been elected at primaries held under circumstances that did not follow party custom in all particulars.[22] Had they been seated, Roosevelt would have controlled the convention, but the Old Guard gave Taft his renomination. That evening Progressives from twenty-two states, including most of the Illinois delegation, at a mass meeting voted to carry on their fight, and under a Bull Moose banner Roosevelt accepted leadership of the new party. They came back to the Coliseum in September for the formal nomination.

At the Democratic national convention, Woodrow Wilson owed his nomination to Roger Sullivan. The Illinois primary had been won by Champ Clark of Missouri, but Sullivan broke a deadlock by voting the delegation for Wilson, who was the second choice.

In November, the Republican split gave the minority Democrats a clean sweep. Roosevelt outpolled Taft but first place went to Wilson by 18,750 votes. At the state level, the Progressives made an even poorer showing. Their candidate for governor finished third, slightly behind Deneen. Roosevelt's followers elected two congressmen, a maneuverable bloc in the legislature, and miscellaneous local officers, but the net result of the Bull Moose campaign was to turn the government over to Wilson at Washington and to Edward F. Dunne at Springfield. Had the Republican factions been able to compose their differences, 1912 would have been a landslide year.

Medill McCormick, who alternated executive control of the *Chicago Tribune* with his brother, Robert R. McCormick, assumed leadership of the twenty-six representatives and one senator who

---

[22] On critical roll calls, the Illinois delegation did not vote solidly for Roosevelt, who had carried the state. Seven supported Taft's choice for temporary chairman and six voted to seat Taft delegates in a crucial California district. Roosevelt had swept the primaries in the other states also, which encouraged the belief that his third party would be successful. Merriam-Overacker, *op. cit.*, pp. 154n, 182.

had Progressive credentials in the legislature. In general, he co-operated with Republicans and, with a realistic assessment of the political facts of life, started to lead his small band back into the G.O.P.[23]

The Ickes faction of the Progressives sought a continued career as a splinter group, but a weak showing in 1914 made it clear that their candidates had a chance only if Roosevelt energetically campaigned at the head of the ticket. The former President declined to run again, although he spoke for Raymond Robins, an Ickes comrade who carried three counties when he ran for senator in 1914. For the next two years McCormick was one of three Progressives in the lower house. From that position he advocated unity in the coming campaign against second terms for Wilson and Dunne.

ANOTHER DEMOCRAT—EDWARD F. DUNNE

Edward Fitzsimmons Dunne, a former mayor of Chicago who had a futile interest in municipal ownership of utilities, replaced Deneen as governor and became a third force among Democratic factions. Twenty years had passed since Altgeld had been the center of a Democratic inaugural celebration at Springfield, and the victors realized that they were fortunate to run in a year when Republicans had not kept the peace. In the new governor's background was a boyhood in Peoria and a college education in Dublin. Dunne was the second Roman Catholic to become governor, and the first since William H. Bissell was elected in 1856. Dunne also had the distinction of having the largest family—thirteen children, of whom ten lived to move into the executive mansion.

Dunne, originally a Bryan man, was serving his third term as a circuit judge when he resigned to become mayor in 1905, the year Harrison stepped aside after four terms. Yerkes had departed, Chicago had voted 5 to 1 in favor of the theory of immediate municipal ownership of traction lines, and Dunne made it his chief plank. He appointed Walter L. Fisher, a former secretary of the interior, as his special traction attorney and together they evolved a plan for the streetcar lines to receive franchises that could be terminated, under terms approved in advance, any time the city could raise the money, which didn't happen until forty years

23 Hutchinson, *op. cit.*, I, 253-260.

432   ILLINOIS: A HISTORY OF THE PRAIRIE STATE

later.[24] Fred A. Busse, a bulky coal dealer and Republican power who succeeded Dunne in the city hall, settled the traction issue with a twenty-year franchise that gave the city 55 percent of the revenue from a five-cent fare and made possible electrification of the cable lines. As mayor, Dunne also appointed an unusually competent school board, with Jane Addams as one of its members.

During his single term as mayor, Busse appointed Charles H. Wacker, a businessman, to head a commission on beautification of Chicago.[25] Daniel H. Burnham, who had made his reputation as architect for the 1893 fair, was placed in charge of large-scale projects that included filling in Lake Michigan to form Grant Park and the construction of a Michigan Avenue bridge that opened up the near north side as a major commercial area. In his final years Burnham also made plans for a boulevard system that included a lakefront drive, a museum, and relocated railroad terminals. An early accomplishment was replacement of the riverside produce market with a boulevard named for Wacker.

The Progressive movement's emphasis on reform forced Busse and Harrison, who succeeded him for a fifth and last term as mayor, to put a damper on Chicago's reputation as one of the nation's more wide-open cities. Congressman James R. Mann of the Hyde Park district, who had been an antiboodling alderman a decade earlier, in 1910 demonstrated that the city was lagging behind national sentiment when he became author of a white slave law. An example of federal legislation to regulate public morals, it prohibited the interstate transportation of women and girls for immoral purposes. When the Chicago Federation of Churches demanded that commercialized vice be cleaned up, Busse appointed the Rev. Walter T. Sumner to head an investigating committee. Its report the next year said five thousand women were involved in red-light activities and estimated the profits at fifteen million dollars a year. The legislature joined in the crusade, and an investigation headed by Barratt O'Hara, the young lieutenant governor in the Dunne administration, joined Sumner in criticizing wages paid by State Street department stores. Girl clerks received

[24] Dunne argues the case for his administration in the second volume of his *Illinois, The Heart of the Nation.* See also *Dunne: Judge, Mayor, Governor,* edited by William L. Sullivan.

[25] Daniel H. Burnham and Edward H. Bennett, *Plan of Chicago.* Edgar Lee Masters, *The Tale of Chicago,* p. 286. Lloyd Lewis and Henry Justin Smith, *Chicago, The History of Its Reputation,* pp. 399-402.

six to seven dollars a week, and the cost of living was fixed at a dollar more. A surplus of immigrant labor made the low wages possible. One of the results of the investigations was the formation of a Morals Court, to be followed by Domestic Relations and Boys branches of the Municipal Court.[26]

It wasn't permanent, but when Harrison entered the mayor's office for the last time he recognized that public sentiment had turned against the family policy of liberalism. The red-light district, mostly in the First Ward, had been wide open since the Busse administration, and the legislature's investigators had identified four thousand active prostitutes. After a period of stalling, he closed the Everleigh Club, an ornate brothel south of the loop, chiefly because the two sisters who operated it had been indiscreet in their advertising. There was a general crackdown that forced prostitutes to scatter temporarily from the levee district to call flats and new houses elsewhere in town. The mayor lost two old-time political allies by ordering Aldermen Michael Kenna and John Coughlin to cancel their annual First Ward Ball, a notorious social event. The mayor frowned on gambling and closed the racetrack at Washington Park, which meant that henceforth horses would run only in the suburbs.

Dunne had worked in moderate harmony with the waning Harrison faction, but inability to get along with Roger C. Sullivan kept coming to the surface. Their troubles were temporarily adjusted in 1912 when Dunne, who had spent five years in law practice after leaving city hall, beat three downstaters in the primary and then, using "jackpot government must go" as his slogan, went ahead to retire Deneen. Two deadlocks opened the new administration.[27] His own inauguration was delayed until February 5 because the Progressive bloc insisted on voting for one of its own members for speaker. The Democrats had fragmented, but on the seventy-seventh ballot Republicans provided most of the votes that placed William McKinley, a first-term Democrat from Chicago, on the rostrum.

Election of two United States senators took more time. The Seventeenth Amendment for direct election of senators had not

26 *Ibid.,* pp. 336-351. John Landesco, *Organized Crime in Chicago: Part III of the Illinois Crime Survey.* Walter C. Reckless, *Vice in Chicago.*

27 Illinois Democrats have received less literary attention than the Republicans. Basic information can be found in Walter A. Townsend, *Illinois Democracy, A History of the Party and Its Representative Members, Past and Present.*

gone into effect and the expulsion of Lorimer had left a two-year vacancy in addition to the full term in the seat Cullom had filled for thirty years. The preferential primaries had been won by James Hamilton Lewis, a free-lance Democrat who had been corporation counsel during Dunne's term as mayor, and Sherman. Neither party had entered candidates for the short term and Sullivan, always attentive to downstate alliances, proposed that Democrats try for both seats, with Charles Boeschenstein of Edwardsville, the national committeeman, as the second candidate. After several weeks of treadmill action, the governor publicly proposed a bi-partisan compromise under which Lewis would take the long term and Sherman the two-year seat. Sullivan and some downstaters objected, but the arrangement was finally worked out at the end of March.

Lewis, a dapper dresser who used pink whiskers and a courtly manner for self-advertising, was promptly made majority whip in the United States senate. Earlier he had served a term in Congress from the state of Washington, and the Wilson legislative program needed his talents at keeping votes in line. Two years later, when Sullivan became a candidate for the first time and sought direct election to the senate, Dunne insisted on supporting Lawrence B. Stringer of Lincoln, a Bryan and Wilson man who was in his first term as congressman-at-large. Sullivan won the nomination, and Democratic factions blamed each other when Sherman won the full term in a close contest.

The governor at the state level had less success than President Wilson but he also attempted a progressive administration, with sponsorship of plans to reorganize state government and construct all-weather highways. Dunne never lost his interest in municipal ownership and successfully backed legislation creating a bipartisan commission to regulate public utilities and to authorize cities and villages to acquire and operate electric and gas plants on the same basis that most of them provided water service. He failed to get approval of a home rule bill that would give Chicago its own utility commission. He also inspired a law, welcomed by the railroads, which outlawed the old and expensive practice of giving free passes to influential riders.

After Secretary of State Harry Woods committed suicide in 1914, Dunne filled the vacancy with the appointment of Lewis G. Stevenson of Bloomington, son of the former Vice President and father of a future governor. A former manager of Hearst mining properties in the Southwest, Stevenson served fifteen months in the state office.

For Chicago, the last hope for meaningful reform vanished in the 1915 mayoral election. In the Democratic primary Harrison lost to County Clerk Robert M. Schweitzer, a genial party wheel-horse who would be the central figure in his own County Building scandal in a few years. The Republicans staged another factional battle in their primary. The Deneen candidate, the respected chief justice of the Municipal Court, lost by a narrow margin to William Hale Thompson. For a few months there was some hope that Thompson would make a good mayor, but prohibition was on the way and gambling and brothels ran wide open under Big Jim Colosimo's protectorate.[28]

28 John Kobler, *Capone: The Life and World of Al Capone*, pp. 38-67. Lloyd Wendt and Herman Kogan, *Lords of the Levee*. Bruce Grant, *Fight for a City: The Story of the Union League Club and Its Times*. Carter H. Harrison, *Stormy Years*, pp. 304-314.

23

WAR AND REORGANIZATION

ILLINOIS HAD MORE THAN SIX MILLION RESIDENTS, TWO-THIRDS of whom were urban dwellers, when the state reached the one hundredth anniversary of its admission into the Union. Two years later, the 1920 census showed a population of 6,485,280, an increase of 15 percent in the decade. Chicago gained 23.6 percent and had 2,701,705 residents. In the increasing urbanization, 56 of the 102 counties had lost population during the ten-year span.[1]

Since the centennial coincided with America's first involvement in a global war, the official observance emphasized the ideals and sacrifices of the civil and military leaders who had founded Illinois and enabled it to grow. One of the ceremonies took place at Chester, the city nearest the place where the Mississippi River in 1881 had swept away the ancient capital of Kaskaskia. At Springfield, officials laid the cornerstone for the Centennial Building, since the state house and the Supreme Court Building, which had been erected in 1904, were not large enough to house all agencies of government. Nearby statues of Lincoln and Douglas were unveiled. The major accomplishment, however, was the publication of a five-volume *Centennial History of Illinois* under the editorship of Clarence W. Alvord.[2]

[1] Helen R. Jeter, *Trends of Population in the Region of Chicago.* Ernest L. Bogart, "The Movement of Population in Illinois, 1870-1910," *Journal of the Illinois State Historical Society,* XXIII (1917), 64-75.

[2] William T. Hutchinson, *Lowden of Illinois,* I, 372-373. The Centennial history

SENDING AN ARMY OVERSEAS

Needlessly, as it turned out, some concern about Illinois accompanied the entry of the United States into the World War that
had been raging two and a half years in Europe. The defeat of
Germany would require the full agricultural and industrial capacity, as well as the fighting manpower, of the big state that
straddled the east-west transportation lines. But Illinois, which had
a history of Copperheadism in the Civil War, also had potential
weaknesses in 1917. It had more German- and Austrian-born
residents than any other state, and Chicago, the world's sixth
largest German city, had a mayor who preached that American
boys should not be sent to overseas battlefields.

To make it clear that opinion was divided, just before hostilities
began twenty-five German-American leaders from Chicago went to
Washington in an effort to convince President Wilson that the
nation should not take the side of Great Britain and France. Jane
Addams as chairman of the new Woman's Peace party had the
support of some prominent men in opposing the war on humanitarian and moral grounds. When the issue was presented to Congress, Illinois representatives provided five of the fifty votes
against a declaration of war. Fred A. Britten of Chicago took a
prominent role against the war resolution and had the backing of
Congressman-at-Large William E. Mason, the former senator who
long had been a leader of lost causes. Mason later opposed draft
legislation. The other antiwar congressmen were downstaters. All
were reelected the next year.

Soon it became evident that Illinois was more united than in the
troubled administration of the first Richard Yates. Public sympathy sided with the Allies, the great bulk of those with Teutonic
blood proved their loyalty, and Governor Frank O. Lowden, who
had been in office three months, would not permit it to be
otherwise. When the Democratic President broke off diplomatic
relations with Germany, the Republican governor immediately
issued a statement that loyalty was the "solemn duty" of all

began with an introductory volume, Solon J. Buck's *Illinois in 1818,* and then chrono-
logically told the state's story in five volumes—Clarence W. Alvord, *The Illinois Country,*
1673-1818; Theodore C. Pease, *The Frontier State, 1818-1848;* Arthur C. Cole, *The Era*
of the Civil War, 1848-1870; Ernest L. Bogart and Charles M. Thompson, *The Industrial*
State, 1870-1893; and Ernest L. Bogart and John M. Mathews, *The Modern Common-*
wealth, 1893-1918.

Americans. Quickly he went before the legislature and, recalling Douglas' support of Lincoln, obtained unanimous adoption of a pledge to back the national administration. For the duration "Win the War" Lowden set an example of being wholly without partisanship in giving first attention to victory.[3]

The nation, although again unprepared, had learned something from the Civil and Spanish-American wars. Congress in 1904 had started the federalization and standardization of the militia, and in 1912 National Guard regiments were seasoned by duty on the Mexican border against Pancho Villa.[4] In a time of military experimentation, Robert R. McCormick, a cavalry major, raised private funds so that his guard outfit could be equipped with the first modern machine guns used in the field by American troops.[5] With abandonment of the old concept of a volunteer army, the entire Illinois National Guard was mobilized. At Camp Logan, Texas, most of its units were amalgamated into the Thirty-Third or Prairie Division, whose men wore a shoulder patch identification of a yellow cross in a black circle. It was the sixteenth American division to reach France. Counting replacements who came from other states, it reported 1,274 killed, 6,266 wounded, and 127 taken prisoner. Part of the guardsmen, with selected units from twenty-five other states, formed the Rainbow Division which Douglas MacArthur commanded at one time.

Lowden had wide support in believing that the manpower needs of a modern war could be met only by conscription and universal military training. A parade in Chicago set the preparedness stage and the legislature asked Congress to make military training compulsory. As the next step, boards hurriedly organized by county officials registered 646,480 men between the ages of twenty-one and thirty-one. Two more registration days were held the next year, and a total of 1,559,586 men between the ages of eighteen and forty-five came under the jurisdiction of the selective service system. A special legislative session set up the machinery for 227 draft exemption boards and for medical and legal advisory groups. Of the Illinois men who learned how to wrap woolen leggings in a spiral around their calves or to sleep in hammocks, more than 56 percent volunteered. One incident of draft resistance, involving a Rockford man, quickly terminated.

3 *Ibid.*, I, 328-329.
4 *Illinois Blue Book, 1915-16*, pp. 329-330.
5 Frank C. Waldrop, *McCormick of Chicago*, pp. 144-145.

Illinois became a training ground for land, sea, and air forces. Two-story wooden barracks were hurriedly erected for Camp Grant, south of Rockford, where draft boards from northern Illinois and southern Wisconsin sent men. Drafted men from southern Illinois went to Camp Zachary Taylor at Louisville. A new policy required that all fighting units be kept at full strength, and most of the men who learned about trench warfare from French and British instructors were used as replacements in divisions already on the fighting line. Fort Sheridan quickly became an officers' training camp at which nine thousand men learned the rudiments of command. Just before the war ended it became a general hospital. The Great Lakes Naval Training Station, which had been opened in 1904 on Lake County land donated by Chicagoans, underwent a major expansion and spread into adjacent woodland as new facilities were erected in which fifty thousand country and small-town boys spent three months before joining the fleet. In mid-1917, Illinois acquired two aviation bases. At Scott Field near Belleville fourteen squadrons organized or trained. Chanute Field at Rantoul became a ground school as well as a flying school from which men were hurried to France.

Illinois sent 314,504 men to the war by enlistment and draft, which was 52,207 more than the state contributed to the longer and bloodier Civil War. The bulk went into the army, but 24,663 served in the navy and 3,678 became marines. The war department tried to keep an outfit from being overloaded with men from one community and did not maintain casualty records on a state-by-state basis.[6]

THE HOME FRONT AND SAMUEL INSULL

In the overseas war, the United States triumphed by a full mobilization of its human and economic resources and, on at least some of the criteria that can be measured statistically, it has been demonstrated that Illinois contributed more and delivered earlier than most states. Millions helped unstintingly and Governor Lowden gave undivided leadership to the cause of victory, but for the

[6] Marguerite E. Jenison, *The War-Time Organization of Illinois*, Vol. 5, and *War Documents and Addresses*, Vol. 6 of *Illinois in the World War*. Frank S. Dickson, "Military Achievements of Illinois in the World War," *Illinois Blue Book, 1919-20*, pp. 82-97. E. L. Bogart and J. M. Mathews, *The Modern Commonwealth, 1893-1918*, pp. 452-461.

Courtesy Illinois State Historical Library

Frank O. Lowden

showing of Illinois the largest amount of individual credit goes to Samuel Insull, chairman of the state council of defense.[7]

When President Wilson asked the states to set up counterparts of a national council of defense, Lowden offered the Illinois chairmanship to Insull, who at the age of fifty-seven was one of the most successful and respected American businessmen. His pioneering policy of cutting utility rates and improving service to attract customers made the Commonwealth Edison Company prosperous in Chicago. In Lake County he had connected a string of villages with a generating plant, something no other man had

---

[7] Forrest McDonald, *Insull,* pp. 162-176. Samuel Insull, "Civilian Achievements of Illinois in the War," *Illinois Blue Book, 1919-20,* pp. 97-103. Bogart-Mathews, *op. cit.,* pp. 461-475.

attempted. He became the father of rural electrification by offering service to all farms within reach of his lines. By taking over small companies he considered inadequately managed, Insull operated widely in adjoining states as well as Illinois. To finance his scattered properties he organized Middle West Utilities Company and developed the holding company technique. Closer to Chicago, he controlled Public Service Company of Northern Illinois and Peoples Gas Light and Coke Company. Because they were his customers for electricity and no one else could run them as well, Insull acquired interurban lines and the long-troubled Chicago elevated system. Insull had been an American citizen since 1896, but his parents still lived in London and he depended on bankers there for assistance with major financing operations. In the European conflict his sympathy was with his native land and he had given secret help before America became involved. Insull furnished a six-story office building and a staff from his utility companies. He raised money among business friends instead of asking the state for an additional appropriation.

As the coordinating agency, the council under Insull's direction ran the home front. It mobilized opinion, anticipated emergencies, and cut red tape while the people accepted the draft, restrictions on food and fuel, longer working hours, curtailed amusements, and a repetitious drive to sell more Liberty bonds and war savings stamps. The council recruited and worked through an estimated eighty thousand volunteers, of whom fifty thousand were spread across downstate, organized as committees and boards on a county and community basis. The women's division had three hundred thousand members.

Insull understood the art of propaganda, and at a well-timed patriotic rally in Chicago President Harry Pratt Judson of the University of Chicago presented resolutions supporting the draft. Mayor Thompson gave necessary assistance in organizing draft boards, but he refused to invite Marshal Joffre of France to visit Chicago. In the general atmosphere of patriotism, the city council rebuked the mayor by adopting resolutions urging that all of the president's actions be upheld. State labor officials endorsed full participation in the war effort and in his final report Insull said that uninterrupted industrial peace was the greatest single contribution to victory. An Insull innovation, soon copied nationally, was the organization of two thousand Four Minute Men, volunteers whose short speeches explaining war policies and exhorting the purchase of more Liberty bonds were part of every theatrical performance and community, union local, and fraternal meeting. Before radio broadcasting, they could reach a weekly audience of seven hundred thousand. With 5.5 percent of the nation's population, Illinois residents and firms bought 7 percent—1.3 billion dollars' worth—of Liberty bonds and war savings stamps. More than 42.5 million dollars was collected for the Red Cross and other war aid and relief organizations.

Without waiting for national leadership, the council took such conservation steps as persuading bakeries to discontinue the practice of taking back unsold day-old bread. Following an early frost in 1917, Insull arranged for Chicago banks to finance a 1.25-million-dollar purchase of seed corn and then carried on an educational campaign so that farmers would not plant untested seed. The demand that the corn belt produce more foodstuffs coincided with a shortage of farm labor. Farmers received a deferred draft classification, their sons got school credit for working at home in busy seasons, and city boys were recruited to help with crops. Production in 1918 was the third greatest in yield and, in terms of money, by far the largest ever harvested in Illinois.

The women knitted for the soldiers, helped make hospital supplies at Red Cross centers, learned to use substitutes in preparing wheatless and meatless meals, and took jobs in factories. Lowden proclaimed special registration days for women to sign up for whatever type of work they had a talent. The women's branch of the council of defense asked "on grounds of economy and justice" that clubs stop serving alcoholic beverages, and the legislature, as another war measure, petitioned Congress to institute daylight-saving time.

Coal was a problem. Lowden had to convince the national food administration that Chicago faced a major crisis of frozen water pipes in unheated apartments because all the anthracite production was being diverted to eastern ports and cities. Relaxation of the order came too late to prevent the underheating of many homes in a cold winter. Owners of Illinois coal mines tripled their prices in sixty days and then made only mild reductions when Lowden, threatening to seize and operate the pits, appointed Supreme Court Justice Orrin N. Carter as state fuel director. Meanwhile a national fuel administration was set up to control distribution and prices, so Carter did not have to take action.[8]

8 McDonald, *op. cit.,* pp. 108-109. Hutchinson, *op. cit.,* I, 335-337.

Due to overseas orders for gun casings and other munitions, the state's heavy industrial plants had partially gone into war production before 1917. Direct war contracts approximated two billion dollars, a third of the state's industrial production, in 1918. Approximately two-thirds of the output came from Cook County.

In downstate cities as well as the metropolis, manufacturing had boomed since 1890, with the result that markets for grain, livestock, and lumber were relatively less important, although those products still flowed into Chicago in prodigious quantities. Outside of Cook County, a compilation just before the war showed important industries in thirty-five cities. Second to Chicago in importance, Peoria had distilleries, breweries, agricultural implement plants, packing houses, and one of the biggest wire factories. In Joliet, steel and rolling mills, blast furnaces, and coke and wire plants lined the railroads and waterway. East St. Louis grew faster than any other Illinois city in the war decade and was a national leader in aluminum and animal feeds products. Other plants were major employers in the packing, rolling mill, chemical, and flour fields and, like many cities, East St. Louis also was known for foundry and machine shops and railroad repair plants. Fifth in value in manufactured products, Rockford had a reputation for knitting, furniture, foundries, agricultural implements, and wagons. Moline, a leader in the agricultural implement field since the John Deere era, was one of the cities in which automobiles were assembled. With the only brass rolling mill west of Connecticut, Alton manufactured cartridges and also was a glass- and bottle-blowing center. Among other downstate cities, Elgin was internationally known for watches and, as the recognized butter market, had a major condensed milk plant. Belleville and Quincy both specialized in stoves but were also important in other fields. Springfield made watches, farm implements, and motor car accessories in some of its ninety plants. Other downstate cities which had industrial plants with sizable payrolls included Rock Island, Granite City, Decatur, Waukegan, Aurora, Pekin, Freeport, Kewanee, Danville, La Salle, Bloomington, Streator, Galesburg, Kankakee, Canton, Jacksonville, Bradley, Peru, Oglesby, Champaign, and North Chicago. Cairo was a major lumber market. Chicago Heights was the home of steel works and other heavy industries, and other suburban cities were expanding as manufacturing centers.[9] The Rock Island arsenal, enlarged in 1917, and a new

[9] Donald C. Ridgley, *The Geography of Illinois,* pp. 224-225. John M. Glenn, "The

ordnance proving ground established up the Mississippi River at Savanna provided war work for 15,400.

Short of labor despite the rapid increase in population, factory managers at East St. Louis encouraged some ten thousand Negroes to migrate from the South. By moving into already overcrowded slums and taking jobs at lower wages than whites, they aggravated racial tensions, resulting in frequent clashes. The same situation existed at Chicago and some other cities with direct rail lines to the South, but conditions at East St. Louis were so bad that Lowden at the request of local officials sent in troops for several weeks.[10] After they left, a group of whites shot at Negro homes, blacks retaliated by killing two white policemen, and in the next twenty-four hours at least thirty-nine Negroes and nine whites died in fighting while 250 buildings and forty loaded freight cars were burned. As some Negroes fled across the bridges, Lowden sent in poorly trained militiamen who did little to stop a battle which the whites seemed to be winning. Lowden and the adjutant general the next day instituted a policy of impartial law and order. Attorney General Edward J. Brundage participated in a grand jury inquiry that resulted in the indictment of 144 men, including five policemen, for crimes ranging from riot to murder and arson, but no convictions were obtained. The grand jury blamed agitators of both races and politicians who allowed slums to be overcrowded.

The Negro population of Chicago more than doubled between 1910 and 1920, by which time some 109,000 were mostly crowded into an area of eight square miles on the south side. Unions rejected Negroes as members, which gave the meat packers a pool of several thousand unorganized men who would work for less than the regular wage scale. Pressure of numbers forced the blacks to edge into white neighborhoods, and the end of the war did not terminate the friction that resulted in the bombing of Negro homes and trouble at recreational areas. In the summer of 1919 a Negro boy floated into a white area on a segregated beach and was stoned to death. When police did not make any arrests, a pitched battle turned into a six-day series of street fights during which two score were killed, hundreds injured, and thousands left

Industrial Development of Illinois," *Transactions of the Illinois State Historical Society*, XXVIII (1921), 55-72.

[10] Elliott M. Rudwick, *Race Riot at East St. Louis, July 2, 1917. Report of the National Advisory Commission on Civil Disorders*, Otto Kerner, chairman, pp. 217-218. Hutchinson, *op. cit.*, I, 337-342.

homeless as a result of fires. The week of violence, which coincided with a streetcar strike, ended when Mayor Thompson finally asked Lowden to send in troops.[11]

The Socialist party opposed the war, and Lowden, anxious to challenge any latent Copperheadism, led the applause when a federal drive resulted in revocation of second-class mailing privileges for its newspaper. A Washington effort to suppress criticism of the war resulted in the conviction of Socialist leaders after supposedly seditious literature had been seized in their Chicago headquarters. On a blanket indictment that they hampered the war effort, 166 members of the Industrial Workers of the World, a labor group with headquarters in Chicago but few members in Illinois, were sentenced to twenty years in prison and given heavy fines.[12] In the Socialist and I.W.W. cases, protests were made that the prosecution had ignored constitutional safeguards. Despite the blanket imputations of disloyalty, a Socialist-backed alderman was reelected in Chicago and in the off-year judicial election a Socialist ticket polled approximately one-third of the vote against a Republican-Democratic coalition of sitting judges.

Pacifist groups held meetings at which Congressman Mason and others braved public displeasure by defending freedom of speech and press. The climax came September 1, 1917, when Thompson helped arrange for the People's Council of America, which had been unable to hire a hall in Minneapolis, to meet in an auditorium on the west side. Troops sent from Springfield by Lowden in an effort to stop the meeting arrived after Mason and others had hurriedly finished their speeches. Mason's persistence in questioning national policy had brought suggestions that he be investigated, but he kept on winning statewide election to Congress until his death in 1921.

Prowar hysteria reached a peak in the lynching of Robert P. Prager of Collinsville, a German-born Socialist who had volunteered for the navy but been turned down for physical shortcomings. Other coal miners suspected that he was disloyal and possibly a spy. Lowden and others demanded that the guilty

---

11 *Ibid.*, II, 404-406. William M. Tittle, Jr., *Chicago in the Red Summer of 1919.* Kerner commission, *op. cit.*, p. 219. Lloyd Lewis and Henry Justin Smith, *Chicago: The History of Its Reputation,* pp. 388-395.

12 Edgar Bernhard, *et al., Pursuit of Freedom, A History of Civil Liberty in Illinois, 1787-1942,* pp. 26-27, 46, 86-91. Melvyn Dubofsky, *We Shall Be All: A History of the Industrial Workers of the World.*

parties be punished, but the trial of eleven men ended with a not guilty verdict.[13]

In the closing months of the war, Thompson sought the Republican nomination for senator with hope that he would be backed by the German population and assorted pacifists and liberals. Denounced by Chicago newspapers, he was badly beaten by Medill McCormick, who in an election six days before the Armistice retired Senator James Hamilton Lewis from public life.

The Illinois troops came home on scattered transports, and Lowden met many at debarkation ports with briefly fervent speeches telling of the state's pride in the men who had been at Belleau Woods, Chateau Thierry, St. Mihiel, and the Argonne. The legislature asked that farm laborers get early discharges. As in all wars, the returning veteran found it difficult to settle down. Many went to St. Louis for the first convention of the American Legion, which had been organized in Paris and which for thirty years would have an active voice in public councils without the one-sided political devotion of the Grand Army of the Republic.

At the 1922 election, a soldiers' bonus bond issue received a large majority. The payments, on a length of service formula, averaged $206.

FRANK O. LOWDEN'S ADMINISTRATIVE CODE

In the first two months after he became governor in 1917, Frank O. Lowden attained national recognition as a miracle man among public administrators by shoving through the legislature a long-needed reorganization of state government.[14] Political scientists praised Lowden, and other states borrowed his blueprints for economy and centralized control.

Especially at the state level, Illinois government for decades had been notorious for its administrative disorganization. More than one hundred officers, boards, agencies, commissions, institutions, and departments had responsibility for administering the laws. The governor could appoint to and remove from office, but in the jumbled lines of authority he found it difficult to keep in touch with subordinates, let alone guide and control their actions.

[13] Donald R. Hickey, "The Prager Affair: A Study in Wartime Hysteria," *Journal of the Illinois State Historical Society,* LXII (Summer, 1969), 117-134.

[14] Hutchinson, *op. cit.,* I, 265-326. *Illinois Blue Book, 1917-18,* pp. 57-62.

The illogical system, which had its roots in the preceding century's fear that a governor could have too much power, had developed haphazardly as legislatures sought to solve the problems of growth by creating new governmental agencies. Some of them had deliberately been kept small so that too much authority would not be concentrated in one place. Others received independent status for patronage reasons or because the sponsors of a new movement wanted it to have the prestige of standing alone or the advantage of being in friendly hands. The multiplicity of administrators, Lowden said in his inaugural message, was bewildering and confusing. Pointing to the fields of education, welfare, agriculture, labor, mining, and health, he noted that in each authority was divided among several boards and commissions, with no means of coordination. The finance administration he called "chaotic, illogical and confused." Occasionally progress had been made, as with the 1909 law creating a central board of administration for charitable institutions, but as the years passed the situation generally became more complicated.

Reform had been recommended by Deneen in his farewell message and actively pursued by Dunne, who in his 1913 inaugural called for creation of a bipartisan legislative commission on efficiency and economy. He also was responsible for the creation of a legislative reference bureau with power to prepare the state's first biennial budget. After a long series of hearings and a year of intensive study supervised by Professor John A. Fairlie of the University of Illinois, the efficiency and economy committee recommended the abolition of more than one hundred independent agencies and the reassignment of their functions to ten administrative departments. Four would be administered by single executives appointed by the governor, the law department would remain under the elective attorney general, and the other five would be headed by commissions. Dunne battled for the reform at the 1915 session, but achieved only the passage of secondary laws creating a new office of state superintendent of printing and requiring a uniform system of state reports. Inertia, political jealousies, the protection of vested interests, and fear of change made it impossible to do more.

Before taking office, Lowden made fundamental decisions. He would push for reorganization where the need was greatest, in those agencies under the governor's theoretical jurisdiction, and not complicate the issue by trying to change the duties and reduce the power of the secretary of state and other elected officials. He would disregard, at least for a time, some of the obviously worthwhile but not primary recommendations of the Dunne commission. He wanted a constitutional convention, but would give it second priority. He would present consolidation as a single omnibus bill and it would be the first business of his new administration, taking precedence over the distribution of patronage.

As a result of changes made in the Fairlie blueprints, Lowden's civil administrative code called for nine departments—finance, agriculture, labor, mines and minerals, public works and buildings, public welfare, public health, trade and commerce, and registration and education. Each was headed by a director who served on the governor's cabinet and provided a direct line of responsibility through bureau chiefs and section heads. The civil service commission retained independent status, but others such as the commerce commission, which regulated railroads and utilities, were attached to departments for budgetary control. The governor insisted that an executive budget be prepared by an expert after all agencies followed uniform accounting procedures. In several cases where commissions had been recommended, Lowden gave authority to one man. The University of Illinois still stood alone with its elected trustees, but the Normal schools fitted into the blueprint as part of the registration and education department.

Dunne in a combined biography and history of the state said that such a revolutionary change could be achieved only by a new governor at the start of his administration.[15] Lowden realized it fully. He vigorously solicited bipartisan support for his code, which quickly cleared the two legislative houses with only two negative votes. Only after final passage on March 1 did the governor give attention to Republicans who scrambled for the reduced number of positions available for distribution as patronage. Several of Lowden's directors came from outside political ranks, and the biggest surprise was the appointment of Charles H. Thorne, former president of Montgomery Ward and Company, as director of public welfare at seven thousand dollars a year.

Meanwhile, a 1917 law and a referendum the next year put more than five hundred private banks under the jurisdiction of the state auditor, a reform that had been agitated for twenty years. Private banking had flourished in Illinois more than any other

15 Edward F. Dunne, *Illinois, The Heart of the Nation,* II, 338.

William Hale Thompson

state and, due in large part to lack of regulation, a sizable number had failed with heavy losses to depositors.

The Lowden reorganization continued in 1919 with creation of a state tax commission attached to the finance department. It took over the work of a state board of equalization—one man elected from each congressional district—which since 1868 had met briefly once a year and supposedly adjusted assessments so that taxation would be uniform. The old board, especially under its last chairman, William H. Malone of Park Ridge, had been accused of being political. When he learned that Lowden was abolishing his job, Malone raised valuations on the Pullman Company and some utilities.

The Lowden system has worked well in Illinois, although the

next governor showed that streamlining did not prevent the political use of governmental machinery. In the following half-century, the blueprints were revised frequently to abolish some departments and add others, with the result that the number has been doubled, but the basic plan for centralized authority is still in effect in Illinois.

BY CHOICE, A ONE-TERM GOVERNOR

Unique among Illinois governors, Lowden decided before his inauguration that he would serve only one term. Development of an extensive farming operation in Arkansas had become a major interest, and the newly elected governor, who had served two terms in Congress, professed to have no desire to return to Washington or to prolong his stay in Springfield.

Lowden had sought to reunite his party after the 1912 split, and when he entered the 1916 gubernatorial primary most Progressives found him more acceptable than Frank L. Smith of Dwight, a downstate power, or Morton D. Hull, a Deneen Chicagoan. All three candidates were millionaires and ran on similar platforms. Lowden, who wore a broad-brimmed Panama hat and made speeches from the rear platform of a private Pullman car, received most of his vote from downstate. His big handicap was the charge, made by Smith, that he was bossed by William Hale Thompson. In the fall campaign the Democratic split between Dunne and Sullivan had not healed, and both Lowden and Charles Evans Hughes carried Illinois.[16]

The new governor wasted no time in breaking with Thompson and Fred Lundin, who had replaced Lorimer as the city hall's kingmaker, wheeler-dealer, and political strategist. Thompson, a rich man's son who had never gone to college but was captain and star tackle of the Chicago Athletic Club's football team, in 1915 settled a streetcar strike and demonstrated a readiness to act in emergencies.[17] James A. Pugh, who had been financial angel of the campaign, wanted Thompson to consolidate streetcar lines and build subways, but Lundin, who knew how to cater to the mayor's

[16] Hutchinson, *op. cit.*, I, 274-291.

[17] John Bright, *Big Bill Thompson.* Lloyd Wendt and Herman Kogan, *Big Bill of Chicago.* William H. Stuart's *The Twenty Incredible Years* is mostly the story of Thompson's three terms as mayor, written by an insider seeking to put "Big Bill" in the most favorable light.

ego, believed a Lorimer-style patronage machine should have first priority and soon shoved Pugh out of the inner circle.

Lundin, a self-effacing political genius, referred to himself as the "poor Swede" or "insignificant me" and avoided the limelight while wearing a flowing Windsor tie, a frock coat, oversized horn-rimmed glasses, and diamond studs. That costume the Swedish immigrant had worn since he peddled Juniper Ade, a temperance drink, from a rickety wagon on the northwest side of Chicago. An early disciple of Lorimer, Lundin was regarded as something of a radical because he believed in such causes as old-age insurance. While turning the city hall into a political machine, he planned to control the state by backing Lowden for governor and Len Small of Kankakee for a second term as state treasurer. That dream went on the sidetrack when Lowden refused to let Lundin handle his patronage.[18]

For the first time since Grant, Illinois in 1920 had a contender for the presidency who received serious consideration at his party's national convention. Lowden watched the situation for several months before entering fights for delegates in several primaries. For a campaign manager he selected Louis L. Emmerson, a Mount Vernon banker and future governor who claimed no knowledge of national political complexities and no acquaintance with Republicans from other states. The primaries brought a series of disappointments as the Illinois candidate failed to forge ahead of General Leonard Wood and Senator Hiram Johnson of California.[19]

Lundin and Thompson had their revenge by denying Lowden the solid support of his home state. In the Illinois primary, Wood carried Chicago and the mayor attempted to stampede the state convention by moving adoption of a platform drafted by Lundin. It hit a popular note by opposing entrance into the League of Nations under any circumstances. It also blamed the war on munitions makers and proposed that excess profits be conscripted. Lowden denounced the proposal and said he would never make a political trade with the mayor.

Emmerson's lack of capacity became a coast-to-coast sensation just before the national convention met in Chicago. Johnson and Democratic newspapers had complained of heavy spending in

[18] Carroll H. Wooddy, *The Case of Frank L. Smith*, pp. 166-183.

[19] Hutchinson, *op. cit.*, II, 408-483.

behalf of Wood, and Lowden authorized his manager to supply any records requested by a special senate subcommittee. Wood had spent four times Lowden's $415,000, of which all but about thirty-five thousand dollars had been paid by the governor and Mrs. Lowden. The subcommittee, which did not include any Lowden supporters, took voluminous testimony about $2,500 checks given to two St. Louis court officials before they were named delegates. Emmerson was vague and under unfriendly interrogation left the impression that he was either naive or dishonest. Unfriendly editors and the Thompson forces spread the impression that all Lowden delegates had been bought and paid for.

The convention balloted for two days with Lowden and Wood running neck and neck but far short of a majority. The governor, who remembered 1904 and wished to avoid a deadlock, released his delegates. Then the Old Guard, operating from a room in the Blackstone Hotel, launched the drive that put Warren G. Harding in the White House. Lowden was the second choice of the Ohio delegation but never received its votes. Had Harding withdrawn from contention and had Thompson's seventeen delegates gone for the Illinois candidate, Lowden might have been the nominee in a landslide year.

WOMEN VOTE IN A DRY STATE

Prohibition came to Illinois before women's suffrage. The sequence might have been reversed had not some of the new stock residents feared that women, if they had the chance, would vote for local option at a time when public opinion was closely divided on the old question of whether intoxicants should be outlawed.

The agitation over legalized drinking had a similarity to Know-Nothingism before the Civil War. Nativists disapproved the new culture, languages, and customs of the immigrants and feared that the Illinois they had known would be drastically changed for the worse if eastern and southern Europeans outnumbered the original Anglo-Saxons. The prohibition issue cut across sectional, political, and religious lines, but under the general rule Chicagoans were inclined to be wet while downstaters had a larger proportion of drys. Republicans were dry, with many exceptions, and the heavy support for temperance came from the evangelical Protestant denominations. In an issue that was closely allied, Chicagoans were apt to be more tolerant about giving women access to the ballot box.

When the 1907 legislature met, the Rev. Clay F. Gaumer, who had been elected to the house as a Prohibitionist from the Danville district, made a major effort in behalf of a constitutional amendment for statewide prohibition. He failed, but the wets were forced to accept a bill for local option on a township basis, under which a majority vote could close all saloons in an area. The result was a series of battles in which the temperance forces succeeded in drying up large sections of downstate and outlying parts of Cook County. Enforcement generally was left to the local community, and in many cases it was nonenforcement.[20]

After Mayor Dunne in 1906 came under heavy criticism for failing to enforce a state law requiring that saloons close at 1 a.m., the opponents of prohibition formed their own pressure group, the United Societies for Local Self-Government. It mobilized Germans, Bohemians, Italians, Poles, Belgians, French, and Hungarians, as well as the bulk of the city's politicians, under a personal liberty banner. Anton J. Cermak, who was a Democratic ward committeeman and state representative, became its secretary and dominant force.[21] Cermak turned out more than forty thousand paraders to protest when Mayor Thompson early in his first term announced he would enforce a Sunday closing law. After several argumentative months, the mayor switched positions and allowed Chicago to revert to its wide-open tradition, but under the strict control of the city hall. In the legislature the drys failed to set up local option on a county basis.

The uncompromising Anti-Saloon League, headed in Illinois by F. Scott McBride of Chicago, used economic as well as moral arguments against the liquor traffic, and with the advent of war added appeals to patriotism. Not only were sober employees essential to maximum efficiency, the drys contended, but grains needed for foodstuffs should not be diverted to distilleries and breweries. Downstate Republicans furnished most of the votes in 1917 when statewide prohibition passed the house of representatives, only to die in the senate. As a wartime measure, Congress a few months later banned the manufacture of whiskey and reduced

20 John D. Buenker, "The Illinois Legislature and Prohibition, 1907-1919," Journal of the Illinois State Historical Society, LXII (Winter, 1969), 363-384. Alex Gottfried, Boss Cermak of Chicago, pp. 53-56, 82-85.
21 Harold F. Gosnell, Machine Politics: Chicago Model, pp. 144-147.

the alcoholic content of beer to 2.75 percent by weight. Cermak forces mobilized when McBride circulated petitions for a referendum on whether Chicago should become dry territory. The vote, delayed until 1919, was a resounding negative, but by that time the issue had been settled.[22]

In the opening weeks of January, 1919, the state legislatures joined in a stampede to ratify the Eighteenth Amendment prohibiting the manufacture, sale, or transportation of intoxicating liquors for beverage purposes. At Springfield, the senate acted January 8 and the house concurred January 14. Ratification was proclaimed at Washington January 29 and, under terms of the amendment, one year from that date the liquor trade became illegal. An Illinois law, effective July 1, 1919, outlawed the liquor trade in dry territory and outside the corporate limits of municipalities. For enforcement, the attorney general received a fifty-thousand-dollar appropriation.

Dwight, which had a busy railroad station, was famous for the Keeley Institute, founded in 1890 for the treatment of alcoholism. For a weekly fee of twenty-five dollars, which included room but not board, anyone who promised to stay a minimum of four weeks received hypodermic injections of what was reputed to be a double chloride of gold. Leslie E. Keeley, a graduate of Rush Medical School who had the then unusual belief that alcoholism was a disease rather than a vice, asserted that his patients within two days lost all desire for alcohol, but his detractors claimed that relapses were frequent and medical associations objected that his methods were commercial. Keeley, who had the blessing of temperance and church workers, told of having achieved hundreds of thousands of cures. He died in 1900, but his institute flourished despite competition from sanitariums.[23]

On June 10, 1919, Illinois tied with Wisconsin and Michigan in a race to be the first state to ratify the Nineteenth Amendment for women's suffrage. For nearly three decades, women had been allowed to cast ballots for some offices at some elections.[24] In 1891, Illinois women, provided they met other qualifications,

22 Gottfried, *op. cit.*, p. 104.

23 George A. Barclay, "The Keeley League," *Journal of the Illinois State Historical Society*, LVII (Winter, 1964), 341-365.

24 Grace W. Trout, "Side Lights on Illinois Suffrage History," *Journal of the Illinois State Historical Society*, XIII (July, 1920), 145-179. *Illinois Blue Book, 1929-30*, p. 632. Bogart-Mathews, *op. cit.*, pp. 351-354. *Illinois Blue Book, 1929-30*, pp. 632-633.

received the right to vote for school board members or any school official except the state superintendent of public instruction and county superintendent of schools. Those two offices were barred on the theory that they had been created by the 1870 constitution, which made no provision for voting by women. Voting for school officials did not give women the right to cast ballots on educational propositions. Women became eligible in 1909 to hold school offices not created by law. The next extension of the right of suffrage came in 1913 and permitted women to vote for offices that could be abolished by the legislature since they did not originate in the constitution.

Mrs. Lucy Flower, a prominent social worker, became the first woman elected on a statewide basis in Illinois. She had a Republican nomination for trustee of the University of Illinois in 1894, the year a state suffragette convention talked both parties into letting women run for the office they could vote for under the 1891 law. Since then the election of women trustees had become routine and four women served on the nine-member board in 1920 when suffrage became universal.

Mrs. Earle Benjamin Searcy of Springfield, the first woman to hold a state administrative office, was elected Supreme Court clerk after she was appointed to the post in 1955 to succeed her late husband. Governor William G. Stratton set a precedent for appointing women to cabinet rank when Vera M. Binks of Cambridge, a county judge, was named director of registration and education in 1953. Governor Otto Kerner appointed Maude Myers of Springfield, who had been chairman of the civil service commission, as state director of personnel in 1961. Dawn Clark of Chicago, an attorney, was made his legal assistant.

Mrs. Winifred Mason Huck of Chicago, the first woman to run for major office, in 1922 was elected congressman-at-large to fill the unexpired term of her father, William E. Mason. In a pacifist tradition, she introduced a resolution for a universal plebiscite upon a declaration of war. Mrs. Ruth Hanna McCormick, widow of Senator Medill McCormick, in 1928 won the Republican nomination for United States senator in what turned out to be a Democratic year. Several women have had extended congressional careers.

Mrs. Lottie Holman O'Neill of Downers Grove became the first woman state legislator in 1922. First in the house and then in the senate, she set a longevity record for women by serving until 1964, except for a two-year gap when she ran for United States senator in 1930. Mrs. Florence Fifer Bohrer of Bloomington, daughter of a governor, was the first woman to enter the senate. Since then there have been from two to eight women in the legislature.

During a literary renaissance that centered on Chicago, three Illinois poets—Carl Sandburg, Vachel Lindsay, and Edgar Lee Masters—received national attention. Miss Harriet Monroe, a Chicagoan who had composed a "Columbian Ode" for the 1893 exposition, as editor of *Poetry, A Magazine of Verse* played a unique role as champion of new writers during the early part of the century. Some came from outside the state and some left for New York when they encountered success, but an unusually large number of poets and novelists spent part of their productive careers in Chicago.[25]

Born of Swedish immigrants at Galesburg in 1878, Sandburg first received recognition thirty-six years later when Miss Monroe printed "Chicago" and other vigorous free verse from his pen. Sandburg, who had an irregular education, had been a journalist and organizer in Wisconsin for the Social-Democratic party before he became a leading figure in the Chicago school of writers. He used colloquialisms in telling of the beauty of the ordinary and the commonplace, and won the first of a series of Pulitzer prizes in 1918. A ballad singer and collector, a novelist and a writer of books for children, he climaxed a long career with a monumental six-volume biography of Abraham Lincoln.

Lindsay, a year younger than Sandburg, hoped to be an artist but evolved a style of rhythmic poetry intended to be half-sung. He tramped through the country, exchanging his verse for food and lodging, before receiving major recognition in 1913 when Miss Monroe's magazine printed "General William Booth Enters Into Heaven" and other poems. A mystic and humanitarian, Lindsay was in demand as a reader of his own verse. His last years were tragic as his poetry declined in power.

Masters, a friend of Lindsay, spent his boyhood at Petersburg and Lewistown and had been a successful lawyer at Chicago for thirty years before he took up writing as an avocation. Most famous of his thirty volumes is the *Spoon River Anthology*, published in 1914-1915, which made him a leading literary figure.

[25] Dale Kramer, *Chicago Renaissance: The Literary Life of the Midwest, 1900-1930.* Bernard I. Duffey, *The Chicago Renaissance in American Letters: A Critical History.* Eleanor Ruggles, *The West Going Heart: A Life of Vachel Lindsay.*

The anthology, in the form of free-verse epitaphs revealing the secret lives of early acquaintances whose identity was not fully concealed, became the center of controversies. Masters also wrote a history of Chicago that emphasized his iconoclastic traits.

For almost two decades, Chicago was a capital of movie-making. Pioneers in a new business turned out several thousand films which were shown after 1900 in nickel theaters which sprang up in the cities. As early as 1905 Colonel William Selig shot a dramatic film, "Tracked by Bloodhounds," in Rogers Park, which then was sparsely settled. His company had indoor and outdoor studios in the city. The Essanay Film Manufacturing Company, founded by George K. Spoor and G. M. Anderson, in 1914 paid Charles Chaplin $1,250 a week to act in its Chicago studio. Ben Turpin and Wallace Beery played in slapstick shows, and Beverly Bayne made four hundred films in Chicago, many of them with Francis X. Bushman as co-star. The era ended in 1918 when Essanay closed its doors. Chaplin had left two years earlier, after producers and actors found that Hollywood had a better climate.

In the early 1920's, the Chicago loop had twenty-three legitimate theaters in which a hundred shows were given each season, but one of the biggest attractions was the International Livestock Exposition. Since 1900 it was staged yearly to demonstrate the interest the owners of the stockyards had in improving market grades of cattle, hogs, and sheep. Held in early winter, it awarded prizes for the best grain and other crops grown on the North American continent, but the major emphasis was on the selection of grand champion steers, singly and in carload lots, that were ready for slaughter. A companion attraction was the national meeting of 4-H club leaders and members. Originally organized as a means of stirring up the vocational interests of rural youngsters, the 4-H clubs later started an expansion into inner-city areas.

24

THE PROHIBITION ERA

MUCH OF THE PROGRESS MADE DURING THE DENEEN, DUNNE, and Lowden administrations proved ephemeral. William Hale Thompson, yachtman, former cowboy, and political showman with a pied piper manner of leading unusual coalitions to the ballot box, may or may not have been the worst-intentioned mayor in Chicago's experience, but he was the most flamboyant. His second term coincided with the arrival of prohibition, which gave entrepreneurs in brothels and gambling the opportunity to get richer through the purveying of illegal booze. Chicago, which retained the wide-open traditions of its comparatively recent frontier beginning, could not have been expected to adhere to the dictates of the national prohibition amendment. Looking backward from the end of the 1920's, Charles E. Merriam commented that almost no known dry had been elected mayor of Chicago or state's attorney of Cook County, while the issue in many campaigns was which candidate was the wettest.[1]

Thompson and Fred Lundin erected their power base on the foundations of campaign buffoonery and a policy of noninterference with the illegal activities of gangsters. Four years earlier Lowden had refused to cooperate, but in 1921 Thompson and Lundin conspired with Governor Len Small in hope that they

[1] Charles E. Merriam, *Chicago, A More Intimate View of Urban Politics*, p. 60.

459

could merge Chicago and state political machines into an unbeatable Tammany.

Lowden's reorganization of the state administrative machinery could well have been extended to the metropolitan area, where a maze of big and little municipalities and other taxing districts provided payroll jobs for some eighty-five thousand persons and leadership posts for possibly 7,700. In Cook County the jumbled table of governmental organization had eight major agencies—the city of Chicago and its board of education, library board, and sanitary district, the county itself, and the Lincoln, West, and South Park districts, all with independent taxing powers.[2] With ability and some luck, a man might build a strong political organization within that complex. Even a chronic loser might keep a toehold while he hoped for better luck at the next election.

CAPONE & COMPANY VERSUS THE LAW

Scattered around Chicago were underworld gangs whose leaders often had more difficulty with rival criminals than they did with law enforcement officials. Most of the prohibition-era hoodlums were bright enough to know that illegal profits and prestige could be shared handsomely if they would abide by territorial treaties. Frequently alliances were formed and pledges made that the proceeds would be divided peacefully, but seemingly the gangsters could no more abide by their own contracts than they could comply with the federal Constitution and state statutes. As a result, the years of prohibition were tumultuous and gory. Their history is a repetitious recital of ambushes and murders, of one-way rides ending on lonely suburban roads, and of garish displays of flowers at funerals attended by judges and aldermen. Chicago earned a notorious reputation, but the thirsty public wanted alcoholic beverages, and in any event there was a certain amount of good-riddance in gangsters killing each other. The dominant name was Alphonse Capone, alias Scarface Al, who in a perversion of the American dream became one of the most successful as well as infamous men to wield power in Illinois.[3]

[2] Alex Gottfried, *Boss Cermak of Chicago*, p. 359. See also Charles E. Merriam, *et al.,* *The Government of the Metropolitan Region of Chicago.*

[3] John Kobler, *Capone: The Life and World of Al Capone.* Fred B. Paisley, *Al Capone: The Biography of a Self-Made Man.*

Shortly before the 1928 election, Frank J. Loesch, a respected spokesman for the city's better element, made a formal trip to Capone's Lexington Hotel headquarters to make an unusual request.[4] President of the Chicago Crime Commission, a member of the National Commission on Law Observance and Enforcement, and counsel for the Pennsylvania Railroad, he asked that the people of Chicago be allowed to elect their own officials without gangster interference. "Will you help us by keeping your damned cutthroats and hoodlums from interfering with the polling booths?"

Capone, who sat at a mahogany desk flanked by portraits of Washington, Lincoln, and Thompson, agreed and kept his word. Seventy police cars rounded up the potential troublemakers. Since prohibition there hadn't been an election in which the good government forces had been so temporarily successful.

Capone was the third man who headed what Chicagoans called the syndicate, an underworld organization with Mafia connections that attained great wealth by illegal means and in civic affairs exerted profound influence for the worst. The business end of the alliance between crime and politics, which dated back to the 1875 era, had earlier come under the control of Big Jim Colosimo. A glad-hander, he organized street sweepers into a social and athletic club, delivered their votes to the Kenna-Coughlin First Ward organization, and in time operated from a well-patronized restaurant in the heart of an empire of gambling halls and red-light houses. Prohibition brought new opportunities for illicit wealth, and that caused competition. Like many later gangsters, Colosimo became the victim of an unsolved assassination and the recipient of a lavish funeral. That happened in 1920, and permitted Johnny Torrio to take over.[5]

The gangsters in self-justification explained that they were only practicing free enterprise when they provided thirsty customers with highly prized beverages. The public's disregard for the law against liquor did nothing to generate a respect for other statutes, with the result that civic morality declined noticeably during the years "Big Bill" Thompson sat in the mayor's office. Torrio, who was a deceptively mild-appearing man, and Capone, who wasn't, had been imported from New York as hired guns, and together

[4] Fletcher Dobyns, *The Underworld of American Politics*, pp. 1-4.
[5] Jack McPhaul, *Johnny Torrio, First of the Ganglords.*

they did much to put the illicit liquor trade on a profitable basis. In Chicago and some of the suburbs they did a conglomerate business in booze, prostitution, gambling, labor racketeering, and shakedowns in which they sold protection from themselves to

Courtesy Illinois State Historical Library

Al Capone

businessmen. Chicago's thirst each week required thousands of barrels of beer, which possibly cost five dollars each and could be retailed at fifty-five dollars. The number of speakeasies—retail outlets which had no advertising expense and scrutinized customers through a one-way mirror before admitting them—was estimated at twelve thousand in 1922 and at twenty thousand in 1926. There were expenses for Torrio and Capone, including bribes to some policemen, bailiffs, court clerks, and prohibition agents, to say nothing of big payments to the higher-ups. Federal investigators estimated that in 1927 the syndicate had a gross revenue of 110 million dollars, of which sixty million dollars came from beer, whiskey, and alcohol cooking; twenty-five million dollars from gambling and dog tracks; fifteen million dollars from labor racketeering, and ten million dollars from vice.

Minor violence escalated and by 1924, a year in which there were fifty gang murders, a penchant for mutual extermination brought the rival gangs to the verge of open warfare. That year Torrio with Capone's help took over the suburb of Cicero by brute force after helping reelect the local officials. About that time Torrio went to the hospital as a gunshot case. He recovered and returned to New York and comparative oblivion. Some authorities on the prohibition era contend that Torrio operated from a distance as the syndicate's absentee brains while Capone stayed on as the front man.

Connivance and official laxity became notorious. Four days before he was to be hanged for a policeman's murder, Thomas (Terrible Tommy) O'Connor escaped from the Cook County jail without leaving a trace. Investigators discovered that special foods, guns, moonshine liquor, and dope had been delivered to inmates. The solution was to appoint a new warden, who within four years was himself serving a federal sentence for allowing two beer barons, while under confinement for contempt, to go home to their wives or to Wisconsin resorts. For those privileges jail officials had been paid two thousand dollars a month.

Gang assassinations, many of them one-way rides, became routine and the public had consolation only in that most of the victims came from the undesirable element. The factional gunfire gradually weakened the enemies of Capone, but there never seemed to be a shortage of men who were willing to take a chance on getting a slice of the illegal profits even if it could mean assassination preceded by torture. Perhaps the most spectacular was the setback received by the Bugs Moran gang, old enemies of Capone, on St. Valentine's Day, 1929. Machine gunners disguised as policemen mowed down six Moran hoodlums and a visitor in a garage on North Clark Street. As usual, officials never established either the motive or the identity of the killers.

Lawlessness was not confined to Chicago, and in much of downstate bootleggers cautiously supplied customers with some form of alcohol, which could be locally produced or imported by truck or car. Any connections with the big city syndicate were camouflaged, and the usual pattern was for the bootlegger and his supplier to take their own risks.

Williamson County, which had a long history of violence, disregarded the law in a different manner. There the Ku Klux Klan took over enforcement of the law in an effort to suppress liquor sales and gambling operations by persons with Italian names. The secret Klan, which was Protestant and against foreigners and Catholics, made its debut in the county in 1923 by visiting a revival service to commend the evangelist.[6]

The Klan imported S. Glenn Young, who had lost an underpaid job as a federal dry agent because of a craving for publicity and a willingness to fight with fists or guns at any excuse. Young recruited Klansmen, had them deputized by a prohibition agent, and staged several raids on the authority of federal court and justice of the peace warrants. Thirteen tumultuous months later, Young, two of his guards, and a deputy sheriff were shot to death in a western-style gunfight in a cigar store at Herrin. During the interval, National Guardsmen tried to keep order while the Klansmen shot up a hospital and carried revolvers and machine guns into courtrooms. The Klan finally expelled Young from membership and paid him one thousand dollars, raised by passing the hat, in an effort to get him to stay out of the county. The last guardsman didn't leave until the summer of 1926, by which time twenty persons had been killed and Young's wife blinded by gunfire. Roadhouses were closed, but bootleggers, some of whom had been fined and sentenced to jail by a federal judge, were still selling alcohol. In other downstate areas, the Klan pushed the cause of bigotry and intolerance, but nowhere else in Illinois did it achieve the influence and notoriety it attained at Herrin.

Herrin's long history of violence had reached an earlier climax with the massacre June 22, 1922, of nineteen strikebreakers, part of a contingent of fifty men brought from Chicago in an effort to operate a mine against the wishes of the United Mine Workers. Local men brought to trial on murder charges were quickly acquitted by Williamson County juries.[7]

6 Paul M. Angle, *Bloody Williamson*, pp. 134-204. Edgar Bernhard, *et al., Pursuit of Freedom*, pp. 135-139.

7 Angle, *op. cit.*, pp. 3-71.

In Williamson and Franklin counties the suppression of the Klan was followed by a gang war in which Charlie Birger, who had been fined and jailed as a result of one of the Young raids, was opposed by three Shelton brothers—Carl, Earl, and Bernie.[8] The action included fourteen murders, with two mayors and a state highway policeman among the victims. Birger was hanged in 1928, shortly before Illinois substituted the electric chair for the gallows. Law and order finally prevailed and State's Attorney Arlie O. Boswell of Williamson County, a Birger ally, was sentenced to two years in jail for conspiracy to violate the national prohibition act. By 1947 the Sheltons were operating through much of downstate, and the next year Bernie Shelton was killed in front of a saloon he owned in Peoria.

LEN SMALL AND BILL THOMPSON

In 1920, the first year women were allowed to vote for all offices, Len Small (no one ever used his full name of Lennington) owed his election to the Harding landslide and the masterminding of Thompson's man Fred Lundin. A physician's son from Kankakee, Small had been in politics since 1894. He almost lost the nomination to John G. Oglesby, who was Lowden's lieutenant governor and a son of the Civil War general. In the November campaign Small fitted into the Harding normalcy theme and kept in tune with Thompson by denouncing the League of Nations.[9] Once in office he acted as the mayor's downstate partner and converted Lowden's centralized code departments into a political machine. Republican opponents of Small and Thompson had been weakened by a perennial rift between the forces of former Governor Deneen and Edward J. Brundage, the new attorney general.

Like Thompson, the governor sought support by emphasis on public works. Small twice set national records for paving highways, but his administration also is remembered because the governor was the defendant in criminal and civil suits at the end of which he was forced to pay $650,000 into the state treasury. That situation grew out of a factional quarrel with Brundage. Small started his administration by vetoing part of an appropriations bill for the attorney general's office and by refusing to sign an Anti-

8 *Ibid.,* pp. 206-266.
9 C. H. Wooddy, *The Case of Frank L. Smith,* pp. 151-166.

Saloon League bill to appropriate $150,000 for prohibition enforcement on the ground that Brundage would use the money to harass the governor's friends in Chicago.

Brundage retaliated, and the Sangamon County grand jury in the summer of 1921 indicted Small and Lieutenant Governor Fred E. Sterling of Rockford on charges of embezzling state funds and conspiring to defraud the state. Small had first been elected treasurer in 1904, but Brundage's case involved only interest on state funds during his second term in 1917-18 and Sterling's 1919-20 term as treasurer. It revolved around the Grant Park Bank, a long-dormant private bank in the Kankakee County village of Grant Park, which had been reactivated in 1917 by State Senator Edward C. Curtis and a brother, who were close friends of the governor. State funds deposited there were loaned to Chicago packers at standard commercial interest rates as high as 6 percent, and the bank paid the state interest at the regular call-money rate of 2 or 3 percent. Brundage disputed the legality of depositing state funds in a private bank and contended that the interest rate differential had been an illegal profit. The governor argued that he had followed both custom and a 1908 law. A change of venue was taken to Lake County, and Small, who was the only defendant to go on trial, was acquitted on the second ballot June 24, 1922.[10]

The governor's critics were dissatisfied with the verdict, but administration men called it persecution when Brundage filed a civil suit to recover the balance of the interest money. The Sangamon County Circuit Court ruled that the governor was liable, the Supreme Court agreed in a split decision, and a master-in-chancery fixed $1,025,434 as the amount due the state. By that time Brundage had been succeeded by Oscar G. Carlstrom of Aledo, who at the moment was on friendly terms with the governor. A compromise was reached and Small on June 15, 1927, settled the account by turning over to the court a check for $650,000. The court record included a stipulation that Small as treasurer had not received any interest money that had not been accounted for and paid into the treasury. Small in a statement

[10] *Ibid.*, pp. 159-162. William H. Stuart, *The Twenty Incredible Years*, pp. 246-247. Neil Garvey, *The Government and Administration of Illinois*, pp. 112-113, 133. Edward F. Dunne, *Illinois, The Heart of the Nation*, II, 406-408. William T. Hutchinson, *Lowden of Illinois*, II, 530. E. L. Bogart and J. M. Mathews, *The Modern Commonwealth*, pp. 242-243. Illinois Supreme Court Reports, *319 Ill. 437-595. Chicago Daily News Almanac*, 1923, p. 732, and 1928, p. 822.

reported that, all told, he had paid 1.1 million dollars interest money to the state, which approximated 5 percent, compared with the usual rate of 3 percent received on public money. The 1.1 million dollars, he added, was more than had been paid by all preceding treasurers during ninety-nine years of statehood.

Fortunately for Small, he could raise the $650,000 and additional sums for campaign nest eggs by taking it from state employees, who were assessed as much as 80 percent of one month's paycheck, and from contractors and suppliers doing business with the state. Before the day of the hundred-dollar-a-plate fund-raising dinner for Republican candidates and the involuntary dues check-off by union members in behalf of Democrats, payroll assessments were an accepted means of political financing, but the public regarded as excessive the amassing of as much as one million dollars for expenditure in a political campaign.

During most of the 1920's, residents of Illinois enjoyed a prosperity that provided a standard of living far in advance of that in any other country, while real wages, the measure of what could be bought with a day's pay, increased until they were the highest in American history. The average man could afford an automobile, think of moving to his own home in the suburbs, and buy his wife overstuffed furniture, an electric refrigerator, and a vacuum cleaner. Farmers were an exception, since their income had not held even with industrial prices in the postwar era. The prosperity and conservatism were good for Republicans, who had no difficulty carrying Illinois in three presidential elections starting with 1920. On a platform of extreme conservatism, Charles Gates Dawes became the second Vice President from Illinois in 1924. Dawes, who had a colorful vocabulary, smoked an underslung pipe, and wore sharp-pointed wing collars, was board chairman of a Chicago bank. He had been a World War I general, chief purchasing agent of the American Expeditionary Force, and director of the federal bureau of the budget. He also received the Nobel Peace Prize for the "Dawes Plan," which reorganized German reparations payments.

Times were bad for union organizers, since workmen shared in the general prosperity and were satisfied with company unions and other benefits provided by employers. At the end of the war John Fitzpatrick, who had started as a horseshoer and became president of the Chicago Federation of Labor, and William Z. Foster, whose career began in the Industrial Workers of the World movement, urged that labor go forward by organizing the steel plants.[11] The American Federation of Labor gave its approval and Foster, who in later years became a communist spokesman, headed a strike which ended in failure, as did an attempt to sign up workers in meat-packing plants. John L. Lewis as national president of the United Mine Workers had urged the steel-organizing drive. When his own men walked out they obtained a wage increase.

Dismal failure also marked a postwar effort by labor leaders to become an independent political force, in emulation of the British Labor party. Labor had been treated with unexpected fairness during the Lowden administration, but President John H. Walker of the state federation and Fitzpatrick were dissatisfied with the AFL policy of political nonpartisanship.[12] They participated in a series of conferences and at Chicago in 1919 helped adopt a platform based on the fundamental thesis that workers and farmers should have controlling power over the economic and political system, with nationalization of public utilities, basic industries, and banks. Parley Parker Christensen of Utah was nominated for President, and the organization adopted the name of Farmer-Labor party in a futile effort to get cooperation from the Nonpartisan League, which had achieved major party success in the Northwest. At the 1920 election Walker as the nominee for governor and Fitzpatrick for senator received only scattered support and polled fewer votes than the Socialist ticket. That took the heart out of the movement. Walker and Fitzpatrick blocked an effort of Foster's left-wing group to capture control of the state and Chicago federations, and in the following years Illinois labor followed the traditional conservatism of the AFL.

Industry countered with an open-shop drive aimed at the building trades unions in Chicago. In a construction boom that followed the war, the affiliates of the Building Trades Council aggressively sought higher pay but were vulnerable to public opinion because of high rents that went with a housing shortage. Building operations were virtually at a standstill in the spring of 1921 when the unions refused to accept a wage reduction and contractors

[11] Eugene Staley, *History of the Illinois State Federation of Labor*, pp. 361-390. Mary Watters, *Illinois in the Second World War*, II, 200-204. George Soule, *Prosperity Decade, From War to Depression*, pp. 200-202, 217. Stuart, *op. cit.*, pp. 145-146. Lloyd Lewis and Henry J. Smith, *Chicago: The History of Its Reputation*, pp. 406-409.

[12] John H. Keiser, "John H. Walker: Labor Leader from Illinois," *Essays in Illinois History* (Donald F. Tingley, ed.), pp. 75-87.

instituted a lockout. Kenesaw Mountain Landis, a colorful federal judge, was chosen to arbitrate the dispute. Landis presumably did not have a big-business bias, since in 1907 he had fined Standard Oil Company of Indiana 29.04 million dollars in a railroad rebate case later reversed by the Appellate Court. He held extended hearings and in three months announced that, except for stone carvers, wages would be reduced in all branches of the building industry.[13] For electricians and bricklayers, the hourly scales would be cut from $1.25 to $1.10, for plumbers from $1.25 to ninety-five cents, and common laborers from one dollar to seventy-two and a half cents. Carpenters, plasterers, painters, and other trade unions which had not signed the arbitration agreement also were ordered to take cuts. To complete the victory for employers, Landis also decreed arbitration of future disputes, outlawed sympathy strikes, and ordered abandonment of regulations that had the effect of increasing construction costs by dictating the use of materials. A state senate investigation charged that labor leaders had been bribed to insure completion of buildings, and the Chamber of Commerce backed members of the Contractors' Association who announced they would hire only members of unions which accepted the Landis award. Under pressure, the Building Trades Council voted to affirm the Landis decision, but some unions refused to go along and demanded a rehearing. None suffered lasting damage to their status or membership rolls, and in time the award was forgotten. The same year Landis resigned from the federal bench to become commissioner of baseball, by appointment of the major league club owners. By strict discipline, he restored public confidence in organized baseball in the wake of the "Black Sox" scandal that followed revelation that eight members of the Chicago American League champions had thrown the 1919 World Series to Cincinnati.[14]

HOW NOT TO AMEND A CONSTITUTION

The state's fifth and longest constitutional convention overlapped the Lowden and Small administrations and, in an atmo-

---

[13] Gottfried, *op. cit.*, p. 104. *Chicago Daily News Almanac,* 1922, p. 730.

[14] David Quentin Voigt, "The Chicago Black Sox and the Myth of Baseball's Single Sin," *Journal of the Illinois State Historical Society,* LXII (Autumn, 1969), 293-306.

Courtesy Illinois State Historical Library

Governor Len Small

sphere of sectionalism and partisanship, ended in failure with a 5 to 1 adverse vote at a special election December 12, 1922.

Agitation for modernization of the 1870 constitution had been building up since adoption of the Australian ballot in 1891 ended the system under which political parties furnished ballots they printed and marked in advance. Since adoption of a proposition required a majority of the total vote cast, a failure to mark one of the official ballots was in effect a negative vote. An attempt to liberalize the process by a "gateway" amendment met defeat in 1892, and Governor Altgeld struck a note which echoed through the state house for decades when he said that revenue problems and the industrialization of Illinois made it necessary to modernize the basic law. A series of other amendment proposals were defeated, although in 1904 Chicago was granted a measure of home rule with the backing of both parties, Governor Yates, and the Chicago newspapers. The basic problems remained, however.

The Lowden administration opened in a climate favorable to reorganization and reform and, at the urging of the new governor, the legislature in 1917 voted overwhelmingly for a convention. [15] The resolution it adopted avoided specifics but stated that the 1870 constitution in many respects was inadequate to meet public needs and also was difficult to amend. The war was a distraction and, in the long delay until a referendum at the 1918 election, Chief Justice Orrin H. Carter of the Supreme Court took over the chairmanship of a bipartisan committee dedicated to keeping alive interest in a cause that had been endorsed by the Chicago city council and the platforms of both parties. At the election the proposition received 57.5 percent of the vote. [16]

Progressive ideology required that the delegates—two from each senatorial district—be nominated at direct primaries, and the political result was that the Republicans had a disproportionate 85 to 17 majority when Lowden called the winners together January 6, 1920. The delegates, a majority of them lawyers, included experienced public officials and men active in civic and community affairs. Perhaps the best known were Joseph W. Fifer, who had been governor thirty years earlier, and David E. Shanahan of Chicago, speaker of the house of representatives. The Democratic minority was shut out when Republicans elected all the officers but did not object that the presidency went to Charles E. Woodward of Ottawa, a close friend of Lowden and chief draftsman of the new civil administrative code.

Sectionalism, in the form of downstate distrust of Chicago and a fear that the industrial metropolis would dominate the traditionally rural counties, soon became a divisive problem. The last reapportionment of the legislative and congressional districts in 1901 had allotted nineteen of the fifty-one senate districts to Cook County, which had continued to grow rapidly and was mathematically entitled to forty-eight of the 102 delegates but had only thirty-eight. Downstaters insisted on retaining the advan-

[15] *Illinois Blue Book, 1917-18,* pp. 63-64.

[16] Janet Cornelius, *A History of Constitution Making in Illinois,* pp. 68-92. *Illinois Blue Book, 1921-22,* pp. 216-253.

tage during long arguments that intensified the geographical cleavage. In the fifteenth month of the convention, after downstaters had repeatedly insisted upon keeping control of both legislative houses, a compromise allowed Cook County to have representation in the house in proportion to its population but limited it permanently to one-third of the senate. The same issue arose in connection with the judicial article. Of the seven Supreme Court justices, only one came from a district encompassing the big counties of Cook, Lake, Du Page, Will, and Kankakee. Downstaters agreed to let that district have three justices, which would increase the size of the court to nine, but stipulated that only two could come from Cook County. Downstate opposition also killed proposals that the constitution provide for the initiative and referendum, one of the holiest concepts among orthodox Progressives, and authority for municipalities to acquire public utilities. Cook County had provided the margin by which those proposals had been endorsed at a referendum held simultaneously with the election of delegates, but men from other districts rejected them out of fear that big city voters in the future could initiate legislation and set statewide policies alien to downstate traditions. That distrust also brought defeat of a proposal, strongly backed by Chicago leaders, that the more controversial parts of the new constitution, including the initiative and referendum, be separately submitted to the voters for adoption or rejection without jeopardizing the rest of the document.

The final draft included permission for Bible reading without comment in public schools, guaranteed civil rights for Negroes, granted increased home rule to Chicago except on revenue matters, retained a general tax by valuation on property, and authorized a state income tax in which the highest rate could not be more than three times the lowest. On a major issue it retained the provisions that made difficult the adoption of constitutional amendments.

The convention finally finished its work September 12, 1922, two years and nine months after the delegates took the oath of office, but during that time they worked only 140 days. Organization was inefficient, committees seldom functioned, summer vacations were taken because of the heat in Springfield, and the delegates, who were paid a salary of two thousand dollars, usually met only two or three days a week because most needed to spend time at their regular occupations. They took a recess of seven weeks in the autumn of 1920, and by December 8 of that year had been in existence twice as long as any other Illinois convention. The longest recess, for fourteen months, kept the convention from meeting at all during 1921 and was utilized by the committee on phraseology and style in meticulously polishing the wordage of a document that was rejected in part because the public lost interest in the convention as delays alternated with debates. During the convention five delegates died, several were elected to legislative and judicial offices, and four vacancies were filled by special elections.

Between adjournment and the final referendum, only three months were allowed for the public to study the proposed constitution, and at an early date it became apparent that ratification was improbable. Without enthusiasm, Lowden endorsed the document, as did Deneen, Senators Medill McCormick and William B. McKinley, and Attorney General Brundage. Justice Carter headed another bipartisan committee of advocates and many downstate newpapers gave support. Chiefly because the downstate majority had been unfair to Cook County, the Chicago papers which had urged the calling of the convention now asked for defeat of its product. Mayor Thompson and Governor Small threw their political influence on the side of the opposition, which aligned them with labor. Former Governor Dunne and Clarence Darrow convinced Chicago Democrats that support of the document would be a mistake, and Harold L. Ickes helped line up liberals from both parties against it. The negative vote was 921,398 to 185,298, while Cook County turned down the constitution by an amazing margin of 19 to 1.[17]

Complaints continued about the 1870 revenue and home rule restrictions, and after the 1930 census downstaters in the legislature again refused to reapportion their districts. Conservatives argued that it would be unwise to attempt constitutional revision in the unstable economic and political atmosphere of the depression, and an attempt to call a convention failed in 1934 because more than half of the voters ignored the proposition ballot.

[17] Staley, *op. cit.,* pp. 427-448. Dunne, *op. cit.,* II, 424-454. Hutchinson, *op. cit.,* I, 323-324. *Illinois Blue Book, 1923-24,* carries the text of the proposed constitution on pp. 293-314 and the convention's Address to the People, pp. 285-292.

THE EMERGENCE OF CERMAK

Fred Lundin had political brains and Mayor Thompson, along with a demagogic ability to attract the masses, had ambition. With Lundin's help, Thompson won a second term as mayor in 1919, but Democrats achieved control of the Chicago city council under a newly enacted reform law that was intended to produce better aldermen by letting them run as theoretical independents without party labels. In the new council, Anton J. Cermak assumed a Democratic leadership post and as wet spokesman for the United Societies did all he could to hamper enforcement of the dry laws. The election of supposedly independent aldermen has helped only the established political organizations since in practice it hampers their opposition. Machine candidates are usually elected at the mayoral primary, when the turnout is light and most get the required 51 percent of the vote without difficulty. Only when the high man has a smaller percentage is there a runoff at the mayoral election.[18]

Unexpected hard luck hit at the 1921 judicial election, which turned out to be a city hall disaster. The Lincoln and West Park boards were appointed by the governor, which under the Thompson-Small alliance meant they were already under Lundin's control. The South Park commission, however, was appointed by the circuit judges, and a thirty-million-dollar program for reclamation of the south shore of the lake had been prepared. To get control of that spending, the Thompson forces refused to slate several judges who were allied with other factions. George E. Brennan, who had advanced to the leadership of Cook County Democrats when Roger Sullivan died the preceding year, cannily entered a strong judicial ticket that included the Republicans dropped by their own party. Brennan's coalition carried the county by a 3 to 2 margin. State's Attorney Robert E. Crowe, a powerful figure, then broke with Thompson. In a new scandal, Lundin and thirty-five others were indicted for defrauding the school system of three million dollars. Clarence S. Darrow, who had acquired a reputation as the leading defense attorney, won an acquittal for Lundin, but

[18] Alex Gottfried's *Boss Cermak of Chicago* and Carroll H. Wooddy's *The Case of Frank L. Smith* are the most valuable works in tracing political trends during the 1920's. The best biographical sketch of Small is found in Wooddy, pp. 156-166. For third-term campaign use, Small issued *Illinois Progress, 1921-1928*, which devoted 382 pages to state activities during his two administrations.

meanwhile the city hall lost control of the election machinery when Edmund K. Jarecki, a Democrat, defeated the Republican incumbent county judge. The mayor, self-styled as "Big Bill the Builder," had implemented much of Burnham's Chicago plan by pushing the construction of large-scale public works, including wide boulevards and lakefront improvements. Contracts could be a source of graft, and the *Tribune* sued the mayor and his closest associates for 2.75 million dollars in fees allegedly overpaid to real estate experts who handled condemnation cases. As the disasters accumulated, Thompson dispiritedly stepped out of public life and let a Democrat, William E. Dever, take over the mayor's office in 1923.

Not once during the 1920's did the Democratic party elect a statewide candidate. Nevertheless steady progress was made toward building a political organization that during the next decade would be able to dominate the state. Big steps were taken in 1919, when Democratic aldermen organized the council's majority, and in 1922, when most Cook County Democrats won and a bipartisan deal enabled the shrewd and industrious Cermak to become president of the county board of commissioners. Brennan made a major advance the next year when he supported Dever, a judge with an independent background. Under Roger Sullivan the Democrats had never been able to elect a mayor, but Brennan's grand strategy permitted him to support a Democrat who did not swear allegiance to the county chairman. Their advance agreement provided that, except for top-level jobs, Brennan could parcel out Dever's patronage. Meanwhile the Democratic leader made bipartisan deals with Thompson and his allies, with the result that the more respectable Republican factions were weakened if not eliminated through a series of defeats.

Mayor Dever, who by all accounts was an honest man, took a neutral position toward prohibition but believed that all laws, including those against liquor, should be enforced. He would not accept the Harrison philosophy that noble intentions and a good cause are sufficient excuse for alliances with grafters and gamblers. Consequently, the new mayor disappointed Cermak by trying to enforce the dry laws, but had little success as gang wars intensified and the casualty lists of undesirables lengthened. During the Dever years, when the police force was less friendly, Capone shifted his base of operations from Chicago to Cicero.

Before the 1924 election, Small brought Lundin, who had

broken with Thompson, to the state house as his private strategist. Lundin's friends got state jobs, a Progressive movement headed by Senator Robert M. LaFollette of Wisconsin fizzled, and Small won reelection but ran behind President Coolidge and Deneen, who had beaten Senator Medill McCormick by an eyelash in the primary. Small's second-term nomination came with 53 percent of the vote even though the Brundage interest suits were a major liability and the governor was under attack for generosity in pardoning convicts. Another fragmentation occurred when, at the start of Small's second term, Thompson staged a big dinner at Springfield to signify that he was planning to run for mayor again. Thompson undiplomatically announced that Attorney General Carlstrom was his choice for governor in 1928. Small, who had his own third-term ambitions, thereafter bypassed Thompson and depended upon Lundin to do his political work in Chicago.[19]

The personal tragedy of Frank L. Smith, a land dealer at Dwight who really didn't want to run for United States senator, in the aftermath of the expensive 1926 primary gave national attention to Samuel Insull's campaign contributions.[20]

Smith, a blacksmith's son who started in the real estate business as a protégé of the Keeley family, had a great ambition to be governor. As a member of Governor Tanner's personal staff during the Spanish-American War, he acquired the title of colonel, which he used during a political career that included a try for nomination as lieutenant governor in 1904 as the Lorimer-Lowden choice and again in 1908, when Deneen forces successfully supported John G. Oglesby. Smith was the Taft manager in the 1912 presidential primary won by Roosevelt, he contributed three thousand dollars to help elect Mayor Thompson in 1915, and the next year he ran third in the primary in which Lowden was nominated for the governorship. In 1918 he finally won an office and served a term in Congress. Two years later he wanted to run for governor, but Lundin picked Small for that office and Smith unwillingly ran for the senate, only to lose to William B. McKinley in the primary.

As a Lundin-Small insider, Smith was Republican state chairman and was suitably rewarded with appointment to a major state position, the chairmanship of the commerce commission that

19 Stuart, *op. cit.*, p. 227.
20 Wooddy, *op. cit.*, includes excellent sketches of Lorimer, Small, Lundin, and Deneen, in addition to Smith.

regulated public utilities. In 1926, the future road to the governorship apparently was still blocked and Smith made a second attempt to beat Senator McKinley, a millionaire who had previously
served in Congress from the Champaign district. McKinley's wealth
came from a utility empire that included electric and gas companies, street railways, and an interurban network. McKinley had
been loyal to the Coolidge administration but lost by one hundred
thousand votes to Smith in a primary swept by the Thompson-
Small candidates whose chief issue was an isolationist dislike for
the World Court. Smith loyally followed the Thompson "America
First" platform and argued that the United States should not
become involved in international affairs.

Unfortunately for Smith, a senate committee had its attention
diverted to Illinois while it was investigating heavy campaign
expenditures in a Pennsylvania primary. The charge was made that
Insull in recent years had poured millions of dollars into primary
campaigns, in part because he did not want his giant utility
companies to deal with unfriendly officials. While defeated
Deneen candidates sought a recount and State's Attorney Crowe
was embarrassed by the gangland murder of an assistant, Senator
James A. Reed of Missouri, a Democrat with great talent as a
prosecutor, held extensive hearings in Chicago. Part of the information he collected about factionalism and campaign expenditures
was that Smith had received $125,000 from Insull and $33,753
from an anti-World Court fund financed by Insull. The commerce
commission chairman had received money from two other utility
executives, and into the primary Insull had poured $238,735,
including fifteen thousand dollars given to Brennan, who was the
Democratic candidate for governor. Utilities were sitting ducks for
venal politicians and Insull, who had been an early advocate of
regulation, kept the peace by contributing money and making
other concessions, such as selling junk at bargain prices to persons
with influence at the city hall. Ward patronage included a pool of
low-paying jobs with privately owned companies which depended
upon the goodwill of public officials.

Insull came under heavy criticism for the donation of funds and
Smith for their acceptance while head of a regulatory agency.
Smith in rebuttal presented evidence that the commission had
reduced utility rates, but questions were raised whether the cuts
had been deep enough for the Insull companies. In a dilemma,
Smith refused to withdraw as a candidate and the November

campaign was complicated by the late entry of an independent, Hugh S. Magill, a former state senator who had become secretary of the National Council for Religious Education. Magill pleaded for higher ethics in government and had the support of a committee of men of prominence and unquestioned integrity. On the prohibition issue, Magill was a known dry, but the Anti-Saloon League made a point of being consistently loyal to its established friends and never wavered in its support of Smith. Brennan meanwhile campaigned vigorously as a wet, but against heavy odds Smith was elected senator by sixty-five thousand votes.

Smith never took the oath of office. Upon McKinley's death the governor appointed him to the short term, but the senate insisted upon long hearings, which were delayed when Smith became ill. In early 1928 the Reed committee reported that Smith's use of utility contributions had been contrary to public policy and was tainted with fraud and corruption. On a 61 to 23 roll call the seat to which he had been elected was declared vacant.

Dever's blue-nosed views about law enforcement failed to appeal to the Chicago electorate and "Big Bill" Thompson reentered the city hall for a third term in 1927. Lorimer had quietly reappeared in an undercover capacity in the mayor's camp and prospects were deceptively bright at the opening of 1928. With strong support from Thompson and Crowe, Small ran for a third term and Smith with a plea for vindication entered the primary for United States senator. Although Deneen had replaced Medill McCormick in the other senate seat four years earlier, his local and state candidates had little chance in the primary. That situation changed, however, when bombs exploded in front of the homes of Deneen and John A. Swanson, his choice for state's attorney. The bombs, of a type popularly known as pineapples, did little damage. The unidentified bomber could have been a Deneen partisan seeking public sympathy. If so, he was successful. The public was tired of Capone gangsters and Thompson buffoonery and a wave of public indignation turned the "pineapple primary" into a rout of the Small-Smith-Crowe ticket. Other Republican factions had achieved unity behind Secretary of State Louis L. Emmerson of Mount Vernon for governor, State Senator Otis F. Glenn of Murphysboro for United States senator, and Swanson for state's attorney. All were nominated. Again without support of Thompson, Lowden sought the Republican nomination for President but withdrew before the convention opened. Herbert Hoover swept the Republican nominees to a landslide victory in the election in which Capone granted Frank Loesch's request that Chicago be allowed to vote without disorders.

In 1928 the lid blew off the Chicago sanitary district, exposing graft that had statewide ramifications and in scope far exceeded the scandals that involved State Auditor Orville E. Hodge in 1956 and Secretary of State Paul Powell in 1971. District officials during a "whoopee era" that lasted for years had looted the public till through payroll padding, phony expense accounts, nepotism, mismanagement, and improper favors, among other mal-practices.[21] Without advertising for bids, outrageous prices had been paid for supplies and materials, and large sums allowed for improper expenses. Personnel practices reached such an extreme that almost anyone could get on the payroll, whether or not he intended to show up for work. The district had overspent an inflated appropriation for payrolls, and the trustees were accused of putting at least two thousand persons, real and imaginary, on the 1928 payrolls for political purposes. A legislative investigation revealed that lawyers had received big fees as special counsel and other politically important persons had drawn pay for such doubt-ful duties as occasionally inspecting the water level of the Illinois River. The scandal was bipartisan, and a Swanson assistant obtained the indictment of seven assorted trustees and four top employees for conspiracy to defraud the district of five million dollars. The money allegedly went for payrolls, a cinder path that cost 1.1 million dollars, a boulevard lighting system that cost fourteen hundred dollars per lamppost, and grossly exorbitant contracts for construction of sewage treatment plants. Charges against Edward J. Kelly, a future mayor who was the district's chief engineer, were dropped as the prosecution ran into diffi-culties. The first judge to whom the case was assigned had a nonworking son on the district's payroll. The chief justice of the Criminal Court refused to permit jurisdiction to be transferred even though the defendants were his close friends. Efforts to disbar the district's legal staff came to naught. One employee went to jail briefly and two trustees received maximum sentences of one to five years, but only one went to prison. With Deneen help,

---

[21] Edward M. Martin, *The Role of the Bar in Electing the Bench in Chicago*, pp. 300-310. Stuart, *op. cit.*, pp. 390-391, 481, 545-547. Gottfried, *op. cit.*, pp. 171, 185-186.

given in exchange for patronage, Cermak meanwhile worked out a bipartisan deal that gave him political control of the board elected in 1928. As part of the arrangement, Deneenites helped with the election of Kelly to the presidency of the politically important South Park system.

With its payrolls pruned, the district turned its attention to a losing battle before the United States Supreme Court, which ruled that only fifteen hundred cubic feet of water per second could be diverted into the Illinois waterway. The case, brought by other Great Lakes states, forced the agency to install expensive locks at the Chicago River's mouth and to erect sewage treatment plants costing $150,000. The excessive withdrawal of water, which endangered the lake level, was wanted by inland water enthusiasts as well as the sanitary district.[22]

Most of those indicted in the sanitary district scandal had Irish names, and the disposition of the charges was part of a sequence of events that enabled Cermak, who had mastered the ramifications of the scrambled governments in the Chicago area, to manipulate them for political benefit. Brennan had died in 1928, and his political heir apparent was Michael L. Igoe, who had been minority leader in the legislature. Sullivan and Brennan had let men from other nationality groups hold some of the offices, but the best jobs and leadership positions were reserved for Irish until Cermak grabbed the opportunity to form a coalition of Jews, Poles, Bohemians, and other non-Irish and have himself elected Democratic county chairman.

As it had in the 1915 primary and 1919 election, the Negro vote provided the winning margin when Thompson was elected the third time in 1927. The migration of blacks from the agricultural South began to assume large proportions about 1915, and grew steadily in spite of the race riot four years later. Overseas immigration had been shut down after the war, the boll weevil cut cotton yields, and the *Chicago Defender,* a colored weekly, took the lead in spreading word that Negroes could find work and political advancement in Chicago. As a result the black population, which was 4.1 percent in 1920, grew to 6.9 percent in 1930. Persistent white hostility squeezed most of the blacks into a narrow strip extending southward from the loop for eight miles. The middle class was small, with teachers and postal workers enjoying social

---

[22] Stuart, *op. cit.,* pp. 392-394. For a chronological account of Chicago's drainage and sanitary problems since the Civil War, see *Illinois Blue Book, 1925-26,* pp. 482-488.

Mayor Anton J. Cermak

prominence, but Negroes since 1882 had attained increasing representation in the legislature.[23] The first black alderman sat in the
Chicago city council in 1915, and in 1928 the south side district
sent to Washington the first Negro congressman since reconstruction. In other northern cities the Negroes had not advanced as fast

[23] Oscar DePriest was the first Chicago black to be elected alderman and congressman. Harold F. Gosnell, *Negro Politicians: The Rise of Negro Politics in Chicago*, 2nd
edition, pp. 163-195. Thompson's relations with the south side black district are covered
on pp. 37-62. There has been at least one Negro in the legislature since 1882, with the
number growing steadily since a second was elected in 1914.

For studies of the Negro population of Chicago, see St. Clair Drake and Horace R.
Cayton, *Black Metropolis: A Study of Negro Life in a Northern City;* Arvarh E.
Strickland, *History of the Chicago Urban League;* Chicago Commission on Race Re-
lations, *The Negro in Chicago;* Allan H. Spear, *Black Chicago: The Making of a Negro
Ghetto, 1890-1920;* and Irving Dilliard, "Civil Liberties Since 1865," *Journal of the
Illinois State Historical Society,* LVI, 3 (Autumn, 1963), 592-624.

politically. In Chicago, they almost solidly voted the Republican ticket, not only because of Lincoln's emancipation but for such later reasons as a belief that the Wilson administration had been unfriendly to black employment.

Thompson courted all minorities, and he had an especially tight grip on the loyalty of the black district. "Big Bill" was criticized for many antics. He used caged rats and a halter as props when he ridiculed campaign opponents, and his threat to "punch King George in the snoot" was part of a vendetta about history books used in the public schools.[24] The mayor considered himself available for the presidency, but expeditions down the Mississippi River in behalf of flood relief and a midcontinental waterway failed to arouse popular enthusiasm. He collapsed physically when litigation over fees to real estate appraisers resulted in a verdict that he and close associates were liable for three million dollars. The Supreme Court later canceled the penalty, but for months city business was transacted by the corporation counsel. The long-range strategy had been to let Thompson have a third term in expectation that he would be so unpopular in 1931 that Chicago would be ready for a Democratic mayor from organization ranks. Sullivan and Brennan had never attempted to run for mayor, but Cermak was ready to try it.

Weak and discredited, Thompson insisted on running again in 1931. Republican support ostensibly went to Judge John H. Lyle, whose anticrime efforts from the bench had aroused little public appreciation.[25] In a split field, Thompson won the nomination. Cermak ran for mayor in the role of a governmental expert who had enough business acumen to tackle the city's financial problems. Some Chicagoans considered they had a difficult choice, but Cermak won with 58 percent of the vote. The native of Bohemia looked forward to being mayor while a world's fair was held in Chicago.

Lyle, alone among judges of the Municipal Court, set one hundred thousand dollars bail in armed robbery cases. He found that the public was apathetic, that more than half of the prisoners obtained reduced bail from other judges, and that only eight

---

[24] Stuart, *op. cit.*, pp. 559ff., in his chronological account of the Thompson years as seen by an insider, does not believe that the mayor offered to "hit King George in the snoot." Stuart was the apologist for the Thompson regime. See Dobyns, *op. cit.*, p. 33.

[25] John H. Lyle, *The Dry and Lawless Years.* Lyle had a low rating with bar leaders, who regarded him as a grandstander.

among some three hundred went to prison. Lyle also set a precedent in 1930 by issuing vagrancy warrants for gang leaders. That widely publicized procedure had the approval of the Chicago Crime Commission, a private agency established twelve years earlier, and of a businessman's antiracketeering agency known as the Secret Six.[26] In that anonymous group only Robert Isham Randolph, president of the Association of Commerce, was identified.

The city and state seemed hopelessly in the grip of gangsters, but the federal government removed Capone from Chicago. Instead of charging murder or dry law violations, officials at Washington obtained the gang leader's indictment for cheating on his income tax, for failing over a five-year period to pay taxes of $215,030 on an unreported income of $1,038,654. Capone, who had expected a short prison term, withdrew a plea of guilty when Judge James H. Wilkerson announced that he would not be bound by a recommendation of the district attorney, George E. Q. Johnson, for a two-and-a-half-year sentence. To thwart jury tampering, at the beginning of the eleven-day trial the judge unexpectedly switched panels of veniremen. Special Prosecutor Dwight H. Green, a future governor, carefully pieced together evidence of illicit income and heavy spending that treasury agents had laboriously assembled. The jury deliberated sixteen hours and, after a verdict of guilty, Judge Wilkerson sentenced Capone to maximum consecutive terms totaling eleven years. The Supreme Court upheld the verdict and on a spring day in 1932 Public Enemy No. 1, at the age of thirty-two, boarded a train for an Atlanta penitentiary. Capone served nearly seven years in federal prisons, but before his release from Alcatraz a syphilitic infection had reached the tertiary stage.[27] He never came back to Chicago, but the crime syndicate continued operations as usual under more obscure and less flamboyant leaders.[28]

[26] Bruce Grant, *Fight for a City*, pp. 231-232.

[27] Kobler, *op. cit.*, pp. 371-375.

[28] Dobyns, *op. cit.*, pp. 10-12. Also see Ovid Demaris, *Captive City, Chicago in Chains*, and Alson J. Smith, *Syndicate City: The Chicago Crime Cartel and What To Do About It*.

25

OUT OF THE MUD, INTO THE AIR

RAILROADS, STEAM AND ELECTRIC

ILLINOIS HAD A SUPERB NETWORK OF RAILROADS, WITH BRANCH lines connecting at junction points with fast trains, but through the first quarter of the twentieth century the dirt roads were poor much of the time and virtually impassable in the rainy months of spring and autumn. By necessity, travelers and freight shippers depended upon train service.

In 1920, Illinois had 12,406 miles of railroad right-of-way which did not count double tracks and yards. Only Calhoun County lacked a railroad, and Nauvoo was the largest town without a depot. With twenty-one trunk lines operating over twenty-eight divisions or routes, Chicago had six busy passenger stations in the downtown area, plus freight houses, classification yards, roundhouses, switching lines, repair shops, coach yards, and other terminal facilities of a magnitude befitting the nation's major railroad center. Downstate also had bustling rail centers, and passenger depots were almost as imposing architecturally as the courthouses in the larger cities. Multiple ticket windows and dining rooms with table cloths were part of the facilities at Peoria's Union Station, two blocks long, which handled passengers on some two hundred trains daily on twelve railroads.[1]

[1] Cary C. Burford, "The Twilight of the Local Passenger Train," *Journal of the Illinois State Historical Society,* LI (Summer, 1958), 161-180.

To survive, a village had to have both train service and a livery stable where a farmer could leave his team of horses. When roads were fairly passable, every farm was within driving distance of a town where freights and local passenger trains stopped. The steam locomotives carried coal and water in tenders and passenger trains had at least two coaches, one of them a smoker, and cars for mail, baggage, and express.

Starting around 1900, electric interurban lines provided a link between town and country and furnished short-haul competition for the steam railroads. While running from town to town they made wayside stops and once inside the cities they followed streetcar lines into the business districts, which was a convenience for traveling salesmen.[2] By frequent transfers, an unhurried traveler could ride from Chicago to St. Louis on electric lines. Before his election to the senate, William B. McKinley developed the Illinois Traction System, the largest interurban network in the Middle West. It provided fast and frequent service over four hundred miles of track extending from St. Louis through Springfield to Peoria and Danville, with another line connecting Decatur and Bloomington with Peoria. Further north, the system operated between Chicago and Princeton. The big cars, dark green until they gave way in 1924 to bright orange, included parlor car and sleeper service from St. Louis to Peoria and Champaign. The McKinley Line built its own bridge over the Mississippi and did a substantial freight business on routes that paralleled steam roads. It operated on an interurban basis until 1956, and two years later removed the overhead electric cables and converted into a diesel-powered freight carrier.

The arrival of the automobile forced the interurbans to retrench, and starting around 1927 many abandoned service. Exceptions were lines radiating from Chicago which competed with the motorcar by giving suburban service in heavily populated areas. Both the Chicago, Aurora, and Elgin and the Chicago, North Shore, and Milwaukee terminated in the loop and had been taken over and revitalized by Samuel Insull. Not until the 1960's did they succumb to the private automobiles, which created congestion on the boulevards and parking problems downtown.

---

[2] The literature of nostalgia has given due attention to the interurbans. See James Davis Johnson, *The Lincoln Land Traction*. Johnson also is author of *Aurora 'n' Elgin*. See also William Middleton, *North Shore: America's Fastest Interurban*. A general view is given by George W. Hilton and John F. Due in *Electric Interurban Railroads of America*.

The motorcar killed off both the trains and the streetcars, which had prospered on a five-cent fare until around 1920. Because of steadily diminishing revenues, many county seats were without streetcar service four decades later. Oil-powered diesels replaced the steam locomotives and enabled railroads to keep alive in a new era of competition from truckers. The long-distance passenger trains began making their last runs as railroads reported deficits and asked commerce commission permission to abandon routes made unprofitable by the internal combustion engine.

THE COMING OF THE HARD ROADS

There were exceptions, but to a great extent roads were as bad in 1918 as they had been in the preceding century. Since first surveyed they had been maintained, inadequately and without coordination, by township commissioners. Able-bodied men between twenty-one and fifty years had the option of paying a tax or temporarily becoming a shovel-wielding member of a road crew. The use of a horse-drawn scraper, which was the standard method of maintaining a smooth surface, was effective only when the dirt was beginning to dry out after a rain. That made an excellent roadway, until it turned to dust or until it rained again. When the rains were prolonged the quagmires deepened and in winter they were frequently frozen into deep ruts. The weather determined whether roads were passable, and highway travel was rough on passengers, wearing on horses, and destructive of vehicles.[3]

A bicycle craze in the 1890's allowed venturesome spirits to explore the countryside away from the railroad tracks and helped stir up interest in the development of a network of roads that were better than cowpaths. In advance of his first campaign for mayor in 1897, young Carter Harrison captured public attention by joining a group of men who had ridden their bicycles one hundred miles in a day. For his first "century," Harrison peddled from his home on Chicago's west side to Waukegan, via Wheeling and Libertyville, and back in nine and a half hours.[4]

Only a few stretches of experimental highways had been built by 1903, when a good roads commission established by the

---

[3] David R. Wrone, "Illinois Pulls Out of the Mud," *Journal of the Illinois State Historical Society,* LVIII (Spring, 1965), 54-78.

[4] Carter H. Harrison, *Stormy Years,* pp. 104-106.

legislature found that dirt roads were inadequate, but township officials and many farmers objected to changing the system. During a growing volume of complaints about gas buggies being mired in mudholes, Representative Homer J. Tice of Greenview, a farmer, made a career out of road legislation.[5] He followed a standard lawmaking procedure of accepting compromises that weakened his original bills, but permitted them to get enough votes for enactment. Then at following sessions he perfected the statute by amendment or, if necessary, by writing a new law. In 1911 another law required that revenue from license fees, which automobile owners were required to pay to the secretary of state, be expended on roads and bridges outside municipalities.

Tice had help from William G. Edens, who had been a national officer of the Brotherhood of Railroad Trainmen before he switched careers and became chairman of the good roads committee of the Illinois Bankers Association. Edens argued that all-weather roads would be an economic asset, and was joined by the Chicago Motor Club in stirring up interest among automobile owners in the metropolitan area. An Illinois Highway Improvement Association, organized at a Peoria convention in 1912 and headed by Edens, mobilized rural and urban sentiment. As a result Governor Dunne, who advocated that convicts be used on road crews, enthusiastically signed a Tice law that switched responsibility for the main routes from the townships to the counties. Each county was required to have a qualified superintendent of highways, responsible to a three-member state highway commission and a state highway engineer. The state would pay half of the construction cost and all of the maintenance expense of county roads. To get the job done promptly, the counties could sell bonds to finance the state-aid roads. Much of the work was done with shovels and teams, and at Mooseheart thirteen hundred volunteers turned out April 15, 1913, to participate in a "road day" promoted by the governor.[6]

The new law worked only in Vermilion County, which after dissension finally built 174 miles of narrow roads, mostly of shallow concrete but some with brick surfacing. Cook, St. Clair,

[5] E. L. Bogart and J. M. Mathews, *The Modern Commonwealth, 1893-1918,* pp. 147-154. John Clayton, *Illinois Fact Book and Historical Almanac,* pp. 350-352.

[6] Edward F. Dunne, *Illinois, The Heart of the Nation,* II, 410-414. *Illinois Blue Book, 1915-16,* pp. 361-363.

and Jackson counties also approved bond issues, but by that time it was obvious that paved highways were a job for the state.[7] Congress in 1916 began to match state expenditures with federal appropriations, and the state highway commission developed a plan to "pull Illinois out of the mud" with a four-thousand-mile system of hard roads. The state had some 340,000 automobile owners, but pay-as-you-go financing would take too long, so Governor Lowden pushed a sixty-million-dollar bond issue, to be retired through automobile license fees. It called for 4,800 miles of pavement and was approved in 1918 by a decisive vote. Under Lowden, routes were graded and bridge work started, but the only pavement laid was an experimental two-mile strip at Bates, west of Springfield, where road designs and materials were tested by heavily loaded trucks. In a period of postwar adjustment,

[7] Wrone, *op. cit.,* pp. 61-67.

Deep mud and slow travel

Courtesy Illinois State Historical Library

bonds were not sold by the governor, who insisted that cement prices had risen too rapidly.[8] Meanwhile cross-country tourists followed routes marked by emblems painted on telephone poles by improvement associations. Red, white, and blue stripes designated the Lincoln Highway, which became U.S. 30. An Ocean-to-Ocean highway ran from Terre Haute, Indiana, to Quincy, and a Red Ball route from Quincy to Chicago. There were some fifty other roads and trails, all supposedly marked, but printed instructions telling which way to turn when distinctive buildings or landmarks came into view were an invaluable aid to motorists.

Under Governor Small's administration, Illinois developed a hard-road system that was the envy of other states. The number of motor vehicles increased, cement prices and wages of laborers dropped, and the governor pushed construction in a belief that roads would be a political as well as an economic asset. If local interests squabbled, Small did not pave in the area, and a six-mile gap in DeWitt County isolated Clinton from the paved roads. When it became apparent that the Lowden bond issue would not finish the job, Small boosted the total mileage of proposed hard roads to 9,900 and won approval for a second bond issue of a hundred million dollars. Year after year, his engineers set records by laying more than one thousand miles of pavement.[9] Every county had at least one paved route, although La Salle County benefited little from the second bond issue, presumably because Senator Thurlow G. Essington of Streator ran against Small in the 1924 primary.[10]

The bond issues and license plate fees failed to bring in enough money, and eventually Illinois became the last state to adopt a motor fuel tax. The first law in 1927 was held unconstitutional, but lawyers in time found out how to comply legally with the insistence of farmers that gasoline used in tractors be exempted. In 1929, at the start of Governor Louis L. Emmerson's term, the state began collecting a three-cent gas tax, with the third cent distributed to the counties for use on their secondary routes.

---

8 William T. Hutchinson, *Lowden of Illinois*, I, 355-360. Also see *Illinois Blue Book, 1917-18*, pp. 67-73. John M. Allswang, *A House for All Peoples: Ethnic Politics in Chicago, 1890-1936.*

9 Even before the Small administration, the biennial *Illinois Blue Book* carried articles telling of the status of road improvements. See also D. C. Ridgley, *The Geography of Illinois*, pp. 243-244.

10 Wrone, *op. cit.*, pp. 73-74.

Emmerson carried on the good roads program, and by 1930 the state had some 7,500 miles under pavement, approximately three-fourths of the primary system. The hard roads were only eighteen feet wide and turns were sharp, but Illinois was well out of the mud on intercity routes. Gravel had been spread on a quarter of the county roads that received state aid, and Emmerson in 1929 recognized that the Chicago area had special problems that required widening the existing routes and constructing grade separations at railroad crossings. Officials for years had been concerned about highway accidents and fatalities, and motorists were urged not to drink before starting their engines. After the legislature had twice refused to set up a state constabulary with search-and-arrest powers, in 1923 it provided for a highway maintenance police unit of not more than a hundred men. With the onset of the hard times of the 1930's, the state filled in the gaps on the Lowden-Small system, but the township roads, which served most farmers, were still to a great extent dirt surfaced.

FAILURES IN CAR MANUFACTURING

That Illinois did not become Michigan's rival as the big automobile-manufacturing state was not the fault of men who invested money and mechanical talent in some 160 highly competitive enterprises in Chicago and downstate communities.

Interest in motoring developed early, and the first American auto race, sponsored by the *Chicago Times-Herald* on Thanksgiving Day, 1895, was won by Frank Duryea, who drove a gas buggy from Jackson Park to Evanston and back in nine hours, which was better than five miles an hour.[11]

Scores of other men began tinkering with engines and gears. At Decatur, Hieronymous A. Mueller modified a Benz in which his son, Oscar, finished third in the *Times-Herald* race.[12] He built five more Muellers and planned to go into the manufacturing business but was killed in a workshop explosion in 1900. The Mueller firm since then has been successful in the brass-forging field. Ten early Chicago companies built electric cars, the most successful being

[11] Duryea and his older brother, Charles, who had a bicycle business in Peoria, feuded the rest of their lives about which one was responsible for the success of the first American automobile. It was built in Springfield, Mass., where Duryea's bicycles were manufactured.

[12] G. N. Georgano (ed.), *Encyclopedia of American Motor Cars*.

the Woods, which sold for as much as $4,500 and stayed on the market from 1899 to 1910. Four Illinois firms manufactured steam-powered cars, but none lasted more than three years. Starting with tiller-steered cycle cars and motor buggies and progressing through light roadsters and high-wheeled sedans with folding tops and side curtains, most of Henry Ford's Illinois rivals depended on the internal combustion engine. A few attempted to turn out motors in their own machine shops, but most were assembled cars, with the manufacturer buying the major parts, including such engines as the Lycoming, Bristol, Continental, and Knight.

The bulk of the short-lived enterprises were located in Chicago. The suburbs of Blue Island, Chicago Heights, and Cicero had one company each, and others were scattered through northern and central Illinois. At different times nine cars were manufactured at Moline, the plow center. Aurora men experimented with six makes of cars, and Decatur, Galesburg, Joliet, Peoria, and Sterling each had three auto companies. An available labor force and access to raw materials were not always prime considerations, and a compilation of Illinois-built cars lists manufacturers at Belvidere, Chrisman, Dallas City, Danville, Detroit (a Pike County community which in 1905 turned out La Petite, a two-seater with a one-cycle engine), East Chicago, Elgin, Freeport, Highland Park, Kankakee, Lanark, Lincoln, Ottawa, Plano, Rochelle, Rock Falls, Rockford, Rock Island, Springfield, Streator, and Waukegan. All were eventually unsuccessful and some were as short-lived as the Kirksell, which Dr. James Selkirk of Aurora planned to market for three thousand dollars. Apparently he turned out only one, in 1907.

The Sears, a high-wheeler available from the Chicago mail-order firm from 1906 to 1911, had a top price of $485 for a closed coupe. The company in 1952 briefly returned to the mail-order business with the Allstate. At Moline, Deere and Company had its own cars in 1906 and 1907 and then in 1909 backed a well-known carriage firm in selling the Velie, which was distributed by Deere plow dealers until 1915. The Velie company began making its own engines in 1922 and stayed on the market six more years. International Harvester Company, another farm equipment manufacturer, started to make a car in Chicago in 1907 but shifted the operation to Ohio.

The Commonwealth, which was assembled at Joliet from 1917 to 1922, ultimately became the Checker taxi. The Shaw was offered for sale in 1920-21 by the Shaw Livery Company, which for years had operated taxicabs in Chicago. It was taken over by the Yellow Cab Company, controlled by John Hertz, and in 1922 was sold as the Ambassador. Starting in 1925, the Hertz was manufactured for self-drive rental, but in 1928 the company switched to standard makes for leasing.

Downstate firms produced some good cars which stayed on the market several years but failed to attract a wide clientele and in time succumbed to competition from Michigan. The Comet, manufactured in Decatur from 1917 to 1922, had consistent sales only in its home area. The Moline, made by the Moline Plow Company, was first produced in 1904 and in 1912 had one of the first long-stroke engines. Later it adopted the Knight sleeve-valve motor, and its successors stayed in business until 1924. The Stephens, made by a Moline company starting in 1916 and from 1922 to 1924 by a Freeport firm, sold nearly twenty-five thousand as a competitor of the Buick in price and appearance.

Preston T. Tucker between 1946 and 1948 provided the most spectacular failure of Illinois auto makers. With a Michigan background, he took over a World War II plant in Chicago for the production of a sedan that had engineering innovations. Charged with fraud and violation of the regulations of the securities and exchange commission, the controversial Tucker won vindication in 1950 but his financial holdings were wiped out. Only a few Tuckers came off the assembly line and in the hands of collectors were reported to be running well.

The automobile increased the demand for all-weather roads and made other profound changes. Farmers and villagers could more easily reach the towns, which speeded the decline of the smaller settlements. An urban blight infected downtown areas when city residents found it possible to live on the outskirts of metropolitan areas, especially after Henry Ford gave impetus to increased purchasing power in 1914 by announcing he would pay a minimum wage of five dollars a day, compared to the going rate of two or three dollars. The housing boom in the suburbs was generated by simultaneous construction of roads along which the petroleum industry placed filling stations. Roadside stands, cabin camps, billboards, and weekend traffic jams appeared as other symbols of the automobile age.

CROSSROADS OF AIR TRAVEL

Starting in 1850, a few balloon pilots got overhead views of the Illinois landscape, and a quarter of a century later Thomas Scott Baldwin of Quincy developed the flexible parachute, which balloonists used as another means of entertaining the crowds that turned out for their ascensions.[13] A different type of man was Octave Chanute, the Chicago engineer who showed the Wright brothers it was theoretically possible to fly a plane with the power of an internal combustion engine. Parisian-born and American-educated, Chanute during a long career had held top construction jobs with several railroads, including the Chicago and Alton. In 1883 he set up shop in Chicago as a consulting civil engineer, but soon was giving most of his time to the study of airfoils and the theory of flight. He presided at an international conference on aerial navigation, one of the scientific events held during the 1893 world's fair, and he studied the reports of the first Europeans who experimented with gliding. Beginning in 1890 he designed gliders, and at the age of sixty made flights from a hill in the Indiana sand dunes, where he made notes on the strength and variability of air currents. Chanute discarded the monoplane used in Europe, experimented with a five-plane glider, and evolved a biplane of novel design, with arched surfaces held together by vertical posts and diagonal wires. Steady in flight, it carried 178 pounds at twenty-three miles an hour and became the model for the plane in which Harold and Orville Wright made the first powered flight at Kitty Hawk, North Carolina, in 1903. The Wrights never failed to acknowledge the help they received from Chanute, who acted as their unofficial spokesman and helped convince skeptics that they really had flown.

By the time Chanute died in 1910, possibly one hundred Chicagoans and thirty more downstaters, all amateurs, worked on the invention of a variety of flying machines. For a quarter of a century several Illinois companies manufactured flimsy planes in a precarious industry that could be wiped out if the inventor-pilot crashed. The planes were used chiefly by exhibition pilots and wealthy sportsmen, and American records for total distance and nonstop flight fell in 1910 as the result of an offer by H. H.

---

[13] This section is based largely on Howard L. Scamehorn, *Balloons to Jets,* and Clayton, *op. cit.,* pp. 375-383.

Kohlsaat of the *Record-Herald* of ten thousand dollars for a flight from Chicago to Springfield. On the first day of the state fair, Walter R. Brookins, a Wright employee, took off before thirty thousand spectators, made brief stops at Gilman and Mt. Pulaski, and reached Springfield in seven hours and twenty minutes. All the well-known American flyers and five Europeans participated in an international aviation meet held in 1911 with Grant Park as the flying field. Harold F. McCormick raised a hundred thousand dollars and guaranteed two dollars for each minute a plane was in the air between 3:30 and 7:00 p.m. during the nine days of the meet. Two men died in crashes, but in a remarkable performance the others logged 206 hours of flying time.

Airmail service began with demonstration flights as early as 1912, and four years later a plane with mail flew from Chicago to New York between sunrise and sunset. Using war surplus planes, a New York-Chicago mail route opened in late 1918, and during 1920 the service was extended to San Francisco, Minneapolis, and New Orleans. Chicago inevitably became an airmail center, and operations shifted from the lakefront to Checkerboard Field, a commercial operation at Maywood, and then to the nearby grounds of Walter Hines Hospital.

Men who had learned to fly at such army bases as Chanute and Scott fields took up barnstorming in surplus planes. As "gypsies," they stopped at any convenient field, gave short rides for fares as low as three dollars, and occasionally did a taxi business to nearby communities. By winter, or earlier if business was bad, they tried their luck elsewhere, but there were fixed-base operators around Chicago and at Sheldon, Aurora, Moline, Springfield, and Monmouth. They made a living from exhibitions, passenger and charter trips, and flight instruction, but during the early 1920's attempts to organize airline service failed. The revenue was in carrying the mail for the government and, by 1926, Chicago was served by four airlines which used open planes and let an occasional passenger sit among the mailbags in the front cockpit.

Single-handedly, Charles A. Lindbergh made the nation aviation conscious in the spring of 1927. A former barnstormer, he flew airmail on the St. Louis-Chicago run, with stops at Springfield and Peoria, as chief pilot for Robertson Aircraft Corporation of St. Louis. The work was pioneering, including the impromptu selection of airfield sites, and dangerous, since fogs at Maywood twice forced him to ditch his plane and land by parachute. Convinced that a flight over the Atlantic would require only a good plane and stamina, he obtained financial backing and landed at Paris thirty-three hours after taking off from New York on a nonstop solo flight that won a twenty-five-thousand-dollar prize and made him an international hero.

In an era of expansion, the mail routes were generally unprofitable, but the post office department distributed subsidies to private operators, and by 1931 eight companies served Chicago on routes totaling 5,072 miles. Most were controlled by four holding companies, with United Air Lines operating the New York-Chicago-San Francisco transcontinental route and a line to Dallas. It was a consolidation of lines formerly operated by Boeing Air Transport, Pacific Air Transport, National Air Transport, and Varney Air Lines. A network from New England to California was operated by American Airways for the Aviation Corporation Company of Delaware. Its properties included Robertson Aircraft and Egyptian Airways, Inc., which operated a flying field in Marion. Cord Corporation owned passenger and express routes radiating from Chicago, but failed to get airmail contracts and in time sold to Aviation Corporation. Transcontinental and Western Air, Inc., served both Chicago and St. Louis as part of its network. On the ground that the mail contracts were the result of fraud and collusion, they were canceled in 1934 by Postmaster General James A. Farley, and for several disastrous months the army air corps flew the mail. The new contracts were awarded after the corporations underwent nominal reorganizations.

The airline expansion continued despite the depression and was only temporarily slowed by World War II, when planes flew at near capacity most of the time. After 1945, the major lines doubled and redoubled passenger traffic and expanded routes. Ozark Airlines, the biggest local service operator in Illinois, began flying in 1950 and at the start was limited to a Chicago-Champaign-Decatur-Springfield-St. Louis route.

The early airports were mostly private ventures. Outside East St. Louis, Oliver L. Parks founded an air college for the training of commercial pilots, and in 1929 sizable airports there and at Glenview were constructed as bases for civil and military planes by the Curtiss-Wright Airports Corporation. The latter was taken over by the navy before World War II. The federal government began to regulate aviation in 1928, but not until 1931 did the legislature create a state commission, which found that in Illinois licenses had been issued to 506 planes, 988 pilots, and 52 airports. Many of the private airport operators went out of business during the depression of the 1930's, but municipalities took their place. They received federal grants for use on projects which would furnish jobs for the unemployed.

Chicago's Municipal Airport, later renamed Midway, was dedicated in 1927 on the southwest side as part of Mayor Thompson's public improvements program.[14] Originally it had a single runway on a tract a quarter of a mile square, but as traffic improved it became the world's busiest and before World War II the Belt Line railway was relocated to permit the construction of nine long runways surrounded by hangars. Eight major airlines served Midway, and United Airlines made its headquarters in Chicago. In 1946 a lakefront airport, on the site of a former world's fair, permitted private pilots to land closer to the loop and was named for Merrill C. Meigs, a publisher who was one of the foremost aviation boosters. Even before the wartime restrictions were lifted, it was obvious that Chicago must have a larger airport, and in 1946 as surplus property the federal government gave the city Orchard Airport, a 1,371-acre tract beside which the Douglas Aircraft Company had assembled C54 Skymaster planes. The city renamed the big field for Lieutenant Edward H. (Butch) O'Hare, a naval hero in South Pacific aerial combat. Federal and state grants enabled the expansion of O'Hare Field to more than ten times the size of Midway, which for several years was closed to traffic.

[14] Mary Watters, *Illinois in the Second World War,* II, 189-194.

26

THE GREAT DEPRESSION

IN THE GENERAL PROSPERITY OF THE 1920's, MOST PEOPLE HAD some money and the far-sighted and thrifty could ride a speculative boom by investing in corporate stocks and bonds readily available in branch brokerage houses. For several years prices of securities rose rapidly and the boom, largely financed on credit, continued after a slight recession in 1927, but in the autumn of 1929 the optimism quickly dissipated. The bull market gave way to a depression and October 24 was Black Thursday, the worst day in a stock market panic that had never been equaled in the peacetime destruction of security values and in capital losses to individuals.[1]

The expansion of Illinois' population, which had been spectacular for a century, almost stopped during the depression decade. Restrictions on immigration checked the flow of new residents from Europe and during the hard times Chicago lost its attraction for the ambitious young and their displaced elders from small towns and the farms. In the stagnation, the population increase was only 266,587 or 3.5 percent during the decade, compared with 17.7 percent during the preceding ten-year period and 10.3 percent between 1940 and 1950. Chicago gained only 20,370 residents during the depression, and the census bureau found that rural Illinois increased 4.6 percent while the urban places grew only 3.1 percent.

[1] George Soule, *Prosperity Decade*, pp. 107-126, 275-314.

GROWING UNEMPLOYMENT AND FINANCIAL SQUEEZES

Factories, stores, and offices laid off help and sometimes closed their doors, and family savings were depleted if not wiped out, but the manufacturing and agricultural diversity of Illinois delayed for a year the full effect of the depression. During 1930 payrolls dropped 30 percent, and unemployment caused alarm that winter. As many as seven hundred thousand were out of work, with the situation most critical in Chicago and the mining counties of Franklin and Williamson. Governor Louis L. Emmerson, whose own bank would soon close, set an example by privately contributing to relief collections. In October, 1930, he appointed a state committee on unemployment and relief, but he still hoped that the people of Illinois could be fed and sheltered without the state becoming directly involved. Within the next year, however, it became obvious that state aid was both imperative and difficult to provide.

Relatives helped relatives and friends tried to look out for neighbors, but before long both private and public resources were exhausted. Chicago was on the verge of bankruptcy. "Big Bill" Thompson's profligacy had been followed by a reassessment of all real estate in Cook County, something that Governor Small had advocated. The reassessment was delayed, however, and the revenue collection machinery thrown off schedule when no taxes were paid in 1929. That caused problems at Springfield, since Cook County was two years delinquent in paying its share of the state levy on property, which for a century had been the state government's main revenue source.[2]

In the sobering situation, the legislature at first took such short-term steps as authorizing nonreferendum bond issues for the Chicago governments, but there was no agreement that the time had come for a state income tax. Special sessions in 1930 and 1931 were devoted in part to the tax collection difficulties in Cook County, one of the steps being establishment of the new office of assessor. The problem of the jobless persisted, and in 1932 and again in 1933, when crises kept arising and majority agreement became difficult to achieve, three special sessions of the legislature met simultaneously. In February, 1932, the lawmakers created a seven-member Illinois Emergency Relief Commission and

[2] William H. Stuart, *The Twenty Incredible Years*, pp. 401-405.

Depression victims

Courtesy Illinois State Historical Library

voted a twenty-million-dollar appropriation in expectation that it would pay the bills for a year, but the money was gone by July.[3] Downstaters pushed stopgap measures for their communities, Cook County was authorized to float a seventeen-million-dollar bond issue, and twice Illinois voters gave overwhelming approval of relief bond issues—twenty-five million dollars in 1932 and thirty million dollars in 1934—with the money to be repaid from future gas tax revenues. Washington provided help and Mayor Cermak arranged for Chicago teachers to be paid with a twenty-million-dollar loan from the Reconstruction Finance Corporation, which had been set up by President Hoover. Some said that Illinois could not avoid a sales tax.

Banking suffered along with other segments of the business world, and Charles G. Dawes, the hard-boiled former Vice President, in the summer of 1932 resigned as president of the Reconstruction Finance Corporation so that he could keep his own bank, the Central Republic of Chicago, from crashing. In violation of his own principles, Dawes accepted a ninety-million-dollar RFC loan. There was no other way to protect 122,000 depositors and 755 correspondent banks in fifteen states which depended upon the Central Republic.[4]

Heavy runs forced some banks on their own initiative to limit withdrawals and, after a mid-February moratorium in Michigan, deposits in Chicago dropped 350 million dollars in two weeks. In the crisis Governor Horner, acting in concert with Governor Lehman of New York, at 3:15 a.m. on President Roosevelt's inauguration day ordered the closing of all banks in Illinois.[5] The Board of Trade stopped operations for the first time in its history, and in two days the new President made the moratorium nationwide. As a substitute for money, some businesses issued scrip which their employees were glad to use as a circulating medium.

Emergency legislation soon enabled national and state examiners to allow the reopening of banks that had liquid assets. Within three months the bulk of the 704 state banks were open for business. The others, mostly small, were under the jurisdiction of William L. O'Connell, a Dunne Democrat who acted as general receiver and had deputies in charge of individual banks. Reorga-

[3] Frank Z. Glick, *The Illinois Emergency Relief Commission.*

[4] Broadus Mitchell, *Depression Decade*, pp. 79-81.

[5] Thomas B. Littlewood, *Horner of Illinois*, pp. 105-106.

nizations continued and some banks were allowed to defer payments to depositors.

Roosevelt's efforts to revive the economy with "blue eagle" codes of fair competition stirred up controversy and put the spotlight on Hugh S. Johnson, a retired army officer who had been general counsel of the Moline Plow Company.[6] He was administrator of the National Industrial Recovery Administration, whose codes were to be enforceable in court. The Illinois Manufacturers Association and the State Chamber of Commerce protested that business was being subjected to a dictatorship, but the legislature passed a bill, requested by Washington, which provided for state policing of the NRA. Blue-eagle emblems appeared in most windows, and advertisements before the Supreme Court held the whole program unconstitutional. Harold L. Ickes went to Washington as secretary of the interior and survived four terms of infighting with New Deal bigwigs.

The financial collapse of Samuel Insull's utility corporations, which produced one-eighth of the nation's electricity and gas, made the depression worse. They had more than four million customers, six hundred thousand stockholders, five hundred thousand bondholders, and combined assets approaching three billion dollars, while Insull's personal fortune was estimated at 150 million dollars. The complex empire survived both the 1929 stock market crash and another downturn in 1931 before it went into receivership as the result of a financial squeeze. Although he had been under fire in 1926, more power and responsibility were being thrust upon Insull. Chicago voters in 1930 approved a unified traction ordinance which would give management control to Insull. That project didn't get off the ground, but Insull, as Chicago's leading citizen, called upon other business leaders to help arrange for the payment of teachers, police, and firemen. His namesake son headed relief drives and privately collected ten million dollars for the city's unemployed.

The mammoth network of interrelated companies inevitably brought financial problems. Uneasy about the purchase of large blocks of stock by Cyrus J. Eaton of Cleveland, Insull during the runaway market of 1928 formed an investment company, Insull Utility Investments, which was designed to perpetuate his manage-

[6] Johnson had been associated with George N. Peek, the company's president, in trying to restore farm prosperity.

ment by pyramiding. The market price, which originally had been set at twelve dollars a share, soon boomed to $150. Before the 1929 crash, Insull made the corporate setup more complex by forming Corporation Securities of Chicago, a second investment trust. The two were interlocking and the second sought to insure control through a voting trust feature.[7]

The squeeze came when Insull bought Eaton's stock for fifty-six million dollars without arranging for permanent financing, which made it necessary to borrow from banking houses on the security of the holding company portfolios. Chicago banks could not finance the entire amount and Insull came into unfriendly New York hands. None of his operating companies collapsed and Insull insisted that his properties were in sound condition, but his Chicago creditors hesitated and then followed the lead of the New Yorkers by refusing to renew his notes. The empire could have been saved at the critical hour by ten million dollars, but by April, 1932, the top companies were in receivership and the savings of thousands of small investors had been wiped out.

Insull resigned his corporate posts and went to Europe on a vacation while losses of the small stockholders became a political issue. State's Attorney John A. Swanson made public a list of insiders, including politicians from both parties, who had been allowed to buy Insull stock at half-price. President Roosevelt, who had once been criticized by Insull's brother Martin, joined in the general denunciation. Indicted by federal and state grand juries, Insull was extradited from Greece. In federal court, where Dwight H. Green prosecuted the case, Insull took the stand and told the long story of a career devoted to bringing electrical and gas service to the midcontinent. "I would do it again," he testified repeatedly. A verdict of acquittal came quickly. Prosecution on state charges also failed.

Chicago politicians financed part of their campaigning by the sale of junk from utility companies. Moe Rosenberg, who long had been a west side power, testified in his own income tax case that he had made bargain purchases of scrap metal from Insull and other companies and in 1929 and 1930 had distributed five hundred thousand dollars to fellow Democrats.

In the fourth year of the hard times, Chicago staged a successful world's fair, a Century of Progress, and repeated it the next year.

[7] Forrest McDonald, *Insull.*

Privately financed through a ten-million-dollar bond issue, the fair opened in 1933 on Northerly Island, which later became the lakefront site of Meigs Field. Its scope did not approach that of the Columbian Exposition, but the new fair had twelve buildings, mostly of futuristic design, in which exhibits showed the world's progress in the last hundred years. A replica of Fort Dearborn recalled Chicago's beginnings, and the new midway contained a spectacular skyride that drew less attention than a sideshow in which Sally Rand, previously unknown, danced in a costume of fans. The fair was a financial success and in two years drew thirty-nine million admissions at fifty cents for adults and twenty-five cents for children.

HENRY HORNER TAKES COMMAND

Anton J. Cermak wanted to run for governor in 1932, but he did not comprehend the scope of the forthcoming Democratic sweep and decided not to risk offending the Jewish support that constituted a major part of the coalition that had made him mayor. As a result, he played it safe and endorsed Henry Horner, judge of the Cook County Probate Court, for the highest office in the state.[8]

Cermak was not certain there would be a repetition of the 1930 landslide in which Republicans salvaged control only of the legislature. The primary that year was another expensive exercise in G.O.P. bloodletting, and Senator Deneen had been beaten by the congresswoman-at-large, Ruth Hanna McCormick of Rockford, widow of Medill McCormick and daughter of Mark Hanna of Ohio. The public disapproved of her heavy spending, the stock market panic further weakened Republicans, and the nomination was worthless. By combining courtly manners with subtle ridicule, James Hamilton Lewis returned to the senate after a twelve-year absence.

Bald, stout, and affable, Horner was a bachelor and collector of Lincolniana who had a reputation for efficient administration of the thousands of estates probated yearly in Chicago. He had entered the primary without waiting for Cermak's approval and,

---

[8] Littlewood, op. cit., pp. 67-86. See also Alex Gottfried, Boss Cermak of Chicago, and Arvarh E. Strickland, "The New Deal Comes to Illinois," Journal of the Illinois State Historical Society, LXIII (Spring, 1970), 55-68.

with organization help, polled half of the vote in a three-man field. Governor Emmerson, who had acquired the same liabilities as President Hoover, wisely decided not to try for a second term. In a field of eight Republicans, Omer N. Custer of Galesburg,[9] a businessman who had Emmerson's support, insisted on running as a dry and finished second to Len Small. Many Republicans refused to support the former governor, and Horner, who became the first Jewish chief executive, received more votes than Roosevelt in the Democratic landslide.

Cermak, the dripping wet, misplayed his cards at the 1932 Democratic convention in the Chicago Stadium. Unsure of the New York governor, Cermak preferred Alfred E. Smith and used Senator Lewis as a favorite son candidate. Roosevelt had approximately a quarter of the Illinois delegation, and when Lewis announced for him, Cermak switched to Melvin A. Traylor, president of the First National Bank of Chicago. Roosevelt won anyway and Cermak faced the danger of White House ostracism.

Horner, the third Democratic governor since the Civil War, had a streak of idealism and independence in his makeup. He owed his position to Cermak, but whether the two men could have worked in harmony is debatable. The new administration at Springfield opened with at least one difference of opinion, over a high-level appointment, before an assassin's bullet released the governor from his political obligation. Hoping to cement an alliance with the President-elect, Cermak had timed a Miami vacation to coincide with a reception for Roosevelt. A bullet fired in the direction of the President's car struck Cermak, who died in nineteen days and was buried as a martyr. Giuseppe Zangara went to the electric chair amid a general belief that he had tried to kill Roosevelt, but some contend his marksmanship was quite accurate. Gambling had flourished in Chicago while Cermak was mayor, and less than two months before the Miami tragedy two police sergeants under unusual circumstances had shot and wounded Frank Nitti, who had a high place in the gangland hierarchy that took over when Capone went to prison. For one, Judge John H. Lyle believed that the crime syndicate had arranged for Zangara to rub out the mayor.[10]

[9] Lowell N. Peterson, "Omer N. Custer: A Biography of a Downstate Political Boss," *Journal of the Illinois State Historical Society,* LX (Spring, 1967), 37-63.

[10] *The Dry and Lawless Years,* pp. 267-268. Ovid Demaris, *Captive City,* pp.

An emergency law, designed to save time and the cost of an election, allowed the city council to name Cermak's successor. The Irish returned to power and the job went to Edward J. Kelly, tall and red-headed, who had started as a rodman with the sanitary district. Colonel Robert R. McCormick of the *Tribune,* a former sanitary district president, was his friend. Kelly shared Democratic leadership with Patrick A. Nash, the county chairman.

Horner believed that only with a sales tax could the state pay its portion of the relief load and meet other governmental expenses. He had been elected on a pledge to reduce the tax load on property owners, and the Illinois Supreme Court had held unconstitutional an income tax law. The strict constructionist judges treated income as property and held that the law's graduated rates and exemptions violated the 1870 constitution's requirement that taxation be uniform.[11]

The constitutional restrictions made it difficult to draft a sales tax bill. A direct tax on sales would be impossible under the 1932 opinion, so the administration proposed an occupational tax on those who sold tangible personal property at retail for final use or consumption. Horner used the full power of his office to force through such a sales tax at a 3 percent rate. Disappointment came quickly when the court invalidated the law because it exempted farm products and motor fuel. A revised bill, for a 2 percent tax without exemptions, required six roll calls but eventually received the two-thirds emergency majority. When the Supreme Court gave its approval, Horner suspended the state's property levy, which yielded nearly thirty-one million dollars. Farmers especially were glad to get rid of the state's portion of the property levy.

At the depression's nadir, some 1.5 million residents of Illinois were unemployed in January, 1933, and the federal government poured as much money into Illinois as it did in New York and Pennsylvania combined.[12] Approximately 277,000 families received relief in amounts hardly sufficient to keep food on tables, with 177,000 in Cook County averaging $29.13 monthly and

117-119, contends that Ted Newberry, who had been Capone's man on the north side, was Cermak's choice to take over the top spot in the underworld syndicate.

[11] Neil F. Garvey, *The Government and Administration of Illinois,* p. 153. Littlewood, *op. cit.,* pp. 109-113.

[12] David J. Maurer, "Unemployment in Illinois During the Great Depression," *Essays in Illinois History* (Donald F. Tingley, ed.), pp. 120-132. Studs Terkel, *Hard Times: An Oral History of the Great Depression.*

downstaters $12.81. The rate of expenditures decreased from North to South, and jobless families in Alexander County (Cairo) averaged $1.83 a month from the federal government. Horner refused to listen to complaints, some alleging favoritism and others reflecting dismay that social workers were so numerous, about the Illinois Emergency Relief Commission, which administered the expenditure of most state and federal funds. Not all of the jobless received financial help, since eligibility required that a family's private resources must first be exhausted, and some six hundred thousand could not qualify in that category. An average of one million received some kind of help until July, 1934. Building construction was at a standstill and boarded-up windows identified half-finished apartments that had gone into receivership.

Communists organized some hunger marches on Springfield and one delegation had an audience with the governor, but most protesters were turned back by police. The public accepted the hard times with patience and no thought of revolution. Police had less trouble with demonstrators than they did with John Dillinger, who celebrated an Indiana parole by going on a sensational crime spree that included bank robberies and escapes in Illinois. Federal Bureau of Investigation agents finally ended his career in an ambush outside a neighborhood movie house in Chicago in 1934.

Harry L. Hopkins, the federal relief administrator, preferred to deal with Chicago Democrats and in the fall of 1933 notified Horner that he would advance additional money to Illinois only on the condition that immediate steps be taken to increase the state's contributions. Horner reminded the legislature, which had been in almost continuous session, that for fifteen months the federal government had carried almost all of the financial burden. He said the alternative would be privation and starvation for 223,000 families, or approximately one million persons. Unwillingly, the legislature accepted the alternative and voted a second relief bond issue, for thirty million dollars, with interest and principal to be paid from the gasoline tax. Most moneyless families received food and clothing, medical services, and rent payment, while about one-fifth worked at less than the prevailing wage on construction and maintenance jobs or at clerical tasks involved in the distribution of supplies. The Civil Works Administration provided work relief for a few months but in 1935 was replaced by the Works Progress Administration, headed by Hopkins. Horner much preferred to deal with Ickes.

The governor, who from economic necessity cut the welfare department's budget 28.5 percent,[13] refused to use his option of restoring the state tax on property and, with Kelly support, raised the sales tax to 3 percent in a 1935 crisis. Relief was costing more, since a new federal policy put a larger share of the burden on the states. Hopkins shut off federal funds in an effort to force Illinois to raise three million dollars a month and the IERC virtually stopped operations. A deadlock continued for months, but Hopkins finally released a stopgap five-million-dollar grant and the legislature agreed to the tax increase.

By Horner's arrangement, the formal repeal of prohibition was a bipartisan ceremony in Illinois. Fifty delegates, equally divided between the two parties and spread geographically over the state, met at Springfield July 10, 1933, and unanimously ratified the Twenty-First Amendment, which less than four months earlier had been submitted to state conventions by Congress. The delegates had been selected by a 4 to 1 margin when only nineteen counties cast majorities for a slate pledged to continue prohibition. The governor, who acted as temporary chairman and keynoter, had opposed delaying the convention until 1934. Public sentiment was on his side, since referenda at the 1930 election gave 2 to 1 majorities for repeal of national and state prohibition and repeal of the Volstead Act.[14] He had recently signed laws repealing the state prohibition and search-and-seizure statutes. Two years earlier similar measures had been vetoed by Emmerson.

Horner had voluntarily given up part of his patronage by approving consolidation of the Chicago park systems, but frequently he disagreed with Kelly. Because the two men clashed, the legal sale of liquor began without a state control law. The governor wanted personal liberty to be tempered with self-control and moderation, and he reminded the legislature that platforms of both parties condemned the old-time saloon. His advocacy of strong state controls was opposed by the mayor, who was interested chiefly in licensing revenue and wanted regulation to be left largely to the cities. Not until May, 1934, was a compromise law passed which divided control between the state and local officials.[15]

[13] See Director A. L. Bowen's report in *Illinois Blue Book, 1935-36,* pp. 631-655.

[14] Walter S. G. Kohn, "Illinois Ratifies the Twenty-First Amendment," *Journal of the Illinois State Historical Society,* LVI (Winter, 1963), 692-712.

[15] Littlewood, *op. cit.,* pp. 134-138.

The incompatibility of Horner and Kelly returned to the surface in 1935 when the mayor pushed through the legislature a bill which would allow Chicago to license handbooks. The badly needed revenue from off-track betting on horse races would go to payment of teachers' salaries, the bill applied only to Chicago, and it had been held constitutional by Attorney General Otto Kerner, a Cermak protégé. Kelly had sent word that the bill was of top importance, but Horner without warning vetoed it with a strong message asserting that public morals could not be protected if the city legalized betting establishments.[16] Kelly's decision to dump Horner from the 1936 ticket was made easier because the sales tax, for which the public held the governor individually responsible, had made "High Tax Henry" unpopular throughout Illinois.

Kelly blundered by slating Dr. Herman N. Bundesen, president of the Chicago board of health, to replace Horner. Several downstaters would have made good candidates, and Bruce A. Campbell, who had run well in the 1932 primary and was an organization loyalist, had a strong following in the rural counties. Bundesen's political asset was that he was widely known as the author of a book on baby care. He wore spats, talked with enthusiasm about the benefits of drinking milk, and in an energetic tour failed to excite the voters.[17]

In retaliation, the governor accused Kelly and Nash of bossism and vote thievery. There had been charges of wholesale ballot box irregularities at the 1934 election, when Democrats completed their take-over of state and local offices, and in 1935 when Kelly was overwhelmingly elected to a full term as mayor. The governor had given no assistance when the League of Women Voters unsuccessfully requested adoption of permanent registration, a system under which voters are required to match signatures kept on file by election officials. After the party organization turned against him, Horner took a ringing stand for honest elections and demanded permanent registration as an antifraud measure. The bill didn't pass until after the 1936 primary, but while it was being delayed Nash was quoted as saying that permanent registration would cost his party two hundred thousand votes.

Horner made bossism his chief issue and became a downstate hero in a bitter and expensive campaign. He gained public sym-

16 *Ibid.*, pp. 151-154.
17 *Ibid.*, pp. 166-193.

Courtesy Illinois State Historical Library
Governor Henry Horner

pathy by a single-handed fight against the big city machine at the same time that he put campaign workers on the state payroll and raised campaign money by assessing state employees and demanding contributions from firms doing business with the state. Few protests were heard about practices which thirty years later would receive severe condemnation from editors and civic groups. Both sides became eligible for blame in a campaign which Thomas B. Littlewood estimated cost the enormous pretelevision sum of three million dollars.[18]   Horner had important help, including County Judge Edmund K. Jarecki, who had administrative control over the Chicago election machinery. Republicans switched pri-

18 *Ibid.,* p. 169.

maries to vote for Horner. The organization meanwhile provided Bundesen with the backing of forty-seven of the fifty Chicago ward committeemen, and some of the orthodox Jewish leaders on the west side were prevailed upon to vote against Horner. From Washington, Harry L. Hopkins threw the political resources of the Works Progress Administration into the fight on the Kelly-Nash side. The primary was a great personal triumph for the governor, who carried every downstate county and eight Chicago wards to win renomination by 161,092.

In the reaction, Horner ran behind the Democratic ticket at the November election, but Republicans were demoralized in the face of Roosevelt's great popularity.[19] The President had provided money and jobs as well as sympathy for the unemployed and his coattails were bigger than party factionalism.

JOHN L. LEWIS EXPANDS HIS POWER

John Llewellyn Lewis, national president of the United Mine Workers, combined a great ego with a willingness to compromise for what he considered the overall good of the soft coal industry, which suffered from a bad case of overproduction at a time when the number of coal diggers exceeded the jobs available. With twenty-nine mines, the Peabody Coal Company set policy in Illinois for the industry and worked closely with the union. The shaggy-browed Lewis in his rise from a Montgomery County local had bypassed the ladder of promotion through the Illinois district, and before the depression he had quarreled with state leaders who were popular with the rank and file. On a financial pretext he took over the district charter and ruled that John H. Walker could not be state president. In the internal row, Walker was reelected at a time when fifty thousand men struck because the operators insisted upon a 30 percent cut in the six-dollar daily wage.[20]

When the miners rejected a 1932 contract that made concessions to the operators, Lewis took over negotiations and wrote one that contained almost identical provisions. Early returns showed a heavy vote to repudiate Lewis, and conflicting versions

[19] The Republican nominee for Vice President was Frank Knox, publisher of the *Chicago Daily News*. Norman Beasley, *Frank Knox, American.*

[20] Dallas M. Young, "Origin of the Progressive Mine Workers of America," *Journal of the Illinois State Historical Society*, XL (Sept., 1947), 313-330. Mary Watters, *Illinois in the Second World War*, II, 218-222.

were given about what happened to the ballots after they had been tabulated in Springfield. Union tellers said they had been stolen on a downtown street, but enemies of Lewis claimed that they had been given to a motorist who drove away. Lewis declared an emergency, announced that the contract was ratified, and ordered his men back to work.

Walker's career had ended but he did not join in a secessionist movement sparked by Scotch and Welsh miners in Macoupin County. At their call, conventions at Benld and Gillespie formed a rival union, the Progressive Miners of America, and adopted a democratic constitution limiting officers to two-year terms and requiring that they return to the pits for four years before being elected again. The Mine Workers District 12, which covered all of Illinois, operated under a Lewis-controlled provisional government during five years of chaos. Employees of Peabody mines stayed loyal to Lewis while bloody warfare broke out in Christian County, at Springfield, and further south. A Progressive caravan from Macoupin County started for southern Illinois in a membership drive, but was met at Mulkeytown, near the Franklin County border, by sheriff's deputies and police. Machine guns and ball bats repelled the invaders, without killing anyone, and the new union thereafter accomplished little in that region.

The Progressives insisted there was collusion between Lewis and the Peabody company. Fratricidal war kept the National Guard on emergency duty and saw men killed on the picket line and in ambushes. Governor Horner failed to mediate the dispute and no one responded when he ordered residents of Christian County to turn in their guns. Black powder bombing of front porches led to dynamiting of tracks and trains of railroads that hauled coal from Peabody mines. The federal government took sides, and in 1937 two-score Progressive leaders were indicted for interference with interstate commerce and the mails and for conspiracy. A special prosecutor from Washington handled the trial in which thirty-six were found guilty. Prison terms took the fire out of the new union, which proved ineffective when it tried to proselyte Kentucky locals, but the two unions divided union miner membership during the following decades.

The Progressives affiliated with the American Federation of Labor in 1936 when Lewis and other insurgent unions on the national scene formed the Committee for Industrial Organization. Ten years later, when Lewis returned the United Mine Workers to

AFL membership, the Progressives withdrew, since their hatred of Lewis would not permit them to belong to the same organization. Lewis-negotiated contracts brought a succession of pay increases and fringe benefits enjoyed by members of both unions. Simultaneously he permitted mechanization of the mines, which enabled the coal industry to survive. The result was that in a period of declining employment a smaller number of miners held better jobs.

On the national scene, the presidents of the craft unions that dominated the American Federation of Labor had neglected the obviously difficult task of organizing the mass production employees of great corporations. The steel mills were among the best customers of the coal mines, and Lewis, in his eagerness to unionize the steel workers, helped force a split in labor's ranks. Disregarding warnings of dual unionism, he joined with seven other unions, including the garment workers, in forming the Committee for Industrial Organization in late 1935. It launched the Steel Workers Organizing Committee, and by early 1937 Carnegie-Illinois, the chief subsidiary of United States Steel, signed up. The new union received a wage increase, an eight-hour day and forty-hour week, vacations with pay, and seniority rights.

City hall still sided with big business against the unions when "Little Steel" was asked to sign a collective bargaining agreement. Commissioner James P. Allman ordered Chicago police to preserve the peace and protect life and property when the Republic Steel plant on the far southeast side was struck May 27, 1937. Mayor Kelly announced that peaceful picketing would be allowed, if limited to a line of ten men at the plant gate. All others would be kept two blocks away. On Memorial Day, a Sunday, strikers at a mass meeting voted to establish a nonviolent picket line and started marching across a field. A riot filmed by a newsreel company showed police firing their pistols apparently without warning into the ranks of the strikers. Tear gas and clubbing completed the action. Ten strikers died of police bullets and thirty were wounded, many in the back. Police injuries were light. The newsreel was suppressed until a showing at Washington by a senate committee.[21]

Federal and state anti-injunction laws gave some protection to

[21] Edgar Bernhard, *et al., Pursuit of Freedom*, pp. 192-194. Barbara W. Newell, *Chicago and the Labor Movement: Metropolitan Unionism in the 1930's.*

labor, but picket lines were often ineffective and the unions developed a new technique, the sit-down or "quickie" strike, which forced immediate recognition of grievances and compelled collective bargaining. Seizure of a company's property violated accepted constitutional precepts, but the strikers contended that their rights to well-paid jobs were equal to the rights of stockholders to receive dividends. In any event, they argued that the stockholders, not the management, owned the plants. In a rash of sit-down strikes, attention centered on the Fansteel Manufacturing Company at North Chicago, which refused to bargain with a CIO affiliate. Workers on February 17, 1937, took possession of two key Fansteel plants and held them for nine days while heat and light were shut off and the sheriff used tear and nauseating gases, guns, and battering rams. The company rejected Horner's proposal that it recognize the union and rehire the men who had been discharged. The hungry and sick miners were arrested when they finally evacuated the plant, with fourteen being fined and jailed and ninety-one discharged. The National Labor Relations Board ordered the men reinstated, but the United States Supreme Court held the strike was illegal.[22]

In the 1936 campaign Lewis as executive committee chairman for Labor's Non-Partisan League had been one of Roosevelt's most energetic and vocal supporters. The Mine Worker president was soon affronted, however, when Roosevelt took "a plague on both your houses" stand of neutrality regarding the issue of industrial unionism. As a result, Lewis returned to the Republican party and made good on a pledge that he would resign CIO leadership if Wendell Willkie was not elected President in 1940.

HORNER'S SECOND-TERM BATTLES

Governor Horner devoted much of his curtailed second term to a renewal of his vendetta with those Democrats who had supported Bundesen in the destructive 1936 primary. He hoped to arrange for the removal of Ed Kelly from the mayor's office but even more he disliked the second-ranking official at Springfield, Lieutenant Governor John H. Stelle. The two were incompatible, and Stelle, who then was state treasurer, just before the primary had held up issuance of the salary warrants of thirty-two thousand

22 *Ibid.*, pp. 191-192.

employees under the governor's jurisdiction. Horner made it no secret that he distrusted Stelle and had no intention of turning the state over to him.

Governmental problems were critical and administrative duties tiring. Frequent special legislative sessions to deal with relief financing were necessary until mid-1939, when the economy recovered under the stimulus of war orders. Horner had the benefit of the increased sales tax, as well as a new tax on utilities, which meant that the state had more revenue than had been at the disposal of the Small and Emmerson administrations. By strict economy in other fields he was able to increase welfare and educational budgets while contributing heavily to the support of the unemployed. Conservatives hesitated to go along with the concept of social security, but unemployment insurance became effective in 1937. Two years earlier the legislature, despite warnings that burdensome tax increases would be necessary before many decades, voted for aid to dependent children and for old age and blind pensions. Horner backed the New Deal programs, although he had political difficulties with Harry L. Hopkins, and he refrained from expressing an evident displeasure with Roosevelt's unsuccessful effort to get favorable rulings from the Supreme Court by enlarging its membership. He arranged for Otto Kerner to be appointed to the federal Court of Appeals, which enabled him to give the vacancy in the attorney general's office to John E. Cassidy of Peoria, who had been beaten by Stelle in the 1936 primary.

The 1938 primary found Democrats again divided, and Horner gained political stature by winning another major victory. He forced the retirement after one term of Senator William H. Dieterich of Beardstown, a Roosevelt loyalist who had made the mistake of being a Kelly-Nash man. Michael L. Igoe, who had become United States attorney at Chicago, wanted to replace Dieterich, but the governor respected the tradition that only one of the two senators should come from Chicago. His choice was Scott W. Lucas of Havana, the chairman of the state tax commission. Both the President and the mayor favored Igoe, but Horner's candidates carried the state largely as a result of another split in Cook County. County Judge Edmund K. Jarecki had supported permanent registration of voters, and Kelly tried to retire him. Lucas benefited when Jarecki used the honest elections issue and won with Horner's help.[23]

The strain of the intraparty fighting started to show in the November election. High-level harmony was restored in time for the Democratic state ticket to win, but Lucas lost downstate and his winning margin was only ninety thousand. Republicans, who had elected a Supreme Court justice in the south-central district in June, won majority control of the house of representatives by five votes. Horner's health had been sapped by the factionalism and the burden of administrative detail, and two days before the election he was stricken with cerebral thrombosis and sent to Miami for a long period of complete rest, not to return until April. Stelle, who was acting governor by terms of the constitution, did not attempt to remove Horner appointees and allowed the executive power to be exercised by a regency of Horner men. The illness canceled whatever plans Horner had to enter a candidate against Kelly in 1939. State's Attorney Thomas J. Courtney, who for months had sent ax squads to raid hundreds of handbooks, ran for mayor and had the support of Jarecki, but Jacob M. Arvey, who was rising from the west side to party leadership, prevented worse outbreaks and Kelly won reelection in a race that was unexpectedly close.

Meanwhile second-term laws limited women to an eight-hour day and made them eligible for jury duty, a public works grant from Ickes enabled Chicago to break ground for a subway system, oil drillers located a productive field in the Centralia-Salem region, and as a result of widespread flooding along the Ohio River some of the residents of Shawneetown decided at last to move, with government assistance, to a dry town site atop a nearby hill.

To work out a Democratic slate for 1940, Kelly and Nash spent two days with other party leaders on the first floor of the executive mansion while messages were relayed to and from Horner's second-floor bedroom. The Chicagoans agreed to drop Stelle and Auditor Edward J. Barrett from a harmony ticket, which enabled Horner to respond with an announcement that he would not seek a third term. He wanted Cassidy to be his successor, but the compromise choice was Harry B. Hershey of

---

[23] Littlewood, *op. cit.,* pp. 201-208. "Recent Acquisitions of the Historical Library," *Journal of the Illinois State Historical Society,* LVIII (Autumn, 1965), 305-307.

Taylorville, a Peabody attorney and the Democratic state chairman. Hopes for party unity were ruined by the formation of an opposition slate by Stelle, Barrett, and Benjamin S. Adamowski, a young Chicagoan who gave up a legislative leadership post to launch a long career as a political maverick. Stelle sought the governorship, Barrett ran again for auditor, and Adamowski opposed James M. Slattery, who had been appointed to the senate upon the death of the colorful J. Ham Lewis.

The Hershey-Slattery slate won the primary, but only after the rebels made vociferous charges that the regency, a "bedside cabinet," had usurped Horner's powers and had made political deals with his enemies.[24] Republicans meanwhile raised constitutional questions about who had the executive power when the governor was disabled. Just before the primary Stelle unsuccessfully tried to discharge Finance Director Samuel L. Nudelman, a leader in the regency. Slattery, who had been Horner's commerce commission chairman, was nicknamed "Strongbox" by the *Chicago Tribune* as part of allegations that the collection of campaign funds had gone beyond ethical bounds. F. Lynden Smith, a Pontiac lumberman who had become state director of public works, had the major voice in handling the treasury of the Iroquois Lincoln League, into which the Hornerites placed payroll deductions and money collected from contractors. Nudelman sought to supplant him, and a bitter feud ended with Smith's death in a hospital bathroom. The rumors of graft were a major handicap and the Democrats were soundly defeated at the November election.

During the spring Horner had rallied occasionally and granted interviews that showed he had some of his old-time determination, if not energy. When a legislative committee wanted to ask questions about state finances, an ambulance on June 2 took the governor to a rented house on Winnetka lakefront. There he died October 5, not knowing that Republicans would return to power largely because Democrat had battled Democrat for much of eight years.

Horner was buried as a martyr, and the public remembered him as a man of integrity and compassion, a Lincoln scholar, and a battler who had refused to quit against political odds that seemed insurmountable. Stelle became governor for ninety-nine days. A lawyer, businessman, and farmer at McLeansboro, he had risen

[24] Littlewood, *op. cit.*, pp. 209-226. Watters, *op. cit.*, II, 456-463.

through the ranks of the American Legion and an alliance with the Chicago organization. As the European situation worsened, he established an emergency defense council and a reserve militia, since the National Guard had been mobilized into federal service. Admirers of Horner inherited his dislike of Stelle, and they called it scandalous when he painted the executive mansion, which had become dingy during eight years as a bachelor's habitat.[25] They accused the Stelles of staging orgies when old friends from southern Illinois were entertained. Without submitting proof, they spread rumors of financial misdealings that were accepted as gospel and never retracted until his death.

[25] *Chicago Sun-Times,* July 8, 1962. Littlewood, *op. cit.,* pp. 232-234. Watters, *op. cit.,* II, 470-471.

27

WAR AND RECOVERY

W̶AR CLOUDS OVER EUROPE STIMULATED THE AMERICAN ECON-
omy, and during 1939 prosperity returned to the land but could
not conceal the existence of a deep ideological split. For two
decades the national mood had been isolationist, and "Big Bill"
Thompson had accurately judged public sentiment when he
demanded that the United States steer clear of overseas entanglements. President Roosevelt in 1936 also favored keeping out of
Europe's troubles. As the months passed, however, a growing
number feared that noninvolvement would be impossible, if not a
mistake. The President moved from neutrality to nonbelligerence
and the next year called for the quarantining of aggressors when
he came to Chicago to dedicate the Outer Drive bridge.

Colonel Robert R. McCormick did not change his views, and
spectators at the bridge dedication ceremony could see a billboard
proclaiming that the *Chicago Tribune* was undominated. The
grandson of Joseph Medill and grandnephew of Cyrus Hall Mc-
Cormick, the newspaper's editor and publisher was an aloof giant
who demonstrated intellectual and financial independence and was
one of the nation's most influential men. After a patrician up-
bringing as the son of a second-level diplomat, McCormick in 1905
at the age of twenty-five first became involved in Chicago affairs
when he was elected president of the sanitary district. A lawyer
and National Guard officer, he became a field artillery colonel in
France. The *Tribune* was the family's property, and under the

colonel it developed the largest circulation in the Middle West and boasted of being the "World's Greatest Newspaper." He expanded news coverage, improved mechanical facilities, and developed pulpwood empires in Canada. As editor he defended freedom of the press, opposed most of the New Deal's programs, believed that the Midwest was the bulwark of Americanism, and directed Easterners to follow the course charted by his editorial page.

In the foreign policy debate, the *Tribune* warned that lend-lease would involve the nation in war, and it raised its voice against extension of the draft. The White House encouraged opposition and a new morning newspaper, the *Chicago Sun,* was launched late in 1941 with millions provided by Marshall Field III, a liberal who recently had come into an inheritance from the estate of his merchant grandfather. Whether the *Sun* could have convinced midwestern readers that the colonel was wrong was never determined. On the fourth day of its publication the Japanese bombed Pearl Harbor. The debate over steps that had been taken was put aside as McCormick and all who agreed with him gave complete support to the two-ocean war.[1]

ONE MILLION ILLINOISANS IN UNIFORM

Mobilization started without fanfare nine months before Pearl Harbor when the National Guard's 33rd Division was inducted into federal service and ordered to Camp Forrest, Tennessee, for training. During the following four years, by enlistment and the draft, probably one million Illinois men and women joined the armed services.

As in the other big war a quarter of a century earlier, the military did not operate on a state basis except for selective service. National melting-pot policies and statistics do not encourage assertions of state superiority or home community heroism, but they do show that 2,922,729 Illinois men of eighteen or more years came under the jurisdiction of the selective service system by registering with 361 local draft boards; 968,055 of

[1] Mary Watters, *Illinois in the Second World War,* II, 472-479. Frank C. Waldrop, *McCormick of Chicago: An Unconventional Portrait of a Controversial Figure.* Walter Trohan, "My Life with the Colonel," *Journal of the Illinois State Historical Society,* LII, 4 (Winter, 1959), 477-502. John Tebbel, *An American Dynasty: The Story of the McCormicks, Medills, and Pattersons.* S. Becker, *Marshall Field III.* John Tebbel, *The Marshall Fields: A Study in Wealth.*

them were above military age and their direct contribution was an exact count of manpower up to sixty-five years. The draft boards, nonpartisan and overworked, had the thankless task of deciding who, because of dependents or needed talents, could stay at home and in what sequence the others would receive orders to report to induction centers for physical examinations. Of those who volunteered, a majority preferred the navy. With a comparatively small number of exceptions, draft dodging was not a problem.[2]

The navy's recruits went to the training station at Great Lakes, the largest of its kind in the nation. Only a guard of forty marines had been left there between 1933 and 1935, but Great Lakes experienced a mushrooming in which the government spent seventy-five million dollars on added barracks and other facilities. Great Lakes provided boot training for more than one million men, which was more than a third of those who served in the navy. Abbott Hall at Northwestern University became the nation's largest school for midshipmen.

For its first induction center the army used Fort Sheridan, where a coast artillery brigade and pioneers in the women's army corps trained. Camp Grant south of Rockford also was reactivated as a reception center. It processed three hundred thousand men by late 1943 and then became the second largest medical replacement center. In the Spoon River country, the army took over 17,750 acres for Camp Ellis, a new army camp that had Galesburg as a rail connection and opened in early 1943 in a sea of mud. The rough terrain had been selected for the training of self-sufficient units for combined operations, anything from engineering regiments to small medical detachments.[3]

Because time and materials were insufficient to build required facilities, the army turned to skyscrapers and took over the Stevens and Congress hotels overlooking Grant Park. There radio operators and air force mechanics were trained. The Stevens, which later became the Conrad Hilton, was the largest hotel in the world with three thousand rooms. The Congress had one thousand rooms, and together they housed fifteen thousand men in scenes of former luxury. Grant Park was their drill field, the Chicago Beach Hotel their hospital, and the old Auditorium Hotel their

[2] Watters, *op. cit.,* I, 95-108. Much of the information in this chapter comes from this two-volume work, published by the Illinois State Historical Library.

[3] *Ibid.,* I, 108-143.

servicemen's center for a year, until the manpower demand was
satisfied. Chanute Field was expanded and became one of the
largest air force technical training schools, graduating 62,433 men
in 1943. With peace, it became a separation center where discharge
papers were issued. Scott Field, where airship pilots and balloon
observers had been training between 1923 and 1938, became the
chief communications school for the air force. Elsewhere big
facilities were hurriedly built, intensively used for a comparatively
brief period, and then closed. One was George Field near Lawrenceville where the army gave advanced flying instruction.

The navy converted two lake steamers into noncombatant aircraft carriers on whose flight decks landed pilots being trained at
the Glenview Air Base. Specialized schools also were conducted on
Navy Pier, in armories, and on campuses and smaller facilities. At
the state fairgrounds, used by the air force as a storage depot,
more than one thousand Chinese troops were trained in the
autumn of 1943.

The home front problems of civilians were increased by the
presence of the military. Some communities were entirely displaced to make room for ordnance plants, while towns such as
Rantoul had insufficient housing for families of noncommissioned
officers and civilian employees who arrived when military operations expanded. Schools were overcrowded and facilities for water
supply, sewage treatment, and electric and telephone service
strained. Recreational accommodations also proved inadequate.
Some local officers had trouble when servicemen became involved
in brawls, and some towns were forced to reform when they were
declared "out of bounds" to men in uniform.

Chicago won an international reputation as a "liberty town."
There were USO lounges at the six busy railroad stations and
smaller facilities elsewhere, but the center of attraction was a
fourteen-story former Elks Club in the loop that had been taken
over by the city before the United Services Organizations was
created nationally to raise a common fund and coordinate the
activities of the Y.M.C.A., Y.W.C.A., Salvation Army, Travelers
Aid, National Jewish Welfare Board, and National Catholic Community Service. All free to servicemen, the downtown club had
dormitories, showers, game rooms, a library, writing rooms, craft
shops, lounges, a cafeteria, two dining rooms, and frequent dances.
It was the pride of Mayor Kelly, whose wife worked as chairman
of the canteen service. Elsewhere in Chicago, twelve bowling alleys

occupied the stage of the historic Auditorium Theater. On smaller scales, downstate cities also went all out to provide hospitality for men who had been stationed nearby or were traveling through the state.[4]

PRAIRIE ARSENALS

In a great expansion of its industrial facilities, Illinois converted to war production and wiped out the last traces of the depression of the 1930's. Unemployment no longer was a problem. Beginning in 1838, some Illinois firms had gained ordnance experience by contracting with British and French purchasing commissions to build tanks and other armaments. While some people dreaded the long-range effects of wartime dislocations and felt that preservation of the status quo would be preferable to immediate profits, the state reacted with immediate loyalty when Pearl Harbor was bombed December 7, 1941.

Major civilian posts went to Illinois men. Donald M. Nelson, who had risen to the top management level at Sears Roebuck, was appointed chairman of the War Production Board by President Roosevelt and given overall responsibility for industrial conversion to a war footing. Harold L. Ickes was petroleum administrator as well as interior secretary in the Roosevelt cabinet, and Colonel Frank Knox, publisher of the *Chicago Daily News,* became secretary of the navy in a preliminary to the third-term campaign of 1940. Others who held top-ranking production jobs included Ralph Budd, president of the Burlington railroad; Merrill C. Meigs, aviation pioneer and publisher of the *Chicago Herald-American,* and B. C. Heacock of Peoria, president of Caterpillar Tractor Company.

Illinois remembered the lessons of 1917-18 and, while a state council of defense again was created at the start of the war, it did not face the succession of emergencies which Samuel Insull handled in World War I. Governor Green was chairman and Murray Baker of Peoria, an industrialist, was vice chairman of the new council of defense.[5] The executive director, who had direct charge of the supervision and coordination of the war effort, was Frank Parker, a retired general.

[4] *Ibid.,* I, 155-166, tells of other liberty towns.
[5] *Illinois Blue Book, 1945-46,* pp. 508-512.

At a time when overseas cities were being bombed, the blueprints called for every Illinois community to be organized for civilian defense, with block captains, air raid wardens, and first-aid facilities. Many thought the idea unnecessary, but Mayor Kelly in early 1941 started Chicago on a program that signed up nine hundred thousand volunteers and trained three hundred thousand for Red Cross duty or other emergencies. A reserve militia, inducted as home guards when the National Guard went to camp, under Adjutant General Leo M. Boyle stood watch over vital facilities, did some strike duty, and helped with sandbags in the severe flood of 1943, when the Illinois River reached a ninety-nine-year peak.

With the government paying the bill, construction records were broken in the erection of several gigantic industrial plants operated by corporations under special contracts.[6] The Dodge plant on Chicago's southwest side cost one hundred million dollars, was rated as the largest factory in the world, and employed more than thirty thousand in assembling engines for Superfortresses. Between March and September, contractors completed the twenty-acre Melrose Park Buick plant, which also turned out airplane engines. Outside Park Ridge, an all-wooden Douglas plant with its own airport assembled C54 Skymasters for aerial freight duty. Sizable factories at Rockford, Moline-Rock Island, Peoria, Springfield, Decatur, East St. Louis, and Alton also became permanent additions to the industrial scene, while hundreds of smaller plants in Cook and downstate counties were built to meet wartime demands. A larger number were expanded. Some war industries took over plants that had been closed during the depression. Prime contractors and subcontractors utilized space in warehouses, garages, and retail stores. Small businesses in some cases started in basements. As part of its amazing versatility, Illinois built ships for the navy. The small community of Seneca in La Salle County acquired new facilities from which landing ship-tanks were floated down the Illinois toward salt water. Western Electric Company at Cicero, where twenty-nine thousand had jobs, helped develop radar. In hundreds of plants, employees and management took equal pride in the army-navy "E" awards, which recognized significant contributions to the war effort.

The feasibility of the atomic bomb was proved in strict secrecy

6 Watters, *op. cit.,* II, 1-136.

at the University of Chicago. The government, alarmed by reports of atom-splitting research in Germany, assembled hundreds of scientists for a series of experiments that included the first weighing of plutonium, a man-made element. In a laboratory concealed under the west stands of Stagg Field they used bricks of graphite, slugs of uranium, and rods of cadmium to set off the first self-sustaining chain reaction. The experiment, which initiated the controlled release of nuclear energy, was conducted by Dr. Enrico Fermi, an Italian-born scientist, under the overall direction of Dr. Arthur H. Compton, one of the Nobel Prize winners on the Midway. The results justified the government's award of contracts for huge plants at Oak Ridge, Tennessee, and Hanford, Washington, to purify uranium and make plutonium. Meanwhile the Stagg Field reactor was moved twenty-five miles westward to the Argonne National Laboratory. On that peaceful, 3,700-acre site along the Des Plaines River, scientists working for the government and the university built bigger and better reactors and made other secret experiments which facilitated the military and civilian uses of atomic energy.

By January, 1945, Illinois led in production of ammunition as well as artillery. The government took over forty thousand acres in Will County near Wilmington for the Kankakee ordnance plant, the first in the nation to produce one billion pounds of TNT, and the Elwood plant, which assembled and loaded shells. Isolated shell-landing facilities and igloos for the storage of explosives occupied large acreages in other plants—Green River near Dixon, Illiopolis east of Springfield, and Crab Orchard west of Marion. In the only major accident, forty-one were killed in an Elwood explosion in 1942. The Western Cartridge plant at East Alton produced three billion cartridges. The expanded Rock Island arsenal manufactured machine guns and artillery mechanisms but specialized in the manufacture, storage, and shipment of spare parts to battlefields. Employment jumped from 2,735 to 18,675 during the war.

Severe sacrificing on the home front made the war production record possible. In a curtailment of civilian activities, twenty thousand retail stores closed because of a reduced supply of consumer goods, and many filling stations went out of business when a shortage of tires and gasoline stopped nonessential travel. The dislocations inevitably brought rationing and price controls. Within a month after the outbreak of hostilities, 101 special boards were set up in Illinois to control the distribution of automobile and truck tires, the theft of which became the equivalent of horse stealing on the frontier. Automobiles, typewriters, sugar, and bicycles also came under rationing, and in fairly rapid succession the boards, which issued coupon books, extended their controls to rubber footwear, fuel oil, coffee, gasoline, heating stoves, and by 1943 to processed foods, shoes, meats, etc. Some people hoarded scarce commodities.

The Office of Price Administration, one of the multitude of agencies with which the Roosevelt administration met its emergencies, meanwhile attempted to keep the lid on the cost of living, but found itself widely criticized at a time when the economic gap widened between consumer income and the supply of goods. Between 1939 and 1943 retail prices advanced 31 percent, twice as much as in the World War I period. After 1943, when controls became effective, the advance slowed. Complaints were loudest about gasoline and tire shortages, and some local boards found they had issued too many "C" cards, which allowed a vehicle to be driven with fair regularity. Racketeers sensed opportunities for profit and, when a point system of rationing was set up to control the distribution of meat, black markets became a threat. Investigators found that some packers and many meat dealers had slaughtered more animals than their quotas allowed and were charging prices higher than the ceiling. Some retailers received unexpected advertising when the OPA charged that the number of steaks sold exceeded the ration points allowed.

Used fats and waste paper were salvaged, children helped collect scrap, Chicagoans as well as downstaters bought seeds and hoes for victory gardens, and high-school teachers gave up vacations so that shops and laboratories could be used for vocational training in war jobs. Illinois eight times oversubscribed its quotas for war bond drives, consumers were educated about the war regime, and child care centers were set up so that mothers could fill gaps in the work force. Kenney, a DeWitt County village of 483, won recognition as the first community in the nation in which every home was participating in the war effort.

Too rapidly, gold stars appeared in windows, and more than twenty-two thousand men did not return to Illinois. After the war the army reported that 18,527 from the state were dead and seventy-four missing, while the navy's statistics were 3,665 killed and eighty-five missing. To care for the wounded, the army opened hospitals at Galesburg, Maywood, and on Chicago's south side. In time men who could not be released were transferred to veterans' administration hospitals, which in Illinois were located at Danville, Downey, Dwight, Hines, and Marion.

Those who returned with able bodies in some cases had difficulty finding jobs, but many corporations adopted a policy of hiring back all of their former employees.

Former Governor John Stelle, who in a few years would be national commander of the American Legion, helped draft a G.I. Bill of Rights, quickly enacted by Congress. Under it ambitious veterans could enter academic or vocational schools on government scholarships. The rush was so great that the University of Illinois established branches on Navy Pier and, for a year after the army no longer needed the eighteen hundred beds, in the Mayo General Hospital buildings at Galesburg. To help the returning

Restored gateway to Fort de Chartres

Courtesy Illinois Department of Conservation

men, Governor Green set up a special agency that became the Illinois Veterans Commission. Illinois increased cigarette and racing taxes to bond itself 385 million dollars to pay a bonus to its veterans. The formula called for ten dollars a month for domestic service, fifteen dollars a month for overseas duty, and nine hundred dollars to the dead's next of kin.

The return of peace found Illinois more firmly established than before as a preeminent industrial state. Heavy industries were growing rapidly and, although the 1950 census would show the state fourth in population, Illinois as a manufacturing state ranked a high third, close behind Pennsylvania. A census in 1947 showed that the value added to raw materials by manufacturing had increased from 2.1 billion dollars in 1939 to 6.68 billion dollars in eight years. Part reflected higher prices, but much was due to a larger volume of business in which both large and small plants participated.

Private corporations took over most of the big war factories built with government funds. International Harvester moved into the Melrose Park Buick plant. Such firms as Western Electric and Reynolds Metal, and many smaller corporations, acquired others, and Preston P. Tucker arranged to use the Chicago Dodge plant for an ill-fated attempt to put a new car on the highways. The city of Chicago took title to the Douglas Aircraft plant and expanded the acreage to make room for its new airport, O'Hare Field, named for a naval aviator. The major loss was that the aircraft and airplane engine business did not stay in the state, but Illinois continued to be the chief producer in radio and electronics and moved rapidly into television production. Chicago continued to be a manufacturing city of remarkable diversity, and the food and clothing industries dropped in their comparative importance. Meat packing became decentralized with the closing of the slaughterhouses around the stockyards and the opening of more efficient plants in smaller towns.

A LEADER IN WARTIME STRIKES

Illinois had more than its proportionate share of manpower shortages and strikes during the war. Possibly because of its large population, the problem became acute in some other places before it did in Illinois and, while manpower controls eventually were established, all hands joined in avoiding a labor draft. Women left their homes to work in factories and mills, men brought home checks fattened with overtime, retired workers returned to their former employers, German and Italian war prisoners helped out, and some twenty thousand Japanese-American evacuees from the west coast became permanent additions to the Chicago melting pot.[7]

The Negro migration speeded up. Such cities as Joliet and Rockford, where personnel managers encountered early difficulty in filling jobs, received sizable reinforcements from southern states, but the biggest impact was in the Chicago area. There 277,731 blacks were reported in the 1940 census and an estimated one hundred thousand were added during the war period. In five years Negro employment in the Chicago area increased from 4.9 to 11.7 percent of the work force. The pay was good, but housing was miserable and usually far from the jobs.

Although unions had been active in the state for more than a half-century, the big steel, packing house, and farm equipment industries had not been organized until the eve of the war, and vociferous protests had not eradicated company unions and open-shop policies. Hundreds of strikes, some of them wildcat stoppages, broke out in defiance of public opinion. Some had national repercussions. When the International Harvester Company, which had important war contracts, encountered trouble at its Rock Falls plant and elsewhere in 1941, President Roosevelt created a National Defense Mediation Board. It adopted a maintenance of membership formula as a step to protect the unions.

Government-administered work relief programs during the depression had been a handicap to union organizers, but labor prospered during the New Deal to the extent that it could afford internal squabbles. The Illinois Federation of Labor in 1936 endorsed John L. Lewis' fight for industry-wide unions. In 1941, when the Congress of Industrial Organizations was three years old, Lewis found that in its Illinois branch the new and militant Farm Equipment and Auto Workers unions had almost as many delegates as the Mine Workers. The next year he withdrew the Mine Workers from CIO membership, and the old custom of membership raiding became more pronounced when he established District 50 as a national catchall for miscellaneous membership. District 50 organizers had little success in Illinois, but carpenters and ma-

[7] *Ibid.*, II, 317-367.

chinists were prominent in jurisdictional disputes that at times resulted in stoppages.

The Mine Workers president, who had been an isolationist before Pearl Harbor, had refused to strike against the government during World War I, but in the military crisis of 1943 he defied the administration. Pearl Harbor had been followed by a labor-management pledge to President Roosevelt that there would be neither strikes nor lockouts, but one thousand miners at Danville left the pits when Lewis insisted that the wage features of his new Appalachian contract be extended to United States Steel captive mines. When the mediation board ruled against the union shop, its effectiveness was destroyed. Three times the government was forced to take over the coal mines and operate them for weeks. In an effort to retaliate against Lewis, Congress passed the Smith-Connally no-strike law and Lewis was accused of trying to increase his own power by wrecking the War Labor Board, the second agency given responsibility for labor peace.

The labor unions prospered under the Democratic President, and many businessmen unwillingly adopted a policy of negotiating the best contracts possible. There were exceptions to that rule, however, and one of the most uncompromising was George P. McNear, Jr., of Peoria, president of the once bankrupt Toledo, Peoria, and Western railroad.[8] McNear had prospered by giving efficient service on the 199-mile carrier, which extended on an east-west line across midstate. Bypassing the crowded Chicago terminal, it enabled shippers to save twenty-four to thirty-six hours. McNear, a hard-liner against featherbedding, fought the powerful railroad brotherhoods and quickly rejected arbitration ordered by the new War Labor Board in a 1941 strike. A federal grand jury indicted three labor men for plotting to dynamite a bridge. McNear obtained an injunction to limit picketing of his trains. After a personal appeal from the President failed, the government took control of the road in 1942. McNear said his money was being wasted and demanded return of the road. After three and a half years, control was surrendered. Thirteen brotherhoods promptly struck, McNear refused to negotiate, two pickets were killed, and shippers asked that a receiver be appointed on the unusual ground that the Toledo, Peoria, and Western, while financially solvent, was physically bankrupt. During prolonged litiga-

[8] *Ibid.,* II, 157-161.

tion there were indications that McNear had triumphed in his long antiunion stand, but after the war he was shot to death outside his Peoria home.

Sewell L. Avery defied the government for a different reason.[9] He insisted that the mail-order firm of Montgomery Ward and Company, of which he was board chairman, was not involved in war work and hence was not subject to the War Labor Board's jurisdiction. At the age of seventy-one he symbolized the business executive's resentment of New Deal interference with free enterprise, and he refused to deal with the United Mail Order, Warehouse, and Retail Employees union, which the NLRB certified as the bargaining agent for the Chicago retail store and warehouse. In 1944, after a two-year dispute, Roosevelt ordered the commerce department to take over and operate the Chicago plant. Avery staged a private sit-down strike until two military policemen carried him out of the building. The government obtained an injunction and surrendered control, after which the union won a collective bargaining election. In a later strike at the Chicago headquarters, the War Labor Board found the situation had "epidemic proportions," since sympathy strikes in war plants were possible. On Roosevelt's orders, the army took possession of Ward plants in seven cities, but this time Avery was left at his desk, isolated from the new management.

The Western Cartridge Company at Alton, which sent more than three billion bullets to the war fronts, was involved in long difficulties over segregation. Its employees successfully insisted that the company continue to hire only whites. One of the most troublesome unions, the United Farm Equipment Workers, had left-wing leadership that reversed its stand and emphasized conciliation when armament shipments to Russia were vital. In 1947, after the Taft-Hartley Act was passed, the union collapsed when its officials refused to sign affidavits disclaiming communist connections.

FARM SURPLUSES AND PRODUCTION MIRACLES

The prairie soil performed new miracles in the Second World War. There were shortages of manpower and equipment, but the men left on the farm worked harder to plant more acres on which

[9] *Ibid.*, II, 368-375.

they grew larger crops, part of which were fed to more hogs, cattle, and chickens. Illinois was first in soybeans, second in corn, hogs, and cheese, fourth in livestock, and important in poultry, dairy products, and fruits and vegetables as the Middle West again responded to calls for increased production of foodstuffs needed to supply larger armies and more allies. McLean County raised more corn than any other county in the United States. Henry County was first in hogs, and Champaign in soybeans. They and ten other counties—La Salle, Iroquois, Livingston, Cook, DeKalb, Bureau, Kane, Vermilion, Ogle, and Sangamon—were listed in a 1945 compilation of the hundred leading counties in value of farm products.[10]

In the turnaround from depression conditions, it again was demonstrated that agriculture's problems were economic rather than technological. When the demand arose, as it had in the Civil and first European wars, the farmer could produce enough grain and livestock to meet both export and domestic demands. Scientists had helped as well as inventors, and the showing in World War II was accomplished by reinforcement of the land's natural fertility with fertilizers and other chemicals, which were part of an agricultural revolution. Had the demand been greater, the rural technology could have geared up to meet it, and a vastly larger population could have been fed with a diet that gave more emphasis to soybeans than to meat and milk. The farmers' difficulties came in peacetime, when a dwindling export market shoved prices downward and led to agitation for reduced plantings. Under those conditions, the world did not need to make full use of the Illinois fertility.

The agricultural revolution between the two wars had many facets. The internal combustion engine made the draft horse obsolete. With adoption of the tractor, another great advance was made in the number of acres a man could plant, cultivate, and harvest. Farmers who earlier had learned the value of spreading manure and limestone on their fields obtained even higher yields by annual applications of nitrogen and other fertilizers. Herbicides took much of the labor out of weed eradication and thus helped reduce the number of mechanical operations during the crop-growing season. Insecticides kept under control the corn borer and other pests which could have caused rural disaster. As a result,

10 *Ibid.*, II, 383-450.

farmers no longer were self-sufficient. The number of farms de-
creased, since each man needed a larger acreage to justify his
investment in specialized machinery. A sizable part of the added
income from increased yields went to distributors of chemicals
and petroleum products.

Horses hadn't entirely been replaced by tractors when the
depression arrived, and many farmers who lacked money for
gasoline and tires used wagons for their infrequent trips to town.
In the process of mechanization that began with the McCormick
reaper, threshers required a better source of power than could be
supplied by draft animals, and belts were turned by early steam
engines which, because of their great weight, were not satisfactory
for field work. Tractors used a heavier version of the automobile
engine and as early as 1902 did farm work. A trend toward small
tractors had started by 1913. The International Harvester Company, which was the result of a merger of McCormick and other
companies, had headquarters in Chicago and made tractors there
and at Rock Island. Deere and Company, the world's largest
manufacturer of plows, went into the tractor business also. The
Caterpillar Company at Peoria, the result of a merger of companies
that made the original crawlers, became a major manufacturer of
earth-moving equipment.

The motor truck was instrumental in changing the system of
livestock marketing. Until about 1920, fattened cattle and hogs
were shipped by rail to Chicago and other markets, either by
feeders, shipping associations, or order buyers. Then the truck
provided faster and more flexible schedules and began diverting
animals to plants in smaller cities. The packing industry had been
in a slow process of decentralization, and the major firms stopped
building new plants in Chicago. Money reserved for modernization
was spent in the smaller towns, many of them west of the
Mississippi River, with the result that the Chicago stockyards lost
customers and importance. One of the by-products was a surplus
of unskilled labor that intensified a public aid financing problem.

Farmers learned that the old ways were not necessarily the best.
Illinois became a leading producer of hybrid seed that was a major
factor in increasing the corn yield. Pioneering research had been
started before World War I by Gene Funk of Bloomington, C. L.
Gunn of DeKalb, and Lester Pfister of El Paso. Their companies,
along with the Iowa firm founded by Henry A. Wallace, were the
largest producers of the new seed. In time the inbreeding process

made it unnecessary for the female rows, which produced the commercial seed, to be detasseled during the pollination season.

With tractors replacing horses, the demand for oats slackened but a more valuable crop with an industrial market was imported from Manchuria. Between the two wars, soybeans became the great second crop, with seeds that contained a high content of excellent protein and oil in demand for edible and industrial uses. Agricultural experiment stations developed new varieties adapted to the Illinois soil and climate, and government and private researchers found a multitude of uses for the oil and meal that were the by-products of hydraulic crushing. Processing plants sprang up along rail sidings, and Decatur became the soybean capital of the nation, with the A. E. Staley Company dominating the industry. The crop was well established when the outbreak of World War II shut off importation of vegetable oils from the Pacific, and soon Illinois farmers harvested one acre of soybeans for every two of corn. With peace, part of the demand disappeared, but the harvest was greater than in the 1930's. Margarine competed with butter, and until 1950 the dairy interests kept Congress from repealing a 10 percent tax on the butter substitute. The next year the housewives won a lobbying battle and the legislature legalized the sale of yellow margarine.

Concern about the topsoil grew in the drought years of 1934 and 1936. Illinois had never experienced a crop failure, for lack of rainfall or other reasons, and the reduced yields were still adequate in view of the carry-over of stored grains, but continuous clouds of dust blew from the great plains and erosion had reached the threatening stage in half of Illinois. Conscious that the soil was not inexhaustible, the legislature in 1937 authorized formation of soil conservation districts. Within a few years they covered most of the state and experts advocated contour plowing, grass waterways, and other steps that would control the runoff. Meanwhile, formation of levee and farm drainage districts had enabled 88.3 percent of the state's total area to be brought under cultivation. No other state had such a high proportion of its land under tillage.

Like urban residents, farmers also suffered in the depression, and many were reduced to a subsistence basis that left only memories of the 1909 to 1914 "parity period" of good crops and stable prices when rural and city people enjoyed equal prosperity. In 1912, farmers began to follow the example of chambers of commerce and bar and medical associations which had organized in the preceding century. At the University of Illinois, Dr. Cyril G. Hopkins preached that a crop rotation emphasizing use of lime, legumes, and phosphates would increase soil fertility and enable farmers to raise eighty bushels of corn and fifty bushels of wheat to an acre. With encouragement from bankers and editors, farmers in DeKalb County in 1912 organized a soil improvement association and hired a soil expert who, while managing the county poor farm, also demonstrated scientific methods and urged a greater use of limestone and clover. Association members purchased limestone on a cooperative basis and formed a subsidiary, the DeKalb County Agricultural Association, which bought and sold commodities and became a major producer of hybrid seed corn. Kankakee County next organized a farm bureau which selected a farm adviser from a list supplied by the University of Illinois. The organized farmers paid part of the county agent's salary and furnished him with a car and an office. Representatives of thirteen county crop improvement associations signed up as the first members of the Illinois Agricultural Association in 1916. The movement spread rapidly and the IAA became the largest and strongest state affiliate of the American Farm Bureau Federation.[11]

During the 1920's farm prices staged a partial and temporary recovery from a setback that followed the war. Many farmers unwisely purchased land, machinery, and livestock at inflated prices. George N. Peck, president of the Moline Plow Company, used an "equality for agriculture" slogan in advocating that grain surpluses be sold abroad at world prices in an effort to stabilize domestic prices at a profitable level. His proposal that the plan be financed through an equalization fee, incorporated in the McNary-Haugen Bill, had strong support from the Illinois Agricultural Association and was twice vetoed by President Coolidge. President Hoover in 1929 created a federal farm board headed by Alexander Legge, president of International Harvester Company, but it failed to achieve the objective of stabilizing prices at a higher level.

In the depression, many farmers were enabled to keep their farms as the result of debt adjustments worked out by a statewide committee appointed by Governor Horner and corresponding committees in each county. The number of foreclosures would have been larger had not the committee helped convince mortgage

[11] John J. Lacey, *Farm Bureau in Illinois.*

Tomb of Abraham Lincoln

holders that the occupants should be left on the land and given a chance to work out their financial troubles.

Earl C. Smith, a Pike County cattle and hog farmer who had faith in cooperative marketing, served as president of the IAA for twenty years starting in 1926. He defended the New Deal farm program and advocated that marginal lands be returned to the public domain. Legislation for production control and acreage reduction was guided through Congress with the help of Henry T. Rainey of Carrollton, a Democrat who early in the Roosevelt administration became the second Illinois man to be speaker of the house of representatives. The Roosevelt administration failed to stabilize the farm economy and by 1941 the agricultural association under Smith's leadership had broken away from the New Deal, leaving the smaller Illinois Farmers Union as a loyal supporter of government controls. The IAA developed cooperative subsidiaries that entered insurance, purchasing, and marketing fields and became increasingly vocal in the advocacy of free enterprise in the marketing system. Charles B. Shuman of Sullivan became the Farm Bureau's national president in 1945, and in 1970 was succeeded by William B. Kuhfuss of Mackinaw.

REPUBLICAN CONTROL—UNTIL 1948

Franklin D. Roosevelt lost the suburbs and downstate when he carried Illinois in his 1940 third-term election. That he had majorities in only twenty-eight counties was due to rural and business dissatisfaction with government controls, to a heartland distrust of foreign policy liberalism, and also to the influence of Colonel McCormick's editorial page. Certainly in the corn belt the Republican revival appeared first and showed the most vitality.

Dwight H. Green, a handsome Republican of exceptional promise, had been a public hero since he helped send Capone to the penitentiary. As a career government lawyer he acted as district attorney for northern Illinois for three years. Then he entered private practice and, drafted by Republicans to run for mayor in 1939, made a good showing by getting three-fourths of Kelly's vote. In 1940 he was elected governor in a campaign that soft-pedaled the isolationist controversy while calling for unity and preparedness.[12] In the resurgency the Republicans stressed claims that high-handed Chicago leaders bossed the Democrats while depending heavily on vote frauds in the river wards. The co-leader of the Republican triumph was C. Wayland Brooks, who took over Slattery's senate seat by a margin less than Green's. Outspoken in his refusal to go along with Rooseveltian policies, "Curly" Brooks

[12] Robert J. Casey and W. A. S. Douglas, *The Midwesterner*, a campaign biography written in 1948 when the governor aspired to be Vice President.

was a young and energetic Chicago lawyer who, with the backing of Colonel McCormick, had made several losing races for statewide office in the 1930's. Brooks, who had made a "This Is Not Our War" speech in the senate just before Pearl Harbor, survived a steady attack from labor and interventionists and won a full term in 1942.

The Green administration opened with a tax reduction, for the only time in the century. In mid-1942 the sales tax was allowed to drop to two cents, canceling the third cent added in 1936 for emergency relief. At the same time, the first cigarette tax was enacted. The unemployment crisis had vanished, and under wartime conditions construction of roads and public buildings had almost halted. Green zealously guarded a treasury surplus that reached one hundred million dollars and boasted that Illinois had never been in better financial condition. Nevertheless government appropriations began a slow but consistent climb. John Stelle had proposed a half-billion-dollar biennial budget when he left the governor's office in 1940, and six years later the legislature for the first time appropriated a billion dollars.[13] A soldiers' bonus added three hundred million dollars to the bonded debt, which was second largest among the states. Officials were under heavy pressure to expand welfare programs, mental hospitals needed modernization, and a heavy demand for improved schools coincided with pleas from farmers and home owners that the state pay more of the cost. Meanwhile local governments argued that, since their home rule powers were curtailed, the legislature should provide part of their revenues.

The opening of a 4.9-mile subway under State Street in 1945, made possible by federal grants of twenty-three million dollars, was followed in two years by a consolidation that solved Chicago's aged transit problem with a variation of the municipal ownership idea. The Surface Lines, which operated streetcars and buses, had a cash surplus of twenty million dollars but went into bankruptcy because they had not been able to renew franchises that expired in 1927 and as a result could not refinance bond issues. The elevated lines, owned by the Rapid Transit Company, each year reported increased deficits. Small in size, the Chicago Motor Coach Company had a profitable bus service with good chances for expansion on the city's fringes. Mayor Kelly and Governor Green joined in

13 *Illinois Blue Book, 1945-46,* pp. 482ff.

establishing the Chicago Transit Authority, which extended into the suburbs. The mayor named four and the governor three members of a board authorized to buy and operate, free from taxation, the transportation systems. Financial difficulties soon overtook the CTA, however, as a result of increasingly higher wage settlements. One feature of the consolidation agreement called for appointment of a circuit judge on wage arbitration panels. There were no strikes because the judicial member consistently voted for higher pay scales, which resulted in increased fares and fewer riders. The unusual Kelly-Green harmony also helped Chicago with congressional reapportionment, slum clearance, and airport legislation.

The midterm reaction against the party in power in 1946 was a disaster for the Democrats. The final fighting had ended in the Pacific and the public wanted an immediate return to peacetime conditions, with the servicemen back at home and plenty of meat on the dinner table. Not since "Big Bill" Thompson had the Republicans made such inroads in city wards, but the Democrats managed to save their most important offices, county judge and county clerk, which controlled the city and suburban election machinery.[14]

Faced with the possibility of losing the city hall in 1947, the Democrats with an instinct for self-preservation ran a reform candidate for mayor. Kelly's public standing had slipped. He denied any knowledge of syndicate crime and big-scale gambling by Capone's successors. More damaging, the school board he had appointed was under attack, and at indignation meetings parents charged that public education was under political control. Kelly was both mayor and Democratic chairman and was ready to announce for a fourth full-term, but Jacob M. Arvey, who had risen far in party leadership, calmly told him that the ward committeemen were consenting to his retirement. The new candidate was Martin H. Kennelly, a self-made businessman whose warehouses and moving vans, as well as his Red Cross work, had made him well known to most Chicagoans. Kennelly received large pluralities and, during eight years in office, avoided leadership by taking a position aloof from the affairs of aldermen, ward committeemen, and syndicate chieftains.[15]

[14] Watters, *op. cit.*, II, 508-509.
[15] *Ibid.*, II, 510-513.

Republicans, who no longer regarded Illinois as a doubtful state, took the road to political disaster. Party leaders attempted to get Green the vice presidential nomination and put him in the spotlight as temporary chairman and keynoter of the 1948 national convention at Philadelphia. To win the nomination it was necessary for Green, a rather pedestrian speaker, to instantly command national attention. The governor's friends paid for a masterful speech, written by a well-known eastern publicist, and then spoiled it by rewriting it several times in the interests of conservatism. As a result the keynote, delivered on a hot day, was a tactical failure, but Green was still the third-term nominee for governor.

Under Arvey's leadership, the Democrats followed their theory that in a bad year it is better to win with a reformer than to lose with an organization man. They gave the top positions to Paul H. Douglas and Adlai E. Stevenson but switched the offices they wanted to run for. Douglas had been an economics professor at the University of Chicago and a maverick alderman. At the age of fifty he enlisted in the marines and was wounded in Pacific fighting. His wife, Emily Taft Douglas, had served one term as congressman-at-large. Stevenson was not well known in Illinois and few voters remembered that his grandfather had been Vice President fifty-six years earlier. His boyhood roots were in Bloomington and he had interrupted a Chicago law practice for extensive service in Washington, where he became acting United States delegate to the commission that selected New York for the United Nations headquarters. Stevenson's travels and experience had been focused on Washington and Douglas presumably would have been preferred to run for governor, but the party organization regarded him as too independent. So Arvey reversed the roles, and Douglas ran for senator and Stevenson for governor.[16]

Green and Brooks were unexpectedly weak as 1948 candidates. The governor's subordinates not only ignored warnings about the unsafe condition of a Centralia mine where 111 were killed in an underground explosion, but they had solicited campaign contributions from its owners. Democrats succeeded in disqualifying a new third party which used the Progressive name, had ties with communist elements, and ran Henry A. Wallace for President. Grant Oakes of the leftist Packinghouse Workers Union was its

---

[16] Douglas in later years said that from the start he privately preferred to be senator, in part because in the governor's office he would have had trouble with the Democratic organization.

candidate for governor. A reporter for the *St. Louis Post-Dispatch,* which supported Stevenson, was arrested and indicted when he attempted to investigate a murder at Peoria, the new headquarters of the old Shelton gang. Green, who in past years had condemned Roosevelt for seeking a third term, now found himself doing the same thing and had no better answer than to plead that Republicans were experienced in government. The state labor federation's executive board endorsed Green, but Brooks had alienated CIO leaders, who organized union locals on a political action basis. President Truman made a back-platform speaking tour through southern Illinois in an underdog role.

Small crowds turned out to hear the Democratic state candidates, but the reaction against the Republicans was strong. Stevenson and Douglas won by landslide majorities, and their momentum was enough to enable Truman to carry Illinois over Thomas E. Dewey.

EDUCATIONAL CONSOLIDATION

Francis G. Blair, who served twenty-eight years as state superintendent of public instruction, reported in 1917 that Illinois was backward about joining a movement, which was gaining momentum elsewhere, for consolidation of school districts. It was costly to have approximately ten thousand one-room country schools, especially when some four thousand had fewer than ten pupils each, but the public had little interest in reorganizing the cumbersome administrative system under which elementary and high schools had separate boards. Small children could walk to a nearby one-room school, and farmers were not enthusiastic about hauling them in wagons over unimproved roads to the center of a consolidated district. Governor Lowden, who assumed that living costs would drop after the First World War, discouraged efforts to increase salaries of teachers. Blair wanted the state to pay 25 percent of the cost of public education, but Finance Director Omar Wright replied that the school districts were becoming too dependent upon the state government.

Others became concerned about inequalities in educational opportunity at a time when tax support varied, many teachers had only probationary certificates, and the state gave official recognition to three classes of high schools, those with two-, three-, and four-year courses of instruction. Fiscal conservatism was a major problem and many schools preferred to hire teachers who would accept the lowest salary. As a result, during the 1920's Illinois lost ground in its comparative position with other states. In an effort to help the districts with low tax assessments, the legislature in 1927 adopted a new state aid formula that was designed to achieve equalization. Each district got a flat grant of nine dollars for each child, computed by averaging attendance, and the low valuation districts were eligible for as much as twenty-five dollars additional each year.

Schools suffered during the depression. Rural teachers gratefully accepted salaries of seventy-five dollars a month, sometimes paid in scrip. Budgets were reduced, many courses discontinued, grades combined, terms shortened, and construction halted. The Illinois Education Association, which drew its membership from teachers, kept up a long campaign for reorganization and higher financial support, and was joined by the Illinois Agricultural Association in a campaign to do whatever might be needed to improve rural education. Most of the one-room schools were still in operation but, as a result of declining rural population, total enrollment in 1942 was one-third of what it had been four decades earlier. Survey laws passed in 1941 and 1945 encouraged formation of rural-urban committees to see what could be done about geographic, administrative, and financial reorganization. Many areas, if they had a population of two thousand and assessment valuations of six million dollars, adopted a new type of community-unit district which operated both grade and high schools. Resistance was encountered in some areas, but by 1948 the number of school districts of all types had been reduced to 6,166, approximately half of the original figure.

In the postwar decades the tax-supported universities expanded until the University of Illinois ranked eighth and Southern Illinois University nineteenth nationally in terms of full-time students. To care for returning veterans, the University of Illinois in 1946 opened branches at Galesburg, where classes were conducted for three years in a vacated army hospital, and at Navy Pier, which for nineteen years was used as an unlikely campus site because of a demand for undergraduate instruction at Chicago. The permanent Chicago Circle campus, at the edge of which the original Hull House was preserved, opened in the winter of 1965. Some alumni had feared that a metropolitan campus would offer strong competition to the Urbana-Champaign institution. Within a decade

Chicago Circle had 60 percent as much enrollment as the downstate student body. Dr. David Dodds Henry, who served longer than any of his predecessors, was president from 1955 to 1971, a period of major physical growth and academic recognition.

Southern Illinois University meanwhile became a double-campus institution and led the way as the former Normal schools achieved university rank. College facilities were nonexistent in much of the lower third of the state, and students who enrolled at the Carbondale campus legally could be trained only to be teachers. The University of Illinois failed to block a series of changes demanded by residents of the southern counties. As a result, the old teachers college in 1943 achieved a limited university status. Four years later it officially became a university. Dr. Delyte W. Morris, who believed that a university legitimately could perform some of the functions of a Chamber of Commerce, during a twenty-two-year career as president of Southern saw its enrollment increase twelvefold while it expanded into the populous St. Clair-Madison county area. Morris had been at Carbondale only a year before opening a residence center for classes at Belleville. In 1957, SIU took over the Shurtleff College campus and gave instruction there and at East St. Louis. The permanent campus outside Edwardsville opened in 1965 and soon had 57 percent as many students as were enrolled at Carbondale. The Normal schools at DeKalb, Macomb, and Charleston also advanced to recognition as state colleges and then as universities, while the original institution at Normal, still specializing in the training of teachers, through a series of name changes became Illinois State University. The state meanwhile created new senior universities at Springfield and Park Forest and took over the teachers' colleges in Chicago.

$$28$$

STILL GROWING, AMID
NEW PROBLEMS

A HEAVILY URBAN POPULATION FACED PROFOUND CHANGES as Illinois moved into the second half of the complex twentieth century. Larger generations born of population explosions were joined in the cities by migrants from the South, from Europe, and from Puerto Rico and Mexico. Population patterns changed in the old melting pot. Chicago began to lose residents, while the adjoining areas experienced a growth as startling as that of a century earlier. Cities and suburbs alike were crowded with children and problems for the coming generation. As taxpayers, the people demanded economy, and as pressure groups they asked for solutions, most of them necessarily expensive, to social problems. In a great ferment of ideas and action, incumbent and aspiring office-holders competed in offering new programs.

ADLAI E. STEVENSON, PRESIDENTIAL NOMINEE

A four-year term as governor was an interlude in the global career of Adlai E. Stevenson, the first presidential nominee from Illinois since Ulysses S. Grant. Like many of his predecessors, Stevenson lacked familiarity with state problems, and some Democrats, including Speaker Paul Powell during the 1949 legislative session, found the patrician governor difficult to understand.

547

Republicans recalled the troubles of the Green administration and leaped at any excuse to proclaim that Stevenson had his own scandals: the superintendent of foods and dairies was fired when it was revealed that horse meat had been sold as beef, and the governor dismissed his executive assistant and campaign manager for buying racetrack stock at bargain basement prices. Nevertheless Stevenson acquired a national reputation for improving the moral climate of Illinois.[1]

The Stevenson administration did little that was innovative. Budget-balancing was not a problem, due to Dwight H. Green's wartime surplus, but highway construction was overdue and Stevenson prevailed upon the legislature in 1951 to increase the gasoline tax and truck license fees drastically.[2] State police were taken out of politics through adoption of a merit system, and the troopers were sent raiding where local officials allowed slot machines to operate. Stevenson imported a professional to be nonpolitical head of the welfare department. Unable to get a constitutional convention called, he helped with passage and ratification of a "gateway" amendment which made it easier to get referendum approval of changes in the basic law.

The governor insisted that he wanted a second term at Springfield, but his intellect and eloquence made it inevitable that the Democratic party, which suffered from a shortage of top-level material in 1952, would consider him for the presidency. Friends organized a draft committee before the convention met in the Chicago Amphitheater.[3] The nomination came on the third ballot, and the acceptance speech, delivered after midnight, started a futile campaign. Whether Stevenson could have been reelected governor is questionable, since State Treasurer William G. Stratton, the surprise winner of the Republican nomination, had prepared an aggressive attack on the governor's Illinois record. Republicans had bounced back from the 1948 setback and in midterm the state had been carried overwhelmingly by Everett M. Dirksen, who went to the senate in place of Minority Leader Scott

---

[1] Most Stevenson biographers concentrate on the presidential campaigns and United Nations career. Little insight into the term as governor is given by such books as Edward P. Doyle (ed.), *As We Knew Adlai: The Stevenson Story by Twenty-Two Friends,* and Elizabeth Stevenson Ives and Hildegard Dolson, *My Brother Adlai.*

[2] The Stratton administration in 1953 canceled the second step in the truck license increase.

[3] Walter Johnson, *How We Drafted Adlai Stevenson.*

W. Lucas. Republicans in 1950 elected several Cook County candidates after Daniel (Tubbo) Gilbert, the Democratic nominee for sheriff, became a target of a crime investigation headed by Senator Estes Kefauver of Tennessee. Gilbert, who for twenty years had been chief investigator for state's attorneys, was known as the "world's richest cop."

Stevenson's great misfortune was to run twice against Dwight D. Eisenhower, who set records by carrying all but four counties in 1952. He lost only five counties in 1956, by which time the former governor had passed to the international scene.[4]

RELAPSES IN GOVERNMENTAL ETHICS

Illinois has never been cited as an example of purity in governmental ethics. Questionable practices began as early as the British period, when military commanders profited from land grants, and the Third General Assembly's switch of position during the Shaw-Hansen election contest is a classic example of high-handed operations in the legislative sector. Complaints about corruption at Springfield reached peaks in the flood of private bills that speeded adoption of the Constitution of 1870, and in the jackpot roll calls of the Lorimer era. Chicago's only successful civic uprising was against the boodling council, and the honest aldermen elected then had short careers. The standard Democratic answer to charges of river ward vote frauds has been to assert that some downstate returns also are shuffled. In recent decades allegations of general vote-buying in the legislature have been occasionally made and never proved. Comparative ethics is an inexact science, but an argument can be made that the rank-and-file membership of the legislature has improved in recent years. The apparent improvement in part could be due to a recent emphasis on investigative reporting by metropolitan newspapers.

Republicans retained control of the state house in 1956 in spite of Orville E. Hodge. One of the beneficiaries of the first Eisenhower landslide, the state auditor soon developed a yearning for

---

[4] There is no evidence that the divorce obtained by Ellen Borden Stevenson was an adverse political factor. She disliked public life and the governor unwillingly consented to the breakup of the marriage. Stevenson was the first governor of Illinois to be divorced. Stratton, his successor, was divorced during his last term as treasurer and afterwards was twice elected governor. The public considered that neither man was responsible for his divorce.

more spending money than was provided by his official salary and minor league real estate business at Granite City. His administrative assistant, Edward A. Epping, figured out how to siphon money from office appropriations so that Hodge could convincingly pose as a rich man. Their most original fraud was to prepare phony warrants, made out to persons who formerly had done business with the state, and have them secretly cashed by Edward A. Hintz, a naive sportsman who was president of a Chicago bank. Hintz thought that all officials had such check-cashing arrangements. With the money thus obtained, Hodge spent lavishly on himself. He acquired an interest in a Florida hotel, secretly invested in financial institutions under his jurisdiction, and let it be known that he expected to become governor.

The Hodge-for-governor dream never could have been realized. While temporarily successful as a secondary elective official, he lacked speaking ability and business acumen, and to campaign for a higher office would have exposed his shortcomings. Besides, his fraudulent operations had to be pyramided to keep up with his appetite for more money. State house insiders wondered why Hodge's office appropriations—the legislature had dealt with him generously—were nearly depleted midway in the fiscal biennium. The situation aroused the curiosity of George Thiem, state house correspondent of the *Chicago Daily News*.[5] When Thiem uncovered evidence of the phony warrants, prosecutors and other newspapers joined in the investigation.

Thiem acted just in time to save the Republican ticket in 1956. Under pressure from Stratton and Attorney General Latham Castle, Hodge in early July signed three resignations—as auditor, second-term nominee for auditor, and national convention delegate. Unable to borrow enough money to cover his thefts, he pleaded guilty to confidence game, embezzlement, and forgery charges and went to Menard penitentiary under concurrent sentences of twelve to fifteen years. The state recovered all of the $1,571,364 taken by Hodge, but the total amount misused, including inflated expense accounts for some employees, came to $2,599,603. Hodge's release on parole came in the winter of 1963. Epping and Hintz served shorter terms.

Stratton, who was not involved in the Hodge scandal, in his campaign stressed that the auditor was independent of the gover-

---

[5] George Thiem, *The Hodge Scandal: A Pattern of American Political Corruption.*

nor and that, once the wrongdoing was uncovered, he had acted forcefully. In the second Eisenhower landslide, Stratton won by 36,877.[6]

Unlike most governors, Stratton was an expert on state government before he took office. The son of a secretary of state, he was elected congressman-at-large at twenty-six, and served two terms in that office and two as state treasurer before his election as governor at the age of thirty-nine. Misjudged by the voters, who regarded him as a politician, Stratton was an administrator who kept a close rein on subordinates and showed a keen judgment of fiscal priorities. His errors were in the political arena. A downstater, Stratton maintained close liaison with Chicago leaders. When construction of badly needed expressways bogged down due to money shortages, the governor revived them with a 245-million-dollar bond issue retired from the gasoline tax. Later he pushed a 415-million-dollar bond issue to finance the 187-mile toll road system in the Chicago area. He helped downstate cities as well as Chicago by removing a restriction that referendum approval had to precede adoption of the city sales tax. That came at the start of Mayor Daley's regime, and 788 municipalities promptly levied a half-cent tax on retailing. Meanwhile the governor kept the lid on state spending until 1959, when the state sales tax was increased a half-cent to get money for schools. He provided beds for inmates who had slept on state hospital floors.

Disregarding the failures of Deneen, Small, and Green in the preceding half-century, Stratton ran for a third term. He won the primary by exerting the full power a governor has over the affairs of his own party. In the 1960 campaign, his experience was an inadequate issue, and almost any other Republican would have made it possible for President Nixon to carry Illinois and for the state house to remain under Republican control.[7]

Stratton won vindication in 1965 when a federal court jury

[6] The Democrats gave Stratton an assist by switching candidates for governor. Herbert C. Paschen, who was Cook County treasurer, resigned the nomination for governor because his office operated a "flower fund" for nonpublic expenses and the party, in the wake of the Hodge scandal, wanted to be circumspect. Paschen was replaced by Richard B. Austin, a judge from Chicago who was largely unknown downstate and didn't have time to campaign. Four years earlier, when Stevenson resigned as nominee for governor, the Democrats split over a replacement. With Stevenson's approval, the position went to Lieutenant Governor Sherwood Dixon, to the displeasure of friends of Secretary of State Edward J. Barrett.

[7] In a final ballot box appearance, Stratton ran for governor and finished third in the 1968 primary.

acquitted him of charges that he had evaded payment of income taxes on campaign contributions. In the climactic testimony, Senator Dirksen said that a governor had ceremonial expenses beyond his salary and that Congress had not taxed contributions. The prosecution made no claim that there had been kickbacks, bribes, or graft during the Stratton administration.

THE LONG CAREER OF RICHARD J. DALEY

In 1955 Richard J. Daley became mayor of Chicago for the first of five consecutive four-year terms, longer than anyone else had held the office. Born in the stockyards ward, the son of a union man, he worked his way up the political ladder, qualified as an authority on municipal finance and procedures, served in the legislature and as Stevenson's revenue director, and in time became Democratic county chairman. His only setback was a 1946 defeat for sheriff, which could have been a dead-end job. Martin H. Kennelly wanted a third term as mayor, but a long list of politicians who preferred someone else was headed by Congressman William L. Dawson, who rated No. 1 in the expanding black wards on the south side. Daley's entire career had been a preparation for the mayor's office, and he had little difficulty winning any of his elections.

As mayor, Daley accumulated political and administrative power. When other cities became bogged down with the problems of growth and inner decay, Daley maintained essential services and made a succession of improvements. Alliances with minority and ethnic leaders helped in the diverse and changing neighborhoods, and downtown business executives showed their appreciation with endorsements every four years. Daley was acclaimed as both the last of the big city Democratic bosses and the most successful of the new generation of mayors.[8]

Cermak had made the Democrats the ruling party in Chicago, but neither he nor Kelly attained the power Daley wielded. In his dual capacity as mayor and county chairman, he dominated the other ward committeemen and their regiments of precinct

[8] Two biographies of Daley have been written. Mike Royko's *Boss: Richard J. Daley of Chicago* became a best seller by attempting to belittle the mayor and to give him a minimum of credit for Chicago's progress. Democratic precinct captains prefer Bill Gleason, *Daley of Chicago: The Man, the Mayor, and the Limits of Conventional Politics.*

workers. Democratic slate-making sessions settled nothing until he spoke. Nonorganization candidates rallied by the Independent Voters of Illinois won occasionally, mostly in pockets of liberal strength along the lakefront. In a few cases black officials maintained freedom of operation after the party organization asserted control over newly occupied areas. The number of Republican aldermen became smaller, and in many wards the Republican organization was a stepchild of the Democrats. Countywide Republicans won some offices at some elections, if they had strong candidates and good issues to turn out a big suburban majority. In the downstate counties Republicans followed Dirksen, but neither Small and Thompson nor any of their successors had unified them into a Chicago-style political organization. Voters became more selective in marking ballots. Meanwhile Democrats from distant counties appreciated the Chicago majorities on election day, and only occasionally would a Democratic legislator vote contrary to city hall instructions. Labor especially was a key ally and had no pretense of nonpartisanship. The big Auto Workers and Steel Workers unions, as well as the reunited state AFL-CIO, supported Democrats and organized their members to register and vote. Stratton had given labor no cause for complaint and Joseph Germano, district chairman of the Steelworkers, in 1960 told his political action committee that "he is a friend of ours," but no votes were produced. The Republican governor told the AFL-CIO state convention that his administration had provided them with protection and services, but the delegates booed him and then voted full support of the Democratic state and national tickets.

In 1960 Daley's precinct workers saved the presidency for John F. Kennedy, who was officially credited with carrying Illinois by only 8,859 votes. Republicans claimed that the election had been stolen, by wholesale frauds and by disenfranchising voters whose registration records were missing from precinct binders. The protest attracted national attention, since a reversal of the Illinois electoral vote would have been followed by an investigation in Texas, and without the two states Kennedy would have been defeated. In Chicago the key Democratic objective had been to prevent a second term for Benjamin S. Adamowski, the Republican state's attorney. He lost by twenty-five thousand votes. The Illinois electoral vote was cast for Kennedy and a recount dragged into March. The court would not rule on thirteen hundred disputed paper ballots before proceeding with a recount of voting machine precincts. Adamowski finally gave up since he could not afford to continue paying $690 a day for recount teams. The tentative results indicated that enough votes had been switched to provide Kennedy's winning margin. Eventually contempt citations against more than six hundred persons, including election judges in 130 precincts, were dismissed on technical grounds.[9]

Under a civil service loophole created when Deneen was governor, thousands of employees of Chicago area governments held temporary appointments, periodically renewed, which permitted them to engage in precinct activity forbidden to permanent employees. The "temporaries" were the backbone of the Democratic organization. Senate Republican Leader W. Russell Arrington charged in 1967 that 40 percent of the Chicago city hall workers were exempt from civil service regulations. Governor Ogilvie in 1969 abandoned a demand for corrective legislation in the face of opposition from downstate Republicans whose conservative views were opposed to civil service in any form.

Republicans repeatedly failed to enact legislation introduced by the Better Government Association in an effort to reorganize the Chicago election machinery and reduce balloting frauds. Democratic discipline kept in line a vital handful who had intended to vote for the bills.

SECTIONALISM AND REAPPORTIONMENT

Until Stratton became governor, legislative districts had not been reapportioned since 1901. Glaring inequities had developed, but state and federal courts declined to order their correction. Congressional districts had been realigned in 1947 only because the alternative would have been a statewide election since both the at-large seat and one of twenty-five districts had been eliminated. Legislative reapportionment seemed an insoluble problem. Cook County, with slightly more than half of the population, had only nineteen of fifty-one districts, and simultaneously there were both big and little districts in Chicago and the downstate counties, while most of the suburbs were a gargantuan district. The situation was blatantly unfair, but sectionalism, based primarily on a downstate fear that liberal and prolabor laws would be enacted if Chicagoans controlled the legislature, preserved the status quo.

9 *Chicago Daily News,* March 17, 1961.

Stratton opened his administration by prevailing upon the legislature to accept a half-a-loaf compromise that gave Cook County its share of representation in the lower house but let downstaters have continued domination of the senate. His constitutional amendment, ratified in 1954, put the house on a one-man, one-vote basis before the Supreme Court promulgated that doctrine. A tripartite provision recognized Democratic Chicago, the Republican suburbs, and downstate as separate political regions, each entitled to its proportionate share of districts without overlapping the Chicago city limits or the Cook County boundary. The amendment froze the senate with eighteen Chicago, six suburban, and thirty-four downstate districts.

The 1960 census showed that Chicago had lost population while the suburbs gained 77 percent in a decade. As a result, reapportionment became part of the struggle for control of the legislature, and Democrats refused to abide by the Stratton formula. It called for two Chicago districts to be transferred to the suburbs, but the Daley men sought to protect their incumbents through the medium of undersized districts in Chicago and big districts in the suburbs. After the Supreme Court's one-man, one-vote edict, they insisted that Chicago districts be extended into the suburbs in a manner that would dilute Republican strength. A reapportionment bill passed in 1963 was vetoed by Governor Kerner because it contained population variations, for which Republicans in this case were responsible. The next step was appointment of a bipartisan commission which deadlocked when Democrats insisted that districts overlap the city limits. That forced an at-large election of all 177 state representatives in 1964. The ground rules called for the winning party to take a two-thirds majority, and Republican county chairmen mistakenly believed that their candidates would sweep the state because Barry Goldwater was the presidential nominee. Instead, by a fairly close margin, Democrats elected their full slate of 118 representatives headed by Adlai E. Stevenson III. Earl D. Eisenhower, the former President's brother, sat with the outnumbered Republicans.

Republicans in the senate canceled the big house majority, and the 1965 session saw more deadlocks. Senate and congressional redistricting was taken over by a three-judge federal court panel on which two Democrats sat, but they drew maps which gave Republicans another senate majority in 1966. A second commission worked on a house map, with the Democrats giving in rather than forcing another at-large election. As a result, the house returned to Republican control after four years.

At the 1970 election Daley almost achieved his goal of wiping out the Republican senate majority. It was a tie, with each party

Restored Old Capitol, 1840-1876

Courtesy State of Illinois, Department of Conservation

electing twenty-nine, but Lieutenant Governor Paul Simon was a Democrat, and Senator Cecil A. Partee, a black leader from Chicago, became president pro tem.[10] Republicans had only a thin edge in the house, and neither party could pass its major bills, but labor had a good session and a minimum wage law was finally passed. The new census was followed by more litigation. Federal judges drew a congressional map that displeased the Democrats. The legislature in 1971 did not attempt to reapportion itself but left the job to a commission dominated by its leaders. They reached a compromise that saw extensive overlapping of county and municipal boundaries.

THE KERNER ADMINISTRATION

Unfortunately for Otto Kerner, the senate had a frustrating Republican majority during his seven plus years as governor. Friendly Democrats ruled the house of representatives at times, but the senate was dominated by conservatives who did not deviate from positions taken at almost daily caucuses. Senator Arrington took major steps to upgrade the legislative branch of government as the senate repeatedly blocked measures advocated by the governor, a loyal Daley man who combined self-confidence with an affable style of downstate campaigning. The son of Horner's attorney general, Kerner had married a Cermak daughter and served as a National Guard general, federal district attorney, and judge of the County Court. During his military and public career his right-hand man was Theodore J. Isaacs, who had been his law partner and campaign manager and who came to Springfield to take the sensitive post of state revenue director.

Kerner's administration began with a reorganization of the judiciary on Daley's terms. Preliminary steps had been taken in Stratton's time by setting up a court administrator and by drastically reducing the number of justices of the peace and putting them on a salary basis. The court system still was compartmentalized and duplicative, however, and heads of the Illinois State and Chicago bar associations wanted the election and tenure of judges taken out of politics. Republicans leaders had agreed with them that new judges should be appointed by the governor

---

[10] For the first time in Illinois elections, the governor and lieutenant governor came from opposing parties.

from nominations by nonpartisan commissions. After years of maneuvering and with Kerner's help, Daley finally got his way and a constitutional amendment was ratified which, in addition to streamlining the courts, retained the traditional system of political nomination and first-term election of judges. The new system required that at the end of their terms judges run against their records, with a favorable vote automatically returning them to the bench. In effect, it provides lifetime tenure to most judges.

Kerner gave major attention to mental health and used the bulk of a 150-million-dollar bond issue, which Stratton had intended for modernization of state hospitals, for the construction of new zone center clinics. A statewide junior college system was created, and a board of higher education charged with coordination of academic programs and budgeting of rival state universities. The governor led trade missions to Europe in 1963 and Asia in 1965. Taxation provided a continual headache. In 1961 he prevailed upon the legislature to add a half-cent to the state sales tax, but not until 1965 was Daley able to double the city sales tax to a full penny. That year the senate turned down Kerner's plea for the state revenue fund to get two-thirds of a proposed three-cent increase in the gasoline tax. Kerner wanted a constitutional convention and, as an alternative, gave conflicting opinions about how the revenue article should be amended and what kind of an income tax levied, if any.

A conflict-of-interest situation almost cost Kerner a second term. In midcampaign it was revealed that Isaacs, the dominant behind-the-scenes personality in the administration, was stockholder and attorney of an envelope company he had organized after the 1960 election and which received considerable state business. Amid alarm in high Democratic circles, Isaacs resigned as campaign manager. Charles H. Percy, who was Kerner's 1964 opponent, had his own troubles, trying to be loyal to the Goldwater presidential ticket without offending Republican liberals. [11] As a result, Percy made only incidental use of the conflict-of-interest issue. Isaacs was indicted for collusion and defrauding the state, but the charges were later dropped.

The political pendulum did not play favorites, and both Percy and Daley were winners in 1966. Percy bounced back and de-

[11] Martha Cleveland, *Charles Percy: Strong New Voice from Illinois.* David Murray, *Charles Percy of Illinois.*

feated Senator Paul H. Douglas, who sought a fourth term. Several Republicans carried Cook County, including Sheriff Richard B. Ogilvie, who became president of the county board of commissioners. Daley's top priority was the election of Democrats to two Supreme Court justiceships that had been transferred from downstate to Cook County as a result of judicial reform. His judges carried by a narrow margin, and within three years a vacancy in southern Illinois enabled the Democrats to obtain a majority on the high court for the first time since the depression era. The mayor's next objective was control of both legislative houses.

The Supreme Court had its own scandal in 1969, and Chief Justice Roy J. Solfisburg of Aurora and Justice Ray I. Klingbiel of East Moline resigned. They had held stock in a Chicago bank which Isaacs had organized, and a special bar commission found that the transactions had the appearance of impropriety. Kerner considered making a third-term campaign, but took an appointment as a federal Court of Appeals judge after resigning and turning the state over to Lieutenant Governor Samuel H. Shapiro. Kerner achieved additional prominence as chairman of a commission appointed by President Johnson to study the civil disorders that reached a climax in the summer of 1967. The group concluded that the United States was "moving toward two societies, one black, one white—separate but unequal."

In the twentieth-century migration of black Americans from the rural South to northern cities, one of the major routes led from Mississippi, Tennessee, Arkansas, and Alabama directly northward to Chicago and its satellites. Restlessness did not observe color lines and the Negroes followed the example of the first whites who poured across the Ohio River to reach new homes. The proportion of blacks in Chicago increased steadily—from 10 percent in 1950 to 14 percent in 1960 and 32.7 percent in 1970. Simultaneously there was a shift of whites to outlying parts of Chicago and then to the suburbs. Neighborhoods changed rapidly as the south side's original black belt expanded and most of the west side was taken over by newcomers who found assimilation problems as difficult as those faced by Irish and east Europeans in previous waves of immigration. John Cardinal Cody, a strong supporter of civil rights and unsegregated housing, encountered resistance when he arrived in 1961 to become spiritual leader of more than 2.25 million Catholics in the world's richest and most populous archdiocese.

The Rev. Martin Luther King, Jr., fresh from successes in the

South, attempted to break down Chicago's segregation pattern in the summer of 1966. He led demonstrators into white neighborhoods on the southwest side but canceled plans for a march into all-white Cicero, although Kerner had promised the protection of the National Guard in a threatened racial war. For weeks rock throwing, looting, and fire bombings were common. King also failed to overturn the establishment when he symbolically seized a white-owned flat building to underscore complaints that absentee landlords were responsible for the deterioration of property. The Rev. Jesse Jackson, who didn't accept a football scholarship at the University of Illinois and didn't get a city hall payroll job when he arrived in Chicago, became the most charismatic of a new breed of black leaders. As head of Operation Breadbasket, the economic arm of King's Southern Christian Leadership Conference, he organized blacks to fight discrimination in employment by withholding purchasing power. Meanwhile a prolonged economic boycott developed into a stalemate at Cairo, where black leaders attempted to imitate Jackson. Blacks also demanded auxiliary programs for the training of apprentices, and Chicago in 1969 saw a long dispute involving the building trades industry. The same issue shut down construction of interstate highways in the East St. Louis vicinity.

Illinois in 1885 had been one of the first states to enact a civil rights law against discrimination in public accommodations. In 1939 black legislators began efforts to create a state fair employment practices commission, but their bills, although supported by Stevenson and Stratton, were defeated until 1961. When the legislature repeatedly refused to prohibit racial discrimination in the sale and rental of private housing, the state Supreme Court gave blanket approval of local ordinances adopted in many cities. By executive order, Kerner in 1967 promulgated a code of fair practices under which state agencies were ordered not to discriminate in the granting of licenses and other legal privileges. Three years later real estate brokers obtained an injunction when the Democratic administration ordered that licenses not be issued to anyone who discriminated in the sale or rental of residences.

Part of a national trend, the Kerner years saw a rapid escalation in public aid costs. Budgeting problems became tougher. The governor's solution in 1961 was to order a 10 percent across-the-board cut in welfare payments, but the appointive public aid commission revolted. Daley took no public action, but Kerner gave in and accepted an alternative he had previously rejected. The legislature established the principle of ceilings on individual grants and replaced the commission with a public aid department under a single executive. So that the governor would not have to sign or veto a bill, by resolution the lawmakers authorized the use of public aid funds for birth control.

RICHARD B. OGILVIE AND THE INCOME TAX

Until his first budget message in 1969, Governor Richard B. Ogilvie gave no hint that he would risk unpopularity by recommending that Illinois adopt a state income tax. As Republican nominee and governor-elect he had talked candidly about the existence of a financial crisis that had been ignored too long. The only solution he recommended was federal tax sharing, the distribution to the states of part of the federal income tax receipts. Other governors supported him, and President Nixon sent a tax-sharing message to Congress. Ogilvie believed that the proper functioning of state government required more money, and he courageously acted where other officials avoided unpopular stands.

Never admitting that federal help might not arrive on time, if ever, Ogilvie made a public relations mistake by imposing strict advance secrecy on his sensational message. Delivered at noon, it asked for the appropriation of an astronomical four billion dollars in the first of the annual budgets. To raise that amount he proposed a sizable package of revenue bills topped by a request for a 4 percent income tax on both individuals and corporations. Word spread quickly, and by sundown Republicans had lost some local elections.

Ogilvie bought support from Daley and other mayors with his own revenue-sharing program. No action had been taken at Washington, but the budget provided for distribution of one-eighth of the state income tax to the cities and counties on a no-strings basis. Democratic legislators privately admired Ogilvie's courage, but they placed the blame for the income tax on his shoulders, even while they made certain that it would get enough votes for passage under a bipartisan agreement. The process took months, during which most of the miscellaneous taxes in his budget were dropped and the income tax rates were set at 2.5 percent for individuals and 4 percent for corporations. The state Supreme

Court, which in recent decades had not hesitated to break away from precedents when the problems of government became critical, promptly held the tax constitutional. Based on a new legal approach, it imposed a tax on the privilege of earning or receiving income in or as a resident of Illinois.

Ogilvie had planned to use the income tax revenue on schools, universities, welfare institutions, mass transportation, recreational facilities, and a long list of other governmental services. He was thwarted, however, because public aid costs kept rising drastically. They soared past the one-billion-dollar-a-year level and forced the governor to retrench. An effort to make selective reductions in aid payments was blocked by a court order in Cook County. As belt tightening became general, university boards were notified that they could not expect funds for expansion. Despite the new tax, at the start of his second-term campaign Ogilvie warned the state that it faced bankruptcy.

Unfortunately for Republicans, Everett McKinley Dirksen, the rumpled minority leader whose oratory fascinated America, died in the first year of his fourth term in the United States senate, where only Shelby M. Cullom had represented Illinois longer.[12] Dirksen, a hard-working legislative technician who did not hesitate to change his position on national and international questions, retired from the house in 1948 because of an eye affliction but two years later won the senate seat from which he attained prominence. Paying a political debt, Ogilvie appointed his downstate campaign manager, House Speaker Ralph T. Smith of Alton, to the Dirksen vacancy. Daley meanwhile shifted positions and backed State Treasurer Adlai E. Stevenson III for the short-term election to the senate. Two years earlier, because he had questioned the Vietnam War, Stevenson had been denied a chance to run against Dirksen. He had been critical of the mayor and Chicago police, whom he called "stormtroopers in blue" for their part in handling street rioters at the 1968 Democratic convention. Stevenson had assumed leadership of a liberal revolt against what he had called the Democratic party's "feudal" system. It was to be launched at a campaign-style picnic, held the day Dirksen died. Daley showed up unexpectedly and endorsed Stevenson, whose slating followed automatically.

[12] Neil MacNeil, *Dirksen: Portrait of a Public Man.* Cullom served five full terms as senator. Lyman Trumbull and Paul H. Douglas served three each.

In the 1970 campaign Smith counted upon a public reaction against campus and ghetto violence and in television commercials emphasized the law-and-order issue. Stevenson countered by moving to the political center, pinning an American flag on his lapel, and calling for an end of violence by his student supporters. The economy was quiet and Smith, the victim of the income tax's unpopularity, failed to adjust to Stevenson's strategy. The resultant Democratic landslide did not end at the state house. At the courthouse level, in several counties Democrats were elected for the first time since the Civil War.

The result might have been different had the public known that Secretary of State Paul Powell, the leading downstate Democrat who died during the campaign, had amassed a three-million-dollar fortune that included racetrack stock and enough one hundred dollar bills to fill several shoeboxes. Powell, the leading downstate Democrat, talked with the twang of his hill-country background and had served three times as speaker of the house of representatives. Several months after the funeral eulogies, the public learned that a cache of eight hundred thousand dollars in big bills was found under mysterious circumstances in his hotel room. Unlike Orville E. Hodge, who was a friend, Powell was not available for explanations and confessions. The Internal Revenue Service took custody of his financial records, and several subordinates and associates were indicted. To protect the state's interest, Attorney General William J. Scott filed court claims against Powell's estate.

During the Powell investigation, which coincided with renewed agitation for a stronger law on governmental ethics, a federal grand jury indicted Kerner and Isaacs for bribery, tax evasion, mail fraud, and conspiracy. They were charged with having profited secretly from the purchase and resale of stock in one of the racetracks under state regulation. Kerner also was charged with perjury when he denied that he had talked to racing officials about preferred racing dates for the track. Three other persons, two of them former Kerner appointees, also were indicted for allegedly arranging for Kerner and Isaacs to make a quick profit.

THE CONSTITUTION OF 1970

The most pressing problems had largely been eliminated before a convention, the sixth in the history of the state, wrote Illinois' fourth constitution. Demand for changes in the basic law had been reduced by adoption, under the gateway procedure, of reapportionment and judicial reform amendments. The revenue article still contained restrictions, however, and the League of Women Voters played a leading role in keeping the "con-con" issue alive. Without fanfare, the legislature in 1967 submitted the question to a referendum. A low-keyed campaign avoided controversial topics, and at the 1968 election the convention was called by a surprisingly large margin, 2,979,977 to 1,135,440.[13] Before the delegates were elected a year later, the Illinois Supreme Court removed another issue by upholding the constitutionality of the new state income tax.

Samuel W. Witwer of Kenilworth, a Republican lawyer who had led previous drives for constitutional reform, was elected convention president when the 116 delegates, two from each senate district, began work in the house chamber December 8, 1969. On a nonpartisan basis they had been nominated September 23 and elected November 18. Despite a poor showing in the suburbs, nominal Republicans held half of the seats but they never functioned as a unit. A major surprise was the election of eight assorted independents in Chicago districts, where only thirty-two of forty-two delegates had been backed by the Democratic organization, and two of those voted independently much of the time. Not all of the independents were liberals and one was the Rev. Francis X. Lawlor, a priest who objected to black infiltration into the southwest side.

The deliberations soon were transferred to the historic Old Capitol, which had been the scene of three earlier conventions. Without party leadership or discipline, the delegates fragmented into nebulous factions and transacted much of their business through temporary alliances. Determined to avoid the long delays of the 1920-1922 convention, in eight months they completed the drafting of a constitution that was ratified, 1,122,425 to 838,168, at a special election November 18, 1970, with the support of major newspapers, several statewide organizations, Governor Ogilvie, Mayor Daley, and most of the major figures in both parties. Most of its provisions became effective the following July 1.

To increase the prospect that the main body of the constitution would be ratified, four controversial points were submitted to the

13 George D. Braden and Rubin G. Cohn, *The Illinois Constitution: An Annotated and Comparative Analysis.* Victoria Ranney (ed.), *Con-Con: Issues for the Illinois Constitutional Convention.*

House of Representatives in the restored Old State Capitol

voters as separate propositions. By a fairly narrow margin, a proposal to lower the voting age from twenty-one to eighteen years was defeated a short time before a United States Supreme Court ruling required that the change be made nationally. By almost 2 to 1, abolition of the death penalty was turned down. The other two propositions maintained the status quo in the selection and retention of judges and in the election of state representatives from multimember districts. The results in both cases represented victories for Daley, whose delegates during the closing days of the convention scored tactical triumphs by dictating the ballot position of alternate proposals.

Witwer, Ogilvie, and the bar association leaders wanted judges to be taken out of politics through appointment from nominations by panels of lawyers and laymen. The mayor insisted upon continuation of the system, in effect since the 1962 amendment, which called for political nomination and selection of judges to their first terms. By the closest margin of any of the separate propositions, the Daley side triumphed, but the results raised a question about public confidence in the metropolitan bench. Cook County voted for appointed judges, with most of the support coming from the suburbs. The issue was decided by many downstaters who wanted to continue election of their local judges. They saved the day for Daley, who was able to keep control of the Cook County judiciary and its patronage. In the other separate proposition, Joseph Medill's unique system of minority representation, which required election of three representatives from each district, carried over the alternate plan for small districts from which only one house member would be chosen. The single-member plan could have benefited Republicans and independents in some areas.

On other issues Daley also was a winner. The new constitution granted extensive home rule, including some taxing authority, to cities of over twenty-five thousand population and made them available to counties of two hundred thousand population. An immediate struggle developed on the question of whether the local governments, as well as the state, should have authority to license and regulate businesses and professions. Metropolitan officials soon took steps toward the adoption of cigarette and gasoline taxes, which in the past could have been done only after passage of enabling legislation at Springfield.

Between the calling of the convention and the election of the delegates, the Supreme Court's approval of the state income tax had eliminated much of the controversy over the 1870 revenue article. Business interests received assurance that the income tax ratio between corporations and individuals could never exceed the existing eight to five. The legislature received authority to levy a true sales tax. Especially in its handling of the personal property tax issue, the convention provided future problems for governmental agencies. It already had been complicated by the adoption at the 1970 election of an amendment to the old constitution eliminating the unpopular and inequitable tax from individuals but not corporations. The delegates required that all personal property taxes must be abolished by 1979. This intensified the problem school districts and other local governments already faced in trying to find replacement sources of revenue. The new constitution apparently paved the way for extensive litigation by requiring that revenues lost by local governments must be replaced by the imposition of statewide taxes, with only real estate exempt, on the persons or corporations relieved of paying the personal property tax. The legislature was authorized to grant homestead exemptions or rent credits, which could be limited to the elderly.

The new constitution required that the legislature meet annually, which it was already doing. It provided that the governor and lieutenant governor must come from the same party, following the federal system. A comptroller was substituted for the auditor, and the state superintendent was abolished as an elected office. From kindergarten to university graduate schools, all education was placed under the jurisdiction of a single board. A bipartisan board was created to supervise elections, and the required residence in the state before voting was reduced from one year to six months. Beginning in 1978, the election of state officers was switched to the nonpresidential years. The governor received authority to reduce appropriations as well as veto them. New sections in the bill of rights called for freedom of discrimination in employment and the sale or rental of property, on the basis of sex, and against the handicapped.

THE CHANGING FACE OF ILLINOIS

When the 1970 census was taken, Illinois was the fifth largest state. Its population had increased 10.2 percent in the decade to a total of 11,113,975, but warmer regions to the southwest and south were growing at a faster rate than the Old Northwest. In the 1950 census Illinois had lost its status as the third largest state to California, and two decades later it also dropped behind Texas. In the new count, Illinois was 82.9 percent urban and 13.6 percent nonwhite.

Urbanization had made great changes in the population pattern of the melting pot as new arrivals from the South were reinforced by immigrants from overseas and from Puerto Rico and Mexico. Chicago was still the nation's second largest city, with 3,366,957 residents, but for two decades it had been losing population. Largely as a result of outmigration to the suburbs, it had 254,005 fewer residents than twenty years earlier. Of those who remained in the city, there was almost exactly one black for every two whites. Spanish signs appeared on public buildings to testify that Chicago was becoming a bilingual city. Latin-Americans composed from 10 to 15 percent of the city's population. In the older, deteriorating neighborhoods, Puerto Ricans were joined by migrants from Mexico and Central and South American countries who sought employment that would permit them to move to better living quarters or, in some cases, to return to a warmer homeland. Chicago, which was building one-hundred-story plus skyscrapers, also had furnished apartments in which migrant native whites camped while they shuttled between city employment and their homeland in the hills of southern Appalachia. Approximately ten thousand persons of Japanese blood, most of whom became Chicagoans in the wartime evacuation of the Pacific coast, had been assimilated easily. More difficulty was encountered by a smaller number of Indians who had left reservations to try city life.

Mobility continued to be an outstanding characteristic of the people and there had been a great movement from the city to the suburbs. As a result, nearly two-fifths of the population of the nation's second largest county lived outside Chicago. The census also revealed that, for the first time since 1920, no longer did a majority of the people of Illinois live in Cook County. As fast as the suburban townships were growing, the rate of growth for twenty years had been approximately twice as great in the 101 counties outside Cook. Rockford with 147,370 residents was the second largest Illinois city, followed by Peoria, Springfield, and Decatur. Of the state's nineteen municipalities of more than fifty thousand population, seven were in the Cook County suburbs— Evanston, Skokie, Cicero, Arlington Heights, Oak Park, Oak Lawn, and Berwyn. Four others—Joliet, Aurora, Waukegan, and Elgin— were in the nearby counties. Downstate growth was largely concentrated in and around the cities and, in a continuation of a century-old trend, forty-nine counties had fewer residents than when the 1960 census was taken. Not all were rural. One of the cities losing population was East St. Louis, which ranked ninth. Its ratio of blacks to whites was approximately 2 to 1, and it had severe problems as the result of a small tax assessment base and a large proportion of unemployed. Cairo, where the blacks constituted a large minority, also lost appreciably.

Almost without warning, environmental protection became a major concern. In 1967 only a mild protest greeted Governor Kerner's veto of a bill which would have outlawed the dumping of dredgings into Lake Michigan. Within two years, however, public sentiment was mobilized, largely due to the work of William J. Scott, the new attorney general. He assumed leadership of an antipollution campaign and gave a decisive push to enactment of laws designed to increase the prospect that future generations might have clean air and water, despite increases in population and development of more complex technologies. To that end, he won court cases against utility companies, steel mills, sanitary districts, and other agencies. Coal from Illinois mines became undesirable because of its high sulphur content, and utilities erected duplications of an atomic-powered electrical generating plant at Dresden. Concern about pollution was not limited to the cities. Agricultural practices that had made bonanza yields possible became suspect when scientists learned that Decatur's water supply might be endangered by fertilizer nitrogen washed from upstream farms. [14] In the background of a debate over the economy and the environment was the recollection that within two thousand years in Illinois two earlier civilizations, the Hopewellian and the Middle Mississippian, had flourished at sophisticated heights and then collapsed.

The people of Illinois remained mobile, with many moving frequently to new jobs or homes. To provide for the families which were leaving Chicago, corporate management rushed the construction of subdivisions and, in some cases, of entire towns. Asphalt parking lots around shopping centers blanketed the soil where corn and truck crops had grown before the population explosion. By 1971 Cook County had 101 suburban municipalities, some of them brand new, and the rest of the metropolitan area seventy-one. Up and down the economic scale, they provided homes for families whose paychecks in most cases came from Chicago. Commuting problems added to traffic congestion and

[14] Barry Commoner, *The Closing Circle: Nature, Man and Technology.*

created a demand for more and wider expressways. Downtown garages and parking lots raised their fees, but the rapid transit lines could not escape deficits.

Chicago, the youngest of the world's ten largest cities, was building skyscrapers over a hundred stories high, and three of them would be among the world's six tallest. New industries, among them insurance, developed in the city that no longer was "hog butcher to the world." Because of racial tensions and increased crime rates, fewer people visited the loop area after business hours and police patrols were reinforced.

Downstate villages disappeared, interstate highways cut wide swaths through farms, hotels failed to meet competition from motels which specialized in convenience for the motoring public, and middle-sized cities experienced downtown decay when housewives drove to outlying shopping centers. In a tragic deforestation, canopies of elms over streets and parks succumbed to a blight that, starting in 1950, spread rapidly through Illinois and left once beautiful villages and farmsteads with an unshaded barrenness. Weston, a farming village in Du Page County, vanished when the Atomic Energy Commission bought land for a 250-million-dollar atom accelerator, the world's largest alternating gradient synchrotron, for basic scientific research.

For three centuries each generation had found that Illinois is a good place in which to live, to work, and to plan confidently for the future. In recognition of the state's rich heritage, a Sesquicentennial Commission headed by Ralph G. Newman in 1968 arranged for a series of observances that included dedication of the restored Old Capitol in the Springfield square. It sponsored publication of a series of books giving the people of Illinois a greater awareness of the struggles and accomplishments of their predecessors. Abraham Lincoln's state has advanced dramatically in the three hundred years since Jolliet and Marquette discovered the Illinois country and in the two centuries since George Rogers Clark made it part of the newly independent nation that became the United States. Illinois still has its central location, its rich soil and invigorating climate, and the other assets that have been utilized by a diverse, intelligent and resourceful people. The roster of heroes is long, with hundreds providing inspiration for the generations to come, in confidence that the story of Illinois has just begun and that the Prairie State will continue to undergo great changes, whatever they might be.

GOVERNORS OF ILLINOIS

Name	Date of Birth	Place of Birth	Inaugurated	County
Shadrach Bond, Dem.	1773	Maryland	Oct. 6, 1818	St. Clair
Edward Coles, Dem.	1786	Virginia	Dec. 5, 1822	Madison
Ninian Edwards, Dem.	1775	Maryland	Dec. 6, 1826	Madison
John Reynolds,[1] Dem.	1788	Pennsylvania	Dec. 6, 1830	St. Clair
William L. D. Ewing,[2] Dem.	1795	Kentucky	Nov. 17, 1834	Fayette
Joseph Duncan, Dem.	1794	Kentucky	Dec. 3, 1834	Morgan
Thomas Carlin, Dem.	1789	Kentucky	Dec. 7, 1838	Greene
Thomas Ford, Dem.	1800	Pennsylvania	Dec. 8, 1842	Ogle
Augustus C. French,[3] Dem.	1808	N. Hampshire	Dec. 9, 1846 Jan. 8, 1849	Crawford
Joel A. Matteson, Dem.	1808	New York	Jan. 10, 1853	Will
William H. Bissell,[4] Rep.	1811	New York	Jan. 12, 1857	Monroe
John Wood,[5] Rep.	1798	New York	Mar. 21, 1860	Adams
Richard Yates, Rep.	1815	Kentucky	Jan. 14, 1861	Morgan
Richard J. Oglesby, Rep.	1824	Kentucky	Jan. 16, 1865	Macon
John M. Palmer, Rep.	1817	Kentucky	Jan. 11, 1869	Macoupin
Richard J. Oglesby,[6] Rep.	1824	Kentucky	Jan. 13, 1873	Macon
John L. Beveridge,[5] Rep.	1824	New York	Jan. 23, 1873	Cook
Shelby M. Cullom,[6] Rep.	1829	Kentucky	Jan. 8, 1877 Jan. 10, 1881	Sangamon
John M. Hamilton,[5] Rep.	1847	Ohio	Feb. 16, 1883	McLean
Richard J. Oglesby, Rep.	1824	Kentucky	Jan. 30, 1885	Macon
Joseph W. Fifer, Rep.	1840	Virginia	Jan. 14, 1889	McLean
John P. Altgeld, Dem.	1847	Germany	Jan. 10, 1893	Cook

John R. Tanner, Rep.	1844	Indiana	Jan. 11, 1897	Clay
Richard Yates, Rep.	1860	Jacksonville	Jan. 14, 1901	Morgan
Charles S. Deneen, Rep.	1863	Edwardsville	Jan. 9, 1905	Cook
			Jan. 18, 1909	
Edward F. Dunne, Dem.	1853	Connecticut	Feb. 3, 1913	Cook
Frank O. Lowden, Rep.	1861	Minnesota	Jan. 8, 1917	Ogle
Len Small, Rep.	1862	Kankakee	Jan. 10, 1921	Kankakee
			Jan. 12, 1925	
Louis L. Emmerson, Rep.	1863	Albion	Jan. 14, 1929	Jefferson
Henry Horner,[4] Dem.	1879	Chicago	Jan. 9, 1933	Cook
			Jan. 4, 1937	
John H. Stelle,[5] Dem.	1891	McLeansboro	Oct. 6, 1940	Hamilton
Dwight H. Green, Rep.	1897	Indiana	Jan. 13, 1941	Cook
			Jan. 8, 1945	
Adlai E. Stevenson, Dem.	1900	California	Jan. 10, 1949	Lake
William G. Stratton, Rep.	1914	Ingleside	Jan. 12, 1953	Grundy
			Jan. 14, 1957	
Otto Kerner,[7] Dem.	1908	Chicago	Jan. 9, 1961	Cook
			Jan. 11, 1965	
Samuel H. Shapiro,[5] Dem.	1907	Estonia	May 22, 1968	Kankakee
Richard B. Ogilvie, Rep.	1923	Missouri	Jan. 13, 1969	Cook

[1] Resigned to become congressman.

[2] Senate president pro tem filled vacancy.

[3] Re-elected under 1848 constitution.

[4] Died in office.

[5] Lieutenant governor filled vacancy.

[6] Resigned to become senator.

[7] Resigned to become federal judge.

UNITED STATES SENATORS

(The line of succession to the two senate seats is designated by letters A and B.)

Jesse B. Thomas	Dem.	1818-1829	A
Ninian Edwards[a]	Dem.	1818-1824	B
John McLean	Dem.	1824-1825	B
Elias Kent Kane[b]	Dem.	1825-1835	B
John McLean[b]	Dem.	1829-1830	A
David J. Baker[c] [b]	Dem.	1830	A
John M. Robinson	Dem.	1830-1841	A
William L. D. Ewing	Dem.	1835-1837	B
Richard M. Young	Dem.	1837-1843	B
Samuel McRoberts[b]	Dem.	1841-1843	A
James Semple	Dem.	1843-1847	A
Sidney Breese	Dem.	1843-1849	B
Stephen A. Douglas[b]	Dem.	1847-1861	A
James Shields	Dem.	1849-1855	B
Lyman Trumbull	Anti-Neb.Dem., Rep.	1855-1873	B
Orville H. Browning[c]	Rep.	1861-1863	A
William A. Richardson	Dem.	1863-1865	A
Richard Yates	Rep.	1865-1871	A
John A. Logan	Rep.	1871-1877	A
Richard J. Oglesby	Rep.	1873-1879	B
David Davis	Ind.	1877-1883	A
John A. Logan[b]	Rep.	1879-1886	B
Shelby M. Cullom	Rep.	1883-1913	A
Charles B. Farwell	Rep.	1887-1891	B
John M. Palmer	Dem.	1891-1897	B

William E. Mason	Rep.	1897-1903	B
Albert J. Hopkins	Rep.	1903-1909	B
William Lorimer[d]	Rep.	1909-1912	B
James Hamilton Lewis	Dem.	1913-1919	A
Lawrence Y. Sherman	Rep.	1913-1921	B
Medill McCormick	Rep.	1919-1925	A
William B. McKinley	Rep.	1921-1927	B
Charles S. Deneen	Rep.	1925-1931	A
(Frank L. Smith)[e]	Rep.		B
Otis F. Glenn	Rep.	1928-1933	B
James Hamilton Lewis[b]	Dem.	1931-1939	A
William H. Dieterich	Dem.	1933-1939	B
James M. Slattery[c]	Dem.	1939-1940	A
Scott W. Lucas	Dem.	1939-1951	B
C. Wayland Brooks	Rep.	1940-1949	A
Paul H. Douglas	Dem.	1949-1967	A
Everett M. Dirksen[b]	Rep.	1951-1969	B
Charles H. Percy	Rep.	1967-	A
Ralph Tyler Smith[c]	Rep.	1969-1970	B
Adlai E. Stevenson III	Dem.	1970-	B

[a] Resigned senate seat.

[b] Died in office.

[c] Appointed by governor.

[d] Expelled by senate.

[e] Elected in 1926 but refused seat by senate.

THE GROWTH OF ILLINOIS

Population by Geographical Divisions in Census Years

Year	Rank	Illinois	Chicago	Suburbs	Cook County	Downstate
1970	5th	11,113,976	3,366,957	2,125,412	5,492,369	5,621,607
1960	4th	10,081,158	3,550,404	1,579,321	5,129,725	4,951,433
1950	4th	8,712,176	3,620,962	887,830	4,508,792	4,203,384
1940	3rd	7,897,241	3,396,808	666,534	4,063,342	3,833,899
1930	3rd	7,630,654	3,376,438	605,685	3,982,123	3,648,531
1920	3rd	6,485,280	2,701,705	351,312	3,053,017	3,432,263
1910	3rd	5,638,591	2,185,283	219,950	2,405,233	3,233,358
1900	3rd	4,821,550	1,698,575	140,160	1,838,735	2,982,815
1890	3rd	3,826,352	1,099,850	92,072	1,191,922	2,634,430
1880	4th	3,077,871	503,185	104,534	607,719	2,470,152
1870	4th	2,539,891	298,977	50,989	349,966	2,189,925
1860	4th	1,711,951	112,172	32,782	144,954	1,566,997
1850	11th	851,470	29,963	13,422	43,385	808,085
1840	14th	476,183	4,470		10,201	
1830	20th	157,445				
1820	24th	55,211				
1810		12,282				

SIGNIFICANT DATES

1673	Jolliet and Marquette discover the Illinois country.
1680	La Salle reaches Illinois, erects Fort Crèvecoeur at Peoria.
1682	La Salle and Tonti reach mouth of Mississippi, build Fort St. Louis atop Starved Rock.
1691	French settlement moved to Fort Pimitoui, on Lake Peoria.
1699	Cahokia settled by Seminarian priests.
1703	Kaskaskia settled by Jesuits.
1717	Illinois country placed under government of Louisiana.
1765	British take possession of Fort de Chartres, two years after French cede possessions east of Mississippi.
1778	George Rogers Clark captures Kaskaskia.
1779	Clark takes Vincennes. Bellefontaine settled by Virginians and Marylanders.
c. 1779	Du Sable arrives at Chicago portage.
1783	Treaty of Paris extends United States boundary to Mississippi.
1787	Northwest Territory organized.
1795	Treaty of Greenville begins cession of Indian lands.
1800	Indiana Territory, which includes Illinois, is formed.
1803	Louisiana Purchase puts Illinois in center of United States.
1809	Illinois becomes a territory.
1812	Fort Dearborn massacre.
1818	Statehood for Illinois.
1820	Vandalia becomes seat of government.
1824	Slavery advocates fail to call a constitutional convention.
1832	The Black Hawk War.
1833	Town of Chicago organized. Indians cede last Illinois land.
1837	Internal Improvements plan for state-owned railroads. John Deere invents steel plow. Elijah P. Lovejoy killed by anti-abolitionist mob.

1840   Seat of government moved to Springfield.
1842   First train on Northern Cross railroad, Meredosia to Springfield.
1846   Mormons leave Nauvoo, two years after mob kills Joseph and Hyrum
        Smith.
1848   Second Constitution ratified. Illinois and Michigan canal opened to
        traffic.
1850   First train on Galena and Chicago Union, first privately owned
        railroad.
1855   Public schools get state tax support.
1856   Illinois Central railroad completed. Republican party wins first elec-
        tion.
1858   Lincoln-Douglas debates.
1862   Defeat of a wartime constitution.
1867   Illinois Industrial University established at Urbana.
1868   Construction of new state house begins.
1870   New constitution adopted.
1871   The Chicago fire.
1886   Haymarket bombing.
1889   Jane Addams founds Hull House.
1891   Women granted suffrage in school elections.
1893   World's Columbian Exposition.
1894   The Pullman strike.
1900   Chicago River reversed.
1917   Civil administrative code adopted.
1918
and
1924   Bond issues for paved roads.
1922   Proposed constitution rejected.
1933   Sales tax adopted to finance unemployment relief.
1936   Permanent registration of voters.
1955   First legislative reapportionment since 1901.
1956   State Auditor Orville E. Hodge imprisoned in fund scandal.
1958   First toll road section opened to traffic.
1964   At-large election of 177 state representatives.
1969   State income tax adopted.
1970   New constitution ratified.

Bibliography

Ackerman, William K. *Early Illinois Railroads.* A paper read before the Chicago Historical Society, Feb. 20, 1883.

Addams, Jane. *A Centennial Reader.* New York, 1960.

―――. *The Second Twenty Years at Hull House.* New York, 1930.

―――. "Social Settlements in Illinois," *Transactions of the Illinois State Historical Society,* XI (1906).

―――. *Twenty Years at Hull House.* New York, 1910.

Aldrich, Darragh. *The Story of John Deere: A Saga of American Industry.* Minneapolis, 1942.

Allen, John W. *It Happened in Southern Illinois.* Carbondale, 1968.

―――. *Legends and Lore of Southern Illinois.* Carbondale, 1963.

―――. "Slavery and Negro Servitude in Pope County, Illinois," *Journal of the Illinois State Historical Society,* XLII (1949).

Allswang, John M. *A House for All Peoples: Ethnic Politics in Chicago, 1890-1936.* Lexington, 1971.

Altgeld, John P. *Live Questions.* Chicago, 1890.

―――. *Our Penal Machinery and Its Victims.* Chicago, 1884.

Alvord, Clarence W. *Cahokia Records, 1778-1790.* Springfield, 1907.

―――. "The Finding of the Kaskaskia Records," *Transactions of the Illinois State Historical Society,* XI (1906).

――― (ed.). *Governor Edward Coles.* Springfield, 1920.

―――. *The Illinois Country, 1673-1818.* Springfield, 1920.

――― (ed.). *Kaskaskia Records, 1778-1790.* Springfield, 1909.

――― (ed.). *Laws of the Territory of Illinois, 1809-1811.* Springfield, 1906.

Alvord, Clarence W., and Clarence E. Carter (eds.). *The Critical Period, 1763-1765.* Springfield, 1915.

――― (eds.). *The New Regime, 1765-1767.* Springfield, 1916.

――― (eds.). *Trade and Politics, 1767-1769.* Springfield, 1921.

American Automobile Association. "Ackia Battleground National Monument," *Southeastern Tour Book, 1957-58.*

Anderson, Theo. J. (compiler). *100 Years: A History of Bishop Hill, Illinois.* Chicago, 1946.

Andreas, Alfred T. *History of Chicago from the Earliest Period to the Present Time.* 3 vols. Chicago, 1884-86.

――――. *History of Cook County, Illinois, from the Earliest Period to the Present Time.* Chicago, 1884.

Andrews, Wayne. *Battle for Chicago.* New York, 1946.

Angle, Paul M. *Bloody Williamson.* New York, 1952.

――――. "Brief History of Chicago," *Illinois Blue Book, 1953-54.*

―――― (ed.). *Created Equal? Complete Lincoln-Douglas Debates of 1858.* Chicago, 1958.

――――. "Egypt in Illinois," *Chicago History*, VII (1965).

―――― (ed.). *The Great Chicago Fire.* Chicago, 1946.

―――― (ed.). *The Great Chicago Fire, Described by Eight Men and Women Who Experienced Its Horrors and Testified to the Courage of Its Inhabitants.* Chicago, 1971.

――――. *"Here I Have Lived": A History of Lincoln's Springfield, 1821-1865.* Springfield, 1935.

――――. "Nathaniel Pope, 1784-1850, A Memoir," *Transactions of the Illinois State Historical Society*, XLIII (1936).

―――― (ed.). *Prairie State: Impressions of Illinois, 1673-1967, By Travelers and Other Observers.* Chicago, 1968.

Anthony, Elliott. *The Constitutional History of Illinois.* Chicago, 1891.

"The Army Led by Col. George Rogers Clark in His Conquest of the Illinois, 1778-9," *Transactions of the Illinois State Historical Society*, VIII (1903).

Arts and Crafts in Old Illinois. Springfield: Illinois State Museum, 1965.

Asbury, Herbert. *Gem of the Prairie, An Informal History of the Chicago Underworld.* New York, 1940.

Atkinson, Eleanor. "The Winter of the Deep Snow," *Transactions of the Illinois State Historical Society*, XIV (1909).

Babcock, Kendric C. "The Expansion of Higher Education in Illinois," *Transactions of the Illinois State Historical Society*, XXXII (1925).

――――. *The Scandinavian Element in the United States.* New York, 1969.

Babcock, Rufus. *Forty Years of Pioneer Life: Memoirs of John Mason Peck, D.D.* Philadelphia, 1854, and Carbondale, 1965.

Baldwin, Leland D. *The Keelboat Age on Western Waters.* Pittsburgh, 1941.

Bale, Florence Gratoit. "Galena's Century Milestone," *Illinois Blue Book, 1927-28.*

Ballance, Charles. *The History of Peoria, Illinois.* Peoria, 1870.

Barclay, George A. "The Keeley League," *Journal of the Illinois State Historical Society*, LVII (1964).

Bardolph, Richard. *Agricultural Literature and the Early Illinois Farmer.* Urbana, 1948.

――――. "Illinois Agriculture in Transition, 1820-1870," *Journal of the Illinois State Historical Society*, XLI (1948).

Baringer, William E. "Campaign Techniques in Illinois—1860," *Transactions of the Illinois State Historical Society*, XXXIX (1932).
————. *A House Dividing: Lincoln as President Elect*. Springfield, 1945.
————. *Lincoln's Vandalia: A Pioneer Portrait*. New Brunswick, 1949.
Barnard, Harry. *Eagle Forgotten: The Life of John Peter Altgeld*. Indianapolis, 1962.
Barnes, James Anderson. "Illinois and the Gold-Silver Controversy, 1890-1896," *Transactions of the Illinois State Historical Society*, XXXVIII (1931).
Barnhart, John D. *Henry Hamilton and George Rogers Clark in the American Revolution, with the Unpublished Journal of Lieut. Gov. Henry Hamilton*. Crawfordsville, 1951.
Bateman, Newton, and Paul Selby. *Historical Encyclopedia of Illinois*, Cook County edition. 2 vols. Chicago, 1901.
Bauxar, J. Joe. "The Historic Period," *Illinois Archaeology*. Urbana, 1950.
Baxter, Maurice G. *Orville H. Browning, Lincoln's Friend and Critic*. Bloomington, Ind., 1957.
Beasley, Norman. *Frank Knox, American: A Short Biography*. Garden City, 1936.
Beck, Lewis Caleb. *A Gazetteer of the States of Illinois and Missouri*. Albany, 1823.
Becker, Stephen. *Marshall Field III, A Biography*. New York, 1964.
Beckner, Earl R. *A History of Labor Legislation in Illinois*. Chicago, 1929.
Beckwith, Hiram W. *Collections of the Illinois State Historical Library*. Vol. I. Springfield, 1903.
————. *The Illinois and Indiana Indians*. Chicago, 1884.
Beecher, Edward. *Narrative of the Riots at Alton*. New York, 1965.
Belcher, Wyatt Winton. *The Economic Rivalry Between St. Louis and Chicago, 1850-1880*. New York, 1947.
Belting, Natalia Maree. *Kaskaskia Under the French Regime*. Urbana, 1948.
Belting, Paul E. "The Development of the Free Public High School in Illinois to 1860," *Journal of the Illinois State Historical Society*, XI (1918-19).
Benneson, Cora Agnes. "The Work of Edward Everett of Quincy in the Quarter-Master's Department in Illinois During the First Years of the Civil War," *Transactions of the Illinois State Historical Society*, XIV (1909).
Bernhard, Edgar, Ira Latimer, and Harvey O'Connor (editorial committee). *Pursuit of Freedom: A History of Civil Liberty in Illinois, 1787-1942*. Chicago, 1942.
Berry, Daniel. "The Illinois Earthquake of 1811 and 1812," *Transactions of the Illinois State Historical Society*, XII (1907).
Berwanger, Eugene H. *The Frontier Against Slavery*. Urbana, 1967.
Billington, Ray A. "The Frontier in Illinois History," *Journal of the Illinois State Historical Society*, XLIII (1950).
Biographies of the State Officers and Thirty-Third General Assembly of Illinois. Springfield, 1883.
Birkbeck, Morris. *Letters from Illinois*. Philadelphia, 1818.
————. *Notes on a Journey in America from the Coast of Virginia to the Territory of Illinois*. Philadelphia, 1817.

Blair, Francis G. "Development and Growth of the Public Schools," *Illinois Blue Book, 1917-18.*

Blatchford, Eliphalet Wickes. *Biographical Sketch of Hon. Joseph Duncan, Fifth Governor of Illinois.* Read before the Chicago Historical Society, Dec. 5, 1905.

Bluhm, Elaine A. *Illinois Archaeology,* Bulletin 1 of the Illinois Archaeological Survey. Urbana, 1959.

Blumberg, Dorothy Rose. *Florence Kelley: The Making of a Social Pioneer.* New York, 1966.

Boewe, Charles. *Prairie Albion: An English Settlement in Pioneer Illinois.* Carbondale, 1962.

Bogart, Ernest Ludlow. "The Movement of Population in Illinois, 1870-1910," *Transactions of the Illinois State Historical Society,* XXIII (1917).

Bogart, Ernest L., and John Mabry Mathews, *The Modern Commonwealth, 1893-1918.* Chicago, 1922.

Bogart, Ernest L., and Charles Manfred Thompson. *The Industrial State, 1870-1893.* Chicago, 1922.

Boggess, Arthur Clinton. *The Settlement of Illinois, 1778-1830.* Chicago, 1908.

Bogue, Allan G. *From Prairie to Corn Belt: Farming on the Illinois and Iowa Prairies in the Nineteenth Century.* Chicago, 1963.

————. *Money at Interest: The Farm Mortgage on the Middle Border.* Lincoln, 1955.

Bogue, Margaret Beattie. *Patterns from the Sod: Land Use and Tenure in the Grand Prairie, 1850-1900.* Springfield, 1959.

————. "The Swamp Land Act and Wet Land Utilization in Illinois, 1850-1890," *Agricultural History,* XXV (1951).

Bolles, Blair. *Tyrant from Illinois: Uncle Joe Cannon's Experiment with Personal Power.* New York, 1951.

Bond, Beverly Waugh. *The Civilization of the Old Northwest: A Study of Political, Social, and Economic Development, 1788-1812.* New York, 1934.

Bonham, Jeriah. *Fifty Years' Recollections, With Observations and Reflections on Historical Events Giving Sketches of Eminent Citizens—Their Lives and Public Services.* Peoria, 1883.

Bowen, A. L. "The Background of the Constitution of Illinois—The Constitution of 1870," *Illinois Blue Book, 1927-28.*

————. "The Illinois Central Case," *Illinois Blue Book, 1927-28.*

————. "Personal Reminiscences of Joseph W. Fifer, An Interview with the Former Governor and a Description of His Times," *Illinois Blue Book, 1925-26.*

————. "The Press of Illinois," *Illinois Blue Book, 1907-08.*

Bowen, Louise De Koven. *Growing Up with a City.* New York, 1926.

Boylan, Josephine. "Illinois Highways, 1700-1848," *Journal of the Illinois State Historical Society,* XXVI (1933).

Braden, George D., and Rubin G. Cohn. *The Illinois Constitution: An Annotated and Comparative Analysis.* Urbana, 1969.

Breese, Sidney. *The Early History of Illinois.* Chicago, 1884.

Bright, John. *Hizzoner, Big Bill Thompson: An Idyll of Chicago.* New York, 1930.
Bronson, Howard G. "Early Illinois Railroads: The Place of the Illinois Central in Illinois History Prior to the Civil War," *Transactions of the Illinois State Historical Society*, XIII (1908).
Bross, William. *History of Chicago: Historical and Commercial Statistics, Sketches, Facts and Figures, Republished from the "Daily Democratic Press."* Chicago, 1876.
————. *Illinois and the Thirteenth Amendment to the Constitution of the United States.* Paper read before the Chicago Historical Society, Jan. 15, 1884.
Brown, D. Alexander. *Grierson's Raid.* Urbana, 1962.
Brown, Donald R. "Jonathan B. Turner and the Land Grant Idea," *Journal of the Illinois State Historical Society*, LV (1962).
Brown, James. *The History of Public Assistance in Chicago from 1833 to 1893.* Chicago, 1941.
Brown, Stuart. "Old Kaskaskia Days and Ways," *Transactions of the Illinois State Historical Society*, X (1905).
Brownell, Baker. *The Other Illinois.* New York, 1958.
Browning, Orville Hickman. *The Diary of Orville Hickman Browning* (Theodore C. Pease and James G. Randall, eds.). 2 vols. Springfield, 1925-1933.
Bruce, Robert. *The National Road.* Washington, 1916.
Brush, Daniel Harmon. *Growing Up with Southern Illinois, 1820 to 1861* (Milo M. Quaife, ed.). Chicago, 1944.
Buck, F. P. *The Cherry Mine Disaster.* Chicago, 1910.
Buck, Solon J. *The Agrarian Crusade: A Chronicle of the Farmer in Politics.* New Haven, 1920.
———— *The Granger Movement, 1870-1880: A Study of Agricultural Organization and Its Political, Economic and Social Manifestations.* Cambridge, 1913.
————. *Illinois in 1818.* Springfield, 1918.
———— (ed.). "Pioneer Letters of Gershom Flagg," *Transactions of the Illinois State Historical Society*, XV (1910).
————. *Travel and Description, 1765-1865, Together with a List of County Histories, Atlases, Biographical Collections and a List of Territorial and State Laws.* Springfield, 1914.
Buder, Stanley. *Pullman: An Experiment in Industrial Order and Community Planning, 1880-1930.* New York, 1967.
Buenker, John D. "The Illinois Legislature and Prohibition, 1907-1919," *Journal of the Illinois State Historical Society*, LXII (1969).
Buley, R. Carlyle. *The Old Northwest: Pioneer Period, 1815-1840.* 2 vols. Indianapolis, 1950.
Burford, Cary Clive. "The Twilight of the Local Passenger Train," *Journal of the Illinois State Historical Society*, LI (1958).
Burnham, Daniel H., and Edward H. Bennett. *Plan of Chicago.* Chicago, 1909.
Burnham, J. Howard, "The Destruction of Kaskaskia by the Mississippi River," *Transactions of the Illinois State Historical Society*, XX (1914).
Burtschi, Mary. *Vandalia: Wilderness Capital.* Decatur, 1963.

Busbey, L. White. *Uncle Joe Cannon: The Story of a Pioneer American*. New York, 1927.

Busch, Francis X. "The Haymarket Riot and the Trial of the Anarchists," *Journal of the Illinois State Historical Society*, XLVII (1955).

Byrd, Cecil K. *A Bibliography of Illinois Imprints, 1814-1858*. Chicago, 1966.

Caldwell, Joseph R. *New Roads to Yesterday: Essays in Archaeology*. New York, 1966.

Caldwell, Norman W. "Fort Massac During the French and Indian War," "Fort Massac: Frontier Post, 1778-1806," and "Fort Massac Since 1805," *Journal of the Illinois State Historical Society*, XLIII (1950), and XLIV (1951).

————. *The French in the Mississippi Valley*. Urbana, 1941.

Calkins, Ernest Elmo. *They Broke the Prairie: Being Some Account of the Settlement of the Upper Mississippi Valley by Religious and Educational Pioneers, Told in Terms of One City, Galesburg, and of One College, Knox*. New York, 1939.

Campbell, Charles B. "Bourbonnais, or the Early French Settlements in Kankakee County, Illinois," *Transactions of the Illinois State Historical Society*, XI (1906).

Carlson, Theodore L. *The Illinois Military Tract: A Study in Land Occupation, Utilization and Tenure*. Urbana, 1951.

Carpenter, Allan. *Illinois: Land of Lincoln*. Chicago, 1968.

Carr, Clark E. *Stephen A. Douglas: His Life, Public Service, Speeches and Patriotism*. Chicago, 1909.

Carriel, Mary Turner. *The Life of Jonathan Baldwin Turner*. Urbana, 1961.

Carter, Clarence E. *Great Britain and the Illinois Country, 1763-1774*. Washington, 1910.

Cartwright, Peter. *Autobiography of Peter Cartwright, the Backwoods Preacher* (W. P. Strickland, ed.). New York, 1857.

Casey, Robert, and W. A. S. Douglas. *The Midwesterner: The Story of Dwight H. Green*. Chicago, 1948.

————. *Pioneer Railroad: The Story of the Chicago and North Western Railroad*. New York, 1948.

Cathedral of the Holy Name. *100 Years: The History of the Church of the Holy Name / The Church That Became a Cathedral and the Story of Catholicism in Chicago*. Chicago, 1949.

Caton, John D. *The Last of the Illinois and a Sketch of the Pottawatomies*. Chicago, 1876.

Cavanagh, Helen M. *Funk of Funk's Grove: Farmer, Legislator and Cattle King of the Old Northwest, 1797-1865*. Bloomington, 1952.

————. *Seed, Soil and Science. The Story of Eugene D. Funk*. Chicago, 1959.

Chamberlain, Henry Barrett. "Elias Kent Kane," *Transactions of the Illinois State Historical Society*, XIII (1908).

Chamberlin, M. H. "Historical Sketch of McKendree College," *Transactions of the Illinois State Historical Society*, IX (1904).

Changnon, Stanley A., Jr. *Climatology of Severe Winter Storms in Illinois*. Urbana: Illinois State Water Survey, 1969.

Chicago Commission on Race Relations. *The Negro in Chicago.* Chicago, 1922.

Christman, Henry M. (ed.). *The Mind and Spirit of John Peter Altgeld.* Urbana, 1965.

Church, Charles A. *History of the Republican Party in Illinois, 1854-1912.* Rockford, 1912.

Clark, George Rogers. *The Conquest of the Illinois* (Milo M. Quaife, ed.). Chicago, 1920.

Clark, John G. *The Grain Trade in the Old Northwest.* Urbana, 1966.

Clark, Neil M. *John Deere: He Gave the World the Steel Plow.* Moline, 1937.

Clayton, John (ed.). *The Illinois Fact Book and Historical Almanac.* Carbondale, 1970.

Cleveland, Martha. *Charles Percy: Strong New Voice from Illinois.* Jacksonville, 1963.

Climate and Man. U.S. Department of Agriculture Yearbook, 1941.

Coates, Robert M. *The Outlaw Years: The History of the Land Pirates of the Natchez Trace.* New York, 1930.

Cole, Arthur C. (ed.). *Constitutional Debates of 1847.* Springfield, 1919.

————. *The Era of the Civil War, 1848-1870.* Chicago, 1922.

Cole, Fay-Cooper, and Thorne Deuel. *Rediscovering Illinois.* Chicago, 1937.

Coleman, Charles H. *Abraham Lincoln and Coles County, Illinois.* New Brunswick, 1955.

Coleman, Charles H., and Paul H. Spence. "The Charleston Riot, March 28, 1864," *Journal of the Illinois State Historical Society,* XXXIII (1940).

Commoner, Barry. *The Closing Circle: Nature, Man and Technology.* New York, 1971.

Congdon, Harriet Rice. "The Early History of Monticello College," *Transactions of the Illinois State Historical Society,* XXXI (1924).

Conger, John Leonard. *History of the Illinois River Valley.* Chicago, 1932.

Converse, Henry A. "The House of the House Divided," *Lincoln Centennial Association Papers.* Springfield, 1924.

Corliss, Carlton J. *Main Line of Mid-America: The Story of the Illinois Central.* New York, 1951.

Cornelius, Janet. *A History of Constitution Making in Illinois.* Urbana, 1969.

Cramer, Clarence H. *Royal Bob: The Life of Robert G. Ingersoll.* Indianapolis, 1952.

————. "Robert Green Ingersoll," *Transactions of the Illinois State Historical Society,* XLVII (1940).

Craven, Avery. *The Coming of the Civil War.* Chicago, 1957.

Cromie, Robert. *The Great Chicago Fire.* New York, 1958.

Cullom, Shelby M. *Fifty Years of Public Service: Personal Recollections of Shelby M. Cullom.* Chicago, 1911.

Culp, Dorothy. "The Radical Labor Movement, 1873-1895," *Transactions of the Illinois State Historical Society,* XLIV (1937).

Cunningham, Joseph Oscar. "The Bloomington Convention of 1856 and Those Who Participated in It," *Transactions of the Illinois State Historical Society,* X (1905).

Currey, J. Seymour. *The Story of Old Fort Dearborn.* Chicago, 1912.

Cushman, Mary Semple Ames. "General James Semple," *Transactions of the Illinois State Historical Society,* X (1905).

Dana, Edmund. *A Description of the Bounty Lands of the State of Illinois; Also All the Principal Roads, by Land and Water, Through the Territory of the United States.* Cincinnati, 1819.

Dante, Harris L. "The Chicago Tribune's Lost Years, 1865-74," *Journal of the Illinois State Historical Society,* LVIII (1965).

David, Henry. *The History of the Haymarket Affair: A Study in the American Social, Revolutionary and Labor Movements.* New York, 1958.

Davidson, Alexander, and Bernard Stuvé. *A Complete History of Illinois from 1673 to 1873, Embracing the Physical Features of the Country; Its Early Explorations; Aboriginal Inhabitants; Conquest by Virginia; Territorial Condition and the Subsequent Civil, Military and Political Events of the State.* Springfield, 1874.

Davis, David J. *History of Medical Practice in Illinois.* Vol. II. Chicago, 1955.

Davis, J. McCan. *The Breaking of the Deadlock, Being an Accurate and Authentic Account of the Contest of 1903-4 for the Republican Nomination for Governor. . . .* Springfield, 1904.

Dearing, Mary R. *Veterans in Politics: The Story of the G.A.R.* Baton Rouge, 1952.

DeBusk, Charles R. "Dickson Mounds Prehistory," *The Explorer,* XI (1969).

Dedmon, Emmett. *Fabulous Chicago.* New York, 1953.

Delanglez, Jean. *Life and Voyages of Louis Jolliet, 1645-1700.* Chicago, 1948.

Demaris, Ovid. *Captive City: Chicago in Chains.* New York, 1969.

Dennis, Charles H. *Victor Lawson, His Time and His Work.* Chicago, 1935.

Deuel, Thorne. *American Indian Ways of Life.* Springfield: Illinois State Museum, 1958.

De Voto, Bernard. *The Course of Empire.* Boston, 1962.

Dickerson, Oliver M. *The Illinois Constitutional Convention of 1862.* Urbana, 1905.

Dilliard, Irving. "Civil Liberties Since 1865," *Journal of the Illinois State Historical Society,* LVI (1963).

Dillon, Merton L. "Abolitionism Comes to Illinois," *Journal of the Illinois State Historical Society,* LIII (1960).

————. *Elijah P. Lovejoy, Abolitionist Editor.* Urbana, 1961.

Dobyns, Fletcher. *The Underworld of American Politics.* Kingsport, Tenn., 1932.

Donaldson, Thomas. *The Public Domain: Its History, With Statistics.* Washington, 1884.

Donnelly, Joseph P. *Jacques Marquette, S.J., 1637-1675.* Chicago, 1968.

————. "Pierre Gibault and the Critical Period of the Illinois Country, 1768-78," *The French in the Mississippi Valley* (John Francis McDermott, ed.). Urbana, 1965.

Dowrie, George W. *The Development of Banking in Illinois, 1817-1863.* Urbana, 1913.

Doyle, Edward P. (ed.). *As We Knew Adlai: The Stevenson Story by Twenty-Two Friends.* New York, 1966.

Drake, St. Clair, and Horace R. Cayton. *Black Metropolis: A Study of Negro Life in a Northern City.* New York, 1945.

Dubofsky, Melvyn. *We Shall Be All: A History of the Industrial Workers of the World.* Chicago, 1969.

Duffey, Bernard I. *The Chicago Renaissance in American Letters: A Critical History.* East Lansing, 1954.

Dunbar, Willis Frederick. *Michigan: A History of the Wolverine State.* Grand Rapids, 1965.

Dunn, Jacob Piatt. "Father Gibault, the Patriot Priest of the Northwest," *Transactions of the Illinois State Historical Society,* X (1905).

Dunne, Edward F. *Dunne: Judge, Mayor, Governor* (William L. Sullivan, ed.). Chicago, 1916.

―――. *Illinois, the Heart of the Nation.* 5 vols. Chicago, 1933.

Eavenson, Howard N. *The First Century and a Quarter of the American Coal Industry.* Pittsburgh, 1942.

Ebert, Roger. *An Illini Century: One Hundred Years of Campus Life.* Urbana, 1967.

Edwards, Ninian W. *History of Illinois from 1778 to 1833; and the Life and Times of Ninian Edwards.* Springfield, 1870.

Eifert, Virginia S. *Louis Jolliet, Explorer of Rivers.* New York, 1961.

―――. *Of Men and Rivers: Adventures and Discoveries Along American Waterways.* New York, 1966.

Eisendrath, Joseph L., Jr. "Chicago's Camp Douglas, 1861-1865," *Journal of the Illinois State Historical Society,* LIII (1960).

Ellis, Mrs. L. E. "The Chicago Times During the Civil War," *Transactions of the Illinois State Historical Society,* XXXIX (1932).

Ernst, Ferdinand. "Travels in Illinois in 1819, Translated from the German Original," *Transactions of the Illinois State Historical Society,* VIII (1903).

Everett, Edward. "Operation of the Quarter-Master's Department of the State of Illinois, 1861-2," *Transactions of the Illinois State Historical Society,* X (1905).

Ewert, A. F. "Early History of Education in Illinois—The Three Oldest Colleges," *Illinois Blue Book, 1929-30.*

Farb, Peter. *Face of North America: The Natural History of a Continent.* New York, 1963.

―――. *Man's Rise to Civilization as Shown by the Indians of North America from Primeval Times to the Coming of the Industrial State.* New York, 1968.

Fehrenbacher, Don E. *Chicago Giant: A Biography of "Long John" Wentworth.* Madison, 1957.

Fishback, Mason McCloud. "Illinois Legislation on Slavery and Free Negroes, 1818-1865," *Transactions of the Illinois State Historical Society,* IX (1904).

Fisher, Miles Mark. "Negro Churches in Illinois: A Fragmentary History with Emphasis on Chicago," *Journal of the Illinois State Historical Society,* LVI (1963).

Flanagan, John T. "James Hall and the Antiquarian and Historical Society of Illinois," *Journal of the Illinois State Historical Society,* XXXIV (1941).

―――. *James Hall, Literary Pioneer of the Ohio Valley.* Minneapolis, 1941.

Flanders, Robert Bruce. *Nauvoo: Kingdom on the Mississippi.* Urbana, 1965.

Flint, Margaret A. "A Chronology of Illinois History, 1673-1962," *Illinois Blue Book, 1961-62.*

Flower, George. *History of the English Settlement in Edwards County, Illinois, Founded in 1817 and 1818 by Morris Birkbeck and George Flower.* Chicago, 1882.

————. *Letters from the Illinois, 1820-1821.* London, 1822.

Ford, Gov. Thomas. *A History of Illinois, from Its Commencement as a State in 1818 to 1847.* . . . Chicago, 1854 and 1945-46.

Fordham, Elias Pym. *Personal Narrative of Travels in Virginia, Maryland, Pennsylvania, Ohio, Indiana, Kentucky; and of a Residence in the Illinois Territory, 1817-1818.* Cleveland, 1906.

Foreman, Grant. "English Settlers in Illinois," *Journal of the Illinois State Historical Society*, XXXIV (1941).

————. *The Last Trek of the Indians.* Chicago, 1946.

Fortier, John, and Donald Chaput. "A Historical Re-examination of Juchereau's Illinois Tannery," *Journal of the Illinois State Historical Society*, LXII (1969).

French, Dr. A. W. "Men and Manners in the Early Days of Illinois," *Transactions of the Illinois State Historical Society*, VIII (1903).

Fuller, M. L. "The Climate of Illinois: Its Permanence," *Transactions of the Illinois State Historical Society*, XVII (1912).

Gara, Larry. "The Underground Railroad in Illinois," *Journal of the Illinois State Historical Society*, LVI (1963).

Gardner, Hamilton. "The Nauvoo Legion, 1840-1845: A Unique Military Organization," *Journal of the Illinois State Historical Society*, LIV (1961).

Garraghan, Gilbert J. *The Catholic Church in Chicago, 1673-1871.* Chicago, 1921.

Garvey, Neil F. *The Government and Administration of Illinois.* New York, 1958.

Gates, Paul W. *Agriculture and the Civil War.* New York, 1965.

————. "Cattle Kings in the Prairies," *Mississippi Valley Historical Review*, XXXV (1948).

————. "Disposal of the Public Domain in Illinois, 1848-1856," *Journal of Economic and Business History*, III (1931).

————. *The Farmer's Age: Agriculture, 1815-1860.* New York, 1960.

————. "Frontier Landlords and Pioneer Tenants," *Journal of the Illinois State Historical Society*, XXXVIII (1945).

————. *The Illinois Central and Its Colonization Work.* Cambridge, 1934.

————. "Large Scale Farming in Illinois, 1830 to 1870," *Agricultural History Journal*, VI (1932).

————. "The Struggle for the Charter of the Illinois Central Railroad," *Transactions of the Illinois State Historical Society*, XL (1933).

Gayler, George R. "The Mormons and Politics in Illinois, 1839-1844," *Journal of the Illinois State Historical Society*, IL (1956).

Georgano, G. N. (ed.). *Encyclopedia of American Motor Cars.* New York, 1968.

Gerhard, Fred. *Illinois As It Is.* Chicago, 1857.

Gertz, Elmer A. "The Black Laws of Illinois," *Journal of the Illinois State Historical Society*, LVI (1963).
Gerwing, Anselm J. "The Chicago Indian Treaty of 1833," *Journal of the Illinois State Historical Society*, LVII (1964).
Gilpin, Alec R. *The War of 1812 in the Old Northwest.* East Lansing, 1958.
Gleason, Bill. *Daley of Chicago: The Man, the Mayor, and the Limits of Conventional Politics.* New York, 1970.
Glenn, John M. "The Industrial Development of Illinois," *Transactions of the Illinois State Historical Society*, XXVIII (1921).
Glick, Frank Ziegler. *The Illinois Emergency Relief Commission.* Chicago, 1940.
Goff, John S. *Robert Todd Lincoln, A Man in His Own Right.* Norman, Okla., 1969.
Goode, J. Paul. *The Geographic Background of Chicago.* Chicago, 1926.
Goodspeed, Thomas Wakefield. *The Story of the University of Chicago, 1890-1925.* Chicago, 1925.
Gosnell, Harold F. *Machine Politics: Chicago Model.* Chicago, 1937 and 1968.
———. *Negro Politicians: The Rise of Negro Politics in Chicago.* Chicago, 1935 and 1967.
Gottfried, Alex. *Boss Cermak of Chicago: A Study of Political Leadership.* Seattle, 1962.
Gove, Samuel K. (ed.). *Illinois Votes, 1900-1958: A Compilation of Illinois Election Statistics.* Urbana, 1959.
Grant, Bruce. *Fight for a City: The Story of the Union League Club and Its Times, 1880-1955.* Chicago, 1955.
Grass. U.S. Department of Agriculture Yearbook, 1948.
Gray, James. *The Illinois.* New York, 1940.
Gray, Wood. *The Hidden Civil War: The Story of the Copperheads.* New York, 1964.
Greene, Evarts Boutell, and Clarence W. Alvord (eds.). *The Governors' Letter-Books, 1818-1834.* Springfield, 1909.
Greene, Evarts Boutell, and Charles M. Thompson. *The Governors' Letter-Books, 1840-1853.* Springfield, 1911.
Griffith, Katherine and Will. *Spotlight on Egypt.* Carbondale, 1946.
Griffith, Will. "Egypt, Illinois," *Illinois Blue Book, 1945-46.*
Grover, Frank Reed. "Indian Treaties Affecting Lands in the Present State of Illinois," *Transactions of the Illinois State Historical Society*, XXI (1915).
Guide to the Geologic Map of Illinois. Urbana: State Geological Survey, 1961.
Guide to Rocks and Minerals of Illinois. Urbana: State Geological Survey, 1959.
Gutman, Herbert G. "The Braidwood Lockout of 1874," *Journal of the Illinois State Historical Society*, LIII (1960).
Gwinn, William R. *Uncle Joe Cannon, Archfoe of Insurgency: A History of the Rise and Fall of Cannonism.* New York, 1957.

Haeger, John D. "The American Fur Company and the Chicago of 1812-1835," *Journal of the Illinois State Historical Society*, LXI (1968).

Hall, Captain Basil. *Travels in North America in the Years 1827 and 1828.* 3 vols. Edinburgh, 1829.

Hamilton, Elisha Bentley, Jr. "The Union League: Its Origin and Achievements in the Civil War," *Transactions of the Illinois State Historical Society,* XXVIII (1921).

Hamilton, Henry Edward. *Incidents and Events in the Life of Gurdon Saltonstall Hubbard, Collected from Personal Narrations and Other Sources, and Arranged by his Nephew, Henry E. Hamilton.* Chicago, 1888.

Hamilton, Raphael N. *Father Marquette.* Grand Rapids, 1970.

————. *Marquette's Explorations: The Narratives Re-examined.* Madison, 1970.

Hamilton, S. M. (ed.). *Writings of James Monroe.* New York, 1898.

Hand, John Pryor. "Negro Slavery in Illinois," *Transactions of the Illinois State Historical Society.* XV (1910).

Hansen, Harry. *The Chicago.* New York, 1942.

Hardin, Thomas L. "The National Road in Illinois," *Journal of the Illinois State Historical Society,* LX (1967).

Harper, Charles A. *Development of the Teachers College in the United States with Special Reference to the Illinois State Normal University.* Bloomington, 1935.

Harris, N. Dwight. *The History of Negro Servitude in Illinois, and of the Slavery Question in That State, 1719-1864.* Chicago, 1904.

Harrison, Carter H. *Growing Up with Chicago.* Chicago, 1944.

————. *Stormy Years: The Autobiography of Carter H. Harrison, Five Times Mayor of Chicago.* Indianapolis, 1935.

Havighurst, Walter. *George Rogers Clark, Soldier of the West.* New York, 1952.

————. *The Heartland: Ohio, Indiana, Illinois.* New York, 1962.

————. *Land of Promise: The Story of the Northwest Territory.* New York, 1946.

————. *The Upper Mississippi.* New York, 1944.

Hayes, William Edward. *Iron Road to Empire: Rock Island Lines.* New York, 1953.

Hicken, Victor. *Illinois in the Civil War.* Urbana, 1966.

————. *The Purple and the Gold: The Story of Western Illinois University.* Macomb, 1970.

————. "The Virden and Pana Mine Wars of 1898," *Journal of the Illinois State Historical Society,* LII (1959).

Hickey, Donald R. "The Prager Affair: A Study in Wartime Hysteria," *Journal of the Illinois State Historical Society,* LXII (1969).

Hildner, Ernest G. "Higher Education in Transition, 1850-1870," *Journal of the Illinois State Historical Society,* LVI (1963).

Hilton, George W., and John F. Due. *The Electric Interurban Railroads of America.* Stanford, 1960.

Hitsman, J. Mackay. *The Incredible War of 1812: A Military History.* Toronto, 1965.

Hodge, Frederick W. *Handbook of American Indians North of Mexico.* 2 vols. Washington, 1907-1910.

Holt, Robert D. "The Political Career of William A. Richardson," *Journal of the Illinois State Historical Society*, XXVI (1933).

Horan, James D. *The Pinkertons: The Detective Dynasty That Made History*. New York, 1967.

Hosmer, Charles Bridgham. *Presence of the Past: A History of the Preservation Movement in the United States Before Williamsburg*. New York, 1965.

Howe, Walter A. (ed.). *Documentary History of the Illinois and Michigan Canal: Legislation, Litigation and Titles*. Springfield, 1956.

Howlett, Michael J. *History of Twenty-Three Auditors of Public Accounts*. Springfield, 1968.

Hubbard, Gurdon Saltonstall. *The Autobiography of Gurdon Saltonstall Hubbard* (Caroline M. McIlvaine, introduction). New York, 1969.

Hull, Denison Bingham. *The Legislative Life of Morton Denison Hull*. Chicago, 1948.

Humphrey, Judge J. Otis. "Dr. John Mason Peck and Shurtleff College," *Transactions of the Illinois State Historical Society*, XII (1907).

Hunter, Joan. "Prairie Splendors Lost," *Living Museum*, XXX (1968).

Husband, Joseph. *The Story of the Pullman Car*. Chicago, 1917.

Hutchins, Capt. Thomas. *A Topographical Description of Virginia, Pennsylvania, Maryland, and North Carolina, comprehending the Rivers Ohio, Kenhawa, Sioto, Cherokee, Wabash, Illinois, Mississippi etc. . . .* London, 1778.

Hutchinson, William T. *Cyrus Hall McCormick*. 2 vols. New York, 1930-35.

————. *Lowden of Illinois: The Life of Governor Frank O. Lowden*. 2 vols. Chicago, 1957.

Ickes, Harold L. *The Autobiography of a Curmudgeon*. New York, 1943.

Illinois: A Descriptive and Historical Guide Compiled and Written by the Federal Writers' Project of the Works Project Administration for the State of Illinois. Chicago, 1939.

Illinois Guide and Gazetteer. Illinois Sesquicentennial Commission. Chicago, 1969.

Inman, D. M. "Professor Jonathan Baldwin Turner and the Granville Convention," *Journal of the Illinois State Historical Society*, XVII (1924).

Isaksson, Olov, and Soren Hallgren. *Bishop Hill: Svensk Koloni pa Prairien / Bishop Hill, Illinois: A Utopia on the Prairie*. Stockholm, 1969.

Ives, Elizabeth Stevenson, and Hildegard Dolson. *My Brother Adlai*. New York, 1956.

Jackson, Donald (ed.). *Black Hawk, An Autobiography*. Urbana, 1964.

James, Edmund James, and Milo J. Loveless, *A Bibliography of Newspapers Published in Illinois prior to 1860*. Springfield, 1889.

James, James Alton (ed.). *George Rogers Clark Papers, 1771-1781*. Springfield, 1912.

————. "Illinois and the Revolution in the West," *Transactions of the Illinois State Historical Society*, XV (1910).

————. *The Life of George Rogers Clark*. Chicago, 1928.

————. "Oliver Pollock and the Winning of the Illinois Country," *Transactions of the Illinois State Historical Society*, XLI (1934).

Jamison, Isabel. "Literature and Literary People of Early Illinois," *Transactions of the Illinois State Historical Society*, XIII (1908).

————. "The Young Men's Convention and Old Soldiers' Meeting at Springfield, June 3-4, 1840," *Transactions of the Illinois State Historical Society*, XX (1914).

Jay, Charles D. *150 Years of Education in Illinois.* Springfield, 1968.

Jenison, Marguerite E. *War Documents and Addresses*, Vol. 6 of *Illinois in the World War.* Springfield, 1923.

————. *The War-Time Organization of Illinois*, Vol. 5 of *Illinois in the World War*, Springfield, 1923.

Jeter, Helen Rankin. *Trends of Population in the Region of Chicago.* Chicago, 1927.

Johnson, Charles B. "The Subscription School and Seminary in Pioneer Days," *Transactions of the Illinois State Historical Society*, XXXII (1925).

Johnson, Charles B. *Growth of Cook County.* Chicago, 1960.

Johnson, Claudius O. *Carter Henry Harrison I.* Chicago, 1927.

Johnson, James D. *Aurora 'n' Elgin.* Wheaton, 1965.

————. *The Lincoln Land Traction.* Wheaton, 1965.

Johnson, Walter. *How We Drafted Adlai Stevenson.* New York, 1955.

Jones, Abner Dumont. *Illinois and the West.* Philadelphia, 1838.

Jones, James P. *"Black Jack": John A. Logan and Southern Illinois in the Civil War.* Tallahassee, 1967.

Jones, Robert Huhn. "Three Days of Violence: The Regulators of the Rock River Valley," *Journal of the Illinois State Historical Society*, LIX (1966).

Jones, Stanley L. "Agrarian Radicalism in Illinois' Constitutional Convention of 1862," *Journal of the Illinois State Historical Society*, XLVIII (1955).

Jordan, Philip D. *The National Road.* Indianapolis, 1948.

Keiser, John H. "John H. Walker: Labor Leader from Illinois," *Essays in Illinois History* (Donald F. Tingley, ed.).

————. "The Union Miners Cemetery at Mt. Olive, Illinois: A Spirit-Thread of Labor History," *Journal of the Illinois State Historical Society*, LXII (1969).

Keller, William E. (ed.). *Illinois Place Names.* Springfield, 1968.

Kellogg, Louise Phelps. *Early Narratives of the Northwest, 1634-1699.* New York, 1917.

Kenney, David. *Basic Illinois Government: A Systematic Explanation.* Carbondale, 1970.

Kenton, Edna (ed.). *The Jesuit Relations and Allied Documents: Travels and Explorations of the Jesuit Missionaries in North America, 1610-1791.* New York, 1954.

Kerrick, L. H. "Life and Character of Honorable Isaac Funk," *Transactions of the Illinois State Historical Society*, VII (1902).

Kersey, Harry A., Jr. *John Milton Gregory and the University of Illinois.* Urbana, 1968.

Kimball, E. L. "Richard Yates: His Record as Civil War Governor of Illinois," *Journal of the Illinois State Historical Society*, XXIII (1930).

Kimball, James L. "The Nauvoo Charter: A Re-interpretation," *Journal of the Illinois State Historical Society*, LXIV (1971).

Kimball, Stanley B. "The Mormons in Illinois, 1838-1846: A Special Introduction," *Journal of the Illinois State Historical Society*, LXIV (1971).

Kincaid, Robert L. *The Wilderness Road*. Harrogate, Tenn., 1955.

King, Willard L. *Lincoln's Manager, David Davis*. Cambridge, 1960.

————. *Melville Weston Fuller, Chief Justice of the United States, 1888-1910*. New York, 1950.

Kinsey, Philip. *The Chicago Tribune: Its First Hundred Years*. 3 vols. New York, 1943.

Kinzie, Mrs. John H. *Wau-Bun, The "Early Day" in the North-West*. New York, 1856, and Chicago, 1932.

Klement, Frank L. *The Copperheads in the Middle West*. Chicago, 1960.

————. "Copperhead Secret Societies in Illinois During the Civil War," *Journal of the Illinois State Historical Society*, XLVIII (1955).

Klose, Nelson. *A Concise Study Guide to the American Frontier*. Lincoln, 1964.

Knight, Robert, and Lucius H. Zeuch. *The Location of the Chicago Portage in the Seventeenth Century*. Chicago, 1920.

Kobler, John. *Capone: The Life and World of Al Capone*. New York, 1971.

Koeper, Frederick. *Illinois Architecture from Territorial Times to the Present*. Chicago, 1968.

Koerner, Gustave. *Memoirs of Gustave Koerner, 1809-1896: Life Sketches Written at the Suggestion of His Children* (Thomas McCormack, ed.). Cedar Rapids, 1909.

Kofoid, Carrie Prudence. "Puritan Influences in the Formative Years of Illinois History," *Transactions of the Illinois State Historical Society*, X (1905).

Kogan, Herman, and Robert Cromie. *The Great Fire: Chicago 1871*. New York, 1971.

Kohlmier, A. L. "Commerce and Union Sentiment in the Old Northwest in 1860," *Transactions of the Illinois State Historical Society*, XXX (1923).

Kohn, Walter S. G. "Illinois Ratifies the Twenty-First Amendment," *Journal of the Illinois State Historical Society*, LVI (1963).

Kramer, Dale. *Chicago Renaissance: The Literary Life of the Midwest, 1900-1930*. New York, 1966.

Krenkel, John H. *Illinois Internal Improvements, 1818-1848*. Cedar Rapids, 1958.

———— (ed.). *Richard Yates, Civil War Governor*. Danville, 1966.

———— (ed.). *Serving the Republic: Richard Yates, Illinois Governor and Congressman, Son of Richard Yates, Civil War Governor; An Autobiography*. Danville, 1968.

Krug, Mark M. *Lyman Trumbull, Conservative Radical*. New York, 1965.

Kyle, Otto R. *Abraham Lincoln in Decatur*. New York, 1957.

Lacey, John J. *Farm Bureau in Illinois: History of the Illinois Farm Bureau*. Bloomington, 1965.

Landesco, John. *Organized Crime in Chicago: Part III of the Illinois Crime Survey, 1929.* Chicago, 1968.

Lansden, John M. *A History of the City of Cairo, Illinois.* Chicago, 1910.

Larson, Orvin. *American Infidel: Robert G. Ingersoll.* New York, 1962.

Latrobe, Charles Joseph. *The Rambler in North America.* 2 vols. New York, 1835.

Lavender, David S. *Climax at Buena Vista: The American Campaigns in Northeastern Mexico, 1846-47.* Philadelphia, 1966.

Leach, Paul R. *That Man Dawes.* Chicago, 1930.

Lee, Henry W. "The Calumet Portage," *Transactions of the Illinois State Historical Society,* XVII (1912).

Lee, Judson Fiske. "Transportation, a Factor in the Development of Northern Illinois Previous to 1860," *Journal of the Illinois State Historical Society,* X (1917).

Leech, Harper, and John Charles Carroll. *Armour and His Times.* New York, 1938.

Leffingwell, Rev. C. W. "Bishop Chase and Jubilee College," *Transactions of the Illinois State Historical Society,* X (1905).

Lentz, Eli G. *Seventy-Five Years in Retrospect, from Normal School to Teachers College to University: Southern Illinois University, 1874-1949.* Carbondale, 1955.

Lewis, Lloyd. *John S. Wright: Prophet of the Prairies.* Chicago, 1941.

Lewis, Lloyd, and Henry Justin Smith. *Chicago: The History of Its Reputation.* New York, 1929.

Lindsey, Almont. *The Pullman Strike: The Story of a Unique Experiment and of a Great Labor Upheaval.* Chicago, 1942.

Linn, James Weber. *Jane Addams: A Biography.* New York, 1935.

Littlewood, Thomas B. *Horner of Illinois.* Evanston, 1969.

Lusk, D. W. *Politics and Politicians: A Succinct History of the Politics of Illinois from 1856 to 1884, with Anecdotes and Incidents, and Appendix from 1809 to 1856.* Springfield, 1884.

Lyle, John H. *The Dry and Lawless Years.* Englewood Cliffs, N.J., 1960.

MacNeil, Neil. *Dirksen: Portrait of a Public Man.* Cleveland, 1970.

McClelland, Clarence P. "The Education of Females in Early Illinois," *Journal of the Illinois State Historical Society,* XXXVI (1943).

————. "Jacob Strawn and John T. Alexander—Central Illinois Stockmen," *Journal of the Illinois State Historical Society,* XXXIV (1941).

McConnel, George M. "Recollections of the Northern Cross Railroad," *Transactions of the Illinois State Historical Society,* XIII (1908).

McCormick, Cyrus. *The Century of the Reaper: Account of Cyrus Hall McCormick and the Invention of the Reaper; of the McCormick Harvesting Machine Company, the Business He Created, and of the International Harvester Company, His Heir and Chief Memorial.* Boston, 1931.

McDermott, John Francis (ed.). *The French in the Mississippi Valley.* Urbana, 1965.

————. *Old Cahokia: A Narrative and Documents Illustrating the First Century of Its History.* St. Louis, 1949.

McDonald, Forrest. *Insull.* Chicago, 1962.

McDowell, Mary E. "A Quarter of a Century in the Stockyards District," *Transactions of the Illinois State Historical Society*, XXVII (1920).

McHarry, Jessie. "John Reynolds," *Journal of the Illinois State Historical Society*, VI (1913).

McMurtrie, Douglas C. *A Bibliography of Chicago Imprints, 1835-1850.* Chicago, 1944.

———. "The Contribution of the Pioneer Printers to Illinois History," *Transactions of the Illinois State Historical Society*, XLV (1938).

McNulty, John W. "Sidney Breese: His Early Career in Law and Politics in Illinois," *Journal of the Illinois State Historical Society*, LXI (1968).

McPhaul, Jack. *Johnny Torrio, First of the Ganglords.* New Rochelle, 1970.

Madden, Betty. "Buildings in a Wilderness," *The Living Museum*, XXIX (1968).

Magdol, Edward. *Owen Lovejoy: Abolitionist in Congress.* New Brunswick, 1967.

Marchkoff, Fred B. "Currency and Banking in Illinois Before 1865," *Journal of the Illinois State Historical Society*, LII (1959).

Marshall, Helen E. *Dorothea Dix, Forgotten Samaritan.* Chapel Hill, 1937.

———. *Grandest of Enterprises: Illinois State Normal University, 1857-1957.* Normal, 1956.

Marshall, James. *Santa Fe: The Railroad That Built an Empire.* New York, 1945.

Martin, Edward M. *The Role of the Bar in Electing the Bench in Chicago.* Chicago, 1936.

Martin, Lorene. "Old Jubilee College and Its Founder, Bishop Chase," *Transactions of the Illinois State Historical Society*, XLI (1934).

Martineau, Harriet. *Society in America.* 3 vols. London, 1837.

Mason, Edward G. *Chapters from Illinois History.* Chicago, 1901.

Masters, Edgar Lee. *The Sangamon.* New York, 1942.

———. *The Tale of Chicago.* New York, 1933.

Maurer, David J. "Unemployment in Illinois During the Great Depression," *Essays in Illinois History* (Donald F. Tingley, ed.).

Mayer, Harold Melvin. *The Railway Pattern of Metropolitan Chicago.* Chicago, 1943.

Mayer, Harold M., and Richard C. Wade. *Chicago: Growth of a Metropolis.* Chicago, 1969.

Meehan, Thomas A. "Jean Baptiste Point du Sable, the First Chicagoan," *Journal of the Illinois State Historical Society*, LVI (1963).

Merriam, Charles Edward. *Chicago: A More Intimate View of Urban Politics.* New York, 1929.

Merriam, Charles E., and Louise Overacker. *Primary Elections.* Chicago, 1928.

Merriam, Charles E., Spencer D. Parrott, and Albert Lapawsky. *The Government of the Metropolitan Region of Chicago.* Chicago, 1933.

Middleton, William D. *North Shore: America's Fastest Interurban.* San Merino, Calif., 1966.

Milton, George Fort. *The Eve of Conflict: Stephen A. Douglas and the Needless War.* Boston, 1934.

Mitchell, Broadus. *Depression Decade from the New Era through the New Deal, 1929-1941.* New York, 1969.

Mitchell, S. Augustus. *Illinois in 1837.* Philadelphia, 1837
Monroe, James. *Writings.* New York, 1898.
Morehouse, Frances M. I. *The Life of Jesse W. Fell.* Urbana, 1916.
Moses, John. *Illinois Historical and Statistical.* 2 vols. Chicago, 1889.
Moses, John, and Joseph Kirkland. *History of Chicago.* 2 vols. Chicago, 1895.
Mowry, George E. *Theodore Roosevelt and the Progressive Movement.* Madison, 1946.
Mumford, Helen W. *The French Governors of Illinois, 1718-1765.* Evanston, 1963.
Murphy, Edmund R. *Henry de Tonty: Fur Trader of the Mississippi.* Baltimore, 1941.
Murray, David. *Charles Percy of Illinois.* New York, 1968.
Musham, Harry Albert. "The Great Chicago Fire, October 8-10, 1871," *Transactions of the Illinois State Historical Society,* XLVII (1940).
————. "Where Did the Battle of Chicago Take Place?", *Journal of the Illinois State Historical Society,* XXXVI (1943).

Neilson, James W. *Shelby M. Cullom: Prairie State Republican.* Urbana, 1962.
Nevins, Allan. *Illinois.* New York, 1917.
————. "Stephen A. Douglas: His Weaknesses and His Strengths," *Journal of the Illinois State Historical Society,* XLII (1949).
Newell, Barbara W. *Chicago and the Labor Movement: Metropolitan Unionism in the 30's.* Urbana, 1961.
Nortrup, Jack. "Richard Yates: A Personal Glimpse of the Illinois Soldiers' Friend," *Journal of the Illinois State Historical Society,* LVI (1963).
Nowlan, James D. (compiler). *Illinois Major Party Platforms, 1900-1964.* Urbana, 1966.

O'Dea, Thomas F. *The Mormons.* Chicago, 1957.
Oliver, William. *Eight Months in Illinois, with Information to Immigrants.* Newcastle Upon Tyne, 1843, and Chicago, 1924.
O'Shaughnessy, Francis. "General James Shields of Illinois," *Transactions of the Illinois State Historical Society,* XXI (1915).
Osman, Eaton G. *Starved Rock: A Historical Sketch.* Ottawa, 1895.
Ostewig, Kinnie A. "Life of Shadrach Bond, the First Governor of Illinois," *Transactions of the Illinois State Historical Society,* XXXVI (1929).
Overton, Richard C. *Burlington West: A Colonization History of the Burlington Railroad.* Cambridge, 1941.
————. *The First Ninety Years: An Historical Sketch of the Burlington Railroad.* Chicago, 1940.
————. *Burlington Route: A History of the Burlington Lines.* New York, 1965.

Page, John I. *Climate of Illinois.* Univ. of Ill. Agricultural Experiment Station Bulletin 532. Urbana, 1949.
Paisley, Fred D. *Al Capone: The Biography of a Self-Made Man.* Garden City, 1930.
Palm, Sister Mary Borgias, S.N.D. *The Jesuit Missions of the Illinois Country, 1673-1763.* Cleveland, 1933.

Palmer, George Thomas. *A Conscientious Turncoat: The Story of John M. Palmer, 1817-1900.* New Haven, 1941.

Palmer, John M. *The Bench and Bar of Illinois, Historical and Reminiscent.* 2 vols. Chicago, 1899.

————. *Personal Recollections: The Story of an Earnest Life.* Cincinnati, 1901.

Parkman, Francis. *La Salle and the Discovery of the Great West.* Boston, 1869.

Paxson, Frederic L. *The History of the American Frontier, 1763-1893.* Boston, 1924.

Pease, Theodore Calvin. *The Frontier State, 1818-1848.* Chicago, 1922.

———— (ed.). *Illinois Election Returns, 1818-1848.* Springfield, 1923.

———— (ed.). *The Laws of the Northwest Territory.* Springfield, 1925.

————. "The Revolution at Crisis in the West," *Journal of the Illinois State Historical Society,* XXIII (1931).

————. *The Story of Illinois* (revised by Marguerite Jenison Pease). Chicago, 1925, 1949, 1965.

Pease, Theodore C., and Marguerite Jenison Pease. *George Rogers Clark and the Revolution in Illinois, 1763-1787.* Springfield, 1929.

Pease, Theodore C., and Raymond C. Werner (eds.). *The French Foundations, 1680-1693.* Springfield, 1934.

Peck, John Mason. *A Gazetteer of Illinois.* Jacksonville, 1834.

————. *A New Guide for Immigrants to the West.* Boston, 1836.

Peckham, Howard H. *Pontiac and the Indian Uprising.* Chicago, 1961.

Perrin, William Henry. *History of Alexander, Union and Pulaski Counties, Illinois.* Chicago, 1883.

Petersen, William J. *Steamboating on the Upper Mississippi.* Iowa City, 1937.

Peterson, Lowell N. "Omer N. Custer: A Biography of a Downstate Political Boss," *Journal of the Illinois State Historical Society,* LX (1967).

Philbrick, Francis S. (ed.). *Laws of the Illinois Territory, 1809-1818.* Springfield, 1950.

———— (ed.). *The Laws of the Indiana Territory, 1801-1809.* Springfield, 1930.

Pierce, Bessie Louise. *A History of Chicago.* 3 vols. New York, 1940.

Pinkerton, Allan. *Strikers, Communists, Tramps and Detectives.* New York, 1882.

Pitkin, William A. "Shelby M. Cullom: Presidential Prospect," *Journal of the Illinois State Historical Society,* XLIX (1956).

Pixton, John E., Jr. "Charles G. Dawes and the McKinley Campaign," *Journal of the Illinois State Historical Society,* XLVIII (1955).

Plochmann, George Kimball. *The Ordeal of Southern Illinois University.* Carbondale, 1959.

Poggi, Edith Muriel. *The Prairie Province of Illinois: A Study of Human Adjustment to Natural Environment.* Urbana, 1934.

Pooley, William V. *The Settlement of Illinois from 1830 to 1850.* Madison, 1908.

Pope, Nathaniel, *Laws of the Territory of Illinois.* Kaskaskia, 1815. Reissued by the Illinois State Historical Society as *Pope's Digest, 1815* (Francis S. Philbrick, ed.). Springfield, 1938.

Pratt, Fletcher. *The Civil War on Western Waters: Story of Union and Confederate River Navies.* New York, 1956.

Pratt, Harry Edward. "Abraham Lincoln, A Chronology," *Illinois Blue Book, 1955-56.*

————. "David Davis, 1815-1886," *Transactions of the Illinois State Historical Society,* XXXVII (1930).

————. "The Great Debates," *Illinois Blue Book, 1953-54.*

Prince, Ezra M. (ed.). *Convention of May 29, 1857, That Organized the Republican Party in Illinois.* Bloomington, 1900.

Putnam, Elizabeth Duncan. "The Life and Services of Joseph Duncan, Governor of Illinois, 1834-1838," *Transactions of the Illinois State Historical Society,* XXVI (1919).

Putnam, James William. *The Illinois and Michigan Canal: A Study in Economic History.* Chicago, 1918.

Quaife, Milo Milton. *Checagou, From Indian Wigwam to Modern City, 1673-1835.* Chicago, 1933.

————. *Chicago and the Old Northwest, 1673-1835: A Study of the Evolution of the Northwestern Frontier, Together with a History of Fort Dearborn.* Chicago, 1913.

————. *Chicago's Highways Old and New: From Indian Trail to Motor Road.* Chicago, 1923.

———— (ed.). *The Development of Chicago, 1674-1914.* Chicago, 1916.

————. *Lake Michigan.* Indianapolis, 1944.

———— (ed.). *The Life of Ma-Ka-Tai-Me-She-Kia-Kiak or Black Hawk . . . Dictated by Himself.* Chicago, 1916.

————. *The Movement for Statehood, 1845-46.* Madison, 1918.

———— (ed.). *Pictures of Illinois One Hundred Years Ago.* Chicago, 1918.

———— (ed.). *The Western Country in the 17th Century: The Memoirs of LaMothe Cadillac and Pierre Liette.* Chicago, 1947.

Radebaugh, William. *The Boundary Dispute Between Illinois and Wisconsin.* An address read before the Chicago Historical Society. Chicago, 1904.

Rammelkamp, Charles Henry. *Illinois College: A Centennial History, 1829-1929.* New Haven, 1928.

Randall, Frank A. *History of the Development of Building Construction in Chicago.* Urbana, 1949.

Randall, Henry S. *Life of Thomas Jefferson.* New York, 1958.

Randall, Randolph C. *James Hall: Spokesman of the New West.* Columbus, 1964.

Ranney, Victoria (ed.). *Con-Con: Issues for the Illinois Constitutional Convention.* Urbana, 1970.

Rauch, Mable Thompson. "Along the Trail of Tears," *Journal of the Illinois State Historical Society,* XLIII (1950).

Raum, Green B. *History of Illinois Republicanism.* Chicago, 1900.

Reckless, Walter C. *Vice in Chicago.* Chicago, 1933.

Rees, Thomas. "Nauvoo, Illinois, Under the Mormon and Icarian Occupations," *Journal of the Illinois State Historical Society*, XXI (1929).

Report of the National Advisory Commission on Civil Disorders (Otto Kerner, chairman). New York, 1968.

Reynolds, John. *My Own Times, Embracing Also the History of My Life.* Belleville, 1855, and Chicago, 1879.

————. *The Pioneer History of Illinois.* Belleville, 1852, and Chicago, 1887.

————. *Sketches of the Country, on the Northern Route from Belleville, Illinois, to the City of New York.* Belleville, 1854.

Richardson, Eudora R. "The Virginian Who Made Illinois a Free State," *Journal of the Illinois State Historical Society*, XLV (1952).

Riddle, Donald W. *Lincoln Runs for Congress.* New Brunswick, 1948.

Ridgley, Douglas Clay. *The Geography of Illinois.* Chicago, 1921.

Rinaker, Thomas. *Gideon Blackburn, the Founder of Blackburn University, Carlinville, Illinois.* Springfield, 1924.

Risser, Hubert E., and Robert L. Major. *History of Illinois Mineral Resources.* Illinois State Geological Survey, Educational Series 10. Urbana, 1968.

Rissler, Howard F. "The State Capitol, 1837-1876," *Journal of the Illinois State Historical Society*, LXI (1968).

Robbins, Roy M. *Our Landed Heritage: The Public Domain, 1776-1936.* Lincoln, 1962.

Roberts, B. H. *The Rise and Fall of Nauvoo.* Salt Lake City, 1965.

Roberts, James H. "The Life and Times of General John Edgar," *Transactions of the Illinois State Historical Society*, XII (1907).

Roberts, Sidney I. "The Municipal Voters League and Chicago's Boodlers," *Journal of the Illinois State Historical Society*, LIII (1960).

Rodnitzky, Jerome Leon. "President James and His Campaigns for University of Illinois Funds," *Journal of the Illinois State Historical Society*, LXIII (1970).

Rohrbough, Malcolm J. *The Land Office Business: The Settlement and Administration of American Public Lands, 1788-1837.* New York, 1968.

Rombauer, Roderick E. "The Life of Hon. Gustave Koerner," *Transactions of the Illinois State Historical Society*, IX (1904).

Roosevelt, Theodore. *The Spread of the English-Speaking Peoples*, Vol. 1 of *The Winning of the West.* New York, 1905.

Rose, James A. "The Regulators and Flatheads in Southern Illinois," *Transactions of the Illinois State Historical Society*, XI (1906).

Rosenberg, Charles E. *The Cholera Years: The United States in 1832, 1849, and 1866.* Chicago, 1962.

Royce, Charles C. *Indian Land Cessions in the United States.* Washington, 1899.

Royko, Mike. *Boss: Richard J. Daley of Chicago.* New York, 1971.

Rudwick, Elliott M. *Race Riot at East St. Louis, July 2, 1917.* Carbondale, 1964.

Ruggles, Eleanor. *The West Going Heart: A Life of Vachel Lindsay.* New York, 1959.

Russell, Nelson Vance. "The French and British at Play in the Old Northwest, 1760-1796," *Journal of the Illinois State Historical Society*, XXXI (1938).

Savelle, Max. *George Morgan, Colony Builder.* New York, 1932.

Scamehorn, Howard L. *Balloons to Jets: 1855-1955, a Century of Aeronautics in Illinois.* Chicago, 1957.

Schafer, Joseph. *The Wisconsin Lead Region.* Wisconsin Domesday Book, General Studies III. Madison, 1932.

Schlarman, Joseph H. *From Quebec to New Orleans: The Story of the French in America.* Belleville, 1929.

Schmidt, Louis Bernard. "The Internal Grain Trade of the United States, 1850-1860," *Iowa Journal of History and Politics,* I (1920).

Schockel, Bernard Henry. "Settlement and Development of the Lead and Zinc Mining Region of the Driftless Area with Special Emphasis upon Jo Daviess County, Illinois," *Mississippi Valley Historical Review,* IV (1917).

Schoolcraft, Henry R. *Travels in the Central Portions of the Mississippi Valley.* New York, 1825.

Schuyler, Robert L. *The Transition in Illinois from British to American Government.* New York, 1909.

Scott, Roy V. *The Agrarian Movement in Illinois, 1880-1896.* Urbana, 1962.

Selby, Paul. "Genesis of the Republican Party in Illinois," *Transactions of the Illinois State Historical Society,* XI (1906).

————. "The Lincoln-Conkling Letter, September 3, 1863," *Transactions of the Illinois State Historical Society,* XIII (1908).

————. "The Part of Illinoisans in the National Education Movement, 1851-1862," *Transactions of the Illinois State Historical Society,* IX (1904).

Severin, Timothy. *Explorers of the Mississippi.* New York, 1967.

Shannon, Fred A. *The Farmer's Last Frontier: Agriculture, 1860-1897.* New York, 1945.

Simon, Paul. *Lincoln's Preparation for Greatness: The Illinois Legislative Years.* Norman, Okla., 1965.

————. *Lovejoy, Martyr to Freedom.* St. Louis, 1964.

Sinclair, Upton. *The Jungle.* New York, 1906.

Small, Len. *Illinois Progress, 1921-1928.* Springfield, 1928.

Smith, Alice E. *George Smith's Money: A Scottish Investor in America.* Madison, 1966.

Smith, Alson J. *Syndicate City: The Chicago Crime Cartel and What to Do About It.* Chicago, 1954.

Smith, George W. *History of Illinois and Her People.* 6 vols. Chicago, 1927.

————. "The Salines of Southern Illinois," *Transactions of the Illinois State Historical Society,* IX (1904).

Smith, Henry Justin. *Chicago, a Portrait.* New York, 1931.

Smith, William Henry (ed.), *The St. Clair Papers.* 2 vols. Cincinnati, 1882.

Snyder, John Francis. *Adam W. Snyder and His Period in Illinois History, 1817-1842.* Virginia, 1906.

————. "The Armament of Fort Chartres," *Transactions of the Illinois State Historical Society,* XI (1906).

————. "Captain Jean Baptiste Saucier at Fort Chartres in the Illinois," *Transactions of the Illinois State Historical Society,* XXVI (1919).

————. "Forgotten Statesmen of Illinois: Hon. Jesse Burgess Thomas,"

Transactions of the Illinois State Historical Society, IX (1904).

————. *John Francis Snyder: Selected Writings* (Clyde C. Walton, ed.). Springfield, 1962.

Soil. U.S. Department of Agriculture Yearbook, 1957.

Solberg, Winton U. *The University of Illinois, 1867-1894: An Intellectual Cultural History.* Urbana, 1968.

Soule, George. *Prosperity Decade, from War to Depression, 1917-1929.* New York, 1968.

Sparks, Edwin Erle. *The Lincoln-Douglas Debates of 1858.* Springfield, 1908.

Spear, Allan H. *Black Chicago: The Making of a Negro Ghetto, 1890-1920.* Chicago, 1967.

Spencer, Donald S. "Edward Coles: Virginia Gentleman in Frontier Politics," *Journal of the Illinois State Historical Society,* LXI (1968).

Staley, Eugene. *History of the Illinois State Federation of Labor.* Chicago, 1930.

Stead, William Thomas. *If Christ Came to Chicago.* Chicago, 1894.

Steck, Francis Borgia. *The Jolliet-Marquette Expedition, 1673.* Washington, 1927.

Stevens, Frank E. *The Black Hawk War.* Chicago, 1903.

————. "A Forgotten Hero: General James Dougherty Henry," *Transactions of the Illinois State Historical Society,* XLI (1934).

————. "Illinois in the War of 1812-14," *Transactions of the Illinois State Historical Society,* IX (1904).

————. "Stillman's Defeat," *Transactions of the Illinois State Historical Society,* VII (1902).

Steward, J. F. *The Reaper: A History of the Efforts of Those Who Justly May Be Said to Have Made Bread Cheap.* New York, 1931.

Stibitz, E. Earle (ed.). *Illinois Poets: A Selection.* Carbondale, 1968.

Storr, Richard J. *Harper's University: The Beginnings, a History of the University of Chicago.* Chicago, 1966.

Strickland, Arvarh E. *History of the Chicago Urban League.* Urbana, 1966.

————. "The New Deal Comes to Chicago," *Journal of the Illinois State Historical Society,* LXIII (1970).

Strong, M. N. *History of the Territory of Wisconsin from 1836-1848.* Madison, 1885.

Stuart, William H. *The Twenty Incredible Years.* Chicago, 1935.

Swanberg, W. A. *Citizen Hearst: Biography of William Randolph Hearst.* New York, 1961.

Swanson, Leslie C. *Canals of Mid-America.* Moline, 1964.

Swift, Louis F., and Arthur Van Vlissingen, Jr. *The Yankee of the Yards: The Biography of Gustavus Franklin Swift.* New York, 1927.

Tarr, Joel A. "President Roosevelt and Illinois Politics, 1901-1904," *Journal of the Illinois State Historical Society,* LVIII (1965).

Taylor, Charles H. *History of the Board of Trade of the City of Chicago.* 3 vols. Chicago, 1917.

Tebbel, John. *An American Dynasty: The Story of the McCormicks, Medills and Pattersons.* New York, 1968.

————. *The Marshall Fields: A Study in Wealth.* New York, 1947.

Tebbel, John, and Keith Jennison. *The American Indian Wars.* New York, 1960.

Temple, Wayne C. *Indian Villages of the Illinois Country.* Springfield: Illinois State Museum, 1958.

———. *The Piasa Bird: Fact or Fiction?* Springfield: Illinois State Museum, 1956.

Terkel, Studs. *Hard Times: An Oral History of the Great Depression.* New York, 1970.

Thiem, George. *The Hodge Scandal: A Pattern of American Political Corruption.* New York, 1963.

Thomas, Benjamin P. "Lincoln and New Salem," *Transactions of the Illinois State Historical Society,* XLI (1934).

———. *Lincoln's New Salem.* Springfield, 1934.

Thompson, Charles M. "A Study of the Administration of Thomas Ford, Governor of Illinois, 1842-1846," in Evarts B. Greene and Thompson, *Governors' Letter-Books, 1840-1853.*

Thompson, Robert Luther. *Wiring a Continent: The History of the Telegraph Industry in the United States, 1832-1866.* Princeton, 1947.

Thornburn, Neil. "John P. Altgeld: Promoter of Higher Education in Illinois," in *Essays in Illinois History* (Donald F. Tingley, ed.).

Thwaites, Reuben Gold. *Early Western Travels, 1748-1846.* 37 vols. Cleveland, 1904-07.

———. *Father Marquette.* New York, 1902.

———. *France in America.* New York, 1905.

———. *How George Rogers Clark Won the Northwest.* New York, 1903.

———. *The Jesuit Relations.* Cleveland, 1899.

———. "Notes on Early Lead Mining in the Fever River Region," *Wisconsin Historical Collections,* XIII (1895).

Tice, Homer J. "The Illinois State Fair," *Illinois Blue Book, 1931-32.*

Tilton, Clint Clay. "John W. Vance and the Vermilion Salines," *Transactions of the Illinois State Historical Society,* XXXVIII (1931).

Tingley, Donald F. (ed.). *Essays in Illinois History in Honor of Glenn Huron Seymour.* Carbondale, 1968.

Tittle, William M., Jr. *Race Riot: Chicago in the Red Summer of 1919.* New York, 1970.

Townsend, Walter A. (ed.). *Illinois Democracy: A History of the Party and Its Representative Members, Past and Present.* Springfield, 1935.

Trohan, Walter. "My Life with the Colonel," *Journal of the Illinois State Historical Society,* LII (1959).

Trout, Grace Wilbur. "Side Lights on Illinois Suffrage History," *Journal of the Illinois State Historical Society,* XIII (1920).

Turner, Fred H. "Misconceptions Concerning the Early History of the University of Illinois," *Transactions of the Illinois State Historical Society,* XXXIX (1932).

Twyman, Robert W. *History of Marshall Field & Co., 1852-1906.* Philadelphia, 1954.

Verlie, Emil Joseph (ed.). *Illinois Constitutions.* Springfield, 1919.

Voegeli, V. Jacque. *Free but Not Equal: The Midwest and the Negro During the Civil War.* Chicago, 1967.

Voigt, David Quentin. "The Chicago Black Sox and the Myth of Baseball's Single Sin," *Journal of the Illinois State Historical Society,* LXII (1969).

Wade, Louise C. *Graham Taylor, Pioneer for Social Justice, 1851-1938.* Chicago, 1964.

————. "The Heritage from Chicago's Early Settlement Houses," *Journal of the Illinois State Historical Society,* LX (1967).

Wagenknecht, Edward. *Chicago.* Norman, 1964.

Waggoner, Madeline S. *The Long Haul West: The Great Canal Era, 1817-1850.* New York, 1958.

Wakefield, Eva Ingersoll (ed.). *Letters of Robert Green Ingersoll.* New York, 1951.

Waldrop, Frank C. *McCormick of Chicago: An Unconventional Portrait of a Controversial Figure.* Edgewood Cliffs, N.J., 1966.

Wallace, Anthony F. C. *Prelude to Disaster: The Course of Indian-White Relations Which Led to the Black Hawk War of 1832.* Springfield, 1970.

Walsh, Justin E. *To Print the News and Raise Hell! A Biography of Wilbur F. Storey.* Chapel Hill, 1968.

Walton, Clyde C. (ed.). *An Illinois Reader.* De Kalb, 1970.

Ward, Estelle Francis. *The Story of Northwestern University.* New York, 1924.

Washburne, Elihu B. (ed.). *The Edwards Papers.* Chicago, 1884.

————. *Sketch of Edward Coles, Second Governor of Illinois, and of the Slavery Struggle of 1823-4.* Chicago, 1882.

Watkins, Sylvestre C., Sr. "Some of Early Illinois' Free Negroes," *Journal of the Illinois State Historical Society,* LVI (1963).

Watters, Mary. *Illinois in the Second World War.* 2 vols. Springfield, 1951, 1952.

Way, Royal B. *The Rock River Valley: Its History, Traditions, Legends and Charm.* 3 vols. Chicago, 1926.

Weaver, John E. *The North American Prairie.* Lincoln, 1954.

Webb, Howard W., Jr. *Illinois Prose Writers: A Selection.* Carbondale, 1968.

Webb, Walter Prescott. *The Great Plains.* New York, 1931.

Wendt, Lloyd, and Herman Kogan. *Big Bill of Chicago.* Indianapolis, 1953.

————. *Give the Lady What She Wants! The Story of Marshall Field & Company.* Chicago, 1952.

————. *Lords of the Levee.* Indianapolis, 1943.

White, Horace. *The Life of Lyman Trumbull.* Boston, 1913.

Windle, Ann. "John Wentworth—His Contributions to Chicago," *Transactions of the Illinois State Historical Society,* XLIV (1937).

Wilson, Bluford. "Southern Illinois During the Civil War," *Transactions of the Illinois State Historical Society,* XVI (1911).

Wilson, F. E. *Arthur St. Clair: Rugged Ruler of the Old Northwest.* Richmond, 1944.

Wilson, Howard E. *Mary McDowell, Neighbor.* Chicago, 1928.

Wilson, Samuel J. "Colonial Fortifications and Military Architecture in the

Mississippi Valley," in *The French in the Mississippi Valley* (J. F. McDermott, ed.).

Wilson, William E. *The Wabash.*

Wiltsee, Herbert. "The Temperance Movement, 1848-1871," *Transactions of the Illinois State Historical Society,* XLIV (1937).

Wish, Harvey. "Governor Altgeld Pardons the Anarchists," *Journal of the Illinois State Historical Society,* XXXI (1938).

——————. "The Pullman Strike: A Study in Industrial Warfare," *Journal of the Illinois State Historical Society,* XXXII (1939).

Wooddy, Carroll H. *The Case of Frank L. Smith: A Study in Representative Government.* Chicago, 1931.

Woods, John. *Two Years Residence on the English Prairie of Illinois* (Paul M. Angle, ed.). Chicago, 1968.

Woolard, Francis M. "Route of George Rogers Clark and His Army from Kaskaskia to Vincennes, 1779," *Transactions of the Illinois State Historical Society,* XLI (1934).

Wright, James E. *The Galena Lead Mining District: Federal Policy and Practice, 1824-1847.* Madison, 1966.

Wrone, David R. "Illinois Pulls Out of the Mud," *Journal of the Illinois State Historical Society,* LVIII (1965).

Yager, Rosemary. *James Buchanan Eads: Master of the Great River.* Princeton, 1968.

Young, Dallas M. "Origin of the Progressive Mine Workers of America," *Journal of the Illinois State Historical Society,* XL (1947).

Yungmeyer, D. W. "An Excursion Into the Early History of the Chicago and Alton Railroad," *Journal of the Illinois State Historical Society,* XXXVIII (1945).

Index

ILLINOIS:
A HISTORY OF THE PRAIRIE STATE
ROBERT P. HOWARD

"There are at least five million people," Paul Angle remarks in his Foreword to this comprehensive history, "who will assert vigorously that Chicago is not Illinois." Robert Howard is certainly one of them.

It is true, of course, that Chicago has played a large and influential role in the development of Illinois and of the entire country. But its story is only part of a larger chronicle; south and west of the Windy City lie the rich agricultural areas that drew the state's early settlers, and that continue to justify its reputation as "The Prairie State." Downstate Illinois made its own, equally significant, contribution to the history of a complex, multi-faceted state.

Robert Howard is a veteran Chicago newspaperman who has traveled to every corner of his home state, and he is uniquely qualified to trace the history of both urban and rural Illinois. The account begins in the seventeenth century, when the land was populated by the Iliniwek and the Iroquois Indians, and is carried through 300 years of the past and into the present. During those years Illinois grew from a sparsely populated frontier state into a leading industrial power; plank roads gave way to iron rails; the state endured and survived war, prohibition, and the great depression.

These recurring social, economic, political, educational, racial, agricultural and industrial trends provide the framework within which Howard's narrative unfolds. But history is much more than abstractions and labels; at bottom, it has to do with people, with particular individuals and personalities. And so Howard writes about people—the famous and the infamous, the prominent and the obscure. Among those who find a place in these pages are George Rogers Clark, Elijah Lovejoy, Stephen Douglas, Abraham Lincoln, Jane Addams, Al Capone, Carl Sandburg, Richard Daley. And scores of others, each of whom—for better or for worse—helped to shape and to define the Prairie State.